THE WAITE GROUP'S

# VISUAL BASIC HOW-TO

ROBERT ARNSON
DANIEL ROSEN
MITCHELL WAITE
JONATHAN ZUCK

**WAITE GROUP
PRESS**
Mill Valley, California

**Development Editor** *Mitchell Waite*
**Technical Editor** *William Potter*
**Design and Production** *Barbara Gelfand*
**Cover Design** *Juan Vargas*
**Production Manager** *Julianne Ososke*
**Editorial Director** *Scott Calamar*

© **1992 by The Waite Group, Inc.**
**Published by Waite Group Press, 100 Shoreline Highway, Suite A-285, Mill Valley, CA 94941.**

Waite Group Press is distributed to bookstores and book wholesalers by Publishers Group West, Box 8843, Emeryville, CA 94662, 1-800-788-3123 (in California 1-510-658-3453).

Printed in the United States of America
92 93 94 95 • 10 9 8 7 6 5 4 3 2 1

The Waite Group's Visual Basic How-To / Robert Arnson ... [et al.].
    p.  cm.
  Includes index.
  ISBN: 1-878739-09-3
  1. BASIC (Computer program language) 2. Microsoft Visual BASIC.
I. Arnson, Robert, 1970-   . II. Waite Group. III. Title: Visual Basic How-To.
QA76.73B3W334 1992
005.26'2--dc20                                  91-45526
                                                      CIP

## DEDICATION

To two pioneers: Alan Cooper, the father of Visual Basic, for his inception of the Visual interface, and Bill Gates for having the vision to develop it and hook it to the most accessible computer language to date.

# ACKNOWLEDGMENTS

It took an amazing amount of synergy to create the book that you are now holding in your hands.

Thanks to Mitch Waite for his ebullient devotion to Visual Basic, innovative vision to develop this book, and tenacity to keep this project evolving until we just about needed a pitbull to loosen it from his caring grasp and deliver it to the printer.

Above all, thanks to the co-authors. Daniel Rosen and Jonathan Zuck are true professionals with whom it was a great pleasure to work. They put in countless months developing their programs, documenting them, and remaining true to the Waite Group vision of this book throughout. A special Star Fleet thanks must go to Robert Arnson, who perservered to the very end, writing and refining and keeping his good spirits when we asked for more, more, and even more. We also thank John Cole for contributing a number of splendid How-Tos to this collection.

The third-party chapter, especially, would not have been possible without the generosity and hard work of a number of people. Thanks to Zane Thomas for writing the incredible Sound Blaster How-Tos and contributing a nifty DLL that raises Visual Basic programming to another plane. Thanks to Mark Novisoff of MicroHelp for providing the great demo VBTools DLL, and to Ethan Winer of Crescent Software for the assembly routines. We also thank Joe Modica of Sheridan for the How-To on 3-D controls and Sheridan's DLL.

Our heartfelt thanks to Bill Potter for his very helpful technical reviews of the Visual Basic code, and special credit to Jim Conger for his assistance with the Windows API chapter. Waite Group Press always appreciates the accommodating folks at Microsoft Corp., especially Nevet Basker and Mike Risse for helping to make this project possible in the first place.

Cheers to Julianne Ososke for her understanding as this book was honed and re-honed. And finally, our praise goes out to Bibi Gelfand and her very talented production crew—lesser people would have had visions of "The Shining" dealing with our brand of perfectionism.

**Scott Calamar**
Editorial Director
Waite Group Press

# TABLE OF CONTENTS

# TABLE OF CONTENTS

# FOREWORD

When Visual Basic was being developed, we immediately thought of The Waite Group. The light touch and high quality of Mitch's books, particularly those on QuickBasic and C, made him an excellent publisher to seed.

Of course we all wondered what the reception to Visual Basic would be, after all the traditional development platform for Windows was C, and Microsoft had thousands of developers working with that language. We were pleased to find that the development community quickly embraced Visual Basic. Quotes from many technical developers and journalists in our industry all agreed: Visual Basic gives "leverage" over Windows programming and provides a full-fledged development system for creating real Windows applications. Compilation is almost instantaneous and the final results are indistinguishable from programs written in C. The core language is based on QuickBasic and modified for the graphics platform with an event-drive programming model which ensures a major host of new programmers can use it.

Rather than write just another tutorial, The Waite Group has given us clever new insights to the Visual Basic language through the extensive use of Windows APIs. The API or Application Programming Interface is the underlying library of over 800 system calls and messages that makes up the Windows programming environment. Visual Basic is designed so that it can easily call these powerful functions. With the *Visual Basic How-To* you will learn how to push the environment to its limits.

We're proud to have book authors and publishers in the Visual Basic add-on community. And we're especially proud of the support of Mitch Waite and The Waite Group. The *Visual Basic How-To* is a valuable source for all kinds of tricks and tips. I think you'll enjoy this book, and at the same time, it will stretch your appreciation of Microsoft's revolutionary new product. With Microsoft Visual Basic and *The Waite Group's Visual Basic How-To*, you can create real Windows applications the fast and easy way.

**Nevet Basker**
Visual Basic Product Manager
Microsoft Corporation

November 1991

# FOREWORD

In 1987 I wrote a program called "Ruby" that delivered visual programming to the average user. When I showed the prototype to Bill Gates, he said "this advances the state of the art." Little did we know at the time just how far forward it would go. More than two years later, as the project evolved, Ruby was married to QuickBasic, and the result was Visual Basic—the first native programming environment for Windows. And you are the beneficiary. For the first time you can write Windows programs from within Windows without the enormous overburden of code needed with C. And they are real programs, for real customers with real application needs.

When people ask me what is the best way to learn programming or how to use a specific language, I tell them to experiment—write as many small programs as you can, as each one will teach you more—and each one will add another trick to your tool bag. Unfortunately, when a simple "Hello, World" program takes four hundred lines of code, as it can when Windows is programmed with the C language, this prescription is nearly impossible to follow. Well now The Waite Group gives us a book that uses that learning method. First, Visual Basic brings the size of Windows programs down to a manageable level, then *The Waite Group's Visual Basic How-To* guides you through dozens of small programs (and some not-so-small) that fulfill the learning prescription admirably.

This book goes considerably beyond reference, without catering to the lowest common denominator of typical tutorials. You can think of it as a guide to enjoyable learning, a mentor for experimentation. The programs in this book are the kind that you can learn with. You can add to them, combine them, extend them and, ultimately, use them in day-to-day computing.

Mitch Waite has been delivering practical, helpful writing for personal computer users since the mid-seventies. He has gathered around him some of the best and most capable writers working today. Their collective expertise with the Basic language and programming in Windows has come together with their understanding of learning and writing. Coupled with Robert Arnson's amazingly strong affinity with Visual Basic, it means the book you now hold in your hands delivers the most useful information available on the subject.

**Alan Cooper**
Director Applications Software
Coactive Computing Corp
Dec. 1991

*(Alan Cooper is considered the father of Visual Basic)*

# INTRODUCTION

## What This Book Is About

If you love Visual Basic and want to do marvelous things with it—things not immediately apparent—this book is for you.

However, if you are looking for a book that shows how to make a beep, tells how to set up a menu with three items in it, or shows how you set the caption of a form, this book may not be for you. For those kinds of things we recommend one of the many introductory books on Visual Basic or the manuals which we think are pretty adequate for first time learners.

## Takes Visual Basic to Its Limits

Rather than rehash the manuals, *Visual Basic How-To* shows you how to take the program to its ultimate limits. We view Visual Basic as a complete stand-alone Windows development system—rivaling the professional Windows SDK used by C programmers. And so we show you how to do things that you would think could only be done in C with the SDK. The bottom line is that our book is chock full of tricks of all kinds.

For example, you'll learn how to size a form's controls automatically, flash title bars, make a button with continuous events, and remember the size and locations of forms so the next time you open them they are in the same place. You'll see how to build a powerful editor that searches for text, make floating pop-up menus, or give an application a NeXT-like graphical interface. There are details on how to scroll objects in a window, align text automatically, ensure numeric-only entry in a text box, even control the rate at which your text caret blinks.

## Uses Windows APIs Extensively

One of the cool things about this book is that it uses many of Windows' built-in Application Programming Interface (API) routines. These powerful routines are what professional Windows developers use to create killer applications. We'll tell you how to use the Windows APIs to draw transparent icons, create a file dialog box, send messages to controls, display the progress of an operation in a bar chart, paint the interiors of complex objects, and build professional line, bar, and pie charts. There is even a complete slide show project that displays Windows bitmaps with special graphics effects.

## Question and Answer Format

The questions and answers are arranged by categories: controls, forms, text and scrolling, mouse and menu, graphics, environment and system, peripherals, custom controls, DLLs, and Windows APIs. Each How-To contains a program solution with complete construction details. All the code, bitmaps, fonts, icons, forms, and DLLs are contained on the enclosed disk.

### Tons of Bundled Third Party Controls

*Visual Basic How-To* provides more than just solutions—the bundled disk contains custom controls from MicroHelp, Crescent, Sheridan Software, and Waite Group Software. You'll find list boxes that allow multiple selections, triggering alarms, and ribbon buttons that work like Excel's toolbar. Beautiful three-dimensional buttons can include custom bitmaps as well as text with raised or etched effects. Finally, a Sound Blaster DLL and three custom controls are provided for creating digitized speech, FM synthesized effects, and playing MIDI tunes from Visual Basic.

### The Fractal DLL

A chapter on Windows DLLs shows how to interface Visual Basic to a custom made Fractal DLL that is written in C++ and supplied with the book. You'll see how to translate the parameters required by a Windows DLL into Visual Basic Declare statements. Finally, an exhaustive appendix explains Microsoft's WINAPI.TXT Declare file for using Windows APIs. The file is also included on the disk so you can merge it into your programs.

### Expected Level of Reader

No, you don't need to be a genius to use this book. It's really designed for all levels of readers—beginner, intermediate, and advanced. What we have done is give each question and its solution a heading that indicates what the "complexity" level is. If you are just starting out with Visual Basic you can use the beginning How-Tos. These almost exclusively use pure Visual Basic code. If you are somewhat experienced in Basic, you can jump to the intermediate level How-Tos which push the use of Basic and in a few cases use simple APIs. If you are experienced in Visual Basic or C and really want to stretch the code, you should check out the advanced level complexity How-Tos. These almost exclusively use APIs and tricks to do their magic.

### What You Need to Use This Book

In order to use this book you will need a computer capable of running Windows and Visual Basic. We recommend a VGA display but an EGA will do fine since Visual Basic can only generate 16 colors on screen (the remaining colors are dithered). You should have a mouse hooked up as well. And you probably should get a copy of *The Waite Group's Visual Basic Super Bible* which provides a comprehensive reference to Visual Basic that goes way beyond the manuals.

## How This Book Is Organized

The book is divided into 9 chapters as follows:

### Chapter 1 Controls

This chapter, Controls, reveals little-known secrets of Visual Basic controls by using several powerful Windows APIs. A firm footing is provided in SendMessage, one of the most powerful APIs which allows you to exploit many control properties not found in Visual Basic. You'll learn how to make a custom check box that uses real checks instead of little Xs, how to add controls at run time, and how to make a file dialog box using APIs. A powerful API-based text editor will be created that allows cut, copy, and paste to the clipboard, as well as a searching list box using APIs. There is a How-To that shows how to make a button with continuous events. Another shows how to set up old-fashioned file dialog boxes that have the directories listed together with the drives.

### Chapter 2 Forms

You will probably want to include the techniques in this chapter to make sure your form is centered automatically, and that its controls are adjusted automatically when the form is resized. You'll also learn to ensure that your program's settings, size and location are saved when you exit the program and restored when you reopen it. This chapter demonstrates ways to attract user attention by flashing the title bar of a form, displaying a hidden or minimized form, and a very cool way of starting your applications with an animated "exploding" look. You will also learn two different ways to secure your programs from unwanted eyes: one to prevent typed text from appearing on the screen, and a method of locking a window or a file so the user needs to enter a password to access it.

### Chapter 3 Text and Scrolling

This chapter presents a number of different techniques for scrolling text and graphics using Windows APIs and native Visual Basic code. You'll find How-Tos that scroll when Visual Basic's AutoRedraw property is either enabled or disabled, line-by-line scrolling or "crawl" scrolling like you see in movie credits, and and how to accomplish those effects with scroll bars or command buttons. You'll find out how to align text horizontally and vertically, instead of simply left-aligned, how to create a README file viewer and a simple text editor that searches for text strings. You'll also see how to accept text strings limited to numbers, how to trim null characters from strings, how to modify the speed at which the cursor blinks, and how to preview screen color combinations with scroll bars. Along the way, we'll corral a few Windows API functions to help make text processing quick and accurate, including the very powerful SendMessage API.

### Chapter 4 Mouse and Menu

This bag-of-tricks chapter shows you how to create more powerful mouse trapping and selection capabilities and how to create more customized, useful, and attractive menus. We will use some very handy Windows APIs to extend Visual Basic's menu-making capabilities: GetMenu, GetSubMenu, GetMenuItem, ModifyMenu. We will also see the versatility of Visual Basic's timer features.

### Chapter 5 Graphics

This chapter provides a collection of projects that show how easy it is for Visual Basic to imitate any "look" you wish—from a modern brushed aluminum NeXT-like interface to a Macintosh-style trash can. You'll see how to fill complex polygon shapes with patterns and colors, how to draw pictures inside your iconized application, and how to build line, bar, and pie charts that work just like the charts in Excel. There is even a powerful slide show that does dissolves and other special effects for presentations. Throughout the chapter powerful APIs are used and carefully explained.

### Chapter 6 Environment and System

This chapter presents techniques for communicating with DOS, running DOS programs from Visual Basic, and determining the state of various aspects of the Windows environment. You'll learn how to use many APIs for finding the amount of available memory, the version of Windows running on your machine, the names of directories, the type of keyboard your user has, and much more. Many important APIs are covered here, including the WinExec function that lets you shell to DOS but doesn't give error messages if the program can't be found. There are also APIs for determining the class name of an application, as well as a great project that simulates the Windows SDK SPY program that gives important information on all applications running under Windows.

### Chapter 7 Peripherals: Screen, Speaker, and Serial Ports

This chapter will show you how to get Visual Basic to control the various hardware extensions of your PC. You will see how to figure out the color capabilities of any user's video display and printer, how to create sound effects and attach them to your programs, how to create a phone dialer that works with a modem and serial port, and how to build your own Visual Basic communications program. Visual Basic lacks the great PLAY statement that came with QuickBASIC so we'll show you a way to simulate PLAY's complete macro language to play music. Many of the familiar hardware-addressing commands of QuickBASIC or DOS have been left out of Visual Basic. This is because Visual Basic programs are written to run in the Windows multitasking environment, where all hardware interrupts must be processed and parceled out by Window. This chapter takes full advantage of a number of Windows APIs to manipulate computer peripherals.

### Chapter 8 Third Party Custom Controls and Functions

This chapter provides How-Tos on using third party controls. Four third party custom control companies—MicroHelp, Crescent, Sheridan, and Waite Group Software—were gracious enough to create special demo versions of their controls for this book. *These controls work just like the fully functional commercial versions except they will not compile to a full EXE program.* This chapter contains three How-Tos for the controls provided by MicroHelp that show you how to make command buttons that contain bitmap graphics, a file dialog box that allows multiple file names to be selected, and a neat alarm that rings like a telephone or a buzzer. There are three projects from Crescent that use assembly routines from their Quick-Pak product, including a way to quickly get a handle to a window, monitor and display the amount of free system resources, and display information in a second monitor. A large project that shows how to make a beautiful 3-dimensional interface using Sheridan's custom 3-D Wigets package is presented. This product gives an outstanding set of controls that have varying degrees of shadowed and raised or recessed text and can make a startling impression on your audience. The last set of three How-Tos show you techniques for making your Visual Basic applications have multimedia capability. Waite Group Software has provided controls for manipulating the Sound Blaster audio board. You'll find controls for playing standard MIDI music files, controlling the 11-voice FM synthesizer, and playing and recording digitized sound effects and even speech so your applications can talk to the end user. Again all the controls for these projects are found on the disk bundled with this book.

### Chapter 9 Visual Basic with DDLs

One of the most powerful aspects of Visual Basic is its ability to use custom dynamic link libraries (DLL) that greatly extend the power of what you can do. This chapter will show you how to take a DLL written in another language, such as C, and get it working for Visual Basic. It will also point out the advantages of a DLL, how they can be used as black boxes, and the power of Visual Basic to serve as an interface that is completely independent of the DLLs operation (adaptive programming). In addition you'll learn how to convert between Visual Basic's data types and the data types found in the C language and the extended data types in Windows.

### Appendix A The Annotated WINAPI.TXT File

Throughout the book, How-To solutions draw on Windows API functions to accomplish tasks that are not built into Visual Basic. Before your Visual Basic program can use a Windows API, the function's parameters, their specific order, and type must be declared in your program. Microsoft supplies a file called WINAPI.TXT that provides all the information you need to use these APIs but the file is cryptic and part of the Visual Basic package. The disk that comes with this book includes WINAPI.TXT, and Appendix A provides explanations about the file to help you more easily use the API functions. Using cut and paste, you can copy specific sections from WINAPI.TXT and put them into your GLOBAL.BAS file.

### Appendix B The Visual Basic How-To Disk

This appendix details the structure and contents of the bundled disk. It lists the directories, subdirectories, and each file.

### What's on the Disk

The disk bundled with *Visual Basic How-To* includes every form, module, control, icon, bitmap, and sound detailed in these pages. All of these files are debugged and ready to run. The disk also includes many powerful add-ons to energize your Visual Basic programs. You'll find the Fractal DLL mentioned in Chapter 9 and the WINAPI.TXT file mentioned throughout the book and detailed in Appendix A. We have also provided a number of demonstration third-party custom controls so you can create every project described in Chapter 8. You'll find add-ons to the Visual Basic Toolbox from MicroHelp, Crescent Software, Sheridan Software, and Waite Group Software. These include some very powerful controls to add Sound Blaster and MIDI-compatible sounds to your programs, gorgeous 3-D buttons, and much more. All told, you'll find over a megabyte of Visual Basic code and add-ons on this disk. Appendix B details the structure and contents of the disk.

### How to Install the Bundled Disk

As shown in Appendix B, the bundled disk is organized by chapter and by numbered How-To. So if you would like to run the project created in How-To 2.2, Size a form's controls automatically, you would navigate to the directory called Chapter 2, and then to the subdirectory called 2.2. Visual Basic links files by looking for the file name on a certain level of directory.

This means that a form may be looking within the same subdirectory for the files it needs, or to the directory a level or two above it. Therefore, when you copy the contents of the floppy to your hard disk, it's very important that the hierarchy of files remains the same as it is organized on the floppy disk. You will notice, for instance, that there is a file called VBHOWTO.BAS within the root directory of the bundled disk. Every *Visual Basic How-To* project that calls that .BAS file has been coded to look two directory levels up for it. Therefore, you will need to use the DOS XCOPY command to create a mirror image of the companion disk on your hard disk.

You will need a hard disk with 1.5 megabytes free to install all of the files on the bundled disk. You will also need a 3.5" drive to read the bundled disk. In the following directions, we will assume that your PC is configured so that your hard disk is the C: drive and your 3.5" floppy drive is labeled B:. Substitute the correct parameters for your machine, for instance you may have a partitioned hard drive and want to copy these files to drive D:, or your 3.5" drive may be drive A:.

Use the Windows File Manager or DOS to create a new directory at the root directory of your hard disk to hold the *Visual Basic How-To* files. We suggest calling the new directory VBHT, but you may name it anything that conforms to directory naming parameters.

To copy the files, you must use the DOS XCOPY command. XCOPY duplicates the directory and subdirectory structure of the floppy disk on your target disk. If you are running Windows, you'll need to switch to the DOS prompt. Make sure that your command prompt shows the disk on which the files are to be copied. For instance, if you are installing the files to drive C:, the DOS prompt should read:

```
C:\>
```

At the prompt type:

**xcopy b: \VBHT /s** (ENTER) (unless there is no ENTER key cap then use RETURN)

Note that b: is the floppy disk drive, \VBHT is the hard drive directory to which you are copying the contents of the floppy disk, and the /s switch means copy all the subdirectories. You may need to change the disk and directory parameters to conform to your particular setup.

You will see the copy process reported on your monitor, and after it's done you will see a message that says

```
265 files copied
```

(Note that this number reflects the number of files at press time, it may vary slightly for the final disk, for example if we add any README files or last-minute goodies.)

After the process is completed, type DIR to verify that the directories, subdirectories, and files have been copied to your hard disk.

### Moving DLL Files

There are a number of Data Link Library (DLL) files on the disk. In order for these files to be found by Windows, they must be moved into the Windows or Windows System directory after installation of the *Visual Basic How-To* disk. We have placed these DLLs in chapter directories, rather than in numbered subdirectories, so they can be easily located and moved.

### Navigational Notes

All files have been tested so that they run from the *Visual Basic How-To* disk in the B:\ drive. If you use another drive, or copy the files to another disk, you may have to re-link a few of the projects for them to run, and change any hard-coded paths. This is especially true for projects that use the VBHOWTO.BAS file (located in the root directory of the floppy disk) or those that call FILEDLG.FRM. If, when running certain projects, you get a PATH NOT FOUND: message, click the OK button. Then go to Visual Basic's File menu and select the Add File… option. Point to the file in its new location, and double-click. Remember to resave the project after you've re-linked it.

Because actual pathnames will vary depending upon your hard disk setup, we have intentionally avoided providing pathnames in each How-To when we tell you to run a project. When you open a project from Visual Basic you will have to navigate to the subdirectory that holds its files.

If you've exactly followed the installation instructions above, after you select Open Project… from Visual Basic's menu, you will have to select the VBHT directory from the Open Project dialog box, then select the Chapter subdirectory (for instance [CHAPTER1]) and then select the subdirectory for the How-To (for instance [1.1]). The .MAK file will be shown under Files; and you can double-click on it.

### Program Note

We have used the <= character to indicate program lines that "overflow" onto more than one line in this book. The overflow character means that you should continue to type that line on one Visual Basic line. Do not type the <= symbol or a carriage return. You'll notice that when native Visual Basic lines overflow, the second and any subsequent lines are indented in this book. However, the overflow from Windows API declaration lines has not been indented because these lines are traditionally very long.

## How to Order Custom Controls

The back of this book includes four ads and order forms for obtaining the commercial versions of the custom controls discussed in Chapter 8 and packaged on the bundled disk. Descriptions, prices, and ordering information can be found on those pages.

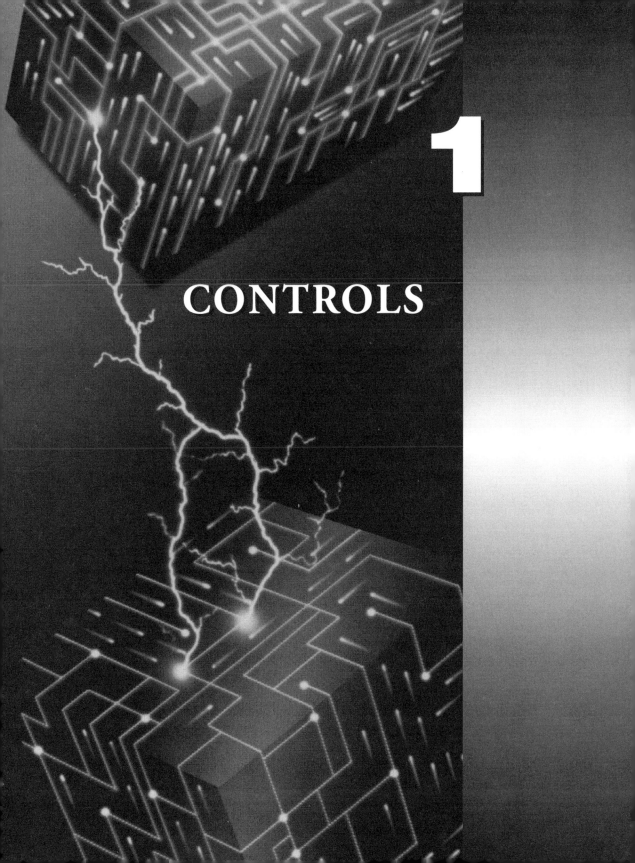

# 1

# CONTROLS

# 1

This chapter, Controls, reveals little-known secrets of Visual Basic controls by using several powerful Windows APIs. A firm footing is provided in SendMessage, one of the most powerful APIs which allows you to exploit many control properties not found in Visual Basic. You'll learn how to make a custom check box that uses real checks instead of little Xs, how to add controls at run time, and how to make a file dialog box using APIs. A powerful API-based text editor will be created that allows cut, copy, and paste to the clipboard, as well as a "searching" list box using APIs. There is a How-

To that shows how to make a button with continuous events. Another shows how to set up old-fashioned file dialog boxes that have the directories listed together with the files.

## Windows APIs Covered

| | | |
|---|---|---|
| ControlhWnd | GetModuleHandle | SendMessage |
| GetFocus | GetWindow | SetWindow |
| GetModule Usage | PutFocus | SetWindowText |

**1.1    Make a custom check box**

You'll begin by learning how to make an Option check box show a real check mark when it's clicked, not just a simple "x." This simple technique can be used to allow any bit-mapped symbol to be used in a check box and uses no APIs.

**1.2    Add controls at run time**

Often you don't know how many of a certain control to put on your form until the program has been run. You'll see how to do this using control arrays.

**1.3    Set up a drive-directory-file list box combination**

**1.4    Quickly send a Windows message to a control**

To fully use Windows APIs with Visual Basic's controls, you need to send messages to the controls. This How-To shows how to use the powerful SendMessage API, which is used in many projects in this book.

**1.5    Quickly clear a list box**

You'll use the SendMessage API described in the previous How-To to make a list box clearing procedure that is much faster than using Visual Basic's RemoveItem method.

**1.6    Make a file dialog box using APIs**

Every program has to open and close files and every program must, therefore, present a File Open and File Save dialog box that lets the user navigate the file system, check for errors, bad file names, and so on. These How-Tos include the pure Visual Basic way to do this, and a more sophisticated method that uses Windows APIs. The API approach gives you greater control over the contents of the files such as letting you see invisible files.

**1.7     Make a powerful text editor using APIs**
The Microsoft manuals include a Text Editor application written in pure Visual Basic. Unfortunately the code is long and complicated, and spread across 3 chapters. This How-To shows how to make a MiniEditor that supports cut, copy, and paste, and a single level of Undo. It uses the SendMessage API to manipulate all the controls on the form, as well as the cursor position in the list box containing the edited text. You'll learn how to use the handles property of a control. A simple DLL is included on the distribution disk that lets you get the handle of any Visual Basic control.

**1.8     Create an old-style file dialog box**
The "new" way to create file dialog boxes in Windows put directory and drive names in different list boxes. In old Windows (pre 3.0) drives were indicated by the letters [-c-], and scrolled just like directory names. The periods (..) were also shown in the scrolling list box. Visual Basic provides the directory, file, and drive controls and expects you to use all three. If you prefer to give users a classic combo directory/drive dialog box, you'll want this How-To.

**1.9     Create multiple entries in the Task List**
Running multiple instances of your Visual Basic application is a great idea and with multiprocessing gives you a nice way to have several tools running at the same time. However Visual Basic will not give you multiple entires in Windows Task List dialog, making it difficult to maneuver in this environment. This API shows how there is a hidden owner window in Visual Basic, and how this owner window can be manipulated to give the right caption for the Task List.

**1.10    Make a simple "searching" list box**
**1.11    Make a "searching" list box using APIs**
Automatic searching of a list box means that a scrolling list zeros in on the matching line as the user types the name. Windows' Help feature works this way, and so do many file dialog boxes that contain lists to select from. These two How-Tos show you how to create this effect in both pure Visual Basic and then using Windows APIs.

**1.12    Make a button with continuous events**
This How-To shows the technique for making a button that will cause a process to continue all the while the mouse button is pressed. The technique for using DoEvents to allow other Windows processes to run and to avoid hogging processing time is revealed.

**1.1    How do I...**

# Make a custom check box?

Complexity: Easy

### Problem

Visual Basic "check boxes" aren't really check boxes; they're X boxes. How can I make a custom check box control where there is a real check mark (✓) in the box?

### Technique

It is possible to create a check box with a real check mark (✓) using Visual Basic's own power. Flipping through a control array of picture boxes will simulate the properties of a check box, with the added ability of being able to use any bitmap for the checked, unchecked, and pressed versions of the box.

None of the icons in Visual Basic's icon library gives the right "look" for the check box, so we provided some on the disk that accompanies this book. Or you can draw your own check box bitmap using the IconWorks sample application provided with Visual Basic.

### Steps

Open and run CUSTOM.MAK. You can click on the check box and observe the three different states of the check box: checked, unchecked, and in the process of being pressed down.

1. Create a new project called CUSTOM.MAK. Create a new form with the objects and properties listed in Table 1-1 and save it as CUSTOM.FRM.

| Object | Property | Setting |
|---|---|---|
| Form | Caption | Custom check box |
| | FormName | CustomCheckbox |
| | BackColor | &HC0C0C0 |
| Label | Caption | Save changes |
| | CtlName | Label1 |
| Picture box | AutoRedraw | False |
| | AutoSize | True |
| | CtlName | Checked |
| | Index | 0 |
| | Picture | CHECKOFF.BMP |
| | Visible | False |

| Picture box | AutoRedraw | False |
| | AutoSize | True |
| | CtlName | Checked |
| | Index | 1 |
| | Picture | CHECKON.BMP |
| | Visible | True |
| Picture box | AutoRedraw | False |
| | AutoSize | True |
| | CtlName | Checked |
| | Index | 2 |
| | Picture | CHECKPRS.BMP |
| | Visible | False |

**Table 1-1** Custom project form's objects and properties

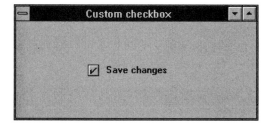

**Figure 1-1** The Custom form in action

The form should look like Figure 1-1 when you're finished creating it. Note how the three picture boxes overlap and appear as one. They only differ by their index number and the bitmap they contain. Figures 1-2, 1-3, and 1-4 show an enlargement of the three bitmaps.

**Figure 1-2**

The "Off" bitmap

**Figure 1-3**

The "On" bitmap

**Figure 1-4**

The "Pressed" bitmap

2. Place the following code in the Click event of any one of the picture boxes. Because the pictures are part of a control array, Visual Basic runs this code in the Checked_Click event subroutine when any of the picture boxes is clicked. (The Index parameter Visual Basic passes will be the Index property of the picture box that is visible. Thus if Index is nonzero, it means the visible picture box is the "checked" picture box so the "unchecked" picture box should become visible.) Otherwise, if Index is zero, it's the "unchecked" picture box that is visible and the "checked" picture box should become visible.

```
Sub Checked_Click (Index As Integer)
   If Index Then
      Checked(0).Visible = -1
      Checked(1).Visible = 0
      Checked(2).Visible = 0
      Print "Changes will not be saved!"
   Else
      Checked(0).Visible = 0
      Checked(1).Visible = -1
      Checked(2).Visible = 0
      Print "Changes will be saved when you exit."
   End If
End Sub
```

3. The following code in the Checked_MouseDown event subroutine causes the "pressed" version of the check box to be displayed while the mouse button is held down.

```
Sub Checked_MouseDown (Index As Integer, Button As Integer, Shift As ⇐
   Integer, X As Single, Y As Single)
   Checked(0).Visible = 0
   Checked(1).Visible = 0
   Checked(2).Visible = -1
End Sub
```

4. Visual Basic runs the following code in the Checked_MouseUp event subroutine when the mouse button is released. The code simply calls the Click event subroutine so the proper picture box is made visible and the "pressed" version is made invisible.

```
Sub Checked_MouseUp (Index As Integer, Button As Integer, Shift As ⇐
   Integer, X As Single, Y As Single)
   Checked_Click (Index)
End Sub
```

**How It Works**

Control arrays come to the rescue. Control arrays have a variety of uses, they often solve problems they were not intented to solve. By making the three possible states of a check box (checked, unchecked, and pressed) elements of a control array, we avoid having to write separate routines for each of the possible states.

Normally, Visual Basic Click events occur when the mouse button is pressed and then released. Because controls must often respond when the mouse button is pressed, Visual Basic provides the MouseDown event. Checked_MouseDown intercepts these mouse button presses and makes only the pressed version of the check box visible. Then, when the mouse button is released, Visual Basic runs Checked_MouseUp, which simply calls Checked_Click to display the proper check box bitmap.

If there are MouseDown or MouseUp event subroutines for a control, they "swallow" up the Click event. Visual Basic will not automatically run the Click event subroutine for that control when the mouse button is released, so that's what Checked_MouseUp does.

Checked_Click checks the Index of the picture box that was clicked, and makes the opposite version the only picture box visible. For this example, we only print a message on the form. In a real application, you might set a global variable to True if the checked picture box is made visible or False if the unchecked picture box is made visible.

### Comment

If you don't want to provide a pressed version of the check box, simply delete the picture box whose Index property is 2 and delete the Checked_MouseDown and Checked_MouseUp event subroutines. Visual Basic will invoke the Checked_Click event subroutine when the mouse button is pressed and released over the picture box.

---

**1.2    How do I...**

# Add controls at run time?

Complexity: Easy

### Problem

When I design forms, I don't always know how many controls will be needed at run time. How can I add or delete controls while an application is running?

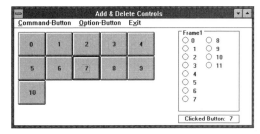

**Figure 1-5** The Addctl form at run time

### Technique

Visual Basic's control arrays are provided for just this type of situation. When a control is declared to be an object of a control array, you can create as many additional copies of that control as needed under program control.

### Steps

Open and run ADDCTL.MAK. Use the Command-Button menu to create or delete Command1 controls. The Option-Button menu adds and deletes Option1 controls. Figure 1-5 shows the form with multiple new controls added. Clicking on any of the individual command buttons or option buttons will identify the selected control in the label.

The Addctl project may be created by entering objects and code as detailed in the following steps.

1. Create a new project called ADDCTL.MAK. Create a new form with the objects and properties shown in Table 1-2 and save it as ADDCTL.FRM. Make sure that the frame is placed on the right-hand side of the form as displayed in Figure 1-5.

| Object | Property | Setting |
|---|---|---|
| Form | FormName | Addctl |
| | Caption | Add and Delete Controls |
| Command button | CtlName | Command1 |
| | Caption | 0 |
| | Index | 0 |
| | Height | 735 |
| | Width | 855 |
| Frame | Ctlname | Frame1 |
| Label | Ctlname | Label1 |
| | Alignment | 2 - Center |
| Option button | CtlName | Option1 |
| | Caption | 0 |
| | Index | 0 |
| | Height | 255 |
| | Width | 735 |

**Table 1-2** Addctl project form's objects and properties

2. Using the Menu Design windows, create a menu for the form with the values in Table 1-3.

| Caption | CtlName | Index | Accelerator |
|---|---|---|---|
| &Command-Button | CB | | |
| – – – –&Add | MenuCmdButton | 0 | Ctrl+A |
| – – – –&Delete | MenuCmdButton | 1 | Ctrl+D |
| &Option-Button | OB | | |
| – – – –&Add | MenuOptButton | 0 | Shift+F1 |
| – – – –&Delete | MenuOptButton | 1 | Shift+F2 |
| E&xit | Quit | | |

**Table 1-3** Addctl menu values

3. Place the following code in the MenuCmdButton_Click event subroutine. This subroutine adds a new command button control to the form or deletes the last one added, depending on the AddDelete parameter.

```
Sub MenuCmdButton_Click (AddDelete As Integer)
Static MaxIndex As Integer              ' # of Command Buttons
Dim CTop As Integer, CWidth As Integer, Cleft As Integer

' AddDelete = 1, Delete the last Command button.
' When adding a new Command button, place to right of previous one.
' If it would overlap frame control, place it at beginning of
'      next line.
' Finally, make control visible; new controls are not visible by default.
   If AddDelete = 1 Then
      If MaxIndex = 0 Then
         MsgBox "Unable to Delete Original Control", 48
         Exit Sub
      End If
'      -----------
      Unload Command1(MaxIndex)      ' Remove the control
'      -----------
      MaxIndex = MaxIndex - 1
   Else
      MaxIndex = MaxIndex + 1
'      -----------
      Load Command1(MaxIndex)        ' Add the control
'      -----------
      CTop = Command1(MaxIndex - 1).Top
      CWidth = Command1(MaxIndex).Width
      Cleft = Command1(MaxIndex - 1).Left + CWidth
      If Cleft + CWidth > Frame1.Left Then
         Cleft = Command1(0).Left
         CTop = CTop + Command1(MaxIndex).Height
      End If
      Command1(MaxIndex).Top = CTop
      Command1(MaxIndex).Left = Cleft
      Command1(MaxIndex).Caption = Str$(MaxIndex)
      Command1(MaxIndex).Visible = -1
   End If
End Sub
```

4. Place the following code in the MenuOptButton_Click event subroutine. This subroutine adds or removes option buttons from Frame1.

```
Sub MenuOptButton_Click (AddDelete As Integer)
Static MaxIndex As Integer
Dim CHeight As Integer, CTop As Integer, CWidth As Integer, ⇐
   Cleft As Integer

' AddDelete = 1, Delete last option button added.
' When adding new option button, place directly below previous one.
' If new button overlaps bottom edge of frame, start a new column.
' Finally, make button visible; new controls are not initially visible.
   If AddDelete = 1 Then
```

```
      If MaxIndex = 0 Then
          MsgBox "Unable to Delete Original Control", 48
          Exit Sub
      End If
'     ------------
      Unload Option1(MaxIndex)          ' Remove control
'     ------------
      MaxIndex = MaxIndex - 1
   Else
      MaxIndex = MaxIndex + 1
'     ------------
      Load Option1(MaxIndex)            ' Add control
'     ------------
      CHeight = Option1(MaxIndex).Height
      CTop = Option1(MaxIndex - 1).Top + CHeight
      CWidth = Option1(MaxIndex).Width
      Cleft = Option1(MaxIndex - 1).Left
      If CTop + CHeight >= Frame1.Height Then
          Cleft = Cleft + CWidth
          CTop = Option1(0).Top
      End If
      Option1(MaxIndex).Top = CTop
      Option1(MaxIndex).Left = Cleft
      Option1(MaxIndex).Caption = Str$(MaxIndex)
      Option1(MaxIndex).Visible = -1
   End If
End Sub
```

5. Place the following code in the Command1_Click event subroutine. Whenever any of the command buttons on the form is clicked, this subroutine will identify which button was selected in the label control.

```
Sub Command1_Click (Index As Integer)
   Label1.Caption = "Clicked Button: " + Str$(Index)
End Sub
```

6. Place the following code in the Option1_Click event subroutine. Whenever any of the option buttons on the form is selected, this subroutine will identify which button was selected in the label control.

```
Sub Option1_Click (Index As Integer)
   Label1.Caption = "Clicked Option:" + Str$(Index)
End Sub
```

7. Place the following code in the Quit_Click menu event. It allows for a graceful exit from the application.

```
Sub Quit_Click ()
   End              ' Exit the Application
End Sub
```

## How It Works

Control arrays are an intrinsic part of Visual Basic and form the basis for a number of features, including the ability to dynamically add controls at run time. A single control is turned into a control array at design time by setting its Index property. In this project we started with an Index of zero for both control arrays.

New controls are added to an array at run time using the Load CtlName(Index) statement. The CtlName must previously exist as a control array on the form, and the Index value must not already be in use for that CtlName. When a new control is added at run time, its Visible property, by default, is turned off, although its position and size will match that of the original control.

In the MenuCmdButton_Click event subroutine, the AddDelete flag indicates whether to add a new control or to delete the previous one. The static variable MaxIndex keeps track of the number of command buttons previously added. Because it is a static variable, MaxIndex retains its value between subroutine calls. When a new control is added, we check whether it can be positioned to the left of Frame1. If it can't, the new control is positioned below the first control of the previous line.

Deleting a control is handled by the Unload CtlName(Index) statement and by reducing the MaxIndex counter.

The MenuOptButton_Click event subroutine is used to add or remove option buttons. The same variable, MaxIndex, is used here as well to keep track of the number of option buttons. Because MaxIndex is declared at the subroutine level, each subroutine keeps its own, nonshared copy, of the variable. Although the command buttons were added from left to right, we have chosen to add the option buttons from top to bottom. This was done to illustrate the ease of positioning an added control.

The two event subroutines, Command1_Click and Option1_Click, demonstrate how Visual Basic lets you know which control in an array the user selected. The Index parameter is used to differentiate each of the control array elements from the others.

## Comment

This project demonstrates how to add at run time just two of Visual Basic's controls, command buttons and option buttons. However, any of the standard controls can be incorporated into a control array— up to a limit of 255 controls per form. Forms, on the other hand, do not have an Index property and cannot be made into a control array.

Note that when a control is already contained within a container, such as the Option1 control is in this example, controls added to that control array will also be positioned in the same container.

**1.3    How do I...**

# Set up a drive-directory-file list box combination?

Complexity: Easy

**Problem**

I'd like to incorporate a file selection box so that users can choose and open up a file to work with. How do I go about getting the various controls involved to work together for this purpose?

**Technique**

The basic functionality for a file selection setup is built into the drive, directory, and file list box objects. All we need to do is enter a little code in the appropriate places to let the individual members of this trio communicate with each other as the user makes changes, and we're up and running! Additionally, we'll add a pattern string so the user can enter the type of files that will be displayed. We'll also include some error checking, so the program won't crash if a user forgets to insert a floppy disk in a drive before selecting it in the drive combo box.

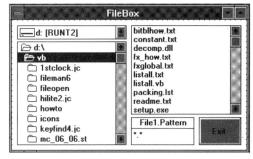

**Figure 1-6** The FileBox project form and its controls at design time

**Steps**

Open and run FILEBOX.MAK. The FileBox project can be created by performing the following steps.

1. Create a new project called FILE-BOX.MAK. Create a new form with the controls shown in Figure 1-6, then set all the properties as listed in Table 1-4. Any properties not specifically mentioned should be left set to their default values. Save it as FILEBOX.FRM.

| Object | Property | Setting |
|---|---|---|
| Form | FormName | MainForm |
| | Caption | FileBox |
| Drive list box | All Properties | All Defaults |
| Directory list box | All Properties | All Defaults |

| File list box | All Properties | All Defaults |
|---|---|---|
| Label | BorderStyle | 1 - Fixed Single |
| | Caption | File1.Pattern |
| Text box | BorderStyle | 1 - Fixed Single |
| | Text | *.* |
| Command button | CtlName | ExitDemo |
| | Caption | Exit |

**Table 1-4** FileBox project form's objects and properties

When they are first dragged onto a form at design time, the contents of drive, directory, and file list boxes reflect the current directory, as would be returned by CurDir$. Thus, the files and directories shown in Figure 1-6 reflect a sample current directory.

2. Place the following code in the Drive1_Change event procedure.

```
Sub Drive1_Change ()
    On Error GoTo Drive1Error
    Dir1.path = Drive1.Drive
Exit Sub                         'This is normal exit from subroutine
Drive1Error:                     'End up here if an error occurs
    Beep
    If Err = 68 Or Err = 71 Then
        Msg$ = "Error #" + Str$(Err) + "  No Floppy in the Drive!"
        MsgBox Msg$, 48
    Else
        Msg$ = "Error #" + Str$(Err)
    End If
    Resume
End Sub
```

3. Place the following code in the Dir1_Change event procedure.

```
Sub Dir1_Change ()
    File1.path = Dir1.path
End Sub
```

4. Place the following code in the Text1_KeyDown event procedure.

```
Sub Text1_KeyDown (KeyCode As Integer, Shift As Integer)
    If KeyCode = 13 Then          'If Enter key is pressed
        File1.Pattern = Text1.Text
    End If
End Sub
```

5. Place the following code in the ExitDemo_Click event procedure.

```
Sub ExitDemo_Click ()
    End
End Sub
```

## How It Works

As mentioned previously, the basic functionality for the file-related list boxes is built in. You don't have to write code to have the drive combo box change to a new drive, to have a directory list box update its display when you double-click on a different directory folder, or to have a file list box highlight the file you click on within its borders. These actions occur automatically, courtesy of Visual Basic. The drive-directory-file list box setup can be thought of as having a hierarchical structure, with the drive combo box located on the highest level, the directory list box on the middle level, and the file list box on the lowest level. (Refer to Figure 1-7.)

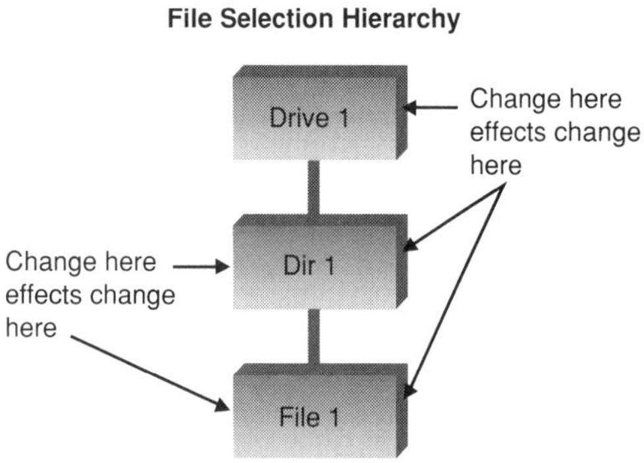

**File Selection Hierarchy**

**Figure 1-7** The file selection list box hierarchy

The small amount of code that must be entered in various event procedures enables the trio of list boxes to stay "in synch" as the user makes changes. A change made on one level generates a Change event for any levels below it. For example, should a user select a different drive in the drive1 combo list box at run time, this will set in motion an updating process courtesy of the Change event procedures for the Drive1combo box and Dir1 list box. When the drive is changed, the path for Dir1 is changed by code in the Drive1_Change event procedure. This action generates a Change event for Dir1, so the Dir1_Change event procedure is called, where code is located to update the path for File1. When a user selects a new directory in Dir1 by double-clicking on it, a Change event is generated for Dir1, so the code in the Dir1_Change event procedure updates the path for File1.

## Comments

If at run time a user selects a floppy drive (such as drive A or B) from the Drive1 combo box, and there is no floppy disk in the drive, the program simply terminates execution (crashes) at that point! By including the error-checking code in the Drive1_Change event procedure, this common pitfall is avoided. With the error-checking code in place, the program displays a dialogue box and does not crash. The user is alerted that there is no floppy disk in the drive and can then insert a disk and click the OK button in the dialogue box to continue executing the application.

The standard method of implementing error-checking code in a procedure is to use the "On Error GoTo" statement (located at the beginning of the procedure, after any variable or constant declarations), with the name of a block of code specifically designed to handle errors. The error-handling code comes at the end of the procedure, after an Exit Sub statement, and is not executed unless an error is generated. If an error is generated and the error-checking code is executed, the "Resume" statement will return execution to the statement in the code that generated the error.

The text box is included in the demo for the purpose of allowing a user to change the Pattern property for the File1 list box. (The Pattern property determines the type of files displayed in a file list box.) When a user types a file specification (which, like the value we entered for Text1.Text at design time, can include DOS wildcards) into the text box and presses Enter while the text box has the focus, the Pattern property of File1 will be set to the text in the text box.

When a user selects Open from the File menu of a Windows application, it is common for the elements of the file selection dialog (drive, directory, and file list boxes, and possibly a Pattern selector) to be displayed on their own form. This demo is set up that way and the code located in the various event procedures takes care of navigating the file system to get a user to a file. Once there a file listed in the file list box could be selected by double-clicking on it. Additional code located in the File1_DblClick event procedure would be needed to actually open and process the file.

```
Sub File1_DblClick ()
    'Code here for application to open and deal with selected file!
End Sub
```

## Quickly send a Windows message to a control?

Complexity: Advanced

### Problem

I'm excited about all the different things you can do with Windows "messages,"—the ones described in the WINDOWS.H file and Microsoft API books. You can do things with these messages that are not available in the Visual Basic environment. Unfortunately there is not a standard subroutine to allow sending custom messages to my controls.

## Technique

Because Visual Basic supports passing a control to subroutines and functions, it is very easy to send a message to a control.

We'll create a function named SendMessageToControl that works just like the API function SendMessage, except that instead of a window handle as the first argument, it accepts a control. We'll use Visual Basic's SetFocus to let the API know which control we want to send a message to.

## Steps

To use the SendMessageToControl function, just add the module VBHOWTO.BAS to any project using Visual Basic's File menu's Add a File option.

1. Create a new module (using the New Module option on the File menu) and add a new function called SendMessageToControl (using the Code menu's New Procedure choice and Alt+F to select Function). Save it as VBHOWTO.BAS. You'll be adding more general functions and subroutine to this module throughout the book.

2. Place the following code in the Declare section of the VBHOWTO.BAS module to declare the GetFocus and SendMessage API functions.

```
Declare Function GetFocusLib "User" () As Integer

Declare Function SendMessageLib "User" (BuyVal hWnd%, ByVal wMsg%, ByVal ⇐
wParam%, ByVal 1Param&) As Integer
```

3. Add the following code to the SendMessageToControl function.

```
Function SendMessageToControl (Ctl As Control, wMsg%, wParam%, lParam&)
    Dim CtlHWnd As Integer

    ' Switch to the control we'll be sending the message to.
    Ctl.SetFocus

    ' Get its handle.
    CtlHWnd = GetFocus()

    ' Send the message to the control.
    I = SendMessage(CtlHWnd, wMsg%, wParam%, lParam&)
End Function
```

## How It Works

SendMessageToControl simply incorporates three steps (SetFocus, GetFocus, and SendMessage) into one.

Note the definition of the Ctl argument. Visual Basic lets subroutines and functions accept a control as an argument by using the "As Control" type. You can pass any kind of control to SendMessageToControl, and the statement

```
Ctl.SetFocus
```

will work just as if you'd used the actual CtlName of the control. This is a great time-saver!

### Comment

Because of the way Visual Basic creates combo boxes, SendMessage-ToControl won't work with them. The problem is not with SendMessage-ToControl itself, but the SetFocus method. After a SetFocus to a combo box, the GetFocus API function won't return a window handle that can accept combo box messages.

---

**1.5 How do I...**

## Quickly clear a list box?

Complexity: Advanced

### Problem

Using Visual Basic's RemoveItem method for clearing a list box is slow. Is there a simple and faster way to do this?

### Technique

Yes, we can use the SendMessageToConrol function to do this. See How-To 1.4 Quickly send a Windows message to a control, for details on how SendMessage works.

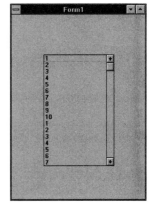

### Steps

Open and run CLEARAL2.MAK. The list box in the form initially loads up to 10 items. If you click once on the form, another 10 items are added to the list box. If you double-click on the form, all the items in the list box are quickly removed using one API call. See Figure 1-8.

**Figure 1-8** The ClearAl2 form in action

1. Create a new project called CLEARAL2.MAK. Create a form with the objects and properties listed in Table 1-5 and save it as CLEARAL2.FRM.

| Object | Property | Setting |
|---|---|---|
| Form | Caption | Form1 |
| | BackColor | &H00C0C0C0& |
| List box | CtlName | List1 |

**Table 1-5** ClearAl2 project form's objects and properties

2. Add the VBHOWTO.BAS module to your project using Visual Basic's File Menu's Add File command. (We've created this module in previous How-To 1.4 Quickly send a Windows message to a control.)Then add the following code to the VBHOWTO.BAS module.

```
Sub ClearListBox (AListBox As Control)
    ' Make sure we're working with a List Box.
    If TypeOf AListBox Is ListBox Then
        ' if so, send the LB_RESETCONTENT message to clear
        I = SendMessageToControl(AListBox, LB_RESETCONTENT, 0, 0)
    End If
End Sub
```

3. Put the following code in the Form_Click event subroutine. This code inserts 10 new items into the list box whenever the form is clicked.

```
Sub Form_Click ()
    For i = 1 To 10
        List1.AddItem Format$(i)   'Put something into List Box.
    Next
End Sub
```

4. Put the following code in the Form_DblClick event subroutine. This code calls the ClearListBox general subroutine whenever you double-click the mouse on the form.

```
Sub Form_dblClick ()
    ClearListBox List1
End Sub
```

5. Put the following code in the Form_Load event subroutine. This code calls the Form_Click event subroutine to insert 10 items into the list box when the form is first loaded.

```
Sub Form_Load ()
    Form_Click
End Sub
```

Figure 1-9 shows the completed ClearAl2 form.

### How It Works

For details about the SendMessageToControl, see the How-To 1.4 Quickly send a Windows message to a control.

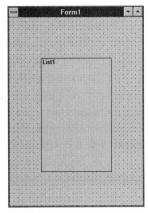

**Figure 1-9** The completed ClearAl2 form

The Windows message to remove all the items from a list box is LB_RESETCONTENT, which the WINDOWS.H file in the Windows SDK defines as WM_USER + 5. WM_USER is defined as 0x400, or &H400 in Visual Basic hexadecimal lingo, so LB_RESETCONTENT boils down to &H405.

The ClearListBox general subroutine first ensures that the parameter that was passed is a list box control. If it is, the SendMessageToControl function uses the LB_RESETCONTENT message to clear out the list box.

The Form_Click event subroutine adds 10 numbered items into the list box whenever you click on the form (outside the list box). You can click on the form as many times as you'd like.

The Form_DblClick event subroutine calls the ClearListBox general subroutine, supplying the List1 list box control as a parameter.

The Form_Load event subroutine just calls the Form_Click event subroutine to add 10 items to the list box when the form is first loaded.

### Comment

Before any control can accept Windows messages, it must be visible. Therefore, if you want to use ClearListBox (or SendMessageToControl itself) in a Form_Load event subroutine, you must first make the form visible using Visual Basic's Show method.

---

**1.6    How do I...**

# Make a file dialog box using APIs?

Complexity: Advanced

### Problem

Although there are purely Visual Basic ways to create a File Open dialog box, Windows must offer a more powerful way to do it with API calls. How can I use those API calls in my Visual Basic applications?

### Technique

The file dialog box in How-To 1.8 Create an old-style file dialog box uses hidden file and directory list boxes to automatically retrieve the file and directory information. Another way to do this uses Windows' messages.

Specifically, Windows list boxes understand a message called LB_DIR, which loads a list box with the file and directory names you specify. You can specify which files to load into the list box two ways. The first is via a wildcard pattern; (you've seen wildcards before like "*.*" at the DOS prompt.) The wildcard pattern "*.*" will load all available files. The second way to specify files to load into the list box is via a file's attributes; DOS keeps track of several bits of information about the files in a directory:

- if a file has been modified
- if a file can't be changed (the file is read-only)
- if a file isn't normally visible (the file is hidden)
- if a file is a system file (the file is part of DOS)
- if a file is actually a directory

The LB_DIR message lets you load a list box with files with any, or with all of these attributes. The LB_DIR message also lets you load a list box with files that have none of those attributes (also called "normal" files).

We can use the LB_DIR message to create a dialog box that acts just like the dialog boxes of other Windows applications, is just as fast, and does things that in pure Visual Basic would take a lot more code.

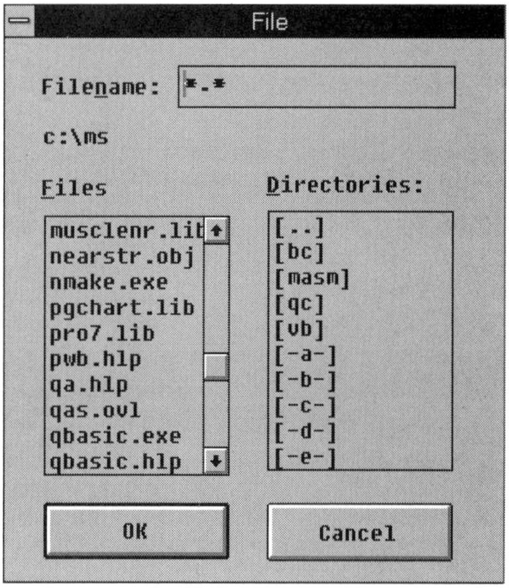

### Steps

Open and run FILEDLG2.MAK. The file dialog box will open up with files in the current directory in the list box on the left, and all the subdirectories, directories, and drives, in the list box on the right. You can negotiate between directories by double-clicking on a directory name in the right-hand list box. The "[..]" entry backs up to the previous directory. You can also get a list of files on a floppy disk by double-clicking on a drive letter like "[-a-]." Figure 1-10 shows a sample of this style file dialog box.

**Figure 1-10** The FileDlg2 form in action

1. Create a new project called FILEDLG2.MAK. Add the VBHOWTO.BAS module using Visual Basic's Add File menu command (created in How-Tos 1.4 and 1.5). This module contains several general functions that the file dialog box form uses.

2. Create a new form with the controls listed in Table 1-6 and save it as FILEDL.G2.FRM. Put the following code in the Declarations section of the form. This code will give the form's subroutines and functions access to the SendMessage API function.

```
Declare Function SendMessage Lib "User" (ByVal hWnd%, ByVal wMsg%, ByVal⇐
wParam%, ByVal lParam$) As Integer

Const WM_USER = &H400
Const LB_DIR = WM_USER + 14
```

| Object | Property | Setting |
|---|---|---|
| Form | Caption | File |
| | FormName | FileDlg |
| | MaxButton | False |
| | MinButton | False |
| | BackColor | &H00C0C0C0& |
| Label | Alignment | 1 - Right Justify |
| | Caption | File&name: |
| | CtlName | Label1 |
| Text box | CtlName | FileEdit |
| | MultiLine | False |
| | ScrollBars | 0 - None |
| | TabStop | True |
| | Text | *.* |
| Label | Alignment | 0 - Left Justify |
| | Caption | c:\ |
| | CtlName | DirLabel |
| Label | Alignment | 0 - Left Justify |
| | Caption | &Files: |
| | CtlName | Label2 |
| List box | CtlName | FileList |
| | Sorted | True |
| | TabStop | True |
| Label | Alignment | 0 - Left Justify |
| | Caption | &Directories: |
| | CtlName | Label3 |

*Table 1-6. continued*

| Object | Property | Setting |
|---|---|---|
| List box | CtlName | DirList |
| | Sorted | True |
| | TabStop | True |
| Command button | Caption | Ok |
| | CtlName | Ok |
| | Default | True |
| | TabStop | True |
| Command button | Caption | Cancel |
| | CtlName | Cancel |
| | Cancel | True |
| | TabStop | True |

**Table 1-6** FileDlg2 project form's objects and properties

3. Put the following code in the UpdateListBoxes general subroutine. The form calls UpdateListBoxes whenever something has changed and the list boxes need to be updated.

```
Sub Update_List_Boxes ()
   Dim CtlHWnd As Integer

   ' Update current directory label.
   DirLabel.Caption = LCase$(CurDir$)

   ' Clear out the file and directory list boxes.
   ClearListBox FileList
   ClearListBox DirList

   ' Switch to the file list box.
   FileList.SetFocus

   ' Get its handle.
   CtlHWnd = GetFocus()

   ' Send the message to the control.
   PathPattern$ = FileEdit.Text
   I = SendMessage(CtlHWnd, LB_DIR, 0, PathPattern$)


   ' Switch to the directory list box.
   DirList.SetFocus
```

```
      ' Get its handle.
      CtlHWnd = GetFocus()

      ' Send the message to the control.
      ' &HC010 = subdirectories + drives only
      I = SendMessage(CtlHWnd, LB_DIR, &HC010, "*.*")

      ' Switch back to the text box.
      FileEdit.SetFocus
End Sub
```

4. Put the following code in the Cancel_Click event subroutine. This code sets the filename text box to the null string and hides the file dialog box.

```
Sub Cancel_Click ()
      ' If we select Cancel, we can hide the dialog, because
      ' we don't need it anymore.
      FileEdit.Text = ""
      FileDlg.Hide
End Sub
```

5. Put the following code in the DirList_DblClick event subroutine. This code changes directories and switches drives depending on the item clicked. There's an error routine in case there's no disk in a floppy drive.

```
Sub DirList_DblClick ()
      Const MB_RETRYANDCANCEL = 5
      Const MB_ICONEXCLAMATION = 48

      On Local Error GoTo UhOh

      ' When you double-click on a directory or drive entry,
      ' check whether the selected item is a drive; if so,
      ' change the current drive.
      If Left$(DirList.Text, 2) = "[-" And Len(DirList.Text) = 5 Then
         oldDir$ = CurDir$
         ChDrive Mid$(DirList.Text, 3, 1)
         A$ = CurDir$     ' Check whether the disk is ready;
      ' otherwise, change the current directory.
      Else
         ChDir Mid$(DirList.Text, 2, Len(DirList.Text) - 2)
      End If

      On Local Error GoTo 0

      Update_List_Boxes
      Exit Sub

UhOh:
      If MsgBox("Unable to switch to drive " + Mid$(DirList.Text, 3, 1) + ⇐
         ":", MB_RETRYANDCANCEL + MB_ICONEXCLAMATION, "Visual Basic - ⇐
         FileDlg") = 2
```

```
Then
   ' If we press Cancel, go back to the previous drive.
         ChDrive Left$(oldDir$, 1)
   End If

   Resume
End Sub
```

6. Put the following code in the FileList_Click event subroutine. This code puts the filename the user clicked on into the text box.

```
Sub FileList_Click ()
   ' Put the selected filename into the Text Box.
   FileEdit.Text = FileList.Text
End Sub
```

7. Put the following code in the FileList_DblClick event subroutine. This code puts the filename the user clicked on in the text box and hides the file dialog box.

```
Sub FileList_DblClick ()
   ' When we double-click on a filename in the List Box,
   ' set the Text Box to the selected filename and
   ' hide the form, because we've picked the filename.
   FileEdit.Text = FileList.Text
   FileDlg.Hide
End Sub
```

8. Put the following code in the Form_Load event subroutine. It shows the form, a requirement of the code in the Update_List_Boxes routine, which Form_Load calls next. Then it hides the form.

```
Sub Form_Load ()
   Show
   Update_List_Boxes
   Hide
End Sub
```

9. Put the following code in the Ok_Click event subroutine. This code checks the text in the text box to see whether it contains the * or ? wildcards. If it does, the Update_List_Boxes routine is called to update the list boxes. Otherwise, Ok_Click closes the dialog box, because the user picked a filename.

```
Sub OK_Click ()
   ' If there are wildcards, just update the List Boxes.
   If InStr(FileEdit.Text, "*") Or InStr(FileEdit.Text, "?") Then
      Update_List_Boxes
   Else
      ' Otherwise, there's a real filename, so we can close up shop.
      FileDlg.Hide
   End If
End Sub
```

10. Create another new form and save it as TESTFDIA.FRM. This form will call the file dialog box to test it and show how it works. There are no controls on the form, but give the form the properties listed in Table 1-7.

| Object | Property | Setting |
| --- | --- | --- |
| Form | Caption | File dialog box test |
|  | CtlName | FileDialogBoxText |

**Table 1-7**  TestFDia project form's objects and properties

11. Create a menu for the form using the Menu Design window:

| Caption | CtlName |
| --- | --- |
| &File | File |
| – – – –&Open… | FileOpen |
| – – – –E&xit | FileExit |

**Table 1-8**  TestFDia form's menu

12. Put the following code in the Declarations section of the form. This Const statement declares a constant for the Show method.

```
Const MODAL = 1
```

13. Put the following code in the FileExit_Click event subroutine. The End statement simply ends the Visual Basic application when you select the Exit menu option.

```
Sub FileExit_Click ()
    End
End Sub
```

14. Put the following code in the FileOpen_Click event subroutine. The code sets up the file dialog box and then shows it modally. Then it displays a message box showing you what you selected.

```
Sub FileOpen_Click ()
    FileDlg.FileEdit.Text = "*.*"
    FileDlg.Show MODAL

    If FileDlg.FileEdit.Text = "" Then
        MsgBox "You click the Cancel button"
    Else
        MsgBox "You selected " + FileDlg.FileEdit.Text
    End If
End Sub
```

### How It Works

The Update_List_Boxes general subroutine updates the contents of all the list boxes as the user changes directories and/or drives. Using the Clear-ListBox subroutine developed in the How-To 1.5 Quickly clear a list box, both the file and directory list boxes are emptied. Since Windows' LB_DIR message is used, the window handle of the list box must be accessed. A SetFocus method sets the focus to the file list box, and the Windows API function GetFocus() returns its window handle.

Then the SendMessage API function sends the LB_DIR message to the file list box. A zero as the wParam parameter tells Windows to load the list box with all "normal" files. (Normal files include all files with no attributes set and ones that have been modified but exclude read-only, hidden, and system files. You can study the WINAPI.TXT file on the distribution disk for the parameter constants to use for other attributes.) For the SendMessage's lParam parameter, the text from the text box is passed. (Note that you can't directly pass the Text property of the text box; although the data type of the Text property is String, Visual Basic won't let an API function change it.)

The same actions are repeated for the directory list box. The difference comes at the SendMessage API function. Instead of passing a zero as the wParam parameter, we pass &HC010, which tells Windows to load the list box with the subdirectories in the current directory and all the available drives in the system. The subdirectories are automatically enclosed in square brackets (for example, [windows]) and the drives are in the format [-x-] where x is the drive letter.

### Catching Errors

The DirList_DblClick event subroutine is executed whenever the user double-clicks on a directory name or drive letter. It catches any errors that come up (most often, an attempt to switch to a floppy drive with no disk in the drive) with an error handler. Visual Basic will invoke the error handler automatically whenever an error occurs, so we don't have to do any special error checking.

The If statement checks whether the item double-clicked starts with [-. If it does, we know that it's a drive letter and the ChDrive statement will switch to the new drive. Otherwise, it's a directory and the ChDir statement will change to the directory.

If there have been no errors so far, the

```
On Local Error GoTo 0
```

statement disables the error handler. Then a call to Update_List_Boxes updates the list boxes with the filenames and directories for the new drive or directory. Then the Exit Sub statement gets us out of the subroutine.

If some error occurred, however, Visual Basic runs the code at line label UhOh. That code assumes that the error was, in fact, a problem that occurred with switching drives. (That's almost guaranteed to be the cause.) So a message box prompts the user to either retry the operation (after the user inserts a disk in the floppy drive) or cancel it. If the user clicks the Cancel button, the ChDrive statement will switch back to the drive that was current before the user tried to switch.

The Resume statement goes back to retry the statement that caused the error. In this case, it's the

```
A$ = CurDir$    ' Check whether the disk is ready.
```

statement, which is there specifically to try to cause an error. If it succeeds, everything went well.

### Strange Form_Load Code

The code in the Form_Load event subroutine may look strange to you. First, a Show method shows the form. Then the Update_List_Boxes subroutine is called to fill in the list boxes. Finally a Hide method hides the form. Why go through the bother of showing, then hiding, the form?

Normally, in Visual Basic, a form if open in the design mode is automatically shown when the program is run. However, we explicitly show the form because Visual Basic only executes the Form_Load event subroutine when it first loads a form. At that point, the form isn't visible yet. However, SetFocus method calls are used as part of getting the window handle to send the LB_DIR messages to the list boxes and (unfortunately) SetFocus will result in an error if the controls aren't yet visible. The Show method is necessary in the Form_Load event subroutine before a call to Update_List_Boxes to avoid this error.

Now given the need for Show, what about Hide? Let's look at how the file dialog box is usually used. The FileOpen_Click event subroutine of the TestFDia form uses the statement

```
FileDlg.Show MODAL
```

to run the file dialog box as a modal form. Let's go through what that entails, step by step.

When Visual Basic executes a Show method, it will load the form if it isn't already loaded. Loading the form triggers its Form_Load event subroutine. The file dialog box's Form_Load event subroutine shows the form as its first statement. For the moment, pretend there wasn't a Hide method call in the file dialog box's Form_Load event subroutine. The form would remain shown. But when Visual Basic goes back to finish executing the Show method from the TestFDia form, it finds that the form is already shown. Because it's illegal in Windows (and therefore Visual Basic) to show a window as a modal window when it's already shown non-modally, Visual Basic will return an error. The Hide method call in the file dialog box's Form_Load event subroutine ensures that the Show method call in TestFDia will succeed.

### Testing the File Dialog

The FileOpen_Click event subroutine in the TestFDia form shows the proper way to use the file dialog box: You can select the files to be displayed in the file list box by setting the Text property of the file text box. You can use any filename, including ones with the DOS wildcards * and ?. If you want all files to be listed, just use *.*. A word processor might use *.DOC to select all files whose extension is .DOC.

Then you should show the file dialog box modally. A constant MODAL equal to 1 is the best way to do that. When the Show method call is complete, you know that the user selected some file or clicked the Cancel button. To determine which actually happened, check the Text property of the file text box. The Cancel_Click event subroutine of the file dialog box sets Text to the null string. If it's not the null string, you know the user selected a filename. You can then use that filename in a Visual Basic Open statement.

### Comment

It's a good idea to set the file dialog box's caption to remind users what they're selecting a file for. In the FileOpen_Click event subroutine, we use

```
FileDlg.Caption = "File open"
```

In a FileSaveAs_Click event subroutine, you might use

```
FileDlg.Caption = "File save as"
```

# Make a powerful text editor using APIs?

Complexity: Advanced

## Problem

Windows controls actually have more features than are made available in Visual Basic. "Messages" are used to access these enhanced features. How do I access the advanced features left out of Visual Basic? Specifically, I am interested in the quickest way to find the current line my cursor is in a text box.

## Technique

It is here that many of the features of Windows controls have been left out of Visual Basic and that accessing those features is accomplished by sending messages.

Nearly all of Visual Basic's control "properties" and "methods" are resolved internally as messages that are sent to the control using the SendMessage API function. However, in order to use messages and the SendMessage API function, we need to pass the "handle" property of a control (called its hWnd property).

Forms in Visual Basic are the only structures that support the hWnd as a property. But actually all controls have hWnds. We will look at two means of determining the hWnd of a control, one of which involves a dynamic link library (DLL) included on the disk.

A DLL is a library of functions, similar to a LIB in QuickBASIC, that can be accessed from Visual Basic. The primary difference between it and a QuickBASIC library function is that DLLs can be linked at run time and as such are never merged into the executable file (.EXE). At this time, Visual Basic is not able to create DLLs. Therefore, CTLHWND.DLL is written in C.

## Steps

The sample program uses a text box to demonstrate the use of SendMessage. The program is the beginning of a utility, similar to Notepad, written almost entirely with the use of messages.

Open and run EDITOR.MAK. You can type text in the editor and the status bar at the bottom will reflect the current line number and the current total number of lines in the editor. [The items in the File menu, such as

Open, Save, etc., do not actually function, but they do determine whether the contents of the editor have changed and prompt you accordingly.] The Editor supports full cut and paste and a single level of UNDO. The Edit menu should function just like the one in Notepad.

To create Editor, perform the following steps:

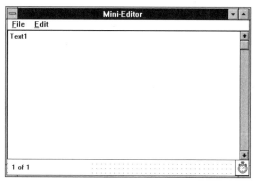

**Figure 1-11** Appearance of the Editor form

1. Create a new project called EDITOR.MAK. Create a new form with the objects and properties in Table 1-9 and save it as EDITOR.FRM. When finished, the form should look like Figure 1-11.

| Object | Property | Setting |
| --- | --- | --- |
| Form | FormName | Mini-Editor |
| Text | CtlName | Text1 |
| | Multiline | TRUE |
| Label | CtlName | Label1 |
| | Caption | 1 of 1 |
| | BorderStyle | NONE |
| Timer | CtlName | Timer1 |
| | Interval | 400 |
| | Enabled | TRUE |

**Table 1-9** Editor project form's objects and properties

2. Build a menu with choices listed in Table 1-10.

| Caption | CtlName | Caption | CtlName |
| --- | --- | --- | --- |
| &File | FileMenu | &Edit | EditMenu |
| &New | FileNew | &Undo | EditUndo |
| &Open | FileOpen | - | Sep2 |
| &Save | FileSave | Cu&t | EditCut |
| – | Sep1 | &Copy | EditCopy |
| E&xit | FileExit | &Paste | EditPaste |
| | | &Delete | EditDelete |

**Table 1-10** The Mini-Editor menu values

3. Create a new module named TEXTBOX.BAS. Insert the following code in TEXTBOX.BAS.

```
DefInt A-Z

Declare Function ControlhWnd Lib "CTLHWND.DLL" (Ctrl As Control)
Declare Function SendMessage& Lib "User" (ByVal hWnd, ByVal Msg, ByVal ⇐
wParam, ByVal lParam As Any)

Declare Function GetFocus Lib "User" ()

'These constants define the messages we will be sending
Const WM_USER = 1024
Const WM_CUT = 768
Const WM_COPY = 769
Const WM_PASTE = 770
Const WM_CLEAR = 771

Const EM_GETMODIFY = WM_USER + 8
Const EM_SETMODIFY = WM_USER + 9
Const EM_LINEINDEX = WM_USER + 11
Const EM_LINEFROMCHAR = WM_USER + 25
Const EM_UNDO = WM_USER + 23
Const EM_GETLINECOUNT = WM_USER + 10

'Now for each routine, we simply send a different message.
Function TextModified (TBox As Control)
   Wnd = ControlhWnd(TBox)
   TextModified = SendMessage&(Wnd, EM_GETMODIFY, 0, 0&) * -1
End Function

Function TextCurLine (TBox As Control)
   Wnd = ControlhWnd(TBox)
   TextCurLine = SendMessage&(Wnd, EM_LINEFROMCHAR, -1, 0&) + 1
End Function

Function TextLineBegin (TBox As Control, LineNum)
   Wnd = ControlhWnd(TBox)
   TextLineBegin = SendMessage&(Wnd, EM_LINEINDEX, LineNum, 0&)
End Function

Sub TextClean (TBox As Control)
   Wnd = ControlhWnd(TBox)
   Ok = SendMessage&(Wnd, EM_SETMODIFY, 0, 0&)
End Sub

Sub EditUndo (TBox As Control)
   Wnd = ControlhWnd(TBox)
   Ok = SendMessage&(Wnd, EM_UNDO, 0, 0&)
End Sub

Sub EditCut (TBox As Control)
   Wnd = ControlhWnd(TBox)
```

```
   Ok = SendMessage&(Wnd, WM_CUT, O, O&)
End Sub

Sub EditCopy (TBox As Control)
   Wnd = ControlhWnd(TBox)
   Ok = SendMessage&(Wnd, WM_COPY, O, O&)
End Sub

Sub EditPaste (TBox As Control)
   Wnd = ControlhWnd(TBox)
   Ok = SendMessage&(Wnd, WM_PASTE, O, O&)
End Sub

Sub EditClear (TBox As Control)
   Wnd = ControlhWnd(TBox)
   Ok = SendMessage&(Wnd, WM_CLEAR, O, O&)
End Sub

Function TextLines (TBox As Control)
   Wnd = ControlhWnd(TBox)
   TextLines = SendMessage&(Wnd, EM_GETLINECOUNT, O, O&)
End Function
```

4. Insert the following code in the Declarations section of Form1.

```
DefInt A-Z

Const MB_CANCEL = 2
Const MB_YES = 6
Const MB_NO = 7
Const CTRL_MASK = 2

Dim OldPos, OldTotal As Integer

Function PromptSave ()
   Title$ = "File has changed"
   Mess$ = "Do you want to save changes?"
   PromptSave = MsgBox(Mess$, 19, Title$)
End Function
```

5. Insert the following code in the FileExit_Click procedure.

```
Sub FileExit_Click ()
   If TextModified(Text1) Then
      Button = PromptSave()
      Select Case Button
         Case MB_CANCEL
            Exit Sub
         Case MB_YES
            'Save file here
      End Select
   End If
   End
End Sub
```

6. Insert the following code in the FileNew_Click procedure.

```
Sub FileNew_Click ()
   If TextModified(Text1) Then
      Button = PromptSave()
      Select Case Button
         Case MB_CANCEL
            Exit Sub
         Case MB_YES
            'Save file here
      End Select
   End If
   Text1.Text = ""
   TextClean Text1
End Sub
```

7. Insert the following code in the FileOpen_Click procedure.

```
Sub FileOpen_Click ()
   If TextModified(Text1) Then
      Button = PromptSave()
      Select Case Button
         Case MB_CANCEL
            Exit Sub
         Case MB_YES
            'Save file here
      End Select
   End If
   Text1.Text = "You have just opened a new file!"
   TextClean Text1
End Sub
```

8. Insert the following code in the FileSave_Click procedure.

```
Sub FileSave_Click ()
   'Save file here
   TextClean Text1
End Sub
```

9. Insert the following code in the EditUndo_Click procedure.

```
Sub EditUndo_Click ()
   EditUndo Text1
End Sub
```

10. Insert the following code in the EditCopy_Click procedure.

```
Sub EditCopy_Click ()
   EditCopy Text1
End Sub
```

11. Insert the following code in the EditCut_Click procedure.

```
Sub EditCut_Click ()
   EditCut Text1
End Sub
```

12. Insert the following code in the EditDelete_Click procedure.

```
Sub EditDelete_Click ()
   EditClear Text1
End Sub
```

13. Insert the following code in the EditPaste_Click procedure.

```
Sub EditPaste_Click ()
   EditPaste Text1
End Sub
```

14. Insert the following code in the Timer1_Timer procedure.

```
Sub Timer1_Timer ()
   CurLine = TextCurLine(Text1)
   TLines = TextLines(Text1)
   If CurLine <> OldPos Or TLines <> OldTotal Then
      Label1.Caption = Str$(CurLine) + " of " + Str$(TLines)
      OldPos = CurLine
      OldTotal = TLines
   End If
End Sub
```

15. Insert the following code in the Text1_KeyDown procedure.

```
Sub Text1_KeyDown (KeyCode As Integer, Shift As Integer)
   If KeyCode = Asc("Y") And Shift  CTRL_MMASK Then
      'Find the current row and where it begins
      CurLine = TextCurLine(Text1) - 1
      Text1.SelStart = TextLineBegin(Text1, CurLine)
      LineLen = TextLineBegin(Text1, CurLine + 1) - Text1.SelStart
      Text1.SelLength = LineLen
      Text1.SelText = ""
   End If
End Sub
```

16. Insert the following code in the Form_Unload procedure.

```
Sub Form_Unload (Cancel As Integer)
   If TextModified(Text1) Then
      Button = PromptSave()
      Select Case Button
         Case MB_CANCEL
            Cancel = -1
            Exit Sub
         Case MB_YES
            'Save file here
      End Select
   End If
End Sub
```

## How It Works

The use of SendMessage is dependent on having the handle property of the control to which you wish to send the message. Internally, Windows keeps track of all the controls you create by their "handle." The handle (or hWnd property) is basically like an ID number for a file, it's needed to link a command with a particular control. Internally, handles are simply pointers. If you want to take advantage of any of the built-in functions of the control that can only be accessed via SendMessage, you need the hWnd of that control. Unfortunately, this property is only available for a form and not for the various other control types. Fortunately, there are a number of ways to use Windows API functions to find the hWnd of a control. The most popular is to use the GetFocus API function to return the hWnd of a Visual Basic control that currently "owns focus." By this we mean the control that is currently active—that is, will receive the next user output. So to send a message to a control that does not have the current forms, you need to determine which control currently owns the focus, save that hWnd, set the focus on the desired control, retrieve its hWnd, and return focus to the original control. A function to return the hWnd of any control might look something like this:

```
DefInt A-Z

Declare Function GetFocus Lib "User" ()
Declare Sub PutFocus Lib "User" Alias "SetFocus" (ByVal hWnd)

Function ControlhWnd (Ctrl As Control)
   Wnd = GetFocus()   'get handle of control with focus
   Ctrl.SetFocus   'sets focus to our control
   ControlhWnd = GetFocus()   'saves return handle of our control
   PutFocus Wnd   'restores focus to original control
End Function
```

In fact, if you create a module that contains this function, add it to your project, and comment out the Declare statement that refers to the external DLL, the program will work exactly the same. This module exists on the distribution disk as HWND.BAS.

However, although we have a working function, there are a number of problems with it. First, it is slow. Why use four lines of code every time we need a property? Second, the function will trigger the LostFocus and GotFocus events of both controls. That's a lot of flag checking if you have to do this with a number of controls that have event handlers for those events.

Third, the function is not always accurate. With combo box styles 1 and 2 this function will return the handle to either the text box or list box portion of the combo box, whichever gets the focus. Therefore, you need additional checking to determine whether the control you receive is a combo box and, if so, which style it is. The fourth disadvantage is that the hWnd Visual Basic of every control is stored in your .EXE file.

There is a function in the Control Development Kit (CDK), available from Microsoft, that enables you to build a DLL function that returns the correct hWnd for *any* control. If you have the CDK, this function is there for your use. The operative line of your DLL function would be:

```
return (VBGetControlhWnd (hCtl);
```

This line looks a lot simpler than the GetFocus approach we just showed. Because this is not a book on C, we have included a custom DLL CTLHWND.DLL, that contains just the ControlhWnd function. The name of the function in the DLL is VBGetControlhWnd and uses the previously described mode line to access it. This is the fastest, safest, and most accurate method of determining the hWnd of a given control.

Finally, once we have the hWnd to a control, we can then use the Windows SendMessage API function to send a message to that control. The SendMessage API function is a generalized function for sending and retrieving information from a control or form. The Declaration of SendMessage looks as follows:

```
Declare Function SendMessage& Lib "User" (Byval hWnd%, ByVal Msg%, Byval ⇐
wParam%, Byval lParam As Any)
```

all on one line, of course. The handle to the control which receives the message is hWnd%. The message number to be sent is Msg%. The meaning of wParam% and lParam vary depending on the message and sometimes are not used at all, as in the Clipboard functions given earlier.

All the parameters to SendMessage are integers with the exception of lParam, which is declared to be As Any. In fact, lParam is always a LONG integer but sometimes we will want to send a string. When a string is sent by using ByVal to a DLL, it is actually a LONG that is placed on the stack. This LONG is a pointer (known as a "long pointer") to an ASCIIZ string, which is not the native format of Visual Basic strings but the form required by most DLL functions.

Keep in mind that by using the As Any directive, you are effectively disabling parameter checking for that variable in your code. Therefore, you must ensure that you are either sending a LONG integer or a string.

Once you get to this point, the rest is easy. It is simply a matter of knowing which messages a control can receive, and the meaning of wParam and lParam in those contexts. You can refer to *The Waite Group's Windows API Bible*, Jim Conger, Waite Group Press, 1992, for information on using the correct messages and parameters. For example, the EM_GETMODIFY message determines whether the contents of a text box have changed. The alternative to using SendMessage would be to create a handler for the Text1_Changed procedure that would set a static variable every time it was triggered. Obviously, this would be a waste, because that same status information is already stored by the text control and can be retrieved and set, only when it is needed.

### How It Works

The WM_ Clipboard messages allow you to perform the standard Clipboard operations on a text control in one step instead of requiring you to make use of Visual Basic's Clipboard object. The EM_UNDO message would be rather complicated to duplicate in vanilla Visual Basic, requiring a large Select Case block. The TextCurLine, TextLineBegin, and TextLines functions would be almost impossible to create in Visual Basic alone.

The code itself is not really that complex and helps to highlight the sophistication of Windows controls. Each of the clipboard commands is ultimately resolved as one message sent to the controls. Because clipboard capability is inherent in a text box control, operations that might take five or six lines of Visual Basic only take one message. The most sophisticated of these is the EM_UNDO message. Duplicating this with pure Visual Basic code would require managing an "undo buffer" along with information about what operation happened last so you could undo it. This capability, however, is native to the text box control so we don't need to worry about it.

The file operations demonstrate the use of a hidden "property" of the text box control not available in native Visual Basic. Text box controls maintain a flag that indicates whether the contents have been changed. In the file menu options, we are checking this flag to determine whether or not to prompt the user to save the work in progress. Duplicating this in Visual Basic would require creating a Text1-Change event handler (which would fire *many* times), setting our own flag, and adding unnecessary overhead to the operation of the control. Using SendMessage we can simply retrieve or set this flag at the appropriate time.

### Comment

As you might guess, another reason to be familiar with these messages is to manipulate the controls in other applications. For example, it would not be difficult to activate Notepad and manipulate the text control that gets focus.

# Create an old-style file dialog box?

Complexity: Intermediate

### Problem

Users often complain about Visual Basic's separate drive, directory, and file list box threesome (see Figure 1-12). Many would prefer the older style, a file dialog box with a single list box that lists both directories and drives (see Figure 1-13). Additionally, how do I prevent errors when users try to change to a floppy drive that doesn't have a disk inserted or has an open door?

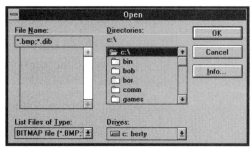

**Figure 1-12** The new, Visual Basic-style file dialog box

### Technique

Visual Basic provides all the tools you need to modify and recreate the old- style dialog box. Visual Basic's file list box will serve, but we need a way to combine directories and drives into a

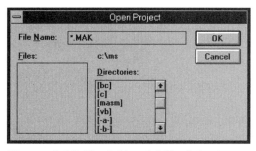

**Figure 1-13** The "old-style" file dialog box

single list box. You might think the Dir$ function would return directory names, but it does not. Also, unfortunately, there is no Windows API function to combine directories and drives. What you can do is copy all the directories from an invisible directory list box, and all the drives from a drive combo box, into a plain list box.

### Steps

Open and run FILEDLG.MAK. You can click on the directories to negotiate the directory tree and click on the drive letters to switch to another drive. You can also double-click on a filename to select that file and close the form. Because this form is ready-to-run, you can simply add it to any project you're working on.

1. Create a new project called FILEDLG.MAK. Create a new form using the properties listed in Table 1-11 and save it as FILEDLG.FRM. Figure 1-13 shows how the form should look when you're finished.

| Object | Property | Setting |
| --- | --- | --- |
| Form | FormName | FileDlg |
| | Caption | File |
| | BorderStyle | 1 - Fixed Single |
| | ControlBox | False |
| | MaxButton | False |
| | MinButton | False |
| | BackColor | &H00C0C0C0& |
| Text box | CtlName | FileEdit |
| Label | Caption | File&name: |
| Label | CtlName | DirLabel |
| Button | CtlName | Ok |
| | Caption | OK |
| | Default | True |
| Button | CtlName | Cancel |
| | Caption | Cancel |
| | Cancel | True |
| File list box | CtlName | File1 |
| Label | Caption | &Files: |
| List box | CtlName | DirList |
| Label | Caption | &Directories: |
| Directory list box | CtlName | Dir1 |
| | Visible | False |
| Drive combo box | CtlName | Drive1 |
| | Visible | False |

**Table 1-11** FileDlg project form's objects and properties

2. Now we're ready to enter the code. Most of this code goes in a subroutine called Update_List_Boxes, which goes in the General section of the form. Other event subroutines in this project call Update_List_Boxes whenever the user clicks in one of the list boxes, so any directory or drive changes are immediately reflected.

```
Sub Update_List_Boxes ()
   ' Update current directory label.
   DirLabel.Caption = LCase$(CurDir$)
```

```
   ' Update Path of file List Box.
   File1.Path = CurDir$

   ' Update Pattern of file List Box (for wildcard searches).
   File1.Pattern = FileEdit.Text

   ' Clear out the directory List Box
   Do While DirList.ListCount
      DirList.RemoveItem 0
   Loop

   ' Add a [..] (parent directory) if we're in a subdirectory.
   If Right$(CurDir$, 1) <> "\" Then DirList.AddItem "[..]"

   ' Update the hidden directory List Box's Path
   ' to match the actual current directory.
   Dir1.Path = CurDir$

   ' Add each directory in the hidden directory List Box
     ' to the "combined" List Box.
   For I = 0 To Dir1.ListCount - 1
      A$ = Dir1.List(I)

      ' The directories in the hidden directory List Box
      ' are absolute paths; that is, they contain the
      ' complete path name, such as c:\visbasic\icons, and
      ' all we're interested in is the last path--icons--
      ' so strip out the rest.
      For J = Len(A$) To 1 Step -1
         If Mid$(A$, J, 1) = "\" Then
            A$ = Mid$(A$, J + 1)
            Exit For
         End If
      Next

      ' Add the path surrounded by brackets, for example, [icons].
      DirList.AddItem "[" + A$ + "]"
   Next

   ' Add the drives in the hidden drive combo box to the
   ' directory List Box.
   For I = 0 To Drive1.ListCount - 1
      DirList.AddItem "[-" + Mid$(Drive1.List(I), 1, 1) + "-]"
   Next
End Sub
```

3. Place the following code in the Click event subroutine of the Cancel button control to unload the form.

```
Sub Cancel_Click ()
   ' If we select Cancel, we can unload the dialog, because
   ' we don't need it anymore.
   FileEdit.Text = ""
```

```
 Hide
End Sub
```

4. Put the following code in the DblClick event subroutine of the DirList list box control. This is where we change directories and switch drives. This is also where we check for errors, because there might not be a disk in a floppy drive.

```
Sub DirList_DblClick ()
    Const MB_RETRYANDCANCEL = 5
    Const MB_ICONEXCLAMATION = 48

    On Local Error GoTo UhOh

    ' When you double-click on a directory or drive entry,
    ' check whether the selected item is a drive; if so,
    ' change the current drive.
    If Left$(DirList.Text, 2) = "[-" And Len(DirList.Text) = 5 Then
        oldDir$ = CurDir$
        ChDrive Mid$(DirList.Text, 3, 1)
        A$ = CurDir$    ' Check whether the disk is ready
    ' Otherwise, change the current directory.
    Else
        ChDir Mid$(DirList.Text, 2, Len(DirList.Text) - 2)
    End If

    On Local Error GoTo 0

    Update_List_Boxes
    Exit Sub

UhOh:
    If MsgBox("Unable to switch to drive " + Mid$(DirList.Text, 3, 1) + ⇐
":", MB_RETRYANDCANCEL + MB_ICONEXCLAMATION, "Visual Basic - FileDlg") = 2
Then
    ' If user presses Cancel, go back to the previous drive.
        ChDrive Left$(oldDir$, 1)
    End If

    Resume
End Sub
```

5. Put the following code in the DblClick event subroutine of the File1 file list box control. We set the text of the text box to the file the user selected and unload the form.

```
Sub File1_DblClick ()
    ' When we double-click on a filename in the List Box,
    ' set the edit control to the selected filename and
    ' close the dialog, because we've picked the filename.
    FileEdit.Text = File1.Filename
    Hide
End Sub
```

6. Put the following code in the Load event subroutine of the form and the Click event subroutine of the OK button to update the various list boxes by calling the Update_List_Boxes routine.

```
Sub Form_Load ()
    Update_List_Boxes
End Sub
Sub OK_Click ()
    Update_List_Boxes
End Sub
```

### How It Works

The Update_List_Boxes procedure updates all the list boxes as the user changes directories or drives. The first Do loop empties out the combined list box. Then we add a double periods entry ".." that lets you "back up" to the previous directory (akin to the DOS (CD ..) command). The first For...Next loop adds the entries of the hidden directory list box to the combined list box. Visual Basic's directory list box lists the complete directory path (for example, C:\VB\ICONS), so we have to extract the last part of the complete directory name (ICONS). That's the part we add to the combined directory list box. The second For...Next loop adds the entries from the hidden drive combo box to the combined list box. We mimic the standard format of [-X-] where X is the drive letter.

The DirList_DblClick subroutine manages the selection of a directory and any possible errors that might come up. Constants are set up for the error message box (that's where the MB_ prefix comes from) and a local error handler is set up for any disk error. The If statement checks for the "[-" added to the drive letters to see if there was a double-click on a drive letter. If so, the program switches to the drive using ChDrive. Otherwise, it's a directory and the program switches to the directory using ChDir.

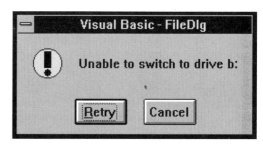

**Figure 1-14** The UhOh message box

Getting this far means there hasn't been any error, so the error handling routine is disabled, Update_List_Boxes is called to make sure the list boxes get updated with the new drive and directory information, and finally we exit from the subroutine.

If there was any error, the code at line label UhOh gets run and a message box is popped up, as shown in Figure 1-14. If the user clicks on Cancel, we ChDrive back to the drive before we tried to switch (which we know was good). Otherwise, we just use Resume to return to where the error occurred.

### Comments

Note how the LCase$ function is used to make the directory label caption lowercase, so it matches the lowercase filenames. You can omit the LCase$ if you'd prefer your directory names to be uppercase.

This project shows one way to create a file dialog box. The file dialog box presented in How-To 1.6 Make a file dialog box using APIs is faster than this one, because it uses Windows messages.

The most common use of this form is to provide a dialog box in response to a File Open menu selection. In that case, you may want to change the form's Caption property to "File Open." You can also use it in response to a File Save As menu selection, in which case you might want to set the caption to "File Save." For example,

```
Sub FileOpen_Click ()
    FileDlg.Caption = "Open a file"
    FileDlg.Show MODAL
End Sub
```

### 1.9    How do I...

# Create multiple entries in the Task List?

Complexity: Intermediate

### Problem

I would like to have multiple instances of my application running with different workspaces. When there are multiple instances of other Windows applications running, such as Notepad, the various entries in the Task List reflect the main window caption (such as Notepad—MYFILE.TXT). However, when I run multiple instances of my Visual Basic application, even though I change the Caption property of my main form, all the entries in the Task List are the same: the name of my .EXE file.

### Technique

Visual Basic has the ability to create what appear to be multiple "ownerless" forms. The way Visual Basic achieves this is to create a hidden window that "owns" all the windows that you create. Although rarely an issue, the ownership does matter here, because the caption of that hidden window must change to change the entry in the Task List. Therefore, we must use the GetWindow API function to retrieve the owner of our main form and then the SetWindowText function to set the caption of that window.

### Steps

To try the sample program, an .EXE file must first be generated from our source code. Open and run TASKS.MAK. Select Make.EXE from the File menu and run the resulting program, TASKS.EXE, from the Program Manager.

You will see that the caption of the program is "My Application: X," where X is the "instance" number of the application. As you load and run more copies of the application, this number will be incremented. Now, if you double-click the desktop to bring up the Task Manager, you will see

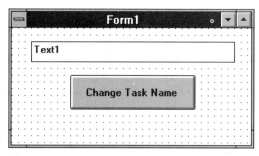

**Figure 1-15** Appearance of the Tasks form

the distinct entries for each instance of the application.

If you enter a new string into the text box on the form and click the command button, you will change not only the caption of the form, but the entry in the Task List.

To create the Tasks project, perform the following steps:

1. Create a new project called TASKS.MAK. Create a new form with the following objects and properties and save it as TASK.FRM. When finished, your form should look like Figure 1-15.

| Object | Property | Setting |
| --- | --- | --- |
| Form | FormName | Form1 |
| Text | CtlName | Text1 |
| Button | CtlName | Command1 |
|  | Caption | Change Task Name |

**Table 1-12** Tasks Project form's objects and properties

2. Insert the following code in the Declarations section of Form1.

```
DefInt A-Z
```

3. Insert the following code in the Command1_Click procedure.

```
Sub Command1_Click ()
    TaskName$ = Text1.Text
    If Len(TaskName$) Then
        SetNewTaskName Form1, TaskName$
        Form1.Caption = TaskName$
    End If
End Sub
```

4. Create a new module called TASKS.BAS and insert the following code.

```
DefInt A-Z
Declare Function GetModuleHandle Lib "Kernel" (ByVal ModuleName$)
Declare Function GetModuleUsage Lib "kernel" (ByVal hModule)
Declare Function GetWindow Lib "user" (ByVal hWnd, ByVal wCmd)
Declare Sub SetWindowText Lib "user" (ByVal hWnd, ByVal WindowText$)

Const GW_OWNER = 4

Sub Main ()
    hModule = GetModuleHandle("TASKS.EXE")
    mCount = GetModuleUsage(hModule)
    TaskName$ = "My Application: " + Str$(mCount)
    Load Form1
    SetNewTaskName Form1, TaskName$
    Form1.Caption = TaskName$
    Form1.Show
End Sub

Sub SetNewTaskName (Frm As Form, TaskName$)
    Wnd = Frm.hWnd
    hOwner = GetWindow(Wnd, GW_OWNER)
    SetWindowText hOwner, TaskName$
End Sub
```

5. Save the form and the project as TASKS.

6. Set Sub Main as the startup form.

7. Create and run the .EXE file.

## How It Works

In Sub Main, GetModuleUsage is used to find the current usage count of the .EXE file, in this case TASKS.EXE. This enables a descriptive task entry to be assigned for each instance of the application that is just in variable TaskName$. The real secret to the technique is in determining that there is a hidden "owner" of the form and that we can use GetWindow to determine the hWnd property of that window. Once we have that information, it is easy to use SetWindowText to assign TextName$ for our Windows caption.

SetNewTaskName is written as a subroutine so it can be called from the form as well as from the module itself.

### Comments

It is indeed possible to use this technique to change the caption and Task List entry for other applications, as well as your own. However, be advised that most applications treat this information dynamically, so your application would have to constantly "check in," using a timer or DoEvents, to see whether another change was warranted.

---

**1.10    How do I...**

# Make a simple "searching" list box?

Complexity: Intermediate

### Problem

I'd like to make a text box/list box combination like the one in Windows Help, where as you type in the text box, the matching entry in the list box is automatically scrolled and selected. How can I do this in Visual Basic?

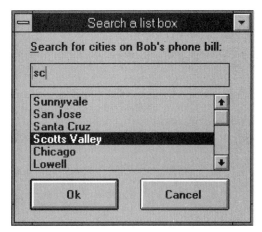

**Figure 1-16** The Search project in action

### Technique

Automatically selecting the entries in a text box while typing is a good timesaver for users. The key to implementing this feature in Visual Basic is to use the text box's Change event. That way you don't have to wait until the user presses Enter or clicks on a button.

Once you detect a Change event you can search the entries of the list box, as shown in Figure 1-16. If there's a match, you can select that item in the list box.

### Steps

Open and run SEARCH.MAK. You can type the first letter or two of the city names in the list box. As you type, the appropriate entry will be highlighted. If two names have a similar letter, the highlight will jump to the name as soon as a match occurs. So as you type

"San" the highlight bar will fall on "San Jose." If the next letter is a "t," it will jump to "Santa Cruz." When you press Enter or click on the OK button, the highlighted list box entry will be displayed in a message box.

1. Create a new project called SEARCH.MAK. Create a new form with the controls and properties listed in Table 1-13 and save it as SEARCH.FRM.

| Control | Property | Setting |
| --- | --- | --- |
| Form | Caption | Search a List Box |
| | MaxButton | False |
| | BackColor | &H00C0C0C0& |
| Label | Caption | &Search for cities on Bob's phone bill |
| Text box | CtlName | Text1 |
| List box | CtlName | List1 |
| Command button | CtlName | Ok |
| | Caption | Ok |
| | Default | True |
| Command button | CtlName | Cancel |
| | Caption | Cancel |
| | Cancel | True |

**Table 1-13** Search project form's controls and properties

2. Put the following code in the Cancel_Click event subroutine.

```
Sub Cancel_Click ()
    End
End Sub
```

3. Put the following code in the Form_Load event subroutine. This code simply adds some default items to the list box.

```
Sub Form_Load ()
    List1.AddItem "Sunnyvale"
    List1.AddItem "San Jose"
    List1.AddItem "Santa Cruz"
    List1.AddItem "Scotts Valley"
    List1.AddItem "Chicago"
    List1.AddItem "Lowell"
    List1.AddItem "Roswell"
    List1.AddItem "Cambridge"
    List1.AddItem "Muskegon"
    List1.AddItem "Agoura"
    List1.AddItem "Englewood"
    List1.AddItem "Bellevue"
    List1.AddItem "Anaheim"
End Sub
```

4. Put the following code in the Ok_Click event subroutine. This statement pops up a message box that displays which list box entry was selected, either by clicking on it with the mouse or by typing in the list box.

```
Sub Ok_Click ()
   MsgBox "You selected " + List1.Text
End Sub
```

5. Put the following code in the Text1_Change event subroutine. This is where the actual matching takes place. The For...Next loop goes through the entries in the list box trying to match with what was entered in the text box. If there's a match, the list box's ListIndex property is set and the For...Next loop is aborted.

```
Sub Text1_Change ()
   Search$ = UCase$(Text1.Text)
   SearchLen = Len(Search$)

   If SearchLen Then
      For I = 0 To List1.ListCount - 1
         If UCase$(Left$(List1.List(I), SearchLen)) = Search$ Then
            List1.ListIndex = I
            Exit For
         End If
      Next
   End If
End Sub
```

**How It Works**

Each time the user makes a change to the text box, by typing another character in the text box, or backspacing, the text box's Change event is triggered. So all the code to do searching is in the Text1_Change event subroutine. When doing this search, you don't want the case of the letters to matter, so the string actually searched for is set to all uppercase by using the UCase$ function.

Because you want the search to get more specific as more and more characters are typed, the SearchLen variable holds the length of the text in the text box. Then you can limit the search to the first SearchLen characters in each list box entry. Notice the first If statement. It ensures that the subroutine won't do any searching unless there is text to search for.

The For...Next loop in the SearchLen subroutine goes through each entry in the list box and compares it to the uppercase search string. A match should be made regardless of case, so the UCase$ function is used. Then, because Visual Basic will only match two string variables if they're identical in content and length, the Left$ function is used to make sure the comparison is between strings of the same length as the search string.

If there is a match, the ListIndex property of the list box is set to the examined entry and the For…Next loop is exited. If there is no match, the currently highlighted item (the ListIndex property) isn't changed. That's all there is to it. You now have a feature in your application that your users will appreciate.

### Comment

Because the Text1_Change event subroutine searches through the entire list box, the list box doesn't have to be sorted (have its Sorted property set to True).

## 1.11 How do I…

# Make a "searching" list box using APIs?

Complexity: Advanced

### Problem

How-To 1.10 Make a simple "searching" list box showed how to build a list box that automatically scrolls as it tries to locate the same text the user types. If it finds a matching prefix, it selects that line. Is there a more powerful way to do this using Windows APIs?

### Technique

By using the SendMessage API function, and some tricks, we can build a faster search function. Our goal is to have a sorted list box "track" characters as they are typed into a text box, so the program starts immediately searching for a corresponding prefix in the list box. This technique of searching allows for partial matches, minimizing the typing the user must do to find a particular entry in the list box. The list box always attempts to find a match for as many characters as have been typed in the edit box. If two entries have similar prefixes, the list will jump to the second one as soon as enough characters have been typed in the edit box to distinguish the entries. If matching text is found in the list, we want that line to become the top line in the list. In addition, we want the text in the text box to change to reflect user selections in the list box, as it does in Windows help.

At first glance, it appears as though a search function of this type can be coded by using the Change event of the text box, then scanning through the list box for matching text and setting the ListIndex property of the list box accordingly. The ListIndex property seems perfectly suited to this task because it can "select" an entry in the list. Unfortunately, setting the ListIndex property in Visual Basic is the same as clicking on the list box. This will trigger another Click event in the list box. Since we would use the Click event handler to change the text in the text box, our application could end up in an endless loop.

The solution is an example of what is known in the object-oriented programming world as "encap-

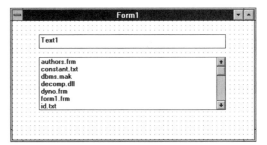

**Figure 1-17** The appearance of the Search form

sulation." Encapulation simply means that an object (or control) contains both data and code. Although the search scheme just outlined treats the list box as a mere passive receptacle of data, in fact, the list box contains a great deal of built-in functionality, or methods. One of these built-in Windows methods is the ability to search for a specified text prefix and select the line that contains it. The SendMessage API function, as described in How-To 1.7 Make a powerful text editor using APIs, is used to access these additional list box functions.. Using the Windows API search function of the list box is not only faster, but also does not generate the Click event, allowing us to process that separately as a "user driven" event. This means we can send another API message to the list box to make our selection the top of the list.

### Steps

Open and run SEARCH.MAK. You will see that the file box is filled with a list of files. Further, the top line of the file list will be selected and the corresponding text copied to the edit control. If you begin to type, the text in the edit control will be replaced with what you type and, with any luck at all, the list box will "track" your keystrokes.

1. Create a new project called SEARCH.MAK. Create a new form with the objects and properties in Table 1-14 and save it as SEARCH.FRM. When finished, your form should look like Figure 1-17.

| Object | Property | Setting |
| --- | --- | --- |
| Form | FormName | Form1 |
| | Caption | Seach a list box |
| Text box | CtlName | Text1 |
| FileList | CtlName | File1 |

**Table 1-14** Search project form's objects and properties

2. Open the Declarations section of Form1 and insert the following code.

```
DefInt A-Z
'Note each Declare statement must fit on one line
Declare Function SendMessage Lib "User" (ByVal hWnd, ByVal wMsg, ⇐
ByVal wParam, ByVal lParam As Any)
Declare Function ControlhWnd Lib "CtlhWnd.DLL" (Ctl as Control)

'Constants from Windows.h
Const WM_USER = 1024
Const LB_SELECTSTRING = WM_USER + 13
Const LB_SETTOPINDEX = WM_USER + 24
```

3. Put this code in the Form_Load procedure.

```
Sub Form_Load ()
   File1.ListIndex = 0
   Text1.SelStart = 0
   Text1.SelLength = Len(Text1.Text)
End Sub
```

4. Put this code in the File1_Click procedure.

```
Sub File1_Click ()
   Text1.Text = File1.FileName
End Sub
```

5. Put this code in the Text1_Change procedure.

```
Sub Text1_Change ()
   FlhWnd = ControlhWnd (File1)
   Search$ = Text1.Text
   If Len(Search$) Then
      Index = SendMessage(FLhWnd, LB_SELECTSTRING, -1, Search$)
      ErrCode = SendMessage(FLhWnd, LB_SETTOPINDEX, Index, 0&)
   Else
      ErrCode = SendMessage(FLhWnd, LB_SETCURSEL, 0, 0&)
      ErrCode = SendMessage(FLhWnd, LB_SETTOPINDEX, 0, 0&)
   End If
End Sub
```

### How It Works

The Form_Load procedure performs an initialization similar to the one used in Windows Help. First, the File1.ListIndex property is set to 0. This is the equivalent of the user clicking on the first row of the file list. Therefore, the File1_Click event handler is triggered. In File1_Click, the Text1.Text property is set to the currently selected FileName in the list. This, in turn, triggers the Text1_Change event. You can see the potential for an endless loop here. What prevents this is that the Text1_Change event handler uses messages instead of the ListIndex property, so it does not trigger a File1_Click event. Finally, the Form_Load procedure selects the text in

Text1. The benefit of mimicking this habit of the help system is that "selected" text is easily replaced by the user just by typing, which deletes the existing text and begins a completely new prefix. This technique can't be used if you wish to allow the user to type into the text box holding a file name.

An important procedure is the Text1_Change event handler. Whenever the user changes the contents of the text control, either by adding or removing characters, Text1_Change attempts to find a matching prefix in File1. The Window handle of the file list is obtained using the ControlhWnd function, as described in How-To 1.7 Make a powerful text editor using APIs. Next, the LB_SELECTSTRING message is sent to the file list. This message searches the list box for the text prefix and makes the first match the current index, all in one operation and without firing the File1.Click event. The LB_SETTOPINDEX message is sent to the file list to put the selected item on top. The Else clause is optional and is added solely to mimic the behavior of Windows Help. If Text1 is empty, the LB_SETCURSEL messages are sent to make the index of the file list the top line. The LB_SETCURSEL message is functionally equivalent to setting the .ListIndex property without triggering the _Click event.

## Comments

The first thing you are likely to notice when trying this How-To is that sometimes the LB_SETTOPINDEX messages seem to malfunction. The reason is that a list box will not allow itself to be scrolled beyond available data. Therefore, if a list box control has ten visible lines, contains 20 lines of text, and your search takes you to line 17, LB_SETTOPINDEX will only move item 17 to visible row seven.

In most cases, you will be searching for matches using a normal list box and not a file list. We used the file list here to simplify populating the list for the example. The only code that would need to be changed to use a normal list box instead would be the line in the File1.Click procedure that refers to the .FileName property. Your code would need to refer to the .Text property instead.

Also, you should note that the example passes a value of (-1) as the wParam when sending the LB_SELECTSTRING message. This parameter refers to the starting point of the search and (-1) means to begin from the top. You may optionally begin from a specific index if, for example, you wanted to step through the list box, finding all matching strings.

There may be times when you want a list to perform a search but not to "select" the match. This is accomplished by sending the LB_FINDSTRING (WM_USER + 16) message in place of the LB_SELECTSTRING message.

Interestingly, this search routine works with combo boxes as well as list boxes and file list boxes.

**1.12    How do I...**

# Make a button with continuous events?

Complexity: Advanced

### Problem

I want the user to be able to hold down a command button with the mouse and while doing so, have the program perform a continuous operation until the mouse button is released. This would let me create my own custom scrolling number boxes for entering values easily. Command buttons in Visual Basic don't seem to work this way. What is the answer?

### Technique

This effect is easily achieved using a picture box and Visual Basic's DoEvents function. Briefly, the DoEvents function simply delays until all the messages waiting to be processed by your application and all others have been handled, before returning. In other words, DoEvents frees up Visual Basic to allow other messages to be processed. This is equivalent to a C program creating a "PeekMessage loop" and allows for cooperative multitasking under Windows. (For a more detailed description of DoEvents refer to *The Waite Group's Visual Basic Super Bible*, Taylor Maxwell and Bryon Scott, Waite Group Press, 1992.)

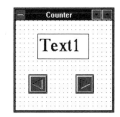

The technique we'll use is to set a static variable to True when the MouseDown event over the button is encountered. Then, the repetitive operation is performed inside a DoEvents loop that checks the status of this global variable to see whether the mouse button is returned down. Finally, the DoEvents loop sets the variable to False when the MouseUp event is encountered.

**Figure 1-18**
Appearance of the Counter form

Our example creates a simple counter that will go up and down when the buttons are held down. Although this is not the most interesting application of this technique, it is the easiest to present clearly here and should point to more creative uses.

### Steps

Open and run COUNTER.MAK. If you hold down the mouse button over one of the picture boxes, the counter will change continuously.

1. Create a new project called COUNTER.MAK. Create a new form with the objects and properties in Table 1-15 and save it as COUNTER.FRM. When finished, your form should look like Figure 1-18.

| Object | Property | Setting |
|---|---|---|
| Form | FormName | Form1 |
| | Caption | Counter |
| Text | CtlName | Text1 |
| Picture | CtlName | Picture1 |
| | AutoSize | True |
| | Index | 0 |
| | Picture | ARW01LT.ICO |
| Picture | CtlName | Picture1 |
| | AutoSize | True |
| | Index | 1 |
| | Picture | ARW01RT.ICO |

**Table 1-15** Counter project form's object and properties

2. Open the Declarations section of Form1 and insert the following code.

```
Dim ButtonDown, Counter As Integer
Const TRUE = -1
Const FALSE = 0
```

3. Put this code in the Picture1_MouseDown procedure.

```
Sub Picture1_MouseDown (Index As Integer, Button As Integer, Shift As ⇐
    Integer, X As Single, Y As Single)
    Increment = Index * 2 - 1
    ButtonDown = TRUE
    While DoEvents() And ButtonDown
        Counter = Counter + Increment
        Text1.Text = Str$(Counter)
    Wend
End Sub
```

4. Put this code in the Picture1_MouseUp procedure.

```
Sub Picture1_MouseUp (Index As Integer, Button As Integer, ⇐
    Shift As Integer, X As Single, Y As Single)
    ButtonDown = FALSE
End Sub
```

## How It Works

The Picture1_MouseDown procedure first determines the increment based on Index passed to the routine. In other words, Increment = Index * 2 - 1 means if Index is 0, Increment is -1; if Index is 1, then Increment is 1. This could just as easily be a Case statement and, in fact, a Case statement is more appropriate for a larger control array, because there would be more than two binary choices of action within the event handler.

The Picture1_MouseDown routine sets the ButtonDown global variable to True. Ultimately, the procedure begins a While...Wend loop that continuously checks both DoEvents and ButtonDown. As stated earlier, we are not checking for any specific value to be returned by DoEvents. The DoEvents function will not return until the message queue under Windows is empty. The very act of checking DoEvents allows all other messages on the system to be processed before continuing, including the MouseUp message.

The MouseUp procedure simply sets ButtonDown to False, causing the test in the While...Wend loop in MouseDown to fail, ending the loop.

## Comments

Windows is based on a system of messages. Every action by the user, and many actions by the system itself, generates messages. If a particular process takes a long time to finish, the messages begin to "queue up." For example, if you open a file, move the mouse, and start typing, Windows queues up each of these events so one can't interfere with another. This is similar to the "type ahead buffer" under DOS. Because Windows, unlike OS/2 Presentation Manager, is not "preemptive," it is possible for applications to misbehave and prevent successful multitasking with other applications. For example, one application can dominate the time slicing so another application doesn't get time to do anything. In fact, if our Picture1_MouseDown routine contained a simple While...Wend loop without the DoEvents function, the application would never free itself up long enough to receive the MouseUp event.

The functionality of DoEvents could be duplicated using a timer but, besides the code being more convoluted, a timer would be slower. The DoEvents loop is the method most often used in Windows programming as it allows the fastest possible execution speed when no other messages are pending.

For this How-To, we used a static variable to hold the state of the buttons. A static variable is available to all the routines within a form. If you choose to use this technique, you might want to add a ButtonDown variable to your global module as you would only need one for each application.

# 2

# FORMS

# 2

Forms are the most fundamental building blocks of Visual Basic—it is impossible to program in Visual Basic without a working knowledge of them. Forms hold control buttons, list boxes, picture boxes, menu bars; they are the multifaceted containers that make Visual Basic programs possible. The tricks and techniques in this chapter are fundamental but versatile. You will probably want to include these techniques in your programs to make sure your form is centered automatically, and that its controls are adjusted automatically when the form is resized. You'll also learn to ensure that your progam's settings, size, and location are saved when you exit the program and restored when you reopen it. This chapter demonstrates ways to attract user attention by flashing the title bar of a form, displaying a hidden or minimized form, and a very cool way of starting your applications with an animated "exploding" look. You will also learn two different ways to secure your programs from unwanted eyes: one to prevent typed text from appearing on the screen, and a method of locking a window or a file so the user needs to enter a password to access it.

Although many of these How-Tos are accomplished with surprisingly few lines of code, this chapter relies heavily on the use of Windows APIs including GetWindowRect, GetWindowLong, ShowWindow, SetWindowLong, and the unbelievably versatile SendMessage.

## Windows APIs Covered

| | | |
|---|---|---|
| BringWindowToTop | GetProfileInt | SendMessage |
| CreateSolidBrush | GetProfileString | SetBkColor |
| DeleteObject | GetWindowRect | SetSysModalWindow |
| FlashWindow | GetWindowLong | SetWindowLong |
| GetDC | Rectangle | ShowWindow |
| GetFocus | Release DC | WritePrivateProfileString |
| GetPrivateProfileInt | SelectObject | WriteProfileString |
| GetPrivateProfileString | | |

### 2.1 Automatically center a form on the screen

It is easy to manually center a form on the screen. But how can you tell if your program's user has a different video resolution from the one you designed in, and automatically center your form accordingly? This very simple How-to checks the form's WindowState property, finds out the height and width of the screen, and divides by two. What could be more simple?

### 2.2 Size a form's controls automatically

Windows users have become accustomed to resizing forms on their screen. A professional-looking program will resize the form's controls proportionately on the fly when the form is stretched or reduced. This simple subroutine builds on the How-To in Chapter 3 that set up a README file reader. It uses the Visual Basic ScaleWidth and ScaleHeight properties to figure out the size of the form and scale its controls.

### 2.3 Save program settings to a file

Sometimes you may want to save your program's settings, like a serial number, to a file so that these settings are restored the next time the file is opened. This How-To uses a number of Windows APIs to take care of the "dirty work" of reading and writing data to an .INI file: GetPrivate-ProfileInt, GetPrivateProfileString, GetProfileInt, GetProfileString, WritePrivateProfileString, and WriteProfileString. In this case, you'll learn how to write your program's settings to the general WIN.INI file.

**2.4**     **Remember the sizes and locations of my forms**

This How-To builds on the previous one to show you how to write additional characteristics of your form to an .INI file. Again we use APIs, in this case GetProfileString and WriteProfileString, but this time we ascertain the size and position of your form's window on the screen. We use Visual Basic's form properties, Left, Top, Width, and Height.

**2.5**     **Flash the title bar of my forms**

A common way to attract a user's attention is to use the PC's speaker to utter a beep, which can eventually become annoying. But there is a more subtle and professional way to draw attention to your form—flash its title bar. By attaching a Windows API, FlashWindow, to Visual Basic's timer event subroutine, you switch back and forth between the title bar's active and inactive colors. Clicking on your form will disable this feature. This HowTo also works on minimized icons.

**2.6**     **Display a hidden form**

Sometimes a form will require attention even if its window is minimized or covered by another application. Two Windows API functions, Show-Window and BringWindowToTop, can display a hidden window under program control. A Timer event will also make the hidden window visible but not active.

**2.7**     **Start my applications with an animated look**

Have you ever noticed the way Macintosh applications "explode" open when they start up? Essentially, they display a quick sucession of gradually increasing zoomboxes before showing the opening window of an application. It is a challenge to duplicate this effect in Visual Basic because the language limits you to drawing objects only on the form itself. This clever How-To uses a number of Windows APIs: GetWindowRect, GetDC, Release DC, SetBkColor, Rectangle, CreateSolidBrush, SelectObject, and DeleteObject to animate a series of expanding boxes on the desktop behind your application. The crucial subroutine in this How-To is written as a separate module so it can be plugged into your other Visual Basic projects.

**2.8** **Prevent text typed in a text box from appearing on the screen**
There may be times when you want to shield user input from curious eyes. Perhaps you want to write a telecommunications program that requests a user's password. You could use Visual Basic's KeyPress event to trap keystrokes but there is a more sophisticated and powerful technique using Windows APIs. This How-To uses GetFocus, GetWindowsLong, SetWindowLong, and SendMessage to allow Windows to intercept and pass messages. When the user types a text character, a tilde (~) appears in the text box.

**2.9** **Prevent user access to a window or file**
Sometimes you may desire more security for your applications than just shielding user input from public view. There may be instances when you want to prevent access to a specific file or window; perhaps you want to create a confidential spreadsheet or document. This intermediate-level How-To uses the APIs we explored in the previous How-To, as well as SetSysModalWindow, to lock a window. This window will not get focus until a user types in the correct password. As an extra precaution, users are only allowed three attempts to type in the password.

---

**2.1    How do I...**

# Automatically center a form on the screen?

Complexity: Easy

### Problem
How can I automatically center my application's form on the screen? I can manually do it when I design the form, but if a user has a different type of screen than I do, the measurements will be off. What can I do?

### Technique
Remember that one can never assume, in Windows, a computer's configuration—especially the type of video display. You must respect Windows' device independence. (Your Visual Basic application can run on any machine that runs Windows, whether it has a CGA, EGA, VGA, or a display with even more colors and higher resolution. Windows manages all the hardware details for you.) Visual Basic provides plenty of statements that you can use to address aspects of the hardware (such as the screen size) in a device-inde-

pendent way. Because we can find out the height and width of the screen and of a form, we can simply divide by two to center the form.

### Steps

Open and run AUTOPOS.MAK. There are no controls on the form, but when it loads, it automatically positions itself in the center of the screen. The form isn't locked in the center (you can move the form), but if you resize it, it automatically moves back to the center.

1. Create a new project called AUTOPOS.MAK. Create a new form with no controls. Save it as AUTOPOS.FRM.

2. Place the following code in the Form_Resize event subroutine. The Form_Resize event subroutine ensures that the form is neither minimized nor maximized by checking the form's WindowState property and if it isn't, moves the form to the center of the screen.

```
Sub Form_Resize ()
    If WindowState = 0 Then
        ' don't attempt if form is minimized or maximized
        Move (Screen.Width - Form1.Width) / 2, (Screen.Height -
Form1.Height) / 2
    End If
End Sub
```

### How It Works

The Form_Resize event subroutine checks whether the form is normal—not minimized and not maximized. Minimized forms can't be moved because they're just icons. Maximized forms can't be moved because they already take up the whole screen.

The Move statement does the magic. Subtracting the width of the form from the total screen width gives us the total amount of space on either side of the form. Dividing that by two gives us the same amount of space on either side of the form, horizontally centering it. The same calculations for height can be performed to center the form vertically.

### Comment

Putting the calculations in the Form_Resize event subroutine will recenter the form whenever the form is resized. If you want to center the form only when you first run the application, just put the calculations in the Form_Load event subroutine.

# Size a form's controls automatically?

Complexity: Easy

### Problem

Window users want to be able to resize forms and have the controls on those forms shrink or stretch proportionately. Windows PaintBrush works this way. For example, if I expand a form, I'd like my list boxes to take advantage of the increased space available. However, when I resize the form, its controls are "clipped."

### Technique

This resizing is easy to accomplish because a control's properties can be changed on the fly. We can easily query a form's controls to find out its current properties, so all we have to do then to resize a list box is query a form's width and height, then set the list box's matching properties proportionately.

### Steps

Open and run AUTOSIZE.MAK. This project is an extension of the FileView project we built in the Text and Scrolling chapter. Scroll bars let you view the entire README file. When you resize a form, the list box resizes right along with it.

1. Create the FileView project as discussed in How-To 3.6 Set up a README file reader, and re-save it as AUTOSIZE.MAK. Then add the following code in the Resize event subroutine of the form object.

```
Sub Form_Resize ()
    List1.Width = ScaleWidth - List1.Left
    List1.Height = ScaleHeight - List1.Top
End Sub
```

### How It Works

The Form_Resize subroutine does all the extra work of resizing the list box. Line 2 of the subroutine sets the Width property of the list box based on the ScaleWidth property of the form, and the current Left property of the list box. This keeps the list box at the current horizontal position but lets it grow toward the right. We used the ScaleWidth property because we want to resize the list box based on the internal width of the form. Line 3 sets the

Height property of the list box based on the ScaleHeight property of the form and the current Top property of the list box. This keeps the list box at the current vertical position but lets it grow downward. Again, we use the ScaleHeight property to measure the interior height of the form.

### Comment

The procedure we just outlined assumes that the list box is the "last" control on the form; in other words, there are no controls below or to the right of the list box. If the list box is not the last control, the list box will cover up those other controls.

When the list box resizes itself, the entries in the list box automatically reformat to fit the new size.

---

**2.3     How do I...**

## Save program settings to a file?

Complexity: Easy

### Problem

I want to save some program settings, such as serial numbers and colors, in a file that will read them back the next time I run my application. How can I do this?

### Technique

Many Windows applications save information like serial numbers or window colors in a file and just read them in when the program starts. Have you ever noticed all the files in your Windows directory that have .INI extensions? That's where Windows applications store those kinds of settings. Windows provides the following API functions to do the dirty work of reading and writing those .INI files for you:

- GetPrivateProfileInt
- GetPrivateProfileString
- GetProfileInt
- GetProfileString
- WritePrivateProfileString
- WriteProfileString

**Steps**

Open and run PROFILE-1.MAK. The first time you run Profile1, the serial number is 1. You can enter a new serial number, then click on Ok. The new serial number is written to the WIN.INI file and the next time you run Profile1, the new serial number will appear in the text box. If you click on Cancel, nothing is written in the WIN.INI file. Figure 2-1 shows the complete form.

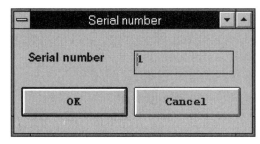

**Figure 2-1** Profile1 form at run time

1. Create a new project called PROFILE1.MAK. Create a new form with the properties listed in Table 2-1 and save it as PROFILE.FRM.

| Object | Property | Setting |
|---|---|---|
| Form | Caption | Serial number |
| Label | Caption | Serial number |
| Text box | CtlName | SerialNumber |
| | Text | <blank> |
| Command button | CtlName | Ok |
| | Caption | Ok |
| | Default | True |
| Command button | CtlName | Cancel |
| | Caption | Cancel |
| | Cancel | True |

**Table 2-1** Profile1 project form's objects and properties

2. Put the following code in the Declarations section of the form. This code defines some constants for use with the API functions that are declared.

```
Const APPNAME$ = "Profile1"
Const KEYNAME$ = "SerialNumber"

Declare Function GetProfileInt Lib "Kernel" (ByVal lpAppName$, ByVal ⇐
lpKeyName$, ByVal nDefault%) As Integer
Declare Function WriteProfileString Lib "Kernel" (ByVal ⇐
lpApplicationName$, ByVal lpKeyName$, ByVal lpString$) As Integer
```

3. Put the following statement in the Load event subroutine of the form. This statement calls the GetProfileInt API function to read the WIN.INI file and get the serial number currently there. If there is none, the value 1 will be returned.

```
Sub Form_Load ()
   SerialNumber.Text = Mid$(Str$(GetProfileInt(APPNAME$, KEYNAME$, 1)), 2)
End Sub
```

4. Put the following code in the Click event subroutine of the Ok button. This code calls the WriteProfileString API function to write the serial number to WIN.INI. If there is an error, a message box is popped up.

```
Sub OK_Click ()
   SerialNum$ = SerialNumber.Text
   If WriteProfileString(APPNAME$, KEYNAME$, SerialNum$) = 0 Then
      MsgBox "Unable to write profile string", 48, APPNAME$
   End If
   End
End Sub
```

5. Put the following code in the Cancel button's Click event subroutine.

```
Sub Cancel_Click ()
   End
End Sub
```

**How It Works**

Luckily, Windows API functions actually do most of the work including reading and writing the WIN.INI file. The Declare Sub statements in the Declarations section give Visual Basic access to the Windows API function DLLs (Data Link Libraries).

The form load event subroutine uses GetProfileInt to retrieve an integer from the WIN.INI file. We then write the string representation of that number into the text box.

The Ok button click event subroutine takes the text and, using WriteProfileString, writes it to the WIN.INI file. If there's a problem, we pop up a message box. Otherwise, we just end the program.

**Comments**

Here we're just using the integer versions of the Windows API functions; there are also API functions to read and write strings. You might also want to record the user's name along with the serial number.

The Windows API functions with "Private" in their name read and write data from individual (private) .INI files, rather than from WIN.INI. Using private .INI files is faster than using WIN.INI. Also, because you must give Windows the path name of your private .INIs, they are especially useful on a network. Each user of your application can store his settings in a private .INI file on a local disk. That way, one user's settings won't overwrite all others'.

## 2.4    How do I...

# Remember the sizes and locations of my forms?

Complexity: Easy

### Problem

My application calls for using multiple forms that users will move around on the screen. I'd like it so when the users quit and then restart the applications the forms appear where they were last.

### Technique

Some Windows applications are "smart" and save and remember the current size and position of their windows. It's easy for you to do the same, using some of Visual Basic's own property keywords.

As mentioned in the previous How-To, Windows supports .INI files—files that store settings on disk so the user doesn't have to enter those settings every time they run an application. One .INI file—WIN.INI—is the "master" .INI file that Windows itself uses to store certain settings, like the type and configuration of your printers. We'll use some Windows API calls to write the size and position of a form to WIN.INI.

**Figure 2-2**  Profile2 form

### Steps

Open and run PROFILE2.MAK. When you close the window, the size and position of the window will be written to WIN.INI under the section titled [Profile2]. Then, whenever you run Profile2, the window will be sized and positioned to the window's size and position the last time it was closed, as shown in Figure 2-2.

1. Create a new project called PROFILE2.MAK. Create a new form and give it a label and a command button captioned Exit!. Save it as PROFILE2.FRM. Put the following code in the Declarations section of the form:

```
Const APPNAME$ = "Profile2"

Declare Function GetProfileString Lib "Kernel" (ByVal lpAppName$, ByVal ⇐
lpKeyName$, ByVal lpDefault$, ByVal lpReturnedString$, ByVal nSize%) ⇐
As Integer
Declare Function WriteProfileString Lib "Kernel" (ByVal
lpApplicationName$, ByVal lpKeyName$, ByVal lpString$) As Integer

Dim iLeft As Single     ' Horizontal size
Dim iTop As Single      ' Vertical size
Dim iHeight As Single   ' Height
Dim iWidth As Single    ' Width
```

2. Put the following code in the Load event subroutine of the form.

```
Sub Form_Load ()
   Temp$ = String$(16, 0)
   i = GetProfileString(APPNAME$, "Left", "1000", Temp$, 16)
   Left = Val(Temp$)

   Temp$ = String$(16, 0)
   i = GetProfileString(APPNAME$, "Top", "1000", Temp$, 16)
   Top = Val(Temp$)

   Temp$ = String$(16, 0)
   i = GetProfileString(APPNAME$, "Width", "1000", Temp$, 16)
   Width = Val(Temp$)

   Temp$ = String$(16, 0)
   i = GetProfileString(APPNAME$, "Height", "1000", Temp$, 16)
   Height = Val(Temp$)
End Sub
```

3. Put the following code in the Unload event subroutine of the form.

```
Sub Form_Unload (Cancel As Integer)
   i = WriteProfileString(APPNAME$, "Left", Str$(iLeft))
   i = WriteProfileString(APPNAME$, "Top", Str$(iTop))
   i = WriteProfileString(APPNAME$, "Width", Str$(iWidth))
   i = WriteProfileString(APPNAME$, "Height", Str$(iHeight))
End Sub
```

4. Put the following code fragment in the Paint event subroutine of the form.

```
Sub Form_Paint ()
   iLeft = Left
   iTop = Top
   iWidth = Width
   iHeight = Height
   Label1.Caption = "Form is" + Str$(iWidth) + "x" + Mid$(Str$(iHeight),
2) + " at" + Str$(iLeft) + "x" + Mid$(Str$(iTop), 2)
End Sub
```

## How It Works

The Windows API functions actually do most of the work for us. The Declare Sub statements in the Declarations section are very important: They give Visual Basic access to the Windows API function DLLs.

Visual Basic's form properties Left, Top, Width, and Height do all the sizing and positioning for us. We use them in the Paint event subroutine to get the size and position of the form. They are saved to the WIN.INI file in the Unload event subroutine, and reset the size and position of the form in the Load event subroutine.

### Comment

You might want to save other window properties also. Check the WindowState property to save the maximized or minimized property of a window, for example.

---

**2.5      How do I...**

# Flash the title bar of my forms?

Complexity: Easy

### Problem

How can I visually attract my users' attention instead of using some annoying bleeping sound from Windows?

### Technique

Windows provides an API function called, appropriately enough, FlashWindow to briefly flash the title bar of a window. You can key FlashWindow to a timer event subroutine to make a form flash at regular intervals.

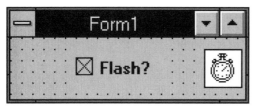

**Figure 2-3** The completed Flash form at design time

### Steps

Open and run FLASH.MAK. The form's title bar will start flashing rapidly. You can stop it from flashing by clicking anywhere on the form. Figure 2-3 shows the completed Flash form.

1. Create a new project called FLASH.MAK. Create a form with the objects and properties shown in Table 2-2 and save it as FLASH.FRM.

| Object | Property | Setting |
|---|---|---|
| Timer | CtlName | Timer1 |
| | Enabled | True |
| | Interval | 250 |
| Check box | CtlName | Check1 |
| | Value | 1 - Checked |
| | Caption | Flash? |

**Table 2-2** Flash project form's objects and properties

2. Put the following code in the Declarations section of the form. This Declare statement lets the program access the FlashWindow Windows API function.

```
Declare Function FlashWindow Lib "User" (ByVal hWnd%, ByVal bInvert%) As ⇐
Integer
```

3. Put the following code in the Check1_Click event subroutine. This code disables the timer that flashes the title bar if the Check Box isn't clicked.

```
Sub Check1_Click ()
   If Check1.Value = 0 Then
      Timer1.Enabled = 0
      I = FlashWindow(Form1.hWnd, 0)
   Else
      Timer1.Enabled = -1
   End If
End Sub
```

4. Put the following code in the Timer1_Timer event subroutine. This call to the FlashWindow API function flashes the title bar every time the timer goes off (every 250 milliseconds) if the Check Box is clicked.

```
Sub Timer1_Timer ()
   I = FlashWindow(Form1.hWnd, 1)
End Sub
```

### How It Works

The FlashWindow API function "flashes" the title bar by switching back and forth between the inactive title bar colors and the active title bar colors. It acts just as if you'd clicked the mouse cursor on another window (which makes your form inactive) and then clicked again on your form (which makes it active).

FlashWindow takes just two arguments: a window handle and a flag called bInvert. The window handle is provided by the hWnd property of the form. If the bInvert flag is nonzero, FlashWindow flashes the title bar to the opposite it is at the time of the call. (active <-> inactive) If the bInvert flag is zero, FlashWindow returns the form to its original state, active.

In the Check1_Click event subroutine, a call to FlashWindow with bInvert 0 makes the form active again. This code disables the timer, if the Check Box has not been clicked, and prevents the form from flashing.

The Timer1_Timer event subroutine calls FlashWindow with bInvert nonzero (1), which inverts the title bar mode. Since the timer is enabled, the next time the timer interval is activated, the title bar will be re-inverted.

### Comment

FlashWindow also works when the form is minimized to an icon, except that instead of the title bar flashing (which the icon doesn't really have), the whole icon flashes. You must restore the icon to a window before you can click on the form to stop it.

---

**2.6     How do I...**

# Display a hidden form?

Complexity: Easy

### Problem

How can I let my users know that a Visual Basic form requires attention if it is minimized or covered by another application's window?

### Technique

The Windows API library has a number of functions that will force Windows to display a hidden window. This project demonstrates how a previously hidden window can be displayed under program control.

**Figure 2-4** Topwin form at design time

### Steps

Open and run TOPWIN.MAK. It will look like Figure 2-4. The form will move itself to the lower right-hand corner of the screen and display the current time. If you hide it by running another Windows application, Topwin will pop through to the top. To exit the application, click anywhere on the form. To create the Topwin project, enter the objects and code in the following steps.

1. Create a new project called TOPWIN.MAK. Enter the following constants and Windows API declarations into the Global module and save it as TOPWIN.BAS.

```
Global Const SW_SHOWNA = 8

Declare Sub BringWindowToTop Lib "User" (ByVal hWnd As Integer)
Declare Sub ShowWindow Lib "User" (ByVal hWnd As Integer, ByVal nCmdShow ⇐
As Integer)
```

2. Create a new form with the objects and properties shown in Table 2-3. Save it as TOPWIN.FRM.

| Object | Property | Setting |
|--------|----------|---------|
| Form | FormName | Topwin |
| | Caption | Make Top Window |
| Timer | CtlName | Timer1 |
| | Enabled | True |
| | Interval | 1000 |
| Label | CtlName | Label1 |
| | Caption | xx:xx:xx xx |

**Table 2-3** Topwin project form's objects and properties

3. Put the following code in the Form_Load event subroutine.

```
Sub Form_Load ()

' Make Label1 fill entire form.
   Label1.Top = 0
   Label1.Left = 0
   Label1.Width = Scalewidth
   Label1.Height = Scaleheight

' Position form in lower right corner of screen.
   Topwin.Top = Screen.Height – Topwin.Height
   Topwin.Left = Screen.Width – Topwin.Width

' Set up crosshair mouse.
   Topwin.MousePointer = 2
End Sub
```

4. Put the following code in the Timer1_Timer event subroutine. On each timer event, this subroutine will make the form visible and display the current time in the Label1 control. The ShowWindow API call makes the form visible but not active. That is, the currently running application will function normally. The WindowState is set to zero to restore the form to its default size from a minimized or maximized state.

```
Sub Timer1_Timer ()
   ShowWindow Topwin.hwnd, SW_SHOWNA
   Windowstate = 0
   Label1.Caption = Time$
End Sub
```

5. Put the following code in the Label1_Click event subroutine. By clicking the mouse anywhere in the Label1 control, the user can exit the application.

```
Sub Label1_Click ()
   End
End Sub
```

### Comments

The ShowWindow API call displays the specified window but doesn't make it active. To activate the window, simply click on the form's caption bar. The BringWindowToTop API call both displays the window and activates it in one step. The declaration for this function is included in the Global module code of Step 1.

You may want to set Topwin's BorderStyle to 0 (None), so that it will take up as little space on the screen as possible.

The form's MousePointer is set to a crosshair as a further indication of when the form is active.

---

**2.7    How do I...**

# Start my applications with an animated look?

Complexity: Intermediate

### Problem

I would like to give my forms an "exploding" look when they are first displayed. How can I do this in Visual Basic?

### Technique

You can make your forms appear to expand at startup by displaying a series of expanding boxes behind each form. This will lend an animated feel to your application's startup. The expanding boxes are displayed with code placed in the form's Load event subroutine. This event is called by Visual Basic before the form is first made visible. The boxes are drawn using the Windows API functions since the Visual Basic methods can only draw objects on the form itself.

**Figure 2-5** The Explode project as a full-sized window

### Steps

Open and run EXPLODE.MAK. Notice how the window grows until it becomes full-sized as shown in Figure 2-5. Clicking on the From Center command button will "explode" the form in all directions from its center. Clicking on the From Corner command button will "explode" it from the upper left-hand corner.

The project may be created by entering the objects and code as detailed in the following steps.

1. Create a new project called EXPLODE.MAK. Create a new form with the objects and properties listed in Table 2-4. Save it as EXPLODE.FRM.

2. Place the following declarations in the Global module and save it as EXPLODE.BAS.

```
Type RECT
   Left As Integer
   Top As Integer
   Right As Integer
   Bottom As Integer
End Type
```

| Object | Property | Setting |
|---|---|---|
| Form | FormName | Explode |
| | BackColor | &HC0& |
| | BorderStyle | 0 - None |
| Command button | CtlName | CmdExit |
| | Caption | Exit |
| | FontSize | 12 |
| Command button | CtlName | CmdCenter |
| | Caption | From Center |
| | FontSize | 12 |
| Command button | CtlName | CmdCorner |
| | Caption | From Corner |
| | FontSize | 12 |

**Table 2-4**  Explode project form's objects and properties

3. Place the following declaration in the Declarations section of the form.

```
Const FALSE = 0
Const TRUE = -1
'
'  Form global flag to expand from corner (false) or
'   center (true).

Dim CenterFlag As Integer
```

4. Place the following code in the CmdExit_Click event subroutine. This command button allows the user to exit gracefully from the application.

```
Sub CmdExit_Click ()
   End
End Sub
```

5. Put the following code in the Form_Load event subroutine to "explode" the form when the application is started.

```
Sub Form_Load ()
   ExplodeForm Explode, CenterFlag
End Sub
```

6. Place the following code in the CmdCenter_Click event subroutine. Setting the CenterFlag variable to True will cause the window to grow from its center.

```
Sub CmdCenter_Click ()
'
' User clicked on from center button, set flag.
' Unload and then load form to trigger Load event.
   CenterFlag = TRUE
   Unload Explode
   Load Explode            ' Simulate startup
End Sub
```

7. Put the following code in the CmdCorner_Click event subroutine. Setting the CenterFlag variable to False will cause the form to expand from its top left corner.

```
Sub CmdCorner_Click ()
'
' User clicked on from corner button, set flag.
' Unload and then load form to trigger Load event.
   CenterFlag = FALSE
   Unload Explode
   Load Explode
End Sub
```

8. Open a new module for this project, using the New Module option from the File menu. This module has the code which gives the form its exploding look at startup. Put the following API declarations into the General section of the module and save the module as EXPLODIT.BAS.

```
Declare Sub GetWindowRect Lib "User" (ByVal hWnd As Integer, lpRect As RECT)
Declare Function GetDC Lib "User" (ByVal hWnd As Integer) As Integer
Declare Function ReleaseDC Lib "User" (ByVal hWnd As Integer, ByVal hDC ⇐
As Integer) As Integer
Declare Sub SetBkColor Lib "GDI" (ByVal hDC As Integer, ByVal crColor As Long)
Declare Sub Rectangle Lib "GDI" (ByVal hDC As Integer, ByVal X1 As ⇐
Integer, ByVal Y1 As Integer, ByVal X2 As Integer, ByVal Y2 As Integer)
Declare Function CreateSolidBrush Lib "GDI" (ByVal crColor As Long) As ⇐
Integer
Declare Function SelectObject Lib "GDI" (ByVal hDC As Integer, ByVal ⇐
hObject As Integer) As Integer
Declare Sub DeleteObject Lib "GDI" (ByVal hObject As Integer)
```

9. Put the following code in the ExplodeForm subroutine of the EXPLODIT.BAS module. This subroutine does the animated drawing on the screen.

```
Sub ExplodeForm (F As Form, CenterFlag As Integer)
Const STEPS = 75
Const TRUE = -1
Dim FRect As RECT
Dim FullWidth As Integer, FullHeight As Integer
Dim I As Integer
Dim X As Integer, Y As Integer, Cx As Integer, Cy As Integer
Dim hDCScreen As Integer, hBrush As Integer, hOldBrush

' If CenterFlag = True, then explode from center of form, otherwise
' explode from upper left corner.
'

' Get current window position (in pixels) and compute width & height.

    GetWindowRect F.hWnd, FRect
    FullWidth = (FRect.Right - FRect.Left)
    FullHeight = FRect.Bottom - FRect.Top

' Get a device context for the whole screen.
' Create brush with Form's background color.
' Select the brush into the device context.

    hDCScreen = GetDC(0)
    hBrush = CreateSolidBrush(F.BackColor)
    hOldBrush = SelectObject(hDCScreen, hBrush)

' Draw rectangles in larger sizes filling in the area to be occupied
' by the form.
    For I = 1 To STEPS
        Cx = FullWidth * (I / STEPS)
        Cy = FullHeight * (I / STEPS)
        If CenterFlag Then
            X = FRect.Left + (FullWidth - Cx) / 2
            Y = FRect.Top + (FullHeight - Cy) / 2
        Else
            X = FRect.Left
            Y = FRect.Top
        End If

        Rectangle hDCScreen, X, Y, X + Cx, Y + Cy

    Next I

' Release the device context and brush to free memory.
' Make the Form visible
    If ReleaseDC(0, hDCScreen) = 0 Then
        MsgBox "Unable to Release Device Context", 16
    End If
    DeleteObject (hBrush)
    F.Visible = TRUE

End Sub
```

## How It Works

The real effort in this program is performed by the ExplodeForm subroutine located in the EXPLODIT.BAS module. This subroutine was written as a separate module so that it can be included in other Visual Basic projects. ExplodeForm draws its series of expanding boxes directly onto the screen, or desktop window. It does this by bypassing the normal window management functions provided by Visual Basic and uses the Windows API directly. It is considered "bad manners" to draw in an area not owned by your application, but, since the area in which we are drawing will eventually be covered by the form itself, potential conflicts are avoided.

To draw on the desktop, we make use of the Windows API functions declared in the General section of the Explodit module. The ExplodeForm subroutine begins by determining the form's size using the GetWindowRect API call. This call loads a form's coordinates into a user-defined structure of type RECT. Each of the elements of RECT: Left, Top, Right, and Bottom, represent the screen coordinates, in pixels, of the form's corners. Because the other API calls in this subroutine use pixels for their drawing coordinates, it is easier to use the GetWindowRect call than to convert Visual Basic's standard unit of measure, twips, to pixels.

To draw a filled object such as a rectangle we must provide Windows with a device context and a brush. The device context identifies on which window the objects will be displayed and their graphics properties, such as the background color. To set a device context's background color, we first create a brush, and then tell Windows to use the brush within a specific device context. Then both the device context and brush must be deleted after use, since Windows can only store internally a limited number of these properties at one time. One of Visual Basic's strengths is that it provides all these functions and services for us when drawing on a form or picture box. However, since Visual Basic's methods cannot be used to draw directly on the desktop, we need to create and delete these items manually.

The GetDC(0) call returns a handle to a device context for the entire screen. With this device context handle, hDCScreen, the Windows API drawing functions can draw anywhere on the display. A brush is created using the API call CreateSolidBrush. Its color is set to match that of the form's background. The SelectObject API call tells Windows to associate the brush with the device context handle passed as the first parameter.

The For...Next loop draws the set of expanding boxes. The variables Cx and Cy contain the width and height, respectively, of each box. If the boxes grow from the center, then the coordinates of the upper left corner, x and y, are set according to Cx and Cy. If the boxes are drawn from the upper left corner, x and y remain fixed.

The Rectangle API function draws a rectangle on the device context passed as its first parameter. The other four parameters are the window coordinates, in pixels, of its four corners. Since the hDCScreen device context has a solid brush associated with it, the rectangles will be drawn with a filled background.

After the boxes are drawn, the device context is released using the ReleaseDC function, and the brush is deleted. If you don't perform these functions, Windows will run out of resources and eventually hang.

To make sure that the form is displayed, the form's Visible property is set to True.

The form exploded on startup as a result of the Form_Load event. When a form is initially loaded, its Form_Load event is called before the form is made visible. Trapping this event and calling the ExplodeForm subroutine lets us get control of the display before Visual Basic initially makes it visible.

The other command button event subroutines takes advantage of the Form_Load event by unloading, and then loading, the Explode form. These actions cause a Form_Load event.

### Comment

If you are entering this code manually, save your code often, and be careful about releasing the hDCScreen device context and deleting the brush. Forgetting to do so will cause Windows to hang and require a system reboot.

---

**2.8     How do I...**

## Prevent text typed into a text box from appearing on the screen?

Complexity: Intermediate

### Problem

When I ask my users for a password or some other confidential information, I'd like to prevent that text from appearing on the screen as users type it in. Is there some way I can do this?

### Technique

A complex way would be to trap keystrokes using the KeyPress event. Luckily, Windows text boxes can do more than Visual Basic lets them do. Windows text boxes respond to a variety of messages, most of which Visual Basic automatically sends when you use a property like SelText. However, you can access the other messages with the API function SendMessage. One of these messages is EM_SETPASSWORDCHAR, which lets you set the character to be displayed.

### Steps

Open and run PAS-SWORD.MAK. It will look like Figure 2-6. Type any text into the text box. Notice that each character

**Figure 2-6** The Password form in action

is echoed as a tilde (~), not the actual character that you typed. When you press Enter or click on Ok, what you actually typed is displayed in a message box.

1. Create a new project called PASSWORD.MAK. Create a form with the objects and properties shown in Table 2-5 and save it as PASSWORD.FRM.

| Object | Property | Setting |
|---|---|---|
| Form | Caption | Enter password |
| | FormName | PasswordForm |
| Text box | CtlName | Text1 |
| | Multiline | False |
| | Text | <none> |
| Command button | Caption | Ok |
| | CtlName | Ok |
| | Default | True |
| Command button | Caption | Cancel |
| | Cancel | True |
| | CtlName | Cancel |

**Table 2-5** Password project form's objects and properties

2. Put the following code in the Declarations section of the form. These Const and Declare statements are used to access the Windows API functions that let us send messages to the text box to change its styles.

```
Declare Function GetFocus Lib "User" () As Integer
Declare Function GetWindowLong Lib "User" (ByVal hWnd%, ByVal nIndex%) ⇐
As Long
Declare Function SetWindowLong Lib "User" (ByVal hWnd%, ByVal nIndex%, ⇐
ByVal dwNewLong&) As Long
Declare Function SendMessage Lib "User" (ByVal hWnd%, ByVal wMsg%, ⇐
ByVal wParam%, ByVal lParam&) As Long
```

```
Const WM_USER = &H400
Const EM_SETPASSWORDCHAR = WM_USER + 28
Const ES_PASSWORD = &H20
Const GWL_STYLE = -16
```

3. Put the following code in the Cancel_Click event subroutine. This subroutine simply ends the program.

```
Sub Cancel_Click ()
    End
End Sub
```

4. Put the following code in the Form_Load event subroutine. This code changes the text box's styles to suppress displaying the characters as they are typed. Then the SendMessage function tells the text box to use the tilde character (~) instead.

```
Sub Form_Load ()
    Dim hWnd As Integer    ' Window handle for the control
    Dim StyleFlags As Long ' Window style for the control

    ' We have to show form before setting focus on Text Box.
    Show

    ' Set focus on the Text Box.
    Text1.SetFocus

    ' Get text box's hWnd.
    hWnd = GetFocus()

    ' Get current style flags.
    StyleFlags = GetWindowLong(hWnd, GWL_STYLE)

    ' Set the password style.
    StyleFlags = StyleFlags Or ES_PASSWORD

    ' Change the style flags.
    StyleFlags = SetWindowLong(hWnd, GWL_STYLE, StyleFlags)

    ' Send message indicating character to print (Chr$(126)=~).
    StyleFlags = SendMessage(hWnd, EM_SETPASSWORDCHAR, 126, 0&)
End Sub
```

5. Put the following code in the Ok_Click event subroutine. This line displays the actual contents of the Text Box in a message box.

```
Sub Ok_Click ()
    MsgBox Text1.Text
End Sub
```

**How It Works**

The Form_Load event subroutine manipulates Windows messages and styles to make a text box display a tilde instead of what the user actually types. Although there are quite a few steps to display multiple lines of text, remember that this is what Visual Basic is doing whenever it encounters a statement like

```
MultiLine = True
```

It's only necessary to resort to sending and processing messages if Visual Basic doesn't provide a keyword to process the text in a non-standard way of your choosing.

Windows sends messages via a window handle, so the GetFocus API function is used to get the window handle of a control.

The Windows message to tell a text box to use another character is EM_SETPASSWORDCHAR, which the WINAPI.TXT file in the Windows SDK defines as WM_USER + 28. WM_USER is defined as 0x400, or &H400 in Visual Basic hexadecimal lingo. Thus, EM_SETPASSWORD-CHAR is actually &H41C.

Windows text boxes have many styles, such as multiple lines. Luckily, most of those styles are selectable by Visual Basic property keywords (such as the Multiline property). One style that Visual Basic doesn't implement is the ES_PASSWORD style, which indicates that a text box will display some character that hides what the user is really typing into the text box.

There might already be several styles applied to the text box, so a call to the GetWindowLong API function returns those styles. The GWL_STYLE constant that is passed as a parameter tells GetWindowLong that all it should return is the current styles of the text box. Visual Basic's bitwise Or operator "adds" the ES_PASSWORD style. Then a call to SetWindowLong updates the text box's styles to include the ES_PASSWORD style.

Once the text box knows a password style is being applied, the box will accept the EM_SETPASSWORDCHAR message, which tells it to change the character it will display as the user types into the text box.

**Comment**

Although the Password form example uses a tilde as the password character, you can use any character you like. Asterisks [Chr$(42)] are common, as are underscores [Chr$(95)].

## 2.9    How do I...

# Prevent user access to a window or file?

Complexity: Intermediate

### Problem

My users would like to keep their confidential information safe from "prying eyes." I'd like to be able to prevent a user from being able to switch to other windows and get into "confidential" files. Can Visual Basic help me accomplish this?

### Technique

Windows can make any window a system modal window. A system modal window is different from a normal modal dialog box in that it is the only window that is allowed to get the focus. Attempts to switch to another by clicking on it with the mouse or pressing Alt+Tab to cycle through the windows will have no effect. Even double-clicking on the desktop or pressing Ctrl+Esc to bring up Windows' Task Manager will do nothing.

You can enhance the Password form from the previous How-To (Prevent text typed into a text box from appearing on screen) to lock the window once the user has typed in a password and only unlock it when the password is typed back in. That way, your users could enter their password to lock the system when they leave for lunch, for example, and reenter the password to unlock the system when they come back.

### Steps

Open and run PASSLOCK.MAK. Be sure to save your work! Enter a password, and don't forget it! The Cancel button will be disabled, so the only way to unlock the system is to enter the correct password and press Enter or click Ok.

1. Create a new project called PASSLOCK.MAK. Create a new form with the objects and properties in Table 2-6 and save it as PASSLOCK.FRM:

2. Put the following code in the Declarations section of the form. These Declare statements are used to access the Windows API functions to make the text box echo back asterisks as the user types the password, and the SetSysModalWindow function, which locks the system.

```
Declare Function GetFocus Lib "User" () As Integer
Declare Function GetWindowLong Lib "User" (ByVal hWnd%, ByVal nIndex%) ⇐
As Long
Declare Function SetWindowLong Lib "User" (ByVal hWnd%, ByVal nIndex%, ⇐
ByVal dwNewLong&) As Long
```

```
Declare Function SendMessage Lib "User" (ByVal hWnd%, ByVal wMsg%, ByVal  ⇐
wParam%, ByVal lParam&) As Long
Declare Function SetSysModalWindow Lib "User" (ByVal hWnd%) As Integer

Const WM_USER = &H400
Const EM_SETPASSWORDCHAR = WM_USER + 28
Const ES_PASSWORD = &H20
Const GWL_STYLE = -16
```

| Object | Property | Setting |
|---|---|---|
| Form | Caption | Unlocked - Enter password to lock |
| | FormName | PasswordForm |
| Text box | CtlName | Text1 |
| | Multiline | False |
| | Text | <none> |
| Command button | Caption | Ok |
| | CtlName | Ok |
| | Default | True |
| Command button | Caption | Cancel |
| | Cancel | True |
| | CtlName | Cancel |

**Table 2-6** PassLock project form's objects and properties

> 3. Put the following code in the Form_Load event subroutine. This code calls the necessary Windows API functions to set up the password text box and lock the form as the only one that can get the focus.

```
Sub Form_Load ()
    Dim hWnd As Integer      ' Window handle for the control
    Dim StyleFlags As Long  ' Window style for the control

    ' We have to show form before setting focus on Text Box.
    Show

    ' Set focus on the Text Box.
    Text1.SetFocus

    ' Get Text Box's hWnd.
    hWnd = GetFocus()

    ' Get current style flags.
    StyleFlags = GetWindowLong(hWnd, GWL_STYLE)

    ' Get the password style.
    StyleFlags = StyleFlags Or ES_PASSWORD
```

```
   ' Change the style flags.
   StyleFlags = SetWindowLong(hWnd, GWL_STYLE, StyleFlags)

   ' Send message indicating character to print (Chr$(42)=*).
   StyleFlags = SendMessage(hWnd, EM_SETPASSWORDCHAR, 42, 0&)

   ' Lock this form as a system modal window.
   I = SetSysModalWindow(PassLockForm.Hwnd)
End Sub
```

4. Put the following code in the Ok_Click event subroutine. This code handles it both when the system is locked and when it's unlocked. When we're locking the system, the Cancel button is disabled, so the only way to unlock the system is by entering the correct password. Also notice how the form's caption is changed to indicate the mode.

```
Sub Ok_Click ()
   Static Password$, Count

   If Password$ = "" Then
      Password$ = Text1.Text
      Text1.Text = ""
      PassLockForm.Caption = "Locked - Enter password to unlock."
      Cancel.Enabled = 0
      Count = 0
   Else
      If Password$ = Text1.Text Then
         Password$ = ""
         Text1.Text = ""
         PassLockForm.Caption = "Unlocked - Enter password to lock."
         Cancel.Enabled = -1
      Else
         Count = Count + 1
         If Count > 3 Then
            MsgBox "Wrong password! Sorry, but you've tried too many ⇐
               times!", 16
            Ok.Enabled = 0
            PassLockForm.Caption = "Locked - Too many mistyped passwords!"
         Else
            MsgBox "Wrong password! Try again, but remember, you" + ⇐
               Chr$(13) + Chr$(10) + "only have" + Str$(3 - Count) + " ⇐
               tries left!", 48
         End If
      End If
   End If
End Sub
```

5. Put the following code in the Cancel_Click event subroutine.

```
Sub Cancel_Click ()
   End
End Sub
```

**How It Works**

See previous How-To 2.8 Prevent text typed into a text box from appearing on screen, for details on how to prevent the characters being typed into the password text box from being displayed.

The SetSysModalWindow API function locks the window whose handle (hWnd) is supplied as a parameter. The only way to unlock it is by unloading the window. The Cancel_Click event subroutine does just that by executing Visual Basic's End statement.

The Ok_Click event subroutine is where the passwords are handled. There is a Password$ variable declared with Visual Basic's Static statement. The Static statement declares variables that are local to the subroutine where they're defined, and retains their values even after the subroutine ends.

The first If statement checks whether Password$ is equal to the null string. If it is, that means that there is no password, so the system isn't locked yet. Therefore, Password$ gets the text in the text box and the Cancel button is disabled.

If there's already a password, that means the system is locked, so the second If statement compares the password that was previously entered (Password$) with what's in the text box. If they match, the system can be unlocked by re-enabling the Cancel button. If they don't match, it means someone either mistyped the password or someone is trying to break into the system. Since someone might be able to guess the password by just trying random combinations, there should be some way to prevent many random guesses. Another static local variable, Count, keeps track of how many mismatched passwords have been entered. If the user has tried less than three times to enter a password, a message box pops up and tells the user that only so many attempts are left. But, if more than three mismatches happen, the OK button is disabled. The Cancel button was disabled when the password was entered, so this means there's no way to unlock the system except by rebooting it.

**Comment**

Remember that a password-protected system is only as secure as the passwords. If your users write their passwords down where other users can find them, someone who wanted to get in could do so easily. A password should be long enough to dissuade the petty hacker yet not so long as to be impossible to remember. Information services like CompuServe and MCI Mail use pronounceable nonsense words like "YAXALUPA" or "HOUSE*DREAM."

As presented, this form can still be closed by double-clicking on the control menu icon in the upper left-hand corner or by pressing Alt+F4. To be extra secure, you should modify the System menu (as shown in How-To 4.4 Modify a form's system menu) to remove the Close item from the system menu.

# 3

# TEXT
# AND
# SCROLLING

# 3

As a programmer, one of the most fundamental aspects of your application to control is the presentation of text. This chapter, Text and Scrolling, provides basic techniques, advanced insight, and programmer's tricks for presenting, receiving, and processing text using Visual Basic. This chapter presents a number of different techniques for scrolling text and graphics using Windows APIs and native Visual Basic code. You'll find How-Tos that scroll when Visual Basic's AutoRedraw property is either enabled or disabled, line-by-line scrolling or "crawl" scrolling like you see in movie credits, and and how to accomplish those effects with scroll bars or command buttons. You'll find out how to align text horizontally and vertically, instead of simply left-aligned, how to create a README file viewer and a simple text editor that searches for text strings. You'll also see how to accept text strings limited to numbers, how to trim null characters from strings, how to modify the speed at which the cursor blinks, and how to preview screen color combinations with scroll bars. Along the way, we'll corral a few Windows API functions to help make text processing quick and accurate, including the very powerful SendMessage API.

## Windows APIs Covered

| | |
|---|---|
| GetCaretBlinkTime | SendMessage |
| GetFocus | SetCaretBlinkTime |
| ScrollDC | SetTextAlign |
| ScrollWindow | UpdateWindow |

### 3.1 Scroll all the objects in a window?

Virtually every professional Visual Basic program needs to move graphics, text, and controls around a form. Often, everything your user needs to see will not fit on the screen at one time. For instance, a text document may have lines that are wider than the window, or you may have a large graphic. This How-To shows how to use the Windows API functions ScrollWindow and UpdateWindow to scroll the contents of an entire screen up, down, left or right.

### 3.2 Scroll text and graphics in a form or picture box

This How-To also demonstrates how the Windows API function library is used to extend Visual Basic. Unlike the APIs used in the previous How-To, theWindows API function ScrollDC allows your program to scroll graphics and text in any of four directions when AutoRedraw is enabled. AutoRedraw saves a bitmap of the screen so that the screen image is refreshed every time an item on the screen is moved, but it takes extra memory and screen painting time. This How-To also allows you to change the position of controls in a window and explains the use of persistent bitmaps.

### 3.3 Make text and graphics roll up the screen

A popular scrolling technique is the slow rolling of text and graphics, similar to "crawling" credits at the end of a movie. This type of scrolling is more gradual and professional looking than scolling text one line at a time because it bases text movement on pixel size, uses a timer, and places a picture box within a picture box. This technique is accomplished using pure Visual Basic code, no Windows APIs are needed. You will learn the subtle power of object containers

**3.4**     **Scroll a text box under program control**

Unlike the previous How-To that allows text to scroll up the screen like movie credits, this project produces smooth scrolling of the contents of a scroll box in any of eight compass directions. Rather than using traditional scroll bars to receive user input about the scroll direction, this project sets up command buttons. The ubiquitous SendMessage Windows API and the GetFocus API are used to receive user input from command buttons to control the direction of text scrolling without the use of scroll bars.

**3.5**     **Align text automatically**

When a Visual Basic program prints text on a screen, that text is always aligned with the left border of the screen. It is relatively easy to use the SetTextAlign Windows API function to vary the location of a text string in relation to the screen. This project will allow you to also center and right justify text, in addition to changing its vertical alignment in one of three ways. This technique uses the x and y properties of a character string to determine and adjust its location.

**3.6**     **Set up a README file reader**

In more "primitive" BASIC dialects, or in languages such as C or Pascal, creating a program to read DOS text requires some sort of input statements, PRINT or printf() statements, and some way to prevent text from scrolling off the screen. Just a very few lines of Visual Basic code will open up a DOS file and put it in a scroll box on the screen.

**3.7**     **Build a simple editor that searches for text**

Many applications can benefit by including a text editor. Visual Basic's text box controls allow a simple text editor that reads text data from a DOS file. A few additional Visual Basic functions can extend this editor's capabilities to load and save files, as well as to search for text. The simplicity of this powerful program, which uses purely native Visual Basic functions and no Windows APIs, shows what a flexible language Visual Basic is.

**3.8**     **Ensure a numeric-only entry in the text box**

Text and data processing account for the most popular computer tasks; word processors, databases, and spreadsheets are routinely used in home and business. Basic to these functions is the processing of user input. For instance, in database field for zip codes, how can you differentiate between text and data to assure that only numeric input is accepted? This How-To uses KeyPress events to limit user input to a restricted range of numbers.

**3.9**  **Trim null characters from a string**

When using Windows API functions to process text strings, a null character CHR$(0) may be added to the string. Visual Basic's LTrim$ and RTrim$ functions are effective for stripping spaces from the left and right end of strings, but not embedded null characters. This How-To demonstrates how to write a general Visual Basic function that will delete those null characters.

**3.10**  **Determine and modify the rate at which a text box's caret blinks**

Drawing user attention to a text box may be accomplished in many ways but generally the more subtle the technique, the more professional it appears. This How-To uses two Windows API functions, SetCaretBlinkTime and GetCaretBlinkTime to provide a variable blink rate for the cursor. Cursor blink speed can be varied through the Windows Control Panel, but this project shows how your Visual Basic application can do the same. A scroll bar is used to select the amount of time between the blinks.

**3.11**  **Use scroll bars to select colors**

This How-To emphasizes the "Visual" aspect of Visual Basic. When you are changing the appearance of your text or graphics display, it is nice to have a "preview" mode that will allow you to see effects before you enable them. This is useful, for instance, to prevent text from being printed on the same color background. If you've ever found yourself in that situation, you know that it is similar to being caught in a perpetual loop and you may have to halt program execution. This How-To uses scroll bars to let you see in advance the different blends of red, green, or blue colors on your monitor. Control arrays make it a very simple task to change color combinations on the fly.

---

**3.1      How do I...**

# Scroll all the objects in a window?

Complexity: Easy

**Problem**

I would like to be able to move all the graphics, text, and controls around my form.

**Technique**

The Windows API function Scroll-Window can be used to solve this problem. ScrollWindow moves the entire contents of a form—graphics, text, and Visual Basic controls—in any of four directions.

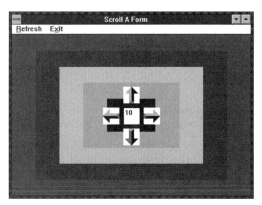

**Figure 3-1** The Scrllwnd form displaying a value of ten screen pixels

### Steps

Open and run SCRLLWND.MAK. Click on any of the four arrows in the center of the screen to scroll the window in the appropriate direction. The value in the centered text box, as shown in Figure 3-1, is the number of screen pixels to scroll on each click. If the value is set to a negative number, the action of the arrows is reversed. Clicking on the Refresh menu item will redraw the background pattern without changing the current position of the controls.

The Scrllwnd project may be created by entering the objects and code as detailed in the following steps.

1. Create a new project called SCRLLWND.MAK. Create a new form with the objects and properties shown in Table 3-1 and save it as SCRLL-WND.FRM. The placement of the controls is shown in Figure 3-1.

| Object | Property | Setting |
| --- | --- | --- |
| Form | FormName | Scroll |
| | Caption | Scroll a Form |
| | BackColor | &H00C0C0C0& |
| Picture box | CtlName | Picture1 |
| | Autosize | True |
| | BorderStyle | 0 - None |
| | Picture | ARROW02UP.ICO |
| | Index | 0 |
| Picture box | CtlName | Picture1 |
| | Autosize | True |
| | BorderStyle | 0 - None |
| | Picture | ARROW02DN.ICO |
| | Index | 1 |
| Picture box | CtlName | Picture1 |
| | Autosize | True |
| | BorderStyle | 0 - None |
| | Picture | ARROW02LT.ICO |
| | Index | 2 |

*Table 3-1. continued*

| Object | Property | Setting |
| --- | --- | --- |
| Picture box | CtlName | Picture1 |
| | Autosize | True |
| | BorderStyle | 0 - None |
| | Picture | ARROW02RT.ICO |
| | Index | 3 |
| Text box | CtlName | Text1 |
| | Text | 10 |

**Table 3-1** Scrllwnd project form's objects and properties

2. Create a menu for the form using the Menu Design window with the values shown in Table 3-2.

| Caption | CtlName |
| --- | --- |
| &Refresh | Repaint |
| E&xit | Quit |

**Table 3-2** Menu items for the Scroll form

3. Enter the following Windows API declarations in the Global module and save as SCRLHWND.BAS.

```
Declare Sub ScrollWindow Lib "User" (ByVal hWnd As Integer, ByVal XAmount ⇐
As Integer, ByVal YAmount As Integer, lpRect As Any, lpClipRect As Any)
Declare Sub UpdateWindow Lib "User" (ByVal hWnd As Integer)
```

4. Place the following code in the Form_Resize event subroutine. This code draws a set of concentric colored boxes, filling the form.

```
Sub Form_Resize ()
Dim I As Integer
'
' Draw concentric, colored boxes.
'
   For I = 5 To 1 Step -1
      Boxwidth = I * ScaleWidth / 5
      BoxHeight = I * ScaleHeight / 5
      BoxTop = (ScaleHeight - BoxHeight) / 2
      BoxLeft = (ScaleWidth - Boxwidth) / 2
      Fillcolor = QBColor(I + 8)
      Line (BoxLeft, BoxTop)-Step(Boxwidth, BoxHeight), Fillcolor, BF
   Next I%
End Sub
```

5. Place the following code in the Repaint_Click event subroutine.

```
Sub Repaint_Click ()
   Form_Resize
End Sub
```

6. Place the following code into the Picture1_Click event subroutine. This subroutine scrolls the form's contents in the direction of the arrow that is clicked.

```
Sub Picture1_Click (Index As Integer)
Dim Delta As Integer, Dx As Integer, Dy As Integer
'
' Scroll window in the direction specified.
'
   Delta = Val(Text1.Text)        ' Number of pixels to move
   Select Case Index
      Case 0: Dy = -Delta         ' Move up
      Case 1: Dy = Delta          ' Move down
      Case 2: Dx = -Delta         ' Move right
      Case 3: Dx = Delta          ' Move left
   End Select
   ScrollWindow Scroll.hwnd, Dx, Dy, ByVal 0&, ByVal 0&
   UpdateWindow Scroll.hwnd
End Sub
```

7. Place the following code in the Quit_Click menu event subroutine. This subroutine allows the user to gracefully exit from the program.

```
Sub Quit_Click ()
   End
End Sub
```

**How It Works**

Scrllwnd uses the Windows API function ScrollWindow to actually move the objects on the screen. When this project is run, the entire window's contents—text, graphics, and objects—are all moved the number of screen pixels specified by the XAmount and YAmount parameters. When XAmount is positive, the window objects are scrolled to the left; when the value is negative, the objects are scrolled to the right. YAmount scrolls the window up when the parameter is negative or down when positive.

Scrolling is performed in the Picture1_Click event subroutine. Because the four picture boxes are part of the same control array, only one event subroutine is needed. The appropriate parameters to the ScrollWindow subroutine, Dx and Dy, are set depending on the Index of the picture box selected.

Note that after a ScrollWindow is called, the UpdateWindow API function statement should be called. This causes Visual Basic to immediately paint the portion of the window exposed by the scrolling action. If Update-

Window is not called, the form will be repainted at an indeterminate time in the future. This may cause subsequent screen updates to be overwritten.

## Comments

ScrollWindow is the easiest and fastest way to move data in a window and is ideal for scrolling a form full of text. However, ScrollWindow should not be used when the form's AutoRedraw property is turned on. AutoRedraw causes a window with custom graphics to be updated each time an object is moved. With AutoRedraw enabled, Visual Basic saves an exact copy of the window in what is called a persistent bitmap. The persistent bitmap is a pixel-for-pixel copy of how the control looks when displayed. Whenever a picture box or form needs to redisplay a previously hidden part of itself, and AutoRedraw is true, Visual Basic simply copies the persistent bitmap to the screen. The cost of enabling AutoRedraw is memory and screen refresh speed. ScrollWindow only affects the on-screen copy, not the persistent bitmap. The repaint that takes place after ScrollWindow is called causes Visual Basic to copy the contents of the bitmap back to the screen, thereby overwriting the intended effects of ScrollWindow. The ScrollDC function is more appropriately used when AutoRedraw is enabled, or if you want to change the positions of the controls in a window. The following How-To uses the ScrollDC function.

---

**3.2    How do I...**

# Scroll text and graphics in a form or picture box?

Complexity: Easy

## Problem

Since I like to include graphics on my form, I prefer to turn on the Auto-Redraw property. How can I scroll text and graphics on my forms and picture boxes?

## Technique

The Windows API library provides much of the functionality that was not included directly in Visual Basic. The API function ScrollDC can be used to scroll graphics and text in any of four directions.

## Steps

Load and run SCROLLDC.MAK. Clicking on the Single Step command button will scroll the text up one line. Clicking on the Continuous com-

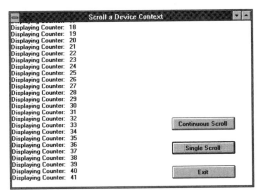

**Figure 3-2** The ScrollDC form in action, showing scrolling text

mand button puts the program into a loop, adding new lines to the bottom of the window while existing data scrolls off the top. Figure 3-2 shows this project while scrolling is in progress.

The ScrollDC project may be created by entering the objects and code as detailed in the following steps.

1. Create a new project called SCROLL-DC.MAK. Create a new form with the objects and properties shown in Table 3-3 and save it as SCROLL-DC.FRM.

| Object | Property | Setting |
| --- | --- | --- |
| Form | FormName | ScrollDC |
| | Caption | Scroll a Device Context |
| Command button | CtlName | Command1 |
| | Caption | Exit |
| Command button | CtlName | Command2 |
| | Caption | Continuous Scroll |
| Command button | CtlName | Command3 |
| | Caption | Single Scroll |

**Table 3-3** ScrollDC project form's objects and properties

2. Place the following declaration in the Global module and save it as SCROLLDC.BAS.

```
Global Const NULL = 0

Type RECT
     Left As Integer
     Top As Integer
     Right As Integer
     Bottom As Integer
End Type

Declare Sub ScrollDC Lib "User" (ByVal hDC As Integer, ByVal dx As ⇐
Integer, ByVal dy As Integer, lprcScroll As RECT, lprcClip As RECT, ⇐
ByVal hRgnUpdate As Integer, lprcUpdate As Any)
```

3. Place the following declaration in the General section of the ScrollDC form. The Continue variable is used to stop the Continuous display.

```
Dim Continue As Integer
```

4. Place the following code in the Resize event subroutine of the form.

```
Sub Form_Resize ()
   For I = 1 To 20
      Print "Sample text for Line: ", I
   Next I
End Sub
```

5. Place the following code in the Command1_Click event subroutine. This command button event permits the user to gracefully exit the application.

```
Sub Command1_Click ()
   End
End Sub
```

6. Place the following code in the Command2_Click event subroutine. This subroutine starts continuous printing and scrolling of the ScrollDC form.

```
Sub Command2_Click ()
Dim Counter As Integer, T As Integer, TxtHeight As Integer
'
'  Loop forever scrolling new lines onto the screen from
'  the bottom.
'
   Scalemode = 3              ' To Pixels
   Continue = -1
   Counter = 0
   TxtHeight = TextHeight("A")
   currenty = scaleheight - TxtHeight
   While Continue
      If currenty > (scaleheight - TxtHeight) Then
         ScrollOneLine
         currenty = scaleheight - TxtHeight
         Currentx = 0
      End If
      Print "Displaying Counter: "; Counter
      Counter = Counter + 1
      T= DoEvents()
   Wend
End Sub
```

7. Place the following code in the Command3_Click event subroutine. This command button event scrolls the form up one line. It also turns off the Continue flag in case continuous scrolling is in effect.

```
Sub Command3_Click ()
   Continue = 0
```

```
    ScrollOneLine
End Sub
```

8. Place the following code into the ScrollOneLine subroutine. This subroutine is called by the command button events to scroll the form window up one line.

```
Sub ScrollOneLine ()
Dim lprcScroll As RECT
'
'  Scroll the Window line line.
'  Use GetClientRect load get window dimensions.
'  Set Scale to 3 – Pixels, dY = text height.
'  Scroll the window and clear out the erased line.
'
    Scalemode = 3
    lprcScroll.Top = 0: lprcScroll.Left = 0
    lprcScroll.Bottom = ScaleHeight
    lprcScroll.Right = ScaleWidth
    dY = TextHeight("A")
    ScrollDC hdc, 0, -dY, lprcScroll, lprcScroll, 0, ByVal 0&
    Line (0, ScaleHeight – dY)-(ScaleWidth, ScaleHeight), BackColor, BF
End Sub
```

### How It Works

Scrolling text in DOS-based applications is an intrinsic capability of most languages. When text is printed on the last line of a screen, previous lines are moved up to make room for the new line. In Windows and Visual Basic, there is no such built-in capability. It is the responsibility of the application's programmer to scroll screen data and make room for incoming lines. The ScrollDC Windows API function provides the mechanism to do this.

When the ScrollDC project is first run, the Form_Resize event subroutine is automatically called. It will print 20 sample text lines so that the scroll effects can be demonstrated. The Command2_Click and Command3_Click event subroutines are used to initiate the scrolling. Before scrolling, the Command2_Click event subroutine checks whether the next line of printed text will fit onto the screen without scrolling. If it won't, The ScrollOneLine subroutine is called to move the window text up by one line.

The ScrollOneLine subroutine first changes the form's ScaleMode to 3-Pixels to be compatible with the ScrollDC call. The RECT structure needed for the lprcScroll and lprcClip parameters are set up to point to the whole window. Table 3-4 lists all of ScrollDC's parameters.

| Parameter | Use |
|---|---|
| hDC | Device context of window to scroll. For forms, use <FormName>.HDC; for PictureBoxes, use <CtlName>.HDC. |
| dx | Number of pixels to scroll horizontally. Positive numbers are used to scroll right, negative numbers to scroll left. |
| dy | Number of pixels to scroll vertically. Positive numbers are used to scroll the window down, negative values to scroll up. |
| lprcScroll | This is a pointer to a RECT structure that defines the size of the scrolling area. For our application, it is set to the entire window. |
| lprcClip | This is a pointer to a RECT structure that will be used to clip the scrolling area. For our application, it is set to the entire window. |
| hRgnUpdate | A handle to an update region. It is not used in our application and is passed as zero. |
| lprcUpdate | If not NULL, the ScrollDC function will update the value of a RECT structure to indicate the area that needs repainting. We don't use this feature, so it is set to NULL. Note the use of the ByVal keyword. |

**Table 3-4** Parameters for the ScrollDC API function

We only want to scroll in the vertical direction, so ScrollDC is called with a zero dX parameter. The dY parameter is set to the text height so that only one line of text is scrolled at a time. ScrollDC moves pixels on the screen as specified but does not clear out the old data. The Visual Basic Line method with the BF (filled box) option clears the area that was occupied by the last screen line.

## Comment

Three Windows API functions can be used to scroll a window. ScrollWindow scrolls everything on a window—controls as well as graphics. However, it does not use a device context and, therefore, can't be used with Visual Basic if AutoRedraw is enabled. The BitBlt routine, like ScrollDC, will also scroll data using the device context, but is slightly slower and more complex to use because of its additional capabilities. ScrollDC will scroll data quickly, and is easy to use.

Be careful in setting the background color of the form when you use this project. When the Line statement draws a box and the background color is not a pure one, the box is bordered in white instead of the background color. Pure colors, other than back or white, are dependent on the type of display card used. Experimentation is required.

**3.3    How do I...**

# Make text and graphics roll up the screen?

Complexity: Easy

### Problem
I would like to add a professional touch to my applications by having text and graphics scroll up the screen, similar to the film credits of a movie. How can I make text and graphics roll upward?

### Technique
This project works by changing the position of a picture box control so that the text and graphics drawn on it will move. With the picture box's border removed and its background color changed to match the color of the surrounding container, the text and graphics appear to float on the screen.

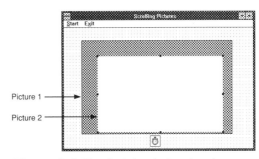

**Figure 3-3** The Scrlpict design time form

To give the program a "film credit" crawl, a Timer control event moves the previously drawn picture box in small increments from the bottom to the top of the screen.

### Steps
Run SCRLPICT.MAK. Select the Start menu option to begin or restart scrolling. Click on the Exit menu to leave the program.

To create the Scrlpict project, enter the objects and code as detailed in the following steps.

1. Create a new project called SCRLPICT.MAK. Create a new form with the objects and properties shown in Table 3-5. Save this form as SCRLPICT.FRM. Note that the Picture2 control must be contained by Picture1 as shown in Figure 3-3. This is done by creating Picture1 first, then drawing Picture2 totally within Picture1's boundaries. When you have done this properly, Picture2 will maintain the same relative position to Picture1 when Picture1 is moved.

| Object | Property | Setting |
|--------|----------|---------|
| Form | FormName | ScrollPicture |
| | Caption | Scrolling Pictures |
| Picture box | CtlName | Picture1 |
| | Backcolor | &HFF00 |
| Picture box | CtlName | Picture2 |
| | Backcolor | &HFFFF80 |
| | Border | 0 - None |
| Timer | CtlName | Timer1 |
| | Enabled | False |
| | Interval | 5 |
| | Tag | 2 |

**Table 3-5** Scrlpict project form's objects and properties

2. Using the Menu Design window, create a menu for the form with the parameters in Table 3-6.

| Caption | CtlName |
|---------|---------|
| &Start | Start |
| E&xit | Quit |

**Table 3-6** Menu Design parameters

3. Put the PrintCenter code in the General section of the form. This code centers and prints a string, Txt, on the specified control.

```
Sub PrintCenter (C As Control, Txt As String)
' Display text in the center of the control.
   C.CurrentX = (C.ScaleWidth - C.TextWidth(Txt)) / 2
   C.Print Txt
End Sub
```

4. Place the Timer1_Timer event subroutine in the form. Each time the timer calls this event, the Picture2 control is moved up a few pixels.

```
Sub Timer1_Timer ()
    Delta = Val(Timer1.Tag)
    Picture1.Scalemode = 3
    If Picture2.Top + Picture2.Height > 0 Then
        Picture2.Top = Picture2.Top - Delta
    Else
       Timer1.Enabled = 0
       Picture1.CurrentY = Picture1.ScaleHeight / 2
       Txt$ = "Finished with Scrolling"
```

```
         Picture1.CurrentX = (Picture1.ScaleWidth - ⇐
            Picture1.TextWidth(Txt$))/2
         Picture1.Print Txt$
      End If
   End Sub
```

5. Put the Start_Click event subroutine in the form. This subroutine starts the action by drawing the text onto Picture2 and enabling Timer1.

```
Sub Start_Click ()
   Timer1.Enabled = 0
   Picture1.Cls
   Picture2.Visible = 0
   Picture2.AutoRedraw = -1
   Picture2.Top = Picture1.ScaleHeight
   Picture2.BackColor = Picture1.BackColor
   Picture2.Height = 5 * Picture1.TextHeight("A")
   Picture2.CurrentY = 0
   PrintCenter Picture2, ""
   PrintCenter Picture2, "Visual Basic"
   PrintCenter Picture2, "makes scrolling"
   PrintCenter Picture2, "of data an easy"
   PrintCenter Picture2, "process"
   Picture2.Visible = -1
   Timer1.Enabled = -1
End Sub
```

6. Place the Quit_Click event subroutine in the form. This routine allows the user to exit the application gracefully by clicking on the Quit menu.

```
Sub Quit_Click ()
   End
End Sub
```

### How It Works

A project like this really highlights the strengths and subtleties of Visual Basic. It takes advantage of object containers to automatically clip windows and selective AutoRedraw to paint text and graphics on nonvisible objects. The program begins when the user clicks on the Start menu, invoking the Start_Click menu event.

Start_Clickbegins by disabling the timer and clearing the outer of the two picture boxes: Picture1. These two steps are necessary in case the Start menu is clicked again while the program is running.

The Picture2 control is then made invisible and its AutoRedraw property turned on. AutoRedraw is a property of form and picture box controls. When AutoRedraw is True—that is, it has a nonzero value—anything drawn or printed to the control is not only displayed on the screen but also is saved in a persistent bitmap. (See How-To 3.1 Scroll all the objects in a window.) The beauty of Visual Basic is that even when a control is invisible, you can still draw and print to its bitmap. In this project we print four lines of centered text to the nonvisible Picture2 control.

At the end of the Start_Click event, the Picture2 control is made visible again. The timer is started, whose event subroutine, Timer1_Timer, slowly moves the Picture2 control from the bottom to the top of the Picture1 control.

When we drew the controls on the Scrlpict form, Picture2 was drawn inside Picture1, making Picture1 a container for Picture2. When an object is contained inside another, it will not be displayed outside the boundaries of the container. In fact, a contained object's position properties, Top and Left, are relative to the origin of the container. An object can be moved anywhere in a container, yet parts of it that fall outside the container are not displayed. In Windows terminology, this is called clipping.

When Timer1 is enabled, Picture2.Top is set to the bottom of its container and no part of Picture2 will be visible. Moving the top of Picture2 slowly toward the top of Picture1 creates the crawl effect. The ScaleMode for Picture1 is set to 3 pixels so that the movement of Picture2 will be made in the smallest of screen increments. As mentioned earlier, without a border or contrasting background color for Picture2, there is no visual frame of reference for its text and graphics.

## Comment

The speed at which Picture2 moves is governed by two factors: the timer interval and the number of pixels to move the picture box for each timer event. We set the interval to 5 milliseconds when building the form. The number of pixels to move is kept in the Tag property of the timer. This lets us quickly change these values without altering the code.

---

**3.4    How do I...**

## Scroll a text box under program control?

Complexity: Intermediate

### Problem

Although my users can scroll the text in a multiline text box using the scroll bars, is there some way my program can scroll the text automatically? That would be another way I could present a rolling "movie credits" screen, for example.

### Technique

Windows text boxes respond to a variety of messages, most of which Visual Basic automatically sends when you use a property like SelText. However, you can access the other messages with the API function SendMessage.

Windows' EM_LINESCROLL message tells the scroll box to scroll the contents of a multiline text box by the specified number of rows and/or columns like in Figure 3-4.

### Steps

Open and run SCROLL.MAK. You can type any text you'd like in the text box. There are eight command buttons covering the eight compass directions: north, northeast, east, southeast, south, southwest, west, and northwest. See Figure 3-5.

1. Create a new project called SCROLL.MAK. Create a new form with the objects and properties from Table 3-7 and save it as SCROLL.FRM.

| Object | Property | Setting |
|--------|----------|---------|
| Form | Caption | Scrolling text |
| | FormName | ScrollText |
| | BackColor | &H00C0C0C0& |
| Text box | CtlName | Text1 |
| | Multiline | True |
| | ScrollBars | Horizontal |
| | Text | <none> |

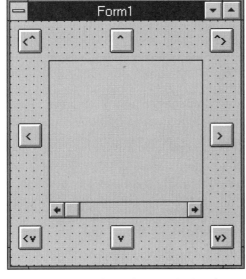

**Figure 3-4** The Scroll form at design time

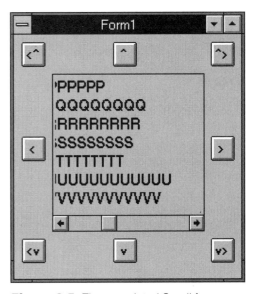

**Figure 3-5** The completed Scroll form

*Table 3-7. continued*

| Object | Property | Setting |
| --- | --- | --- |
| Command button | CtlName | Scroll |
| | Caption | <^ |
| | Index | 0 |
| Command button | CtlName | Scroll |
| | Caption | ^ |
| | Index | 1 |
| Command button | CtlName | Scroll |
| | Caption | ^> |
| | Index | 2 |
| Command button | CtlName | Scroll |
| | Caption | > |
| | Index | 3 |
| Command button | CtlName | Scroll |
| | Caption | v> |
| | Index | 4 |
| Command button | CtlName | Scroll |
| | Caption | v |
| | Index | 5 |
| Command button | CtlName | Scroll |
| | Caption | <v |
| | Index | 6 |
| Command button | CtlName | Scroll |
| | Caption | < |
| | Index | 7 |

**Table 3-7** Scroll Project form's objects and properties

2. Put the following code in the Declarations section of the form. These Const and Declare statements let the program access the Windows API functions.

```
DefInt A-Z

Declare Function SendMessage Lib "User" (ByVal hWnd%, ByVal wMsg%, ByVal ⇐
wParam%, ByVal lParam&) As Integer
Declare Function GetFocus Lib "User" () As Integer

Const WM_USER = &H400
Const EM_LINESCROLL = WM_USER + 6
```

3. Put the following code in the Form_Load event subroutine. This code simply loads some strings you created on the form into the text box.

```
Sub Form_Load ()
    For I = 1 To 26
        Text1.Text = Text1.Text + String$(I, 64 + I) + Chr$(13) + Chr$(10)
    Next
End Sub
```

4. Put the following code in the Scroll_Click event subroutine. This code handles the clicks for all the command buttons and scrolls the text in the text box via the SendMessage API function.

```
Sub Scroll_Click (Index As Integer)
    Dim hWnd As Integer, lParam As Long

    Text1.SetFocus
    hWnd = GetFocus()

    Select Case Index
        Case 0
            hScroll = -1    ' Left
            vScroll = -1    ' Up
        Case 1
            hScroll = 0
            vScroll = -1    ' Up
        Case 2
            hScroll = 1     ' Right
            vScroll = -1    ' Up
        Case 3
            hScroll = 1     ' Right
            vScroll = 0
        Case 4
            hScroll = 1     ' Right
            vScroll = 1     ' Down
        Case 5
            hScroll = 0
            vScroll = 1     ' Down
        Case 6
            hScroll = -1    ' Left
            vScroll = 1     ' Down
        Case 7
            hScroll = -1    ' Left
            vScroll = 0
    End Select

    lParam = 65536 * hScroll + vScroll
    I = SendMessage(hWnd, EM_LINESCROLL, 0, lParam)
End Sub
```

## How It Works

Once again, control arrays come to the rescue. Rather than having eight command button event subroutines, one will do the job. The way the form was designed, the Index of each command button increases by one step each clockwise.

Because Windows sends messages via a window handle, the GetFocus API function is used to get the window handle of a control.

The Windows message that scrolls a text box is EM_LINESCROLL, which the WINAPI.TXT file in the Windows SDK defines as WM_USER + 6. WM_USER is defined as 0x400, or &H400 in Visual Basic hexadecimal lingo. So EM_LINESCROLL is equal to &H406.

The Form_Load event subroutine code loads the text box with multiple strings of varying length, some of which are wider than the width of the text box. This gives the feel of scrolling both vertically and horizontally.

The Scroll_Click event subroutine gets a parameter that's the Index of the command button that was clicked. (Remember that the Index goes from 0 to 7, starting at the upper left-hand corner and going clockwise.) Since a command button has the focus when the Scroll_Click event subroutine is executed, the Text1.SetFocus statement moves the focus to the text box. Then the GetFocus API function returns the window handle of the text box.

The Select Case statement block goes through each of the possible Index values for the command button. Each index value sets the hScroll and vScroll variables to -1, 0, or 1. A value of -1 means to scroll up vertically or left horizontally. The value 0 means no scrolling in either direction. 1 either means to scroll down vertically or right horizontally. Depending on which command button was pressed, either or both hScroll and vScroll variables are set.

The diagonal scroll command buttons (northeast, southeast, southwest, and northwest) set both of the variables, since scrolling diagonally is the same as scrolling vertically and horizontally at the same time. For example, to scroll northeast one position is the same as scrolling north one position and east one position. The "straight" scroll command buttons (north, east, south, and west) only set one variable and set the other to zero.

The EM_LINESCROLL message expects the number of columns to scroll in the high-order word of the message lParam and the number of rows to scroll in the low-order word. (See Figure 3-6.) Because lParam is a Long integer, multiplying by 65536 will move the hScroll value into the high-order word. There's

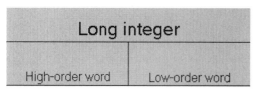

**Figure 3-6** An lParam Long integer packed with two pieces of information

nothing special required to put a value in the low-order word, so it's just added in.

### Comment

Notice in Figure 3-5 that the text box has a horizontal scroll bar. If a multiline text box doesn't have a horizontal scroll bar, Visual Basic automatically wraps the text at the right edge of the text box, meaning that there is nothing to be scrolled horizontally.

---

### 3.5    How do I...

# Align text automatically?

Complexity: Easy

### Problem

The Visual Basic Print method always left justifies text at the current location. To center or right justify a string requires calculating a new position using the TextWidth method. Is there any way to do this automatically?

### Technique

The Windows API library includes a function, SetTextAlign, for automatically aligning text. Calling SetTextAlign before printing will provide your applications with a variety of horizontal and vertical alignments.

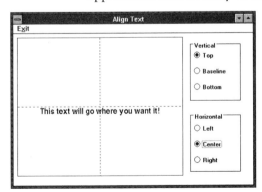

**Figure 3-7** The Aligntxt form with sample text

### Steps

Open and run ALIGNTXT.MAK. A line of sample text will be displayed at the center of the picture box as shown in Figure 3-7. The intersection of the dashed lines indicates the alignment point. Click on the different option buttons to have SetTextAlign change the alignment of the sample text. This project can be created by entering the objects and code in the following steps.

1. Create a new project called ALIGNTXT.MAK. Create a new form with the objects and properties listed in Table 3-8. Save it as ALIGN-TXT.FRM.

| Object | Property | Setting |
|---|---|---|
| Form | FormName | AlignText |
| | Caption | Align Text |
| Picture box | CtlName | P |
| Frame | CtlName | Frame1 |
| | Caption | Vertical |
| Frame | CtlName | Frame2 |
| | Caption | Horizontal |

**Table 3-8** Aligntxt project form's objects properties

2. Place the option buttons listed in Table 3-9 inside the Frame1 control.

| Object | Property | Setting |
|---|---|---|
| Option button | CtlName | VertOpt |
| | Caption | Top |
| | Index | 1 |
| Option button | CtlName | VertOpt |
| | Caption | Baseline |
| | Index | 2 |
| Option button | CtlName | VertOpt |
| | Caption | Bottom |
| | Index | 3 |

**Table 3-9** Frame1 control's objects and properties

3. Place the option buttons listed in Table 3-10 inside the Frame2 control.

| Object | Property | Setting |
|---|---|---|
| Option button | CtlName | HorzOpt |
| | Caption | Left |
| | Index | 1 |
| Option button | CtlName | HorzOpt |
| | Caption | Center |
| | Index | 2 |
| Option button | CtlName | HorzOpt |
| | Caption | Right |
| | Index | 3 |

**Table 3-10** Frame2 control's objects and properties

4. Create the menu listed in Table 3-11 for the form using the Menu Design window.

| Caption | CtlName |
|---------|---------|
| Exit | Quit |

**Table 3-11** Menu items for the ALIGNTXT form

5. Enter the following declarations into the Global module and save it as ALIGNTXT.BAS.

```
' Text alignment options.
Global Const TA_LEFT = 0
Global Const TA_RIGHT = 2
Global Const TA_CENTER = 6

Global Const TA_TOP = 0
Global Const TA_BOTTOM = 8
Global Const TA_BASELINE = 24
Declare Sub SetTextAlign Lib "GDI" (ByVal hDC As Integer, ByVal wFlags ⇐
As Integer)
```

6. Enter the following code in the Form_Paint event subroutine. This subroutine will draw and align the sample text.

```
Sub Form_Paint ()
Dim wFlags As Integer, HFlag As Integer, VFlag As Integer
    P.Cls
    P.FontSize = 12
    P.DrawStyle = 2
    P.Line (0, P.ScaleHeight / 2)-Step(P.ScaleWidth, 0)
    P.Line (P.ScaleWidth / 2, 0)-Step(0, P.ScaleHeight)

    If VertOpt(1).Value Then VFlag = TA_TOP
    If VertOpt(2).Value Then VFlag = TA_BASELINE
    If VertOpt(3).Value Then VFlag = TA_BOTTOM
    If HorzOpt(1).Value Then HFlag = TA_LEFT
    If HorzOpt(2).Value Then HFlag = TA_CENTER
    If HorzOpt(3).Value Then HFlag = TA_RIGHT
    wFlags = VFlag Or HFlag

    P.Currentx = P.ScaleWidth / 2
    P.Currenty = P.ScaleHeight / 2
    SetTextAlign P.Hdc, wFlags
    P.Print "This text will go where you want it!"
End Sub
```

7. Enter the following code in the VertOpt_Click event subroutine. This subroutine will redraw the sample text whenever one of the VertOpt option buttons changes.

```
Sub VertOpt_Click (Index As Integer)
   Form_Paint
End Sub
```

8. Place the following code in the HorzOpt_Click event subroutine. This subroutine will redraw the sample text whenever one of the HorzOpt option buttons changes.

```
Sub HorzOpt_Click (Index As Integer)
   Form_Paint
End Sub
```

9. Put the following code in the Quit_Click menu event subroutine to allow the user to gracefully exit the application.

```
Sub Quit_Click ()
   End
End Sub
```

### How It Works

When you print text in Visual Basic, it is always displayed relative to the CurrentX and CurrentY properties of the object. The leftmost edge of the text starts at the CurrentX position and the top of the characters align with the CurrentY value. To horizontally center or right justify text, you need to use the TextWidth property as illustrated here:

```
A$ = "Text to Print"
L% = TextWidth(A$)
CurrentX = CurrentX - L%/2%          ' For Centered Text
CurrentX = CurrentX - l%             ' For Right-justified Text
Print A$
```

The Windows API provides a function, SetTextAlign, that automatically justifies all subsequent print statements. In addition to handling horizontal justification, SetTextAlign also permits you to change the vertical alignment of printed text. Figure 3-8 shows the three possible vertical alignments.

The Visual Basic default is to print the top of the character at the CurrentY position. The SetTextAlign function with the TA_BASELINE option is useful when there are multiple sizes of fonts on a line. That function will keep your lines from having a jagged look. The TA_BOTTOM option displays characters with the bottom of the character at the CurrentY position. Be aware that the Visual Basic function, TextHeight, returns the distance between the top and bottom of a character. There is no built-in VB method to retrieve the baseline offset.

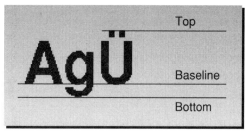

**Figure 3-8** Vertical character alignment alternatives

The SetTextAlign function takes two parameters, the hDC of the object on which to print, and an integer flag word. The flag word specifies the desired alignment options. The Form_Paint event code shows how the vertical and horizontal alignment options are formed to make the flag word.

### Comments

The alignment capability of the SetTextAlign function will not work properly when you are printing multiple strings in one statement. A Print statement such as Print A$; B$ is treated by Visual Basic as two distinct print commands. This results in unexpected centering or right-justified alignment. To center the two strings, use the Print A$ + B$ statement. This concatenates the strings prior to printing, ensuring that VB and SetTextAlign will treat the entire string as one object.

The hDC property can change whenever VB exits a subroutine, or calls the DoEvents function. Therefore, the SetTextAlign function should be called in each subroutine that needs to align text.

---

**3.6    How do I...**

## Set up a README file reader?

Complexity: Easy

### Problem

As I finish my latest application, I realize that I must provide a way for my users to read late-breaking information after they've installed my application. Normally in DOS you just create the README file on the disk, but this is so unfriendly. What is a better way?

### Technique

This is easy to solve. Simply load the lines of text from a file into a list box. When there are more lines in a list box than will fit on screen, Windows automatically provides scroll bars to let the user view the entire file.

### Steps

Open and run FILEVIEW.MAK. You can then click on any filename (as long as it is an ASCII file).

1. Create a new project called FILEVIEW.MAK. Create a new form using the objects and properties shown in Table 3-12 and save it as FILEVIEW.FRM. It will look like Figure 3-9.

| Object | Property | Setting |
|--------|----------|---------|
| Form | Caption | FileViewer |
| | BackColor | &H00C0C0C0& |
| Button | Caption | Close |
| | CtlName | Cancel |
| List box | FontName | Helv |

**Table 3-12** The FileView project form's objects and properties

2. Put the following code in the Cancel_Click event subroutine of the Cancel button.

```
Sub Cancel_Click ()
     End
End Sub
```

3. Put the following code in the Form_Unload event subroutine of the form.

```
Sub Form_Unload (Cancel As Integer)
     End
End Sub
```

4. Put the following code in the Form_Load event subroutine of the form. This code reads the README file into the list box.

```
Sub Form_Load ()
   fileNum = FreeFile
   Open "README" For Input As #fileNum

   Do Until EOF(fileNum)
      Line Input #fileNum, lin$
      List1.AddItem lin$
   Loop

   Close #fileNum
End Sub
```

### How It Works

The Form_Load subroutine simply opens the README file and reads it, line by line, into the list box using the AddItem method in a Do loop. Notice that we use the FreeFile function to ensure that we have an available file number.

### Comment

You can also use this form as a general-purpose file viewer by just adding a call to a file dialog box (like the FileDlg form).

**3.7    How do I...**

# Build a simple editor that searches for text?

Complexity: Easy

### Problem

I would like to incorporate a file editor in my application. It should follow standard Windows editing techniques for user ease.

### Technique

With Visual Basic, most of the editing functions are provided by the text box control. All you need to do is to load a text box with a copy of a file to provide the standard Windows editing features your users desire. This project also copies entire contents of the text box back to disk to save edits made by the user. Figure 3-10 shows the Editor project.

### Steps

Open and run EDITOR.MAK. Selecting the File menu displays options that allow you to Open and Save a file or Exit the program. The Search menu selection helps you to locate text. To create the Editor project, enter the objects and code as detailed in the following steps.

1. Create a new project called EDITOR.MAK. Create a new form with the objects and properties shown in Table 3-13 and save it as EDITOR.FRM.

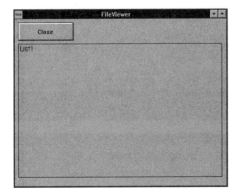

**Figure 3-9** The FileView form that displays ASCII text

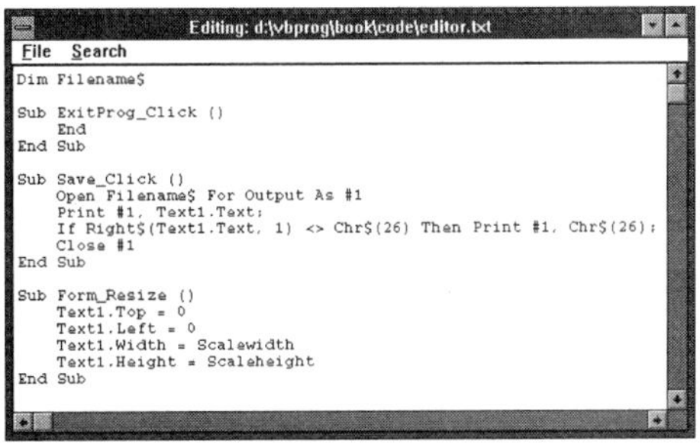

**Figure 3-10** The Editor in action

| Object | Property | Setting |
|--------|----------|---------|
| Form | FormName | Editor |
| | Caption | Edit a File |
| Text box | CtlName | Text1 |
| | FontBold | False |
| | FontName | Courier |
| | FontSize | 10 |
| | MultiLine | True |
| | Text | (blank) |
| | ScrollBars | 3 - Both |

**Table 3-13** Editor project form's objects and properties

2. Create a menu for the form using the Menu Design window.

| Caption | CtlName |
|---------|---------|
| &File | FileMenu |
| – – – –&Open | Openfile |
| – – – –&Save | Save |
| – – – –E&xit | ExitProg |
| &Search | Search |

**Table 3-14** Menu design characteristics

3. Place the following code in the OpenFile_Click event subroutine. This code opens the file using the Open_Dlg form, checks the file length, reads its contents, and then loads it into the text box.

```
Sub OpenFile_Click ()
   Open_Dlg.Show 1
   Filename$ = Open_Dlg.Tag
   If Filename$ = "" Then Exit Sub
   Editor.Caption = "Editing: " + Filename$
   Open Filename$ For Binary As #1
   Filelength = LOF(1)
   If Filelength > 40000 Then
      MsgBox "File Too Long to Edit", 16
      Exit Sub
   ElseIf Filelength = 0 Then
      MsgBox "File: " + Filename$ + " not found or empty", 16
      Exit Sub
   End If
   Tmp$ = String$(LOF(1), 0)
   Get #1, , Tmp$
```

```
   Text1.Text = Tmp$
   Close #1
   Tmp$ = ""
End Sub
```

4. Place the following code in the ExitProg_Click event subroutine.

```
Sub ExitProg_Click ()
   End
End Sub
```

5. Place this code in the Save_Click event subroutine. It copies the contents of the text box control back to the file.

```
Sub Save_Click ()

' If no filename, prompt use for one.
   1 Filename$ = Open_Dlg.Tag
   If Filename$ = "" Then
      Filename$ = InputBox$("Enter new filename")
      If Filename$ = "" Then
         MsgBox "Filename blank, file not saved.", 48
         Exit Sub
      End If
   Open_Dlg.Tag = Filename$
   End If

' Print TextBox to file.
' Append EOF Chr$(26), if not last char in TextBox

   Open Filename$ For Output As #1
   Print #1, Text1.Text;
   If Right$(Text1.Text, 1) <> Chr$(26) Then Print #1, Chr$(26);
   Close #1

End Sub
```

6. The Form_Resize event subroutine changes the size of the Text1 control to fully cover the face of the form. Because the Resize event is also called when a form initially loads, the Text1 control is expanded at application startup as well.

```
Sub Form_Resize ()
   Text1.Top = 0
   Text1.Left = 0
   Text1.Width = Scalewidth
   Text1.Height = Scaleheight
End Sub
```

7. No text editor could be considered complete without the ability to search for text. The Search_Click event subroutine prompts the user to enter a search string. If the search string is found, the matching text is left selected.

```
Sub Search_Click ()
   Static Searchstring As String, Newsearchstring As String
```

```
'
' Default to previous search string.
' If match is found, leave matching text selected.
'

    Newsearchstring = InputBox$("Enter search string", "", Searchstring)
    If Newsearchstring = "" Then Exit Sub
    Searchstring = Newsearchstring
    T% = InStr(Text1.Selstart + 1 + Text1.Sellength, Text1.Text,
Searchstring)
    If T% Then
        Text1.Selstart = T% - 1
        Text1.Sellength = Len(Searchstring)
    End If
End Sub
```

8. Open a second form for this project using the New Form selection from Visual Basic's File menu. This form is an Open Dialog box that allows the user to point and choose a file to edit. Enter the objects and properties for this form as listed in Table 3-15 and save the form as OPEN_DLG.FRM. The layout of the controls in shown is Figure 3-11.

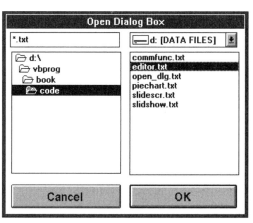

**Figure 3-11** The Open_Dlg form in action

| Object | Property | Setting |
| --- | --- | --- |
| Form | FormName | Open_Dlg |
| | BorderStyle | 3 - Fixed Double |
| | ControlBox | False |
| | MaxButton | False |
| | MinButton | False |
| Command button | CtlName | Command1 |
| | Cancel | True |
| | Caption | Cancel |
| | FontSize | 12 |
| Command button | CtlName | Command2 |
| | Caption | OK |
| | Default | True |
| | FontSize | 12 |

| Dir list box | CtlName | Dir1 |
| --- | --- | --- |
| Drive list box | CtlName | Drive1 |
| File list box | CtlName | File1 |
| Text box | CtlName | Text1 |
| | Borderstyle | 1 - Fixed Single |
| | Text | *.* |

**Table 3-15** Open_Dlg project form's objects and properties

9. Put the following code in the Drive1_Change event subroutine of the Open_Dlg form. When the user changes drives, this event will send a message to the Dir1 control indicating the new drive.

```
Sub Drive1_Change ()
   Dir1.Path = Drive1.Drive
End Sub
```

10. Put the following code in the Dir1_Change event subroutine of the Open_Dlg form. When the user changes directories, this event will send a message to the File1 control requesting a new directory display.

```
Sub Dir1_Change ()
   File1.Path = Dir1.Path
End Sub
```

11. Put the following code in the File1_DblClick event subroutine of the Open_Dlg form. This code causes a double-click event in the File1 control to be processed the same as clicking on the OK button.

```
Sub File1_DblClick ()
   Command2_Click
End Sub
```

12. Put the following code in the Text1_Change event subroutine of the Open_Dlg form. By responding to changes in the Text1 control, the user can alter which filenames will be displayed by the File1 control.

```
Sub Text1_Change ()
   File1.Pattern = Text1.Text
End Sub
```

13. Put the following code in the Command1_Click event subroutine of the Open_Dlg form. The Command1 button is the Cancel button. This code simply clears the return variable and hides the form.

```
Sub Command1_Click ()
   Open_Dlg.Tag = ""
   Open_Dlg.Hide
End Sub
```

14. Put the following code in the Command2_Click event subroutine of the Open_Dlg form. This is the OK command button which will return the drive, directory, and filename to the calling form.

```
Sub Command2_Click ()
    If File1.Listindex < 0 Then
        MsgBox "No File Selected", 48
        Exit Sub
    End If
    Open_Dlg.Tag = Dir1.Path
    If Right$(Open_Dlg.Tag, 1) <> "\" Then
        Open_Dlg.Tag = Open_Dlg.Tag + "\"
    End If
    Open_Dlg.Tag = Open_Dlg.Tag + File1.List(File1.Listindex)
    Open_Dlg.Hide
End Sub
```

15. Put the following code in the Form_Load event subroutine of the Open_Dlg form. This code positions the dialog form in the center of the screen and sets the default file match pattern.

```
Sub Form_Load ()
    Open_Dlg.Top = (Screen.Height - Open_Dlg.Height) / 2
    Open_Dlg.left = (Screen.Width - Open_Dlg.Width) / 2
    File1.Pattern = Text1.Text
End Sub
```

### How It Works

The text box control provides just the kind of basic editing functions that we need to build a text editor. By adding a few additional functions to load and save a file, and to search for text, our editor becomes fully functional. This program exploits the similarity between the format of text data in a DOS file and how data is kept in a text box Text property. Both are stored as lines of characters, each line ending with carriage return and line feed characters. With a few short lines of code, Visual Basic can copy the contents of a file into a text box control or, conversely, can transfer the text box Text back to a disk file.

The Openfile_Click event subroutine uses binary input/output to read the entire file with a single Get statement. The user selects the file to open using the Open_Dlg form. After the file is opened, its size is determined using the Lof function (LOF stands for Length of file). The Tmp$ variable is extended to match the size of the file so that the Get statement will read the entire file in one operation. Copying Tmp$ into Text1.Text moves the data to the text box control and displays it. Tmp$ is cleared so that its memory can be reused by other variables in the form.

Saving the data is even easier. All you need to do is to print the contents of the text box control back to the file. The end-of-file marker [Chr$(26)] is appended to the text.

The Search_Click event subroutine scans from the current position in the text box for characters matching the search string. If a match is found, the text is selected using the SelStart and SelLength text box properties. Note that the InStr function counts characters starting from one, but the SelStart property uses zero to indicate the first character of the Text property.

See How-To 1.7 Make a powerful text editor using APIs for a more full-featured, sophisticated text editor.

### Comment

Because of memory limitations in Visual Basic, the maximum size of a string variable in this program is approximately 40,000 bytes, which limits the maximum size of text files that can be edited. In any event, the maximum number of characters in a text box is limited to 65,000 bytes by Windows itself.

---

**3.8**  **How do I...**

## Ensure a numeric-only entry in a text box?

Complexity: Easy

### Problem

I need to make sure that a text box control will accept numeric input only. I would also like to restrict input to a specific range of numbers.

### Technique

The KeyPress event for a text box control lets your program process each incoming character as it is typed. Nonnumeric keys and out-of-range values can be rejected.

### Steps

Open and run NUMINPUT.MAK or create it according to the following steps.

1. Create a new project called NUMINPUT.MAK. Create a new form with the objects and properties shown in Table 3-16 and save it as NUMINPUT.FRM. A sample of the form appears in Figure 3-12.

| Object | Property | Setting |
|---|---|---|
| Form | FormName | Numinput |
| | Caption | Numeric Input |
| Command | CtlName | Command1 |
| | Cancel | True |
| | Caption | &Exit |
| | Fontsize | 12 |
| Label | CtlName | Label1 |
| | Alignment | 1 - Right justify |
| | Caption | Numeric Only |
| | Fontsize | 14 |
| Text box | CtlName | Text1 |
| | Fontsize | 12 |

**Table 3-16** Numinput project form's objects and properties

2. Put the following code in the Text1_KeyPress event subroutine. The code will analyze each typed character before displaying the character in the text box. If the character is not numeric or would cause the value of the text box to exceed the established minimum and maximum bounds, the character is not passed on for display.

```
Sub Text1_KeyPress (Keyascii As Integer)
Const DECIMAL_OK = -1               ' 0 = no, -1 = YES
Const MIN_VALUE = -999              ' Minimum value
Const MAX_VALUE = 999               ' Maximum value
   Key$ = Chr$(Keyascii)            ' Convert to string
   Select Case Key$
     Case "0" To "9", "-"           ' Numbers and minus signs
       Newvalue = Val(Left$(Text1.Text, Text1.Selstart) + Key$ + ⇐
           Mid$(Text1.Text, Text1.Selstart + Text1.Sellength + 1))
       If Newvalue > MAX_VALUE Or Newvalue < MIN_VALUE Then
          Keyascii = 0
       End If
     Case "."
       If DECIMAL_OK = 0 Or InStr(Text1.Text, ".") Then
          Keyascii = 0
       End If
     Case Chr$(8)                    ' Backspace
     Case Else
       Keyascii = 0
   End Select
   If Key$ = "-" And (InStr(Text1.Text, "-") Or Text1.Selstart <> 0) Then
      Keyascii = 0
   End If
End Sub
```

3. Place the following code in the Text1_GotFocus event subroutine. When the text box receives the focus, the current contents of the control are selected. The first character typed by the user will then overwrite the contents.

```
Sub Text1_GotFocus ()
   Text1.Selstart = 0
   Text1.Sellength = Len(Text1.Text)
End Sub
```

4. Put the following code in the Command1_Click event subroutine to provide a graceful method for ending the application.

```
Sub Command1_Click ()
   End
End Sub
```

### How It Works

The message-based architecture of Windows and Visual Basic makes this type of low-level handling of keyboard input a snap. Each time the user presses a key on the keyboard, a series of messages is sent to the control that has the focus. In Visual Basic, these messages can be trapped and processed as KeyDown, KeyPress, and KeyUp events. The KeyDown and KeyUp events operate at a very low level and would require a lot more work to code. However, the KeyPress event subroutine provides exactly the right data needed for this project.

The Text1_KeyPress event subroutine is called for every printable character typed. Its KeyAscii parameter holds the character's numeric ASCII value. If the KeyPress subroutine changes the value of Keyascii to zero and exits, the character will not be placed into the text box.

Using a Select Case statement, the code first checks whether the incoming character is numeric (0 to 9) or a minus sign. If the character is either numeric or the minus sign, a simulated insert of the character is made into the text box, and the character's value is taken and compared with the range constants MIN_VALUE and MAX_VALUE. If the new value is out of range, the KeyAscii variable is set to zero, thereby stopping the character from being placed into the text box.

This simulated insert emulates how a text box control actually inserts a character into the Text property. When characters are inserted into a text box, they all

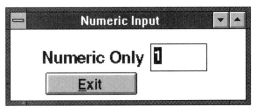

**Figure 3-12** Numinput form displaying a numeric character

are placed at the insertion point (marked on the display by a vertical bar) and any currently selected text is replaced by the new character. The text box property SelStart can determine or set the current insertion point. The value of SelStart is the number of characters in the text box that precede the insertion point. The SelLength property keeps count of the number of selected characters. The simulated insert is performed by concatenating the text box characters up to the insertion point with the incoming character (Key$), then appending the remainder of the text box that is not selected. Note that the currently selected characters are not included in the test for the Newvalue.

A quick check is also made to ensure that multiple decimal points and minus signs are not passed on to the text box. The Case Else statement processes all characters that slipped through prior Case statements by setting KeyAscii to zero. The Case Chr$(8) statement is needed so that backspaces are processed.

It is a standard in Windows programs to select the contents of a text box when it receives the input focus. The Text1_GotFocus event subroutine selects all the characters in the control so that the first numeric character the user types overwrites the current contents.

### Comment

If you have multiple text boxes for which you want to have numeric-only input, this routine could be rewritten as a Form-level subroutine with the text box control name passed as a parameter.

---

### 3.9    How do I...

## Trim null characters from a string?

Complexity: Easy

### Problem

When I use Windows API functions that accept and modify strings, those functions put null characters [Chr$(0)s] into the strings. How can I strip those Chr$(0)s out of the strings?

### Technique

Visual Basic has the LTrim$ and RTrim$ functions to strip extra spaces from the left and right ends of a string, but they don't strip embedded

Chr$(0)s. Instead we can write a Visual Basic general function called VBHTTrim$ that will remove them.

### Steps

To use the VBHTTrim$ function, add the module VBHOWTO.BAS to any project using the Visual Basic File menu's Add a file... option. (See How-To 1.4 Quickly send a Windows message to a control, for how to create VBHOWTO.BAS.) You call the VBHTTrim$ function exactly like you call LTrim$ and RTrim$.

1. Create a new module (with the File menu's New Module option) and add a new function called VBHTTrim$ to it (using the Code menu's New Procedure, Alt+F, to select a function).

2. Add the following code to the VBHTTrim$ function.

```
Function VBHTTrim$ (Incoming$)
    Temp$ = Incoming$
    I% = InStr(Temp$, Chr$(O))
    If I% Then Temp$ = Left$(Temp$, I% - 1)
    Temp$ = LTrim$(RTrim$(Temp$))
    VBHTTrim$ = Temp$
End Function
```

### How It Works

The first line in the VBHTTrim$ function copies the string parameter supplied to the function to a temporary string Temp$.

The second line uses the InStr function to see if there's an embedded Chr$(0). If there is, the third line chops the string at the character immediately before the Chr$(0) using the Left$ function.

The fourth line uses Visual Basic's LTrim$ and RTrim$ functions to trim off any spaces on the left and right ends of the string.

Finally, the last line makes the trimmed temporary string the return value of the function.

### Comment

The VBHTTrim$ function will work with both fixed- and variable-length strings.

**3.10    How do I...**

# Determine and modify the rate at which a text box's caret blinks?

Complexity: Intermediate

### Problem

I would like to draw my user's attention to a text box by making the cursor blink faster. How can I do this?

### Technique

Your users can pick the cursor blink speed by using the Control Panel's Desktop icon. The Control Panel uses an API function—SetCaretBlinkTime—to change the blink speed to whatever you set it to. A Visual Basic application can do the same thing.

**Figure 3-13** The Blink form features a horizontal scroll bar to control cursor speed

### Steps

Open and run BLINK.MAK. A scroll bar shows the current setting of the cursor blink time. If you change the value, the cursor speed is changed too, through a call to SetCaretBlinkTime.

1. Create a new project called BLINK.MAK. Create a new form with the objects and properties shown in Table 3-17 and save it as BLINK.FRM. See the completed form in Figure 3-13.

| Object | Property | Setting |
|---|---|---|
| Form | Caption | Cursor blink rate |
| | FormName | CursorBlinkForm |
| Horizontal scrollbar | CtlName | BlinkRate |
| | LargeChange | 50 |
| | Max | 1000 |
| | Min | 1 |

**Table 3-17** Blink form's controls and properties

2. Put the following code in the Declarations section of the form. These Declare statements let the form access the GetCaretBlinkTime and SetCaretBlinkTime API functions.

```
Declare Function GetCaretBlinkTime Lib "User" () As Integer
```

```
Declare Sub SetCaretBlinkTime Lib "User" (ByVal wMSeconds As Integer)
```

3. Put the following code in the Form_Load event subroutine. This code will be executed when the form is first loaded, to get the current cursor blink speed and change the scroll bar's value and the form's caption to match it.

```
Sub Form_Load ()
   BlinkRate.Value = GetCaretBlinkTime()
   CursorBlinkForm.Caption = "Cursor blink rate is" +
Str$(BlinkRate.Value) + " milliseconds"
End Sub
```

4. Put the following code in the BlinkRate_Change event subroutine. This code will be executed whenever the user changes a scroll bar value, whether by clicking on the scroll arrows or moving the scroll thumb. This code sets the blink speed based on the new value of the scroll bar and changes the form's caption.

```
Sub BlinkRate_Change ()
   SetCaretBlinkTime (BlinkRate.Value)
   CursorBlinkForm.Caption = "Cursor blink rate is" + ⇐
      Str$(BlinkRate.Value) + " milliseconds"
End Sub
```

### How It Works

One thing to remember is that, in proper Windows terminology, the cursor in a text box is called a caret. So the various Windows API functions that deal with the cursor have "caret" in the name. The (real) cursor is the mouse pointer. Because most people think of the cursor as the blinking rectangle on the screen, that's what we'll call it.

The GetCaretBlinkTime API function returns the time, in milliseconds, between flashes of the cursor. Actually, what is measured is the length of time that the cursor is on, and the length of time it's off.

The parameter supplied to the SetCaretBlinkTime function sets the cursor blink time, in milliseconds.

You can set the blink speed to a value between 1 and 32,767 (the largest possible integer). A blink speed of 1 is dizzying, and one of 32,767 means that the cursor blinks about every 32 seconds.

### Comment

Note that the Control Panel's scroll bar that changes the cursor blink speed is backward from how this application does it. The Control Panel bases the scroll bar on how fast the cursor should blink, but this application bases it on the delay between blinks.

**3.11      How do I...**

# Use scroll bars to select colors?

Complexity: Intermediate

### Problem

Although I understand the RGB (red/green/blue) color scheme of Windows and Visual Basic, it's still confusing to select a unique color other than the primary colors. How can I visualize the way certain combinations of red, green, and blue will turn out?

### Technique

As with many aspects of a visual development environment, the easiest way to work with colors is to visualize them. Any color in Visual Basic can be specified by the amount of red, green, and blue it contains. Each component color can have a range of 0 to 255, making it perfect to be represented by a scroll bar. Figure 3-14 shows a monochrome picture of a selected color.

**Figure 3-14**  The ColorScr form in action

### Steps

Open and run COLORSCR.MAK. There are three scroll bars and three text boxes, each of which is red, green, or blue to show which color the scroll bar controls. (Unfortunately, scroll bar color is controlled by Windows and the Control Panel, so the color can't be changed by an application.) Click on the scroll bars or type a number in the text box, and the background color of the form will change to match the RGB color you specified.

1. Create a new project called COLORSCR.MAK. Create a new form with the objects and properties listed in Table 3-18 and save it as COLORSCR.FRM.

| Object | Property | Setting |
|---|---|---|
| Form | BackColor | &H00000000& (Black) |
| | Caption | Color scroll bars |
| | FormName | ColorScrollBars |
| Scroll bar | CtlName | ColorBar |
| | Index | 0 |
| | LargeChange | 16 |
| | Max | 255 |

| | | |
|---|---|---|
| | Min | 0 |
| | SmallChange | 1 |
| Text box | BackColor | &H000000FF& (Red) |
| | CtlName | ColorText |
| | Index | 0 |
| | Text | 0 |
| Scroll bar | CtlName | ColorBar |
| | Index | 1 |
| | LargeChange | 16 |
| | Max | 255 |
| | Min | 0 |
| | SmallChange | 1 |
| Text box | BackColor | &H0000FF00& (Green) |
| | CtlName | ColorText |
| | Index | 1 |
| | Text | 0 |
| Scroll bar | CtlName | ColorBar |
| | Index | 2 |
| | LargeChange | 16 |
| | Max | 255 |
| | Min | 0 |
| | SmallChange | 1 |
| Text box | BackColor | &H00FF0000& (Blue) |
| | CtlName | ColorText |
| | Index | 2 |
| | Text | 0 |

**Table 3-18** ColorScr project form's objects and properties

2. The code is extremely simple; the form does most of the work. Place the following code in the ColorBar_Change event subroutine. Whenever the scroll bar is moved, this subroutine is executed. Because our scroll bars are elements of a control array, Visual Basic passes the Index of the scroll bar. The code updates the text of the corresponding text box, then uses the RGB function to change the background color of the form with the new value.

```
Sub ColorBar_Change (Index As Integer)
    ColorText(Index).Text = Str$(ColorBar(Index).Value)
    ColorScrollBars.BackColor = RGB(ColorBar(0).Value, ColorBar(1).Value, ⇐
    ColorBar(2).Value)
End Sub
```

3. Visual Basic runs the following code in the ColorText_Change event subroutine whenever the user types any character in any of the text boxes. If the new value in the text box is within range, we change the value of the scroll bar to that value. This invokes the ColorBar_Change event subroutine to update the background color. If the new value is greater than 255, though, the text is changed to 255 to avoid Visual Basic run-time errors.

```
Sub ColorText_Change (Index As Integer)
   Select Case Val(ColorText(Index).Text)
      Case Is < 0
         ColorText(Index).Text = "0"
      Case 0 To 255
         ColorBar(Index).Value = Val(ColorText(Index).Text)
      Case Else
         ColorText(Index).Text = "255"
   End Select
End Sub
```

### How It Works

This example shows how easy control arrays can make some programming tasks. By using control arrays, we avoid having to write three almost identical routines for both the scroll bars and the text boxes. Visual Basic tells us which scroll bar or text box has been changed with the Index parameter, which is the same as the Index property.

Visual Basic runs the code in the ColorBar_Change event subroutine whenever the scroll bar is changed, either by clicking on the scroll arrows or moving the scroll thumb. Also, the scroll bar is changed in the ColorText_Change event subroutine when the user types in one of the text boxes.

The code updates the Text property of the corresponding text box to the Value property of the scroll bar. This will give a running value of the red, green, and blue components of the form's background color.

Finally, ColorText_Change calls the RGB function with the value of each scroll bar and assigns the number that RGB returns to the form's BackColor property.

Visual Basic runs the code in the ColorText_Change event subroutine whenever the user types any character in any of the text boxes. Normally, the form would have an OK button to press before the changes take effect. Using the Change event, though, makes the changes take effect immediately, as the user types them, without having to click on a button or press Enter.

Because the component red, green, and blue colors must be within the range from 0 to 255, there's an If statement in the code to ensure that the user doesn't try to exceed that range. If the text box's value is okay, the Value property of the corresponding scroll bar is changed to that value. Changing a scroll bar's value automatically invokes its Change event subroutine. In this example, the ColorBar_Change event subroutine updates the background color.

If the user tries to enter a text box value for a color component greater than 255, the If statement sets the Text property of the text box to "255" so Visual Basic won't complain with an Overflow error.

### Comment

Certain color combinations result in pure colors. For example, RGB(0,0,0) creates black and RGB(255,255,255) creates white. Other combinations like RGB(255,128,255) should give a nice mauve shade on a monitor that supports it. Unfortunately, Visual Basic doesn't support more than 16 colors, so Windows will attempt to dither a matching color. (Dithering means to make a dot pattern that closely matches the requested color.)

# 4

# MOUSE
# AND MENU

# 4

Windows includes many improvements over the DOS operating system, but the most noticeable is the beauty of the user interface. And it has not taken long for faithful DOS command-line users to appreciate the ease of use of the graphical user interface. Most essential to a good user interface are mouse-driven user input and command menus. While Visual Basic makes interface programming a snap with its toolbox and control array features, in some cases this young language is limited. This bag-of-tricks chapter shows you how to create more powerful mouse trapping and selection capabilities and how to create more customized, useful, and attractive menus. We will use some very handy Windows APIs to extend Visual Basic's menu-making capabilities: GetMenu, GetSubMenu, GetMenuItem, and ModifyMenu. We will also see the versatility of Visual Basic's timer features.

## Windows APIs Covered

| | |
|---|---|
| DeleteMenu | GetSystemMenu |
| GetMenu | ModifyMenu |
| GetMenuItem | TrackPopupMenu |
| GetSubMenu | |

### 4.1 Draw an animated bounding box

Ease of the user interface is an important issue in a graphically-oriented language such as Visual Basic. You may notice that various Windows paint or draw programs use a rotating dashed line to show rectangular areas selected with a mouse. This clever How-To uses the timer to simulate an animated bounding box (or the "marching ants" effect, as it's known to Macintosh programmers). No APIs are required.

### 4.2 Trap both Click and DoubleClick events

Many mouse users are accustomed to clicking and double-clicking to select items, open and close menus, and run applications. Amazingly enough, Visual Basic's capabilities allow you to either trap single Click events or a DoubleClick event, but not both in one application! One reason for this is that Visual Basic has a hard time distinguishing between two single clicks or one double-click. Waiting for the second-half of a double click can slow up your application's performance. This How-To uses the timer to distinguish between the events and allows you to build a more flexible user interface. This project also includes a gauge to display the performance hit that's caused by distinguishing between Click and DoubleClick events.

### 4.3 Make a floating pop-up menu

Visual Basic allows you to easily create menu bars at the top of a form. However, it does not provide the power to create "floating" menus that pop up anywhere at the click of a mouse. This How-To shows you how to use the Windows API functions GetMenu, GetSubMenu, and TrackPopupMenu to display a pop-up menu that allows you to choose a form's background color. This menu will appear anywhere on your screen. You'll also see how to make Windows API functions interpret Visual Basic's "twips" measurement.

**4.4    Modify a form's system menu**

Visual Basic's toolbox allows you to modify most menus, but the System menu seems sacrosanct—it cannot be changed with ordinary Visual Basic control arrays. Sometimes you may want to disable some options of the System menu so users of your program have limited choices. For instance, you may want to restrict the way your users can close an application or to prevent your application from ever being minimized. The Windows APIs GetSystemMenu, ModifyMenu, and DeleteMenu are used in this How-To to get a handle to the System menu and use that handle to delete menu items.

**4.5    Draw a bitmapped picture in a menu**

Visual Basic is a relatively flexible language when it comes to creating menus but it does have its limitations. One restraint is that you cannot put a bitmapped graphic image in a menu with purely native Visual Basic code. Sometimes, however, you may want to spruce up your menus to include icons or custom graphics. For example, a telephone icon could appear next to the word "Dial." This How-To uses the Windows API functions GetMenu, GetSubMenu, and GetMenuItem ID to place a bitmapped graphic in a menu, including .BMP (bitmap), .ICO (icon), or .WMF (window metafile) file types.

**4.6    Place font typefaces in a menu**

The high-resolution look of Windows 3.0 and 3.1 is causing users to expect a higher standard in the way applications look on the screen. Windows word processors are being touted for their WYSIWYG (What You See Is What You Get) capabilities; you can preview a printed page on your monitor and see them style and size of a font, for instance. The previous How-To demonstrated how to include bitmapped graphics on your menus; this How-To goes further to create a Font menu that displays bitmapped images of the actual font typefaces. Again, the multipurpose Windows APIs GetMenu, GetSubMenu, GetMenuItem, and ModifyMenu API are used for this effect.

**4.1 How do I...**

# Draw an animated bounding box?

Complexity: Easy

### Problem

I want to offer my users a way to select an area on a form with their mouse. How can I display a rotating bounding box around the area they select?

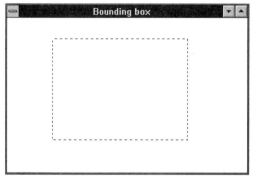

**Figure 4-1** The Bounding form in action

### Technique

A timer object is useful when you are doing animation. Dotted line boxes can create an optical illusion of movement, as shown in Figure 4-1. Each time the timer goes off, the line can be inverted, which creates the illusion of the box rotating.

### Steps

Open and run BOUNDING.MAK. You can draw boxes by holding down the mouse button and dragging. Once you release the mouse button, the box will remain rotating on the screen until you drag it on another area. Notice that the box rotates even as you draw it.

1. Create a new project called BOUNDING.MAK. Create a new form with the objects and properties listed in Table 4-1. Save it as BOUND-ING.FRM.

| Object | Property | Setting |
|--------|----------|---------|
| Form | FormName | BoundingBox |
| | Caption | Bounding box |
| | BackColor | &H00FFFFFF& (White) |
| Timer | CtlName | Timer1 |
| | Interval | 100 |
| | Enabled | True |

**Table 4-1** Bounding project form's objects and properties

2. Place the following code in the Declarations section of the form to define some constants for drawing and global variables.

```
Const DOTSTYLE = 2
Const SOLIDSTYLE = 0
Const INVERTMODE = 6
Const COPYPENMODE = 13
Dim X1 As Single, Y1 As Single, X2 As Single, Y2 As Single
```

3. Put the following code in the form's MouseDown event subroutine to set the box's coordinates to the point where the mouse was clicked. As the user moves the mouse, the coordinates of the lower right-hand corner (X2 and Y2) of the box will change.

```
Sub Form_MouseDown (Button As Integer, Shift As Integer, X As Single, Y ⇐
    As Single)
    X1 = X
    Y1 = Y
    X2 = X
    Y2 = Y
End Sub
```

4. The form's MouseMove event subroutine first checks whether a mouse button is being held down. If so, it erases the previously drawn box, then draws a dotted box at the new coordinates of the mouse with this code.

```
Sub Form_MouseMove (Button As Integer, Shift As Integer, X As Single, Y ⇐
    As Single)
    If Button Then
        DrawStyle = SOLIDSTYLE
        DrawMode = COPYPENMODE
        Line (X1, Y1)-(X2, Y2), BoundingBox.BackColor, B
        X2 = X
        Y2 = Y
        DrawStyle = DOTSTYLE
        Line (X1, Y1)-(X2, Y2), , B
    End If
End Sub
```

5. Timer1's Timer event subroutine draws the inverted dotted box around the current coordinates set by the MouseDown and MouseMove event subroutines.

```
Sub Timer1_Timer ()
    DrawStyle = SOLIDSTYLE
    DrawMode = INVERTMODE
    Line (X1, Y1)-(X2, Y2), , B
End Sub
```

### How It Works

The code in the MouseDown and MouseMove event subroutines handles drawing the box as the user moves the mouse. In the MouseMove event subroutine, the Line statement draws a box using a solid DrawStyle and a dotted DrawMode in the background color of the form. Using the background color erases the last box before drawing the box with the new size.

The key to simulating animation is to be able to invert the box often enough to stimulate continuous motion. A timer causes a timer interrupt to occur every 100 milliseconds, at which point it causes the inverse of the current box to be drawn. Since we used a dotted DrawMode, the inverse of the dot-space pattern will become space-dot. Doing that often enough gives the illusion of a rotating box.

### Comments

Although the MouseMove event subroutine uses a dotted DrawStyle, you could just as easily use another DrawStyle (a dashed box—DrawStyle = 1— also looks attractive). Note that using many timers running on short intervals will slow down your whole system. Be sure to disable timers as soon as you're finished using them. You can safely increase the timer interval, and the bounding box will simply "rotate" more slowly.

---

**4.2        How do I...**

# Trap both Click and DoubleClick events?

Complexity: Intermediate

### Problem

I have seen a number of programs that do one thing when users click on an object and another when users double-click. I can't seem to get this to work in Visual Basic. I can trap either the Click event or the DoubleClick event, but not both. When I create an event procedure for both, the Click handler gets launched in both instances, and my program never hears about the DoubleClick. I know that my DoubleClick procedure works, because if I disable the Click procedure, the DoubleClick procedure works fine. Is there anything I can do?

### Technique

This issue is, in fact, a sore spot with no easy answer for the developers of Visual Basic without a real performance hit. The problem is this: a double-click is technically a series of two clicks in rapid succession. Just how rapid is determined by the system "DoubleClick Time," which can be set by a program, as we will do later in this project, or by using the Control Panel.

When Windows receives the first mouse click, it has no way of knowing whether this will ultimately become a double-click or will remain a single click, so it simply passes on the Click message. (In reality, Windows passes the MouseDown followed by the MouseUp message.) Now, if another click arrives within the specified interval, it is considered the second half of a double-click and the DoubleClick message is sent.

Theoretically, Windows could wait for the duration of the double-click interval before sending the Click message. However, when you consider that the user generates many more clicks than double-clicks, it doesn't make sense to slow the whole system down to make it easier for the few programs that need to trap both events.

The good news is that you can perform this operation yourself, using a timer. The technique is to enable your timer, the interval of which is set to be equal to the "DoubleClick Time," within your Click event handler. Within the Timer event handler, you must first disable the timer and then build in the processing that would normally be contained in the Click event handler. From within the DoubleClick event handler, you simply disable the timer and proceed with normal double-click processing.

### Steps

Open and run CLICKS.MAK. There is a button labeled "Try It!" that you can either click or double-click with the left mouse button. The caption of the form will change to reflect your action as either "Clicked" or "Double-Clicked." As shown in Figure 4-2, the scroll bar is used to set the "Double-Click Time" and thus the speed with which you must double-click the mouse to have the action register as a double-click in the pro-gram. The number below the scroll bar reports the current double-click time in milliseconds. The smaller the number, the faster you have to double-click on the button for it to register as a double-click in the program.

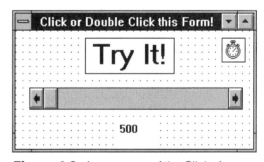

**Figure 4-2** Appearance of the Clicks form

To see that the system-wide double-click time is actually being set, move all the way left on the scroll bar, minimize Clicks, and see whether you can restore it, or try to open any other application by double-clicking it. Luckily, you can select Restore from the System menu to get back into Clicks. When you exit from Clicks, the previous setting for the double-click time is restored. To create the Clicks program, perform the following steps:

1. Create a new project called CLICKS.MAK. Create a new form with the objects and properties shown in Table 4-2, and save it as CLICKS.FRM.

| Object | Property | Setting |
|--------|----------|---------|
| Form | FormName | Form1 |
|  | Caption | Click or DoubleClick |
|  | BackColor | &H00FFFFFF& (White) |
| Picture | CtlName | Picture1 |
|  | Caption | Try It! |
|  | BorderStyle | Fixed Single |
| Timer | CtlName | Timer1 |
|  | Interval | 200 |
|  | Enabled | FLASE |
| Scroll | CtlName | HScroll1 |
|  | LargeChange | 10 |
|  | Max | 2000 |
|  | Min | 100 |
|  | SmallChange | 1 |
| Label | CtlName | Label1 |
|  | Caption 500 | |

**Table 4-2** Clicks project form's objects and properties

2. Insert the following code in the Declarations section of Form1.

```
DefInt A-Z

Declare Function GetDoubleClickTime Lib "User" ()
Declare Sub SetDoubleClickTime Lib "User" (ByVal wCount)

Const TRUE = -1
Const FALSE = 0

Dim OldInterval As Integer
```

3. Insert the following code in the Form_Load procedure.

```
Sub Form_Load ()
   OldInterval = GetDoubleClickTime()
   Timer1.Interval = 500
   HScroll1.Value = 500
End Sub
```

4. Insert the following code in the Form_Unload procedure.

```
Sub Form_Unload (Cancel As Integer)
   SetDoubleClickTime OldInterval
End Sub
```

5. Insert the following code in the Label1_Click procedure.

```
Sub Label1_Click ()
   Timer1.Enabled = TRUE
End Sub
```

6. Insert the following code in the Label1_DblClick procedure.

```
Sub Label1_DblClick ()
   Timer1.Enabled = FALSE
   Form1.Caption = "DoubleClicked!"
End Sub
```

7. Insert the following code in the Timer1_Timer procedure.

```
Sub Timer1_Timer ()
   'Click processing here!
   Form1.Caption = "Clicked!"
   Timer1.Enabled = FALSE
End Sub
```

8. Insert the following code in HScroll1_Change procedure.

```
Sub HScroll1_Change ()
   NewInterval = HScroll1.Value
   SetDoubleClickTime NewInterval
   Timer1.Interval = HScroll1.Value
   Label2.Caption = Str$(HScroll1.Value)
End Sub
```

### How It Works

A click is defined as a MouseDown followed by a MouseUp within the same region. After Visual Basic has received both of these messages, it triggers the Click event for a given control. If another Click occurs within the Double-Click Time, Windows sends the DoubleClick message to your application, and the message gets translated into the DblClick event.

What we are doing here is setting a timer, the Interval of which is the same as the DoubleClick Time, which we enable in the Click event handler. This frees up the system quickly enough to avoid swallowing the DblClick event. If the DblClick event occurs within the specified interval, we immediately disable the timer and process the DblClick event. However, if the timer gets a chance to fire, it means that a second click did not manage to occur within the DoubleClick Time, so we process the first click by itself.

### Comments

You can see by scrolling the interval gauge all the way to the right just what sort of performance slowdown can result from always trapping both events. This is why this sort of trapping is not supported natively in the Windows API. However, it is not too complicated to implement such a feature for your own use.

One issue that might arise is that you want to be able to trap both events for a number of controls. This is most easily accomplished with a control array. If the controls are all in an array, then the index of the array could simply be saved in a static variable. This way, when the Timer event occurs, it can execute specific code based in the index in the static variable.

---

**4.3      How do I...**

# Make a floating pop-up menu?

Complexity: Intermediate

### Problem

Is there any way to make my menus pop up anywhere on the screen at the touch of a mouse button? Pop-up menus are a nice way to let users select an object, then click a mouse button rather than having to select a menu item from the top of the form.

### Technique

Although in Windows the menu bar is fixed at the top of the form, individual menus can be popped up anywhere you'd like, even off your form. Windows API functions allow this.

There are API functions that let you get a menu handle (the Windows identification of a menu and its items). Once you have that handle you can use it to manually pop up a menu. You press the mouse button in conjunction with another key and then slide down the menu to select an item. You can also control where you want it to pop up. For this example, we'll pop the menu up at the current mouse position.

### Steps

Open and run FLOATING.MAK. Click and hold down the left mouse button. The Color menu will appear next to your mouse pointer. Move the mouse to select a color and release the button. The background color of the form will change.

1. Create a new project called FLOATING.MAK. Create a new form with the objects and properties listed in Table 4-3, and save it as FLOAT-ING.FRM.

| Object | Property | Setting |
|--------|----------|---------|
| Form | FormName | FloatingPopupMenu |
| | Caption | Floating popup menu |

**Table 4-3** Floating project form's objects and properties

2. Create a menu for the form, as shown in Table 4-4, using the Menu Design window.

| Caption | CtlName | Index |
|---------|---------|-------|
| &Color | ColorMenu | |
| B&lack | Colors | 0 |
| &Blue | Colors | 1 |
| &Green | Colors | 2 |
| &Cyan | Colors | 3 |
| &Red | Colors | 4 |
| &Magenta | Colors | 5 |
| &Yellow | Colors | 6 |
| &White | Colors | 7 |
| - | Separator | |
| E&xit | ColorExit | |

**Table 4-4** FloatingPopUpMenu menu items

3. Put the following code in the Declarations section of the form. This code declares several API functions and a global variable.

```
DefInt A-Z
Declare Function GetMenu% Lib "User" (ByVal hWnd%)
Declare Function GetSubMenu% Lib "User" (ByVal hMenu%, ByVal nPos%)
Declare Function TrackPopupMenu% Lib "User" (ByVal hMenu%, ByVal wFlags%, ⇐
ByVal X%, ByVal Y%, ByVal nReserved%, ByVal hWnd%, ByVal lpReserved&)
Dim TwipPixelRatio As Single
```

4. Once you've created the menu, you can add the code that goes with the menu items. Put the following code in the ColorExit_Click event subroutine.

```
Sub ColorExit_Click ()
    End
End Sub
```

5. Put the following code in the Colors_Click event subroutine.

```
Sub Colors_Click (Index As Integer)
    BackColor = QBColor(Index)
End Sub
```

6. Because the Windows API functions we're using don't understand twips (Visual Basic's "logical" measurement), the Form_Load event subroutine calculates the ratio of twips to screen pixels by changing the ScaleMode property from twips to pixels, getting the width of the form in pixels, then switching back to twips, and finally getting the form width in twips.

```
Sub Form_Load ()
    ScaleMode = 3   ' Use pixel measures
    PixelWidth = ScaleWidth
    ScaleMode = 1   ' Switch back to twips
    TwipPixelRatio = ScaleWidth / PixelWidth
End Sub
```

7. The Form_MouseDown event subroutine is used to call the API functions to pop up the menu. Because Visual Basic automatically passes to MouseDown event subroutines, we'll convert the x- and y-coordinates to pixels using the figure we calculated in the Form_Load event subroutine.

```
Sub Form_MouseDown (Button As Integer, Shift As Integer, X As Single, Y ⇐
    As Single)
    PopupX = (X + Left) / TwipPixelRatio
    PopupY = (Y + Top) / TwipPixelRatio
    hMenu = GetMenu(hWnd)
    hSubMenu = GetSubMenu(hMenu, 0)
    I = TrackPopupMenu(hSubMenu, 0, PopupX, PopupY, 0, hWnd, 0)
End Sub
```

## How It Works

Figure 4-3 shows what the pop-up Colors menu will look like at run time. The Declare statements in the Declarations section give Visual Basic access to the Windows API functions we'll need. Note also that we declare a variable called TwipPixelRatio. Unfortunately, the Windows API functions don't understand Visual Basic's twips measurement; they expect x- and y-coordinates to be in pixels, so we must convert down to the API functions' level. (A twip, by the way, stands for a twentieth of a point. A point, used by typographers, is 1/72nd of an inch. So a twip is 1/1440th of an inch. How-

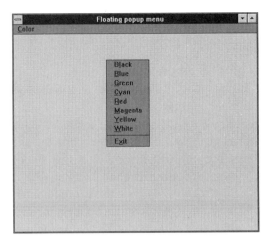

**Figure 4-3** The FloatingPopupMenu form showing a menu to select color

ever, in Visual Basic, an inch on the screen depends on what size and resolution monitor is attached. On a printer, though, an inch is an inch.)

The Form_Load event subroutine is a good place to calculate the ratio of twips to pixels, so that ratio will be available anytime after the form is loaded.

We use a control array's index value to our advantage. The indexes from the Colors menu will be from zero to seven, which correspond exactly to the first eight color codes that QuickBasic uses. Visual Basic has the QBColor function to convert from the QuickBasic color codes to the RGB codes that Visual Basic itself uses. So we'll use it to change the background color of the form by simply saying BackColor = QBColor(Index).

The Form_Load event subroutine calculates the ratio between twips and pixels for the video screen the program's running on at the time. Remember, you can never assume what kind of video adapter a user will have. Thus, TwipPixelRatio will be different as your resolution changes. We end up with a TwipPixelRatio variable that we'll use later in the MouseDown event subroutine.

The Form_MouseDown event subroutine calls up the Colors menu. First, the location of the mouse pointer must be calculated using the twips-to-pixels ratio calculated in Form_Load. Then Windows' requirement to get a handle on everything must be satisfied by using the GetMenu and GetSubMenu API functions. Finally, the TrackPopupMenu API pops up the menu and lets you select an item. Notice that even though we're using a Windows API function to call the menu, Visual Basic still intercepts the menu access and calls the Colors_Click event subroutine just as if the menu were at the top, where it normally is.

**Comment**

Note that the menus are still available, as you'd expect, from the menu bar at the top of the form. The menu only pops up when you click on the "surface" of the form.

**4.4    How do I...**

# Modify a form's system menu?

Complexity: Intermediate

### Problem

Not all the features of the System menu (the square in the upper left-hand corner of windows) are needed for my application. I would like to both remove some System menu items and modify others, like Visual Basic's

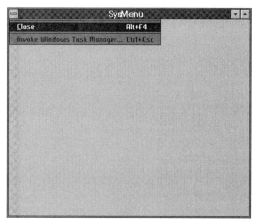

toolbox does. Although I can modify a form's normal menu items using control arrays, that method doesn't seem to work on the System menu. I'd like to prevent the user from closing the application except through the File menu's Exit option, as shown in Figure 4-4.

**Figure 4-4** The SysMenu form and menu

### Technique

Once again, you can use Windows API functions to extend the power of Visual Basic. The API GetSystemMenu is a function that returns a handle to the System menu. Remember, handles are integer values (IDs) that Windows uses to identify elements like menus and windows. Once we have a handle for the System menu, we can use other API functions like ModifyMenu and DeleteMenu to modify it.

### Steps

Open and run SYSMENU.MAK. You'll be presented with a blank form once you access System menu. You'll see the changes that Form_Load has made to the System menu.

1. Create a new project called SYSMENU.MAK. Create a new form with no controls on it, and save it as SYSMENU.FRM.

2. Add the following Declare statements to the Declarations section of the form. They declare the Windows API functions that will be used later.

```
DefInt A-Z
Declare Function GetSystemMenu Lib "User" (ByVal hWnd, ByVal bRevert)
Declare Function ModifyMenu Lib "User" (ByVal hMenu, ByVal nPosition, ⇐
ByVal wFlags, ByVal wIDNewItem, ByVal lpNewItem$)
```

```
Declare Function DeleteMenu Lib "User" (ByVal hMenu, ByVal nPosition, ⇐
ByVal wFlags)
```

3. Put the following code in the Form_Load event subroutine. It declares constants to use in the API function calls. It gets a handle to the System menu and then uses the handle to change the menu and delete some menu items.

```
Sub Form_Load ()
    Const MF_BYCOMMAND = 0
    Const MF_BYPOSITION = &H400
    Const SC_TASKLIST = &HF130
    Const ICON_STOP = 16

    Dim hSysMenu As Integer

    hSysMenu = GetSystemMenu(hWnd, 0)

    NewMenuItem$ = "Windows Task Manager--" + Chr$(9) + "Ctrl+Esc"
    If ModifyMenu(hSysMenu, SC_TASKLIST, MF_BYCOMMAND, SC_TASKLIST, ⇐
        NewMenuItem$) = 0 Then
        MsgBox "Can't modify system menu item!", ICON_STOP
    End If

    For I = 0 To 4
        If DeleteMenu(hSysMenu, 0, MF_BYPOSITION) = 0 Then
            MsgBox "Unable to delete system menu item!", ICON_STOP
        End If
    Next
End Sub
```

### How It Works

The Declare statements in the Declarations section of the form provide access to the Windows API functions. GetSystemMenu is the API function that returns a handle to the System menu. ModifyMenu lets you change the text of a menu item. DeleteMenu deletes items from a menu, not the whole menu as its name would imply.

The Form_Load subroutine manages the modification process for the System menu. The first couple of lines define some Windows constants for the various API functions. (The MF_ prefix means "menu flags," and SC_ means "system menu commands.") MF_BYCOMMAND specifies to modify a menu item based on its message ID, whereas SC_TASKLIST is the actual message ID of the Switch To item on the System menu. MF_BY-POSITION indicates that a menu item should be modified based on its position within the menu.

We call the GetSystemMenu to get the handle of the System menu. We use Visual Basic's hWnd property to give the form's window handle, which GetSystemMenu requires.

Note the use of Chr$(9), the tab character; a tab is used in this menu item to tab over to the right side of the menu. In the Windows interface, that's where you tell users what key to press to get the same result as selecting the menu item. Here, we specify Ctrl+Esc to get to the SwitchTo selection.

By using MY_BYCOMMAND and the same message ID (SC_TASK-LIST) in the call to the ModifyMenu function, we're telling Windows not to change the message ID, just the text of the menu item. If ModifyMenu returns 0, Windows was for some reason unable to make the requested change, so we display a message box with the error. (Windows should always be able to change a menu, unless very little memory is available, but it's better to be safe than sorry.)

The For...Next loop deletes five of the standard System menu items. Actually, we specify to delete by position (MF_BYPOSITION), item 0 five times. Because item 0 is always the topmost item, Visual Basic deletes the top five items. DeleteMenu also returns 0 if there was an error, so we check for it and display a message box if necessary.

## Comments

If you're modifying the text on the System menu, you should always be sure to put the keyboard equivalent in the text. In the previous example, the Form_Load event subroutine uses Chr$(9) + "Ctrl+Esc" because that was the original key of the Switch to item.

Be aware that if you delete an item from the System menu, you won't be able to do the function performed by the deleted item. For example, if you delete the Move item, you won't be able to move it around the screen with either the mouse or the keyboard.

---

**4.5    How do I...**

# Draw a bitmapped picture in a menu?

Complexity: Intermediate

## Problem

I want to make my application as graphical as possible. Unfortunately, the part of my application my users must deal with the most is lackluster text: the menu. What can I do to spice up this menu?

## Technique

The use of graphical icons is very important in today's applications. Fortunately, there is a way to place bitmap images into a menu using Windows APIs.

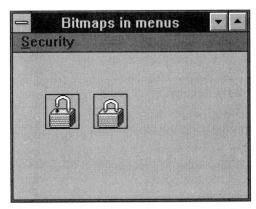

**Figure 4-5** The BitMapMenu form at design time

**Steps**

Open and run BITMAPS.MAK. Notice the two picture boxes (as shown in Figure 4-5). They will be hidden when you run the application. Select the Security menu and see how it looks when you mix text and graphics on the same menu.

1. Create a new project called BIT-MAPS.MAK. Create a new form with the objects and properties listed in Table 4-5, and save it as BITMAPS.FRM.

| Object | Property | Setting |
|---|---|---|
| Form | FormName | BitmapMenu |
| | Caption | Bitmaps in menus |
| | BackColor | &H00C0C0C0& (50% gray) |
| Picture box | CtlName | Unlocked |
| | AutoSize | True |
| | Picture | \VB\ICONS\MISC\SECUR02A.ICO |
| | Visible | False |
| Picture box | CtlName | Locked |
| | AutoSize | True |
| | Picture | \VB\ICONS\MISC\SECUR02B.ICO |
| | Visible | False |

**Table 4-5** BitMap project form's objects and properties

2. Create a menu for the form as shown in Table 4-6, using the Menu Design window.

| Caption | CtlName |
|---|---|
| &Security | SecurityMenu |
| O&ff | SecurityOff |
| O&n | SecurityOn |
| E&xit | SecurityExit |

**Table 4-6** Bitmaps menu

3. Because we need to declare some API functions and API constants, put the following code in the Declarations section of the Form object.

```
DefInt A-Z

Declare Function GetMenu% Lib "User" (ByVal hWnd%)
Declare Function GetSubMenu% Lib "User" (ByVal hMenu%, ByVal nPos%)
Declare Function GetMenuItemID% Lib "User" (ByVal hMenu%, ByVal nPos%)
Declare Function ModifyMenu% Lib "User" (ByVal hMenu%, ByVal nPosition%, ⇐
ByVal wFlags%, ByVal wIDNewItem%, ByVal lpNewItem&)

Const MF_BYCOMMAND = 0
Const MF_BITMAP = 4
Const MF_CHECKED = 8
Const FALSE = 0, TRUE = Not FALSE
```

4. The Form_Load event subroutine manages placing the bitmaps in the menu. Because Windows only allows changes to a menu via its menu handle (an integer number that Windows uses to identify menus), you'll need to use the GetMenu and GetSubMenu API functions to access those handles from Visual Basic. Also, you'll need to use the Get-MenuItemID API function to be able to put a bitmap in the individual menu item.

```
Sub Form_Load ()
    ' Get the form's menu handle.
    hMenu = GetMenu(hWnd)

    ' Get the menu's Security (submenu 0) submenu handle.
    hSubMenu = GetSubMenu(hMenu, 0)

    ' Make sure Picture gets the bitmap handle from Image property.
    UnLocked.Picture = UnLocked.Image
    ' Get the Windows menu message ID of Off item.
    menuId = GetMenuItemID(hSubMenu, 0)
    ' Put the "unlocked" bitmap into the menu.
    J = ModifyMenu(hMenu, menuId, MF_BYCOMMAND Or MF_BITMAP Or ⇐
        MF_CHECKED, menuId, UnLocked.Picture)

    ' Make sure Picture gets the bitmap handle from Image property.
    Locked.Picture = Locked.Image
    ' Get the Windows menu message ID of On item.
    menuId = GetMenuItemID(hSubMenu, 1)
    ' Put the "locked" bitmap into the menu.
    J = ModifyMenu(hMenu, menuId, MF_BYCOMMAND Or MF_BITMAP, menuId, ⇐
        Locked.Picture)
End Sub
```

5. Put the following code in the SecurityExit_Click event subroutine.

```
Sub SecurityExit_Click ()
    End
End Sub
```

6. Place the following code in the SecurityOff_Click and SecurityOn_Click event subroutines. This code simply prints a message and then puts a check mark next to the menu item you picked.

```
Sub SecurityOff_Click ()
    Print "Security has been deactivated"
    SecurityOn.Checked = FALSE
    SecurityOff.Checked = TRUE
End Sub

Sub SecurityOn_Click ()
    Print "WARNING: Security has been activated"
    SecurityOn.Checked = TRUE
    SecurityOff.Checked = FALSE
End Sub
```

### How It Works

The Declare and Const statements in the Declarations section give Visual Basic access to the various Windows API functions that we'll be using to manipulate the menu.

The Form_Load event subroutine does the work of placing the bitmaps from the hidden picture boxes into the menus. The Picture property of a picture box is what Windows is expecting as a handle to a bitmap.

Windows uses handles extensively. A Windows handle is just an integer that Windows uses to identify elements like menus and bitmaps. In the Form_Load event subroutine, a call to the GetMenu and GetSubMenu API functions gets the handles to the main menu and the Security menu.

The Windows API functions don't let you change the properties of a menu item without knowing its message ID (something that we Visual Basic programmers don't have to fuss with), so we call GetMenuItemID to get it and store it in a variable. Next, we give the handle back to Windows in the ModifyMenu call.

Notice the expression MF_BYCOMMAND Or MF_BITMAP Or MF_CHECKED. These are all constants (defined in the Declarations section) that tell Windows how to process the change in the menu. (The MF_ prefix stands for menu flags.) MF_BYCOMMAND tells Windows we want to identify the menu item with its message ID. MF_BITMAP says we're going to be providing a handle to a bitmap rather than the plain text that was there. MF_CHECKED tells Windows to place a check mark next to the bitmap to show that it's selected. We could have modified the Checked property as we do in the SecurityOn_Click and SecurityOff_Click event subroutines; either method works. Also notice how we use the Or operator with the menu flag expressions. Here, Or is a bitwise operator that combines the bits of all three constants, so Windows knows we want to combine them. In other words, the Or expression doesn't mean one MF_ constant or another, it means all three bits are used.

## Comment

Although in this How-To the bitmaps are preloaded into the form, we could also use the LoadPicture function to load any .BMP bitmap file, .ICO icon file, or .WMF metafile into the picture boxes. That way you could display any graphic you wanted to at run time.

### 4.6 How do I...

# Place font typefaces in a menu?

**Figure 4-6** Fonts in a menu

Complexity: Intermediate

## Problem

Many users would like to see samples of the fonts before they select them from a menu. Is there any way that Visual Basic can plan font typefaces in a menu?

## Technique

As shown in How-To 4.5 Draw a bitmapped picture in a menu, you can place simple icons into a menu. Using the same techniques, we can place graphical text in a menu.

## Steps

Open and run FONTSIN.MAK. After a short pause that occurs while Visual Basic creates the menu with all the fonts in your system, you'll be presented with a blank form. Click on the menu of fonts. Your screen should resemble the menu shown in Figure 4-6. You may select any font from the menu as you would normally expect, and a brief message will be printed in the font you selected.

1. Create a new project called FONTSIN.MAK. Create a new form with the objects and properties listed in Table 4-7, and save it as FONTSIN.FRM.

| Object | Property | Setting |
|---|---|---|
| Form | FormName | MenuFontsForm |
| | Caption | Fonts in a menu |
| | FontBold | False |
| | FontSize | 12 |
| Picture box | AutoRedraw | True |
| | BackColor | &H80000004& |
| | CtlName | FontPicture |
| | FontBold | False |
| | FontSize | 9.75 |
| | ForeColor | &H80000008& |
| | Index | 0 |
| | Visible | False |

**Table 4-7** FontsIn project form's objects and properties

2. Using the Menu Design window, give the form a menu with the characteristics in Table 4-8.

| Caption | CtlName | Index |
|---|---|---|
| F&ont | FontMenu | |
| First font | FontMenuList | 0 |

**Table 4-8** FontsIn project form characteristics

3. Put the following code in the Declarations section to declare the required Windows API functions and the constants that those functions use.

```
DefInt A-Z

Declare Function GetMenu% Lib "User" (ByVal hWnd%)
Declare Function GetSubMenu% Lib "User" (ByVal hMenu%, ByVal nPos%)
Declare Function GetMenuItemID% Lib "User" (ByVal hMenu%, ByVal nPos%)
Declare Function ModifyMenu% Lib "User" (ByVal hMenu%, ByVal nPosition%, ⇐
ByVal wFlags%, ByVal wIDNewItem%, ByVal lpNewItem&)

Const MF_BYCOMMAND = 0
Const MF_BITMAP = 4
Const MF_CHECKED = 8
Const FALSE = 0, TRUE = Not FALSE
```

4. Place the following code in the FontMenuList_Click event subroutine to switch to the font you selected from the menu and print a brief message.

```
Sub FontMenuList_Click (Index As Integer)
    FontName = Screen.Fonts(Index)
    Print "You have selected " + FontName
End Sub
```

5. The Form_Load event subroutine does all the magic. First, it uses API functions to get menu handles, because those handles are required by the other API functions used to put the fonts in the menu. Second, the first For...Next loop creates enough new elements in the menu and picture box control arrays to hold all the fonts in your system.

Then, the second For...Next loop goes through each font and prints the name of that font in the picture box, adjusting the width and height of the box to fit. Then, because the ModifyMenu API function needs to know the menu message ID, a call to the GetMenuItemID API function gets it. Finally, a call to ModifyMenu tells Windows to put the font bitmap from the picture box into the menu.

```
Sub Form_Load ()
    ' switch to hourglass cursor
    Screen.MousePointer = 11

    ' get the form's menu handle
    hMenu = GetMenu(hWnd)

    ' get the menu's Font (submenu 0) submenu handle
    hSubMenu = GetSubMenu(hMenu, 0)

    ' create new menu items and picture boxes
    For I = 1 To Screen.FontCount - 1
        Load FontMenuList(I)
        Load FontPicture(I)
    Next

    For I = 0 To Screen.FontCount - 1
        ' switch font
        FontPicture(I).FontName = Screen.Fonts(I)
        ' set width & height to match
        FontPicture(I).Width = FontPicture(I).TextWidth(Screen.Fonts(I))
        FontPicture(I).Height = FontPicture(I).TextHeight(Screen.Fonts(I))
        ' and print font name in picture box
        FontPicture(I).Print Screen.Fonts(I)
        ' make sure Picture gets the bitmap handle from Image property
        FontPicture(I).Picture = FontPicture(I).Image
        ' get the Windows menu message ID of current item
        menuId = GetMenuItemID(hSubMenu, I)
        ' put the font bitmap into the menu
```

```
    J = ModifyMenu(hMenu, menuId, MF_BYCOMMAND Or MF_BITMAP, menuId,
CLng(FontPicture(I).Picture))
    Next

    ' switch to normal cursor
    Screen.MousePointer = 0
End Sub
```

### How It Works

The Declare statements in the Declarations section of the form provide access to the Windows API functions. GetMenu is the API function that returns a handle to the menu. GetSubMenu gets a handle to an individual top-level menu (Fonts, in this example). GetMenuItemID gets the message ID that Windows uses for each menu item (something Visual Basic takes care of for us). ModifyMenu lets you change a menu item; the Form_Load event subroutine will use it to put the font bitmap in the menu.

Notice that we use the ByVal modifier for all the parameters, which instructs Visual Basic to simply pass the actual value of the parameter, rather than the address of a variable (the default). Note the declaration for ModifyMenu, which declares the last parameter ByVal lpNewItem$. When Visual Basic sees ByVal next to a string parameter, it passes (in C lingo) a long pointer to a null-terminated string, the type of string that Windows normally expects. Luckily, that's not something we have to worry about—Visual Basic takes care of it.

The Form_Load event subroutine does all the work of putting the fonts into the Font menu. It uses the GetMenu and GetSubMenu API functions to get the requisite menu handles.

You'll notice that both the picture box and font menu item are defined as elements in a control array, because their Index property is 0, instead of just being left blank. This was necessary because it's impossible to know at design time how many fonts are available on your users' machines. With font managers such as Adobe Type Manager (ATM), it's possible to have dozens of fonts. (Refer again to Figure 4-5.)

The first For...Next loop creates enough new elements in the control arrays to hold all the fonts in the user's system using Visual Basic's Load statement.

The second For...Next loop goes through each screen font, switches to the font, and prints the name of that font in the Picture box that holds the fonts before they go in the menu. The loop's code then adjusts the width and height of the box to fit using the picture box's TextHeight and TextWidth properties. The TextHeight and TextWidth properties are very useful, because they let you adjust the width of the picture box before there's any text printed there. Windows automatically adjusts the width of the entire menu to fit the largest width of all the fonts in the menu, but it won't change the height of individual fonts in the menu.

The ModifyMenu API function expects a handle to a bitmapped image (an HBITMAP), which the picture box provides in its Image property.

Finally, because ModifyMenu needs to know the menu message ID, a call to the GetMenuItemID API function gets it. A call to ModifyMenu tells Windows to put the font bitmap from the picture box into the menu. Notice the two menu flag (MF_) constants, MF_BYCOMMAND and MF_BITMAP. They tell Windows that we're modifying the menu by its menu message ID with a bitmapped image.

## Comment

On a system that includes a large number of fonts, it can take a fair amount of time for the Form_Load event subroutine to go through all the fonts. It may take 25 seconds for 33 fonts. You might display a "please wait—fonts loading" message to assure your user that nothing is wrong. Notice the use of the hourglass cursor in the Form_Lode() subroutine.

# 5

# GRAPHICS

# 5

If you really want your applications to make a lasting impression, turn your attention to graphics. This chapter provides a collection of projects that show how easy it is for Visual Basic to imitate any "look" you wish—from a modern brushed aluminum NeXT-like interface to a Macintosh-style trash can. You'll see how to fill complex polygon shapes with patterns and colors, how to draw pictures inside your iconized application, and how to build line, bar, and pie charts that work just like the charts in Excel. There is even a powerful slide show that does dissolves and other special effects for presentations. Throughout the chapter powerful APIs are used and carefully explained.

## Windows APIs Covered

| | | |
|---|---|---|
| ArrangeIcons | DeleteDC | ReleaseDC |
| BitBlt | EmptyClipBoard | SelectObject |
| CloseClipBoard | GetDesktopWindow | SendMessage |
| CreateCompatibleBitmap | OpenClipBoard | SetClipBoardData |
| CreateCompatibleDC | Polygon | SetPolyFillMode |
| CreateDC | | |

**5.1**   **Make a brushed aluminum NeXT™ interface**

**5.2**   **Give my application a three-dimensional look**

One of the first things you'll want to do with Visual Basic is create an interface. If you wish that interface to be modern and "sexy", then you should examine these two How-Tos. The first shows how simple it is to make a interface that mimics the look of the NeXT computer by simply passing a control to a subroutine that draws a line around it. The second How-To takes that idea further and creates a more general application that lets you control more details of the 3D look, including such things as the width of the bezel around each control and whether the frame is recessed or raised.

**5.3**   **Draw pictures into an iconized running application**

This How-To reveals how easy it is to change the default icon that Visual Basic gives your application while the program is running. This can be used to notify your user that some process has completed even though the icon is minimized.

**5.4**   **Draw a transparent picture or icon on a form**

One of the first things you might discover about Visual Basic is that when you put a picture box on a form, any graphics or text underneath it are covered and won't show through. Unfortunately picture boxes in Visual Basic are opaque and there is no property for making them transparent…unless you know how to use the BitBlt API. This How-To shows you a simple way to make pictures and icons that are transparent, so you can write games, for instance, that let the background show through. It teaches you the concept of how the pixels in your image can be combined in many different ways with the pixels in the background.

**5.5**    **Preview the DrawMode settings**

There 16 different ways that you can draw graphics on a form or picture box. Trying to visualize the effects of all these modes is not easy. This How-To lets you experiment with the different modes and see how they affect your bitmaps.

**5.6**    **Separate the red, green, and blue components of a color**

When programming color into your applications you'll frequently run across a long integer value that represents a color. This How-To presents a project that lets you enter the long integer and see immediately what red, blue, and green components of the color are. You'll also learn about hexidecimal math in this How-To.

**5.7**    **Make a screen capture from my running program**

While it is easy to capture screens to the clipboard in Windows using Alt-Print Screen there is no way to capture a section of your running Visual Basic application. This How-To shows how to capture a screen while your program is running. This could be useful if there are graphics that you want your user to save for manipulating in a Paint program or if you wish to make your own Visual Basic screen capture program. This How-To uses a variety of APIs, such as OpenClipBoard and SelectObject, and also gets you familiar with the concept of Windows Device Contexts.

**5.8**    **Arrange the icons on the Windows desktop**

Normally you can use the Task Manager to arrange the icons on a cluttered desktop and you could devise a way to use SendKeys so that your Visual Basic application could handle this for you. However the Task Manager is slow and when it suddenly pops up it might confuse users of your program. This project shows how to use the ArrangeIconicWindows API.

**5.9**    **Make a Macintosh-style trash can**

You've heard that Windows is close to the Macintosh interface; here is a project that puts a Macintosh trash can on the desktop. Using pure Visual Basic this How-To lets you drag files to the trashcan and delete them from a menu. This How-To will teach you a lot about dragging icons and Drag-Drop events.

**5.10**    **Display the progress of an operation**

Do you wish you could have a progress bar appear on your form while an operation is busy; one that lets the user know the percentage of the operation that has completed? Here is a How-To project that does just that. Again using the Windows BitBlt API, this project presents a colored bar that grows as the operation is progressing. The center of the bar displays the percentage of the operation that has been completed while the bar grows.

**5.11 Fill complex objects**

Visual Basic has powerful graphics functions that let you fill a circle or a rectangle, but there is no built-in function for filling a complex object like a polygon. This How-To uses the Polygon and SetPolyFillMode APIs to let you fill any object with any color. This same routine is used in the pie and bar chart How-Tos that follow.

**5.12 Build a line chart**

**5.13 Build a bar chart**

**5.14 Build a pie chart**

Did you know Visual Basic can create charts just like Excel? This trio of How-Tos reveals all you need to build line, bar, and pie charts into your projects. They feature automatic scaling, text labels, centered legends, custom patterns, colors, and line markers. Multiple series are allowed in the line and bar charts so you can compare sets of data. The polygon and SetPolyFillMode APIs are utilized to do the drawing and filling of patterns in these charts. Values to be plotted are passed in arrays so communication from your application is very simple.

**5.15 Build a video-based slide show**

Here is the ultimate Visual Basic weekend project: a slide show that lets you make a custom video presentation with custom transition effects between screens, and variable delays between each slide. The program can present Microsoft .BMP or .WMF files. There is an editor for arranging and previewing the sequence and a display module that shows the actual simulated slides. A File Open dialog box from the How-To "Build an editor that searches for text" is also used to make locating files a breeze. The BitBlt and SendMessage APIs are used in this How-To.

**5.1    How do I...**

# Make a brushed aluminum NeXT™ interface?

Complexity: Easy

### Problem

I want to create a Visual Basic application with a modern NeXT-like computer interface. But Visual Basic offers only the old-fashioned (pre-Windows 3) kind of buttons. I want the slick, metal-on-metal look, where the light seems to fall on one side and the buttons seem to be raised off a steel or gunmetal gray panel. (Even Microsoft has adopted the NeXT interface look; compare Word for Windows 1.1 to 1.0.) I also want to have important text on my screen appear like cool blue light is being emitted, similar to a glowing LED. Is there a simple way to do this?

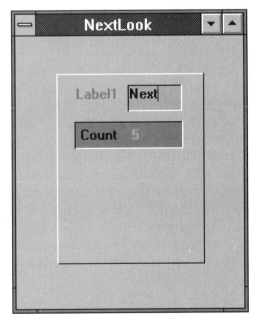

**Figure 5-1** A NeXTized interface in VB

### Technique

It is actually very easy to create a NeXT-like interface in Visual Basic as the simple example shows in Figure 5-1. For those who are not familar with the NeXT computer, it was created by Steve Jobs, founder of Apple computer, as the "next-step" after the Macintosh. Whether that event ever comes to pass, no one knows, but one thing Jobs did do is alter forever how a computer screen looks. Buttons, text input boxes, labels, and the like resemble a gray slick, brushed-metal look. The NeXT computer has raised and recessed panels, soft blue text, red text for warning, yellow for caution, and cleverly uses subtle shades of gray to achieve its stunning effect.

There are a few secrets to achieving this effect using Visual Basic. One of the main tricks is to use a 50 percent gray background. With such a gray background and a white line to draw the left and top border of a box as well as a black line to draw the right and bottom of a box, the box will appear to sit above the background, with light brightening up the left and top side, and the right and bottom sides in shadow. It will seem that there is light shining on your screen at a 45-degree angle from the button's corner.

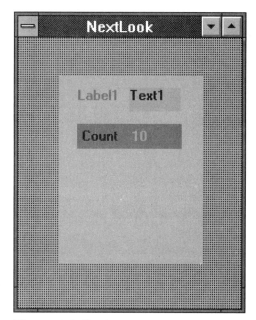

**Figure 5-2** The NextLook Form and
Controls at design time

To reverse the effect and make the box look like it is below the surface of the background (recessed), simply reverse the algorithm: Create the black line on the left and top, and the white line on the right and bottom. The blue light-emitting-diode look can be achieved by using cyan for the forecolor of your text, and a dark gray for the backcolor.

The trick to this is to recognize that we can turn off the borders of various objects such as text boxes, pictures, and labels. Then we can draw our own borders. We use Visual Basic's Line method (which is just like QuickBasic 4.5's Line statement) to draw four lines around the perimeter of a rectangular object, such as a picture box, using the right colors (black or white).

To NeXTize an object, you need to be able to turn off all its borders and set its background color carefully. In some cases, such as a label, the background color will be the same as the form or picture it is on, and with no border it is hard to see when you want to select it. See Figure 5-2. Clicking on the object and adjusting its position might not always prove worthy of a NeXT approach. You'll have to be the judge of that.

Another important point about setting up examples with controls is the use of picture controls for frames. Microsoft provided the frame object as a way to create a collection of controls so you can move them around as a group. Unfortunately, the frame does not work as advertised and has coloring and positioning limitations. Instead you can use a picture control, which is not only well behaved but also allows you to insert bitmaps, something a frame can't do.

## Steps

Open and run NEXT.MAK and examine its code. If you run the project (press F5), you will get the interface shown in Figure 5-1. To build the form from scratch, do the following, using Figure 5-2 as your guide.

1. Create a new project called NEXT.MAK. Create a new form, give it dimensions of about 2 inches wide and 3 inches tall as shown in Figure 5-2. Save it as NEXT.FRM.

2. Add the objects and properties shown in Table 5-1 to this form. If a property is not listed, its effect is not important and the default is assumed.

| Object | Property | Setting | |
|---|---|---|---|
| Form | FormName | Form_Next_Look | Root Control Frame (RCF) |
| | Caption | NextLook | |
| | BackColor | &H00C0C0C0& (50% gray) | |
| Picture box | CtllName | Picture1 | |
| | BackColor | &H00C0C0C0& | |
| | BorderStyle | 0 = None | |
| Label | CtlName | Label1 | RCF Left Top Control |
| | Caption | Label1 | |
| | BackColor | &H00C0C0C0& | |
| | ForeColor | &H00808080& (dark gray) | |
| | BorderStyle | 0 = None | |
| Text box | CtlName | Text1 | RCF Right Top Control |
| | Text | Text1 | |
| | BackColor | &H00FFFF00& (cyan) | |
| | ForeColor | &H000000000& (black) | |
| | BorderStyle | 0 = None | |
| Picture box | CtlName | Picture2 | Bottom Control Frame (BCF) |
| | Caption | Label1 | |
| | BackColor | &H00808080& (dark gray) | |
| | BorderStyle | 0 = None | |
| Label | CtlName | Label2 | BCF Left |
| | Caption | Count | |
| | ForeColor | &H000000000& (black) | |
| | BackColor | &H00808080& (dark gray) | |
| | BorderStyle | 0 = None | |
| Text box | CtlName | Text2 | BCF Right |
| | Text | 10 | |
| | ForeColor | &H00FFFF00& (cyan) | |
| | BackColor | &H00808080& (dark gray) | |
| | BorderStyle | 0 = None | |

**Table 5-1** NEXT project objects and properties

3. Add a new module called NEXT.BAS. We will put the two routines BoderBox and BorderBoxRaised in it. By placing this code in a .BAS file, you can easily move it to other projects and it is accessible to all forms in the project. Open the NEXT.BAS form for editing and type the following code in it. You should end up with two individual functions.

```
Sub BorderBox (source1 As Control, source2 As Control)
   'note we can't draw inside a text box so these controls
   'must get their outline drawn on the from or picture
   'box they are inside
   BLeft% = source1.Left - 20  'Get coordinates
   BTop% = source1.Top - 20
   BWide% = source1.Width + 15
   BHigh% = source1.Height + 15

   ' Draw a recessed border around Source1 control
   source2.Line (BLeft%, BTop%)-Step(BWide%, 0), 0
   source2.Line -Step(0, BHigh%), &HFFFFFF
   source2.Line -Step(-BWide%, 0), &HFFFFFF
   source2.Line -Step(0, -BHigh%), 0
End Sub

Sub BorderBoxRaised (source1 As Control, source2 As Form)
   BLeft% = source1.Left - 20  'Get coordinates and shrink them
                               'to make up for the border
   BTop% = source1.Top - 20
   BWide% = source1.Width + 15 'Make up for existing border on
     BHigh% = source1.Height + 15

   ' Draw a recessed border around Source control.
   source2.Line (BLeft%, BTop%)-Step(BWide%, 0), &HFFFFFF
   source2.Line -Step(0, BHigh%), 0
   source2.Line -Step(-BWide%, 0), 0
   source2.Line -Step(0, -BHigh%), &HFFFFFF
End Sub
```

4. Put this code in the Form_Load procedure of the form.

```
Sub Form_Load ()
   BorderBoxRaised Picture1, Form_Next_Look
   BorderBox Text1, Picture1
   BorderBox Picture2, Picture1
End Sub
```

### How It Works

Examine the first routine called BorderBox. The routine is passed two controls, Source1 and Source2. Thus, we would call the routine with

```
BorderBox Text1, Picture1
            or
BorderBox Picture2, Picture1
```

The first statement passes a text control that is sitting inside a picture control while the second statement passes a picture control that is sitting inside another picture control.

The next four lines set up four variables (BLeft% to BHigh%) for drawing a rectangle around the first control, using the second control as the drawing surface. The drawing is done a few pixels outside the inner control, because you can't draw on a text control with the Line statement (which may be the first control passed to the procedure). So source1.Left% - 20 puts the line to the left of the first control, and so on. The next four lines actually draw the Next rectangle. Refer to *The Waite Group's QuickBasic Bible*, Waite, Arnson, Gemmel and Henderson, Microsoft Press, 1990, for details on how the Line statement works. The first statement draws a line on the control source2 (source2.Line) using the parameters derived from the four variables, BLeft% to BHigh%. The Step option of Line is used to control the width of the box. At the end of each Line statement a value that follows the comma is the color for the line. Here we use 0 for black and &HFFFFFF for white. Thus, we draw a black line on top, a white line on the right side, a white line on the bottom, and a black line on the left side. This makes our box appear to be recessed in the panel.

The next procedure is called BorderBoxRaised. This works like the previous routine except it changes the order of the colors drawn so that the box appears to be white on the left and black on the right. Thus, the box appears to be raised, rather than recessed.

The Form_Load produced simply calls the routines when the program is started and passes the correct names of the parts to the procedures.

## Comment

You don't have to worry about redrawing the form if it is covered with another form or window. Windows remembers the way the screen looks and will repaint things just right.

## 5.2 How do I...

# Give my application a three-dimensional look?

Complexity: Easy

### Problem

In How-To 5.1 Make brushed aluminium NeXT™ interface, you show a simple technique for making 3-D buttons and controls. Is there a more powerful and more general way to do this, one that gives me better control over the details like the thickness of frames?

### Technique

Adding depth to controls is done using simple optical effects. Light edges on the top and left of an object with corresponding darker colored edges on the bottom and right gives the control a raised appearance, like those in Figure 5-3. Reversing the light and dark edges causes an object to appear recessed into the form, like those in Figure 5-4. To enhance the effect, coloring the form and object with the same background color gives the edges higher contrast.

### Steps

Open and run 3D.MAK. Click on the Raise Frame button to give all the objects on the form a raised look. Click on the Recess Frame button to have the objects appear recessed. The width of the sculpted frame may be changed by clicking on the horizontal scroll bar arrows. The text box indicates the width, in pixels, of the frames. The three-dimensional project can be created by entering objects and code as detailed in the following steps.

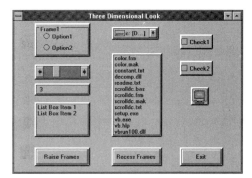

**Figure 5-3** 3D project with raised controls

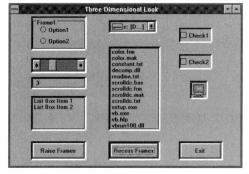

**Figure 5-4** 3D project with recessed controls

1. Create a new project called 3D.MAK. Create a new form with the objects and properties shown in Table 5-2, and save it as 3D.FRM. Note that one each of the standard Visual Basic objects has been included in this form to demonstrate how it looks in a sculpted frame.

| Object | Property | Setting |
| --- | --- | --- |
| Form | FormName | Form3D |
| | Caption | Three Dimensional Look |
| Command button | CtlName | Command1 |
| | Caption | Raise Frame |
| Command button | CtlName | Command2 |
| | Caption | Recess Frame |
| Command button | CtlName | Command3 |
| | Caption | Exit |
| List box | CtlName | List1 |
| Frame | CtlName | Frame1 |
| Option button | CtlName | Option1 |
| Option button | CtlName | Option2 |
| HScrollBar | CtlName | HScroll1 |
| | Min | 0 |
| | Max | 10 |
| Text box | CtlName | Text1 |
| Drive list box | CtlName | Drive1 |
| File list box | CtlName | File1 |
| Check box | CtlName | Check1 |
| Check box | CtlName | Check2 |
| Picture box | CtlName | Picture1 |
| | AutoRedraw | True |
| | AutoSize | True |
| | Picture | ..\VB\ICONS\COMPUTER\MONITOR01.ICO |

**Table 5-2** 3D project form's objects and properties

2. Select the Global module, enter the following code and save it as 3D.BAS.

```
Global Const CTLRECESSED = 0    ' Frame is recessed.
Global Const CTLRAISED = -1     ' Frame is raised.
Global Const BKGNDGRAY = 192    ' Background Gray.
Global Const DARKGRAY = 64      ' Dark Gray
Global Const LIGHTGRAY = 255    ' Light Gray (white).
```

```
Global Const DEFAULTWIDTH = 3     ' Default Frame Width
Global FrameWidth As Integer      ' Width of 3d frame (in pixels).
```

3. Put the following code in the Form_Load event subroutine. This code sets the form's background color, puts sample data into the text box control, and initializes the default FrameWidth.

```
Sub Form_Load ()
   BackColor = RGB(BKGNDGRAY, BKGNDGRAY, BKGNDGRAY)
   FrameWidth = DEFAULTWIDTH
   HScroll1.Value = FrameWidth
   List1.AddItem "List Box Item 1"
   List1.AddItem "List Box Item 2"
End Sub
```

4. Put the following code in the PaintFrames subroutine in the General section of the form. This subroutine is used to specify which controls have frames around them.

```
Sub PaintFrames (InOut As Integer)

' Convert All forms to Single View.
   Cls  ' Remove Old Frames
   InitCtl Frame1, InOut
   InitCtl HScroll1, InOut
   InitCtl Text1, InOut
   InitCtl List1, InOut
   InitCtl Command1, InOut
   InitCtl Command2, InOut
   InitCtl Command3, InOut
   InitCtl Drive1, InOut
   InitCtl File1, InOut
   InitCtl Check1, InOut
   InitCtl Check2, InOut
   InitCtl Picture1, InOut

' Other elements that need initialization.
   Option1(0).BackColor = BackColor
   Option1(1).BackColor = BackColor
   Picture1.Refresh            ' Repaint Picture Box
End Sub
```

5. Put the following code into the InitCtl subroutine in the (General) section of the form. InitCtl eliminates run-time errors in setting the background color of a scroll bar.

```
Sub InitCtl (C As Control, InOut As Integer)
   If TypeOf C Is HScrollBar Then     ' No BackColor for Scroll bars
   Else
      C.BackColor = C.Parent.BackColor ' Set to Form's Backcolor
   End If
   HighLight C, InOut
End Sub
```

6. Enter the following code into the Form_Paint event subroutine. This subroutine is called automatically at application startup or whenever the system needs to repaint the contents of the form.

```
Sub Form_Paint ()
   PaintFrames CTLRAISED
End Sub
```

7. Place the following code in the Command1_Click event subroutine.

```
Sub Command1_Click ()
   PaintFrames CTLRAISED
End Sub
```

8. Place the following code in the Command2_Click event subroutine.

```
Sub Command2_Click ()
   PaintFrames CTLRECESSED
End Sub
```

9. Place the following code in the HScroll1_Click event subroutine. Clicking the scroll bar arrows will change the width of the sculpted frames from 0 to 10 pixels.

```
Sub HScroll1_Change ()
   FrameWidth = HScroll1.Value
   Text1.Text = Str$(FrameWidth)
End Sub
```

10. Place the following code in the Command3_Click event subroutine. This button allows the users a graceful way to exit the application.

```
Sub Command3_Click ()
   End
End Sub
```

11. Create an additional module for this project by selecting New Module from the File menu. Put the following subroutine in the General section of the module and save the module as 3D_DRAW.BAS. This subroutine draws the sculpted frame around the control passed as the first parameter. The InOut parameter indicates whether the frame is to be raised or recessed.

```
Sub HighLight (C As Control, InOut As Integer)

' Convert ScaleMode of form to pixels.
' Set up colors for borders on InOut. For recessed control:
'     top & left = dark, bottom & right = left
'     opposite for raised controls.
   C.Parent.scalemode = 3
   If InOut = CTLRAISED Then
      TLShade& = RGB(LIGHTGRAY, LIGHTGRAY, LIGHTGRAY)
      BRShade& = RGB(DARKGRAY, DARKGRAY, DARKGRAY)
```

```
    Else
        TLShade& = RGB(DARKGRAY, DARKGRAY, DARKGRAY)
        BRShade& = RGB(LIGHTGRAY, LIGHTGRAY, LIGHTGRAY)
    End If

' Now draw the Frame Around the Control, on the Parent Form.
    For I% = 1 To FrameWidth
        T% = C.Top - I%
        L% = C.Left - I%
        H% = C.Height + 2 * I%
        W% = C.Width + 2 * I%
        C.Parent.Line (L%, T%)-Step(0, H%), TLShade&        ' Left side
        C.Parent.Line (L%, T%)-Step(W%, 0), TLShade&        ' Top
        C.Parent.Line (L% + W%, T%)-Step(0, H%), BRShade& ' Right side
        C.Parent.Line (L%, T% + H%)-Step(W%, 0), BRShade& ' Bottom
    Next I%
End Sub
```

## How It Works

Sculpted frames are easy to draw once you understand how they are formed. The HighLight subroutine does the work of drawing a sculpted frame around any control. Its first parameter is the name of the control to frame; the second parameter is a constant that determines whether the frame is raised or recessed.

HighLight's first task is to set the ScaleMode of the control's parent, or Form, to 3 - pixel mode. Using the parent property enables the HighLight subroutine to work in multiform projects. ScaleMode "3" is used, because a screen pixel is the smallest visible unit of measure. This ensures that each frame line will be drawn directly adjacent to the previous one. The TLShade& (Top-Left Shading) and BRShade& (Bottom-Right shading) variables are set to the appropriate gray colors. Note that equal levels of red, green, and blue for the RGB function will always produce a gray shade. Higher values for each color result in lighter shades.

The global variable FrameWidth specifies the number of lines in each frame. Starting at the existing object border, a successive series of frame lines is drawn on each of the object's four edges. Each frame line is two pixels longer then the previous one giving the frame a beveled look.

The PaintFrames subroutine initiates the drawing for each of the controls on the form. If you add or remove a control from the form, the PaintFrames code will need to be updated.

## Comments

You can change the size of the frame by clicking on the horizontal scroll bar. If you pick an extremely wide frame, greater than six or seven pixels, the frame effect will be exaggerated, creating less visual appeal. When you lay out a form with sculpted frames, be sure to leave enough blank space around each control to draw the frame.

Because of the way Visual Basic is designed, you cannot draw sculpted frames around objects in a container, such as a frame or picture box. In this example, note that the option buttons inside Frame1 do not have a sculpted outline.

**5.3     How do I...**

## Draw pictures into an iconized running application?

Complexity: Intermediate

### Problem
If a user minimizes my application's form, how can I change the icon that appears at the bottom of the screen from the default "form with shadow" icon that Visual Basic puts there for me?

### Technique
There are several ways to change a form's icon. The first is to specify an .ICO icon file for the Icon property when you design your form. Then, when you make an .EXE executable file using the Visual Basic File menu's Make EXE File option, you can pick an icon for the entire application.

The second is to use the LoadPicture function. You can assign the return value of the LoadPicture function to a form's Icon property, like this:

```
Icon = LoadPicture(NET11.ICO)
```

There is another option, related to the second. Let's say a form was processing some lengthy job and didn't need any user input (for example, an accounting application has to post numerous general ledger entries to a chart of accounts). You would probably want to perform such a job in the background so the user could continue doing other work. It would make sense to minimize the form that is doing the work and place it out of the way when the user switches to other forms or applications. But you'd want to notify the user how the job is progressing and when it is complete. How can you do that when the form is minimized (iconized) at the bottom of the screen?

Visual Basic, of course, provides the option of drawing on the surface of the icon, regardless of its size (icons for a standard VGA screen are 32 by 32 pixels). Assigning the return value of the LoadPicture function with no arguments to a form's Icon property will clear out the form's icon and let you draw on it as if it were a normally sized form.

## Steps

Open and run DRAWICON.MAK. This is a simple example of some graphical output tied to a timer control. Note that the graphics continue to be drawn, even if you click the icon and bring up its System menu.

1. Create a new project called DRAWICON.MAK. Create a new form with the controls and properties shown in Table 5-3, and save it as DRAW-ICON.FRM.

| Control | Property | Setting |
|---------|----------|---------|
| Timer | CtlName | Timer1 |
|  | Interval | 50 |

**Table 5-3**   DrawIcon form's controls and properties

2. Put the following code in the Declarations section of the form. The DefInt statement ensures all variables will be integers and the Dim statement defines some variables that will be shared with subroutines in that form.

```
DefInt A-Z

Dim X, Y, Z, Clr
```

3. Put the following code in the Form_Load event subroutine. This code prepares the form's icon to be drawn on, minimizes the window, then finally sets two of the form variables declared in the Declarations section.

```
Sub Form_Load ()
   Icon = LoadPicture()     ' clear out icon
   WindowState = 1          ' iconize window
   Show                     ' show the form so we can
   X = ScaleWidth           ' get the width of the icon
   Clr = 1                  ' start with blue
End Sub
```

4. Put the following code in the Timer1_Timer event subroutine. This code simply draws lines that approach each other from opposite corners of the icon. Once the lines meet, the color used to draw the lines is changed.

```
Sub Timer1_Timer ()
   Line (Z, 0)-(0, Z), QBColor(Clr)
   Line (X - Z, X)-(X, X - Z), QBColor(Clr)
```

```
    Z = (Z + 2) Mod X
    If Z = 0 Then Clr = (Clr + 1) Mod 16
End Sub
```

### How It Works

Normally, Visual Basic provides an icon for every form. This icon is unaffected by Cls; it's always in the background. A special feature of the LoadPicture function lets you blank out a form's icon. If you put

```
Icon = LoadPicture()
```

somewhere in your application, that form's icon will be blank. Then you can use normal graphics statements to draw small graphics on the icon.

The WindowState property controls whether a form is normal size (the size that you gave it when you designed the form), maximized (full-screen), or minimized (to an icon).

The statement

```
WindowState = 1
```

is the same as clicking on the down-arrow minimize button in the upper right corner.

Although most icons are 32 by 32 pixels (the standard icon size for VGA monitors), icons for different monitors (like CGA, EGA, or 8514/a monitors) are different sizes. It's important, therefore, to adapt your program to whatever the current icon size is. The Show code displays the icon on the screen, which is necessary before your application tries to get its width with the ScaleWidth property.

The Clr variable keeps track of the color used to draw the current line. In the Timer1_Timer event subroutine, the QBColor function converts the Clr variable to the RGB color that Visual Basic is expecting. The first Line method draws a line in the upper left corner and the second Line method draws a line in the lower right corner. These lines approach and meet each other in the center of the icon.

The first Mod operator is used to prevent Z from overflowing the X width of the icon.

The second Mod operator prevents Clr from going beyond 15, which is the highest value that the QBColor function expects.

The Timer Interval property is set to 50, which causes the lines to be drawn very quickly. You can set the Interval property to whatever value you'd like.

## Comment

You can also use Print methods to print text on the icon; just be sure to set the CurrentX and CurrentY properties to values that are within the width and height of the icon. (CurrentX=0 and CurrentY=0 indicate the upper left corner of the icon.)

| 5.4 | How do I... |

# Draw a transparent picture or icon on a form?

Complexity: Intermediate

### Problem

I want to draw an icon or picture on the screen, but when I do, the picture always appears as an opaque rectangle covering everything under it. Is there any way around this?

### Technique

The normal way of displaying icons won't work if what you want is transparency. Figure 5-5 shows several Microsoft Pencil icons drawn on a complex bit map. The rectangular 32 x 32 area that surrounds all icons would normally be erased if we used Visual Basic's built-in commands to draw an icon. Instead, these were drawn with Window's BitBlt library functions, which are faster and more powerful than any of the graphics keywords built into Visual Basic.

BitBlt lets us blast color bitmaps from one location to any other location on any picture or form. BitBlt needs the size and name of its destinations, and other details, but it essentially draws images. BitBlt comes with a large number of possible options that control how it copies the bits when there are existing bits in a background. The secret of drawing without erasing the background is to use the exclusive OR (XOR) mode for the copying.

When using XOR with BitBlt, you must first create a mask of the icon. There will be two icons for each image: the full color image and the mask of the image. All pixels in the original image that are to be reproduced like the original are set to black in the mask. All pixels in the original image that are to be transparent are set to white in the mask. All the pixels in the original that are to be transparent should be made black. So, the original white area around the pencil is changed to black.

Once you have the mask, you are ready to draw your image. You first draw the mask using SCRAND logic. Next you draw the original image using SCRINVERT logic. Using AND for a black (0) pixel in the mask

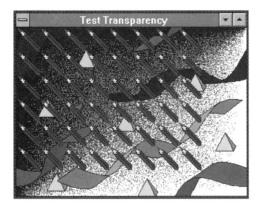

**Figure 5-5** The pencil icon drawn with BitBlt

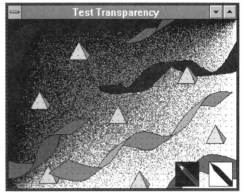

**Figure 5-6** The form for the BitBit project

image with any pixel in the background turns that pixel to black. Using AND for any white pixel in the mask does not affect the pixel in the background. So after we draw the mask, the area around the pencil will be unaffected, while the area defined by the pencil will be black.

Next when we OR the original image with the changed background, any pixels that are black in the image will allow the pixels in the background to show through. Thus, the entire area around the pencil will show. Any colored pixels in the original image that are ORed will appear on the background. In this case, the pencil area is all black, so the pixels become those of the original image. It actually sounds more complicated than it really is.

**Steps**

Open and run MASK.MAK. When you click on the form 48 little red pencil icons will be drawn on top of the background as shown in Figure 5-5.

1. Create a new project called MASK.MAK and a new form as shown in Figure 5-6. Save the form as MASK1.FRM. There are two icons to be placed on the form and a background bitmap that is supplied with Windows called PARTY.BMP. This can be any bitmap you want, including any of the wallpaper bitmaps supplied with Windows.

   Set the properties and objects on it as shown in Table 5-4.

| Object | Property | Setting |
| --- | --- | --- |
| Form | FormName | MaskForm1 |
|  | Caption | Test Transparency |
|  | Picture | PARTY.BMP |
|  | Scalemode | 3 - Pixel |

*Table 5-4. continued*

| Object | Property | Setting |
|--------|----------|---------|
| Picture box | CtlName | Pencil_Image |
| | Visibility | False |
| | autoSize | True |
| | autoRedraw | True |
| Picture box | CtlName | Pencil_Image_Mask |
| | Visibility | False |
| | autoSize | True |
| | autoRedraw | True |

**Table 5-4** BitBlt project form's objects and properties

Select an icon to use for our test. It should be one with a lot of uncluttered background so that we can see behind it and so it's easy to modify and make a mask for. We chose one of the pencil icons that is stored in the Visual Basic WRITING subdirectory (PENCIL9.ICO). We renamed it as PENCILA.ICO and then moved it to the same directory as our Visual Basic How-To.

2. Open this icon into an icon editor program, like ICONWRKS that comes with Visual Basic, or into a paint program like PBRUSH.EXE that is supplied with Windows. Duplicate the pencil icon in a new file and store it as PENCILB.ICO. This will be our Mask icon. You can do this from Windows using the COPY command or you can do it by saving under a new name in ICONWRKS.

3. Now fill in all the white areas around PENCILA.ICO with black. Make all the colored areas of PENCILB.ICO black; leave the white areas white. According to the technique we'll use, anything that is black in the image, and white in the mask will allow the background to show though. Figure 5-7 shows the pencil image after its outer areas have been painted black, and Figure 5-8 shows how the mask for the pencil icon should look.

**Figure 5-7** The PENCILA.ICO icon

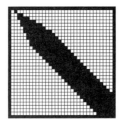

**Figure 5-8** The PENCILA.ICO mask icon

4. Now you will add the necessary code. The main code will go in the Form_Click procedure of the form.

```
Sub Form_Click ()
    'Draw the Image With XOR.
    Cls
    For Y = 1 To Height \ 20 Step 32
    For X = 1 To Width \ 20 Step 32
    R = BitBlt(MaskForm1.hdc, X, Y, 32, 32, Pencil_Mask.hdc, 0, 0, SRCAND)
    R = BitBlt(MaskForm1.hdc, X, Y, 32, 32, Pencil_Image.hdc, 0, 0, SRCINVERT)
    Next X, Y
End Sub
```

5. Put the following code in the General procedure of the form object.

```
DefInt A-Z
Declare Function BitBlt Lib "Gdi" (ByVal destHdc, ByVal X, ByVal Y, ByVal ⇐
w, ByVal h, ByVal srcHdc, ByVal srcX, ByVal srcY, ByVal rop As Long)
Const SRCCOPY = &HCC0020
Const SRCAND = &H8800C6
Const SRCINVERT = &H660046
```

6. Put the following code in the Load procedure of the form object.

```
Sub Form_Load ()
    'Center the window,
    Move (Screen.Width - Width) \ 2, (Screen.Height - Height) \ 2
    DesPicture.Width = 32: DestPicture.Height = DestPicture.Width
End Sub
```

7. Now run the project by pressing F5. When you click on the form, a matrix of icons will appear as shown in Figure 5-5. Notice how only the pencil covers the background.

**How It Works**

The code is amazingly simple. When the form is started up, it is centered on the screen by the routine in the Form_Load procedure. Use this code in all your applications.

The code for defining the BitBlit function so that Visual Basic can use it is placed in the General procedure of the form object. The ByVal keywords tells Windows that the values will be passed by value, not by reference. (See page 211 of *The Waite Group's QuickBASIC Primer Plus*, Prata and Henderson, Microsoft Press, 1991.) Passing by value ensures that the actual value in our Visual Basic program is altered by the function call. If we passed by reference, the default manner of passing an argument, the values in our code would not be altered. The Const statements set up the hex values needed for simulating the proper mode of the BitBlt. These Const statements come from the file WINAPI.TXT that is documented in Appendix A of this book, "Using Windows APIs."

In the Form_Click procedure, we have a simple For...Next loop that increments the variables X and Y, between 1 and the Height and Width of the Form divided by 20. The reason for dividing is to convert twips to pixels. The loop thus gives us a matrix of 32 x 32 icons.

## Comments

You can repeat the experiment with larger drawing objects, and you can have overlapping regions with transparency working in all layers. As long as you use the SRCAND and SRCINVERT modes with a mask, this process will work.

---

### 5.5    How do I...

# Visualize the DrawMode settings?

Complexity: Intermediate

## Problem

When drawing on forms and picture boxes with Visual Basic, you can set the DrawMode property to control how pixels in the drawn object interact with the pixels on the form or picture box. While the default mode simply copies pixels onto the form, there are a total of 16 different modes with strange names like Whiteness, Merge Pen Not, and so on. Is there some simple way to learn what these modes mean?

## Technique

A good way to see the effect of these different modes is to draw a bitmap onto the entire form with the different DrawModes selected from a menu. The Visual Basic LoadPicture function can be used to load a bitmap, icon, or metafile into a picture box. The 16 menu items can be a single menu array and the value of the index will exactly correspond to the mode value!

## Steps

Open and run DRAWMODE.MAK. Select File Open to load a bitmap into the large picture box. Try one of the wallpaper bitmaps provided with Windows. You can then select any item from the DrawMode

**Figure 5-9** The DrawMode form

menu to see what effect that DrawMode setting has. File Restore reverses any changes you've made.

1. Create a new project called DRAWMODE.MAK. Create a new form with the objects and properties listed in Table 5-5, and save it as DRAW-MODE.FRM. See Figure 5-9 for what this form will look like.

| Object | Property | Setting |
|---|---|---|
| Form | FormName | Draw_Mode |
| | Caption | DrawMode |
| | BackColor | &H00C0C0C0& |
| Picture box | CtlName | Picture1 |

**Table 5-5** DrawMode project form's objects and properties

2. Create a menu for the form using the Menu Design window.

| Caption | CtlName | Index |
|---|---|---|
| &File | FileMenu | |
| &Open... | FileOpen | |
| &Restore | FileRestore | |
| E&xit | FileExit | |
| &DrawMode | DrawModeMenu | |
| Blackness | Mode | 1 |
| Not Merge Pen | Mode | 2 |
| Mask Not Pen | Mode | 3 |
| Not Copy Pen | Mode | 4 |
| Mask Pen Not | Mode | 5 |
| Invert | Mode | 6 |
| Xor Pen | Mode | 7 |
| Not Mask Pen | Mode | 8 |
| Mask Pen | Mode | 9 |
| Not Xor Pen | Mode | 10 |
| Nop | Mode | 11 |
| Merge Not Pen | Mode | 12 |
| Copy Pen | Mode | 13 |
| Merge Pen Not | Mode | 14 |
| Merge Pen | Mode | 15 |
| Whiteness | Mode | 16 |

**Table 5-6** The DrawMode project menu

3. Put the following code in the Declarations section of the form.

```
Const MODAL = 1
Dim BitMap$
```

4. Put the following code in the LoadBitMap subroutine in the General section of the form.

```
Sub LoadBitMap ()
    Caption = "DrawMode: " + BitMap$
    Picture1.Picture = LoadPicture(BitMap$)
End Sub
```

5. Put the following code in the FileExit_Click event subroutine.

```
Sub FileExit_Click ()
    End
End Sub
```

6. The following code in the FileOpen_Click event subroutine calls up the FileDlg form (from How-To 1.4 Make a file dialog box using APIs.) Make another type of file dialog box to get a bitmap to load into the picture box.

```
Sub FileOpen_Click ()


    FileDlg.FileEdit.Text = "*.BMP"
    FileDlg.Show MODAL
    BitMap$ = FileDlg.FileEdit.Text
    If InStr(BitMap$, "*") = 0 Then LoadBitMap
End Sub
```

7. Put the following code in the Click event subroutine of the FileRestore button.

```
Sub FileRestore_Click ()
    LoadBitMap
End Sub
```

8. If you resize the DrawMode form, its Form_Resize event changes the width and height of the picture box to match the form's. (See How-To 2.2 Size a form's controls automatically, for more details.) Put the following code in the Form_Resize event subroutine.

```
Sub Form_Resize ()
    Picture1.Height = Draw_Mode.ScaleHeight – Picture1.Top * 2
    Picture1.Width = Draw_Mode.ScaleWidth – Picture1.Left * 2
End Sub
```

9. The Mode_Click event subroutine handles all the various DrawMode settings. Because the menu is a control array, the Index parameter tells us the DrawMode setting.

```
Sub Mode_Click (Index As Integer)
    Picture1.DrawMode = Index
    Picture1.Line (Picture1.ScaleLeft, Picture1.ScaleTop)- ⇐
    (Picture1.ScaleLeft + Picture1.ScaleWidth, Picture1.ScaleTop + ⇐
    Picture1.ScaleHeight), , BF
End Sub
```

### How It Works

It's no coincidence that we're using a control array for the menu items. The Index property for each menu item represents the numeric value of a DrawMode setting. When you click the menu item, the corresponding control array index sets the picture box's DrawMode property. Then a filled box is drawn using Line,,BF.

The FileOpen_Click event subroutine calls up the file dialog box from How-To 1.6 Make a file dialog box using APIs. When you click on the file dialog box's OK button, FileOpen_Click calls the LoadBitMap subroutine, which loads the file into the picture box using Visual Basic's LoadPicture function.

We cheat a little bit for the Restore button. Instead of undoing the changes that might have been made, we just call the LoadBitMap subroutine again to reload the unchanged picture file from disk.

### Comment

Although the file dialog box defaults to using .BMP bitmap files, you can also load .ICO icon files and .WMF metafiles. Visual Basic's LoadPicture function used in the LoadBitMap subroutine understands all three formats.

---

**5.6    How do I...**

## Separate the red, green, and blue components of a color?

Complexity: Easy

### Problem

Visual Basic gives us the RGB function that lets you specify values for a color. However, given a combined color made of a single long integer, how do you separate its individual red, green, and blue values?

### Technique

A color value is a long integer that contains the separate red, green, and blue color components. It's a fairly straightforward mathematical operation to separate the three colors from the composite color value. The color value can best be represented as a hexadecimal number, like this:

```
&Hrrggbb
```

where rr is the red color component, gg the green, and bb the blue.

### Steps

Open and run COLORVAL.MAK. You can enter a color value in the text box (as a long decimal integer) and a message box will display the red, green, and blue color components it represents.

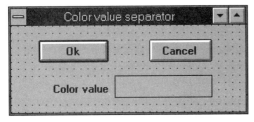

**Figure 5-10** The ColorVal form design

1. Create a new project called COLOR-VAL.MAK. Create a new form with the objects and properties shown in Table 5-7, and save it as COLORVAL.FRM. See Figure 5-10 for the form's design.

| Object | Property | Setting |
|---|---|---|
| Form | Caption | Color value separator |
| | FormName | ColorValue |
| | BackColor | &H00C0C0C0& |
| Command button | CtlName | Ok |
| | Caption | Ok |
| | Default | True |
| Command button | CtlName | Cancel |
| | Caption | Cancel |
| Label | CtlName | Label1 |
| | Alignment | Right justify |
| | Caption | Color Value |
| Text box | CtlName | ColorText |

**Table 5-7** Controls and properties

2. Put the following code in the GetRed general function. This code retrieves the red color component from the combined color value.

```
Function GetRed (ColorValue As Long) As Integer
   GetRed = (ColorValue And &HFF0000) \ 65536
End Function
```

3. Put the following code in the GetGreen general function. This code retrieves the green color component from the combined color value.

```
Function GetGreen (ColorValue As Long) As Integer
   GetGreen = (ColorValue And &HFF00&) \ 256
End Function
```

4. Put the following code in the GetBlue general function. This code retrieves the blue color component from the combined color value.

```
Function GetBlue (ColorValue As Long) As Integer
   GetBlue = ColorValue And &HFF&
End Function
```

5. Put the following code in the Cancel_Click event subroutine. The End statement simply ends the application.

```
Sub Cancel_Click ()
   End
End Sub
```

6. Put the following code in the Ok_Click event subroutine. This code gets the value of the text in the text box and retrieves the color components using the GetRed, GetGreen, and GetBlue general functions. Then a MsgBox statement displays the different component values.

```
Sub Ok_Click ()
   Static ColorVal As Long, R As Integer, G As Integer, B As Integer

   CRLF$ = Chr$(13) + Chr$(10)
   ColorVal = Val(ColorText.Text)
   R = GetRed(ColorVal)
   G = GetGreen(ColorVal)
   B = GetBlue(ColorVal)
   MsgBox "Red component=" + Format$(R) + CRLF$ + "Green component=" +
Format$(G) + CRLF$ + "Blue component=" + Format$(B)
End Sub
```

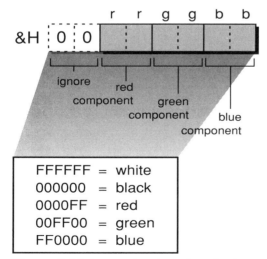

**Figure 5-11** Interpreting the color value long integer

**How It Works**

A combined color value is a long integer that contains the separate red, green, and blue color components packed in a simple format as shown in Figure 5-11. By representing the color value as a hexadecimal number like &Hrrggbb, you can see that each color component ranges from 0 to 255 (or &H00 to &HFF in hexadecimal) and occupies different positions in the long hexadecimal value. You can separate out the component colors by using Visual Basic's bitwise And operator. (See *The Waite Group's Visual Basic Super Bible*, Maxwell and Scott, Waite Group Press, 1992.) The bitwise And operator works like shown in Figures 5-12 and 5-13.

| AND | | |
|:---:|:---:|:---:|
| A | B | C |
| 0 | 0 | 0 |
| 0 | 1 | 0 |
| 1 | 0 | 1 |
| 1 | 1 | 1 |

| | decimal | hex | binary |
|:---:|:---:|:---:|:---:|
| | 300 | 12C | 100101100 |
| AND | 255 | FF | 011111111 |
| | 44 | 2C | 000101100 |

**Figure 5-13** And-ing multidigit numbers

**Figure 5-12** Bitwise And logic

To extract the red component, the color value is And-ed with &H00FF0000 to zero out the green and blue components. For example, a color value of 16,777,215 is &HFFFFFF, which is the color white. If we bitwise And &H00FF0000 and &HFFFFFF, you'll get &H00FF0000, or 16,711,680, not &HFF. Unfortunately, the bitwise And operator zeros out the green and blue components and leaves the red component in the same place. Dividing the value by 65536 (&H10000) will move the red component to the low-order byte.

The same problem applies for the green color component. When you bitwise And the color value with &H0000FF00, the red and blue components are zeroed out, but the green component isn't in the low-order byte. Simply dividing by 256 will move it there.

Luckily, the blue component is already in the low-order byte, so simply bitwise And-ing the color value with &H000000FF will remove the red and green components.

### Comment

You might want to add the GetRed, GetGreen, and GetBlue functions to a separate module of your most-used functions and add that module to your projects using the Visual Basic File menu's Add File... options. (We use VBHOWTO.BAS for the functions in this book.)

Using these functions will make it easy for you to increase, say, the amount of red in a color.

**5.7    How do I...**

# Make a screen capture from my running program?

Complexity: Easy

### Problem

In Windows, it's a litle known secret that pressing Alt-PrintScreen copies the current active window to the Clipboard. The Clipboard can then be viewed with the Windows' CLIPBRD.EXE utility. But suppose I want to capture a specific x/y area of the screen while my Visual Basic application is running. Is that possible?

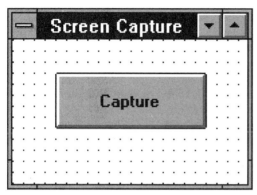

**Figure 5-14** Appearance of the ScrnCap form

**Technique**
Making such a screen capture is actually quite easy from Visual Basic. The key is to get Windows to provide a display context (DC) for the whole screen. A Display Context is a sort of data structure that contains important information about your particular video hardware. This can be accomplished using the CreateDC API function and passing "DISPLAY" as the driver name. Once you receive the display context, you can manipulate the screen just as you would any other bitmap.

**Steps**
Open and run SCRNCAP.MAK. Alternatively, you may create a stand-alone .EXE file and run ScrnCap from the Program Manager. We set up our example so it captures the entire screen, but you can change the rectangle's corner values to capture any area. To capture the screen to the Clipboard once the program is running , simply click on the Capture button. To create the screen capture utility, simply do the following:

1. Create a new project called SCRNCAP.MAK. Create a new form with the objects and properties in Table 5-8, and save it as SCRNCAP.FRM. When finished, the form should look like Figure 5-14.

| Object | Property | Setting |
|---|---|---|
| Form | FormName | Form1 |
| | Caption | Screen Capture |
| | BackColor | &H00FFFFFF& |
| Command button | CtlName | Command1 |
| | Caption | Capture |

**Table 5-8** Scrncap form's objects and properties

2. Insert the following code in Declarations section of Form1.

```
DefInt A-Z

Declare Sub ReleaseDC Lib "User" (ByVal hWnd, ByVal hDC)
Declare Sub OpenClipBoard Lib "User" (ByVal hWnd)
Declare Sub EmptyClipBoard Lib "User" ()
Declare Sub SetClipBoardData Lib "User" (ByVal CBFormat, ByVal hBitMap)
Declare Sub CloseClipBoard Lib "User" ()
Declare Sub SelectObject Lib "GDI" (ByVal hDC, ByVal hObj)
Declare Sub DeleteDC Lib "GDI" (ByVal hDC)
Declare Sub BitBlt Lib "GDI" (ByVal DestDC, ByVal X, ByVal Y, ByVal ⇐
BWidth, ByVal BHeight, ByVal SourceDC, ByVal X, ByVal Y, ByVal Constant&)

Declare Function CreateDC Lib "GDI" (ByVal Driver$, ByVal Dev&, ByVal ⇐
0&,_ByVal Init&)
Declare Function CreateCompatibleDC Lib "GDI" (ByVal hDC)
Declare Function CreateCompatibleBitmap Lib "GDI" (ByVal hDC, ⇐
ByValBWidth,_ByVal BHeight)

Const TRUE = -1
Const FALSE = 0

Sub ScrnCap (Lt, Top, Rt, Bot)
   rWidth = Rt - Lt
   rHeight = Bot - Top
   SourceDC = CreateDC("DISPLAY", 0, 0, 0)
   DestDC = CreateCompatibleDC(SourceDC)
   BHandle = CreateCompatibleBitmap(SourceDC, rWidth, rHeight)
   SelectObject DestDC, BHandle
   BitBlt DestDC, 0, 0, rWidth, rHeight, SourceDC, Lt, Top, &HCC0020
   Wnd = Screen.ActiveForm.hWnd
   OpenClipBoard Wnd
   EmptyClipBoard
   SetClipBoardData 2, BHandle
   CloseClipBoard
   DeleteDC DestDC
   ReleaseDC DHandle, SourceDC
End Sub
```

3. Insert the following code in the Command1_Click procedure.

```
Sub Command1_Click ()
   Form1.Visible = FALSE
   ScrnCap 0, 0, 640, 480  'Use appropriate dimentions
   Form1.Visible = TRUE
End Sub
```

### How It Works

The bulk of the work for the program is in the ScrnCap procedure. Firs,t a "Source" device context is created called SourceDC. This is used to create a copy of the DC for manipulation. This is accomplished with the Create-CompatibleDC API function. You then need to create a bitmap in memory.

You want this bitmap to be of the same size and palette as the display context that you want to copy. The easiest way to accomplish this is with the Create-CompatibleBitmap API function, which returns a handle to an empty bitmap. SelectObject closes this bitmap as the object of the device context. You can then use BitBlt to copy the contents of the screen display context to the memory bitmap in DestDC.

Now that you have memory bitmap that contains the contents of the screen, it is a simple matter to assign this bitmap to the Clipboard. First, a handle to the currently active screen form is obtained. Then OpenClipboard establishes our application as the "owner" of the Clipboard and allows accessing of the information stored there. A call is made to EmptyClipboard to ensure that the Clipboard is empty of information left there by other applications. The Clipboard can store multiple data formats—such as text, bitmaps, or metafiles. We then use the SetClipboardData API function to assign the application's memory bitmap handle to the Clipboard. The bitmap is now owned by the the Clipboard. Finally, the Clipboard is closed, the device context is deleted, and the various handles to these devices are released.

## Comments

Since ScrnCap takes a number of parameters: x, y, Width, and Height, it is easy to copy any portion of the screen to the Clipboard.

In addition, you should note that you are free to "draw" on the screen as well as copy, although this is not considered "well behaved." This technique is used by screen-capture programs and screen-saver programs. For example, you might want to use the SetCapture function (described in How-To 6.16 Simulate SPY in Visual Basic) to allow the user to "select" a portion of the screen and then copy just that portion to the Clipboard.

If you wanted to create a screen saver, you would want to create a "backup" of the screen image with the memory bitmap, as described earlier when we used the CreateCompatibleBitmatp and the BitBlt functions. You could then use all of the normal GDI functions on the screen to create pictures, animation, and so on. Then, when the user pressed a key, clicked something, or used some other standard exit technique, you would restore the original contents of the screen.

**5.8    How do I...**

# Arrange the icons on the Windows desktop?

Complexity: Easy

### Problem

When users iconize my Visual Basic applications and move other icons around the screen, the desktop window can become cluttered. Is there any way I can write code that would automatically arrange all those icons?

### Technique

The first solution that comes to mind is to use SendKeys and the Task Manager to do this from Visual Basic. If you double-click on the desktop (background or wallpaper) window or press Ctrl+Esc, the Windows Task Manager pops up. The Task Manager has a command button captioned "Arrange Icons." That button does what you want, so you could use the Visual Basic SendKeys statement, like this:

```
SendKeys "^{ESCAPE}%A"
```

This statement sends the Ctrl+Esc key sequence (which will bring up the Task Manager) and the Alt+A, which is the shortcut key for the Arrange Icons button. The big disadvantage to doing this is that it takes several seconds for the Task Manager to load, and when it does you will see the Task Manager's window flash briefly on the screen.

A better way is to use the Windows API function called Arrange-IconicWindows which, naturally, arranges all the icons in a given window. Because we want to arrange all the icons on the desktop window, the API function GetDesktopWindow returns the window handle to the desktop window.

### Steps

Open and run ARRANGE.MAK. When you click on the Arrange Desktop Icons button, all the icons on the desktop will be arranged neatly at the bottom of the screen. Figure 5-16 indicates the "before" icon arrangement, and Figure 5-17 the "after."

**Figure 5-15** The Arrange Icons form

1. Create a new project called ARRAN-GE.MAK. Create a form with the controls and properties listed in Table 5-9 and save it as ARRANGE.FRM. Figure 5-15 shows the completed form.

| Object | Property | Setting |
|---|---|---|
| Form | Caption | Arrange desktop icons |
| | FormName | ArrangeIcon |
| | BackColor | &H00C0C0C0& |
| Command button | CtlName | Arrange |
| | Caption | Arrange desktop icons! |
| | Default | True |

**Table 5-9** Arrange project form's and properties

**Figure 5-16** The desktop before arranging the icons

**Figure 5-17** The desktop after arranging the icons

2. Put the following code in the Declarations section of the form. The Declare statements declare the Windows API functions ArrangeIconic-Windows and GetDesktopWindow.

```
Declare Function ArrangeIconicWindows Lib "User" (ByVal hWnd As Integer) ⇐
As Integer
Declare Function GetDesktopWindow Lib "User" () As Integer
```

3. Put the following code in the Arrange_Click event subroutine.

```
Sub Arrange_Click ()
   DesktopHWnd = GetDesktopWindow()
   If ArrangeIconicWindows(DesktopHWnd) = 0 Then
      MsgBox "There are no icons on the desktop window to arrange!"
   End If
End Sub
```

### How It Works

In this case, Windows APIs encapsulate a lot of the work for us. In the Arrange_Click event subroutine, a call to GetDesktopWindow gets the window handle to the desktop window, which is then stored in the DesktopHWnd variable.

The DesktopHWnd is passed in the call to ArrangeIconicWindows, which tells Windows to arrange all the icons on the desktop window. ArrangeIconicWindows returns 0 if there were no icons to arrange, so a call to Visual Basic's MsgBox statement tells the user that.

### Comment

You might want to give your form a Window menu, with an Arrange Icons option, and the following event subroutine.

```
Sub WindowArrangeIcons_Click ()
    DesktopHWnd = GetDesktopWindow()
    If ArrangeIconicWindows(DesktopHWnd) = 0 Then
        MsgBox "There are no icons on the desktop window to arrange!"
    End If
End Sub
```

### 5.9    How do I...

# Make a Macintosh-style trash can?

Complexity: Intermediate

### Problem

I like the way the Macintosh file managing system uses a trash can. You simply drag the program or document icon you wish to delete over the trash can icon, then select the Empty Trash menu item. Can this be simulated in my Visual Basic application?

### Technique

The Drag method can be used along with the DragDrop and DragOver events to make the trash change its appearance according to user actions. Moving an item from one list box to another is another underlying function of implementing the trash can.

### Steps

Open and run TRASHCAN.MAK. The Trashcan project can be created by performing the following steps.

1. The trash can in this project is an icon-sized picture box, and our first step will be to create the different icons necessary for the various states the trash can will have: empty, empty-darkened, full, and full-darkened. Start with the icon for the empty state and modify it for the other three.

   The icon used in the project is located in the ICONS subdirectory of the VB directory, …VB\ICONS\COMPUTER\Trash01.ICO. If this icon is not available to you, substitute another trash icon or make one of your own, using the figures shown below as a guide. Open this icon into an icon editor (IconWorks is a great icon editor and comes with Visual Basic), and save it as Empty.ICO to the project directory. Then, to make the job of creating the other icons easier, trim off the shadow in the lower right portion of the icon and save again so it looks like Figure 5-18.

**Figure 5-18** (left) The trash can icon Trash01.ICO before it's modified (Empty.ICO)
**Figure 5-19** (right) The Dark trash can icon (Dark.ICO)

2. Fill in the interior of the trash can until it is completely black, as in Figure 5-19, and save the new, dark icon as Dark.ICO.

3. Open Empty.ICO back in the Editor, save it as Full.ICO, and modify it so it has a bulging appearance, as in Figure 5-20.

4. Now save Full.ICO as Darkfull.ICO and fill in the interior of the fattened trash can until it is completely black, as in Figure 5-21.

   You should now have a set of four icons, which will ultimately be used to represent the four trash can states: empty, empty-darkened, full, and full-darkened.

**Figure 5-20** (left) The trash can icon modified so it appears full (Full.ICO)
**Figure 5-21** (right) The dark trash can (Darkfull.ICO)

5. Create a new form, place on it the controls shown in Figure 5-22, then set all the properties as listed in Table 5-10. Save the form as MAINFORM.FRM.

| Object | Property | Setting |
|--------|----------|---------|
| Form | FormName | MainForm |
| | Caption | TrashCan Demo |
| | BackColor | &H00E0E0E0& (Light Gray) |
| | BorderStyle | 1 - Fixed Single |
| | ControlBox | False |
| | Icon | Empty.ICO |
| List box | CtlName | SourceList |
| | DragIcon | …VB\ICONS\COMPUTER\Key06.ICO |
| | Sorted | True |
| | Tag | SourceList |
| Command button | CtlName | ExitDemo |
| | Caption | Exit Demo |
| Picture box | CtlName | EmptyTrash |
| | BackColor | &H00E0E0E0& (Light Gray) |
| | BorderStyle | 1 - Fixed Single |
| | DragIcon | Dark.ICO |
| | Height | 495 (twips) |
| | Picture | Empty.ICO |
| | Visible | False |
| | Width | 495 (twips) |
| Picture box | CtlName | FullTrash |
| | BackColor | &H00E0E0E0& (Light Gray) |
| | BorderStyle | 1 - Fixed Single |
| | DragIcon | Darkfull.ICO |
| | Height | 495 (twips) |
| | Picture | Full.ICO |
| | Visible | False |
| | Width | 495 (twips) |
| Picture box | CtlName | TrashCan |
| | BackColor | &H00E0E0E0& (Light Gray) |
| | BorderStyle | 0 - None |
| | Height | 495 (twips) |
| | Picture | Empty.ICO |
| | Visible | True |
| | Width | 495 (twips) |

**Table 5-10** Trashcan project objects and properties in the MainForm form

6. Create another new form, place on it the controls shown in Figure 5-23, then set all the properties as listed in Table 5-11. Save this form as TRASHFRM.FRM.

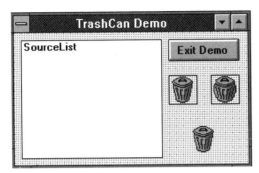

**Figure 5-22**  The MainForm form and its controls at design time

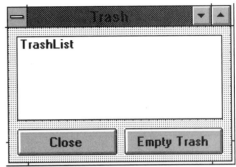

**Figure 5-23**  The TrashForm form and its controls at design time

| Object | Property | Setting |
|---|---|---|
| Form | FormName | TrashForm |
| | Caption | Trash |
| | BackColor | &H00E0E0E0& (Light Gray) |
| | BorderStyle | 1 - Fixed Single |
| | ControlBox | False |
| | Icon | Empty.ICO |
| List box | CtlName | TrashList |
| | DragIcon | …VB\ICONS\COMPUTER\Key06.ICO |
| | Sorted | True |
| | Tag | TrashList |
| Command button | CtlName | Action |
| | Caption | Close |
| | Index | 0 |
| Command button | CtlName | Action |
| | Caption | Empty Trash |
| | Index | 1 |

**Table 5-11**  TrashForm project form's objects and properties

7. Place the following code in the MainForm.Form_Load event procedure.

```
Sub Form_Load ()
    TrashForm.TrashList.DragIcon = SourceList.DragIcon
    For i = 1 To 12
```

```
        Number$ = Format$(i, "00")
        SourceList.AddItem "Source_" + Number$
    Next i
    SourceList.ListIndex = 0           'Highlight first item in list
End Sub
```

8. Place the following code in the MainForm.SourceList_DragDrop event procedure.

```
Sub SourceList_DragDrop (Source As Control, X As Single, Y As Single)
    If Source.Tag <> "SourceList" Then
        SourceList.AddItem Source.List(Source.ListIndex)
        If SourceList.ListIndex = -1 Then  'If no item highlighted,
            SourceList.ListIndex = 0           'highlight first item
        End If
        SetIndex Source
    End If
End Sub
```

9. Place the following code in the MainForm.ExitDemo_Click event procedure.

```
Sub ExitDemo_Click ()
    End
End Sub
```

10. Place the following code in the MainForm.SourceList_MouseDown event procedure.

```
Sub SourceList_MouseDown (Button As Integer, Shift As Integer, X As ⇐
    Single, Y As Single)
    If SourceList.ListCount > 0 Then     'If list not empty
        If Button = 2 Then             'If right button down,
            SourceList.Drag 1          'Begin dragging
        End If
    End If
End Sub
```

11. Place the following code in the MainForm.TrashCan_DblClick event procedure.

```
Sub TrashCan_DblClick ()
    TrashForm.Show
End Sub
```

12. Place the following code in the MainForm.TrashCan_DragDrop event procedure.

```
Sub TrashCan_DragDrop (Source As Control, X As Single, Y As Single)
    If Source.Tag <> "TrashList" Then
        TrashForm.TrashList.AddItem Source.List(Source.ListIndex)
        If TrashForm.TrashList.ListIndex = -1 Then
```

```
                TrashForm.TrashList.ListIndex = 0
        End If
        SetIndex Source
    Else
        Beep    'If Source = TrashList
    End If
    If TrashCan.Picture <> FullTrash.Picture Then
        TrashCan.Picture = FullTrash.Picture
    End If
End Sub
```

13. Place the following code in the MainForm.TrashCan_DragOver event procedure.

```
Sub TrashCan_DragOver (Source As Control, X As Single, Y As Single, ⇐
    State As Integer)
    Select Case State
        Case 0        'If dragged control enters
            If TrashForm.TrashList.ListCount = 0 Then
                TrashCan.Picture = EmptyTrash.DragIcon
            Else
                TrashCan.Picture = FullTrash.DragIcon
            End If
        Case 1        'If dragged control leaves
            If TrashForm.TrashList.ListCount = 0 Then
                TrashCan.Picture = EmptyTrash.Picture
            Else
                TrashCan.Picture = FullTrash.Picture
            End If
    End Select
End Sub
```

14. Place the following code in the TrashForm.TrashList_DragDrop event procedure.

```
Sub TrashList_DragDrop (Source As Control, X As Single, Y As Single)
    If Source.Tag <> "TrashList" Then
        If MainForm.TrashCan.Picture <> MainForm.FullTrash.Picture Then
            MainForm.TrashCan.Picture = MainForm.FullTrash.Picture
        End If
        TrashList.AddItem Source.List(Source.ListIndex)
        If TrashList.ListIndex = -1 Then 'If no item highlighted
            TrashList.ListIndex = 0      'Highlight first item
        End If
        SetIndex Source
    End If
End Sub
```

15. Place the following code in the TrashForm.TrashList_MouseDown event procedure.

```
Sub TrashList_MouseDown (Button As Integer, Shift As Integer, X As ⇐
```

```
Single, Y As Single)
     If TrashList.ListCount > 0 Then        'If list not empty
          If Button = 2 Then                'If right mouse button down
               TrashList.Drag 1             'Begin dragging
          End If
     End If
End Sub
```

16. Place the following code in the TrashForm.Action_Click event procedure.

```
Sub Action_Click (Index As Integer)
     If Index = 1 Then                      'Empty Trash button clicked
          If TrashList.ListCount <= 0 Then  'If trash is empty
               Beep
               Exit Sub
          End If
          Screen.MousePointer = 11          'Hourglass
          For i = 1 To TrashList.ListCount
               TrashList.ListIndex = 0
                    'Code here to deal with items in list.
                    'This code just clears items from list.
               TrashList.RemoveItem 0
          Next i
          MainForm.TrashCan.Picture = MainForm.EmptyTrash.Picture
          Screen.MousePointer = 0           'Back to prior value
     Else                                   'Close button was clicked on
          Action(0).SetFocus                'Set default button to 'Close'
          TrashForm.Hide
     End If
End Sub
```

17. Now create a new module, save it as Gencode.MOD, and add this code to its General declarations.

```
Sub SetIndex (Source As Control)
     If Source.ListIndex > 0 Then           'If not removing first item in list
          Source.ListIndex = Source.ListIndex - 1
          Source.RemoveItem Source.ListIndex + 1
     Else                                    'If removing first item in list
          Source.RemoveItem Source.ListIndex
          If Source.ListCount > 0 Then 'If list not empty
               Source.ListIndex = 0         'Keep first item highlighted
          End If
     End If
     If Source.Tag = "TrashList" Then
          If Source.ListCount = 0 Then
               MainForm.trashCan.Picture = MainForm.emptyTrash.Picture
          End If
     End If
End Sub
```

## How It Works

Our example allows you to drag items from a scrolling list box into the trash can. A list box responds to a click over an item in its list by highlighting that item and setting its ListIndex property to correspond to that item's position in the list. (The first item in a list box corresponds to a ListIndex value of 0.) Setting SourceList's DragMode property to Automatic would not be a good idea, because once a drag operation on a control is underway all mouse events are ignored. Hence, anytime SourceList was clicked on, dragging would begin, and the ListIndex property could not be changed. Indeed the basic functionality of a list box is impaired by setting its DragMode to Automatic!

Thus, in our example, we left the DragMode property for SourceList set to the default value of Manual. When a user clicks and holds down the *right* mouse button while the mouse cursor is over SourceList, dragging is invoked by code in SourceList's MouseDown event procedure (if the list is not empty). If dragging were simply invoked whenever the user clicked the list box with the left button, then, with a DragMode setting of Manual, the ListIndex property would be set before dragging began. However, a user would not be able to scroll a list by dragging the mouse up and down over its items! Again, basic functionality of the list box would be impaired.

### The Right Mouse Button Drag Trick

Clicking on and dragging the SourceList list box with the right mouse button will begin a drag operation. By itself it won't change the item highlighted in the list (set the ListIndex property of the list box). In this project our drag operations are designed to move the highlighted item in a list box, so the user can first highlight an item with the left mouse button by clicking on it, then drag it with the right mouse button or, because of the way in which a list box deals with MouseDown events, can do both at once by clicking on an item and dragging with both the right and left mouse buttons down. When both buttons are held down, the list box will first process the left mouse button, highlighting an item and setting the ListIndex property, and then the right mouse button, initiating dragging as per our code in the MouseDown event procedure.

The Picture property of the TrashCan picture box is set to the Empty.ICO icon at design time, so that, when our program first appears, the trash can will have the proper look. The appearance of the trash can will change at run time according to whether it's empty and whether a control being dragged passes over it. We need to be able to set the Picture property of the trash can to reflect a total of four different states, so we use the Picture and DragIcon properties of the two picture boxes, FullTrash and Empty-Trash (which are not visible at run time), as storage containers for the four images necessary to accomplish this. Code in the TrashCan picture box's DragOver and DragDrop event procedures changes the look of the trash can by setting TrashCan's Picture property. (As you refer to this code, remember the darkened trash can images are "stored" in the DragIcon properties of our "storage containers.")

### Using the Darkened Icons

If the user drags over the trash can, the picture is darkened according to whether it is empty. If the user then lets up the mouse button while it is still over the trash can, a DragDrop event is generated. Code in the trash can's DragDrop event procedure will remove an item from the SourceList, add an item to the TrashList list box, and change the appearance of the trash can to look full. If the user drags off of the trash can without releasing the mouse button, code in the trash can's DragOver event procedure will reset the Picture property to the proper nondarkened state.

The code located in the SourceList and TrashList's DragDrop event procedures moves an item from one list to the other. Our SetIndex procedure contains code that resets the ListIndex property of a list box after an item has been removed, in a manner befitting the remaining contents of the list box. If this were not done, ListIndex would default to a value of -1 after removal of the highlighted item, and no item in the list would be highlighted. Code in a user defined procedure is local to the form with which it is associated, but code located in a module is global in scope. Thus, we created a new module in which to locate SetIndex so that it could be called from any event procedure in the project, regardless of the parent form.

### Comment

The MainForm_Load event procedure added a number of items to the SourceList, for the purpose of providing items to drag to demonstrate the basic principles of a Macintosh style trash can. Were this an actual application, the items in the SourceList might be filenames of existing files. To fully "empty" the trash, additional code would be needed in the Action_Click event procedure to process the deletion. Our code only removes the items from the TrashList.

## 5.10    How do I...

# Display the progress of an operation?

Complexity: Intermediate

### Problem

A lot of Windows applications use a bar-like horizontal gauge to graphically display the completed percentage of an operation in progress, such as when software is being installed, a file downloaded, or a group of files copied. The shaded portion of the gauge grows to show the progress of the operation, and often text displayed in the gauge (10 percent done, and so on) changes color as the shaded portion passes over it. How can I make such a gauge to include in my own Visual Basic creations?

### Technique

The key to making such a gauge lies with the Windows BitBlt function. You can use it to combine the content of an invisible picture box with that of a visible picture box, which will appear to a user as a gauge being constantly updated.

### Steps

Open and run GAUGE.MAK. It should appear as in Figure 5-24. The Gauge project can be created by performing the following steps.

1. Create a new project called GAUGE.MAK, and create a new form called GAUGE.FRM. Place the controls shown in Figure 5-25 on the form,

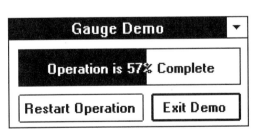

**Figure 5-24** Output of the Gauge project at run time

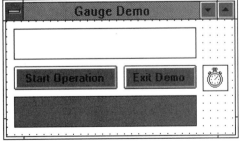

**Figure 5-25** The Gauge project form and its controls at design time

then set all the properties as listed in Table 5-12. Any properties not specifically mentioned should be left set to their default values. As you can see by comparing the run-time to design-time forms (as shown in Figures 5-24 and 5-25), at run time the gauge's form is resized by code in the Form_Load event procedure around the visible controls.

| Object | Property | Setting |
|---|---|---|
| Form | FormName | MainForm |
| | Caption | Gauge Demo |
| | BorderStyle | 1 (Fixed Single) |
| | ControlBox | False |
| Picture box | CtlName | Gauge |
| | AutoRedraw | True |
| | BackColor | &H00FFFFFF& (White) |
| | ForeColor | &H00000000& (Black) |
| Command button | CtlName | StartOp |
| | Caption | Start Operation |
| Timer | CtlName | Timer1 |
| | Enabled | False |
| | Interval | 1 (millisecond) |
| Command button | CtlName | ExitDemo |
| | Caption | Exit Demo |
| Picture box | CtlName | InvisGauge |
| | AutoRedraw | True |
| | BackColor | &H00FF0000& (Blue) |
| | ForeColor | &H00FFFFFF& (White) |
| | Visible | False |

**Table 5-12** Gauge project objects and properties

2. Place the following code in the Global module.

```
Global Const TRUE = -1
Global Const FALSE = 0
Declare Function BitBlt% Lib "Gdi" (ByVal destDC%, ByVal X%, ByVal Y%, ⇐
    ByVal W%, ByVal H%, ByVal srcDC%, ByVal xSrc%, ByVal ySrc%, ⇐
    ByVal RasterOp&)
Global Const SRCCOPY = &HCC0020
```

3. Place the following code in the General section of the Form object.

```
Sub GaugeDisplay (HowMuch!)
    Percent$ = "Operation is " + Format$(HowMuch!, "0%") + " Complete"
    Gauge.Cls                      'Clears previous content
```

```
        InvisGauge.Cls
        Gauge.CurrentX = (Gauge.Width - Gauge.TextWidth(Percent$)) / 2
        InvisGauge.CurrentX = Gauge.CurrentX        'Can do because same size
        Gauge.CurrentY = (Gauge.Height - Gauge.TextHeight(Percent$)) / 2
        InvisGauge.CurrentY = Gauge.CurrentY
        Gauge.Print Percent$                'Prints same string in both Picture
        InvisGauge.Print Percent$           'Boxes in same relative location
        OldScaleMode% = Gauge.Parent.ScaleMode
        Gauge.Parent.ScaleMode = 3          'Set to Pixels for BitBlt call
        R% = BitBlt(Gauge.Hdc, 0, 0, InvisGauge.Width * HowMuch!,
        InvisGauge.Height, InvisGauge.Hdc, 0, 0, SrcCopy)
        Gauge.Parent.ScaleMode = OldScaleMode%      'Resetting to prior value
End Sub
```

4. Place the following code in the Form_Load event procedure.

```
Sub Form_Load ()
            'This code will shrink the form around the
            'controls that are visible at run time.
        MainForm.Width = (Gauge.Left * 2) + Gauge.Width
        MainForm.Height = StartOp.Top + (StartOp.Height * 2)
            'This Code insures the two Picture boxes will
            'be exactly the same size
        InvisGauge.Width = Gauge.Width
        InvisGauge.Height = Gauge.Height
End Sub
```

5. Place the following code in the ExitDemo_Click event procedure.

```
Sub ExitDemo_Click ()
        End
End Sub
```

6. Place the following code in the StartOp_Click event procedure.

```
Sub StartOp_Click ()
        StartOp.Enabled = FALSE
        StartOp.Caption = "In Progress "
        Timer1.Enabled = TRUE
End Sub
```

7. Place the following code in the Timer1_Timer event procedure.

```
Sub Timer1_Timer ()
        Static Counter As Integer       'Initial value of 0 when declared
        HowMuch! = Counter / 100        'Percentage of operation completed
        GaugeDisplay HowMuch!
        Counter = Counter + 1
        If Counter = 101 Then
            StartOp.Enabled = TRUE          'Resetting Command Button
            StartOp.Caption = "Restart Operation"
            Timer1.Enabled = FALSE          'This procedure won't be called
            Counter = 0                     'until StartOp is clicked on again
        End If
End Sub
```

## How It Works

In a working application, a gauge is updated as an operation is in progress. In this demo, we simply use a timer to update our gauge by 1% every time the timer's Timer event procedure gets called. The basic principles involved to actually create the gauge itself in either case are identical. Later you will see how the code would differ for a more practical implementation, where you would actually be following an event's progression.

The event procedure of the project's timer is called as long as the timer's Enabled property is set to True. We set the Enabled property to False at design time, so that at run time we can selectively enable the timer by clicking on the StartOp command button. This button has code in its Click event procedure to set the timer's Enabled property to True.

In the Timer event procedure, we declared the integer variable Counter as a Static variable so that it will retain its value in between procedure calls. When initially declared, Counter has a value of 0 and is incremented by 1 each time the procedure gets called. When Counter's value reaches 101, the code in the If...Then loop at the end of the procedure will be executed, resetting the timer's Enabled property to False and Counter's value to 0. The net effect is that whenever the timer is enabled, its Timer event procedure will be called while Counter's value cycles through the range 0-100.

Within the Timer event procedure, the user-defined subroutine GaugeDisplay is called, with HowMuch! (calculated as the percentage of the operation completed at the time of the call) passed as its sole parameter. Code in GaugeDisplay formats HowMuch! into a character string and incorporates it into the string Percent$, then prints Percent$ centered horizontally and vertically in the Gauge and InvisGauge picture boxes. Because the picture boxes are exactly the same size, the relative position of the text string within each picture box is the same.

The last line of code in GaugeDisplay is a call to the Windows API Function BitBlt (declared in the Global module), which copies a section of Invis-Gauge to Gauge. In the call, the width of InvisGauge is multiplied times HowMuch! to determine the size (percentage) of the section to copy. Remember that Gauge has a BackColor of white, and ForeColor (the color that text is painted in) of black. InvisGauge has a blue BackColor and a white ForeColor. Because the content of both picture boxes is identical except for the color, the white letters of the text in the section copied from InvisGauge to Gauge by the BitBlt call mesh seamlessly with the black letters in Gauge.

Were this an actual application that used a gauge to graphically track an operation's progress, HowMuch! would represent the percentage of the operation completed at the time of the call to GaugeDisplay. For example, if the Gauge were tracking the progress of a copy operation involving a number of files, after each file was copied a call could be made to GaugeDisplay, as in the following code:

```
Sub CopyFiles (SourceFile$(), FileCount)
    Dim BufSize As Long
    Dim FilePosition As Long
    Dim FileSize As Long
    Dim FileSizeLeft As Long

    Screen.MousePointer = 11        'HourGlass (Waiting)
    GaugeDisplay(0)                 'initially displays gauge
                                    'with 0% completed

    For i = 1 To FileCount
        Open SourceFile$(i) For Binary Access Read As #1
        Open DestFile$ For Binary Access Write As #2
        FileSize = LOF(1)
        FileSizeLeft = FileSize
        FilePosition = 1
        While FileSizeLeft >= 0
            If FileSizeLeft > 16384 Then
                BufSize = 16384
            ElseIf FileSizeLeft = 0 Then
                BufSize = 1
            Else
                BufSize = FileSizeLeft
            End If
            Buffer$ = String$(BufSize, " ")
            Get #1, FilePosition, Buffer$
            Put #2, FilePosition, Buffer$
            FilePosition = FilePosition + BufSize
            FileSizeLeft = FileSize - FilePosition

        Wend
        Close #1
        Close #2
        GaugeDisplay(i/FileCount)   'Displays gauge with shaded amount
                                    'proportional to amount of
                                    'operation completed
    Next i
    Screen.MousePointer = 0         'Back to prior value
End Sub
```

## Comments

The Windows BitBlt function is extremely versatile and can be used to copy a source bitmap (or portion thereof) to a destination bitmap in a variety of ways. The exact manner in which the copy is performed is specified by the RasterOp% (last) parameter of the call. Our demo simply did a straightforward copy of a section of InvisGauge to Gauge by using the constant SRCCOPY (defined in the Global module) in the BitBlt call as the value of the RasterOp$ parameter.

The height and width parameters in a BitBlt call specifying the dimensions of the source and destination bitmaps need to be in units of pixels. The value of the ScaleMode property of the parent of a control (the form on which the control is located) determines the units in which the Width and Height properties of the control are given. You can verify this at design time by noting the values of the Width and Height properties of a control, say Gauge, then changing the value of the ScaleMode property of the parent of Gauge, MainForm, to Pixels, and then again noting the values of Gauge's Width and Height properties. They will have changed!

Code in GaugeDisplay first saves the value of the ScaleMode property of the parent of the two picture boxes (Gauge and InvisGauge) involved in the BitBlt call in the variable OldScaleMode%, then sets it to Pixels just prior to the call. After the BitBlt call, the ScaleMode property is reset to Old-ScaleMode%, its value prior to the change. In this way, regardless of the value of the parent form's ScaleMode property at run time, we can rest assured that at the time of the call to BitBlt it will be Pixels.

The Interval property of the timer was set to the minimum possible value (1 millisecond) at design time. Since our demo uses the timer as a stand-in for an actual operation, this insures that the gauge will be updated as quickly as the CPU on which the project is running can execute all the code (including the call to GaugeDisplay) located within the Timer event procedure.

A certain amount of overhead is involved when a Gauge is used to display an operation's progress. The total time of the operation is increased by the amount of time it takes to update the Gauge times the total number of times the Gauge is updated throughout the course of the operation.

## 5.11    How do I...

# Fill complex objects?

Complexity: Intermediate

### Problem

Visual Basic has powerful graphing functions and ability to draw rectangles and circles filled with any color or pattern. But there are no routines to fill any other kind of closed shape. Is there a way to do this?

### Technique

It's true that Visual Basic's drawing tools are limited to the Circle and Line statements. Luckily, more complex objects can be drawn using the Polgygon function found in the Windows API library.

### Steps

Open and run POLY-GON.MAK. This program draws five filled objects on the picture box as shown in Figure 5-26. Click Exit on the menu to leave the application.

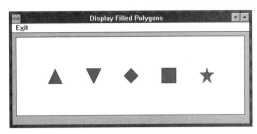

**Figure 5-26** The Polygon project's filled polygons

The project can be built by entering the code and objects as detailed in the following steps.

1. Create a new project called POLYGON.MAK. and create a new form with the objects and properties listed in Table 5-13. Save the form as POLY-GON.FRM.

| Object | Property | Setting |
|---|---|---|
| Form | FormName | PolyGon |
| | BackColor | &H00C0C0C0 |
| Picture box | CtlName | P |

**Table 5-13** Polygon project form's objects and properties

2. Create a menu for the form using the Menu Design window with the attributes shown in Table 5-14.

| Caption | CtlName |
|---|---|
| E&xit | Quit |

**Table 5-14** Polygon form menu attributes

3. Select the Global module, enter the following code and save it as POLY-GON.BAS. This defines the constants, data structures, and Windows API calls needed to draw the Polygons.

```
Type POINTAPI
     X As Integer
     Y As Integer
End Type

' PolyFill() Modes
Global Const ALTERNATE = 1
```

```
Global Const WINDING = 2

Declare Sub Polygon Lib "GDI" (ByVal hDC As Integer, lpPoints As POINTAPI, ⇐
ByVal nCount As Integer)
Declare Sub SetPolyFillMode Lib "GDI" (ByVal hDC As Integer, ByVal ⇐
nPolyFillMode As Integer)

'   Shape constants
Global Const PG_TRIANGLE = 1
Global Const PG_INV_TRIANGLE = 2
Global Const PG_DIAMOND = 3
Global Const PG_SQUARE = 4
Global Const PG_STAR = 5
```

4. Enter the following code into the picture box's Paint event subroutine. Whenever Visual Basic needs to paint the picture box, this subroutine will draw the five predefined shapes.

```
Sub P_Paint ()
Dim FColor As Long, Size As Integer
    FColor = QBColor(13)
    P.ScaleMode = 3
    Size = 30

    P.CurrentY = P.ScaleHeight / 2
    P.CurrentX = P.ScaleWidth / 6
    DrawPolygon P, PG_TRIANGLE, Size, FColor

    P.CurrentY = P.ScaleHeight / 2
    P.CurrentX = 2 * P.ScaleWidth / 6
    DrawPolygon P, PG_INV_TRIANGLE, Size, FColor

    P.CurrentY = P.ScaleHeight / 2
    P.CurrentX = 3 * P.ScaleWidth / 6
    DrawPolygon P, PG_DIAMOND, Size, FColor

    P.CurrentY = P.ScaleHeight / 2
    P.CurrentX = 4 * P.ScaleWidth / 6
    DrawPolygon P, PG_SQUARE, Size, FColor

    P.CurrentY = P.ScaleHeight / 2
    P.CurrentX = 5 * P.ScaleWidth / 6
    DrawPolygon P, PG_STAR, Size, FColor
End Sub
```

5. Enter the following code into the Quit_Click menu event subroutine to allow the user to exit the application gracefully.

```
Sub Quit_Click ()
    End
End Sub
```

6. Create a new module by clicking on the File menu's New Module option. Enter the following line of code in the Declarations section and then save the module as POLYLINE.BAS.

```
Dim Ply(10) As POINTAPI
```

7. Enter the following code into the (General) section of the Polyline module. This subroutine will draw the shape on the specified picture box control.

```
Sub DrawPolygon (P As Control, Shape As Integer, Size As Integer, FColor ⇐
    As Long)
Dim nPoints As Integer

'   Draws Different shapes at current location using polygons
'
'   Save current Scalemode, and Scale Attributes
    SSMode = P.ScaleMode
    SSTOP = P.ScaleTop: SSLeft = P.ScaleLeft
    SSWidth = P.ScaleWidth: SSHeight = P.ScaleHeight

'   Set up Pixel ScaleMode, Fill style, etc.
    P.ScaleMode = 3         ' PolyGon needs everything in pixels
    P.FillStyle = 0         ' Sold fill
    P.fillcolor = FColor    ' Fill color
    P.Drawwidth = 1         ' Border width in pixels

' Call subroutine to build coordinates for shape
    Select Case Shape
      Case PG_TRIANGLE
        DrawTriangle Size, nPoints

      Case PG_INV_TRIANGLE
        DrawInvertTriangle Size, nPoints

      Case PG_DIAMOND
        DrawDiamond Size, nPoints

      Case PG_SQUARE
        DrawSquare Size, nPoints

      Case PG_STAR
        DrawStar Size, nPoints
    End Select

' Adjust Points to center shape at current point
' Set PolyFillMode to fill whole shape
' Draw polyGon
    For I = 1 To nPoints
      Ply(I).X = Ply(I).X + P.CurrentX - Size / 2
      Ply(I).Y = Ply(I).Y + P.CurrentY - Size / 2
    Next I
```

```
    SetPolyFillMode P.Hdc, WINDING
    Polygon P.Hdc, Ply(1), nPoints
' Restore old ScaleMode
    P.ScaleMode = SSMode
    P.ScaleTop = SSTOP: P.ScaleLeft = SSLeft
    P.ScaleHeight = SSHeight: P.ScaleWidth = SSWidth
End Sub
```

8. Enter the following code in the General section of the Polyline module. This code loads the coordinates for a triangular object.

```
Sub DrawTriangle (Size As Integer, nPoints As Integer)
    Ply(1).X = Size / 2
    Ply(1).Y = 0

    Ply(2).X = Size
    Ply(2).Y = Size

    Ply(3).X = 0
    Ply(3).Y = Size

    nPoints = 3
End Sub
```

9. Enter the following code into the General section of the Polyline module. This code loads the coordinates for an inverted triangle.

```
Sub DrawInvertTriangle (Size As Integer, nPoints As Integer)
    Ply(1).X = 0
    Ply(1).Y = 0

    Ply(2).X = Size
    Ply(2).Y = 0

    Ply(3).X = Size / 2
    Ply(3).Y = Size

    nPoints = 3
End Sub
```

10. Enter the following code into the General section of the Polyline module. This code loads the coordinates for a diamond shaped object.

```
Sub DrawDiamond (Size As Integer, nPoints As Integer)
    Ply(1).X = Size / 2
    Ply(1).Y = 0

    Ply(2).X = Size
    Ply(2).Y = Size / 2

    Ply(3).X = Size / 2
    Ply(3).Y = Size

    Ply(4).X = 0
    Ply(4).Y = Size / 2
```

```
    nPoints = 4
End Sub
```

11. Enter the following code in the General section of the Polyline module. This code loads the coordinates for a square shaped object.

```
Sub DrawSquare (Size As Integer, nPoints As Integer)
    Ply(1).X = 0
    Ply(1).Y = 0

    Ply(2).X = Size
    Ply(2).Y = 0

    Ply(3).X = Size
    Ply(3).Y = Size

    Ply(4).X = 0
    Ply(4).Y = Size

    nPoints = 4
End Sub
```

12. Enter the following code in the General section of the Polyline module. This code loads the coordinates for a five-pointed star.

```
Sub DrawStar (Size As Integer, nPoints As Integer)
    Ply(1).X = Size / 2
    Ply(1).Y = 0

    Ply(2).X = 4 * Size / 5
    Ply(2).Y = Size

    Ply(3).X = 0
    Ply(3).Y = Size / 3

    Ply(4).X = Size
    Ply(4).Y = Ply(3).Y

    Ply(5).X = Size - Ply(2).X
    Ply(5).Y = Size

    nPoints = 5
End Sub
```

### How It Works

To draw graphical shapes, Visual Basic provides you with two methods: Line and Circle. The Line method can be used to draw straight lines or, when used with the BF option, will produce a filled rectangle. More complex objects, with straight edges, can be made up of multiple line segments, but filling the object using Visual Basic statements is tedious and slow. However, the Windows API has a function, Polygon, for drawing and filling complex objects.

The Polygon function takes three parameters as shown in Table 5-15.

| Parameter | Description |
| --- | --- |
| hDC | Device context on which the polygon will be drawn. This could be Form.hDC or, as shown in this project, PictureBox.hDC |
| lpPoints | An array of a user-defined data type, POINTAPI, which specifies the vertices of the Polygon. lpPoints has two elements, X and Y, which are the coordinates, in pixels, relative to the upper left corner of the device context. |
| nCount | The number of vertices in the PolyGon. |

**Table 5-15** Parameters of the Polygon function

The DrawPolygon subroutine in the Polyline module is used to draw one of the five predefined shapes in a picture box at the current cursor location. Putting the DrawPolygon subroutine into a separate module makes it easy to incorporate it into other projects, such as a Linegrph in How-To 5.12 Build a line chart. Table 5-16 lists the parameters to the DrawPolygon subroutine.

| Parameter | Description |
| --- | --- |
| P | Picture box control onto which the shape will be drawn. |
| Shape | One of five predefined shapes: 1 - Triangle, 2 - Inverted Triangle, 3 - Diamond, 4 - Square, and 5 - Star. |
| Size | Height and Width of the Polygon, in Pixels. |
| FColor | Background FillColor for the object. |

**Table 5-16** Parameters of the DrawPolygon subroutine

DrawPolgygon starts by saving the picture box's current ScaleMode and scale parameters. These values will be restored after displaying the Polygon, just before the subroutine exits. Because the Polygon function uses pixels for its coordinates, the ScaleMode for the control is set to 3 - Pixels. A Select Case statement determines the shape of the object. Each object has its own subroutine to load the coordinates of the polygon's verticies.

Using DrawTriangle as an example, the three corners of the shape are stored in the Ply array. The parameter nPoints is returned with the number of corners, or vertices. Note that DrawTriangle doesn't actually draw the object, it only stores the object's coordinates. The For...Next loop adjusts the returned coordinates so that the object is centered around the current position in the picture box. If we didn't do this, the object would always be drawn in the picture box's upper left corner.

The Windows API function SetPolyFillMode determines how complex polygons are filled in. Its second parameter can take one of two values, WINDING or ALTERNATE. The WINDING value specifies that the entire polygon is to be filled in; ALTERNATE only fills in every other enclosed surface. To see the effect of this parameter, change the WINDING constant to ALTERNATE and notice how the five-pointed star (Shape = 5) fill has changed.

DrawPolygon is called from the picture box's Paint event subroutine. Using the Paint event to draw not only displays the shapes automatically at application startup, but also whenever the picture box becomes visible after being minimized or hidden.

### Comments

For nonfilled polygons, the Windows API function, Polyline, can be used instead. It has the same parameters as Polygon.

When an application calls the Polygon function, the entire array of Points needs to be passed as a parameter. To do this with a user-defined data type, you simply use the first element as the function parameter.

---

### 5.12    How do I...

## Build a line chart?

Complexity: Intermediate

### Problem

How can I draw a Line Chart in Visual Basic similar to the ones created by my Windows spreadsheet program?

### Technique

Visual Basic provides an excellent vehicle for creating all kinds of professional-looking business graphics. The Visual Basic drawing and print methods are used to draw the text, grids, and lines for this application. The Windows API Polygon function in How-To 5.11 Fill complex objects, is used to create the graphical symbols.

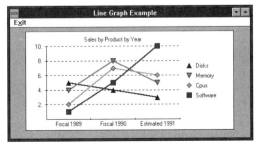

**Figure 5-27** The Linegrph business graphic

### Steps

Open and run LINEGRPH.MAK. It will draw a sample line chart as shown in Figure 5-27. Click on the Exit menu to leave the application.

The project may be created by entering the objects and code as detailed in the following steps. This project makes use of the code in the Polyline module, entry of which is described in Steps 6 through 13 of the Polygon project.

1. Create a new project called LINEGRPH.MAK. Create a new form with the objects and properties listed in Table 5-17, and save it as LINE-GRPH.FRM.

| Object | Property | Setting |
|---|---|---|
| Form | FormName | LineGraph |
| | BackColor | &H00C0C0C0& |
| Picture box | CtlName | P |

**Table 5-17** Linegraph project form's objects and properties

2. Using the Menu Design window, create a menu for the form with the attributes from Table 5-18.

| Caption | CtlName |
|---|---|
| Exit | Quit |

**Table 5-18** Linegraph menu attributes

3. Select the project's Global module, enter the following code, and save it as LINEGRPH.BAS. This defines the constants, data structures, and Windows API calls needed to draw the graphic symbols.

```
Type POINTAPI
     X As Integer
     Y As Integer
End Type

'  PolyFill() Modes
Global Const ALTERNATE = 1
Global Const WINDING = 2

Declare Sub Polygon Lib "GDI" (ByVal hDC As Integer, lpPoints As POINTAPI, ⇐
ByVal nCount As Integer)
Declare Sub SetPolyFillMode Lib "GDI" (ByVal hDC As Integer, ByVal ⇐
nPolyFillMode As Integer)

'   Shape constants
Global Const PG_TRIANGLE = 1
Global Const PG_INV_TRIANGLE = 2
Global Const PG_DIAMOND = 3
```

```
Global Const PG_SQUARE = 4
Global Const PG_STAR = 5
```

4. Place the following constant in the Declarations section of the form. The POLYSIZE constant specifies the height and width, in pixels, of the graphical symbols.

```
Const POLYSIZE = 10
```

5. Put the following subroutine in the General section of the LineGraph form. This subroutine contains the data and descriptions used to draw the line graph.

```
Sub Display_Graph ()
Const CATEGORIES = 3
Const Series = 4
Const MAX_VALUE = 10

Static Desc$(CATEGORIES), Values(CATEGORIES, Series), ⇐
   Series_names$(Series)
   P.MousePointer = 11
   Desc$(1) = "Fiscal 1991"
   Desc$(2) = "Fiscal 1992"
   Desc$(3) = "Estimated 1993"
   Display_grid "Sales by Product by Year", CATEGORIES, Desc$(), 5, MAX_VALUE

   Values(1, 1) = 5: Values(1, 2) = 4: Values(1, 3) = 2: Values(1, 4) = 1
   Values(2, 1) = 4: Values(2, 2) = 8: Values(2, 3) = 7: Values(2, 4) = 5
   Values(3, 1) = 3: Values(3, 2) = 5: Values(3, 3) = 6: Values(3, 4) = 10
   Display_Lines CATEGORIES, Values(), Series, MAX_VALUE

   Series_names$(1) = "Disks"
   Series_names$(2) = "Memory"
   Series_names$(3) = "Cpus"
   Series_names$(4) = "Software"
   Display_Legend Series, Series_names$()
   P.MousePointer = 0
End Sub
```

6. Place the following subroutine in the General section of the LineGraph form. This subroutine draws the graphical legend at the right side of the line chart.

```
Sub Display_Legend (NSeries As Integer, Sname() As String)
   P.Fillstyle = 0                        ' Solid blocks
   Theight% = P.TextHeight(Sname(1)) ' Get text height

'   Center Legend in the middle of the Graph height.
'   For each item in the series, draw a small box and the description.
'   Legends are seperated by 1.5 times the text height.

   StartY = 50 + (Theight% * 1.5 * NSeries) / 2
   For Series% = 1 To NSeries
      P.FillColor = QBColor(Series% + 8)
      P.CurrentX = 107
```

```
      P.CurrentY = StartY - 4
      DrawPolygon P, Series%, POLYSIZE, QBColor(Series% + 8)

      P.CurrentY = StartY
      P.CurrentX = 112
      P.Print Sname(Series%)
      StartY = StartY - Theight% * 1.5
   Next Series%
End Sub
```

7. Place the following subroutine in the General section of the LineGraph form. This subroutine draws the background grid.

```
Sub Display_grid (Title As String, NCategory As Integer, Description() ⇐
As String, Nvalues As Integer, Maxvalue As Single)
Dim I As Integer

'  Set scale so graph portion is scaled 0-100 on x- and y-axes.
'  Print title in center of the graph grid.
'  Draw x-axis and y-axis lines.

   P.Scale (-15, 120)-(140, -15)
   P.CurrentX = (100 - P.TextWidth(Title)) / 2
   P.CurrentY = 105 + P.TextHeight(Title)
   P.Print Title              ' Print bar graph title
   P.Line (0, 0)-(0, 100)     ' Draw x-axis
   P.Line (0, 0)-(100, 0)     ' Draw y-axis

'  For each of the grid values, draw a solid tick mark to the left of axis.
'  Then draw solid dashed line across entire graph width (0-100).
'  Print value of grid line right justified next to tick marks.

   For I = 1 To Nvalues       ' Draw grid lines
      P.Drawstyle = 0
      Yvalue% = 100# * I / Nvalues
      P.Line (-1, Yvalue%)-(0, Yvalue%)    ' y-axis tick marks
      P.Drawstyle = 2
      P.Line (0, Yvalue%)-(100, Yvalue%)   ' y-axis grid dashed grid lines
      Value$ = Format$(Maxvalue * I / Nvalues, "#,##0.#")
      P.CurrentX = -3 - P.TextWidth(Value$)          ' Right justify text
      P.CurrentY = Yvalue% + P.TextHeight(Value$) / 2 ' Center veritcally
      P.Print Value$;                      ' y axis values
   Next I

'  For each category, draw a small tick mark on x-axis.
'  Center and print category description.

   For I = 1 To NCategory     ' Print category descriptions
      P.Drawstyle = 0
      Xvalue = 100 * I / NCategory
      P.Line (Xvalue, -1)-(Xvalue, 2) ' x-axis tick marks
      P.CurrentY = -2
      P.CurrentX = Xvalue - 50 / NCategory - P.TextWidth(Description(I)) / 2
      P.Print Description(I)
   Next I
End Sub
```

8. Place the following subroutine in the General section of the LineGraph form. It will compute the line positions and draw them on top of the grid.

```
Sub Display_Lines (NCategory As Integer, Values(), NSeries As Single, ⇐
    Maximum As Single)
  Dim Series As Integer, Cat As Integer
    P.Fillstyle = 0

' For each series in the PictureBox, P, draw the connecting line from
'  previous category to current category.
' Position x-coordinate in center of category, y-coordinate based on value
'  for the point.
' Then draw the ploygon shape to denote the series at left-side of line segment.
' Finally, draw the last shape on a line.
'
    P.DrawWidth = 1
    For Series = 1 To NSeries
      PreviousX = 50 / NCategory
      PreviousY = Values(1, Series) * 100 / Maximum
      For Cat = 2 To NCategory
        NewX = PreviousX + 100 / NCategory
        NewY = Values(Cat, Series) * 100 / Maximum
        P.DrawWidth = 2
        P.Line (PreviousX, PreviousY)-(NewX, NewY), QBColor(Series + 8)
        P.CurrentX = PreviousX
        P.CurrentY = PreviousY
        DrawPolygon P, Series, POLYSIZE, QBColor(Series + 8)
        PreviousX = NewX
        PreviousY = NewY
      Next Cat
      P.CurrentX = PreviousX
      P.CurrentY = PreviousY
      DrawPolygon P, Series, POLYSIZE, QBColor(Series + 8)
    Next Series
End Sub
```

9. Place the following subroutine in the Paint event subroutine of the Line-Graph form. The line graph will be displayed whenever the picture box needs to be painted.

```
Sub Form_Paint ()
   Display_Graph
End Sub
```

10. Place the following subroutine in the Quit menu event subroutine of the LineGraph form. This subroutine allows for graceful exit from the application.

```
Sub Quit_Click ()
   End
End Sub
```

11. Add the POLYLINE.BAS file from the directory using the Add File option from Visual Basic's File menu. This module contains the drawing routines for the symbols used on the graph and legend. The code for this module is detailed in steps six through twelve of How-To 5.11 How do I fill complex objects?

**How It Works**

The Display_Graph subroutine is used to set up the data, category, and series descriptions, and invoke the drawing subroutines. These subroutines, Display_grid, Display_Lines, and Display_Legend, all draw their respective components on a picture box, called "P," forming the complete line graph.

Data in the Display_Graph subroutine is kept by series within each category. Each series is represented by a single line, while categories are sections on the x-axis. In this example, the four series represent sales by class of product while the three categories are fiscal years. Data is stored in the Values array; with category as the first subscript and series as the second.

The Display_grid subroutine draws the background grid, chart title, and category descriptions. Using Visual Basic's custom scaling capability enables us to draw the graph on any sized picture box. The lines of the graph are drawn within a 100 by 100 unit area, with point 0,0 at the intersection of the x- and y-axes. The actual scaling parameters are set from -15 to 140 for the width and -15 to 120 for the height. The additional scaling units leave room for drawing the chart title, category descriptions, legend, and so on. The subroutine's comments explain the use of each parameter.

The Display_Lines subroutine draws the colored graph lines, one for each of the series. Each line is drawn as a series of lines starting and ending in the middle of each category. The DrawPolygon subroutine draws the graphical symbols. The size of the graphical symbols is determined by the POLYSIZE constant. You can change this constant to alter the symbol size without affecting the rest of the line chart. Note that the values for the QBColor function start at nine to produce a brighter, more colorful graph.

The Display_Legend subroutine also uses the DrawPolygon subroutine to create the graphical symbols.

**Comments**

The width of the lines on the chart can be changed by adjusting the number in the P.DrawWidth = 2 statement in the Display_Lines subroutine.

If the drawing is to be done on a monochrome device, you may want to set the DrawStyle property for each series line instead of changing the line's color.

**5.13    How do I...**

# Build a bar chart?

Complexity: Intermediate

### Problem
Now that I've seen how to do a line chart, I'm ready for a bar graph, one that allows series to be charted. How can I do this?

### Technique
A bar graph is made up of three components: a background grid, the bars themselves, and a legend. Visual Basic's capability to accurately draw and position text, lines, and boxes in a picture box provides all the capabilities needed for this project.

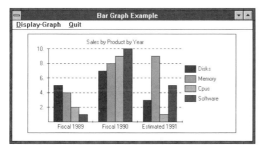

**Figure 5-28** Bargraph project at run time

### Steps
Open and run BARGRAPH.MAK. Click on the Display-Graph menu item to draw the sample graph as shown in Figure 5-28. To change the sample data, alter the code in the Display_Graph_Click event subroutine. The Bargraph project may be created by entering the objects and code in the following steps.

1. Create a new project called BARGRAPH.MAK. Create a new form with the objects and properties shown in Table 5-19, and save it as BARGRAPH.FRM.

| Object | Property | Setting |
|--------|----------|---------|
| Form | Caption | Bar Graph Example |
| | FormName | Bargraph |
| Picture box | AutoRedraw | True |
| | CtlName | P |
| | FontBold | False |
| | FontName | Helv |

**Table 5-19** Bargraph project form's objects and properties

2. Create a menu for the Bargraph form using the Menu Design window with the captions and control names shown in Table 5-20.

| Caption | CtlName |
| --- | --- |
| &Display-Graph | Display_Graph |
| &Quit | Quit |

**Table 5-20** Bargraph menu

3. Put the following code in the Display_Graph_Click event subroutine of the form. This is the name of the routine the menu Display-Graph will call. This subroutine defines all the values that will be drawn, including their descriptions and titles. The constant, CATEGORIES, indicates how many different sets of data will be displayed. In this example, there are three categories, corresponding to the three fiscal years displayed. The SERIES constant is used to specify how many bars will appear in each category. The constant, MAX_VALUE, is used to scale the bars.

```
Sub Display_Graph_Click ()
Const CATEGORIES = 3
Const SERIES = 4
Const MAX_VALUE = 10

Static Desc$(CATEGORIES), Values(CATEGORIES, SERIES),
    Series_names$(SERIES)
    Desc$(1) = "Fiscal 1989"
    Desc$(2) = "Fiscal 1990"
    Desc$(3) = "Estimated 1991"
    Display_grid "Sales by Product by Year", CATEGORIES, Desc$(), 5, MAX_VALUE

    Values(1, 1) = 5: Values(1, 2) = 4: Values(1, 3) = 2: Values(1, 4) = 1
    Values(2, 1) = 7: Values(2, 2) = 8: Values(2, 3) = 9: Values(2, 4) = 10
    Values(3, 1) = 3: Values(3, 2) = 9: Values(3, 3) = 1: Values(3, 4) = 5
    Display_bars CATEGORIES, Values(), SERIES, MAX_VALUE

    Series_names$(1) = "Disks"
    Series_names$(2) = "Memory"
    Series_names$(3) = "Cpus"
    Series_names$(4) = "Software"
    Display_Legend SERIES, Series_names$()
End Sub
```

4. Put the following code in the Display_grid subroutine located in the General section of the form. It will draw the graph's grid, title, and category descriptions in the picture box control.

```
Sub Display_grid (Title As String, Ncategory As Integer, Description() ⇐
    As String, Nvalues As Integer, Maxvalue As Single)
```

```
Dim I As Integer

' Set scale so graph portion is scaled 0-100 on x- & y-axis.
' Print title in center of the graph grid.
' Draw x- & y-axis lines.

   P.Scale (-15, 120)-(140, -15)
   P.Currentx = (100 - P.TextWidth(Title)) / 2
   P.Currenty = 105 + P.TextHeight(Title)
   P.Print Title                ' Print bar graph title
   P.Line (0, 0)-(0, 100)       ' Draw x-axis
   P.Line (0, 0)-(100, 0)       ' Draw y-axis

' For each of the grid values, draw a solid tick mark to the left of axis.
' Then draw solid dashed line across entire graph width (0-100).
' Print value of grid line right justified next to tick marks.

   For I = 1 To Nvalues           ' Draw grid lines
      P.Drawstyle = 0
      Yvalue% = 100# * I / Nvalues
      P.Line (-1, Yvalue%)-(0, Yvalue%)    ' y-axis tick marks
      P.Drawstyle = 2
      P.Line (0, Yvalue%)-(100, Yvalue%)   ' y-axis grid dashed grid lines
      Value$ = Format$(Maxvalue * I / Nvalues, "#,##0.#")
      P.Currentx = -3 - P.TextWidth(Value$)    ' Right justify text
      P.Currenty = Yvalue% + P.TextHeight(Value$) / 2  ' Center vertically
      P.Print Value$;   ' y-axis values
   Next I

' For each category, draw a small tick mark on x-axis.
' Center and print category description.

   For I = 1 To Ncategory                   ' Print category descriptions
      P.Drawstyle = 0
      Xvalue = 100 * I / Ncategory
      P.Line (Xvalue, -1)-(Xvalue, 2)  ' x-axis tick marks
      P.Currenty = -2
      P.Currentx = Xvalue - 50 / Ncategory - P.TextWidth(Description(I)) / 2
      P.Print Description(I)
   Next I
End Sub
```

5. Put the following code in the Display_bars subroutine of the General section of the form. This subroutine draws the bar on picture box, P. Increasing the SEPARATION constant's value will put additional space between each of the category groups.

```
Sub Display_bars (Ncategory As Integer, Values(), Nseries As Single, ⇐
   Maximum As Single)
   Const SEPARATION = 25                    ' Percentage to separate bars
   Dim Series As Integer, Cat As Integer
   Catwidth = 100 / Ncategory
   Barwidth = Catwidth * (100 - SEPARATION ) / (100 * Nseries) ⇐
```

```
    P.Fillstyle = 0
' For each category compute the starting x position.
' Line function leaves CurrentX at right side of box
' so each bar will display adjacent to the previous one.

    For Cat = 1 To Ncategory
        P.Currentx = Catwidth * Cat - Catwidth / 2 - (Barwidth * Nseries) / 2
        For Series = 1 To Nseries
            P.Currenty = 0               ' Reset to graph baseline
            P.Fillcolor = QBColor(Series + 8)' Bright colors
            P.Line Step(0, 0)-Step(Barwidth, Values(Cat, Series) * 100 / ⇐
    Maximum), , B
        Next Series
    Next Cat
End Sub
```

6. Put the following code in the Display_Legend subroutine of the General section of the form. This code draws the legend to the left of the bar graph.

```
Sub Display_Legend (Nseries As Integer, Sname() As String)
    P.Fillstyle = 0                          ' Solid blocks
    Theight% = P.TextHeight(Sname(1))           ' Get text height

' Center Legend in the middle of the Graph height.
' For each item in the series, draw a small box, followed by the
' description.
' Legends are separated by 1.5 times the text height.

    Starty = 50 + (Theight% * 1.5 * Nseries) / 2
    For Series% = 1 To Nseries
        P.Fillcolor = QBColor(Series% + 8)
        P.Line (102, Starty)-Step(8, -Theight%), , B   ' Legend Box
        P.Currenty = Starty
        P.Currentx = 112
        P.Print Sname(Series%)
        Starty = Starty - Theight% * 1.5
    Next Series%
End Sub
```

7. Put the following code in the Quit_Click event subroutine so that the user can gracefully exit the program.

```
Sub Quit_Click ()
    End
End Sub
```

## How It Works

This project demonstrates the ease with which Visual Basic can position and draw lines, boxes, and text. The user-defined scale prevents us from having to worry about physical screen dimensions; all graphic and text positioning is performed relative to our own scale.

To keep the project manageable, the program has been divided into four subroutines:

- Display_Graph_Click sets up the values to be graphed, as well as category and series descriptions. It then calls the following three functions.
- Display_grid draws the background axis, title, and category description.
- Display_bars graphs the bars.
- Display_legend displays the legend to the right of the bar graph.

The Display_Graph_Click subroutine is called from the menu. It sets up three data elements: Category descriptions, Series descriptions, and Data values. Categories are groups of data. In our example, there are three categories, each representing a different fiscal year of data. Category descriptions are kept in the Desc$ array. You can change the number of categories by altering the CATEGORIES constant.

The SERIES constant identifies the number of different bars that will be drawn in each category. One example has four series, each representing a different type of computer commodity. The series descriptions are kept in the Series_names$ array.

Each category and series combination requires a data value, to be kept in the Values array. The first subscript is the category number, the second is the series number.

The Display_grid subroutine sets up a user-defined scale so that all positioning of text, lines, and boxes can be done without regard to the picture box's physical screen dimensions. The actual graph portion is scaled to 100 by 100 units. The additional areas on the top, left, bottom, and right are for the graph title, y-axis values, category names, and bar legend, respectively. The balance of the Display_grid function draws the x- and y-axes with solid lines, and grids as dashed lines. The Nvalues parameter determines the number of grid lines to draw. In the example, five grid lines are drawn. The Maxvalue parameter is the maximum y-axis value.

The Display_bars subroutine displays each of the bars by series within category. The SEPARATION constant is the percentage of the category width to leave between bar groups. The example value of 25 percent means that one-quarter of the category width will be blank. The remaining three-quarters will be occupied by the bar graphs. Increasing SEPARATION will shrink the width of the bars and increase the amount of blank area between each category. Bar colors are picked by using a different QBColor value for each series. QBColors 8 to 15 are used because this will produce brightly shaded bars.

The Display_Legend subroutine draws the legend on the right side of the graph. The legend is centered between the top and bottom of the y-axis. The colors for each series match those used in the Display_bars subroutine.

### Comment

Unfortunately, if the resulting bar graph is to be printed on a black-and-white device (such as a laser printer), the colors will print black. In this case, you might want to include the following code line in the Series% For...Next loop of the Display_bars and Display_Legend subroutines to create different types of fill patterns within the bars.

```
P.Fillstyle = Series%
```

## 5.14    How do I...

# Build a pie chart?

Complexity: Intermediate

### Problem

I would like to be able to display pie charts as part of my Visual Basic applications. How can this be done without purchasing an add-on graphics package?

### Technique

The Circle function can be used not only to draw complete circles but also to create segments or slices of a circle. By drawing slices of appropriate sizes and filling them with different colors, we can use Visual Basic to draw pie charts.

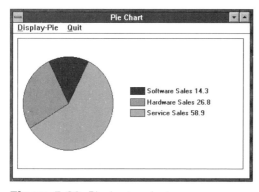

**Figure 5-29**  Piechart project

### Steps

Open and run PIECHART.MAK. Click on the Display-Pie menu item to draw the sample chart as shown in Figure 5-29. To change the sample data, alter the code in the Display_Graph_Click event subroutine. The Piechart project may be created by entering the objects and code in the following steps.

1. Create a new project called PIECHART.MAK. Create a new form with the objects and properties shown in Table 5-21, and save it as PIECHART.FRM.

| Object | Property | Setting |
|---|---|---|
| Form | Caption | Pie Chart |
| | FormName | Piechart |
| Picture box | AutoRedraw | True |
| | CtlName | P |

**Table 5-21** Piechart project form's objects and properties

2. Create a menu for the form as shown in Table 5-22 using the Menu Design window.

| Caption | CtlName |
|---|---|
| &Display-Pie | Display_Pie |
| &Quit | Quit |

**Table 5-22** Piechart project menu

3. Place the following constant declaration for PI in the General section of the form.

```
Const PI = 3.141593
```

4. Put the following code in the Display_Pie_Click event subroutine. This subroutine sets up the descriptions and values that will be graphed. The SLICES constant defines the number of segments to chart. The Desc and Values arrays should be changed to reflect the data you want to plot.

```
Sub Display_Pie_Click ()
Const SLICES = 3
Static Desc(SLICES) As String, Values(SLICES) As Single
   Desc(1) = "Software Sales": Values(1) = 8
   Desc(2) = "Hardware Sales": Values(2) = 15
   Desc(3) = "Service Sales": Values(3) = 33
   Draw_circle SLICES, Values(), Desc()
End Sub
```

5. Enter the code for the Draw_circle subroutine. This code calculates the percentages for each slice and draws the slices. It also appends each slice's percentage to its description for display by the Draw_legend subroutine.

```
Sub Draw_circle (Ndata As Integer, Values() As Single, Desc() As String)
Static Newdesc(10) As String          ' Description with percentages
Dim Total As Single, Startr As Single
Dim N As Integer
```

```
   P.Cls
   P.Refresh
   P.Fillstyle = 0
   Total = 0
   Startr = PI / 2
' Calculate total so we can compute percentage for each pie slice.
' Calculate percentage of slice, add to description.
' Draw each slice starting with center of first slice at the top.
   For N = 1 To Ndata
      Total = Total + Values(N)        ' Need total for whole of pie
   Next N
   For N = 1 To Ndata
      Percentage = Values(N) / Total
      Newdesc(N) = Desc(N) + " " + Format$(100 * Percentage, "##0.0") + ""
      Radians = 2 * PI * Percentage
      If N = 1 Then
         Startr = PI / 2 - Radians / 2
         Endr = PI / 2 + Radians / 2
      Else
         Startr = Endr
         Endr = Startr + Radians
      End If
      P.Fillstyle = 0          ' Solid block
      P.Fillcolor = QBColor(N + 8)
      Startr = Adjust_Radians(Startr)
      Endr = Adjust_Radians(Endr)
'
' Center of Circle is halfway from top, and a little more than one-fifth in.
' This will leave room for the legend on the right. Radius is one-fifth ⇐
' of picture box width.
      P.Circle (P.Scalewidth / 4.5, P.Scaleheight / 2), P.Scalewidth / 5,
, -Startr, -Endr
   Next N
   Display_legend Ndata, Newdesc$()
End Sub
```

6. Enter the code for the Display_legend subroutine. This subroutine draws legend boxes and displays the description for each of the pie segments.

```
Sub Display_legend (Nseries As Integer, Sname() As String)
Dim Theight As Integer, N As Integer
' Draws the legend to the left of the circle, centered with the circle.
' Legends spaced 1.5 times textheight apart.
   P.Fillstyle = 0
   Theight = P.TextHeight(Sname(1))
   Starty = P.Scaleheight / 2 - (Theight * 1.5 * Nseries) / 2
   For N = 1 To Nseries
      P.Fillcolor = QBColor(N + 8)
      P.Line (P.Scalewidth / 2, Starty)-Step(P.Scalewidth / 16, ⇐
Theight),   , B
      P.Currenty = Starty
      P.Currentx = P.Scalewidth / 2 + P.Scalewidth / 14
      P.Print Sname(N)
```

```
      Starty = Starty + Theight * 1.5
   Next N
End Sub
```

7. Enter the code for the Adjust_Radians function. This function converts radians that are less than zero or greater than 2*PI into a range of 0 to 2*PI.

```
Function Adjust_Radians (Radian As Single) As Single
Dim Pi2 As Single

'  Convert values <0 or > 2 * PI back to be between 0 and 2 * PI
'  If radian = 0 then adjust to small value, circle doesn't like zero
'  radians.

   Pi2 = 2 * PI
   If Radian >= Pi2 Then Radian = Radian - Pi2
   If Radian < 0 Then Radian = Radian + Pi2
   If Radian < .001 Then Radian = .001
   Adjust_Radians = Radian
End Function
```

8. Enter the code for the Quick_Click event subroutine. This function allows a user to exit from the application.

```
Sub Quit_Click ()
   End
End Sub
```

### How It Works

Visual Basic is an excellent tool for developing all kinds of business oriented graphs. This project uses the Circle function to draw the multiple slices of a pie chart in a picture box.

The program starts when the user clicks on the Display-Pie menu. The subroutine associated with this event, Display_Pie_Click, sets up the description and values for each of the pie's slices. The SLICES constant defines the total number of slices to be drawn. Calling the Draw_circle subroutine will actually draw the pie chart.

The real work in this program is handled in the Draw_circle subroutine. Its first order of business is to set up some constants. The constant PI (3.14159) is used extensively in this program and is defined in the General section of the form. The Total variable is set to the sum of the individual values, and will be used to compute the percentages of each slice.

The For...Next loop draws each of the pie slices, putting the center of the first slice at the top of the circle. Because the Circle statement expects its parameters in radians, all arithmetic is performed in that unit of measure. There are 2*PI (6.2832) radians in a circle. If you normally think in degrees, zero degrees is equivalent to zero radians, and 360 degrees is equivalent to 2*PI radians. For the Visual Basic Circle statement, zero radians points to the three o'clock position. Increasing radians move counterclockwise around the circle.

The circumference of each slice is its percentage of the total divided into the circumference of the entire circle, 2*PI radians. The starting position of the first pie slice is centered around the top of the circle, which is PI/2 radians. Each successive slice begins where the previous one left off.

The Circle statement's radian parameters must lie in the range of zero to 2*PI. Remember, because radians are points on a circle, -PI/2 radians is equivalent to 3*PI/2 radians. The Adjust_Radians function brings the Startr and Endr parameters into range if needed. When you draw a pie slice with the Circle statement, note that the radians must be expressed as negative numbers. This is a required feature of the Visual Basic Circle statement when filling in parts of a circle. For each pie slice, the Fillcolor is set to a different color using the QBColor function. Values 8 through 15 produce attractive, bright colors.

The Display_Legend subroutine draws the legends starting in the right half of the picture box. Like the Draw_circle subroutine, it too adjusts its positioning parameters based on the actual dimensions of the picture box.

### Comment

The Circle statement accepts single-precision floating-point values for the radian parameters. That is why, all radian-oriented variables have been declared as Single.

Unfortunately, if the resulting pie chart is to be printed on a black-and-white device (such as a laser printer), each slice will print as a solid black. In this case, you might want to include the following code line after the P.FillColor= statement in the Draw_circle and Display_legend subroutines. This will create different types of fill patterns within each pie slice.

```
P.FillStyle = N%
```

---

**5.15    How do I...**

# Build a video-based slide show?

Complexity: Intermediate

### Problem

I would like to create a video-based business presentation. The presentation should have that professional look with different types of transition effects between screens, and variable delays between each slide. The program should be able to open Microsoft .BMP or .WMF metafiles.

### Technique

Visual Basic can load and display the graphical image files created by most Windows text, drawing, and paint programs. Using Visual Basic in conjunction with the Windows API function BitBlt, we can manage the way these images are drawn to create a professional-looking presentation.

### Steps

Open and run SLIDSHOW.MAK. A form like that shown in Figure 5-30 will be displayed. Click on the Add command button to bring up a File Open dialog box. Select a graphic file, either bitmap or metafile, to include in the slide show. There are four metafiles on the destribution disk you can practice with. If you are building this from scratch, you could use the PARTY.BMP or CHESS.BMP bitmaps in your Windows' directory. To change a slide's sequence in the list box, delay, or transition, select one of the entries in the list box and alter the appropriate text box or choose a new transition radio button. The new values are posted to the list box by clicking on the Modify button. To remove an item from the list box, select it and then click on the Remove button.

To start the slide show, click on the Start-Show command button. Each slide will be drawn on a full screen in the same order as displayed in the list box. The Slideshow form will appear again after the current slide is finished being drawn. To stop the show, click the left-hand mouse button at anytime.

To create the Slideshow project, enter the objects and code as detailed in the following steps. There are three forms involved in this project: the Slide Show form that is used for designing and editing the slide sequence, the display form that shows the actual images, and a File Open dialog box from How-To 3.7 Build a simple editor that searches for text.

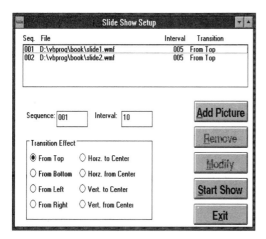

**Figure 5-30** The Slidshow project in action

1. Create a new project called SLID-SHOW.MAK and a form with the objects and properties shown in Table 5-23. The appearance of the form should match the one in Figure 5-30. Note that a picture box control, Picture1, is not visible. You may place it anywhere on the form as long as it does not cover another control. Its size is not important. Save the form as SLIDSHOW.FRM.

| Object | Property | Setting |
| --- | --- | --- |
| Form | FormName | Slideshow |
| | Caption | Slide show setup |
| Label | CtlName | Label1 |
| | AutoSize | True |
| | Caption | Seq ... File ... Interval .. Transition |
| Label | CtlName | Label2 |
| | Caption | Interval |
| | AutoSize | True |
| Label | CtlName | Label3 |
| | Caption | Sequence: |
| | AutoSize | True |
| List box | CtlName | List1 |
| | Sorted | True |
| Text box | CtlName | TxtSeq |
| | Text | 001 |
| Text box | CtlName | TxtInt |
| | Text | 010 |
| Frame | CtlName | Frame1 |
| | Caption | Transition Effect |
| Command button | CtlName | CmdAdd |
| | Caption | &Add Picture |
| | FontSize | 14 |
| Command button | CtlName | CmdRemove |
| | Caption | &Remove |
| | FontSize | 14 |
| Command button | CtlName | CmdModify |
| | Caption | &Modify |
| | FontSize | 14 |
| Command button | CtlName | CmdStart |
| | Caption | &Start-Show |
| | FontSize | 14 |
| Command button | CtlName | CmdExit |
| | Caption | E&xit |
| | FontSize | 14 |
| Picture box | CtlName | Picture1 |
| | Visible | False |

**Table 5-23** SlideShow project form's objects and properties

2. Place the option buttons as shown in Table 5-24 inside Frame1. This is done by selecting Frame1 on the form, choosing the option button control from the toolbox, and then drawing the option buttons inside the Frame1. The option buttons are drawn correctly if they move as a group with their surrounding frame.

| Object | Property | Setting |
|---|---|---|
| Option button | CtlName | Option1 |
| | Caption | From Top |
| | Index | 0 |
| Option button | CtlName | Option1 |
| | Caption | From Bottom |
| | Index | 1 |
| Option button | CtlName | Option1 |
| | Caption | From Left |
| | Index | 2 |
| Option button | CtlName | Option1 |
| | Caption | From Right |
| | Index | 3 |
| Option button | CtlName | Option1 |
| | Caption | Horz to Center |
| | Index | 4 |
| Option button | CtlName | Option1 |
| | Caption | Horz from Center |
| | Index | 5 |
| Option button | CtlName | Option1 |
| | Caption | Vert to Center |
| | Index | 6 |
| Option button | CtlName | Option1 |
| | Caption | Vert from Center |
| | Index | 7 |

**Table 5-24** Filefind transition option button controls

3. Select the Global module, enter the following code, and save it as SLIDSHOW.BAS. This defines the API functions and constants as well as Visual Basic variables that are shared between the forms in this project.

```
'
'   API Declarations.
```

```
'
Declare Sub BitBlt Lib "GDI" (ByVal hDestDC As Integer, ByVal X As ⇐
Integer, ByVal Y As Integer, ByVal nWidth As Integer, ByVal nHeight As ⇐
Integer, ByVal hSrcDC As Integer, ByVal XSrc As Integer, ByVal YSrc As ⇐
Integer, ByVal dwRop As Long)
Declare Function SendMessage Lib "User" (ByVal hWnd As Integer, ByVal ⇐
wMsg As Integer, ByVal wParam As Integer, lParam As Any) As Long
Declare Function GetFocus Lib "User" () As Integer
Global Const WM_USER = &H400
Global Const LB_SETTABSTOPS = (WM_USER + 19)
Global Const SRCCOPY = &HCC0020 ' (DWORD) dest = source
'
' Visual Basic Declarations.
'
Global TransDesc(7) As String
Global TB As String
Global Const TRUE = -1
Global Const FALSE = 0
```

4. Enter the following code into the Form_Load event subroutine. This code sets up the global values used by the forms.

```
Sub Form_Load ()
'
' Load constant strings at startup.
   CmdStart.Enable = FALSE
   TB = Chr$(9)
   TransDesc(0) = "From Top"
   TransDesc(1) = "From Bottom"
   TransDesc(2) = "From Left"
   TransDesc(3) = "From Right"
   TransDesc(4) = "Hz to Center"
   TransDesc(5) = "Hz from Center"
   TransDesc(6) = "Vt to Center"
   TransDesc(7) = "Vt from Center"
End Sub
```

5. Enter the following code into the Form_Paint event subroutine. This routine sets up the tab stops in the list box.

```
Sub Form_Paint ()
ReDim ListTabs(3) As Integer
Dim Retval As Long, List1hWnd As Integer
'
' Set tab stops in the list box.
' Disable command buttons that can't be used at this time.
'
   ListTabs(1) = 20
   ListTabs(2) = 180
   ListTabs(3) = 200
   List1.SetFocus
   List1hWnd = GetFocus()
   Retval = SendMessage(List1hWnd, LB_SETTABSTOPS, 3, ListTabs(1))
   CmdRemove.Enabled = FALSE
```

```
    CmdModify.Enabled = FALSE
End Sub
```

6. Enter the following code into the CmdAdd_Click event subroutine. This subroutine calls the Open_dlg form to let the user select a file to include in the slide show. The file is checked to ensure that Visual Basic can read it as a picture file.

```
Sub CmdAdd_Click ()
'
'  Add a new filename to the ListBox using the Dialog box.
'  If LoadPicture() gives error, then file isn't an icon, metafile, or bitmap.
'  Default to 10 seconds and Vertical from Center transition.
'
    Open_dlg.Show 1
    If Open_dlg.Tag = "" Then Exit Sub
    On Error Resume Next
    Picture1.Picture = LoadPicture(Open_dlg.Tag)
    If Err Then
       MsgBox "Selected File is not a Picture", 48
       Exit Sub
    End If
    TxtSeq.Text = Format$(List1.ListCount * 10 + 10, "000")
    List1.AddItem TxtSeq.Text + TB + Open_dlg.Tag + TB + TxtInt.Text + ⇐
      TB + TransDesc(7)
 CmdStart.Enable = TRUE
' Disable the Remove and Modify CommandButtons until user selects new entry.
'
    CmdRemove.Enabled = FALSE
    CmdModify.Enabled = FALSE
End Sub
```

7. Enter the following code into the List1_Click event subroutine. This handles the processing when the user selects an item in the list box.

```
Sub List1_Click ()
'
'  User has selected an entry to remove or modify.
'  Enable Command Buttons.
'  Parse the current entry into components and load controls.
'  Notice how we set the correct OptionButton.
'
    CmdRemove.Enabled = TRUE
    CmdModify.Enabled = TRUE
    Slide$ = List1.List(List1.ListIndex)
    Firsttab = InStr(Slide$, TB)
    Secondtab = InStr(Firsttab + 1, Slide$, TB)
    Thirdtab = InStr(Secondtab + 1, Slide$, TB)

    TxtSeq.Text = Left$(Slide$, Firsttab - 1)
    TxtInt.Text = Mid$(Slide$, Secondtab + 1, Thirdtab - Secondtab - 1)

    For I = 0 To 7
```

```
      If Mid$(Slide$, Thirdtab + 1) = TransDesc(I) Then
         Option1(I).Value = TRUE
      End If
   Next I
End Sub
```

8. Enter the following code into the CmdModify_Click event subroutine. This routine updates the currently selected slide with the values from the text box and option button controls.

```
Sub CmdModify_Click ()
'
'  Re-write current value of controls back to list box.
'  If nothing selected then exit the subroutine.
'
   If List1.ListIndex < 0 Then Exit Sub
   Slide$ = List1.List(List1.ListIndex)
   FirstTab = InStr(Slide$, TB)
   Secondtab = InStr(FirstTab + 1, Slide$, TB)
   Thirdtab = InStr(Secondtab + 1, Slide$, TB)
   File$ = Mid$(Slide$, FirstTab, Secondtab - FirstTab + 1)
   List1.RemoveItem List1.ListIndex
   For I = 0 To 7
      If Option1(I).Value Then
         Desc$ = TransDesc(I)
      End If
   Next I
'
'  Reformat sequence number.
'  Rebuild the slide record.
'
   TxtSeq.Text = Format$(Val(TxtSeq.Text), "000")
   Slide$ = TxtSeq.Text + File$ + TxtInt.Text + TB + Desc$
'
'  Add item back to Listbox.
'  Calculate new sequence numbers.
'  Disable Remove and Modify controls.
'
   List1.AddItem Slide$
   ReorderList
   CmdRemove.Enabled = FALSE
   CmdModify.Enabled = FALSE
End Sub
```

9. Enter the following code into the CmdRemove_Click event subroutine. This routine deletes the currently selected line from the list box.

```
Sub CmdRemove_Click ()
'
'  Delete selected item from List box.
'
```

```
    If List1.ListIndex >= 0 Then
       List1.RemoveItem List1.ListIndex
       CmdRemove.Enabled = FALSE
       CmdModify.Enabled = FALSE
       ReorderList
    End If
End Sub
```

10. Enter the following code into the CmdStart_Click event subroutine. This routine starts the slide show.

```
Sub CmdStart_Click ()
'
'  Show other form for show. Use Modal option.
'
    Slidescreen.Show 1
End Sub
```

11. Enter the following code into the CmdExit_Click event subroutine. This code allow the users a graceful way to exit the application.

```
Sub CmdExit_Click ()
    End
End Sub
```

12. Put the following code in the ReorderList subroutine located in the General section of the form. It will update the list box with new sequence numbers.

```
Sub ReorderList ()
Dim I As Integer, FirstTab As Integer
'
' Change the sequence numbers in the List box.
' Increment each line by 10.
'
    For I = 0 To List1.ListCount - 1
       Slide$ = List1.List(I)
       FirstTab = InStr(1, Slide$, TB)
       OldSequence$ = Left$(Slide$, FirstTab - 1)
       NewSequence$ = Format$(I * 10 + 10, "000")
       If OldSequence$ <> NewSequence$ Then
          List1.RemoveItem I
          Slide$ = NewSequence$ + Mid$(Slide$, FirstTab)
          List1.AddItem Slide$, I ' Specify index to not reorder list.
       End If
    Next I
If List1.ListCount = 0 then CmdStart.Enable = FALSE
End Sub
```

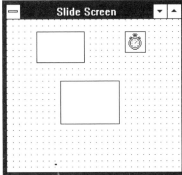

**Figure 5-31** Slidescr form

13. Open a second form for this project, using the New Form option from the File menu. This form is used to display the video graphics. Enter the objects and properties for this form as listed in Table 5-25 and save the form as SLIDESCR.FRM. The layout of the controls is shown in Figure 5-31, however, their size and placement are not important.

| Object | Property | Setting |
|---|---|---|
| Form | FormName | Slidescreen |
| | BorderStyle | 0 - None |
| Picture box | CtlName | P1 |
| Picture box | CtlName | P2 |
| Timer | CtlName | Timer1 |

**Table 5-25** Slidescr project form's objects and properties

14. The following code in the Declarations section of the Slidscrn form defines the shared variables.

```
Dim SlideCounter As Integer
Dim Transition As String
```

15. Enter the following code into the Form_Load event subroutine of the Slidescr form. This code expands the form and picture boxes to cover the entire screen.

```
Sub Form_Load ()
'
'  Resize form to fill entire screen.
'  Set background to black.
'
    SlideScreen.Top = 0
    SlideScreen.Left = 0
    SlideScreen.Width = Screen.Width
    SlideScreen.Height = Screen.Height
    SlideScreen.BackColor = &H0
'
'  Set PictureBoxes to fill entire screen.
'  P1 is setup box, P2 is display box.
'  P1 is invisible but has a bitmap.
'  P2 is visible but has no bitmap.
```

```
'  Set PictureBox scales to 3 - Pixels.
'
   P1.Visible = FALSE
   P1.AutoRedraw = TRUE
   P1.Top = 0
   P1.Left = 0
   P1.Width = SlideScreen.ScaleWidth
   P1.Height = SlideScreen.ScaleHeight
   P1.ScaleMode = 3
   P1.BackColor = &H0              ' Black

   P2.Top = 0
   P2.Left = 0
   P2.Width = SlideScreen.ScaleWidth
   P2.Height = SlideScreen.ScaleHeight
   P2.ScaleMode = 3
   P2.BackColor = &H0              ' Black
'
' Disable Timer and set SlideCounter.
'
   Timer1.Enabled = FALSE
   SlideCounter = 0
End Sub
```

16. Enter the following code into the Form_Paint event subroutine of the Slidescr form. This code starts the slide show.

```
Sub Form_Paint ()
'
'  Always start at first slide.
'  Timer1_Timer event does the transition. No delay to first slide.
'
   SlideCounter = -1
   Timer1_Timer
End Sub
```

17. Enter the following code into the Timer1_Timer event subroutine of the Slidescr form. This subroutine extracts the next slide name from the list, retrieves the picture, and calls the CopyPicture subroutine to display the slide.

```
Sub Timer1_Timer ()
'
'  Disable Timer so we aren't interrupted.
'  Retrieve next slide from list. Wrap to beginning at end.
'
   Timer1.Enabled = FALSE
   SlideCounter = SlideCounter + 1
   If SlideCounter >= Slideshow.List1.ListCount Then
      SlideCounter = 0
   End If
   Slide$ = Slideshow.List1.List(SlideCounter)
'
'  Parse List into Filename$, Interval, and Transition fields.
```

```
' Load P1 (invisible one) with picture.
'
    Tab1 = InStr(Slide$, TB) + 1
    tab2 = InStr(Tab1, Slide$, TB) + 1
    Tab3 = InStr(tab2, Slide$, TB) + 1
    Filename$ = Mid$(Slide$, Tab1, tab2 - Tab1 - 1)
    Timer1.Interval = Val(Mid$(Slide$, tab2, Tab3 - tab2)) * 1000
    Transition = Mid$(Slide$, Tab3)
    P1.Picture = LoadPicture(Filename$)
'
' Copy the picture from P1 to P2 using transitions.
' Enable Timer for next picture.
'
    CopyPicture
    Timer1.Enabled = TRUE
End Sub
```

18. Put the following code in the CopyPicture subroutine located in the General section of the form. It will copy the new slide to the screen using the desired transition.

```
Sub CopyPicture ()
Dim Pixels As Integer, Row As Integer, Column As Integer, J As Integer
'
' Subroutine to copy from invisible PictureBox (P1) to visible one (P2).
' All routines use BitBlt to copy a line or row at a time.
' Because Windows copies rows faster than vertical lines, Pixels are
' doubled for vertical transitions.
'
    Pixels = 2
    Select Case Transition
      Case TransDesc(0):              ' From Top
        For Row = 0 To P2.ScaleHeight Step Pixels
           BitBlt P2.hDC, 0, Row, P2.ScaleWidth, Pixels, P1.hDC, 0, Row, SRCCOPY
        Next Row

      Case TransDesc(1):              ' From Bottom
        For Row = P2.ScaleHeight To 0 Step -Pixels
           BitBlt P2.hDC, 0, Row, P2.ScaleWidth, Pixels, P1.hDC, 0, Row, SRCCOPY
        Next Row

      Case TransDesc(2):              ' From Left
        Pixels = 2 * Pixels
        For Column = 0 To P2.ScaleWidth Step Pixels
           BitBlt P2.hDC, Column, 0, Pixels, P2.ScaleHeight, P1.hDC, ⇐
                Column, 0, SRCCOPY
        Next Column

      Case TransDesc(3):              ' From Right
        Pixels = 2 * Pixels
        For Column = P2.ScaleWidth To 0 Step -Pixels
           BitBlt P2.hDC, Column, 0, Pixels, P2.ScaleHeight, P1.hDC, ⇐
             Column, 0, SRCCOPY
```

```
      Next Column

    Case TransDesc(4):            ' Horizontal to Center
      Pixels = 2 * Pixels
      For Column = 0 To (P2.ScaleWidth + Pixels) / 2 Step Pixels
        J = P2.ScaleWidth - Column
        BitBlt P2.hDC, Column, 0, Pixels, P2.ScaleHeight, P1.hDC, ⇐
            Column, 0, SRCCOPY
        BitBlt P2.hDC, J, 0, Pixels, P2.ScaleHeight, P1.hDC, J, 0, SRCCOPY
      Next Column

    Case TransDesc(5):            ' Horizontal from Center
      Pixels = 2 * Pixels
      For Column = P2.ScaleWidth / 2 To 0 Step -Pixels
        J = P2.ScaleWidth - Column
        BitBlt P2.hDC, Column, 0, Pixels, P2.ScaleHeight, P1.hDC, ⇐
            Column, 0, SRCCOPY
        BitBlt P2.hDC, J, 0, Pixels, P2.ScaleHeight, P1.hDC, J, 0, SRCCOPY
      Next Column

    Case TransDesc(6):            ' Vertical to Center
      For Row = 0 To (P2.ScaleHeight + Pixels) / 2 Step Pixels
        J = P2.ScaleHeight - Row
        BitBlt P2.hDC, 0, Row, P2.ScaleWidth, Pixels, P1.hDC, 0, Row, SRCCOPY
        BitBlt P2.hDC, 0, J, P2.ScaleWidth, Pixels, P1.hDC, 0, J, SRCCOPY
      Next Row

    Case TransDesc(7):            ' Vertical from Center
      For Row = P2.ScaleHeight / 2 To 0 Step -Pixels
        J = P2.ScaleHeight - Row
        BitBlt P2.hDC, 0, Row, P2.ScaleWidth, Pixels, P1.hDC, 0, Row, SRCCOPY
        BitBlt P2.hDC, 0, J, P2.ScaleWidth, Pixels, P1.hDC, 0, J, SRCCOPY
      Next Row
    End Select

End Sub
```

19. Enter the following code into the P2_Click event subroutine of the Slidescr form. This subroutine allows the user to stop the slide show by clicking the mouse.

```
Sub P2_Click ()
'
' Use clicks anywhere on screen to stop the show.
'
   Unload SlideScreen
End Sub
```

20. Add the OPEN_DLG.FRM file from the SLIDSHOW directory. This form is a general-purpose File Open dialog box. Specifications of this form's object, properties, and code are detailed in steps 10 through 17 of How-To 3.7 Build a simple editor that searches for text.

## How It Works

Visual Basic has some exceptional capabilities which enable your application to load and display graphics from bitmap files and Windows metafiles. These graphical files can be created by many Windows applications or even by Visual Basic itself using its SavePicture function. This project enables the user to build a video-based slide show by setting up a list of these graphical files, along with the length of time to display each file, and the transition effect to use between slides. Included in the Visual Basic directory SLIDE-SHOW are four graphics files, SLIDE1.WMF through SLIDE4.WMF, which can be used with this project.

### Start with the Slideshow Form

When the application starts, the Slideshow Form_Load event subroutine loads the global constants. The Form_Paint event subroutine sets the tab stops in the list box and disables the Remove and Modify command button controls.

When the user clicks the Add button, the CmdAdd_Click event subroutine transfers control to a File Open dialog box. This lets the user select an image file to include in the slide show. An attempt is made to load the selected file into the picture box, Picture1. If an error is not received during the LoadPicture function, the file is considered a valid graphic and it, along with the default interval and transition, is added as a single entry to the list box. Because Picture1 is not visible, this processing takes place without the user noticing it.

To change the sequence number, interval, or transition effect, the user selects one of the items in the list box. The List1_Click event subroutine traps this event and loads the values from the selected item into the text boxes and appropriate radio button. The Remove and Modify controls are then enabled, indicating that the selected item may be deleted or modified. If the Modify button is clicked, the CmdModify_Click event subroutine updates the current list box item with the new values from the controls. When the list is modified or an item removed, the ReorderList subroutine is called to create a new set of sequence numbers for the list.

### Transferring Control to the Display Form

The slide show is started by clicking on the Start button, which transfers control to the Slidescr form. The form is started with the Modal option so that it keeps control until the show is terminated by the user.

There are two picture boxes on the Slidescr form: P1 and P2. Both of these picture boxes and the form itself are expanded in the Form_Load event to fill the entire screen. Note that P1 is made invisible but has its AutoRedraw property enabled. With AutoRedraw turned on, pictures loaded into P1 are stored by Windows in memory even if they aren't displayed on screen.

The Form_Paint event sets the SlideCounter variable and calls the Timer1_Timer event subroutine to display the next slide. The Timer1_Timer event subroutine retrieves the next slide description from the SlideShow form list box. The data is parsed into the Filename, Interval, and Transition fields. The nonvisible picture box, P1, is loaded with the image from the file, and CopyPicture is called to transfer the image from the nonvisible picture box to P2, the visible picture box.

The CopyPicture subroutine moves the image from picture box P1 to P2 using the BitBlt Windows API function. BitBlt is used to copy rectangular areas from one device context to another. Because P1's AutoRedraw is enabled, the device context handle returned by Visual Basic, P1.hDC, points to the in memory copy of the picture. Each transition effect has its own For…Next Loop and BitBlt call. The parameters for BitBlt are shown in Table 5-26.

| Parameter | Description |
|-----------|-------------|
| hDestDC | Device context of the destination |
| nX | Upper left corner of destination rectangle. Value in pixels |
| nY | Top of the destination rectangle. Value in pixels |
| nWidth | Width of the rectangle to be copied, in pixels |
| nHeight | Height of the rectangle to be copied, in pixels |
| hSrcDC | Device context of the source |
| nXSrc | Upper left corner of source rectangle. Value in pixels |
| nYSrc | Top of the source rectangle. Value in pixels |
| dwRop | Operation to perform. SRCCOPY is the operation code used to perform a pixel-for-pixel copy from the source to the destination device context |

**Table 5-26** The BitBlt API parameters

### Comment

In the CopyPicture subroutine, each of the different transition effects loops by row or column, copying pixels in picture box P1 to the same location in P2. The Pixels variable determines the copying speed by varying the width of the rectangle being copied. The value of Pixels is doubled when the subroutine is transferring by column, because Windows performs copies by column slower than it does by row. The doubling keeps the copy speed approximately the same for all the different transitions. You may want to experiment with different values for this variable.

# 6

# ENVIRONMENT AND SYSTEM

# 6

This chapter presents techniques for communicating with DOS, running DOS programs from Visual Basic, and determining the state of various aspects of the Windows environment. You'll learn how to use many APIs for finding the amount of available memory, the version of Windows running on your machine, the names of directories, the type of keyboard your user has, and much more. Many important APIs are covered here, including the WinExec function that lets you shell to DOS but doesn't give error messages if the program can't be found. There are also APIs for determining the class name of a application, as well as a great project that simulates the Windows SDK SPY program that gives important information on all application running under Windows.

## Windows APIs Covered

| | | |
|---|---|---|
| CreatePen | GetModuleFilename | GetWindowText |
| DeleteObject | GetModuleHandle | IsWindow |
| ExitWindows | GetModuleUsage | Rectangle |
| FindWindow | GetNumTasks | ReleaseCapture |
| GDIHeapInfo | GetParent | ReleaseDC |
| GetActiveWindow | GetStockObject | SelectObject |
| GetClassName | GetSystemDirectory | SetActiveWindow |
| GetClassWord | GetVersion | SetCapture |
| GetFreeSpace | GetWindowDC | SetROP2 |
| GetHeapSpaces | GetWindowRect | UserHeapInfo |
| GetKeyboardType | GetWindowsDirectory | WindowFromPoint |
| GetMessagePos | GetWinFlags | WinExec |

**6.1**   **Run a DOS program and find out when it's done**

One of the most popular uses of Visual Basic is to create interfaces for DOS applications, especially those DOS programs that are crude and expect parameters to be entered on the command line. One of the hurdles that comes up with this approach is communications between your DOS program and the Visual Basic program running under Windows. How do you know, for example, if the DOS program has finished executing some task? This How-To shows a simple way to find the answer to this question using the GetNumTasks API function.

**6.2**   **Use a more sophisticated method to monitor a DOS program**

While the previous How-To showed that monitoring a DOS process for completion is simple, there are some dangers to using the IsWindow API. This How-To illustrates a technique that will guarantee that your Visual Basic application will accurately detect when the DOS process is finished regardless of the number of running applications. Furthermore you will learn how to communicate command line parameters to a DOS process and learn a little about ray tracing along the way. The GetActiveWindow and IsWindow APIs are used.

**6.3    Exit Windows and return to DOS**

Suppose you want to allow your Visual Basic application to shut down Windows completely, say because you detect the presence of a virus or you just like the idea of an emergency shut down. This How-To shows off the ExitWindows API to immediately leave Windows and enter DOS.

**6.4    Prevent Windows from shutting down**

When exiting from Windows, many running applications will first ask you if you wish to save your work before Windows quits. Unfortunately, Visual Basic applications do not automatically ask if you want to save and your user will lose all their work if Windows is shut down. This How-To shows a simple way around that. You can use this method with the previous How-To for a safe, emergency shutdown technique.

**6.5    Search an entire disk for a file**

Here is an amazingly useful project that will search the entire hard disk for any file or files specified with a search mask. It builds on the capability of the standard Visual Basic directory list box. As the project searches the file system it automatically adds the files that match the entered specification to a scrolling text box as well as the directories that they are found in. This is a pure Visual Basic project.

**6.6    Use the Shell function without causing run-time errors**

Visual Basic's Shell function allows you to run a DOS program. But if the DOS program is not in the directory you expect it to be you'll get an error message. Then you have to build On Error code into your program to deal with this or else a message will pop up File Not Found and stop your application. Many times you want to shell and not have to write all that code to check for errors. This How-To uses a neat API called WinExec that will not give an error if the DOS application can't be found.

**6.7    Run a DOS internal command**

Unfortunately the Visual Basic Shell function will not run a built-in DOS command like DIR or TYPE. This How-To presents a trick that lets you directly manipulate the DOS command processor and send it specific parameters that let it run a DOS command. The Environ$ function is used for this purpose along with the COMSPEC setting so this How-To will teach you a lot about DOS.

**6.8    Prevent multiple program instances from being loaded**

While Windows allows multiple copies of a single application to be run, there are many cases when you would not want a second copy of your application to be started. For example if you're doing telecommunications, a second copy of your application could cause the first to disconnect from the serial port. This How-To shows a safe method that uses the GetModule-Handle and GetModuleUsage APIs to prevent more than one copy of a Visual Basic program to be run.

**6.9    Find other running applications**

Often you will want to be able to locate other Windows applications and manipulate them from Visual Basic, perhaps via the SendKeys statement. Normally you will enable these applications with the AppActivate statement. However AppActivate relies on the title in the title bar of your window to find its target. Since users can modify this title with a .PIF file your program could lose the target application. This How-To shows how to use the FindWindow and WndPeek APIs to determine the location of a Windows application using the Windows "classname" rather than its title. This is a much more reliable way of activating applications since a program's classname can't be altered.

**6.10    Determine how many function keys are on my user's keyboard**

A popular way to make your application slick is to enable the function keys on the keyboard to access different features, for instance, F1 enables Help, F9 captures the screen to a disk file, and so on. Unfortunately there are several types of keyboards on the market and the number of keys function keys can vary from ten to twelve. There are other differences between keyboards, and some may or may not include the numeric keypad, the Home key, Page Up and Page Down and so on. This How-To shows how easy it is for your Visual Basic program to determine just what kind of keyboard is installed in your user's computer. It uses the GetKeyboardType API.

**6.11    Determine the directory where Windows is installed**

Suppose you are writing an installation routine for your great Visual Basic application. You need to make sure the user has VBRUN100.DLL installed on their hard disk for your Visual Basic application to run, and that the DLL is installed in their Windows directory. How do you find out the name of the Windows directory and the hard disk drive name? This How-To shows how to do that using the GetWindowsDirectory and GetSystem-Directory APIs.

**6.12    Determine how much memory is available**

Often you will want to know how much total RAM memory is available in the user's computer system. This How-To uses the GetFreeSpace API to answer that question and produces an icon that sits on your desktop monitoring memory usage.

**6.13    Determine system resources**

Windows shows a figure called the Free System Resources in the About... dialog box. This figure reflects how much memory is available for storing objects such as controls and windows in Visual Basic. If the amount of space allocated for these system resources falls below a certain point, Visual Basic will be unable to load in more controls. This How-To reveals how to determine the amount of available to your application via the GetHeapSpaces API.

**6.14    Determine which version of Windows my application is running on**

Microsoft is constantly improving and adding features to Windows. In many cases there are features in newer Windows versions that you would want to access in your Visual Basic programs, yet you don't want to make your application depend on a certain version. The way to handle this is to make your program recognize the version of Windows that is running. Then you can enable or disable features in your program accordingly. This How-To shows how to do that using the GetVersion API.

**6.15    Find everything about the system configuration**

In the previous How-Tos you saw how to determine the type of keyboard, where the Windows directory is stored, and what version of Windows is running. This How-To creates a single project that summarizes all these functions and provides information on whether a 286 or 386 processor is installed, whether enhanced or standard mode is being run, and whether a math chip is installed in the user's system.

**6.16    Simulate SPY in Visual Basic**

SPY is a very useful utility that ships with the Windows Software Development kit. It is used to trace messages sent to controls and windows so you can debug your program. Most importantly SPY helps you find the class and parent of a window as well as track mouse messages within your form. This How-To builds a program similar to SPY called WndPeek that gives much of the same information. It also highlights windows as the mouse passes over them. Besides being educational, the WndPeek project will help you gauge if you are using too many controls in your application. WinPeek uses the largest number of API calls in this book and is an example of how a Visual Basic program can deftly manipulate Windows as well as any program written in C.

# Run a DOS program and find out when it's done?

Complexity: Easy

### Problem
Visual Basic is supposed to allow me to wrap a beautiful GUI around a DOS interface. Suppose I have a DOS utility that I have to run occasionally from Windows. I don't want to force users to deal with a Shell to DOS and have to use the command line. What I would like them to be able to do is click on a button and have the DOS utility fire up and do its thing. Also, on the same subject, once I run the DOS process, how do I let my Visual Basic application know that the DOS process is done, in other words how do I communicate between the programs?

### Technique
Being able to wrap a shell round a DOS utility or complex application is a great use for Visual Basic. But there are a number of issues to contend with when communicating between DOS and Windows via Visual Basic. Let's make an example that illustrates some of the caveats.

First, we make a batch file called SHELL.BAT that contains the commands:

```
DIR | SORT /+16 > DIR.TXT
```

This command says do a DIRectory listing on the current drive, then "pipe" the output of the listing into the SORT filter. Results are sorted using the letter in the 16th column, then the output redirected into the file DIR.TXT. The 16th column is the file size column, so this means the files will be sorted by size in the text box.

Next, Shell to this batch file from Visual Basic and run the program as an icon in its minimized state. Then, open the file DIR.TXT from Visual Basic and read its lines into a list box. To the unsuspecting user it appears that Visual Basic did all the work!

However, there is a problem. If we immediately open the file after doing the Shell, the file is empty. This happens because when Visual Basic returns

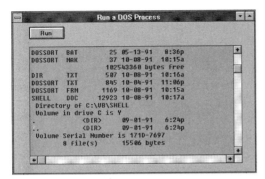

**Figure 6-1** The VB interface for testing the DOS Sort batch file puts the results of the DOS sort into the listing box.

from running the DOS process with Shell, it blindly moves on and executes the next line of code *before* the DOS process is done. We need some way to tell Visual Basic to wait until the DOS process is done (the Shell doesn't offer this—it only tells us if the shell was successful). One simple solution is a Windows API called GetNumTasks. Its use relies on one constraint: that you never begin a second task under Windows until the DOS process run from Visual Basic finishes. That is not really an unrealistic constraint for most users. We'll show you a way around this later.

### Steps

Open and run SHELL.MAK. It should look like Figure 6-1 after it's run, assuming all files are in the proper directories.

1. Create a new project called SHELL.MAK. and a form called SHELL.FRM. Give the form the dimensions of about 4 inches wide and 3 inches tall as shown in Figure 6-1 and save it .

2. Add the objects and properties shown in Table 6-1 to this form. If a property is not listed, its effect is not important and the default is assumed.

| Object | Property | Setting |
| --- | --- | --- |
| Form | FormName | Run_DOS |
| | Caption | Run a DOS Process |
| | BackColor | &H00C0C0C0& (50% gray) |
| | Filename | SHELL.FRM |
| Timer | CtlName | Timer1 |
| | Enabled | False |
| | Interval | 1000 |
| Command button | CtlName | Cmd_Run |
| | Caption | Run |
| List box | CtlName | Text1 |
| | ScrollBars | 3 - Both |

**Table 6-1** Shell project form's objects and properties

3. Now make a .PIF file with the Windows PIF editor. This is important if you expect the Shell styles feature to work. We will specify that the DOS process is minimized and with focus.

The .PIF file filename should be the same as the batch file, with the .PIF extension: SHELL.PIF. The name of the window for the program should be DOS Sort Batch and the startup directory should be set to where the file is located in your system; for instance, C:\VB\SHELL. The Display Usage button should be set to Windowed and Execution set to Background. If you leave this .PIF out, the running DOS batch process will take over the whole screen.

4. Put the following code in the Declarations section of the general object.

```
Declare Function GetNumTasks Lib "kernel" () As Integer
Dim NumTasks%
```

5. Put this code in the Cmd_Click procedure of the form:

```
Sub Cmd_Run_Click ()
   NumTasks% = GetNumTasks()        'Checks num of tasks running now
   Text1.Text = ""
   ChDir ("c:\vb\shell")
   x% = Shell("shell.bat", 2)
   Timer1.Enabled = -1              'Timer monitors running tasks
End Sub
```

6. Put this code in the Timer1_Timer procedure of Timer1:

```
Sub Timer1_Timer ()
   If GetNumTasks%() <> NumTasks% Then
      Exit Sub
   Else
   ' Slow DOS is finished and we can open the file.
      Open "DIR.TXT" For Input As #1
      Do Until EOF(1)
         Line Input #1, oneLine$
         Text1.SelText = Text1.SelText + oneLine$ + Chr$(13) + Chr$(10)
      Loop
      Close #1
      Timer1.Enabled = 0            ' Disable timer
   End If
End Sub
```

## How It Works

The Declare statement sets up the GetNumTasks API and it defines an integer variable called NumTasks that will be global to the form.

Examine the procedure in the single button called Cmd_Run_Click. When the button is clicked, this procedure executes the GetNumTasks API, which returns an integer number that represents the number of tasks running at this moment. Next it clears out any text in the list box and switches to the directory containing our batch file.

Next the Shell command runs the SHELL.BAT file with the window style of 2, which means minimized and focused. This could be a style of 7 also, which is minimized and unfocused; both 2 and 7 work. Finally, the timer is enabled so it starts operating. At this point the DOS process will make a little icon appear on your desktop with the title given by the .PIF file you made. If you would rather your users didn't see this icon you can extend the form so it's larger than the icon, and make the style 7 (unfocused) in the Shell command, so it doesn't pop up on top of the window covering it.

Now examine the code in the Timer1_Timer procedure. This procedure is run every 1000 milliseconds, or 1 second, as set by the value in the timer duration property. The first statement is an If…Then loop that simply examines the current number of tasks with the value stored when we did the Shell. If the number is the same, we can assume that the task is still operating, exit from the subroutine, and do nothing. However, if the task is finished, GetNumTasks will return a lower number than is stored, and the loop will fall through to the next statement. The code that follows is a loop that simply opens the file DIR.TXT for input and reads each line into a variable called oneLine$. The SelText property gives you the current text in the box, so the long statement:

```
Text1.SelText = Text1.SelText + oneLine$ + Chr$(13) + Chr$(10)
```

simply appends a single line to the end of the text block and attaches a carriage return and linefeed character to it.

Next we close the file and disable the timer so it doesn't keep checking and we are done!


## Comment

There is a small danger that if the DOS process was a long slow one, your user could go off and start a new program. The SHELL batch file would end, and our program would enter the Timer1 loop looking for the processes to be the same as when we first started the DOS process. But this won't occur until we quit the new application, so for all that time the Visual Basic program would be hung up.

# Use a more sophisticated method to monitor a DOS program?

Complexity: Easy

**Problem**

In How-To 6.1 Run a DOS program and find out when it's done, you mention that there could be a problem if another task starts up while the DOS process task is running under Windows. I'd like to know a safer and more sophisticated way to run a process and avoid this hangup. And while we're on the subject of controlling DOS processes, can you give me some tips on running and using Windows and DOS programs in concert? I am particularly interested in making it look like an application is a real Windows application, not a DOS application being run from a shell.

**Technique**

There is a better, safer way to know that DOS has finished a process. There are two APIs that can be used: GetActiveWindow and IsWindow. GetActiveWindow returns a handle to the currently active window, the one with the focus. IsWindow returns True if the window exists and False if it no longer exists. Thus, if we use the handle returned by GetActiveWindow for our active DOS process, we can use IsWindow in a loop to check on whether the window is still open. When it is no longer open, the process must have ended, and we can do our next step in Visual Basic, accessing the results from DOS. The DoEvents statement is placed inside the loop that uses IsWindow, so that processing time is given back to Windows. Without DoEvents other processes would not get priority.

We needed a simple interface to control a ray-tracing DOS program called Persistence of Vision Ray Tracer, or just PV. This has all the features of most DOS programs: it is powerful and has an awful interface.

**A Bit About Ray Tracing**

A little bit about PV will help you see what we are doing. PV is a ray-tracing program—you feed it a text file that contains a description of a world of objects, spheres, planes, cylinders, light sources, and so on, specified with a simple descriptive language. Objects have locations in a three-dimensional space, have colors and textures, and so on. PV takes light coming from specified light sources and traces how each ray of it would bounce off and pass through the objects in the world. You set up a camera location that represents where your eye is located in a coordinate system of floating point numbers called the universe.

PV makes a 24-bit color Targa (.TGA) file of the image. You can convert this image to a beautiful 256 color .GIF or .PCX file with a shareware program such as PicLab, you can view the GIF or PCX with PicLab or any popular file viewer. Ray tracing, or rendering, is one of the more important requirements in making photo realistic scenes and is employed by animation houses that make logos, multimedia presentations, engineering studies, and so on. There is great interest in this subject today, because any 386 machine and a good VGA can perform ray tracing that rivals the computers of Lucas Films, the people that made the movie Star Wars.

We won't explain the details of PV and its descriptive language (you can find out more about PV in *Image Lab*, Tim Wegner, Waite Group Press, 1992). Our goal here is to show you how to run PV from a Visual Basic interface, so that you can extend the idea to any DOS program you like.

PV, as it exists at the time of this writing, has only a command line interface. You enter the name of the data file you wish to trace, followed by parameters for the ray tracing, such as resolution, antialiasing, and the name of the description file. You have to create the description file with any editor.

All this works well if you are willing to do a little typing and have a good memory, however, the ideal interface for PV would enable you to open any of the description language text files, edit them on screen, set the resolution of the ray tracing, save the file, and tell the ray tracer to run.

In our example we'll make sure the DOS process runs in a window by setting up a .PIF file, and we'll use the two APIs to monitor when the process has finished. A batch file for PV will also be used that not only runs PV, but also sends the 24-bit Targa output from PV into PicLab and converts it into a 234-color .GIF file that is suitable for viewing under any GIF viewer. Using 234 colors in the map instead of the full 256 means Windows can use the remaining colors for its own interface. If you don't allow for this , you'll get little black holes in your image as Windows steals those colors for its own palette. If you use 234 colors Windows is smart enough to figure out what remaining colors to reserve. Once PicLab finishes the DOS process will end.

At this point we want Visual Basic to bring a GIF viewer—in this case we use the program Fractint for Windows—to the top of the desktop, then automatically open the .GIF file that was just created. This can be done with Visual Basic's SendKeys statement.

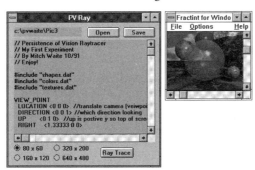

**Figure 6-2** The PV ray tracer with data file opened and Fractint for Windows displaying the ray tracing for this data file

Figure 6-2 shows the interface we made for PV and the Fractint for Windows program revealing the small preview of the ray traced scene in file PIC3.DAT. In this How-To we show the exact program names that were used for the PV interface. On the disk provided with this book we substituted batch files that accomplish the same results by simulating the processes without PV.

**Steps**
Several files make up this project, as shown in Table 6-2. These files must be in the right directories for this project to work. Besides PV.MAK and PV.FRM, there are PV.BAT and the WINFRACT.BAT batch files, as well as a PV.PIF file.

| C:\CHX\HTX directory | |
|---|---|
| PV.MAK | |
| PV.FRM | |
| PV.BAT | This is a dummy that represents your DOS program. |
| WINFRACT.BAT | This is a dummy that represents the WINFRACT program. |
| | |
| WINDOWS directory | |
| PV.PIF | This .PIF file is needed to make your DOS process run in a window. |

**Table 6-2** PV Files

1. Create a new project called PV.MAK, and a form called PV.FRM. Make the form about 4 inches wide and 4 inches tall.

2. Add the objects and properties listed in Table 6-3 to this form. If a property is not listed, its effect is not important and the default is assumed. The radio buttons are arranged as an array, with the first button selected by default by setting its Value property to True. The remaining Value properties are set to False.

| Object | Property | Setting |
|---|---|---|
| Form | FormName | PV_Ray |
| | Caption | PV Ray |
| | BackColor | &H00C0C0C0& (50% gray) |
| Command button | CtlName | CmdOpen |
| | Caption | Open |
| Command button | CtlName | CmdSave |
| | Caption | Save |

| Command button | Ctlname | CmdRunPV |
|---|---|---|
| | Caption | Ray Trace |
| Text box | CtlName | FldPicName |
| | BackColor | &H00FFFF00& |
| | FontName | Helv |
| | FontBold | True |
| Text box | CtlName | TxtListing |
| | BackColor | &H00FFFF00& |
| | FontName | Helv |
| | FontBold | True |
| | ScrollBars | 3 - Both |
| | Text | Listing for the DAT file here |
| Option button | Ctlname | OptReso |
| OptReso(0) | Index | 0 |
| | Caption | 80 x 60 |
| | Value | True |
| OpReso(1) | Index | 1 |
| | Caption | 160 x 120 |
| OptReso(2) | Index | 2 |
| | Caption | 320 x 200 |
| OptReso(3) | Index | 3 |
| | Caption | 640 x 480 |

**Table 6-3** PV project form's objects and properties

3. Now make a .PIF file with the Windows PIF editor and call it PV.PIF. The file, which must be made to use the Shell statement's styles, will be saved in the Windows directory. The DOS process run by Shell has a style of 2, which means a minimized window (iconized) and with focus.

The .PIF file's filename should be the same as the DOS program, in this case PV.BAT, with the .PIF extension: PV.PIF. Fill out the PIF form as follows: the name of the window for the program should be PV Ray Tracer. The Start-up Directory should be set to where the target file is located in your system, in mine it was C:\VB\SHELLBETR. The Display Usage button should be set to Windowed and Execution set to Background.

4. Put the following code in the Declarations section of the form. This sets up general variables global to the form and initializes the APIs.

```
DefInt A-Z
Declare Function GetActiveWindow Lib "user" ()
Declare Function IsWindow Lib "user" (ByVal hwnd)
Dim NumTasks%
```

```
Dim w As String
Dim h As String
Dim d As String
Dim v As String
Declare Function WinExec Lib "Kernel" (ByVal lpCmdLine As String, ByVal ⇐
nCmdShow As Integer) As Integer
Dim crlf As String
Dim safe As Integer
```

5. Put the following code in the Form_Load procedure of the form.

```
Sub Form_Load ()
   crlf = Chr$(13) + Chr$(10)
   'set default values to 80 x 60 no display verbose mode
   w$ = "80": h$ = "60": d$ = "-d": v$ = "+v"
   'if you don't have winfract substitute a different niewer.
    Er% = WinExec("c:\winfract\winfract.exe",
    safe = 0  'set safe to false
End Sub
```

6. Put the following code in the button CmdRunPV. It is responsible for runing the DOS program that does the actual ray tracing.

```
Sub CmdRunPV_Click ()

   PV_File$ = "PV.BAT"
   PV_Para$ = FldPicName.text + " " + w + " " + h + " " + d + " " + v
   X = Shell(PV_File$ + " " + PV_Para$, 1) ' 1 = window with focus, 2 = ⇐
   'minimzed w/focus
   HwndShell = GetActiveWindow()
   While IsWindow(HwndShell)
      X = DoEvents()
   Wend
   ' wait until IsWindow tells us that the iconized DOS window is a
   ' finished process. DoEvents prevents our program from
   ' hogging the system.

   OpenFractint
End Sub
```

7. Put the following code in a procedure called OpenFractint in the Declarations section of the form. This is called whenever the DOS process is finished and control is returned to Visual Basic.

```
Sub OpenFractint ()
   ' Makes Fractint come to top of desktop
   AppActivate "Fractint for Windows - Vers 16.11"
   SendKeys "%(FO)"      'Alt-F Opens File Menu, Alt-O Opens Open Menu
   ' FldPicName.Text is the name in the file box
   SendKeys FldPicName.text + ".gif"  ' This is what Piclab made
   SendKeys "{ENTER}" 'Open the file and display it with Fractint
End Sub
```

8. Put the following code the OptReso_Click radio button. Since this is a button array, there is only one Click routine.

```
Sub OptReso_Click (Index As Integer)
   Select Case Index
   Case 0
      w$ = "80": h$ = "60"
   Case 1
      w$ = "160": h$ = "120"
   Case 2
      w$ = "320": h$ = "200"
   Case 3
      w$ = "640": h$ = "480"
   End Select
End Sub
```

9. Put the following code in the CmdOpen button subroutine.

```
Sub CmdOpen_Click ()
   TxtListing.text = ""     'clear out the listing box
   Open FldPicName.text + ".DAT" For Input As #1
   Do Until EOF(1)
      Line Input #1, oneLine$
      TxtListing.SelText = TxtListing.SelText + oneLine$ + crlf$
   Loop
   Close #1
   safe = -1  'now okay to save
End Sub
```

10. Put the following code the CmdSave button subroutine.

```
Sub CmdSave_Click ()
   If safe = 0 Then
      Beep
      Exit Sub
   End If
   SFile$ = FldPicName.text + ".DAT"
   Open SFile$ For Output As #1
      Print #1, TxtListing.text
   Close #1
End Sub
```

### How It Works

The code in the Declarations section of the form sets up the two APIs, as well as several variables global to the form. The WinExec API works just like Visual Basic's Shell command, except it will not make your program halt if an error returned.

The Form_Load code uses the WinExec API to load the program called WINFRACT.EXE when the Visual Basic application starts. You can replace this with WINFRACT.BAT if you just want to test the routine. The

WinExec API will not report an error if the file is missing and therefore will not interrupt your program with an error message as Shell does. After opening Fractint for Windows a global variable safe is set to False, which is used later to make sure we don't try to save a program that is empty (which would happen if you pressed Save immediatey after opening the program and running it).

The Form_Load code also sets up the default values for the four important variables that control PV from the command line: w$ which is the entry for ray-tracing width, h$ which is the ray-tracing height variable, d$ is the display on or off option, and v$ , the verbose on or off option.

The PV DOS program is set up so a minus sign (-) in front of an option turns it off, while an addition sign (+) turns it on. So "-d" means the display is turned off (graphics would conflict with Windows), and "+v" means the verbose text output mode is enabled.

### Editing Files

The data files that describe the ray-tracing world are simple ASCII files that can be easily modified. To make it possible to edit the files in Visual Basic we simply have to load the file contents into a text box. We set its scrollbar property to 3 - Both, so there is both a vertical and horizontal scroll bar. As a quick and dirty way to open and close files, we used a somewhat crude but simple approach. The name of the file is typed into a text box along with its path. When the Open button is clicked the CmdOpen_Click procedure is called. It attempts to open the file named in the text box, adding the extension .DAT to the file. If the file is found, each line of the file is read one at a time into the list box. When EOF is detected the loop ends and file is closed.

The Save button has a similar function but it does the reverse. Clicking on Save takes the entire text box and saves its contents to a serial file with the Print # statement. The routine checks that there has already been a file loaded so that it does not save an empty file. The danger with this approach is that if the filename is wrong the program halts and must be restarted. The next step would be to add a file open and save dialog using one of the several described in this book.

### Doing It

The main code for running the program occurs in the CmdRunPV button. The file name that will be Shelled to is defined as PV.BAT. Next the parameters that will be sent to the PV program are assembled in a string. Finally the Shell statement is executed with the file name PV.BAT and the parameter string. The DOS process is started in a window with focus (that's the purpose of the 2 at the end of the Shell statement). This will let you watch the DOS process run, and will let you interact with it.

Next a handle to the window for this DOS process is obtained in HwndShell, and a DoUntil loop is entered. This loop continues until IsWindow returns False for the active window HwndShell. During the time that the DOS (or icon) window is still active, the DoEvents function assures the Visual Basic program does not hog its Windows multitasking allotment.

At this point, on a 386 computer, you could stop Visual Basic, and your DOS process would keep running. In fact, you may, if it's not a protected mode application, spawn another copy of the DOS process and run two versions of your program at the same time. Once the DOS process stops, the procedure called OpenFractint is called.

### Open My Application or Bring It to the Top

The code for OpenFractint brings the Fractint program to the top of the desktop and instruct it to open our newly created .GIF file. Recall the .PIF file opened earlier in this project. That file must contain the name of the program. The Visual Basic AppActivate function is used to make the program come to the top of the desktop. The name in the string has to exactly match the name in the .PIF file Next, SendKeys is used to tell Fractint to pull down its File menu and open a file. The extension .GIF is now added to the name of the file in the filename text box (the file we ray traced complete with path). This name is then entered into the name field of Fractint's open file dialog box again using SendKeys. This is followed by sending an Enter keypress, and the image is loaded and displayed.

The OptReso_Click procedure is the way we set the resolution for w$ and h$ variables. A simple Case statement just puts different values in these variables. When the Ray Trace command button is pushed the parameter file is assembled with the current values.

### Comment

Communicating the output of a DOS process to a Visual Basic program running under Windows is not simple. The simple way to accomplish this is by writing information from the DOS process to a file and then reading it with Visual Basic. Another less known way to communicate between a DOS and a Visual Basic program is by using the DOS Intra Application Communications area (IAC) located at 0040:00F0 to 0040:00FF. A single POKE and PEEK DLL would allow Visual Basic to access this area.

## 6.3     How do I...

# Exit Windows and return to DOS?

Complexity: Easy

### Problem

I've written an application that determines whether a virus has attacked a Windows system. If it detects a virus, I'd like to inform the user and then shut down Windows so the virus can't do any damage. Is this possible?

**Figure 6-3** The ShutDown project design

### Technique

Visual Basic's End statement simply terminates the current application. It can't terminate Windows. Luckily, there is a Windows API function—ExitWindows—that will terminate Windows and return to DOS.

Using ExitWindows won't cause you to lose any data. All the applications you have running at the time have the chance to say: "Hey, gimme a minute to save my files!" before Windows will shut down.

### Steps

Open and run SHUTDOWN.MAK. Click on the Exit Windows! button. If all the other applications running agree to terminate, Windows will shut down and you'll be returned to the DOS prompt.

1. Create a new project called SHUTDOWN.MAK. and a new form with the controls and properties shown in Table 6-4. Save the form as SHUT-DOWN.FRM. See Figure 6-3 for the appearance of the completed form.

| Object | Property | Setting |
|---|---|---|
| Form | Caption | Exit Windows |
| | FormName | ExitWindowsForm |
| | BackColor | &00HC0C0C0& |
| Command button | CtlName | ExitWin |
| | Caption | Exit Windows! |
| | Default | True |

**Table 6-4** Shutdown project form's controls and properties

2. Put the following code in the Declarations section of the form. This Declare statement gives the form access to the ExitWindows API function.

```
Declare Function ExitWindows Lib "User" (ByVal dwReserved As Long, ⇐
wReturnCode As Integer) As Integer
```

3. Put the following code in the ExitWin_Click event subroutine.

```
Sub ExitWin_Click ()
    If ExitWindows(0, 0) = 0 Then
        MsgBox "Sorry; another application says not to terminate!"
    End If
End Sub
```

This is a call to the ExitWindows API function. If ExitWindows returns 0, a message box pops up and informs the user that another application won't let Windows terminate.

### How It Works

The Windows API function ExitWindows is used to shut down Windows and all the running applications. In Windows 3.0, ExitWindows will not terminate DOS windows, so if there are any DOS windows, ExitWindows won't shut down all of Windows. ExitWindows tells all Windows applications that someone has requested that Windows be shut down. Those applications can then save any open files. (For example, a word processor would ask the user to save a document.) An application can tell Windows that it can't be terminated at this time, in which case Windows won't shut down.

If all Windows applications agree to terminate, Windows will shut down and you will be returned to the DOS prompt.

The first parameter of the ExitWindows call, dwReserved, isn't used by this version of Windows and must be zero. The second parameter, wReturnCode, is the return code that Windows will pass back to DOS. If you started Windows from a batch file, you can check this return code by using the IF ERRORLEVEL command.

### Comment

You can tell when your Visual Basic application is being terminated by checking for the form's Unload event. If you have some code in the Form_Unload event subroutine, that code will be executed before your application is terminated. For example, you could pop up a message box giving the user a chance to change his mind or to save files.

| 6.4 | How do I... |
| --- | --- |

# Prevent Windows from shutting down?

Complexity: Easy

## Problem

If my users exit Windows (by selecting Exit from the Program Manager's File menu), my Visual Basic application will be shut down without a chance to save any work the user has done. Is there some way I can prevent this?

## Technique

Before Windows shuts down, it gives all the running applications a chance to say "Hey! I'm not finished yet." If an application tells Windows not to shut down, Windows stays active at that application.

Usually the reason you won't want Windows to shut down your Windows application is that there is some data that hasn't been saved to a file yet. The most common approach to preventing data loss is to pop up a message box saying "Save this file?" If the user clicks on Yes to save the file, the application saves it, and then tells Windows it's okay to shut down.

In Visual Basic, the event that's triggered by a potential Windows shutdown is the Form_Unload event. (Note that this event is also triggered by the Unload statement.) You can include a call to your form's file save routine in the Form_Unload event subroutine. For example, if you have a File menu with a Save option that saves a file, you might use the following Form_Unload event subroutine:

```
Sub Form_Unload (Cancel As Integer)
    FileSave_Click
End Sub
```

It's traditional Windows practice to ask users whether they really want to save their changes, so you should include a MsgBox function call, too, as follows:

```
Sub Form_Unload (Cancel As Integer)
    If MsgBox("Do you want to save?", 4 + 32) = 6 Then FileSave_Click
End Sub
```

The "4 + 32" parameter in the MsgBox function call tells Visual Basic to include Yes and No buttons (4) and the question mark icon (32). If MsgBox returns a six, the user selected Yes, so a call to the FileSave_Click event subroutine will save the file.

But what if you don't want Windows to shut down? Some Windows applications give the user the option of aborting the shutdown and to continue working on their applications. You can achieve the same thing in Visual Basic by using a message box with a Cancel button, as follows:

```
Sub Form_Unload (Cancel As Integer)
    Select Case MsgBox("Do you want to save?", 3 + 32)
        Case 6
            FileSave_Click
        Case 2
            Cancel = 1
    End Select
End Sub
```

The "3 + 32" parameter in the MsgBox function call tells Visual Basic to include Yes, No, and Cancel buttons (3) and the question mark icon (32). If MsgBox returns a six, the user selected Yes, so a call to the FileSave_Click event subroutine will save the file. Otherwise, if MsgBox returns a 2, the user selected Cancel. Then we set the Cancel parameter to tell Windows to abort the attempted shutdown. Your application will continue to run as if Windows never tried to shut down.

### Comment

As mentioned, the Unload event occurs in several circumstances. You shouldn't assume that Windows is shutting down; it may just be that your user closed your application somehow (by double-clicking on the system menu icon or by using the End Task button on the Task Manager window, for example).

**6.5    How do I...**

## Search an entire disk for a file?

Complexity: Intermediate

### Problem

Although I try to keep my hard drive organized, sometimes files get placed in the wrong directory. Is there any way to have my Visual Basic application search the whole disk for specific files?

### Technique

You are probably accustomed to searching directories manually using Visual Basic's directory list box control. This project also uses this control but automatically steps it through the directory structure under program control. As each directory is found, the filenames in the directory are scanned against a search mask. Those that match are displayed in a list box on the form.

### Steps

Open and run FILEFIND.MAK. Enter a filename search mask in the file spec text box. Select the disk drive and starting directory, then click on the Go command button. All directories and any matching filenames are displayed in the list box.

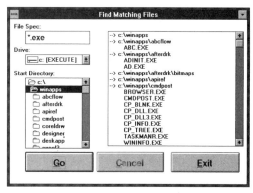

**Figure 6-4** The Filefind project in action

To create the Filefind project, enter the objects and code as detailed in the following steps.

1. Create a new project called FILE-FIND.MAK. Create a new form with the objects and properties shown in Table 6-5, and save it as FILE-FIND.FRM. The appearance of the form should match Figure 6-4. Note that because the Dir2 control is never visible, its size and placement on the form is not critical.

| Object | Property | Setting |
| --- | --- | --- |
| Form | FormName | Filefind |
| | Caption | Find Matching Files |
| | MaxButton | False |
| Label | CtlName | Label1 |
| | Caption | File Spec: |
| | Autosize | True |
| Label | CtlName | Label2 |
| | Caption | Drive: |
| | Autosize | True |
| Label | CtlName | Label3 |
| | Caption | Start Directory: |
| | Autosize | True |
| | Alignment | 1 - Right Justify |
| Text box | CtlName | Text1 |
| | FontSize | 12 |
| | Text | *.* |
| Drive list box | CtlName | Drive1 |
| Directory list box | CtlName | Dir1 |
| Directory list box | CtlName | Dir2 |
| | Visible | False |

| Command button | CtlName | CmdGo |
|---|---|---|
| | Caption | &Go |
| | FontSize | 14 |
| | Default | True |
| Command button | CtlName | CmdCancel |
| | Caption | &Cancel |
| | FontSize | 14 |
| | Enabled | False |
| | Cancel | True |
| Command button | CtlName | CmdExit |
| | Caption | E&xit |
| | FontSize | 14 |
| List box | CtlName | List1 |

**Table 6-5** Filefind project form's objects and properties

2. Place the following variable declaration in the General section of the form.--

```
Dim Abort As Integer                   ' Common Abort flag
```

3. Put the following code in the Dir2_Change event subroutine. This subroutine scans the current directory and all of its subdirectories for matching filenames.

```
Sub Dir2_Change ()
Dim DirCount As Integer, I As Integer, T As Integer
Dim Filename As String, Searchpath As String
'
'  Display directory name in list box.
'  Build Searchpath string, root directory already has "\".
'
   List1.AddItem "--> " + Dir2.Path    ' Show directory
   Searchpath = Dir2.Path
   If Right$(Searchpath, 1) <> "\" Then Searchpath = Searchpath + "\"
   Searchpath = Searchpath + Text1.Text
'
'  Search and display matching files in current directory.
'
   Filename = Dir$(Searchpath)          ' Set initial search string
   Do While Filename <> ""
      List1.AddItem "       " + Filename
      Filename = Dir$                   ' No arguments to find next match
   Loop
'
'  Save all the directory names in current directory.
'
   DirCount = Dir2.ListCount
```

```
ReDim Dirlist(DirCount) As String
   For I = 0 To DirCount - 1
      Dirlist(I) = Dir2.List(I)
   Next I
'
'  For each directory in the list, processes their subdirectories.
'  This may take a while, so processes events in case user aborts.
   For I = 0 To DirCount - 1
      T = DoEvents()
      If Abort Then Exit Sub          ' Stop if requested
      Dir2.Path = Dirlist(I)
   Next I
End Sub
```

4. Put the following code in the Driv1_Change event subroutine. This code passes a drive change event to the Dir1, directory list box control.

```
Sub Drive1_Change ()
'
'  If we change the drive then we change the directory.
'
   Dir1.Path = Drive1.Drive
End Sub
```

5. Put the following code in the CmdGo_Click event subroutine. This code clears the list box of its contents and begins a new search.

```
Sub CmdGo_Click ()
Dim I As Integer
'
' Disable all controls (except CmdCancel) during the search.
'
   CmdGo.Enabled = 0
   Text1.Enabled = 0
   Drive1.Enabled = 0
   Dir1.Enabled = 0
   CmdCancel.Enabled = -1

' Clear ListBox. Let user know what we are doing.
'
   List1.Visible = 0
   CurrentX = List1.Left
   CurrentY = List1.Top + List1.Height / 2
   Print "Clearing List Box"
   For I = List1.ListCount - 1 To 0 Step -1
      List1.RemoveItem I
   Next I
   List1.Visible = -1

   Abort = 0             ' Clear abort flag from prior run
'
'  Dir2_Change does recursive decent through directories.
```

```
' If Dir2 pointing to current directory, we need to trigger
' the change event ourselves.
'
   If Dir2.Path = Dir1.Path Then
      Dir2_Change
   Else
      Dir2.Path = Dir1.Path
   End If
'
' Enable controls after the search.
'
   CmdGo.Enabled = -1
   Text1.Enabled = -1
   Drive1.Enabled = -1
   Dir1.Enabled = -1
   CmdCancel.Enabled = 0
   CmdGo.SetFocus           ' Reset focus to Go button
End Sub
```

> 6. Put the following code in the Text1_GotFocus event subroutine. This code selects the search string when Text1 gets the focus.

```
Sub Text1_GotFocus ()
' Highlight all the contents of the TextBox.
   Text1.SelStart = 0
   Text1.SelLength = Len(Text1.Text)
End Sub
```

> 7. Put the following code in the CmdCancel_Click event subroutine. It sets a global variable, Abort, which will stop an active file search.

```
Sub CmdCancel_Click ()
   Abort = -1              ' Set abort flag
End Sub
```

> 8. Put the following code in the CmdExit_Click event subroutine. This button allow the users a graceful way to exit the application.

```
Sub CmdExit_Click ()
   End
End Sub
```

### How It Works

Although Visual Basic has the Dir$ function to return the filenames in a directory, there is no equivalent statement to return the list of directories on a drive. This project takes advantage of the way the Directory list box control works to have it inspect the branches of a directory tree.

The program begins the search process when the user clicks on the Go button invoking the CmdGo_Click event subroutine. We first disable the controls that were used to set up and initiate the search. If the controls were not disabled, parameters could be changed while a search was in progress, yielding misleading results. The Cancel button is enabled allowing the user to stop the search.

The list box containing the results from the prior search is cleared. Because this process can take a few seconds, the list box is made invisible, and an informational message is printed in its place. When the box is empty, it is made visible again covering the informational message.

This program uses two directory list box controls, Dir1 and Dir2. Dir1 is visible on screen and is used to select the starting directory branch for the search. Using Figure 6-4 as an example, the search would start at the selected subdirectory, C:\WINAPPS. Dir2 retrieves the directory names for us. Even though it is not visible on screen, it can still be manipulated and return data to the Visual Basic program.

The scan of directories begins with a Dir2_Change event. Note that in the Cmd_Go event subroutine we check whether Dir2 is already pointing to the selected directory. If it is, the Dir2_Change event subroutine is called directly. If not, the program initiates the directory change event by setting Dir2.Path to the desired starting point.

The Dir2_Change event subroutine searches the current directory and its subdirectories for filenames that match the search string. The current directory is searched for matching files using the Dir$ function. Dir$ is loaded with the name of the directory being searched and the file search mask located in the text box. Note the If...Then statement that is needed to handle the root directory. Subsequent Dir$ calls, with no parameters, will return the next matching file name. All matching files are displayed in the list box.

Looking at Figure 6-4, notice how subdirectories are displayed underneath the current directory. Each of the subdirectory names is copied from the directory list box to the DirList array. The property Dir2.ListCount returns the number of subdirectories. Finally, the Dir2_Change event subroutine changes the current path to each of the subdirectories, which will trigger a Dir2_Change event for the subdirectory and its subdirectories. This is called a recursive subroutine, because it calls itself to do additional work.

On a large and complex hard drive, a complete search can take quite a few seconds. The user can abort the process by clicking on the Cancel button. This action sets a global Abort flag that is checked by Dir2_Change and will cause it to exit the subroutine. The DoEvents function allows Visual Basic to respond to user actions while the search is progressing.

**6.6      How do I...**

# Use the Shell function without causing run-time errors?

Complexity: Intermediate

### Problem

Using Visual Basic's Shell function will cause a run-time error if the command to be executed can't be found. Is there some way to prevent these run-time errors without using On Error Goto?

### Technique

There's no way around the run-time error a Shell function causes if it can't find the program specified, unless you use an On Error Goto error-handling routine. The Shell function must be a file with an extension of .COM, .EXE, .BAT, or .PIF. Shell will look for a file in the following directories:

- The current directory
- The Windows directory (by default, C:\WINDOWS)
- The Windows system directory (by default, C:\WINDOWS\SYSTEM)
- The directories on your path

If Shell can't find a file in any of those directories, it will cause a Visual Basic run-time error. If your application doesn't have an active On Error Goto error-handling routine, the run-time error will cause Visual Basic to pop up a message box with a "File not found" error message. Then the program will abort—not a very user-friendly response.

Luckily, the Windows API library offers a function named WinExec, which works almost exactly the same as Visual Basic's Shell function, except it won't cause a run-time error. We can add a function that calls WinExec to the VBHOWTO.BAS module.

### Steps

Open and run VBSHELL.MAK. Type a command into the text box and press Enter or click on the Execute button. You can try running both DOS and Windows applications.

1. Create a new project called VB-SHELL.MAK. Create a new form with the controls and properties listed in Table 6-6 and save it as VB-SHELL.FRM. See Figure 6.5 for its appearance.

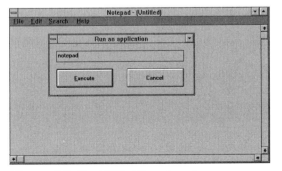

**Figure 6-5** The VBShell form in action

| Control | Property | Setting |
|---------|----------|---------|
| Form | Caption | Run an application |
| | MaxButton | False |
| | BackColor | &H00C0C0C0& |
| Text box | CtlName | Text1 |
| | Text | <blank> |
| Command button | CtlName | Execute |
| | Caption | Execute |
| | Default | True |
| Command button | CtlName | Cancel |
| | Caption | Cancel |
| | Cancel | True |

**Table 6-6** VBShell project form's objects and properties

2. Add the following to the Declarations section of the module. This is the declaration for the WinExec API function.

```
Declare Function WinExec Lib "Kernel" (ByVal lpCmdLine As String, ByVal ⇐
nCmdShow As Integer) As Integer
```

3. Add the following code to the VBHOWTO.BAS module.

```
Function VBHTShell (lpCmdLine$, nCmdShow As Integer)
   VBHTShell = WinExec(lpCmdLine$, nCmdShow)
End Function
```

4. Add the following code to the Cancel_Click event subroutine.

```
Sub Cancel_Click ()
   End
End Sub
```

5. Put the following code in the Execute_Click event subroutine. This code calls the VBHTShell function to execute the command the user entered in the text box.

```
Sub Execute_Click ()
   Cmd$ = Text1.Text
   Er% = VBHTShell(Cmd$, 1)
   If Er% < 32 Then
      MsgBox "Error" + Str$(Er%) + " executing your command!", 48
   End If
End Sub
```

**How It Works**

The WinExec API function is almost identical to Visual Basic's Shell function. It even uses the same numbers for the second parameter (except that Shell calls the parameter "WindowStyle%" and WinExec calls it "nCmdShow").

Both Shell and WinExec return a number; Microsoft calls the number that Shell returns the "task ID." That ID is never used by any other Windows function, so it can be ignored. If WinExec returns a number less than 32, there was an error; if the number is greater than 32, it's the mythical task ID. Don't worry about storing this task ID.

### Comment
Unlike Visual Basic's Shell function, VBHTShell requires the second window style parameter. The default value for Shell is 1, so you could pass a 1 as the second parameter to VBHTShell to get the same effect as Visual Basic's Shell function.

---

**6.7        How do I...**

# Run a DOS internal command?

Complexity: Intermediate

### Problem
Visual Basic's Shell function and the VBHTShell function that we've created won't execute an internal (non EXE) DOS command like DIR or TYPE. Is there any way to run these commands within my applications?

### Technique
In the previous How-To Use the Shell function without causing run-time errors, we created a custom shell called VBHTSHELL. Both the native Visual Basic Shell function and the WinExec API function (that our custom VBHTShell depends on) will only run .COM, .EXE, .BAT, and .PIF files. DOS commands like DIR and TYPE aren't any of these types of files. Instead they're internal to the DOS command processor COMMAND.COM.

Is there some way to get COMMAND.COM to execute its internal commands? A quick look at a DOS manual confirms that you can get COMMAND.COM to do just that by using the following format:

```
COMMAND /C command
```

In other words, we can write COMMAND/C DIR and we'll get a directory listing. So, are we all set? Unfortunately, no. DOS has always supported the ability to replace COMMAND.COM with another command processor. A shareware COMMAND.COM replacement/enhancement, 4DOS, is quite popular. Its filename is 4DOS.COM, so if we were to execute COMMAND.COM, and 4DOS was running instead, our program would still not work. How can you determine the name of the command processor so we run the correct one?

In DOS an environment variable named COMSPEC holds the name of the actual command processor being used by the system. You can get the value of the COMSPEC environment variable and execute it with the /C option of COMMAND.COM. (4DOS supports this option, too.) So, how can we get the COMSPEC environment variable value? The Visual Basic function Environ$ will return the value of a specified environment variable.

### Steps

Open and run DOSSHELL.MAK. You can type a DOS command in the text box and click Execute, the command processor will be invoked, and the command in the text box will be executed. If you don't type anything in the text box, a new DOS shell will be started. Then you can type multiple commands. Type EXIT and press Enter to close the shell.

1. Create a new project called DOSSHELL.MAK and a new form with the controls and properties listed in Table 6-7. Save the form as DOS-SHELL.FRM.

| Control | Property | Setting |
| --- | --- | --- |
| Form | Caption | Do a DOS command |
| | MaxButton | False |
| Text box | CtlName | Text1 |
| | Text | <blank> |
| Command button | CtlName | Execute |
| | Caption | Execute |
| | Default | True |
| Command button | CtlName | Cancel |
| | Caption | Cancel |
| | Cancel | True |

**Table 6-7** DosShell project form's objects and properties

2. Add the VBHOWTO.BAS module to the project. We created this module in How-To 1.4 Quickly send a Windows message to a control, and added the VBHTShell function in the previous VBHOWTO.BAS which contains the VBHTShell function (created in the previous How-To).

3. Put the following code in the Cancel_Click event subroutine.

```
Sub Cancel_Click ()
    End
End Sub
```

4. Put the following code in the Execute_Click event subroutine. This subroutine gets the name of the command processor from the COMSPEC

environment variable, and then uses the /C option to execute the command in the text box, if there is one. Finally, a call to VBHTShell executes the command.

```
Sub Execute_Click ()
    DOSShell$ = Environ$("COMSPEC")

    If DOSShell$ = "" Then DOSShell$ = "COMMAND.COM"
    Cmd$ = DOSShell$
    If Len(Text1.Text) Then Cmd$ = Cmd$ + " /C " + Text1.Text

    Er% = VBHTShell(Cmd$, 1)
    If Er% < 32 Then
        MsgBox "Error" + Str$(Er%) + " executing your command!", 48
    End If
End Sub
```

### How It Works

A call to the Environ$ function returns the name of the command processor, including the directory. If there is no COMSPEC setting, Environ$ will return a null string, so we check for it and assume that the user is using COMMAND.COM. Then, if there's some text in the text box Text1, that command gets added to the command being executed. If there is no text, the command will just be the name of the command processor, which will start a DOS window where you can enter multiple commands. You must type "EXIT" to close the DOS window and return to your Visual Basic application.

### Comment

The settings in your _DEFAULT.PIF file will partially determine how the DOS window looks. If you're running Windows in 386 Enhanced mode, you can set up _DEFAULT.PIF to run either full screen or in a window. You can also change the appearance of the window with the nCmdShow parameter in the VBHTShell function call. See your Visual Basic documentation or the online Help for details on that second parameter.

---

**6.8     How do I...**

## Prevent multiple program instances from being loaded?

Complexity: Advanced

### Problem

I would like to be able to prevent multiple instances of my Visual Basic application from being loaded but this has proven to be more difficult than I had imagined. There appear to be a number of solutions, all of which are less than ideal, such as dynamic data exchange (DDE) and temporary files.

Is there an easier way? Using the FindWindow API function requires that the application must never change the caption on the main window.

### Technique

There are a number of approaches, as you mention, including DDE, temporary files, and FindWindow. All of these are less than ideal, so we will examine a couple of alternatives. FindWindow seems to be the immediate choice, but it falls short of our needs here. This is because all Visual Basic forms have the same classname—ThunderForm—so using FindWindow will not do, unless we are willing to leave the main form's caption alone.

One possibility is simply to check the number of running instances of our application. There are two pertinent Windows API functions for this, GetModuleHandle and GetModuleUsage.

However, to get a little fancier, FindWindow can be broken down to manually step through the "window list." We can step through the window list using the GetWindow and GetNextWindow API functions.

### Steps

There are two examples for this How-To and, in each case, they must be run as .EXE files to test their functionality. Therefore, load the file MIP1.MAK into the Visual Basic editor and select Make EXE from the File menu. Just accept the defaults and click OK. Now do the same thing with the file MIP2.MAK. You now have two .EXE files that you can add to the Program Manager: MIP1.EXE and MIP2.EXE.

In both cases the idea is to simply try to launch each one more than once. Launch MIP1.EXE and then minimize the resulting form. Now, try to launch it again from the Program Manager. You should see a message box, similar to the one used by the File Manager, that says that the application is already loaded. The second instance of MIP1.EXE will then terminate.

When you launch MIP2.EXE, for the second time, there is no message box. Instead, the "original" instance of MIP2.EXE will be restored before the second instance terminates. Use the technique that better suits your needs.

To create MIP1, perform the following steps:

1. Create a new project called MIP1.MAK. and a new form with the objects and properties in Table 6-8.

| Object | Property | Setting |
| --- | --- | --- |
| Form | FormName | Form1 |
|  | Caption | MIP |

| Picture box | CtlName | Picture1 |
|---|---|---|
| | Caption | I'm Here! |
| | BorderStyle | None |

**Table 6-8** Mip project form's objects and properties

2. Select New Module from the File menu.

3. Insert the following code in the new module.

```
DefInt A-Z

Declare Function GetModuleHandle Lib "Kernel" (ByVal lpProgName$)
Declare Function GetModuleUsage Lib "Kernel" (ByVal hModule)

Sub Main ()
   hModule = GetModuleHandle("MIP1.EXE")
   Count = GetModuleUsage(hModule)
   If Count > 1 Then
      MsgBox "Application Already Loaded!"
      End
   Else
      Form1.Show
   End if
End Sub
```

4. Select Save File from the File menu and save the form and the module as MIP1.FRM and MIP1.BAS, respectively. Save the project as MIP1.MAK.

5. Select Sub Main as your startup form. Create the .EXE file and run the application.

To create MIP2.EXE, perform the following steps:

1. Create a new form same as above with the one label.

2. Insert the following code in the Form_Resize procedure.

```
Sub Form_Resize ()
   Label1.Caption = "I'm Back!"
End Sub
```

3. Create a new module named MIP2.BAS. Insert the following code into MIP2.BAS.

```
DefInt A-Z

Declare Sub ShowWindow Lib "User" (ByVal hWnd, ByVal nCmd)
Declare Sub SetActiveWindow Lib "User" (ByVal hWnd)

Const SW_SHOWNORMAL = 1
```

```
Sub Main ()
   Wnd = SearchWindow("multi")
   If Wnd <> 0 Then
      ShowWindow Wnd, SW_SHOWNORMAL
      SetActiveWindow Wnd
      End
   Else
      Form1.Show
   End If
End Sub
```

4. Create a new module and name it WNDFIND.BAS. and insert the following code.

```
DefInt A-Z

Declare Function FindWindow Lib "User" (ByVal Class&, ByVal Caption&)
Declare Function GetWindow Lib "User" (ByVal hWnd, ByVal wCmd)
Declare Function GetNextWindow Lib "User" (ByVal hWnd, ByVal wCmd)

Declare Function GetWindowText Lib "User" (ByVal hWnd, ByVal Buf$, ⇐
ByVal lBuf)

Const GW_HWNDFIRST = 0
Const GW_HWNDNEXT = 2

Dim Capt As String * 256

Function SearchWindow (Search$)
   Dest$ = UCase$(Search$)
   Wnd = FindWindow(0, 0)
   Wnd = GetWindow(Wnd, GW_HWNDFIRST)
   While Wnd <> 0
      TChars = GetWindowText(Wnd, Capt, 256)
      If TChars > 0 Then
         Source$ = UCase$(Left$(Capt, TChars))
         If InStr(Source$, Dest$) > 0 Then
            SearchWindow = Wnd
            Exit Function
         End If
      End If
      Wnd = GetNextWindow(Wnd, GW_HWNDNEXT)
   Wend
   SearchWindow = 0
End Function

Function WndCaption$ (hWnd)
   TChars = GetWindowText(hWnd, Capt, 256)
   WndCaption$ = Left$(Capt, TChars)
End Function
```

5. Set Sub Main as the startup form. Save the form and project as MIP2 and create the .EXE file.

**How They Work**

MIP1 works by first finding the module handle of MIP1.EXE. Because code is reused under Windows, the module handle for both instances (if there are two) of the application will be the same. Therefore, it is a simple matter to find how many instances of the application are currently running by using the GetModuleUsage function. If there is more than one, the application crashes.

MIP2 is a little more sophisticated; we end up with the "other" instance of our application being restored. This is possible because the SearchWindow function returns the hWnd property of the main window of the other application. Using this value we can use the SetActiveWindow (equivalent to AppActivate but uses an hWnd) API function to activate the old instance of the application. Then to get really fancy, we use the ShowWindow API function to "restore" the other instance.

SearchWindow works by stepping through the system's window list of top-level windows. FindWindow is used to simply get a valid handle to any window. With each hWnd retrieved with GetWindow and GetNext-Window, the GetWindowText API function is used to retrieve the caption of that window (just as we do in WndPeek). Then Instr is used to find a match with the search string and, if one is found, it returns that hWnd as the function's result.

**Comments**

You may notice that within the SearchWindow function we check whether TChars is greater than zero. GetWindowText returns the number of characters that were actually copied into our string buffer. There are, in fact, a number of hidden windows on the system at all times, and it is quicker to eliminate them numerically than by using Instr.

An additional function in WNDFIND.BAS returns the caption of a window, based on its hWnd. Although not used in the sample, this is useful if you want to use AppActivate or you want to present a selection for the user.

Finally, it should be obvious that SearchWindow could also easily find the window of another application instead of using FindWindow with the classname. SearchWindow might prove more useful if, for example, you wanted, not only to find any instance of Notepad, but the one that contained a particular file.

**6.9    How do I...**

# Find other running applications?

Complexity: Advanced

**Problem**

I would like to be able to locate other applications so that I can send keystrokes to those applications. Of course, SendKeys sends keystrokes to the active application. Presumably, I should use AppActivate to make the desired "target application" the active one. However, AppActivate requires an explicit Window title. Very often, applications change the Window title to reflect the current workspace, making it impossible to predict what the current window title is for a particular application.

**Technique**

You need to break a high-level function down into its component parts to accomplish this task. Most of the functions of Visual Basic are derived from one or more functions of the Windows API. Further, many of the high-level functions in the API are built using a number of low-level functions, also in the API. For example, by using SendMessage to send the LB_DIR message to a "normal" list box, you can populate the control with a list of files matching a specification, thus creating a File list. Visual Basic's DoEvents function is just a wrapper around the PeekMessage API function.

The AppActivate function is simply a combination of the FindWindow and SetActiveWindow API functions. Using these two functions instead of AppActivate gives more flexibility when searching for the window of another application, when used in tandem with the WndPeek utility, covered in How-To 6.16 Simulate SPY in Visual Basic. Using WndPeek, we can determine the "classname" of a window and with FindWindow, you have the choice to search for a window based on its class, rather than its caption.

Because the class of a window will not change based on the current workspace of an application, this is a consistent way to search for a window.

**Steps**

Open and run FINDAPP.MAK. In the text box, simply enter the classname of the window for which you want to search (such as Notepad). The classname is not case sensitive. Then either press Enter or

**Figure 6-6** Appearance of the FindApp form

click on the Search button. If FindApp finds a match, it displays the window handle (hWnd) in the caption bar and activates the corresponding window, much the same way the Visual Basic AppActivate function does, using the caption.

To determine the classname of a particular window you can use WndPeek. Table 6-9 lists a few classnames to get you started. (Note that the classname used by WINVER.EXE and SETUP.EXE is the same)

| Classname | Application |
|---|---|
| SciCalc | CALC.EXE |
| CalWndMain | CALENDAR.EXE |
| Cardfile | CARDFILE.EXE |
| Clipboard | CLIPBOARD.EXE |
| Clock | CLOCK.EXE |
| CtlPanelClass | CONTROL.EXE |
| Session | MS-DOS.EXE |
| Notepad | NOTE.EXE |
| pbParent | PBRUSH.EXE |
| Pif | PIFEDIT.EXE |
| PrintManager | PRINTMAN.EXE |
| Recorder | RECORDER.EXE |
| Reversi | REVERSI.EXE |
| #32770 | SETUP.EXE |
| Solitaire | SOL.EXE |
| Terminal | TERMINAL.EXE |
| WFS_Frame | WINFILE.EXE |
| MW_WINHELP | WINHELP.EXE |
| #32770 | WINVER.EXE |
| MSWRITE_MENU | WRITE.EXE |

**Table 6-9** Determining the classname of a window

To create FindApp, perform the following steps:

1. Create a new project called FINDAPP.MAK. and a new form with the objects and properties in Table 6-10. Save the form as FINDAPP.FRM. When complete, the form should resemble Figure 6-6.

| Object | Property | Setting |
|---|---|---|
| Form | FormName | Form1 |
| | Caption | Find an App |

*Table 6-10. continued*

| Object | Property | Setting |
|---|---|---|
| Label | CtlName | Label1 |
| | Caption | Enter Class Name |
| Text box | CtlName | Text1 |
| Button | CtlName | Command1 |
| | Caption | Searh |
| | Default | TRUE |

**Table 6-10** FindApp project form's objects and properties

2. Insert the following code in the Declarations section of Form1.

```
DefInt A-Z

Declare Function FindWindow Lib "User" (ByVal lpClassName As Any, ByVal ⇐
lpCaption As Any)
Declare Sub SetActiveWindow Lib "User" (ByVal hWnd)

Const NULL = 0&
```

3. Insert the following code in the Command1_Click procedure.

```
Sub Command1_Click ()
    ClassName$ = Text1.Text
    FoundhWnd = FindWindow(ClassName$, NULL)
    If FoundhWnd <> 0 Then
        Form1.Caption = "Found: " + Str$(FoundhWnd)
        SetActiveWindow (FoundhWnd)
    Else
        Form1.Caption = ClassName$ + " not found!"
    End If
End Sub
```

**How It Works**

The FindWindow function will search for a window based either on its caption or its classname. It then returns the hWnd property of the window if there is a match, or a zero if there is no match. By passing a classname with a NULL for a caption, we tell FindWindow that all captions should match. You can think of it like a file specification, where you can search for a file based on its extension or its filename.

**Comments**

It is interesting to note that FindWindow is described in the Windows API reference as taking two "long pointers to strings" for parameters. Normally, this would imply that two strings must be passed using the ByVal directive. However, declaring the function with ByVal in Visual Basic prevents passing a NULL pointer. If we were to pass a "null string" (that is, "") to this function, we would be passing a pointer to a "null string" and not a "null pointer." This would imply that we were searching for a window that had no caption or no classname. Instead we need to pass a LONG with a value of zero, hence our NULL constant.

We accomplish this by declaring the parameters to FindWindow "As Any," thereby disabling parameter checking by Visual Basic. Use the As Any parameter type with care, because if you place an invalid variable type on the stack, your application will almost certainly visit the Twilight Zone.

---

**6.10    How do I...**

# Determine how many function keys are on my user's keyboard?

Complexity: Easy

### Problem

I'd like to offer function keys for some of the common operations in my application (like saving a file, or printing a document). But different keyboards have a different number of function keys. How can I adapt my program to the type of keyboard a user has?

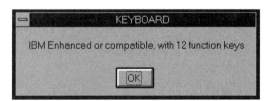

**Figure 6-7** The Keyboard project in action

### Technique

Although you should avoid making your Windows applications hardware-specific, if you can adapt it to take advantage of the complete range of hardware present, that will make the application perform better.

You can determine how many function keys your user's keyboard includes by using the Windows API function GetKeyboardType. GetKeyboardType can return the make and model of keyboard installed for Windows (for example, the original PC keyboard, with the 10 function keys along the left or the Enhanced keyboard, with 12 function keys along the top) and can also return the number of function keys on that keyboard.

If the call to GetKeyboardType determines that the user has a keyboard with 12 function keys, for example, you can check in a KeyDown or KeyUp event subroutine for presses of function key F11 or F12, and respond accordingly.

### Steps

Open and run KEYBOARD.MAK. When you click on the form, a message box describing your keyboard will appear. See Figure 6-7 for an example of the message box.

1. Create a new project called KEYBOARD.MAK. and a new form. There are no controls on this form. Save the form as KEYBOARD.FRM. Put the following code in the Declarations section of the form. This Declare statement gives the form access to the GetKeyboardType API function.

```
Declare Function GetKeyboardType Lib "Keyboard" (ByVal nTypeFlag As ⇐
Integer) As Integer
```

2. Put the following code in the Form_Click event subroutine. This code calls GetKeyboardType to get the make and model of keyboard, and then again to get the number of function keys on the keyboard. Then it pops up a message box with that information.

```
Sub Form_Click ()
    Select Case GetKeyboardType(0)
        Case 1
            Msg$ = "IBM PC/XT or compatible"
        Case 2
            Msg$ = "Olivetti M24"
        Case 3
            Msg$ = "IBM AT or compatible"
        Case 4
            Msg$ = "IBM Enhanced or compatible"
        Case 5
            Msg$ = "Nokia 1050 or compatible"
        Case 6
            Msg$ = "Nokia 9140 or compatible"
    End Select

    FKeys = GetKeyboardType(2)

    MsgBox Msg$ + ", with" + Str$(FKeys) + " function keys"
End Sub
```

## How It Works

The GetKeyboardType API function returns some relatively low-level information about the keyboard that the user specified when installing Windows. The keyboard type may be changed by running the Windows Setup program.

GetKeyboardType accepts a parameter, nTypeFlag, that specifies what information about the keyboard GetKeyboardType is to return. If nTypeFlag is 0, GetKeyboardType returns a code indicating the make and model of the keyboard. (See the Form_Click event subroutine for details on which code indicates which keyboard type.)

If nTypeFlag is 1, GetKeyboardType returns the "subtype" of the keyboard. This subtype is defined in the keyboard driver by the keyboard manufacturer. Unless you have specific information from the keyboard manufacturer, the subtype is meaningless.

If nTypeFlag is 2, GetKeyboardType returns the number of function keys on the installed keyboard. You may be thinking that it's redundant to have a separate call for the keyboard type when an nTypeFlag of 1 will tell you the keyboard type. However, the Olivetti keyboard, for example, can have either 12 or 18 function keys, and there's nothing stopping a keyboard manufacturer from coming out with a keyboard that's identical to an Enhanced keyboard, except with another row of 12 function keys, for a total of 24. If that manufacturer provided an updated keyboard driver for Windows, a call to GetKeyboardType with an nTypeFlag of 2 would properly reveal the presence of 24 function keys.

### Comment

To interpret the KeyCode parameter passed to a KeyDown or KeyUp event subroutine, you'll need to use the key codes defined in the CONSTANT.TXT file from your Visual Basic disks.

---

**6.11    How do I...**

# Determine the directory where Windows is installed?

Complexity: Intermediate

### Problem

As I write my application's installation program, I realize that there are several auxiliary files that I must include, like the VBRUN100.DLL and several custom control VBX libraries. These files must be placed someplace where Windows can find them when the user goes to start my application. How do I find out the best place to put the files?

### Technique

Store files with DLL and .VBX extensions in either the main Windows directory or Windows' own system directory. The default names for these directories are WINDOWS and WINDOWS\SYSTEM, respectively. However, the user is free to change the main Windows directory name, and can install Windows on any hard drive in the system, so using C:\WINDOWS as the directory name won't always work.

Luckily, the Windows API offers two functions—GetWindowsDirectory and GetSystemDirectory—that return the names of the two Windows directories regardless of what the user called them. Your installation program could call these API functions and then copy all the needed .DLL and .VBX files to either of those two directories.

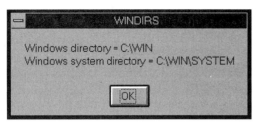

**Figure 6-8** The WinDirs project in action

**Steps**

Open and run WINDIRS.MAK. When you click on the form, a message box appears that shows the names of the two Windows directories. See Figure 6-8 for an example of that message box.

1. Create a new project called WIN-DIRS.MAK. and a new form. There are no controls on this form. Save the form as WINDIRS.FRM.

2. Add the VBHOWTO.BAS module to the project. VBHOWTO.BAS contains the VBHTTrim$ function used in the Form_Click event subroutine. (This VBHTTrim$z function was added to the module in How-To 3.9 Trim null characters from a string.)

3. Put the following code in the Declarations section of the form. These Declare statements provide the form access to the Windows API functions.

```
Declare Function GetWindowsDirectory Lib "Kernel" (ByVal lpBuffer As ⇐
String, ByVal nSize As Integer) As Integer
Declare Function GetSystemDirectory Lib "Kernel" (ByVal lpBuffer As ⇐
String, ByVal nSize As Integer) As Integer
```

4. Put the following code in the Form_Click event subroutine. This code calls the GetWindowsDirectory and GetSystemDirectory API functions and uses the MsgBox statement to show them to the user. GetWindowsDirectory and GetSystemDirectory return 0 if there was an error, so we check for that and display a message box indicating there was an error.

```
Sub Form_Click ()
   WinDir$ = Space$(144)
   WinSysDir$ = Space$(144)

   If GetWindowsDirectory(WinDir$, 144) = 0 Or
GetSystemDirectory(WinSysDir$, 144) = 0 Then
      MsgBox "Unable to determine Windows directories", 16
   Else
      WinDir$ = VBHTTrim$(WinDir$)
      WinSysDir$ = VBHTTrim$(WinSysDir$)
      MsgBox "Windows directory = " + WinDir$ + Chr$(13) + Chr$(10) +
"Windows system directory = " + WinSysDir$
   End If
End Sub
```

## How It Works

First, the Form_Click event subroutine initializes the WinDir$ and WinSysDir$ variables to 144 spaces, which is the theoretical maximum length of the Windows directory names.

The GetWindowsDirectory and GetSystemDirectory API functions return 0 if there was some error processing the Windows directory names, so the If statement calls GetWindowsDirectory and GetSystemDirectory and compares their return values with zero. If either return value is zero, the MsgBox statement pops up a message.

This If statement is a little trick you can use if the return value of any function indicates an error condition. Normally, you might use code similar to the following:

```
I = GetWindowsDirectory(WinDir$, 144)
If I = 0 Then
   MsgBox "Unable to determine Windows directories", 16
   Exit Sub
End If

I = GetSystemDirectory(WinSysDir$, 144)
If I = 0 Then
   MsgBox "Unable to determine Windows directories", 16
   Exit Sub
End If
```

But if all you're doing is checking whether an error occurred and you won't be using the function's return value for anything else, you can call the function as the condition part of an If statement. You can even combine multiple calls using the logical Or operator, as in the Form_Click event subroutine.

If the GetWindowsDirectory and GetSystemDirectory API functions were both successful, a call to the VBHTTrim$ function removes the extra spaces from the strings, and the null characters that API functions put into strings.

## Comment

The GetWindowsDirectory and GetSystemDirectory API functions do not add a backslash at the end of the directory names, which can be useful when you need to copy files. The only directory name that the functions terminate with a backslash is the root directory, for example, C:\. The following code will ensure that the directory name ends in a single backslash.

```
If Right$(WinDir$, 1) <> "\" Then WinDir$ = WinDir$ + "\"
```

## 6.12    How do I...

# Determine system resources?

Complexity: Advanced

**Problem**

The About... dialog box of the Program Manager contains a value labeled Free System Resources. What are "resources?" I thought that resources included icons, bitmaps, and dialog boxes contained in program files. "System resources" seem to be something else. I know that when they get too low, applications cannot be loaded even though there is a lot of "Free Memory." How do I determine how many resources there are and how many my application needs?

**Technique**

There are two different contexts in which the issue of resources comes up. When you discuss an .EXE file, resources refers to noncode or data such as icons, bitmaps, metafiles, dialog boxes, and cursors stored in the .EXE file. The number of these resources in a particular .EXE has absolutely no bearing on "System Resources."

System resources, however, refer to a number of objects that can be created by the system. There are two types of system resources—those in USER.EXE and those in the Graphics Device Interface DLL (GDI.EXE). USER.EXE is the system dynamic link library that manages the creation of windows and controls. Accordingly, "User" resources refer to the number of windows and controls that can be created. GDI.EXE is the system DLL that manages the creation of graphical objects such as brushes, pens, and display contexts (hDC).

One of the greatest benefits of Windows 3.0 is its virtual memory management, which allows for unlimited virtual RAM. Virtual RAM enables you to store local data and documents that are "larger than memory" with little or no special effort by using the hard disk to store sections of RAM. However, Windows 3 also introduced an incredible limitation in the form of system resources. Simply put, User and GDI create arrays to hold the handles of different resources as they are created. Therefore, the entire system is limited to the number of elements in each of these arrays.

Determining the percentage of remaining system resources requires a call to an undocumented API function, GetHeapSpaces, which returns a long integer. The high-order word contains the total number of resources that can be created and the low-order word contains the number already in use. With their values we can determine the number of remaining resource "elements" as a percentage of the total. We can check available resources for both User and GDI. The number displayed by the Program Manager is the lower of these two percentages.

**Figure 6-9** System Resource Monitor at run time

Resources

**Figure 6-10** The minimized icon showing system resource status

However, it is important to note that these figures are independent of each other. It is possible to "run out" of one sort of resource while plenty of the other remains. In fact, this is what almost always happens. Because windows and controls are more often used than graphic objects, the Program Manager is nearly always displaying the percentage of free User resources as the percentage of free GDI resources is almost always much higher.

This How-To creates a generalized function that returns the percentage of free resources for a given module (User or GDI). Our form will display both figures, as shown in Figure 6-9. Finally, when minimized, our utility will periodically check the system resources and paint the result on the icon, as you can see in Figure 6-10.

**Steps**

Open and run RESOURCE.MAK. You will see the remaining resources in both User and GDI; the one that is smaller will be selected. When you minimize the utility, the little monitor icon will be updated with the current resource percentage available. To recreate the example, perform the following steps:

1. Create a new project called RESOURCE.MAK. Create a new form with the following objects and properties from Table 6-11, and save it as RESOURCE.FRM.

| Object | Property | Setting |
|---|---|---|
| Form | FormName | Form1 |
| | Caption | Resources |
| | Icon | COMPUTER\MONITR01.ICO |
| | ScaleMode | Pixels |
| Radio button | CtlName | User |
| | Caption | User |
| Radio button | CtlName | GDI |
| | Caption | GDI |
| Timer | CtlName | Timer1 |
| | Interval | 2000 |
| | Enabled TRUE | |

**Table 6-11** Resource project form's objects and properties

2. Insert the following code in the Declarations section of the form.

```
DefInt A-Z
Declare Function GetModuleHandle Lib "Kernel" (ByVal ModName$)
Declare Function GetHeapSpaces& Lib "Kernel" (ByVal hModule)

Function GetFreeResources (ModuleName$)
   rInfo& = GetHeapSpaces&(GetModuleHandle(ModuleName$))
   Totalr& = HiWord&(rInfo&)
   FreeR& = LoWord(rInfo&)
   GetFreeResources = FreeR& * 100 \ Totalr&
End Function

Function HiWord& (LongInt&)
   Temp& = LongInt& \ &H10000
   If Temp& < 0 Then Temp& = Temp& + &H10000
   HiWord& = Temp&
End Function

Function LoWord& (LongInt&)
   Temp& = LongInt& Mod &H10000
   If Temp& < 0 Then Temp& = Temp& + &H10000
   LoWord& = Temp&
End Function

Function Min (P1, P2)
   If P1 < P2 Then Min = P1 Else Min = P2
End Function
```

3. Insert the following code in the Form_Paint event handler.

```
Sub Form_Paint ()
   UserFree = GetFreeResources("User")
   GDIFree = GetFreeResources("GDI")
   User.Caption = "User: " + Str$(UserFree) + "%"
   GDI.Caption = "GDI:  " + Str$(GDIFree) + "%"
   If UserFree < GDIFree Then
      User.Value = -1
   Else
      GDI.Value = -1
   End If
End Sub
```

4. Insert the following code in the Form_Resize procedure.

```
Sub Form_Resize ()
   If WindowState = 1 Then
      Timer1.Enabled = -1
   Else
      Timer1.Enabled = 0
   End If
End Sub
```

5. Insert the following code in the Timer1_Timer procedure.

```
Sub Timer1_Timer ()
     TFree = Min(GetFreeResources("User"), GetFreeResources("GDI"))
     If TFree <> OldTotal Then
        Text$ = Format$(TFree, "00") + "%"
        Cls
        CurrentX = 7
        CurrentY = 8
        Print Text$
        OldTotal = TFree
     End If
End Sub
```

### How It Works

Once you know about the undocumented GetHeapSpaces API function, the rest of the program is fairly straightforward. First a handle to the "module" for the library we are examining is required. We find this via the GetModuleHandle API function.

You might think it strange that our Visual Basic HiWord& and LoWord& functions are defined as long integer functions. This is because the only way to represent an "unsigned" integer is with a long integer. An unsigned integer is one that is always positive. As you know, the valid range of a signed integer is -32,767 to +32,768. However, the range of an unsigned short integer is 0 to 65,535. The only way to represent numbers greater than 32,768 in Visual Basic is with a long integer.

The Form_Paint procedure simply makes calls to GetFreeResources for User and GDI, fills in the caption properties of the corresponding radio buttons, and "clicks" the one that is smaller. Because the Form_Paint event will occur when the form is restored from an iconic posting, this information will be automatically updated whenever the resources icon is restored.

The Form_Resize procedure will be invoked whenever the form is resized either by directly manipulating the size border or by minimizing, restoring, or maximizing the form. Here we check whether the form is minimized (WindowState = 1) and if so, enable the timer, and if not, disable it.

The Timer1_Timer procedure begins determining the percentage of free system resources. Again, the Min function was constructed to make the code more readable. The value of TFree is compared to a static variable called OldTotal. Only if they are different do we proceed. This is just a small detail but it does serve to minimize flicker and, more importantly, drain on the CPU.

Cls clears our icon back to its original state so that we have a "clean slate," as it were, to draw our text. We then use CurrentX and CurrentY to position the "text cursor" to an appropriate location in our icon. (Note the values are hard-coded and may differ in if you use another icon.) Finally, we use Print to print out the percentage of free resources.

## Comments

Resources are one of the most serious limitations of Windows 3.0, but much less serious under Windows 3.1 because the menus (one of the largest resource consumers) have been seperated into their own array. In addition, Program Manager has been rewritten to mitigate its resource consumption.

In addition, the GetHeapSpaces function, although undocumented in version 3.0, is part of a documented TOOLHELP.DLL in version 3.1.

There are two relevant functions: GDIHeapInfo and UserHeapInfo, which fill record variables with information about the appropriate heaps.

```
Type HeapInfoStruc
    dwSize as Long
    wHeapFree as Integer
    wMaxHeap as Integer
    percentFree as Integer
    hSegment as Integer
End Type

DefInt A-Z

Declare Sub GDIHeapInfo Lib "ToolHelp.DLL" (HeapInfo as HeapInfoStruc)
Declare Sub UserHeapInfo Lib "ToolHelp.DLL" (HeapInfo as HeapInfoStruc)

Dim HeapInfo as HeapInfoStruc

GDIHeapInfo HeapInfo
GDIFree = HeapInfo.percentFree
UserHeapInfo HeapInfo
UserFree = HeapInfo.percentFree
FreeResources = Min (UserFree, GDIFree)
```

Strangely enough, like DOS, the undocumented function GetHeapSpaces appears to still work in Windows 3.1, but it reflects inaccurate information because the nature of resource usage has changed in Windows 3.1. It is therefore, better to make use of the documented API in future Windows releases.

The best way for you to control resource consumption in your application is to minimize the number of controls you use and the the number of loaded forms. For example, you gain huge resource savings by using Print, along with CurrentX and CurrentY, instead of label controls.

## 6.13    How do I...

# Determine how much memory is available?

Complexity: Intermediate

### Problem

I'd like my application to be able to tell the user how much memory is available in the system, like Windows' Program Manager. There is no Visual Basic function that gives the amount of memory. What can I do?

### Technique

Although QuickBASIC for DOS gives you the FRE function to check how much memory is in the system, Microsoft left that function out of Visual Basic. However, you can turn to the Windows API GetFreeSpace function, which returns the amount of available memory, in bytes.

**Figure 6-11**
The Memory project in action

### Steps

Open and run MEMORY.MAK. The Memory application runs itself as an icon and prints the amount of memory available on the top line of the icon as shown in Figure 6-11. Try opening another application and watch how the number goes down.

1. Create a new project called MEMORY.MAK. and a new form with the objects and properties shown in Table 6-12. Save the form as MEMORY.FRM.

| Object | Property | Setting |
|--------|----------|---------|
| Form | BackColor | &H00000000& |
| | Caption | Free memory |
| | FontBold | False |
| | ForeColor | &H00FFFFFF& |
| | FormName | MemoryForm |
| | MaxButton | False |
| | MinButton | False |
| Timer | CtlName | Timer1 |
| | Enabled | True |
| | Interval | 1000 |

**Table 6-12** Memory project form's objects and properties

2. Put the following code in the Declarations section of the form. This Declare statement gives the form access to the GetFreeSpace API function.

```
Declare Function GetFreeSpace Lib "Kernel" (ByVal wFlags As Integer) As Long
```

3. Put the following code in the Form_Load event subroutine. This code clears the icon that would normally be displayed, then iconizes the form.

```
Sub Form_Load ()
   Icon = LoadPicture() 'clears default icon for form
   WindowState = 1      'sets form to minimized icon state
End Sub
```

4. Put the following code in the Timer1_Timer event subroutine. This code updates the display of the icon with the amount of free memory at the time the timer control triggered.

```
Sub Timer1_Timer ()
   Static OldFreeSpace As Long, FreeSpace As Long

   FreeSpace = GetFreeSpace(0)

   If OldFreeSpace <> FreeSpace Then
      OldFreeSpace = FreeSpace
      Cls
      Print Format$(FreeSpace \ 1024);
   End If
End Sub
```

### How It Works

The GetFreeSpace API function returns the amount of memory in bytes Windows has available for use. The wFlags parameter is only used in Real mode Windows, which Visual Basic doesn't support. (Visual Basic applications and Visual Basic itself require Standard or 386 Enhanced mode Windows.)

The form has a timer control with an interval of 1000 (measured in milliseconds). The code in the timer's Timer event subroutine updates the icon's display of how much memory is available, if necessary. The code keeps a variable that stores how much memory was available the last time the icon's display was updated. If that variable and the current amount of available memory match, there's no reason to waste the time it would take to update the icon's display.

Because that variable is declared using the Static statement, Visual Basic initializes it to zero. GetFreeSpace will always return more than zero, so the two variables don't match the first time the timer is triggered and the amount of available memory will be printed on the icon's display.

The Cls method clears the icon to the background color (which was set with the BackColor property when the form was designed) and sets the CurrentX and CurrentY properties to zero.

The Print method then prints the amount of available memory on the icon, in kilobytes. Because the FontSize property of the form was set to 8.25, there is just enough room for the maximum number of digits that could appear.

### Comment

Note the use of the integer division operator(/) in the Timer1_Timer event subroutine. Because the GetFreeSpace API function returns a long integer, you can speed up your calculations by using pure integer operations on it, rather than the floating point division operator(/).

---

**6.14    How do I...**

# Determine which version of Windows my application is running on?

Complexity: Intermediate

### Problem

My application will be run on a variety of machines. I'd like to ensure compatibility with future versions of Windows. If I could determine the current version of Windows, I could use certain features only if they exist in the version of Windows running on the machine.

### Technique

The Windows API library contains a function called GetVersion that returns the version number of Windows. You can use this function to restrict your program's use of certain features. For example, Windows 3.1 provides some common file dialog boxes in a DLL that you can access. If the user is running your application under Windows 3.0, though, those dialog boxes won't be available and you'll have to provide them yourself. If, however, GetVersion reveals that Windows 3.1 is running, you are free to make those calls.

**Figure 6-12**
The Version project in action

### Steps

Open and run VERSION.MAK. This project is based on the Memory project in How-To 6.13 Determine how much memory is available, but adds the Windows version number in the icon below the amount of available memory shown in Figure 6-12.

1. Create a new project called VERSION.MAK. and a new form with the objects and properties listed in Table 6-13. Save the form as VERSION.FRM.

| Object | Property | Setting |
|--------|----------|---------|
| Form | BackColor | &H00000000& |
| | Caption | Windows version |
| | FontBold | False |
| | ForeColor | &H00FFFFFF& |
| | FormName | VersionForm |
| | MaxButton | False |
| | MinButton | False |
| Timer | CtlName | Timer1 |
| | Enabled | True |
| | Interval | 1000 |

**Table 6-13** Version project form's objects and properties

2. Put the following code in the Declarations section of the form. This Declare statement gives the form access to the GetFreeSpace and GetVersion API functions and declares some variables.

```
Declare Function GetFreeSpace Lib "Kernel" (ByVal wFlags As Integer) As Long
Declare Function GetVersion Lib "Kernel" () As Integer

Dim MajorVersion As Integer, MinorVersion As Integer
```

3. Put the following code in the Form_Load event subroutine. This code clears the icon that would normally be displayed, then iconizes the form and gets the Windows version number using the GetVersion API function.

```
Sub Form_Load ()
   Icon = LoadPicture()
   WindowState = 1
   Version% = GetVersion()
   MajorVersion = Version% And &HFF
   MinorVersion = (Version% And &HFF00) \ 256
End Sub
```

4. Put the following code in the Timer1_Timer event subroutine. This code updates the display of the icon with the amount of free memory every one second and redisplays the Windows version number that was determined in the Form_Load event subroutine.

```
Sub Timer1_Timer ()
   Static OldFreeSpace As Long, FreeSpace As Long

   FreeSpace = GetFreeSpace(0)

   If OldFreeSpace <> FreeSpace Then
```

```
        OldFreeSpace = FreeSpace
        Cls
        Print Format$(FreeSpace \ 1024); "K"
        Print "Win"; Format$(MajorVersion); "."; Format$(MinorVersion)
    End If
End Sub
```

### How It Works

See How-To 6.13 Determine how much memory is available, for more information about the GetFreeSpace API function.

The GetVersion API function takes no arguments and just returns the Windows version number. The version is a fractional number, however. The number before the decimal point is called the major version number; the number after the decimal point is the minor version number. So, for example, for version 3.0, the major version number is 3 and the minor version number is 0.

GetVersion puts the major version number in the low-order byte of its return value, and the minor version number in the high-order byte. The Form_Load event subroutine plucks out the major and minor version numbers and stores them in the MajorVersion and MinorVersion variables.

Then in the Timer1_Timer event subroutine, the Windows version number is printed after the current amount of available memory. Because there is very little extra space on the icon, the Format$ function strips out the extra spaces.

### Comment

If you want your application to decide whether it should use the features of another version of Windows, the best place to check the Windows version number is in the Form_Load event subroutine. So you might have code like this:

```
Sub Form_Load ()
    Version% = GetVersion()
    MajorVersion = Version% And &HFF
    MinorVersion = (Version% And &HFF00) \ 256

    If MajorVersion = 3 And MinorVersion = 1 Then
        ' do Windows 3.1 stuff
    Else
        ' stick with Windows 3.0 stuff
    End If
End Sub
```

## 6.15 How do I...

# Find out everything about the system configuration?

Complexity: Advanced

### Problem

A well-behaved application should know about the system on which it is running. Information such as the version of Windows, the total available memory, and current directory is extremely helpful. How can I obtain this information in Visual Basic?

### Technique

This How-To ties together the previous couple of How-Tos in one larger project. In QuickBasic, it is possible to retrieve a lot of system information by using a "CALL Interrupt" construct. Interrupts, under DOS, are roughly equivalent to API calls under Windows. Unfortunately, although the Windows API is much richer than the DOS API, a huge number of functions that are present in DOS were omitted from Windows. Therefore, until an equivalent to CALL Interrupt is made available to Visual Basic programmers, much of the system information will remain unavailable, except through the use of dynamic linked libraries written in other languages.

However, there are a number of Windows API functions devoted to interrogating the system that can be used here. The available system information is sort of a mixed bag, and the importance of each piece of information is dependent on the application you have in mind. We will proceed a little differently in this How-To and put our system functions in a separate Visual Basic module that can then be included in any Visual Basic application.

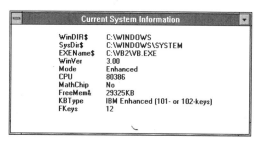

**Figure 6-13** Appearance of the Sysinfo form

### Steps

Open and run SYSINFO.MAK. You will see a dump of system information, as shown in Figure 6-13. The information is updated every time the screen is repainted, so if you minimize SysInfo, load a collection of programs, and restore SysInfo, you will see the changes to memory that result.

1. Create a new project called SYSINFO.MAK. Create a new module called SYSINFO.BAS. Insert the following code in that module.

```
DefInt A-Z
Declare Function GetWindowsDirectory Lib "Kernel" (ByVal Buff$, ⇐
ByVal sizeBuf)
Declare Function GetSystemDirectory Lib "Kernel" (ByVal Buff$, ⇐
ByVal sizeBuf)
Declare Function GetClassWord Lib "User" (ByVal hWnd, ByVal nIndex)
Declare Function GetModuleFileName Lib "Kernel" (ByVal hModule, ⇐
ByVal Buff$, ByVal sizeBuf)
Declare Function GetVersion Lib "Kernel" ()
Declare Function GetFreeSpace& Lib "Kernel" (ByVal wFlags)
Declare Function GetWinFlags& Lib "Kernel" ()
Declare Function GetKeyBoardType Lib "Keyboard" (ByVal nFlag)

'From Win.INI
Const GCW_HMODULE = -16

Const WF_CPU286 = &H2
Const WF_CPU386 = &H4
Const WF_CPU486 = &H8
Const WF_STANDARD = &H10
Const WF_ENHANCED = &H20
Const WF_8087 = &H400

'From CONSTANT.TXT
Const TRUE = -1
Const FALSE = 0

Function EXEName$ ()
   Wnd = Screen.ActiveForm.hWnd
   hModule = GetClassWord(Wnd, GCW_HMODULE)
   Buff$ = Space$(255)
   TChars = GetModuleFileName(hModule, Buff$, 255)
   EXEName$ = Left$(Buff$, TChars)
End Function

Function WinDir$ ()
   Buff$ = Space$(255)
   TChars = GetWindowsDirectory(Buff$, 255)
   WinDir$ = Left$(Buff$, TChars)
End Function

Function SysDir$ ()
   Buff$ = Space$(255)
   TChars = GetSystemDirectory(Buff$, 255)
   SysDir$ = Left$(Buff$, TChars)
End Function

Function WinVer ()
   Version = GetVersion()
   WinVer = ((Version Mod 256) * 100) + Version \ 256
End Function

Function FreeMem& ()
   FreeMem& = GetFreeSpace(0)

End Function
```

```
Function CPU ()
   Flags& = GetWinFlags&()
   Match = 1
   Select Case Match
     Case (Flags& And WF_CPU486) \ WF_CPU486
        CPU = 486
     Case (Flags& And WF_CPU386) \ WF_CPU386
        CPU = 386
     Case Else
        CPU = 286
   End Select
End Function

Function Mode ()
   Flags& = GetWinFlags&
   If Flags& And WF_ENHANCED Then
     Mode = WF_ENHANCED
   Else
     Mode = WF_STANDARD
   End If
End Function

Function MathChip ()
   Flags& = GetWinFlags&
   If Flags& And WF_8087 Then
     MathChip = TRUE
   Else
     MathChip = FALSE
   End If
End Function

Function FKeys ()
   FKeys = GetKeyBoardType(2)
End Function

Function KBType ()
   KBType = GetKeyBoardType(0)
End Function

Function KBSubType ()
   KBSubType = GetKeyBoardType(1)
End Function
```

2. Create a new form and save it as SYSINFO.FRM.

3. In the Declarations section of the form, insert the following:

```
DefInt A-Z

Const WF_STANDARD = &H10
Const WF_ENHANCED = &H20

'Custom Constants
Const KB_XT = 1
```

```
Const KB_M24 = 2
Const KB_AT = 3
Const KB_Enhanced = 4
Const KB_N1050 = 5
Const KB_N9140 = 6
```

4. In the Form_Paint procedure, insert the following:

```
Sub Form_Paint ()
    Form1.Cls
    Print
    Print , "WinDIR$", WinDir$()
    Print , "SysDir$", SysDir$()
    Print , "EXEName$", EXEName$()
    Print , "WinVer", Format$(WinVer() / 100, "##.00")
    Print , "Mode",
    Select Case Mode()
        Case WF_ENHANCED
            Print "Enhanced"
        Case WF_STANDARD
            Print "Standard"
    End Select
    Print , "CPU", Format$(80000 + CPU())
    Print , "MathChip",
    If MathChip() Then
        Print "Yes"
    Else
        Print "No"
    End If
    Print , "FreeMem&", Format$(FreeMem&() \ 1024); "KB"
    Print , "KBType",
    Select Case KBType()
        Case KB_XT
            Print "IBM PC/XT, or compatible (83-key)"
        Case KB_M24
            Print "Olivetti M24 'ICO' (102-key)"
        Case KB_AT
            Print "IBM AT or similar (84-key)"
        Case KB_Enhanced
            Print "IBM Enhanced (101- or 102-keys)"
        Case KB_N1050
            Print "Nokia 1050 or similar"
        Case KB_N9140
            Print "Nokia 9140 or similar"
    End Select
    Print , "FKeys", Format$(FKeys())
End Sub
```

5. Run the application. Minimize the application, open some applications, and restore your Sysinfo utility. You'll see the information on the form is updated.

## How It Works

Most of the API calls used in the SYSINFO.BAS module are self-explanatory but we will discuss those that are not. Essentially this is a semi-random assortment of system functions that can be called from any application that includes SYSINFO.BAS. You may add SYSINFO.BAS to a project by selecting Add File... from the File menu in Visual Basic.

### Name of the Currently Running Application

The EXEName$ function is a little tricky, but this information can be exceptionally useful to use from within an application. EXEName$ is the name of the currently running application, including the path in which the .EXE file can be found. This is useful for two reasons. First, the path eases the search for support, configuration, and data files that are found in the same directory as the .EXE file. Often an .EXE file will be launched without a change to the current directory. This happens when the program's directory is in the path and when the calling program uses an explicit path to your application. Normally, this is not a problem, but if you need to find other files in the same directory, your application needs some way to determine the directory in which it resides. Second, the name of the .EXE is useful when you want to provide special functionality based on the name that has been given to your program. For example, you might need the correct EXE name to find other instances of your application running on the system.

The EXEName$ function first finds the hWnd property of the currently active window. This allows the function to be used more generically. Then GetClassWord is used to determine the current instance handle. This is the handle to the application itself, that is created when the application is launched by Windows. It is this handle that must be passed to the GetModuleFileName function to retrieve the exact name of the currently running process. The result of the function is the number of characters in the name, and this is used to assign the EXEName$ function result.

### Windows and SYSTEM Path Names

WinDir$ and SysDir$ are just shells around the Windows API functions GetWindowsDirectory and GetSystemDirectory. WinDir$ is the full path of the directory from which Windows was run. This is useful when you are trying to locate a support or initialization file stored there. SysDir$ returns the current "system" directory. This directory is usually named SYSTEM and branches off of the WinDir$ directory. This directory most often contains dynamic link libraries and support utilities.

### Windows Version, Flags, and Keyboard Type

The GetVersion API function returns an integer value for the version of Windows that is currently running. The high-order byte contains the "minor" version and the low-order byte contains the "major" version. The Mod function is used to retrieve the remainder of a division by 256, which returns the "major" version. The minor version, or "high byte," is retrieved through simple integer division. We multiply the major version by 100 so that the entire result can be expressed as an integer. This makes comparisons much faster. In other words, if you wanted to make sure that the current Windows version was at least 3.1 you could just check to see if WinVer => 310.

The GetWinFlags API function provides a wealth of information in a single long integer. The result contains a number of True/False values that correspond to bits in the number. CPU, Mode, and MathChip are simply checking the status of the relevant bits in Flags&.

The FKeys, KBType, and KBSubType are all shells around the API function, GetKeyBoardType, but with different parameters. Note that this function is found in a special kind of DLL called a driver. KEYBOARD.DRV will be specific on each system to the installed hardware. However, all keyboard drivers under Windows contain this function to retrieve the keyboard type.

SYSINFO.FRM is not very sophisticated but provides a means to display current system information. In the Declarations section of the Form, we have simply created some constants to make the code more readable.

The work is done in the Form_Paint event handler because this guarantees that the information will be updated when the Form is restored after being minimized. The code in Form_Paint is fairly self-explanatory.

### Comments

Note that, unlike QuickBasic, Visual Basic does not require you to declare routines that are in separate modules in your project. The Declare statement is reserved for the use of truly external routines contained in DLLs.

Note also that Format$ is often used instead of Str$. This prevents the addition of a leading space at the beginning of the created string.

---

**6.16    How do I...**

## Simulate SPY in Visual Basic?

Complexity: Advanced

### Problem

A number of tricks involve knowing more about the windows in applications other than mine. To use FindWindow, SendMessage, and some other API calls, I need the name of the window class, its handle, and so on. I have seen an application that ships with the Software Development Kit (SDK) called SPY that accomplishes this. Can I accomplish the same thing using Visual Basic?

### Technique

While somewhat involved, this is certainly possible in Visual Basic. In fact, in the process of accomplishing this, we will examine a number of Windows API calls and their functions, many of which can be used in other contexts.

SPY is one of the most useful utilities that ships with the Software Developers' Kit. Its primary purpose is to trace messages sent to various controls at run time to help you test an application. While we will not be duplicating this functionality, we can duplicate its ability to "look at" other windows and determine their class and parent. Using the Class name, we can use the FindWindow API function to find another control at run time. It is also educational to see the overuse of controls and their effect on resources.

The key issue, tracking the mouse movements outside of your form, is also the easiest. While Visual Basic can only track mouse messages within your forms directly, when an API function called SetCapture is enabled, every mouse action on the system is sent to your window. This technique, used by screen capture programs and many specialized applications, will be central to WndPeek.

In tracking the mouse movements, we need a way to find the current mouse location and learn whether it is over any windows. This is accomplished through calls to the GetMessagePos and WindowFromPoint API calls.

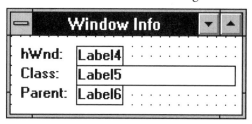

**Figure 6-14** Appearance of the Wndpeek form

As the mouse pointer moves across different windows, the application can make a number of API calls to get information about each window.

Finally, you can add an aesthetic feature that "highlights" the window as the mouse cursor passes over it. This allows you to see just how many windows a number of applications contain.

### Steps

To try the example, run the WNDPEEK.EXE file from the Program Manager. The utility will automatically go into "peek" mode, so just start to move the mouse cursor around the screen. You should see various windows becoming highlighted and their details displayed in WndPeek's information box. You might want to load your favorite application before loading WndPeek so that you can examine the windows of that application. When you click the mouse, WndPeek releases the mouse and exits. To recreate the demo, perform the following steps:

1. Create a new project called WNDPEEK.MAK. Create a new form with the objects and properties in Table 6-14, and save it as WND-PEEK.FRM. It will look like Figure 6-14.

| Object | Property | Setting |
| --- | --- | --- |
| Form | FormName | Form1 |
| | Caption | Window Info |
| Label | CtlName | Label1 |
| | Caption | hWnd: |
| Label | CtlName | Label2 |
| | Caption | Class: |
| Label | CtlName | Label3 |
| | Caption | Parent: |
| Label | CtlName | Label4 |
| | Caption | Label4 |
| Label | CtlName | Label5 |
| | Caption | Label5 |
| Label | CtlName | Label6 |
| | Caption | Label6 |

**Table 6-14** Wndpeek project form's objects and properties

2. Open the Declarations section of Form1 and insert the following code.

```
DefInt A-Z

'Subs in USER.EXE
Declare Sub SetCapture Lib "User" (ByVal hWnd)
Declare Sub ReleaseCapture Lib "User" ()
Declare Sub GetWindowRect Lib "User" (ByVal hWnd, MyRect As Rect)
Declare Sub ReleaseDC Lib "User" (ByVal hWnd, ByVal hDC)

'Functions in USER.EXE
Declare Function GetMessagePos& Lib "User" ()
Declare Function WindowFromPoint Lib "User" (ByVal MPos&)
Declare Function GetParent Lib "User" (ByVal hWnd)
Declare Function GetClassName Lib "User" (ByVal hWnd, ByVal Buff$, ⇐
ByVal sizeBuff)
Declare Function GetWindowText Lib "User" (ByVal hWnd, ByVal Buff$, ByVal ⇐
sizeBuff)
Declare Function GetWindowDC Lib "User" (ByVal hWnd)

'Subs in GDI.EXE
Declare Sub SetROP2 Lib "GDI" (ByVal hDC, ByVal DrawMode)
Declare Sub SelectObject Lib "GDI" (ByVal hDC, ByVal hPen)
Declare Sub Rectangle Lib "GDI" (ByVal hDC, ByVal X1, ByVal Y1, ByVal ⇐
X2, ByVal Y2)
Declare Sub DeleteObject Lib "GDI" (ByVal hPen)

'Functions in GDI.EXE
Declare Function CreatePen Lib "GDI" (ByVal pStyle, ByVal pWidth, ⇐
ByVal pClr&)
```

```
Declare Function GetStockObject Lib "GDI" (ByVal nIndex)

Const R2_NOT = 6
Const PS_InsideFrame = 6
Const Null_Brush = 5

Dim OldWnd As Integer
Dim MyRect As Rect

Sub BoxWindow (Wnd)
    GetWindowRect Wnd, MyRect
    TargetDC = GetWindowDC(Wnd)
    SetROP2 TargetDC, R2_NOT
    hPen = CreatePen(PS_InsideFram, 5, 0)
    SelectObject TargetDC, hPen
    SelectObject TargetDC, GetStockObject(Null_Brush)
    X2 = MyRect.Right - MyRect.Left
    Y2 = MyRect.Bottom - MyRect.Top
    Rectangle TargetDC, 0, 0, X2, Y2
    ReleaseDC Wnd, TargetDC
    DeleteObject (hPen)
End Sub
```

3. In the Form_Load procedure, insert the following code.

```
Sub Form_Load ()
    SetCapture hWnd
End Sub
```

4. In the Form_MouseMove procedure , insert the following code.

```
Sub Form_MouseMove (Button As Integer, Shift As Integer, X As Single, ⇐
    Y As Single)
    MyPos& = GetMessagePos&()
    Wnd = WindowFromPoint(MyPos&)
    If Wnd <> OldWnd Then
        Label4.Caption = Str$(Wnd)
        Label6.Caption = Str$(GetParent(Wnd))
        Class$ = Space$(255)
        TChars = GetClassName(Wnd, Class$, 255)
        Class$ = Left$(Class$, TChars)
        Label5.Caption = Class$
        Capt$ = Space$(255)
        TChars = GetWindowText(Wnd, Capt$, 255)
        If TChars > 0 Then
            Form1.Caption = Left$(Capt$, TChars)
        Else
            Form1.Caption = "(No Caption)"
        End If
        BoxWindow OldWnd
        BoxWindow Wnd
        OldWnd = Wnd
    End If
End Sub
```

5. In the Form_MouseUp procedure, insert the following code.

```
Sub Form_MouseUp (Button As Integer, Shift As Integer, X As Single, ⇐
    Y As Single)
    BoxWindow OldWnd
    ReleaseCapture
    Unload Form1
End Sub
```

6. Place the following record variable declaration in the global module. It is required for the GetWindowRect API function to work. This function is used by the BoxWindow routine to draw a box around the window that currently has mouse focus in WndPeek.

```
Type Rect
    Left As Integer
    Top As Integer
    Right As Integer
    Bottom As Integer
End Type
```

Now, save the global module as MNDPEEK.GLB.

7. Now compile the program to a stand-alone .EXE for best results. Add your program as a Program Manager icon.

8. (Optional) Launch the program you want to examine.

9. Launch WndPeek, using File Open in Program Manager.

As you move the mouse around the screen, you should see the WndPeek form updated with the information corresponding to the window below the cursor, including the background.

If you use WndPeek to examine the Program Manager, you will see very quickly why so many "User" resources are gone before you load any programs!

## How It Works

There are a number of interesting things going on in WndPeek. First, in the Form_Load procedure we are making a call to the Windows API function SetCapture. This function, when passed a valid hWnd, informs Windows that all following mouse messages should be sent to our window. This enables us to process these messages as though the mouse were inside our own form.

This technique is often used in applications like WndPeek—for example, SPY—that allow the user to dynamically select a window to examine.

The real work in WndPeek is done in the Form_MouseMove event handler. First, the GetMessagePos API function is used to retrieve the current mouse cursor location. GetMessagePos returns the location of the mouse cursor, the last time a message was generated. In this case, the last message was generated by the MouseMove event. At first glance, it might appear more efficient to use the X and Y parameters passed to the MouseMove procedure, but there are a couple of disadvantages to this approach. First, these figures are relative to the position of the form. In other words, if the form is in the lower right-hand corner of the screen and the mouse is in the upper left, X and Y will both be negative. Finding the true screen coordinates is then based on the location of the form on the screen.

Second, using GetMessagePos, we are able to more easily use the WindowFromPoint function. WindowFromPoint is actually expecting a record variable of the type POINT, used in a number of Windows Graphics Device Interface (GDI) routines.

```
Type PointStruc
     X as Integer
     Y as Integer
End Type
```

Normally, this record variable structure would have to be typed in the global module, and an instance of it dimensioned (Dim MyPoint As PointStruc) for use by the form. However, two short integers make a long integer, so a LONG can be passed to this routine as well. Conveniently, GetMessagePos returns a long integer with the X position in the LoWord and the Y position in the HiWord—in other words, identical to the POINT structure expected by WindowFromPoint. Therefore, using GetMessagePos will increase speed dramatically compared to the X and Y parameters passed to us by Visual Basic.

### Returning the Windows' Handle

WindowFromPoint, as its name implies, returns the hWnd (or handle) of the window currently at the location specified in POINT. In our case, this is the current mouse cursor position. Obviously, this function would be of great value in the "drag 'n drop" situation as well.

Before going any further, we check to make certain that the hWnd that we are "over" is different from the last one we were examining. We compare Wnd to OldWnd, a static variable that we continuously update with our current window handle. This is done to increase program speed and reduce flicker.

Whenever the mouse moves to a new window, the window is updated. The hWnd of the current window is shown. This information is useful if you want to try to send messages to a specific window. Next, the parent of the current window is found and displayed. The parent of any window can be retrieved using the GetParent API call. To find the main window of an application, you should look for the window that does not have a parent.

Next the "Class name" of the window being examined is retrieved. The Class name is perhaps the most useful information, retrieved by WndPeek because it is the most accurate way to locate a window, using the FindWindow API call. The use of FindWindow is explained in How-To 6.9 Find other running applications. The GetClassName API function requires that you send it a buffer in which to place the classname, and the function returns the number of characters actually copied to the buffer. It is essential to preallocate space in strings being passed to API functions declared in this way. If the string is not big enough to hold all of the characters that will be copied to it by the GetClassName function, the result will be truncated.

Next, to make sure that the cursor is placed correctly, the Caption of the current window is retrieved and displayed.

Finally, the box around the old window is erased and a box is drawn around the new window being examined.

The Form_MouseUp event handler cleans up by releasing the mouse capture, using the ReleaseCapture API routine, erasing the last box we drew, and exiting from our application.

The BoxWindow routine is a self-contained procedure that draws a box around a window. This routine is purely aesthetic, but the box allows the user to see which window is being examined at a particular time. The GetWindowRect API function determines the coordinates of the window in question. BoxWindow is implemented this way, so that a second call to the routine with the same hWnd erases the box that was previously drawn.

GetWindowDC is a specialized function that retrieves the display context of the entire window. You will use GetWindowDC very seldom, because most often you only need the display context of the client region of the window. However, because we want to enclose the entire window in a box, we need the display context of the whole window.

**Drawing Windows**

SetRop2 is equivalent to setting DrawMode for an object in Visual Basic. In our case, we want to set it to R2_NOT, which is equivalent to DrawMode 2 in Visual Basic, or more specifically, inverting the current colors of the screen. This drawing mode is preferable to using specific color, for two reasons. First, it is practically guaranteed to be visible on almost any background. Second, it facilitates erasing the box, because the box can simply be "inverted" to its original color.

Next, we create a pen with which to draw the box. The PS_INSIDEFRAME pen style draws a box inside of the window, without having to calculate a different position for the box. We can simply pass the coordinates of the window as retrieved by the GetWindowRect procedure. This is identical to setting the DrawStyle property of a control or form in Visual Basic to Inside_Solid.

Then the project calls the SelectObject API function to tell Windows to use the objects we specify when painting on the specified display context. First, we specify that our newly created pen should be used. Next, a NULL_BRUSH should be used to paint on TargetDC. This would normally be the handle to a brush, of a certain color, that was created with the CreateBrush function. However, in this case, we don't want the rectangle to be filled in, so we select one of Windows' "stock objects" as NULL (or invisible) brush. This is functionally equivalent to setting the FillStyle for a particular control to Invisible in Visual Basic.

Next our rectangle is drawn using the Rectangle API procedure. We calculate our width and height parameters and call Rectangle to draw the box. This is equivalent to using the Line method in Visual Basic.

Finally, the project's cleanup is handled, releasing the display context of the window and deleting the pen that the project created.

## Comments

The most important purpose of WndPeek as a utility is to find the class name of the window of a particular application so that it can be used in a call to FindWindow. It is also instructive to see how many windows various applications are creating to accomplish their tasks. You can see which applications are resource monsters and how. Everytime, WndPeek highlights a new area on the desktop, it is revealing the location of another window or control. Each one of these consumes valuable resources. Program Manager, for example, uses seperate controls to display icons and their labels. It is also useful to examine your own application and attempt to minimize the number of controls that you use on your forms and the number of forms that are loaded at one time.

However, WndPeek demonstrates a number of important techniques, including the tracking of the mouse outside of your application, drawing on windows of other applications, even the desktop, and calling API functions.

In addition, we have looked here at a number of Windows API equivalents to Visual Basic functions—how they differ and how they are used. Although Visual Basic supplies equivalents to many functions in GDI (actually, Visual Basic is calling these functions) the Visual Basic routines are very specific to use with Visual Basic controls and forms. Therefore, if you want to accomplish some of the same functionality outside of your application, you need to use the equivalent API calls.

Note that the speed of BoxWindow could be increased if the pen was created only once and the Null_BRUSH was retrieved only once. Their handles could be stored in static variables by the Form_Load procedure and the pen could be released in the Form_Unload routine. BoxWindow was created to be self contained, in this instance for simplicity and to facilitate its use in other applications.

# 7

# PERIPHERALS: SCREEN, SPEAKER, AND SERIAL PORTS

# 7

Your computer's peripherals—the monitor, printer, speaker, and serial port—may be thought of as its arms, legs, and voice. They allow your programs to communicate with the outside world. This chapter will show you how to get Visual Basic to control these various hardware extensions of your PC. You will see how to figure out the color capabilities of any user's video display and printer, how to create sound effects and attach them to your programs, how to create a phone dialer that works with a modem and serial port, and how to build your own Visual Basic communications program. Visual Basic lacks the great PLAY statement that came with QuickBASIC so we'll show you a way to simulate PLAY's complete macro language to play music.

Many of the familar hardware-addressing commands of QuickBasic or DOS have been left out of Visual Basic. This is because Visual Basic programs are written to run in the Windows multitasking environment, where all hardware interrupts must be processed and parceled out by Windows. This chapter takes full advantage of a number of Windows APIs to manipulate computer peripherals.

## Windows APIs Covered

| | | |
|---|---|---|
| BuildCommDCB | OpenComm | SetVoiceNote |
| CloseComm | OpenSound | SetVoiceQueueSize |
| CloseSound | ReadComm | SetVoiceSound |
| CountVoiceNotes | SetCommState | StartSound |
| GetCommError | SetVoiceAccent | WriteComm |
| GetDeviceCaps | | |

**7.1    Determine the color capabilities of a screen or printer**

There is no straightforward way to guarantee the monitor or printer display characteristics of your users' systems and, therefore, that your program will generate the output you intend. This How-To shows how to determine the number of colors that a system can display or print. Since Visual Basic does not include this capability, we use the GetDeviceCaps Windows API to ascertain the number of bits per pixel and bits per color plane, which can then be used to figure out the colors available for display and hard-copy printing. These values are found in the device drivers that come with each video card and printer.

**7.2    Make a replacement for QuickBasic's SOUND statement**

**7.3    Make music in Visual Basic**

Visual Basic's forerunner, QuickBASIC, includes sophisticated sound commands that can add fun and realism to your games and other applications. But the powerful Visual Basic language only includes a BEEP statement. Sound generation is dangerous in a multitasking environment like Windows because no appliction should directly access any hardware, including the speaker. Indeed, all messages to hardware should be directed by Windows to prevent more than one application from controlling the same hardware at the same time. How-To 7.2 uses four Windows APIs: OpenSound, CloseSound, SetVoiceSound, and StartSound, to produce a siren effect. The process shown can be modified to create a myriad of different sounds. How-To 7.3 expands the previous technique to play music just like Quick-BASIC's original PLAY statement using the additional Windows APIs SetVoiceQueueSize, SetVoiceAccent, and SetVoice Note. All of the APIs found in a special Windows device driver called SOUND.DRV. The sample program demonstrates how to set voices, octaves, notes, sound duration, and accents—all the elements of standard music. You can add this module to any of your Visual Basic programs and it will process sound in the background.

**7.4    Create a phone dialer in Visual Basic**

Serial port communications is a hot topic in every programming language.

This How-To uses Visual Basic's file I/O techniques to create a simple phone dialer that can be used with a modem and COM2 port. An interesting aspect of this How-To is that DOS does all the work—you will see that Windows still uses DOS file operations!

**7.5     Perform Serial I/O in Visual Basic**

Once again, we delve into the magical Winows Application Interface library to build a simple  serial commuinications program that allows you to choose a serial port, transmission speed, and communications parameters. Windows gives you a number of built-in functions for these purposes: OpenComm, SetCommState, ReadComm, WriteComm, CloseComm, BuildCOmmDCB, and GetCommError. Using Windows APIs for serial communications is superior to using Visual Basic's I/O statements because, as mentioned in How-To 7-4, simple I/O functions are still routed through DOS, which does not queue characters. This will cause characters to be lost in a multi-tasking environment, or using high transmission rates such as 2400 baud.

**7.1     How do I...**

# Determine the color capabilities of a screen or printer?

Complexity: Easy

### Problem

My applications will be used with systems that have different display and printer characteristics. I need to determine the number of colors that can be displayed or printed for any given system.

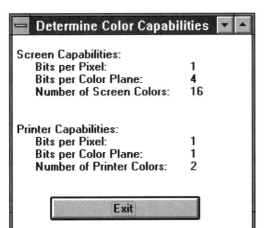

**Figure 7-1** The GetColor form displays screen and printer color parameters

### Technique

Visual Basic has no built-in statement or facility to determine a device's color capability, but a Windows API function can be used to provide your program with this data.

### Steps

Open and run GETCOLOR.MAK. The form will display the color parameters of the screen and default print as shown in Figure 7-1.

The GetColor project may be created by entering the objects and code as detailed in the following steps.

1. Create a new project called GETCOLOR.MAK. Create a new form with the objects and properties shown in Table 7-1, and save it as GET-COLOR.FRM.

| Object | Property | Setting |
|---|---|---|
| Form | FormName | GetColor |
| | Caption | Determine Color Capabilities |
| Command button | CtlName | Command1 |
| | Caption | Exit |

**Table 7-1** GetColor project form's objects and properties

2. Place the following code in the Declarations section of the form.

```
Const BITSPIXEL = 12        '  Number of bits per pixel
Const PLANES = 14           '  Number of planes
Declare Function GetDeviceCaps Lib "GDI" (ByVal hdc As Integer, ByVal ⇐
nIndex As Integer) As Integer
```

3. Place the following code in the Form_Paint event subroutine. Because Form_Paint is automatically called when a form is initially loaded, the user does not have to perform any action to display the data.

```
Sub Form_Paint ()
   Cls
'
' Get and display screen color capabilities.
'
   BPP = GetDeviceCaps(GetColor.hdc, BITSPIXEL)
   CPlanes = GetDeviceCaps(GetColor.hdc, PLANES)
   Print
   Print " Screen Capabilities:"
   Print Tab(5); "Bits per Pixel: "; Tab(32); BPP
   Print Tab(5); "Bits per Color Plane: "; Tab(32); CPlanes
   Print Tab(5); "Number of Screen Colors:"; Tab(32); (2 ^ BPP) ^ CPlanes
'
'  Get and display printer color capabilities.
'
   BPP = GetDeviceCaps(Printer.hdc, BITSPIXEL)
   CPlanes = GetDeviceCaps(Printer.hdc, PLANES)
   Print
   Print
   Print " Printer Capabilities:"
   Print Tab(5); "Bits per Pixel: "; Tab(32); BPP
   Print Tab(5); "Bits per Color Plane: "; Tab(32); CPlanes
   Print Tab(5); "Number of Printer Colors:"; Tab(32); (2 ^ BPP) ^ CPlanes
End Sub
```

4. Place the following code in the Command1_Click event subroutine to allow for a graceful exit from the program.

```
Sub Command1_Click ()
    End
End Sub
```

### How It Works

Color in Windows can be a tricky issue. The capabilities differ for various display cards, printers, and other Windows-supported devices. Each device has an associated device driver that provides information about many of the supported capabilities, including number of colors. The screen or display drivers are defined in the SYSTEM.INI file, and the printer drivers can be selected through the Control Panel. We use the Windows API function GetDeviceCaps to have a device driver return information about its capabilities.

The two values from GetDeviceCaps that determine color capabilities are number of bits per pixel and number of color planes. The number of bits per pixel specifies how many bits are used in each color plane. The number of color planes determines the types of colors that a device can represent. The total number of shades per color is 2 raised to the bits per pixel. The total number of colors is this value raised to the number of color planes.

For instance, a standard VGA display has one bit per pixel and four color planes—red, green, blue, and intensity. This gives us a total of 16 pure colors. Nonpure or dithered colors are used when an RGB value specifies something other than these 16.

GetDeviceCaps retrieves information about a device by passing it the handle to a previously created device context, hDC. Visual Basic makes readily available two useful device contexts for us: the form's device context, GetColor.hDC; and the printer's device context, Printer.hDC. The second parameter to GetDeviceCaps is a constant that specifies which piece of information to return.

### Comment

Making sense of the bits per pixel and number of color planes can be a bit confusing. Table 7-2 lists the values for some common Windows device drivers.

| Device | Bits Per Pixel | Number of Color Planes | Total Colors |
|---|---|---|---|
| Standard VGA | 1 | 4 | 16 |
| 256 Color VGA | 8 | 1 | 256 |
| Mono Adapter | 1 | 1 | 2 |
| LaserJet | 1 | 1 | 2 |
| Postscript Printer | 1 | 1 | 2 |
| HP PaintJet | 1 | 3 | 8 |

**Table 7-2** Color capabilities for selected Windows devices

## 7.2    How do I...

# Make a replacement for QuickBasic's SOUND statement?

Complexity: Intermediate

### Problem

My QuickBasic programs have some marvelous sound effects like police sirens and bloop sounds. Visual Basic, on the other hand, has only a Beep statement. What can I do?

### Technique

Sound is complicated in Windows because you can have many different programs running simultaneously. It would wreak havoc on your computer if any program could access hardware like the PC's speaker, so Windows programs have to cooperate with Windows to get access to the speaker and sound hardware. There are four Windows API functions that produce sound: CloseSound, OpenSound, SetVoiceSound, and StartSound. All these functions are stored in the SOUND.DRV device-driver DLL that comes with Windows.

### Steps

Open and run SOUND.MAK. There are no controls on this form. Just click on the form to produce a siren glissando effect. This project may be created by following these steps.

1. Create a new project called SOUND.MAK. Create a new form with no objects or properties and save it as SOUND.FRM. Put the following code in the Declarations section of the form. These Declare statements give access to the various sound functions needed to produce sounds in a Windows application.

```
DefInt A-Z

Declare Function CloseSound Lib "Sound.Drv" () As Integer
Declare Function OpenSound Lib "Sound.Drv" () As Integer
Declare Function SetVoiceSound Lib "Sound.Drv" (ByVal nSource%, ByVal ⇐
Freq&, ByVal nDuration%) As Integer
Declare Function StartSound Lib "Sound.Drv" () As Integer
```

2. Put the following code in the general Sound subroutine. These statements call the SetVoiceSound and StartSound functions to play the specified tone for the specified duration.

```
Sub Sound (ByVal Frequency As Long, ByVal Duration As Integer)
   Frequency = Frequency * 65536
   I = SetVoiceSound(1, Frequency, Duration)
```

```
   I = StartSound()
End Sub
```

3. Put the following code in the Form_Click event subroutine. This code produces a police siren sound effect whenever you click on the form. (Dividing the frequency by 880 causes the higher frequencies to last longer, which produces a more realistic siren sound effect.)

```
Sub Form_Click ()
   For Freq& = 440 To 880 Step 4
      Call Sound(Freq&, Freq& / 880)
   Next

   For Freq& = 880 To 440 Step -4
      Call Sound(Freq&, Freq& / 880)
   Next
End Sub
```

4. Put the following code in the Form_Load event subroutine. This code calls the OpenSound function to tell Windows that the program will use sound.

```
Sub Form_Load ()
   I = OpenSound()
End Sub
```

5. Put the following code in the Form_Unload event subroutine. This code calls the CloseSound function to tell Windows that the program is done using sound. It's important to call this function so Windows can let other applications use sound.

```
Sub Form_Unload (Cancel As Integer)
   I = CloseSound()
End Sub
```

### How It Works

Creating sound in Windows applications is much more complex than it is in DOS applications, primarily because Windows is a multitasking environment that runs multiple applications simultaneously. Something the computer generally only has one of—like the speaker and sound hardware—must be requested and addressed by Windows to prevent several applications from trying to grab the same thing at the same time.

There are four steps involved in creating sound under Windows:

1. Request access to the sound hardware by calling OpenSound. (The Form_Load event subroutine does this.)

2. Enter a note to be played into Windows' sound queue. Windows maintains a queue of sounds that are to be played sequentially. (If you are

familiar with QuickBasic programming, this is similar to the queue used by the Play statement.)

3. Tell Windows to actually play the note that was entered into the sound queue.

4. Repeat steps 2 and 3 for as many notes as you want to play. Then tell Windows you're finished using sound by calling CloseSound. (The Form_Unload event subroutine does this.)

The general Sound subroutine is called for each note you want to play. First, it moves the frequency you passed it as a parameter into the high-order word, since that's how Windows expects it. Because the frequency of each note is limited to a single word, the frequency can be anywhere between 0 and 32,767 hertz. Since most humans only hear between 20 and 20,000 hertz, that shouldn't be a problem.

## Comment

Be aware that after the OpenSound and before the CloseSound functions are called, no other application can use sound.

---

**7.3    How do I...**

# Make music in Visual Basic?

Complexity: Intermediate

### Problem

Visual Basic offers a number of functions that make the interface easier to use and to make programs fun for the user, including sophisticated graphics functions. In QuickBasic, however, I can make sound effects, using the Sound and Play functions. Is Visual Basic really two steps forward and one step back, or can I have the best of both worlds? I would like to be able to create sound effects at various times in my application and to reuse all those QuickBasic PLAY macros I spent so much time typing in.

### Technique

Don't delete those macros yet! Visual Basic can produce some very interesting sound effects, because of the sophisticated sound support built into the Windows API. The sound functions are contained in a device driver, which is a special DLL called SOUND.DRV. It can be called from Visual Basic, because the functions in a device driver can be accessed in the same way as functions in a normal DLL by just declaring them as external functions.

Under DOS, a program must jump through a lot of hoops to run the speaker, including speeding up the timer. This is certainly not a good idea under Windows for a number of reasons, not the least of which is that a lot of functions depend on the timer. With multiple applications running on the system at the same time, it is certainly not "well behaved" to speed up the timer. For this reason many device drivers exist that provide a layer between the application and the hardware and standardize the hardware access method.

### Steps

The sound effects sample, PLAYTEST.MAK, uses two subroutines that control the sound driver functions: a specialized replacement for the MsgBox function and a simple implementation of the Play statement. Each subroutine is in a separate module file, so you can use either one in your own programs.

Open and run PLAYTEST.MAK. If you click the button labeled "Music," the program will play a few bars from "Greensleeves." You will notice that you can minimize the application and even switch to another application, without disrupting the music. If you click on the button labeled "Error," you will see a specialized message box and hear music you can use in error situations.

Unlike many How-Tos in this book, we will first create separate module files that can be called from any Visual Basic program. Then to demonstrate them we'll build a new form that makes music.

1. Create the file EBOX.BAS, the module that provides support for the "enhanced" message box, and insert the following code.

```
DefInt A-Z

'Sound.DRV DLL routines.

Declare Function OpenSound Lib "SOUND.DRV" ()
Declare Sub CloseSound Lib "SOUND.DRV" ()
Declare Sub SetVoiceNote Lib "SOUND.DRV" (ByVal Voice, ByVal Note, ⇐
ByVal Length, ByVal Dots)
Declare Sub StartSound Lib "SOUND.DRV" ()

Function ErrBox (Message$, BoxType, Title$)
   CloseSound
   Voices = OpenSound()
   For I = 1 To 10
     SetVoiceNote 1, 40, 16, 0
     SetVoiceNote 1, 41, 16, 0
     SetVoiceNote 1, 40, 16, 0
     SetVoiceNote 1, 37, 16, 0
```

```
    Next I
    StartSound
    ErrBox = MsgBox(Message$, BoxType + 48, Title$)
    CloseSound
End Function
```

The ErrBox function is used exactly like the MsgBox function, with one exception. ErrBox automatically adds 48 to the box type that you specify to produce the exclamation point icon in the message box. Your application need only specify the base message box type. ErrBox returns the same values as the MsgBox function does, referring to the button that the user has selected. While the user reads the message box, the musical theme is playing in the background. The music is stopped, using the CloseSound function, as soon as the user makes a selection. This is a fairly simple implementation of sound from Visual Basic, but it is a good warmup for our implementation of Play.

The following code creates the PLAY.BAS module, which you can include in your applications to add this sound functionality. The majority of the relevant code is simply parsing the string that is passed to it. Note that there are a number of occasions in which a number must be parsed from the string; the GoSub GetNote is used for this purpose. In addition, many characters in the PLAY macro do not immediately require a sound driver function to be called. For example, when the program sees a letter corresponding to a note on the scale, the code waits to find the length of the note and the number of dots before making a call to the SetVoice-Note function. Therefore, the SendNote subroutine is used to submit all the current information to the queue when a new note is encountered.

2. Insert the following code in a new file called PLAY.BAS.

```
DefInt A-Z

'Sound.DRV DLL routines.

Declare Function OpenSound Lib "SOUND.DRV" ()
Declare Sub CloseSound Lib "SOUND.DRV" ()
Declare Sub SetVoiceQueueSize Lib "SOUND.DRV" (ByVal Voice, ByVal Bytes)
Declare Sub SetVoiceAccent Lib "SOUND.DRV" (ByVal Voice, ByVal Tempo,_ ⇐
ByVal Volume, ByVal Mode, ByVal Pitch)
Declare Sub SetVoiceNote Lib "SOUND.DRV" (ByVal Voice, ByVal Note,_ ⇐
ByVal Length, ByVal Dots)
Declare Sub StartSound Lib "SOUND.DRV" ()

Const Range$ = "PCzDzEFzGzAzB"
Const Numbers$ = "0123456789"

Const TRUE = -1
Const FALSE = 0
```

```
Sub Play (Song$)
   Voices = OpenSound()
   SetVoiceQueueSize 1, 1024
   SongString$ = UCase$(Song$)
   TChars = Len(SongString$)
   Tempo = 120
   Music = 0
   Octave = 3
   Length = 4
   NewNote = FALSE
   NewAccent = TRUE
   CharOff = 1
   Do
     Char$ = Mid$(SongString$, CharOff, 1)
     Select Case Char$
        Case "A" To "G", P
          GoSub SendNote
          Pitch = InStr(Range$, Char$) - 1
          NewNote = TRUE
        Case "+", "#"
          Pitch = Pitch + 1

        Case "-"
          Pitch = Pitch - 1

        Case "."
          Dots = Dots + 1

        Case "1" To "9"
          GoSub GetNum
          NoteLength = TempNum

        Case ">"
          GoSub SendNote
          Octave = Octave + 1

        Case "<"
          GoSub SendNote
          Octave = Octave - 1

        Case "M"
          GoSub SendNote
          CharOff = CharOff + 1
          Char$ = Mid$(SongString$, CharOff, 1)
          Select Case Char$
             Case "N"
               Music = 0
             Case "S"
               Music = 2
             Case "L"
               Music = 1
          End Select
          NewAccent = TRUE

        Case "N"
```

```
            GoSub SendNote
            CharOff = CharOff + 1
            GoSub GetNum
            Pitch = TempNum
            NewNote = TRUE
            GoSub SendNote

        Case "O"
            GoSub SendNote
            CharOff = CharOff + 1
            GoSub GetNum
            Octave = TempNum

        Case "T"
            GoSub SendNote
            CharOff = CharOff + 1
            GoSub GetNum
            Tempo = TempNum
            NewAccent = TRUE

        Case "L"
            GoSub SendNote
            CharOff = CharOff + 1
            GoSub GetNum
            Length = TempNum

        Case Else
      End Select
      CharOff = CharOff + 1
   Loop Until CharOff > TChars
   GoSub SendNote
   StartSound
Exit Sub

   SendNote:
   If NewAccent Then SetVoiceAccent 1, Tempo, 1, Music, 0
   If NewNote Then
   If Pitch > 0 Then Pitch = (Pitch + (Octave * 12)) - 1
      If NoteLength Then
         PlayLength = NoteLength
         NoteLength = 0
      Else
         PlayLength = Length
      End If
      SetVoiceNote 1, Pitch, PlayLength, Dots

      Dots = 0
   End If
   NewNote = FALSE
   NewAccent = FALSE
Return

GetNum:
   TempNum = Val(Mid$(SongString$, CharOff, 1))
   If CharOff < TChars Then
     TestChar$ = Mid$(SongString$, CharOff + 1, 1)
```

```
   If InStr(Numbers, TestChar$) > 0 Then
      TempNum = TempNum * 10 + Val(TestChar$)
      CharOff = CharOff + 1
   Else
         Return
   End If
End If
If CharOff < TChars Then
   TestChar$ = Mid$(SongString$, CharOff + 1, 1)
   If InStr(Numbers, TestChar$) > 0 Then
      TempNum = TempNum * 10 + Val(TestChar$)
      CharOff = CharOff + 1
   End If
End If
Return
End Sub
```

To make use of PLAY.BAS, simply add it to your application, using the Add File option of the File menu. You can then call the Play statement, passing a macro, similar to the one in QuickBasic. The only exception is that all music is played in the background, so MF and MB are simply ignored. If you want to force the sound driver into foreground mode, you can simply call the WaitSoundState sound driver function, like this:

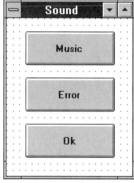

**Figure 7-2** Appearance of the Playtest form

```
WaitSoundState 0
```

However, it is recommended that you do not tie up the system in this way. To create the demo program shown in Figure 7-2, perform the following steps:

3. Create a new project called PLAYTEST.MAK. Create a new form with the following objects and properties and save it as PLAYTEST.FRM.

| Object | Property | Setting |
| --- | --- | --- |
| Form | FormName | Form1 |
| | Caption | Sound |
| | BackColor | &H00FFFFFF& (White) |
| Button | CtlName | Command1 |
| | Caption | Music |
| Button | CtlName | Command2 |
| | Caption | Error |
| Button | CtlName | Command3 |
| | Caption | OK |

**Table 7-3** Playtest objects and properties

4. Using the Add File option on the File menu, add the EBOX.BAS and PLAY.BAS files to your project.

5. Insert the following code in the Declarations section of Form1.

```
DefInt A-Z

Declare Sub CloseSound Lib "SOUND.DRV" ()
```

6. Insert the following code in the Form_Unload procedure.

```
Sub Form_Unload (Cancel As Integer)
   CloseSound
End Sub
```

7. Insert the following code in the Command1_Click procedure to actually make music.

```
Sub Command1_Click ()
   Part1$ = "E8G4A8MLB8.>C16.MN<B8A4F#8MLD8.E16.MNF#8G4E8"
   Part2$ = "MLE8.D#16.MNE8F#4.<B4>"
   Green$ = "T24Oo2" + Part1$ + Part2$
   Play Green$
End Sub
```

8. Insert the following code in the Command2_Click procedure.

```
Sub Command2_Click ()
   Title$ = "You shouldn't have done that!"
   Mess$ = "You are now entering "
   Button = ErrBox(Mess$, 0, Title$)
End Sub
```

9. Insert the following code in the Command3_Click procedure.

```
Sub Command3_Click ()
   Unload Form1
End Sub
```

### How It Works

Although the Windows sound driver is still underdeveloped, to say the least, enough functions are operational to mimic the functionality of Sound and Play. The sound driver operates on a system of queues, much like Windows itself. You open a "voice" of the sound driver and insert notes, and other information, in the queue, then instruct the sound driver to begin processing the queue. The sound driver then processes the sound in the background, allowing your application to continue with other tasks.

You open a "voice queue" using the OpenSound function. This function returns the number of available voices. Currently, only one voice can be opened at once, but the API allows for future enhancements. If there is an error opening a queue, or the sound driver is already in use, OpenSound will return a -1. The SetVoiceQueueSize function is used to tell the sound driver to reserve enough space for the notes that you want to play. Determining the correct value to use is still a bit of a black art, but 1024 seems to do the trick in most cases.

The functions that allow us to place information in the voice queue are SetVoiceNote and SetVoiceAccent. SetVoiceNote enables us to place a note in the queue. This note corresponds to the number used in the N directive in BASIC's PLAY macro language. It is a value of 1 through 84, corresponding to the 84 keys—7 octaves—on a piano keyboard. A value of 0 is considered a pause. SetVoiceNote also enables us to set the length of the note we insert into the queue. These lengths, again, are specified the same way they are in BASIC. For example, 1 is a whole note, 2 is a half note, and 16 is a sixteenth note. You specify the reciprocal of the duration of the note. Finally, SetVoiceNote allows us to set the number of "dots" following the note directly.

SetVoiceAccent enables us to set the tempo, volume (not implemented), mode, and pitch. Again, tempo is specified exactly the way it is in BASIC, with values ranging from 32 to 255 and a default of 120.

When you are finished filling the queue, you start the sound driver processing the queue using the StartSound function.

## Comments

One nice aspect of the Windows 3 sound driver is the music can be processed in the background, even when the current task is modal. Such is the case with the message box example for this project.

As noted earlier, it is not wise to force the sound driver into foreground mode. If you want to keep the CPU free yet pause your program until the music has finished playing, insert the following code after each call to PLAY:

```
While DoEvents () and CountVoiceNotes (1) > 0
Wend
```

Of course, you will need to include the additional declaration for CountVoiceNotes in the Declarations section of the form:

```
Declare Function CountVoiceNotes Lib "Sound.DRV" (nVoice%)
```

The CountVoiceNotes will return the number of notes in the specified voice queue put there by the SetVoiceNote function. As always, the DoEvents function will allow other applications to proceed while your application pauses. This enables you to have the best of both worlds: foreground music and a "well-behaved" Windows application.

In addition, you will probably see a number of ways to improve on the string parsing in the Play subroutine. This routine is presented primarily for educational purposes and was written for readability. Perhaps the most important speed optimization enhancement would be to compare integers in the Select Case loop rather than strings. Integer comparisons are much faster than string comparisons. However, it is easier to see what is going on from the letters. Your new Select Case block would look something like this:

```
Select Case ASC (Char$)
    Case 65 - 71, 80
    etc.
```

This code will certainly improve the speed of your string parsing. Another technique that this implementation of Play uses is to create a look-up table, for note values, using a string constant, PCzDzEFzGzAzB. The Instr function is used to find which "note" should be inserted in the queue based on the character's position in this table. One possible alternative would be to create a look-up array, whose subscripts correspond to the ASC values of the characters. The result might look something like this:

```
NoteTable(65) = 10 ' A
NoteTable(66) = 12 ' B
NoteTable(67) = 1  ' C
NoteTable(68) = 3  ' D
NoteTable(69) = 5  ' E
NoteTable(70) = 6  ' F
NoteTable(71) = 8  ' G
```

So, as you can see, there are a number of places to go from here, but this should get you started.

## 7.4    How do I...

# Create a phone dialer in Visual Basic?

Complexity: Easy

### Problem
I would like to create a simple phone dialer in Visual Basic, but Visual Basic doesn't seem to include communications functions. Is this true? Is there a way to access a modem from within Visual Basic?

### Technique
This can be accomplished using simple file I/O techiniques. While it is possible to create a full terminal emulation program in Visual Basic using the Windows communications API, this is not necessary for creating a simple phone dialer, as shown in Table 7-4.

### Steps

To try the sample program, open and run DIALER.MAK. Type a phone number into the text control and click the command button. Dialer will then dial the phone number and change the caption of the command button to Hangup. Once the other party has answered, and you have picked up the extension, you should click Hangup to hang up the modem.

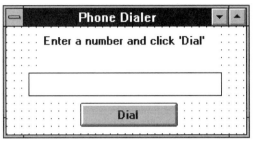

**Figure 7-3** Appearance of the Dialer form

The port is set to COM2 as a program default, because most people install their mouse on COM1. If your modem is on another port, simply change that line in the source code.

To create Dialer, perform the following steps:

1. Create a new project called DIALER.MAK. Create a new form with the following objects and properties and save it as DIALER.FRM. When finished, the form should look like Figure 7-3.

| Object | Property | Setting |
| --- | --- | --- |
| Form | FormName | Form1 |
| | Caption | Phone Dialer |
| Label | CtlName | Label1 |
| | Caption | Enter a number and click 'Dial' |
| Text box | CtlName | Text1 |
| Button | CtlName | Command1 |
| | Cation | Dial |

**Table 7-4** Dialer project form's objects and properties

2. Insert the following code in the Command1_Click procedure.

```
Sub Command1_Click ()
   If Command1.Caption = "Dial" Then
      If Text1.Text <> "" Then
         Num$ = "ATDT" + Text1.Text
         Open "Com2" For Output As #1
         Print #1, Num$
         Label1.Caption = "Pick up the phone and click 'Hangup'"
         Command1.Caption = "Hangup"
      End If
   Else
      Num$ = "ATH"
```

```
      Print #1, Num$
      Close #1
      Label1.Caption = "Enter number and click 'Dial'"
      Command1.Caption = "Dial"
   End If
End Sub
```

### How It Works

The process is fairly simple. We open the communications port as a standard device supported by DOS. We then send command strings to the "file" using the Print # statement. This technique automatically appends the necessary carriage return to our command string.

A Hayes-compatible modem string is constructed by combining the phone number and the standard ATDT prefix of the Hayes command set. If your phone line is pulse dial, than the prefix would be ATDP.

The port then remains open until the user clicks the Hangup button. The label of the Command button is set and checked to determine whether to dial or hang up the phone.

### Comment

The most interesting aspect of this sample is that DOS does all the work. In fact, file operations are one of the few things that Windows still uses DOS to accomplish. While the DOS file system leaves quite a bit to be desired, it does have the capability to address a number of devices, including a communications port, as though it was a file. This technique is used to redirect output dynamically in a DOS application.

Although this simplistic example can be accompished without using the standard Windows communications, we would have to move beyond these techniques to create something like a terminal emulation package. The functions exist in the Windows API to check for a modem and, in fact, to create an entire communications package.

<br>

**7.5      How do I...**

# Perform serial I/O in Visual Basic?

Complexity: Advanced

### Problem

I need to transfer data between a Visual Basic application and our corporate minicomputer using serial communcations. When I use the standard input/ output functions such as Open, Get, and Put, with a communication port, my program often loses characters.

### Technique

Using standard I/O calls for serial communications has never worked properly, either under DOS or Windows. DOS-based applications usually require the assistance of a third party's programming library to assist in serial communications. Fortunately, Windows comes with a built-in serial communications library that Visual Basic applications can access.

**Figure 7-4** The Commfunc form in action

### Steps

The Commfunc project demonstrates the use of the Windows communication functions by emulating a dumb terminal.

Open and run COMMFUNC.MAK. Check that the Commstring constant in Declarations section of the form is set for the desired port, speed, and communication parameters. Change it to suit your particular hardware configuration.

Click on the Start menu to open the serial communications port. Characters entered from the keyboard will be sent to the COM port. Any characters received will be displayed on the form. Click on the End menu item to close the port, and exit the program.

1. Create a new project called COMMFUNC.MAK. Create a new form with the properties and settings shown in Table 7-5, and save it as COMM-FUNC.FRM. The layout of the form will appear similar to Figure 7-4.

| Object | Property | Setting |
|--------|----------|---------|
| Form | AutoRedraw | False |
| | Caption | Communication Port Closed |
| | FormName | Commfunc |

**Table 7-5** Commfunc project form

2. Create a menu for the form using the Menu Design window with the captions and controls shown in Table 7-6.

| Caption | CtlName |
|---------|---------|
| &Start | Start |
| &End | End_Comm |

**Table 7-6** Menu for Commfunc form

3. Place the following constants and declarations in the Global module. Save them as COMMFUNC.BAS. The constants defined in this module are returned error codes. The user-defined types, DCB and COMSTAT, are passed as parameters to some of the API communications routines.

```
' Error Flags
Global Const CE_RXOVER = &H1        ' Receive Queue overflow
Global Const CE_OVERRUN = &H2       ' Receive Overrun Error
Global Const CE_RXPARITY = &H4      ' Receive Parity Error
Global Const CE_FRAME = &H8         ' Receive Framing error
Global Const CE_BREAK = &H10        ' Break Detected
Global Const CE_CTSTO = &H20        ' CTS Timeout
Global Const CE_DSRTO = &H40        ' DSR Timeout
Global Const CE_RLSDTO = &H80       ' RLSD Timeout
Global Const CE_TXFULL = &H100      ' TX Queue is full
Global Const CE_PTO = &H200         ' LPTx Timeout
Global Const CE_IOE = &H400         ' LPTx I/O Error
Global Const CE_DNS = &H800         ' LPTx Device not selected
Global Const CE_OOP = &H1000        ' LPTx Out-of-Paper
Global Const CE_MODE = &H8000       ' Requested mode unsupported

Global Const IE_BADID = (-1)        ' Invalid or unsupported ID
Global Const IE_OPEN = (-2)         ' Device Already Open
Global Const IE_NOPEN = (-3)        ' Device Not Open
Global Const IE_MEMORY = (-4)       ' Unable to allocate queues
Global Const IE_DEFAULT = (-5)      ' Error in default parameters
Global Const IE_HARDWARE = (-10)    ' Hardware Not Present
Global Const IE_BYTESIZE = (-11)    ' Illegal Byte Size
Global Const IE_BAUDRATE = (-12)    ' Unsupported BaudRate

        Type DCB
        Id As String * 1
        BaudRate As Integer
        ByteSize As String * 1
        Parity As String * 1
        StopBits As String * 1
        RlsTimeout As Integer
        CtsTimeout As Integer
        DsrTimeout As Integer
        Bits1 As String * 1
        Bits2 As String * 1
        XonChar As String * 1
        XoffChar As String * 1
        XonLim As Integer
        XoffLim As Integer
        PeChar As String * 1
        EofChar As String * 1
        EvtChar As String * 1
        TxDelay As Integer
End Type

Type COMSTAT
        Bits As String * 1
```

```
      cbInQue As Integer
      cbOutQue As Integer
End Type

' COMM declarations
Declare Function OpenComm Lib "User" (ByVal lpComName As String, ByVal ⇐
wInQueue As Integer, ByVal wOutQueue As Integer) As Integer
Declare Function SetCommState Lib "User" (lpDCB As DCB) As Integer
Declare Function ReadComm Lib "User" (ByVal nCid As Integer, ByVal lpBuf ⇐
As String, ByVal nSize As Integer) As Integer
Declare Function WriteComm Lib "User" (ByVal nCid As Integer, ByVal lpBuf ⇐
As String, ByVal nSize As Integer) As Integer
Declare Function Closecomm Lib "User" (ByVal nCid As Integer) As Integer
Declare Function BuildCommDCB Lib "User" (ByVal lpDef As String, lpDCB ⇐
As DCB) As Integer
Declare Function GetCommError Lib "User" (ByVal nCid As Integer, lpStat ⇐
As COMSTAT) As Integer

' Functions for Scrolling a Window
'
Declare Sub ScrollWindow Lib "User" (ByVal hWnd As Integer, ByVal XAmount ⇐
As Integer, ByVal YAmount As Integer, lpRect As Any, lpClipRect As Any)
Declare Sub UpdateWindow Lib "User" (ByVal hWnd As Integer)
```

4. Enter the following code into the Declarations section of the form. The Commstring constant, which is in DOS mode format, should be changed to reflect the communication parameters of your hardware configuration. The example below is read as, COM port 2, 2400 baud, no parity, 7 data bits, and 1 stop bit.

```
Dim LpDCB As DCB
Dim nCid As Integer
Const Commstring = "COM2:2400,n,7,1"
```

5. Place the following code in the General section of the Commfunc form. This code, which is called from the Start_Click event subroutine, opens the communication port and sets the port parameters to those specified in the Comstring.

```
Sub Comm_open (Commstring$)
  Dim T As Integer
'------------------------------------------------
' -- Close any previously open communication ports
'
   T = Closecomm(1)
   T = Closecomm(2)
'------------------------------------------------
' -- Open the communication port, get nCid
' -- nCid < 0 if error, refer to IE_ constants.
' -- -2 = port already open, try closing it anyway.
'
   Commport$ = Left$(Commstring$, InStr(Commstring$, ":") - 1)
```

```
    nCid = OpenComm(Commport$, 1024, 1024)
    If nCid < 0 Then
        MsgBox "Unable to Open Comm Device: " + Str$(nCid), 16
        If nCid = -2 Then T = Closecomm(1)
        End
    End If

'------------------------------------------------
' -- Load the CommDCB with parameters from Commstring
'
    If (BuildCommDCB(Commstring$, lpDCB)) Then
        MsgBox "Unable to Build Comm DCB", 16
        End
    End If

'------------------------------------------------
' -- Set the port state
'
    lpDCB.Id = Chr$(nCid)
    If (SetCommState(lpDCB)) Then
        MsgBox "Unable to set Comm State", 16
        End
    End If
End Sub
```

6. Place the following code into the General section of the Commfunc form. This code, will constantly check for incoming characters. If any are found, they will be sent to the Print_to_form subroutine for printing.

```
Sub Poll_comm ()
  Dim Nchars As Integer, Commerr As Integer, T As Integer
  Dim Readbuff As String * 1024, Lpstat As COMSTAT
    Do While nCid
        Nchars = ReadComm(nCid, Readbuff, Len(Readbuff))  ' Read buffer
        If Nchars < 0 Then Nchars = -Nchars                ' Ignore errors
        If Nchars Then Print_to_form Left$(Readbuff, Nchars)  ' Display data
        Commerr = GetCommError(nCid, Lpstat)           ' Need to poll for errors
        T = DoEvents()                                 ' Let other people run
    Loop
End Sub
```

7. Place the following code into the General section of the Commfunc form. This subroutine closes the communication port.

```
Sub Close_comm ()
  Dim Ret As Integer
    Ret = Closecomm(nCid)
    If Ret < 0 Then
        MsgBox "Unable to Close comm port: " + Str$(Ret), 16
        End
```

```
    Else
        nCid = 0                    ' Clear nCid to stop Poll_comm
    End If
End Sub
```

8. Enter the following code into the Form_KeyPress event subroutine. This subroutine sends characters entered from the keyboard to the communications port.

```
Sub Form_KeyPress (KeyAscii As Integer)
  Dim Ret As Integer, T As Integer
  Dim Lpstat As COMSTAT                ' Communication status block
  Static Buffer$
    If nCid = 0 Then Exit Sub
    Buffer$ = Buffer$ + Chr$(KeyAscii)
    T = GetCommError(nCid, Lpstat)   ' Get current stats
    If Lpstat.cbOutQue < 1024 Then   ' Space left in buffer?
        Ret = WriteComm(nCid, Buffer$, Len(Buffer$)) ' Place chars in buffer
        If Ret <= 0 Then Ret = -Ret    ' Ret has # of chars output,
                                       ' <0 indicates error (ignored)
        Buffer$ = Mid$(Buffer$, Ret + 1)    ' Remove xmited chars from buffer
    End If
End Sub
```

9. Put the following code in the Start_Click menu event subroutine. This subroutine opens the COM port and changes the caption on the form to indicate that the port is open. The Poll_comm subroutine is then called to read incoming characters from the COM port.

```
Sub Start_Click ()
    Comm_open Commstring$
    If nCid Then Commfunc.Caption = "Communication Port Open"
    Poll_comm
End Sub
```

10. Put the following code in the End_Comm_Click menu event subroutine. It closes the COM port and exits the application.

```
Sub End_Comm_Click ()
    Close_comm
    Commfunc.Caption = "Communication Port Closed"
    End
End Sub
```

11. Place the following subroutine in the General section of the Commfunc form. This subroutine is used to print characters on the form. Unlike the standard Visual Basic Print statement, this code emulates the scrolling action of a dumb terminal. As a new line is printed at the bottom of the form, the previous lines are scrolled up to make room.

```
Sub Print_to_form (Buffer As String)
  Dim Yamount As Integer, Cnt As Integer
    Scalemode = 3                      ' Set to pixels
    Yamount = TextHeight("a")          ' Height of character
    For Cnt = 1 To Len(Buffer)         ' Process all characters
        C$ = Mid$(Buffer, Cnt, 1)
      If C$ = Chr$(10) And Currenty >= Scaleheight - 2 * Yamount Then ' do  ⇐
            we scroll?
          ScrollWindow hwnd, 0, -Yamount, ByVal 0&, ByVal 0&
          UpdateWindow hwnd
          T% = DoEvents()
          Currentx = 0
      ElseIf C$ = Chr$(13) Then        ' Carriage returns reset line position
          Currentx = 0
      Else
          Commfunc.Print C$;
      End If
    Next Cnt
End Sub
```

### How It Works

Using Windows communication functions isn't difficult once you realize how much of the work Windows does for you. If you try to open a communication port, such as COM1, and use standard I/O statements—such as Get and Put—on the port, your communications will be unreliable. Incoming characters are likely to be dropped, especially at line speeds of 2400 baud or greater. In addition, if Windows switches to another application, all characters received while the second application is in control will be lost. The reason is that Visual Basic I/O relies on DOS to do the work. DOS's COM port drivers were not designed for high-speed lines or multitasking environments like Windows.

The Windows communication functions are "interrupt driven." This means that incoming characters briefly interrupt the current program so that Windows can receive the character from the communication port. The character is then stored away in a queue, maintained by Windows, for later reading by the application.

Writing characters works much the same way. Windows takes the characters from your application program and stores them in its queue. When the communication port is ready to transmit the next character, Windows will transmit it for you. All this happens behind the scenes, very quickly, and without direct involvement on your part.

If you are familiar with the standard Visual Basic I/O statements, using the communications functions provided by the Window's API will not be much different. In fact, the important communication port API calls look very similar to the standard Visual Basic I/O statements, as Table 7-7 shows.

| VB I/O Statement | Communications API Name | Function Performed |
| --- | --- | --- |
| Open | OpenComm | Open a communication port |
| Close | CloseComm | Close a communication port |
| Get | ReadComm | Read data from receive buffer |
| Put | WriteComm | Write data to the COM transmit buffer |
| Err | GetCommError | Check for communication errors |
| n/a | SetCommState | Set COM port characteristics |
| n/a | BuildCommDCB | Build a Data Control Block |

**Table 7-7** Visual Basic's I/O statements and communication port API calls compared

Our sample terminal program starts by opening a communcation port with the OpenComm API call. The three parameters to OpenComm are the communication port name (such as COM2) and the sizes, in number of bytes, of the receive and transmit queues. These sizes are limited to 32,767 bytes per queue, although typical values range from 1K to 16K bytes. The OpenComm function returns a variable, nCid, which is used in subsequent communications API calls. The nCid variable is similar to a file number in the Visual Basic I/O statements. If the returned nCid is less than zero, then the COM port was not opened, and nCid represents an error code instead. The global constants IE_ will identify the type of error. For example, a returned value of (-2) is an IE_OPEN error, "Device Already Open."

Because a communications port is a hardware device, it has many different configurable attributes. Items like baud rate, parity, and bits per character can be set and changed. The functions BuildCommDCB and SetCommState are used to configure the COM port. The SetCommState function actually sets the communication port attributes. Its only parameter is a user-defined data type called the DCB, which contains all the information needed to configure the operation of the communication port and API functions. SetCommState is called with the DCB as its single parameter. The first byte of the DCB is set to the nCid value returned by OpenComm. The other bytes of the DCB can be set manually or by calling BuildCommDCB. The BuildCommDCB function interprets a standard DOS mode-style string into the proper byte and bit settings in the DCB.

### Processing Incoming Characters
The Poll_com subroutine processes incoming characters from the COM port. The ReadComm API function takes three parameters: the nCid from the OpenComm call, a string to store the incoming characters, and the total number of characters that the string can store. Its return value is the actual

number of incoming characters transferred to the string parameter. If the returned value is negative, an error was detected, although the magnitude of the returned value still indicates the number of characters transferred.

We can ignore the sign of ReadComm's return value, because Get-CommError is always called after each read. GetCommError not only returns communication errors, but also clears any internal error indicators with the communication API functions. Until these indicators are cleared, ReadComm will not return additional characters to your application. GetCommError return values are set according to the CE_ constant flags defined in the Global declarations. Note that these are bit flags; each bit in the return code corresponds to a different error. The lpStat contains the number of characters present in the receive and transmit buffer queues.

The Poll_comm subroutine calls DoEvents after each read to ensure that other Windows functions can process.

The Form_KeyPress event subroutine handles keyboard activity. As each character is typed, it is appended to a buffer within the subroutine itself. The GetComm function is called to determine whether any room is left in the communication port's output buffer. The variable lpStat.cbOutQue is checked against the maximum buffer size to ensure that there is some space left. The WriteComm function moves the number of characters specified in the third parameter to the transmit queue. Windows will then take care of sending these characters to the communication port. WriteComm returns the number of characters actually moved to the transmit queue. These characters can then be removed for the Buffer$ string.

Although it doesn't use a communications API function, the Print_to_form subroutine does make a different use of the Windows API. The purpose of the Print_to_form subroutine is to provide a scrolling window, much like you would see on a CRT or at the DOS command line. When the cursor is at the bottom of the screen and a line feed is received, the entire contents of the screen are scrolled up by one line. The ScrollWindow API function scrolls the window's contents vertically by the number of pixels specified in the third parameter, Yamount. Yamount is set to the height of a single line of text using Visual Basic's TextHeight function. Because the Scalemode was previously set to "3 - Pixels," Yamount will already be expressed in terms of screen pixels. Since we want the text to scroll up the screen, a negative value for Yamount is used in the ScrollWindow call. The UpdateWindow and DoEvents calls ensure that the scrolling takes place before the characters on the new line are printed.

## Comments

Although the code in this project will work for many communications applications, a truly robust and reliable system will require a more thorough understanding of the DCB than was presented in this project.

The ScrollWindow API function will not work properly if the Auto-Redraw property of the form is set to True. For additional information about this API function, see the Scrllwnd project in How-To 3.1 Scroll all the objects in a window.

To test this project, your system will need to be connected via a communcation port to another device, such as a modem, minicomputer, or printer. If so, insure that the port and connection are operating properly using a commercial communications package such as the Terminal program supplied with Microsoft Windows. This step lets you isolate hardware, interface, and cabling issues prior to debugging the Commfunc project code.

# 8

# THIRD PARTY
# CUSTOM
# CONTROLS AND
# FUNCTIONS

# 8

One of Visual Basic's most exciting features is its ability to use custom controls and functions provided by parties other than Microsoft. When you purchase custom controls you usually get a .DLL or .VBX file that is placed in your Windows directory. When you load a project .MAK file, Visual Basic loads any .VBX files in that project and adds custom controls in those .VBXs to the Toolbox.

When Visual Basic is first loaded it automatically reads any DLLs or .VBX files that are included for it, and then it extends the toolbar to hold these controls. You'll actually see new tools at the bottom of the bar.

Of course this would not be a very "hands on" book if we just presented a survey of available third party controls. Fortunately, four third party custom control companies—MicroHelp, Crescent, Sheridan, and Waite Group Software—were gracious enough to create special demo versions of their controls for this book. *These controls work just like the fully functional commercial versions except they will not compile to a full EXE program.* In other words you can run these controls and play with them to your heart's content, even going beyond things described in this book, but you can only use them in the Visual Basic environment. If you select Make .EXE from the File menu, the resulting .EXE file will not run. Only the .MAK file will work with these controls. If you like any of these controls and wish to purchase the complete product, special order forms are provided for doing that in the back of this book.

This chapter contains three How-Tos for the controls provided by MicroHelp that show you how to make command buttons that contain bitmap graphics, a file dialog box that allows multiple file names to be selected, and an alarm that rings like a telephone or a buzzer. There are three projects from Crescent that use assembly routines from their QuickPak Professional for Windows product, including a way to quickly get a handle to a window, monitor and display the amount of free system resources, and display information in a second monitor. A large project that shows how to make a beautiful three-dimensional interface using Sheridan's custom 3-D Wigets package is presented. This product gives an outstanding set of controls that have varying degrees of shadowed and raised or recessed text to make a startling impression on your audience. The last set of three How-Tos shows you techniques for making your Visual Basic applications have multimedia capability. Waite Group Software provides controls for manipulating the Sound Blaster audio board. You'll find controls for playing standard MIDI music files, controlling the 11 voice FM synthesizer, and playing and recording digitized sound effects and speech so your applications can talk. Again all the controls for these projects are found on the disk bundled with this book.

## Windows APIs Covered

SendMessage

### 8.1 Make command buttons with graphics

While Visual Basic provides a nice collection of command, option, and radio buttons, it still has some limitations. For example, you can't customize the command buttons to have pictures or icons on them, instead you can only put text on the buttons' faces. Also you can't control the placement of the text exactly where you want it. Using MicroHelp's VBTools buttons (supplied on the disk) this How-To shows how to specify a .BMP bitmap,

.WMF metafile, or an .ICO icon for the up and the down positions of the button. Also we'll show you how to make an Excel-like icon bar by using the VBTools StateButton property so that the buttons stay in when pressed.

**8.2      Make a file dialog box that accepts multiple filenames**
While Windows allows multiple files to be selected in a list box (with the Shift Click technique), for some reason the designers of Visual Basic left this feature out. This How-To shows how to use the MicroHelp MhTag custom list box that allows multiple filenames to be selected by just clicking on them. You'll build a complete file selection dialog box that lets you navigate the file system.

**8.3      Make an attention-getting alarm**
If you are constantly in front of your computer, one way to always be on time to appointments is to set up an alarm system. This How-To is based on MicroHelp's MhAlarm control. This control can be configured to run as an icon and to look and sound like a telephone, an alarm clock, or a wrist watch. At a certain time the alarm will ring, or buzz, or beep—a big improvement over Visual Basic's wimpy beep statement.

**8.4      Send a Windows message to a control**
The next three How-Tos use the Crescent set of add-on assembly language routines. This particular How-To uses the QuickPak library ControlHWnd function to quickly return a windows handle. Written in assembly language, this How-To shows that instead of using Visual Basic's slow RemoveItem statement in a loop you can instantly clear items in a list box.

**8.5      Monitor and display the amount of free system resources**
System resources are controls, bitmaps, windows, icons, and so on. Too many of these will eat into the system resource memory and eventually give a system error. Since the pool of RAM memory devoted to system resources can't be changed, some way is needed to monitor system resource memory and alert you when it is getting low. This How-To creates a small icon in the shape of a pie chart that visually displays how much system resource memory is available. When it dips below 50% the icon turns red. It's based on the Crescent QuickPak's GetSystemResources function.

**8.6      Display information on a secondary monitor**
If you are a serious developer you want to be able to view the Immediate window while your program is running. But often other forms and windows

will obscure this small window. This How-To presents a simple routine from Crescent called MonoPrint that lets you display information on a second monitor. This How-To uses MonoPrint to display the 44 properties of the current form in a tabular format.

## 8.7 Create a state-of-the-art 3-D grayscale look

Sheridan Software makes a set of controls called 3-D Wigets that includes six controls to give a neat grayscale look to buttons and text like those found in sophisticated computer systems such as the NeXTStep interface. Check boxes, option buttons, frames, and command buttons provide an outstanding shadowed effect with text that appears like it is etched or raised from the surface of the form. You can use the frames to hold other controls in a 3-D box. The option buttons have an unusual circular appearance while check boxes have an actual X mark with a slight shadow. A special Ribbon button control lets you create a group of buttons that mimic the functionality of the ribbon button in Microsoft Excel. The Panel control can be used to display text with a 3-D effect, or to wrap around list boxes, combo boxes, and scroll bars to give them a 3-D feeling. This How-To presents a demo project that shows off all these controls by letting you set document preferences.

## 8.8 Play MIDI music using the Sound Blaster

The next three How-Tos use a set of controls called SoundBytes from Waite Group Software. These controls allow you to set up forms that play music on a Sound Blaster or Sound Blaster compatible board. (Sound Blaster is also fully compatible with the Adlib board used in many PC games.) In case you never heard of it, the Sound Blaster has become the standard sound board for PC-based games. It can play digitized sounds, complex MIDI music, or it can give you complete control over its built-in FM tone generators, allowing incredible sound effects. PC games use it for everything from machine guns and laser blast sounds to playing beautiful classical music. It can even reproduce full speech so your applications can talk. This particular How-To shows how to use the music control. When placed on your form, this control lets you play MIDI music from files saved in the standard MFF (Midi File Format). The project has scroll bars that let you change the tempo and scale of a Bach fugue or a neat Scott Joplin piano tune.

## 8.9 Use the Sound Blaster's FM synthesizer

One of the real powers of the Sound Blaster is its ability to make sound effects. It comes with a built-in 11-voice FM music synthesizer. This is what the MIDI drivers use to make the music you heard in the previous How-To.

In this How-To we will show you how easy it is to manipulate the FM synthesizer directly. Each channel of the synthesizer has an operator cell and a modulator cell. One makes the basic carrier tone and the other modulates this tone. The parameters for each cell are enormous including attack, decay, sustain, and release (ADSR), envelope type, volume, frequency, vibrato, tremolo, and so on. All of these parameters in this project are controlled by scroll bars and check boxes so you can custom design the sound you want.

**8.10    Play and record voice using the Sound Blaster**

This last How-To shows you how to record voice and other digitized sound and play it back with the Sound Blaster. Files are stored in the Creative Voice file format. You can use this method for adding voice narrations to specific screens or animations. The digitized speech or sound effects play in the background so screen activity is not affected. Five properties associated with the control allow selecting a filename, pause, playback, record, and sampling rate. You'll need a microphone or audio sound source for this project.

**8.1    How do I...**

# Make command buttons with graphics?

Complexity: Easy

### Problem

I'd like to make my dialog boxes as attractive as those provided in programs such as Borland's Resource Workshop. (See Figure 8-1.) I'd also like to provide an icon ribbon such as that provided in Microsoft's Word for Windows. (See Figure 8-2.) How can I do this?

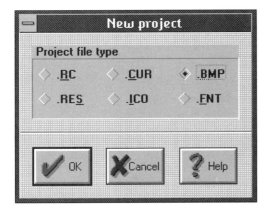

**Figure 8-1** (left) Bitmapped buttons from Borland's Resource Workshop.

**Figure 8-2** (above)  Icon ribbon from Microsoft's Word for Windows

### Technique

VBTools from MicroHelp provides a number of custom controls to extend Visual Basic. Figure 8-3 shows the Visual Basic Toolbox with the MicroHelp VB Tools custom controls. This How-To, and How-Tos 8.2 and 8.3, show how to use the MhButton, the MhTag, and the MhAlarm tools. MhButton lets you specify a picture (bitmap, metafile, or icon) for a button. You can specify pictures for both the "up" position—when the button isn't being pressed—and the "down" position—when the mouse button is held down on the button. Figure 8-4 shows the tool that corresponds to the MhButton tool.

### Bitmapped Buttons

When you use bitmapped buttons, you have the additional responsibility of making sure that your buttons look good. The standard "look" for Windows 3 is three dimensional, so your buttons should also be three dimensional. The easiest way to make an "up" button look three dimensional is to place a border around it. The top and left sides of the border should be white and the bottom and right sides should be dark grey. To make the "down" button three dimensional you can either reverse those to make a depressed button—make the top and left sides white and the bottom and right sides dark grey—or you can use a "flat" button—no border at all. The "face" of the button should be light gray.

You can create your button bitmaps using Windows Paintbrush or a resource editor like Borland's Resource Workshop. Buttons should be large enough to display the glyph (icon) and any text, but small enough so they fit nicely on the form. In Paintbrush you can set the size of the bitmap using the Options menu's Image Attributes... command. In Resource Workshop, when you create a new bitmap project, you're prompted for the size of the bitmap. You can change the size of the bitmap after you've created it using the Bitmap menu's Size And Attributes... command.

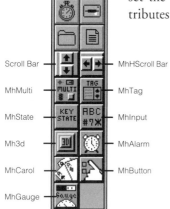

Scroll Bar — MhHScroll Bar

MhMulti — MhTag

MhState — MhInput

Mh3d — MhAlarm

MhCarol — MhButton

MhGauge

**Figure 8-3** (far left) The Visual Basic Toolbox with the MicroHelp VBTools custom controls.
**Figure 8-4** (left) The MhButton tool from the Visual Basic Toolbox

The VBTools button PictureUp and PictureDown properties both accept a .BMP bitmap, .WMF metafile, or .ICO icon file for the pictures of the up and down states of the button. Both Paintbrush and the Resource Workshop create .BMP bitmap files.

In this How-To project, we use a bitmap of a printer for the button that prints a copy of the form, and a red X for the Cancel button. The Print button uses the Caption property for the "Print the form" caption, but the Cancel button has the word "Cancel" drawn on the button graphically. Drawing the text lets you position it exactly, while using the Caption property lets VBTools position the text, which may not place it exactly where you'd expect.

### Icon Bars

An icon bar works like a series of graphical radio buttons: When you press one, the others are "popped out." In a word processor like Word for Windows, an icon bar lets you set attributes like boldface, italics, and underlining. That's exactly what we do in this How-To project.

The same design rules (above) apply to the bitmaps of an icon bar as they do to VBTools command buttons.

VBTools buttons have a StateButton property to specify that the button is a toggle; when you press it once, it stays in until you press it again.

In this project, we use a bold letter B for the bold button, an italicized letter I for the italicize button, an underlined U for the underlining button, and a struckthru S for the strikethru button.

**Figure 8-5** The MhButton project in action

### Steps

Open and run MHBUTTON.MAK. As shown in Figure 8-5, the four buttons in a row along the top of the form let you set the style of the text in the Text box. The "Print the form" button prints a copy of the form on the printer using Visual Basic's PrintForm method.

All the bitmaps needed to create this form are available on the disk accompanying this book.

1. Create a new project called MHBUTTON.MAK and add the VBTools demo .VBX file (VBTDEMO.VBX) to the project.

2. Create a new form with the controls and properties listed in Table 8-1. Save it as MHBUTTON.FRM.

| Control | Property | Setting |
|---------|----------|---------|
| Form | Caption | Bitmapped buttons |
| Text box | CtlName | Text1 |
| | FontBold | False |
| | FontItalic | False |
| | FontStrikethru | False |
| | FontUnderline | False |
| | FontName | Helv |
| | FontSize | 20.25 |
| | Text | Visual Basic How-To |
| MhButton | Alignment | 2 - Center |
| | Autosize | True |
| | Caption | Bold |
| | CtlName | Bold |
| | Multiline | True |
| | PictureDown | BOLDDOWN.BMP |
| | PictureUp | BOLDUP.BMP |
| | StateButton | True |
| MhButton | Alignment | 2 - Center |
| | Autosize | True |
| | Caption | Italic |
| | CtlName | Italic |
| | Multiline | True |
| | PictureDown | ITALDOWN.BMP |
| | PictureUp | ITALUP.BMP |
| | StateButton | True |
| MhButton | Alignment | 2 - Center |
| | Autosize | True |
| | Caption | Strike |
| | CtlName | Strikethru |
| | Multiline | True |
| | PictureDown | STRKDOWN.BMP |
| | PictureUp | STRKUP.BMP |
| | StateButton | True |
| MhButton | Alignment | 2 - Center |
| | Autosize | True |
| | Caption | Under |
| | CtlName | Underline |

| | | |
|---|---|---|
| | Multiline | True |
| | PictureDown | ULINDOWN.BMP |
| | PictureUp | ULINUP.BMP |
| | StateButton | True |
| MhButton | Alignment | 2 - Center |
| | Autosize | True |
| | Caption | Print the form |
| | CtlName | FormPrint |
| | Multiline | True |
| | PictureDown | PRINTDWN.BMP |
| | PictureUp | PRINTUP.BMP |
| | StateButton | False |
| MhButton | Alignment | 2 - Center |
| | Autosize | True |
| | Caption | Cancel |
| | CtlName | Cancel |
| | Multiline | True |
| | PictureDown | CANCELDN.BMP |
| | PictureUp | CANCELUP.BMP |
| | StateButton | False |

**Table 8-1** The MhButton form's controls and properties

3. Put the following lines of code in the Click event subroutine of the four buttons that make up the icon bar. Each line sets the corresponding font property of the text box.

```
Sub Bold_Click ()
   Text1.FontBold = Bold.Value
End Sub

Sub Italic_Click ()
   Text1.FontItalic = Italic.Value
End Sub

Sub Strikethru_Click ()
   Text1.FontStrikethru = Strikethru.Value
End Sub

Sub Underline_Click ()
   Text1.FontUnderline = Underline.Value
End Sub
```

4. Put the following code in the Cancel_Click event subroutine. The End statement just ends the Visual Basic application.

```
Sub Cancel_Click ()
    End
End Sub
```

5. Put the following code in the FormPrint_Click event subroutine. Calling the form's PrintForm method simply prints a copy of the form to the current printer.

```
Sub FormPrint_Click ()
    PrintForm
End Sub
```

### How It Works

Like many of the projects that use custom controls, this How-To project has very little code associated with it. Most of the complexity is handled by VBTools buttons with little extra work on our part. The two bitmapped buttons act exactly like normal Visual Basic Command buttons except they contain graphics: When the button is pressed and released, it generates a Click event.

The icon bar is constructed using several VBTools buttons with their StateButton property set to True. When StateButton is true, VBTools sets the button's Value property to True when the button is depressed and False when the button is up. Since a Text box has several Font... properties that you can set to True or False, we just set each property to the value of the corresponding icon bar button.

### Comment

VBTools buttons are more flexible than standard Visual Basic buttons, even if you're not using bitmapped buttons. VBTools buttons have Alignment and MultiLine properties that let you control the position of the Caption of the button.

**8.2        How do I...**

## Make a file dialog box that accepts multiple filenames?

Complexity: Intermediate

### Problem

I'm writing an application that lets users copy and move files around in their directories. Rather than make the user select files one at a time, I'd like to let them select multiple files at a single time. But all the file dialog boxes I've seen only let the user select a single file. Is there something I can do?

### Technique

**Figure 8-6**
The MhTag
tool from the
Visual Basic
Toolbox

Most file dialog boxes only allow selecting a single file because the list boxes they use only support selecting a single file. Although Windows supports *multiple selection* list boxes, Visual Basic doesn't offer one on the Toolbox. Naturally, a custom control can offer this feature. The MicroHelp MhTag custom control in VBTools offers this feature, and others. Figure 8-6 shows what the MhTag tool looks like in the Visual Basic Toolbox.

This file dialog box is based on the project presented in How-To 1.6 Make a file dialog box using Windows messages. It uses the Windows message LB_DIR to fill the VBTools list box with filenames and directory names.

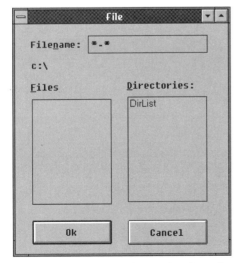

**Figure 8-7** The MFileDlg project in action

### Steps

Open and run the MFILEDLG.MAK project. Select the File menu's Open... option. The file dialog box will open up and list the files in the current directory in the list box on the left, and all the subdirectories and drives in the list box on the right. You can negotiate between directories by double-clicking on a directory name in the right-hand list box. The "[..]" entry backs up to the previous directory. You can also get a list of files on a floppy disk by double-clicking on a drive letter like "[-a-]." You can select multiple files simply by clicking them. Figure 8-7 shows a sample of this style file dialog box.

1. Create a new project and save it as MFILEDLG.MAK. Add the VB-HOWTO.BAS module using Visual Basic's Add File menu command. This module was first created in How-To 1.4 Quickly send a Windows message to a control, and modified throughout the book to contain several general functions that the file dialog box form uses. Since this project uses VBTools, add the VBTools demo .VBX file (VBTDEMO.VBX) to the project.

2. Create a new form, add the controls listed in Table 8-2, and save it as MFILE-DLG.FRM.

| Object | Property | Setting |
|---|---|---|
| Form | Caption | File |
| | FormName | FileDlg |
| | MaxButton | False |
| | MinButton | False |
| Label | Alignment | 1 - Right Justify |
| | Caption | File&name: |
| | CtlName | Label1 |
| Text box | CtlName | FileEdit |
| | MultiLine | False |
| | Scroll bars | 0 - None |
| | TabStop | True |
| | Text | *.* |
| Label | Alignment | 0 - Left Justify |
| | Caption | c:\ |
| | CtlName | DirLabel |
| Label | Alignment | 0 - Left Justify |
| | Caption | &Files: |
| | CtlName | Label2 |
| MhTag | CtlName | FileList |
| | Sorted | True |
| | TabStop | True |
| | SingleSelect | False |
| | ExtendedSelect | True |
| Label | Alignment | 0 - Left Justify |
| | Caption | &Directories: |
| | CtlName | Label3 |
| List box | CtlName | DirList |
| | Sorted | True |
| | TabStop | True |

| Command button | Caption | Ok |
|---|---|---|
| | CtlName | Ok |
| | Default | True |
| | TabStop | True |
| Command button | Caption | Cancel |
| | CtlName | Cancel |
| | Cancel | True |
| | TabStop | True |

**Table 8-2** The MFileDlg project form's objects and properties

3. Put the following code in the Declarations section of the form. This code will give the form's subroutines and functions access to the SendMessage API function.

```
Declare Function SendMessage Lib "User" (ByVal hWnd%, ByVal wMsg%, ByVal ⇐
wParam%, ByVal lParam$) As Integer

Const WM_USER = &H400
Const LB_DIR = WM_USER + 14
```

4. Put the following code in the UpdateListBoxes general subroutine. UpdateListBoxes updates the list boxes that list the files and directories. The form calls UpdateListBoxes whenever something has changed and the list boxes need to be updated.

```
Sub Update_List_Boxes ()
    Dim CtlHWnd As Integer

    ' update current directory label
    DirLabel.Caption = LCase$(CurDir$)

    ' clear out the file and directory list boxes
    FileList.ClearBox = 1   ' use VBTools property to clear
    ClearListBox DirList

    ' switch to the file list box
    FileList.SetFocus

    ' get its handle
    CtlHWnd = GetFocus()

    ' send the message to the control
    PathPattern$ = FileEdit.Text
    I = SendMessage(CtlHWnd, LB_DIR, 0, PathPattern$)

    ' switch to the directory list box
    DirList.SetFocus

    ' get its handle
    CtlHWnd = GetFocus()
```

```
' send the message to the control
' &HC010 = subdirectories + drives only
I = SendMessage(CtlHWnd, LB_DIR, &HC010, "*.*")

' switch back to the text box
FileEdit.SetFocus
End Sub
```

5. Put the following code in the Cancel_Click event subroutine. This code sets the filename text box to the null string and hides the file dialog box.

```
Sub Cancel_Click ()
' If we select Cancel, we can hide the dialog, because
' we don't need it anymore.
FileEdit.Text = ""
FileDlg.Hide
End Sub
```

6. Put the following code in the DirList_DblClick event subroutine. This code changes directories and switches drives depending on the item clicked. There's an error routine in case there's no disk in a floppy drive.

```
Sub DirList_DblClick ()
    Const MB_RETRYANDCANCEL = 5
    Const MB_ICONEXCLAMATION = 48

    On Local Error GoTo UhOh

    ' When you double-click on a directory or drive entry,
    ' check whether the selected item is a drive; if so,
    ' change the current drive.
    If Left$(DirList.Text, 2) = "[-" And Len(DirList.Text) = 5 Then
        oldDir$ = CurDir$
        ChDrive Mid$(DirList.Text, 3, 1)
        A$ = CurDir$    ' Check whether the disk is ready;
    ' otherwise, change the current directory.
    Else
        ChDir Mid$(DirList.Text, 2, Len(DirList.Text) - 2)
    End If

    On Local Error GoTo 0

    Update_List_Boxes
    Exit Sub

UhOh:
    If MsgBox("Unable to switch to drive " + Mid$(DirList.Text, 3, 1) + ⇐
        ":", MB_RETRYANDCANCEL + MB_ICONEXCLAMATION, "Visual Basic - ⇐
        FileDlg") = 2 Then
    ' If we press Cancel, go back to the previous drive.
        ChDrive Left$(oldDir$, 1)
    End If

    Resume
End Sub
```

7. Put the following code in the FileList_DblClick event subroutine. This code hides the file dialog box.

```
Sub FileList_DblClick ()
   ' When we double-click on a filename in the list box,
   ' hide the form, because we've picked the filename.
   FileDlg.Hide
End Sub
```

8. Put the following code in the Form_Load event subroutine. It shows the form, a requirement of the code in the Update_List_Boxes routine, which Form_Load calls next. Then it hides the form.

```
Sub Form_Load ()
   Show
   Update_List_Boxes
   Hide
End Sub
```

9. Put the following code in the Ok_Click event subroutine. This code checks the text in the text box to see whether it contains the * or ? wildcards. If it does, the Update_List_Boxes routine is called to update the list boxes. Otherwise, Ok_Click closes the dialog box because the user picked a filename.

```
Sub OK_Click ()
   ' If there are wildcards, just update the list boxes.
   If InStr(FileEdit.Text, "*") Or InStr(FileEdit.Text, "?") Then
      Update_List_Boxes
   Else
      ' Otherwise, there's a real filename, so we can close up shop.
      FileDlg.Hide
   End If
End Sub
```

10. Create another new form and save it as TESTFDIA.FRM. This form will call the file dialog box to test it and show how it works. There are no controls on the form, but give the form the properties listed in Table 8-3.

| Object | Property | Setting |
|---|---|---|
| Form | Caption | File dialog box test |
| | CtlName | FileDialogBoxText |

**Table 8-3** The TestFDia form's objects and properties

11. Create a menu for the form using the Menu Design window and the information listed in Table 8-4.

| Caption | CtlName |
|---------|---------|
| &File | File |
| &Open... | FileOpen |
| E&xit | FileExit |

**Table 8-4** The menu for the TestFDia form

12. Put the following code in the Declarations section of the form. This Const statement declares a constant for the Show method.

```
Const MODAL = 1
```

13. Put the following code in the FileExit_Click event subroutine. The End statement simply ends the Visual Basic application when you select the Exit menu option.

```
Sub FileExit_Click ()
    End
End Sub
```

14. Put the following code in the FileOpen_Click event subroutine. The code sets up the file dialog box and then shows it modally. Then it displays a message box showing you what you selected.

```
Sub FileOpen_Click ()
    FileDlg.FileEdit.Text = "*.*"
    FileDlg.Caption = "File open"
    FileDlg.Show MODAL

    If FileDlg.FileEdit.Text = "" Then
        MsgBox "You hit the Cancel button"
    Else
        temp$ = ""
        For I = 0 To FileDlg.FileList.ListCount
            If FileDlg.FileList.Tagged(I) Then temp$ = temp$ + Chr$(13) +
Chr$(10) + FileDlg.FileList.List(I)
        Next

        MsgBox "You selected " + temp$
    End If
End Sub
```

## How It Works

The Update_List_Boxes general subroutine updates the contents of all the list boxes as the user changes directories and/or drives. Using the ClearListBox subroutine developed in How-To 1.5 Quickly clear a list box, the directory list box is emptied. Since VBTools list boxes have a ClearBox property that, when set to any number, empties the list box, that property is used instead for the file list box. Then, because the Windows LB_DIR message is used, we need to get the window handle of the list box. (The SendMessageToCtrl function from How-To 1.5 can't be used because that function expects numeric arguments and we'll be passing a string.) A SetFocus method sets the focus to file list box, and the Windows API function GetFocus returns its window handle.

Then the SendMessage API function sends the LB_DIR message to the file list box. A zero as the wParam parameter tells Windows to load the list box with all "normal" files. (Normal files include all files with no attributes set and ones that have been modified but exclude read-only, hidden, and system files.) For the lParam parameter, we pass the text from the text box. (Note that you can't directly pass the Text property of the text box; although the data type of the Text property is String, Visual Basic won't let an API function change it.)

The same actions are then repeated for the directory list box. The difference comes at the SendMessage API function. Instead of passing a zero as the wParam parameter, we pass &HC010, which tells Windows to load the list box with the subdirectories in the current directory and all the available drives in the system. The subdirectories are automatically enclosed in square brackets (for example, [windows]) and the drives are in the format [-x-] where x is the drive letter.

The DirList_DblClick event subroutine is executed whenever the user double-clicks on a directory name or drive letter. It catches any errors that come up (most often, an attempt to switch to a floppy drive with no disk in the drive) with an error handler. Visual Basic will invoke the error handler automatically whenever an error occurs, so we don't have to do any special error checking.

The If statement checks whether the item double-clicked starts with [-. If it does, we know that it's a drive letter and the ChDrive statement will switch to the new drive. Otherwise, it's a directory and the ChDir statement will change to the directory.

If there have been no errors so far, the statement

```
On Local Error GoTo 0
```

disables the error handler. Then a call to Update_List_Boxes updates the list boxes with the filenames and directories for the new drive or directory. Then the Exit Sub statement gets us out of the subroutine.

If some error occurred, however, Visual Basic runs the code at line label UhOh. That code assumes that the error was, in fact, a problem that occurred with switching drives. (That's almost guaranteed to be the cause.) So a message box prompts the user to either retry the operation (after the user inserts a disk in the floppy drive) or cancel it. If the user clicks the Cancel button, the ChDrive statement will switch back to the drive that was current before the user tried to switch.

The Resume statement goes back to retry the statement that caused the error. In this case, it's the

```
A$ = CurDir$    ' Check whether the disk is ready.
```

statement, which is there specifically to try to cause an error. If it succeeds, everything went well.

The code in the Form_Load event subroutine may look strange to you. First, a Show method shows the form. Then the Update_List_Boxes subroutine is called to fill in the list boxes. Finally, a Hide method hides the form. Why go through the bother of showing, then hiding, the form?

First, let's look at why we need to show it. Normally, a form is automatically shown. We explicitly show it because Visual Basic executes the Form_Load event subroutine only when it is first loading a form. At that point, the form isn't visible yet. However, SetFocus method calls are used as part of getting the window handle to send the LB_DIR messages to the list boxes and (unfortunately) SetFocus will result in an error if the controls aren't yet visible. The Show method is necessary in the Form_Load event subroutine before a call to Update_List_Boxes.

Now given the need for Show, what about Hide? Let's look at how the file dialog box is usually used. The FileOpen_Click event subroutine of the TestFDia form uses the statement

```
FileDlg.Show MODAL
```

to run the file dialog box as a modal form. Let's go through what that entails, step by step.

When Visual Basic executes a Show method, it will load the form if it isn't already loaded. Loading the form triggers its Form_Load event subroutine. The file dialog box's Form_Load event subroutine shows the form as its first statement. For the moment, pretend there wasn't a Hide method call in the file dialog box's Form_Load event subroutine. The form would remain shown. But when Visual Basic goes back to finish executing the Show method from the TestFDia form, it finds that the form is already shown. Because it's illegal in Windows (and, therefore, Visual Basic) to show a window as a modal window when it's already shown nonmodally, Visual Basic will return an error. The Hide method call in the file dialog box's Form_Load event subroutine ensures that the Show method call in TestFDia will succeed.

The FileOpen_Click event subroutine in the TestFDia form shows the proper way to use the file dialog box: You can select the files to be displayed in the file list box by setting the Text property of the file text box. You can use any filename, including ones with the DOS wildcards * and ?. If you want all files to be listed, just use *.*. A word processor might use *.DOC to select all files whose extension are .DOC.

Then you should show the file dialog box modally. A constant MODAL equal to 1 is the best way to do that. When the Show method call is complete, you know that the user selected some file or clicked the Cancel button. To determine which actually happened, check the Text property of the file text box. As you saw, the Cancel_Click event subroutine of the file dialog box sets Text to the null string. If it's not the null string, you know the user selected at least one filename.

The FileOpen_Click event subroutine of the TestFDia form uses the Tagged property of the VBTools list box to check each of the entries in the list box. If the Tagged property is set for an entry, that means the file was selected.

### Comment

It's a good idea to set the file dialog box's caption to remind users what they're selecting a file for. In the FileOpen_Click event subroutine, we use

```
FileDlg.Caption = "File open"
```

In a FileSaveAs_Click event subroutine, you might use

```
FileDlg.Caption = "File save as"
```

---

**8.3    How do I...**

# Make an attention-getting alarm?

Complexity: Easy

### Problem

I'm writing an application that tracks appointments. I'd like to be able to remind the user when there's an upcoming appointment. If the user has iconized my application, how can I still attract their attention?

### Technique

When an application is iconized, it can still receive Timer events. You could set up a Timer event subroutine to check the current time using the Visual Basic

**Figure 8-8**
The
MhAlarm
tool from the
Visual Basic
Toolbox

Time$ function. When the current time is the time you're checking for (say ten minutes before the appointment time), you can notify the user.

But what's the best way to notify the user? You could use the Beep statement, but that's not very distinctive and might get confused as coming from another application. Luckily, MicroHelp's VBTools has an alarm control called MhAlarm that can be configured to look like a telephone, an alarm clock, or a wrist watch. Better yet, the alarm "ring" matches what the control looks like; so if the alarm control is a telephone, the ring sounds like a telephone ringing, the alarm clock makes you want to reach for the snooze button, and the wrist watch beeps. Figure 8-8 shows what the MhAlarm tool looks like in the Visual Basic Toolbox.

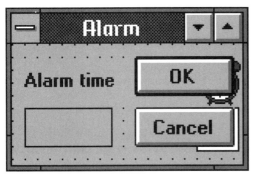

**Figure 8-9** The Alarm form at design time

**Steps**

Open and run ALARM.MAK. Enter a time in 24-hour format; for example, 8:00 PM is 20:00. Press Enter or click the OK button. The form automatically minimizes. When it's that time, the icon changes to that of a ringing wind-up alarm clock and starts "ringing." Double-click on the icon and press the Cancel button to shut off the alarm.

1. Create a new project and save it as ALARM.MAK. Add the VBTools demo .VBX file (VBTDEMO.VBX) to the project. Create a new form with the controls and properties listed in Table 8-5 and save it as ALARM.FRM. Figure 8-9 shows what the form looks like; note that the timer and MhAlarm controls are "hidden" behind the two command buttons.

| Control | Property | Setting |
|---|---|---|
| Form | AutoRedraw | True |
| | Caption | Alarm |
| | Icon | VB\ICONS\CLOCK04.ICO |
| Label | Caption | Alarm time |
| Text Box | CtlName | AlarmText |
| Command button | Caption | OK |
| | CtlName | Ok |
| | Default | True |

| Command button | Caption | Cancel |
|---|---|---|
| | CtlName | Cancel |
| | Cancel | True |
| Timer | CtlName | Timer1 |
| | Interval | 10000 |
| | Enabled | False |
| MhAlarm | Autosize | True |
| | CtlName | MhAlarm1 |
| | Style | 1 - Clock |
| | Visible | False |

**Table 8-5** The Alarm project form's controls and properties

2. Add the following code to the Cancel_Click event subroutine. The End statement just ends the application.

```
Sub Cancel_Click ()
   End
End Sub
```

3. Put the following code in the Form_Load event subroutine. This code puts the current time (without the seconds) into the Text Box, to provide a default alarm time.

```
Sub Form_Load ()
   AlarmText.Text = Left$(Time$, 5)
End Sub
```

4. Put the following code in the Form_Resize event subroutine. This If statement ensures that if you restore the form from its iconized state then the MhAlarm control is also "informed" that it's no longer on an icon.

```
Sub Form_Resize ()
   If WindowState = 1 Then
      MhAlarm1.WindowState = 1
   Else
      MhAlarm1.WindowState = 0
   End If
End Sub
```

5. Put the following code in the Ok_Click event subroutine. When the user presses Enter or clicks the OK button, this code iconizes the form and the MhAlarm control and then enables the Timer and executes the Timer event subroutine to check the time.

```
Sub Ok_Click ()
   AlarmForm.WindowState = 1
```

```
    MhAlarm1.WindowState = 1
    Timer1.Enabled = 1
    Timer1_Timer
End Sub
```

6. Put the following code in the Timer1_Timer event subroutine. This code gets executed every 10,000 milliseconds (10 seconds) to check the current time against the time entered in the Text Box to see if the alarm should be rung.

```
Sub Timer1_Timer ()
    If Left$(Time$, 5) = AlarmText.Text Then
        MhAlarm1.RingOn = 2
    End If
End Sub
```

## How It Works

Setting the form's Icon property to one of the supplied Visual Basic icons provides the default icon that will be displayed when the alarm isn't ringing.

Since it's not a good idea to slow down the whole system waiting for the alarm time to arrive, the Timer interval is set to 10,000 milliseconds, or only every ten seconds. This means it's possible that the alarm won't start ringing exactly on the minute. Don't worry; the latest it could be is ten seconds.

Setting the MhAlarm WindowState property to 1 (minimized) means that when the form is minimized and the alarm is ringing, its icon will take the place of the default icon. MhAlarm icons are animated; the alarm clock striker moves, the telephone shakes while ringing, and the wristwatch flashes.

The RingOn property is set to two for continuous ringing. A value of one means only a single ring and zero means no ring at all, which is the value until the alarm time is reached.

## Comment

The Style property sets which icon set is used, as follows:

- 0: Telephone
- 1: Alarm clock
- 2: Wrist watch

## 8.4    How do I...

# Send a Windows message to a control?

Complexity: Easy

### Problem

Does a third party offer a function to help me send Windows messages to my form's controls? Using SetFocus and GetFocus as outlined in How-To 1.4 Quickly send a Windows message to a control, seems awfully slow.

### Technique

Crescent's QuickPak Professional for Windows library provides a number of custom controls written in Assembly language. Figure 8-10 shows the Visual Basic Toolbox with the QuickPak custom controls. This and the next two How-To projects show how to use the ControlHWnd, Get System-Resources, and Monoprint functions.

How-To 1.5 Quickly clear a list box, discussed a method of using a Windows message and the SendMessageToControl function developed in How-To 1.4 Quickly send a Windows message to a control to clear the contents of a list box. We can improve that method by using a function from Crescent's QuickPak Professional for Windows library.

Using Visual Basic's SetFocus method followed by a call to the Windows API function GetFocus to return a window handle can be slow. Luckily, QuickPak has a function called ControlHWnd that returns a control's window handle with only a few lines of assembly language code.

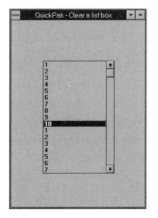

### Steps

Open and run CLEAR-LST.MAK. The list box in the form initially loads up 10 items in it. If you click once on the form, another

CurTime
QPVScroll
CSText
CSTime
CSDouble
CSLabel

QPHScroll
QPList
CSDate
CSLong
CSCurrency
CSGroupBox

**Figure 8-10** (left) The Visual Basic Toolbox with the Crescent QuickPak Professional for Windows custom controls **Figure 8-11** (above) The ClearLst form in action

10 items are added to the list box. If you double-click on the form, all the items in the list box are removed. See Figure 8-11.

1. Create a new project called CLEARLST.MAK. Create a form with the objects and properties listed in Table 8-6 and save it as CLEARLST.FRM.

| Object | Property | Setting |
|--------|----------|---------|
| Form | Caption | QuickPak - Clear a list box |
| List box | CtlName | List1 |

**Table 8-6** ClearLst project form's objects and properties

2. Add the QUICKPAK.BAS module to your project using the Visual Basic File menu's Add File command. Add the following code to the Declarations section of the QUICKPAK.BAS module. The Declare statement accesses a function from the QuickPak demo DLL (QPRODEMO.DLL).

```
Declare Function ControlHWnd% Lib "QPRODEMO.DLL" (Ctrl As Control)

Declare Function SendMessage Lib "User" (ByVal hWnd%, ByVal wMsg%, ⇐
ByVal wParam%, ByVal lParam&) As Integer

Const WM_USER = &H400
Const LB_RESETCONTENT = WM_USER + 5
```

3. Add the following code to the general subroutine SendMessage ToControl in the QUICKPAK.BAS module. This code uses the QuickPak function ControlHWnd to retrieve the list box's window handle.

```
Function SendMessageToControl (Ctl As Control, wMsg%, wParam%, lParam&)
   I = SendMessage(ControlHWnd(Ctl), wMsg%, wParam%, lParam&)
End Function
```

4. Add the following code to the general subroutine ClearListBox in the QUICKPAK.BAS module.

```
Sub ClearListBox (AListBox As Control)
   ' Make sure we're working with a list box.
   If TypeOf AListBox Is ListBox Then
      ' if so, send the LB_RESETCONTENT message to clear
      I = SendMessageToControl(AListBox, LB_RESETCONTENT, 0, 0)
   End If
End Sub
```

5. Put the following code in the Form_Click event subroutine. This code inserts 10 new items into the list box whenever the form is clicked.

```
Sub Form_Click ()
   For i = 1 To 10
      List1.AddItem Format$(i)   'Put something into list box.
   Next
End Sub
```

6. Put the following code in the Form_DblClick event subroutine. This code calls the ClearListBox general subroutine whenever you double-click the mouse on the form.

```
Sub Form_dblClick ()
   ClearListBox List1
End Sub
```

7. Put the following code in the Form_Load event subroutine. This code calls the Form_Click event subroutine to insert 10 items into the list box when the form is first loaded.

```
Sub Form_Load ()
   Form_Click
End Sub
```

### How It Works

The Windows message to remove all the items from a list box is LB_RESETCONTENT, which the WINDOWS.H file in the Windows SDK defines as WM_USER + 5. WM_USER is defined as 0x400, or &H400 in Visual Basic hexadecimal lingo so LB_RESETCONTENT is &H405.

The ClearListBox general subroutine first ensures that the parameter that was passed is a list box control. If it is, the SendMessageToControl function uses the LB_RESETCONTENT message to clear out the list box.

The Form_Click event subroutine adds 10 numbered items into the list box whenever you click on the form (outside of the list box). You can click on the form as many times as you'd like.

The Form_DblClick event subroutine calls the ClearListBox general subroutine, supplying the List1 list box control as a parameter.

The Form_Load event subroutine just calls the Form_Click event subroutine to add 10 items to the list box when the form is first loaded.

### Comment

Before any control can accept Windows messages, it must be visible. Therefore, if you want to use ClearListBox (or SendMessageToControl itself) in a Form_Load event subroutine, you must first make the form visible using Visual Basic's Show method.

## 8.5 How do I...

# Monitor and display the amount of free system resources?

Complexity: Intermediate

### Problem

I've noticed the Program Manager About box tell me about "free system resources." Sometimes that percentage is extremely low, even though I have several megabytes of memory. What exactly does this percentage mean and how can I make sure I don't run out of memory?

### Technique

Resources in Windows are things like bitmaps, windows, icons, etc. When you have several applications open, and if those applications have many bitmaps or windows, they consume resource memory. Unfortunately, in Windows 3.0, resource memory is separate from "normal" memory, and fixed in size. So even though you may have several megabytes of normal memory free, you can still run out of resource memory.

The Program Manager also takes up its own chunk of resource memory, so you usually start out with between 60-70% free system resources. Graphic-intensive applications like Microsoft Excel or Word for Windows can take up large chunks of resouce memory themselves. If you try to exceed your remaining resource memory, Windows will give you an error message.

Crescent's QuickPak Professional for Windows contains a function called GetSystemResources that returns the percentage of free system resources. We can use that function to create an application that runs as an icon in the background, continuously displaying the amount of free system resources as a pie chart. If it dips too low, we can warn the user with a visual cue, such as turning the pie chart red.

**Figure 8-12** The SysRes icon showing amount of free system resources

### Steps

Open and run SYSRES.MAK. An icon with a pie chart indicating the percentage of free system resources will appear as shown in Figure 8-12. Try starting several Windows applications to see how free system resources will decrease.

1. Create a new project called SYSRES.MAK. Create a new form with the controls and properties from Table 8-7 and save it as SYSRES.FRM.

| Control | Property | Setting |
| --- | --- | --- |
| Form | BorderStyle | 1 - Fixed Single |
| | Caption | <blank> |
| | MaxButton | False |
| Timer | CtlName | Timer1 |
| | Interval | 1000 |

**Table 8-7** The SysRes project form's controls and properties

2. Put the following code in the Declarations section of the form. This code declares some constants and defines GetSystemResources from the QuickPak DLL.

```
DefInt A-Z
Declare Function GetSystemResources% Lib "QPRODEMO.DLL" ()
Const Pi = 3.141592653
Dim X, Y, oldFreeResources%
```

3. Put the following code in the Form_Load event subroutine. This code sets up a blank icon.

```
Sub Form_Load ()
   Icon = LoadPicture()
   WindowState = 1
End Sub
```

4. Put the following code in the Form_Paint event subroutine. This code ensures that the icon gets repainted when necessary.

```
Sub Form_Paint ()
   oldFreeResources% = 0
End Sub
```

5. Put the following code in the Form_Resize event subroutine. Although you don't resize icons, this code calculates the size of the icon when Windows first creates it (after the Form_Load event subroutine is run).

```
Sub Form_Resize ()
   X = ScaleWidth \ 2
   Y = ScaleHeight \ 2
   oldFreeResources% = 0
End Sub
```

6. Finally, put the following code in the Timer1_Timer event subroutine. This code draws a pie chart on the icon when the timer triggers (every 1000 milliseconds). When percentage of free system resources falls below 50%, it paints the pie chart in red to attract attention.

```
Sub Timer1_Timer ()
   FreeResources% = GetSystemResources%()
   If oldFreeResources% <> FreeResources% Then
      Form1.Caption = Format$(FreeResources%) + "% free resources"
      Form1.Cls

      If FreeResources% < 50 Then
         Form1.FillColor = RGB(255, 0, 0)
      Else
         Form1.FillColor = RGB(255, 255, 255)
      End If

      Form1.FillStyle = 0
      Form1.Circle (X, Y), X, , -.02 * (100 - FreeResources%) * Pi, -.01
      oldFreeResources% = FreeResources%
   End If
End Sub
```

### How It Works

As discussed in How-To 5.3 Draw pictures into an iconized running application, in the Form_Load event subroutine the icon is blanked out by using the LoadPicture function, since we'll be drawing our own graphics on it. Then the form is iconized by changing its WindowState property.

GetSystemResources returns an integer number that's the percentage of free system resources. To avoid unnecessarily repainting the pie chart, a global variable is declared in the Declarations section of the form. That variable keeps track of the percentage of free system resources from the last time the timer was triggered. If it hasn't changed, we don't bother repainting the pie chart.

If the percentage of free system resources has changed since the last time the timer was triggered, the icon is updated. First, the caption is updated to tell the user the exact percentage of free system resources. Then we check to see if there's less than 50% free system resources. If so, the RGB function is used to set the color of the pie chart to red. Otherwise, it's set to white.

Then the "start" and "end" parameters of the Circle method draw a pie segment. Visual Basic itself supports pie segments when you specify the right start and end parameters. For more information about pie charts, see How-To 5.14 Build a pie chart.

The last step in the Timer1_Timer event subroutine is to set the global variable so it isn't unnecessarily updated the graphic the next time through.

### Comment

The Interval property for the timer in this project is set to 1000 milliseconds (one second), but can be set to any value you'd like. The higher the interval, the longer it will take the project to "realize" that the percentage of free system resources has changed.

# Display information on a secondary monitor?

Complexity: Intermediate

### Problem

The Immediate window that comes up when I start my Visual Basic applications within the Visual Basic environment is handy, but it can be cluttered. Is there any way I can get some information displayed on my secondary monitor?

### Technique

Although the Immediate window is convenient, if your application has many forms, it can be difficult to see your windows and the Immediate window. But strategically placed Debug.Print methods can be a boon to debugging. What to do?

If you have two monitors, one color and one monochrome, you usually can't use them both simultaneously. One (usually the color monitor) is the primary monitor and the other (usually monochrome) is secondary. Some Windows applications like Microsoft's CodeView or Borland's Turbo Debugger for Windows can use the secondary monitor while running your application on the primary monitor. But that doesn't really help us, since neither CodeView nor Turbo Debugger can debug Visual Basic applications.

Luckily, Crescent's QuickPak Professional for Windows offers a routine called MonoPrint that you can use to display information on the secondary monitor. In this project, we create a replacement for Visual Basic's Debug.Print method call that uses the secondary monitor, not the Immediate window.

| AutoRedraw | 0 | BackColor | &H80000005& | BorderStyle | &H2& |
|---|---|---|---|---|---|
| Caption | "Form1" | ControlBox | −1 | CurrentX | 0 |
| CurrentY | 0 | DrawMode | 13 | DrawStyle | 0 |
| DrawWidth | 1 | Enabled | −1 | FillColor | &H0& |
| FillStyle | 1 | FontBold | −1 | FontItalic | 0 |
| FontName | "Helv" | FontSize | 8 | FontStrikethru | 0 |
| FontTransparent | −1 | FontUnderline | 0 | ForeColor | &H80000008& |
| FormName | Not available | hDC | 3558 | Height | 2100 |
| hWnd | 3644 | Icon | 12582 | Image | 2998 |
| Left | 1770 | LinkMode | 1 | LinkTopic | "Form1" |
| MaxButton | −1 | MinButton | −1 | MousePointer | 0 |
| Picture | Not available | ScaleHeight | 1695 | ScaleLeft | 0 |
| ScaleMode | 1 | ScaleTop | 0 | ScaleWidth | 3615 |
| Tag | "" | Top | 1140 | Visible | −1 |
| Width | 3735 | WindowState | 0 | | |

**Figure 8-13** Example output from the MONOPRNT project

**Steps**

Open and run MONOPRNT.MAK. Click on the command button to display property information about the form. If you have a secondary monitor, the information will appear there. See Figure 8-13 for an example of the output.

1. Create a new project called MONOPRNT.MAK. Create a new form with the controls and properties listed in Table 8-8 and save it as MO-NOPRNT.FRM.

| Control | Property | Setting |
|---------|----------|---------|
| Command button | CtlName | Command1 |
| | Caption | Print property information! |

**Table 8-8** The MonoPrint form's controls and properties

2. Add the QUICKPAK.BAS general module to the project using Visual Basic's File menu's Add File option. Then add the following Declare statement to the Declarations section of the module.

```
Declare Sub MonoPrint Lib "QPRODEMO.DLL" (Text$, ByVal Row%, ByVal Col%, ⇐
ByVal Attr%)
```

3. Create a new general subroutine in the QUICKPAK.BAS module and add the following code to it.

```
Sub DebugPrint (ByVal What$)
   Static Y

   If Y = 0 Or Len(What$) \ 80 > 25 - Y Then GoSub DebugCls
   Call MonoPrint(What$, Y, 1, 7)
   GoSub AdjustRow
   Exit Sub

DebugCls:
   Y = 1
   Call MonoPrint(Space$(2000), Y, 1, 7)
   Return

AdjustRow:
   Y = Y + Len(What$) \ 80 + 1
   If Y > 25 Then GoSub DebugCls
   Return
End Sub
```

4. Create a general function for the form and add the following code to it. This is a function to help provide tabular output for integer values.

```
Function RJustI$ (Title As String, ByVal Number As Integer)
   RJustI$ = Title + Space$(23 - Len(Title) - Len(Format$(Number))) + ⇐
      Format$(Number) + "  "
End Function
```

5. Create a general function for the form and add the following code to it. This is a function to help provide tabular output for long integer values.

```
Function RJustL$ (Title As String, ByVal Number As Long)
   RJustL$ = Title + Space$(20 - Len(Title) - Len(Hex$(Number))) + "&H" ⇐
      + Hex$(Number) + "& "
End Function
```

6. Create a general function for the form and add the following code to it. This is a function to help provide tabular output for single precision values.

```
Function RJustS$ (Title As String, ByVal Number As Integer)
   RJustS$ = Title + Space$(23 - Len(Title) - Len(Format$(Number))) + ⇐
      Format$(Number) + "  "
End Function
```

7. Create a general function for the form and add the following code to it. This is a function to help provide tabular output for strings.

```
Function RJustT$ (Title As String, ByVal Strng As String)
   RJustT$ = Title + Space$(21 - Len(Title) - Len(Strng)) + Chr$(34) + ⇐
      Strng + Chr$(34) + "  "
End Function
```

8. Finally, the code to actually display the property information for the form is located in the Command1_Click event subroutine.

```
Sub Command1_Click ()
   DebugPrint RJustI$("AutoRedraw", Form1.AutoRedraw) + ⇐
      RJustL$("BackColor", Form1.BackColor) + RJustL$("BorderStyle", ⇐
      Form1.BorderStyle)
   DebugPrint RJustT$("Caption", Form1.Caption) + RJustI$("ControlBox", ⇐
      Form1.ControlBox) + RJustS$("CurrentX", Form1.CurrentX)
   DebugPrint RJustS$("CurrentY", Form1.CurrentY) + RJustI$("DrawMode", ⇐
      Form1.DrawMode) + RJustI$("DrawStyle", Form1.DrawStyle)
   DebugPrint RJustI$("DrawWidth", Form1.DrawWidth) + RJustI$("Enabled", ⇐
      Form1.Enabled) + RJustL$("FillColor", Form1.FillColor)
   DebugPrint RJustI$("FillStyle", Form1.FillStyle) + ⇐
      RJustI$("FontBold", Form1.FontBold) + RJustI$("FontItalic", ⇐
      Form1.FontItalic)
   DebugPrint RJustT$("FontName", Form1.FontName) + RJustI$("FontSize", ⇐
      Form1.FontSize) + RJustI$("FontStrikethru", Form1.FontStrikethru)
   DebugPrint RJustI$("FontTransparent", Form1.FontTransparent) + ⇐
      RJustI$("FontUnderline", Form1.FontUnderline) + ⇐
      RJustL$("ForeColor", Form1.ForeColor)
   DebugPrint "FormName Not available  " + RJustI$("hDC", Form1.hDC) + ⇐
      RJustS$("Height", Form1.Height)
```

```
      DebugPrint RJustI$("hWnd", Form1.hWnd) + RJustI$("Icon", Form1.Icon) + ⇐
          RJustI$("Image", Form1.Image)
      DebugPrint RJustS$("Left", Form1.Left) + RJustS$("LinkMode", ⇐
          Form1.LinkMode) + RJustT$("LinkTopic", Form1.LinkTopic)
      DebugPrint RJustI$("MaxButton", Form1.MaxButton) + ⇐
          RJustI$("MinButton", Form1.MinButton) + RJustI$("MousePointer", ⇐
          Form1.MousePointer)
      DebugPrint "Picture  Not available " + RJustS$("ScaleHeight", ⇐
          Form1.ScaleHeight) + RJustS$("ScaleLeft", Form1.ScaleLeft)
      DebugPrint RJustS$("ScaleMode", Form1.ScaleMode) + ⇐
          RJustS$("ScaleTop", Form1.ScaleTop) + RJustS$("ScaleWidth", ⇐
          Form1.ScaleWidth)
      DebugPrint RJustT$("Tag", Form1.Tag) + RJustS$("Top", Form1.Top) + ⇐
          RJustI$("Visible", Form1.Visible)
      DebugPrint RJustS$("Width", Form1.Width) + RJustI$("WindowState", ⇐
          Form1.WindowState)
End Sub
```

### How It Works

While QuickPak's MonoPrint subroutine does the job of displaying the text on the secondary monitor, it isn't very smart; it wants us to tell it where to print the text. To make it act more like the Immediate window, we use the DebugPrint subroutine.

In DebugPrint, a static variable Y is defined. Since it's static, Y will keep its value even after DebugPrint is finished, so it's there the next time it's called. That lets DebugPrint keep track of where the cursor is on the screen, so you don't have to tell it each time.

The first time you execute DebugPrint, Y will be zero; the first If statement checks for that and calls the DebugCls GoSub routine if necessary. DebugCls clears the screen and sets Y to one so text will start appearing at the top of the screen (line one).

DebugPrint also knows how to keep track of lines longer than 80 characters that wrap to multiple lines on the secondary monitor. If necessary, it will call DebugCls to clear the screen so a long text string will fit.

DebugPrint then displays the text string by calling QuickPak's MonoPrint. A GoSub routine called AdjustRow then makes sure to count up the lines if the text string took up more than one. Then an Exit Sub statement ends DebugPrint and returns to the statement that called it.

The MONOPRNT.FRM form is an example of printing the names and values of all the properties of a form. Since there are 44 form properties and most monochrome monitors only display 25 lines, we have to use a tabular layout so everything will fit on one screen. The RJust…$ functions left justify the property names and right justify the property values in a column 24 characters wide. That way we can easily fit three columns of information on the monochrome monitor.

The Command1_Click event subroutine passes the name and value of every property a form has, three to a line. This information might be useful to have when diagnosing a form-related bug.

### Comment

The DebugPrint subroutine has another advantage over the Immediate window and Debug.Print: The Immediate window is available only when you run your application under Visual Basic; it's not there when you compile your application to an .EXE executable file. MonoPrint (and DebugPrint) work either way.

The only thing Debug.Print can do that DebugPrint can't is accept numeric arguments. If you need to pass a numeric value to DebugPrint, you must first use the Str$ or Format$ function to turn it into a string.

---

**8.7    How do I ...**

# Create a state-of-the-art 3-D grayscale look on my Visual Basic forms?

Complexity: Easy

### Problem

I'd like to create Visual Basic forms that have a state-of-the-art 3-dimensional look similar to the NeXTStep interface. Ideally, this 3-D look should involve no special Visual Basic code on my part, and should include 3-D versions of the standard controls I'm already used to working with, such as check boxes and option buttons.

### Technique

Sheridan Software has a set of Custom Controls called 3-D Widgets/1 which includes 3-D versions of several standard Visual Basic controls, as well as some new ones. 3-D Widgets/1 includes 6 controls which provide the basic tools necessary to create a variety of 3-D grayscale looks. Figure 8-14 shows the Visual Basic Toolbox with Sheridan's custom controls.

This How-To project describes the steps required to produce the Document Preferences form shown in Fig-

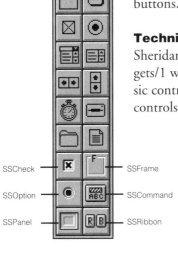

SSCheck

SSOption

SSPanel

SSFrame

SSCommand

SSRibbon

**Figure 8-14** The Visual Basic Toolbox with the Sheridan 3-D Widgets custom controls

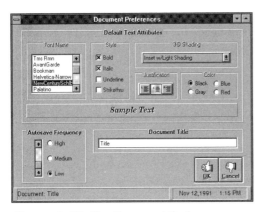

**Figure 8-15** The Document Preferences Screen

ure 8-15. This form has a sampling of the kinds of visual elements we'd like to have as part of our 3-D look. Without 3-D Widgets in our 'bag of tricks', the form would be difficult if not impossible to create.

### 3-D Grayscale Look Overview

The 3-D grayscale look, which is relatively new in Windows applications, has been in use for several years on Unix-based machines such as the NeXT. User interfaces based on this look tend to be very effective because they provide an unobtrusive (but very sexy!) background on which to present an application. And because the look tends to promote the selective (i.e., non-garish) use of color, the interface doesn't get in the way of the application, and it tends to generate a more consistent feel across screens.

### 3-D Widget Controls Summary

In keeping with the grayscale look, 3-D Widgets are designed to be used on Visual Basic forms that have the BackColor property set to light gray (&H00C0C0C0&). The BackColor property on most of the Widgets themselves is set to light gray and is not variable. This allows the controls to look as though they are part of the screen.

3-D Widgets that have a Caption property also have a Font3D property which controls the amount and type of 3-D shading effect to be applied to the Caption text. By changing the setting of the Font3D property at design time or at runtime via code, Caption text can be shaded to appear either raised or inset, and the shading can be light or heavy. The Font3D property works in conjunction with all the standard Visual Basic Font properties. Heavy shading (whether inset or raised) tends to look better with bigger bolder fonts. The Font3D property and the resultant 3-D feel that can be applied to screen text is one of those little details that really adds to the impact of a Visual Basic form without being distracting to the user. We will make use of the Font3D property on our form to subtly highlight key areas. Here is a brief overview of the 3-D Widgets controls we will be using to create our Document Preferences form.

### Check Boxes and Option Buttons

The 3-D Widgets check boxes and option buttons emulate the functionality of their Visual Basic counterparts, while sporting a 3-D look and a text

Alignment property. The appearance of the buttons is definitely 3-D, but they retain the basic feel of the standard Visual Basic buttons.

### Frames

The 3-D Widget frame works just like the standard Visual Basic frame. It can have other controls placed inside it and can optionally have a caption. In addition, there is an Alignment property which allows the caption text to be aligned left, right, or center.

### Command Buttons

The 3-D Widget command button has all the functionality of the standard Visual Basic command button with some interesting additions. Bitmap and icon images can be placed on the button, with or without text. And we can give the text a 3-D look by manipulating the button's Font3D property. In addition, the width of the button's beveled edges can be varied to finetune the 3-D look of the button.

### Ribbon Buttons

The 3-D Widget ribbon button will enable us to create a group of buttons that emulate the functionality of the Ribbon in Microsoft Excel or the Toolbar in Word for Windows. We will implement the three Justification options on the Document Preferences form with ribbon buttons. Think of ribbon buttons as looking like command buttons but acting like option buttons—when one button in a group is selected, the previously selected button in the group (if any) is de-selected.

One of the things that makes ribbon buttons so effective is that a number of choices can be presented in a relatively small amount of space. Unlike option buttons which have a caption to describe the option being selected, ribbon buttons use pictures instead. By assigning a carefully designed bitmap to the Picture property of the button, three justification choices can be fit in the same space that a single option button would occupy. Of course, you still need option buttons for those situations where pictures can't effectively convey the meaning of an option.

One of the convenient aspects of the 3-D Widget ribbon button is that the control can draw a beveled border, which gives the button its 3-D look. In addition, a bitmap does not need to be specified for the down (pressed) state of the button. When a bitmap isn't specified for the PictureDn property, the ribbon button will create one automatically, based on the bitmap specified for the PictureUp property. It does this by dithering or inverting (your choice via another property setting) the up bitmap, and offsetting it with proper shadow lines. So creating the three pictures for our Justification Options is as simple as drawing just three bitmapped images without borders or shadows.

**Panels**

The panel is basically a 3-D rectangular area of variable size. It can be as large as the form itself, or just large enough to display a single line of text. The panel is definitely the most versatile 3-D Widget. Panels can be used in a variety of ways:

- To display text (plain or 3-D) on a 3-D background (as we will do to display the sample text on our Document Preferences form)

- To group other controls on a 3-D background as an alternative to the Frame control (as with the Ok and Cancel buttons on our form)

- To lend a 3-D appearance to standard controls such as list boxes, combo boxes, scroll bars, etc. (as with the 3D Shading combo box, the Font Name list box, and the Autosave scroll bar on our form)

While dramatic 3-D effects can be created with the panel, the panel itself only has four basic visual properties—BevelOuter, BevelInner, BevelWidth, and BorderWidth. By combining these properties in different ways, interesting backgrounds for text and/or controls can be generated.

**Steps**

Open and run 3DWIGET.MAK to get a hands-on feel for the project and the 3-D controls. The form is designed to allow three categories of Document Preferences to be set—Default Text Attributes, Autosave Frequency, and Document Title. As the various Default Text Attributes are set, the sample text is modified to reflect the new settings.

When the Autosave Frequency option buttons are set, the adjacent scroll bar is updated to reflect the new setting. Conversely, when the Frequency is changed via the scroll bar, the appropriate option buttons is set. If the document title is changed, the updated text is reflected in the status bar at the bottom of the screen. All the bitmaps needed to create this form are available on the disk accompanying this book. The completed form should look like that in Figure 8-15.

1. Create a new project and call it 3DWIGETS.MAK. Add the 3-D Widgets demo VBX file SS3DDEMO.VBX to the project using the File menu's Add File command.

2. On the project's default form (Form1) create the controls listed in Table 8-9 with properties set as shown, and in the order listed. Using Figure 8-15 as a guide, be sure to create the controls in the proper sequence; for example, you should create the Default Text Attributes Frame control (SSFrame1)

before you create the Font Name Frame control (SSFrame2), since the Font Name Frame must be placed on top of the Default Text Attributes Frame.

| Control | Property | Setting |
|---------|----------|---------|
| Frame | Alignment | 2 - Center |
| | Caption | Default Text Attributes |
| | CtlName | SSFrame1 |
| | Font3D | 1 - Raised w/light shading |
| | FontBold | True |
| | ShadowStyle | 1 - Raised |

*The following frame should be placed over SSFrame1*

| Control | Property | Setting |
|---------|----------|---------|
| Frame | Alignment | 2 - Center |
| | Caption | Font Name |
| | CtlName | SSFrame2 |
| | Font3D | 1 - Raised w/light shading |
| | FontBold | False |
| | ShadowStyle | 0 - Inset |

*The following frame should be placed over SSFrame1*

| Control | Property | Setting |
|---------|----------|---------|
| Frame | Alignment | 2 - Center |
| | Caption | Style |
| | CtlName | SSFrame3 |
| | Font3D | 1 - Raised w/light shading |
| | FontBold | False |
| | ShadowStyle | 0 - Inset |

*The following frame should be placed over SSFrame1*

| Control | Property | Setting |
|---------|----------|---------|
| Frame | Alignment | 2 - Center |
| | Caption | 3-D Shading |
| | CtlName | SSFrame4 |
| | Font3D | 1 - Raised w/light shading |
| | FontBold | False |
| | ShadowStyle | 0 - Inset |

*The following frame should be placed over SSFrame1*

| Control | Property | Setting |
| --- | --- | --- |
| Frame | Alignment | 2 - Center |
| | Caption | Font Name |
| | CtlName | SSFrame2 |
| | Font3D | 1 - Raised w/light shading |
| | FontBold | False |
| | ShadowStyle | 0 - Inset |

*The following frame should be placed over SSFrame1*

| Control | Property | Setting |
| --- | --- | --- |
| Frame | Alignment | 2 - Center |
| | Caption | Justification |
| | CtlName | SSFrame5 |
| | Font3D | 1 - Raised w/light shading |
| | FontBold | False |
| | ShadowStyle | 0 - Inset |

*The following frame should be placed over SSFrame1*

| Control | Property | Setting |
| --- | --- | --- |
| Frame | Alignment | 2 - Center |
| | Caption | Color |
| | CtlName | SSFrame6 |
| | Font3D | 1 - Raised w/light shading |
| | FontBold | False |
| | ShadowStyle | 0 - Inset |
| Frame | Alignment | 2 - Center |
| | Caption | Autosave Frequency |
| | CtlName | SSFrame7 |
| | Font3D | 1 - Raised w/light shading |
| | FontBold | True |
| | ShadowStyle | 1 - Raised |
| Frame | Alignment | 2 - Center |
| | Caption | Document Title |
| | CtlName | SSFrame8 |
| | Font3D | 1 - Raised w/light shading |
| | FontBold | True |
| | ShadowStyle | 1 - Raised |

*The following panel should be placed over SSFrame2*

| Control | Property | Setting |
|---------|----------|---------|
| Panel | BevelInner | 0 - None |
| | BevelOuter | 1 - Inset |
| | BevelWidth | 2 |
| | Caption | N/A |
| | CtlName | SSPanel1 |

*The following panel should be placed over SSFrame4*

| Control | Property | Setting |
|---------|----------|---------|
| Panel | BevelInner | 0 - None |
| | BevelOuter | 2 - Raised |
| | BevelWidth | 2 |
| | Caption | N/A |
| | CtlName | SSPanel2 |

*The following panel should be placed over SSFrame5*

| Control | Property | Setting |
|---------|----------|---------|
| Panel | BevelInner | 0 - None |
| | BevelOuter | 2 - Raised |
| | BevelWidth | 2 |
| | Caption | N/A |
| | CtlName | SSPanel3 |

*The following panel should be placed over SSFrame7*

| Control | Property | Setting |
|---------|----------|---------|
| Panel | BevelInner | 0 - None |
| | BevelOuter | 1 - Inset |
| | BevelWidth | 2 |
| | Caption | N/A |
| | CtlName | SSPanel4 |

*The following panel should be placed over SSFrame8*

| Control | Property | Setting |
|---------|----------|---------|
| Panel | BevelInner | 0 - None |
| | BevelOuter | 1 - Inset |
| | BevelWidth | 2 |
| | Caption | N/A |
| | CtlName | SSPanel5 |

*The following panel should be placed over SSFrame8 (continued)*

| Control | Property | Setting |
|---------|----------|---------|
| Panel | BevelInner | 0 - None |
| | BevelOuter | 1 - Inset |
| | BevelWidth | 2 |
| | Caption | N/A |
| | CtlName | SSPanel6 |

*The following list box should be placed over SSPanel1*

| Control | Property | Setting |
|---------|----------|---------|
| List box | BackColor | White |
| | CtlName | FontList |
| | FontBold | False |

*The following four check boxes should be placed over SSFrame3*

| Control | Property | Setting |
|---------|----------|---------|
| Check box | Alignment | 0 - Text To The Right |
| | Caption | Bold |
| | CtlName | StyleBold |
| | Font3D | 0 - None |
| | FontBold | False |
| Check box | Alignment | 0 - Text To The Right |
| | Caption | Italic |
| | CtlName | StyleItalic |
| | Font3D | 0 - None |
| | FontBold | False |
| Check box | Alignment | 0 - Text To The Right |
| | Caption | Underline |
| | CtlName | StyleUnderline |
| | Font3D | 0 - None |
| | FontBold | False |
| Check box | Alignment | 0 - Text To The Right |
| | Caption | Strikethru |
| | CtlName | StyleStrikethru |
| | Font3D | 0 - None |
| | FontBold | False |

*The following combo box should be placed over SSPanel2*

| Control | Property | Setting |
| --- | --- | --- |
| Combo box | BackColor | Light Gray -&H00C0C0C0& |
| | CtlName | Text3DStyle |
| | FontBold | False |
| | Style | 2 - Dropdown List |

*The following three tibbon buttons should be placed over SSPanel3*

| Control | Property | Setting |
| --- | --- | --- |
| Ribbon button | CtlName | JustifyLeft |
| | GroupAllowAllUp | False |
| | PictureUp | JUSTIFYL.BMP |
| Ribbon button | CtlName | JustifyCenter |
| | GroupAllowAllUp | False |
| | PictureUp | JUSTIFYC.BMP |
| Ribbon button | CtlName | JustifyRight |
| | GroupAllowAllUp | False |
| | PictureUp | JUSTIFYR.BMP |

*The following four option buttons should be placed over SSFrame6*

| Control | Property | Setting |
| --- | --- | --- |
| Option button | Alignment | 0 - Text To The Right |
| | Caption | Black |
| | CtlName | ColorBlack |
| | Font3D | 0 - None |
| | FontBold | False |
| Option button | Alignment | 0 - Text To The Right |
| | Caption | Gray |
| | CtlName | ColorGray |
| | Font3D | 0 - None |
| | FontBold | False |
| Option button | Alignment | 0 - Text To The Right |
| | Caption | Blue |
| | CtlName | ColorBlue |
| | Font3D | 0 - None |
| | FontBold | False |

*The following four option buttons should be placed over SSFrame6 (continued)*

| Control | Property | Setting |
|---|---|---|
| Option button | Alignment | 0 - Text To The Right |
| | Caption | Red |
| | CtlName | ColorRed |
| | Font3D | 0 - None |
| | FontBold | False |

*The following panel should be placed over SSFrame1*

| Control | Property | Setting |
|---|---|---|
| Panel | BevelInner | 0 - None |
| | BevelOuter | 2 - Raised |
| | BevelWidth | 1 |
| | Caption | N/A |
| | CtlName | Sample |

*The following scroll bar should be placed over SSPanel4*

| Control | Property | Setting |
|---|---|---|
| Scroll bar | CtlName | AutosaveScroll |
| | LargeChange | 1 |
| | Max | 2 |
| | Min | 0 |
| | SmallChange | 1 |

*The following three option buttons should be placed over SSFrame7*

| Control | Property | Setting |
|---|---|---|
| Option button | Alignment | 0 - Text To The Right |
| | Caption | High |
| | CtlName | AutoSave |
| | Font3D | 0 - None |
| | FontBold | False |
| | Index | 0 |
| Option button | Alignment | 0 - Text To The Right |
| | Caption | Medium |
| | CtlName | AutoSave |
| | Font3D | 0 - None |
| | FontBold | False |
| | Index | 1 |

| Option button | Alignment | 0 - Text To The Right |
|---|---|---|
| | Caption | Low |
| | CtlName | AutoSave |
| | Font3D | 0 - None |
| | FontBold | False |
| | Index | 2 |

*The following text box should be placed over SSPanel5*

| Control | Property | Setting |
|---|---|---|
| Text box | BackColor | White |
| | CtlName | DocTitle |
| | FontBold | False |
| | Text | N/A |

*The following two command buttons should be placed over SSPanel6*

| Control | Property | Setting |
|---|---|---|
| Command button | Caption | &OK |
| | CtlName | SSCommand1 |
| | Font3D | 3 - Inset w/Light Shading |
| | Picture | THUMBSUP.BMP |
| Command button | Caption | &Cancel |
| | CtlName | SSCommand2 |
| | Font3D | 3 - Inset w/Light Shading |
| | Picture | THUMBSDN.BMP |
| Panel | BevelInner | 0 - None |
| | BevelOuter | 2 - Raised |
| | BevelWidth | 1 |
| | Caption | N/A |
| | CtlName | SSPanel7 |

*The following two panels should be placed over SSPanel7*

| Control | Property | Setting |
|---|---|---|
| Panel | BevelInner | 0 - None |
| | BevelOuter | 1 - Inset |
| | BevelWidth | 2 |
| | Caption | N/A |
| | CtlName | StatusDocTitle |

*The following two panels should be placed over SSPanel7 (continued)*

| Control | Property | Setting |
|---------|----------|---------|
| Panel | BevelInner | 0 - None |
| | BevelOuter | 1 - Inset |
| | BevelWidth | 2 |
| | Caption | N/A |
| | CtlName | StatusDate |

**Table 8-9** The Document Preferences Form controls and properties

3. Put the following code in the Form_Load event subroutine.

```
Sub Form_Load ()

' INITIALIZE THE FONT NAME LIST BOX
    for i% = 0 To screen.fontcount - 1
        fname$ = screen.fonts(i%)
    FontList.AddItem fname$
    Next i%

' INITIALIZE THE TEXT 3D STYLE COMBO BOX
    Text3DStyle.AddItem "None"
    Text3DStyle.AddItem "Raised w/Light Shading"
    Text3DStyle.AddItem "Raised w/Heavy Shading"
    Text3DStyle.AddItem "Inset w/Light Shading"
    Text3DStyle.AddItem "Inset w/Heavy Shading"
    Text3DStyle.listindex = 0


' INITIALIZE VARIOUS FIELDS
    JustifyCenter.Value = TRUE
    StyleBold.Value = TRUE
    ColorBlack.Value = TRUE
    Autosave(1).Value = TRUE
    doctitle.text = "Title"
    sample.caption = "Sample Text"

    datetime# = Now
    statusdate.caption = Format$(datetime#, "mmm d,yyyy   h:mm AM/PM")
End Sub
```

4. Place the following code in the specified event subroutines. For example, the code in the Text3DStyle_Change Sub should be placed in the Change event of the Text3DStyle control.

```
Sub Autosave_Click (index As Integer, Value As Integer)
    AutosaveScroll.Value = index
End Sub

Sub AutosaveScroll_Change ()
```

```
    i% = AutosaveScroll.Value
    Autosave(i%).Value = TRUE
End Sub

Sub ColorBlack_Click (Value As Integer)
    sample.ForeColor = RGB(0, 0, 0)
End Sub

Sub ColorBlue_Click (Value As Integer)
    sample.ForeColor = RGB(0, 0, 128)
End Sub

Sub ColorGray_Click (Value As Integer)
    sample.ForeColor = RGB(128, 128, 128)
End Sub

Sub ColorRed_Click (Value As Integer)
    sample.ForeColor = RGB(128, 0, 0)
End Sub

Sub DocTitle_Change ()
    StatusDocTitle.caption = "Document: " + doctitle.text
End Sub


Sub FontList_Click ()
    sample.fontname = FontList.text
End Sub


Sub JustifyCenter_Click (Value As Integer)
    sample.Alignment = 7
End Sub

Sub JustifyLeft_Click (Value As Integer)
    sample.Alignment = 1
End Sub

Sub JustifyRight_Click (Value As Integer)
    sample.Alignment = 4
End Sub

Sub SSCommand1_Click ()
    Unload form1
End Sub

Sub SSCommand2_Click ()
    Unload form1
End Sub

Sub StyleBold_Click (Value As Integer)
    sample.FontBold = Value
End Sub
```

```
Sub StyleItalic_Click (Value As Integer)
    sample.FontItalic = Value
End Sub

Sub StyleStrikethru_Click (Value As Integer)
    sample.FontStrikethru = Value
End Sub

Sub StyleUnderline_Click (Value As Integer)
    sample.FontUnderline = Value
End Sub

Sub Text3DStyle_Change ()
    sample.Font3D = Text3DStyle.listindex
End Sub
```

5. Place the following code in the Declarations section of the form.

```
Const FALSE = 0
Const TRUE = -1
```

### How It Works

Getting the various controls to interact with 3-D Wigets, such as the ribbon buttons used for the Justification options, is no more difficult than with standard controls. In fact, all the coding techniques used here to support the various controls are applicable to standard controls as well. For example, using a control array to handle the Autosave option buttons makes the coding for the interaction between the buttons and the scroll bar very clean.

### Comment

3D Widgets enable us to spend more time refining our application's look and feel, and less time writing Visual Basic code to achieve the 3-D look. This is much like the philosophy behind Visual Basic itself—concentrate more on the creation of your application rather than the implementation of it.

---

**8.8     How do I ...**

## Play MIDI music using the Sound Blaster?

. . . . . . . . . . . . . . . . . . . . . . . . . . . . . . . . . . . . . . . . . . . . . . . . . . . . . . . . . . . . . . . . . . . . .

Complexity: Intermediate

### Problem

I have a Sound Blaster card and would like to use Visual Basic to play MIDI music through it. It would be ideal if the music could be played directly from a standard MFF (MIDI File Format) file and required minimal attention from my program. I have heard that these MFF files exist on many

Channel

Music

Voice

**Figure 8-16** The Visual Basic Toolbox with Waite Group Software's SoundBytes custom controls

network services, such as CompuServe in the MIDI forum, where you can find an enormous range of songs and tunes.

## Technique

Waite Group Software offers a set of custom controls called SoundBytes which provide a simple way to control the capabilites of the Sound Blaster and Sound Blaster compatibles. The SoundBytes package includes controls for playing MIDI files, recording and playing voice, and utilizing the FM Synthesizer on the Sound Blaster. These files will play in the background while your Visual Basic application runs, and will only steal a small amount time from the processor because it uses an interrupt routine to supervise the play of MIDI files. Thus you can add interesting and attractive tunes to your opening screens, that will hold the attention of your user much longer than just a simple visual effect. Figure 8-16 shows the Visual Basic Toolbox with Waite Group Software's SoundBytes custom controls.

This How-To describes the steps required to play MIDI files, change the tempo at which the music is played, and transpose the key in which it is played. We'll also list the properties of the Music control that plays these MIDI tunes.

### Music Control Overview

Waite Group Software's Music control has properties that allow you to select a file to be played, change the tempo and key of the music, pause and continue playing, and control volume by fading in and out. Table 8-10 defines the properties of the control.

| Property | Meaning |
|---|---|
| Fade | Starts fading as determined by the following fade properties |
| FadeEnd | Percentage of original music volume to end fading |
| FadeIncrement | Change in percentage at each interval |
| FadeInterval | Tenths of seconds between application of the fade increment |
| FadeStart | Percentage of original music volume to start fading |
| Filename | Determines what MIDI file the music control plays |
| Pause | Suspends the current play |
| Play | Starts playing when TRUE, stops playing when FALSE |

*Table 8-10. continued*

| Property | Meaning |
| --- | --- |
| Tempo | Used to modify the tempo at which a piece is played |
| Transpose | Used to modify the key in which a piece is played |

**Table 8-10** Waite Group Software's Music control properties

In addition there is an event PlayEnd that occurs when the music file has played to completion. These properties allow you to simply start playing a MIDI file by setting the filename and the play properties. The music will play until completed with no further intervention or support from within your code.

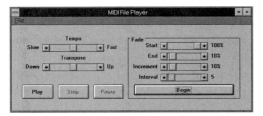

**Figure 8-17** The MIDI Play form for this project

**Steps**

Open and run MUSIC.MAK to get a hands-on feel for the music control. Once the form has loaded use the File menu's Open command to select a MIDI file from the project directory, then press the Play button to begin playing the piece. Figure 8-17 shows the form for this project.

On the left side of the form there are two scroll bars that control the tempo and key of the piece being played, and three buttons which start, stop, and pause the player.

On the right side of the form there is a frame with the caption Fade. Inside the frame are four scroll bars and a button used for fade in and out effects. The top scroll bar is used to set the starting volume of a fade effect. The starting volume is displayed as a percentage, when the Begin Fade button is clicked the volume of the music is set to this percentage of the original volume of the piece. The music will fade until it reaches the percentage set by the Stop scroll bar and then hold this volume level. There are two more scroll bars which are used to set fade properties. The Interval scroll bar is used to control the rate of FadeInterval property. FadeInterval ranges from 0 to 100 tenths of a second. The Increment scroll bar controls the amount by which the volume is either increased or decreased (as a percentage of the original volume) when each interval of time is reached. In summary then, the effect of the fade controls is that when the Begin button is pushed the volume is set to Start percentage of the original volume, and in steps of time given by Interval the volume is changed by Increment percent of the original volume until End percentage is reached.

1. Create a new project called MUSIC.MAK and add the SoundBytes demo VBX file WGSDEMO.VBX to the project using the File menu's Add File command.

2. Using the Menu Design Window, add the File menu as shown in Table 8-11.

| Caption | CtlName |
|---------|---------|
| &File | FileMenu |
| &Open… | FileOpen |
| - | FileBar1 |
| &Exit | FileExit |

**Table 8-11** Menu Design Window settings

3. Create a new form with the controls listed in Table 8-12 with the properties set as shown and save it as MUSIC.FRM. When adding the fade control scroll bars and labels, select the appropriate tool from the tool bar, move the mouse pointer to the interior of Frame1 and then click the left button. Do not create the control by double-clicking on the tool bar since Visual Basic will not establish the proper relationship between the control and the Frame causing the new control to disappear behind the frame the next time the frame is selected.

| Control | Property | Setting |
|---------|----------|---------|
| Form | Caption | MIDI File Player |
| | FormName | Player |
| Music | CtlName | Music1 |
| Horizontal scroll bar | CtlName | Tempo |
| | LargeChange | 10 |
| | Max | 200 |
| | Min | 0 |
| | SmallChange | 1 |
| | Value | 100 |
| Label | Alignment | 2-Center |
| | Caption | Tempo |
| Label | Alignment | 0-Left |
| | Caption | Fast |
| Label | Alignment | 1-Right |
| | Caption | Slow |

*Table 8-12. continued*

| Control | Property | Setting |
|---------|----------|---------|
| Horizontal scroll bar | CtlName | Transpose |
| | LargeChange | 4 |
| | Max | 24 |
| | Min | -24 |
| | SmallChange | 1 |
| | Value | 0 |
| Label | Alignment | 2-Center |
| | Caption | Transpose |
| Label | Alignment | 0-Left |
| | Caption | Up |
| Label | Alignment | 1-Right |
| | Caption | Down |
| Command button | Caption | Play |
| | CtlName | PlayMusic |
| Command button | Caption | Stop |
| | CtlName | StopMusic |
| Command button | Caption | PauseMusic |
| | CtlName | Pause |
| Frame | Caption | Fade |
| | CtlName | Frame1 |
| Horizontal scroll bar | CtlName | StartBar |
| | LargeChange | 10 |
| | Min | 0 |
| | Max | 100 |
| | Value | 100 |
| Horizontal scroll bar | CtlName | EndBar |
| | LargeChange | 10 |
| | Min | 0 |
| | Max | 100 |
| | Value | 100 |
| Horizontal scroll bar | CtlName | IncrementBar |
| | LargeChange | 5 |
| | Min | 0 |
| | Max | 100 |
| | Value | 5 |

| Horizontal scroll bar | CtlName | IntervalBar |
|---|---|---|
| | LargeChange | 5 |
| | Min | 0 |
| | Max | 100 |
| | Value | 1 |

**Table 8-12** Music project form's controls and properties

4. Add the following code to the Click event subroutine of the PlayMusic command button. When the PlayMusic command button is clicked, the music is started by setting the Play property to -1. The PlayMusic button is then disabled, and the PauseMusic and StopMusic buttons are enabled.

```
Sub PlayMusic_Click ()
'
' Start playing selected file, change button enables
'
    Music1.play = -1
    PlayMusic.enabled = 0
    StopMusic.enabled = -1
    PauseMusic.enabled = -1
End Sub
```

5. Place the following code in the Click event subroutine of the StopMusic command button. When the StopMusic command button is clicked, the music is turned off by setting the Play property to 0. The PlayMusic button is enabled and the StopMusic and PauseMusic buttons are disabled.

```
Sub StopMusic_Click ()
'
' Stop playing selected file, change button enables
'
    Music1.play = 0
    PlayMusic.enabled = -1
    StopMusic.enabled = 0
    PauseMusic.enabled = 0
    PauseMuis.caption = "Pause"
End Sub
```

6. Place the following code in the Click event subroutine of the Pause command button. When this button is clicked, the value of the Pause property is tested. If the current value is 0, the music is not paused, so the pause property is set to -1 to pause the music, and the button caption is changed to Continue. If the current value of Pause is -1, the music has been paused, then we change it to 0 to continue the music and change the button caption back to Pause.

```
Sub Pause_Click ()
'
' Pause or Continue current piece (if any)
'
   If Music1.pause = 0 Then
     Music1.pause = -1
     PauseMusic.caption = "Continue"
   Else
     Music1.pause = 0
     PauseMusic.caption = "Pause"
   End If
End Sub
```

7. Add the following code to the Change event subroutine of the Tempo scroll bar.

```
Sub Tempo_Change ()
'
' Set tempo using the value of the Tempo scroll bar
'
   Music1.tempo = Tempo.value
End Sub
```

8. Add the following code to the Change event subroutine of the Transpose scroll bar.

```
Sub Transpose_Change ()
'
' Set transposition using the value of the Transpose scroll bar
'
   Music1.transpose = Transpose.value
End Sub
```

9. Add the following code to the Click event subroutine of FileOpen.

```
'
' User wants to select file   run file open dialog
'
Sub FileOpen_Click ()
   FileForm.Show
End Sub
```

10. Add the following code to the Click event subroutine of SelectExit.

```
Sub SelectExit_Click ()
'
' File Exit selected   we're done
'
   Music1.Play = 0
   End
End Sub
```

11. Add the following code to the Change event subroutine of the StartBar, EndBar, IncrementBar, and IntervalBar scroll bars. When one of these scroll bars is changed, it updates the corresponding label caption.

```
Sub StartBar_Change ()
   StartLabel.caption = Str$(StartBar.value) + "%"
End Sub

Sub EndBar_Change ()
   EndLabel.caption = Str$(EndBar.value) + "%"
End Sub

Sub IncrementBar_Change ()
   IncrementLabel.caption = Str$(IncrementBar.value) + "%"
End Sub

Sub IntervalBar_Change ()
   IntervalLabel.caption = Str$(IntervalBar.value)
End Sub
```

12. Add the following code to the Click event subroutine of the BeginFade command button.

```
Sub BeginFade_Click ()
   Music1.FadeStart = StartBar.value
   Music1.FadeEnd = EndBar.value
   Music1.FadeIncrement = IncrementBar.value
   Music1.FadeInterval = IntervalBar.value
   Music1.Fade = -1
End Sub
```

13. Add the following code to the form's Load event subroutine.

```
Sub Form_Load ()
   '
   ' Initialize fade value display labels
   '
   StartLabel.caption = Str$(StartBar.value) + "%"
   EndLabel.caption = Str$(EndBar.value) + "%"
   IncrementLabel.caption = Str$(IncrementBar.value) + "%"
   IntervalLabel.caption = Str$(IntervalBar.value)
   '
   ' Initialize all buttons to disabled
   '
   PlayMusic.enabled = 0
   PauseMusic.enabled = 0
   StopMusic.enabled = 0
End Sub
```

14. Use New Form from Visual Basic's file menu to add a new form to the project. Save the file as FILEOPEN.FRM. Add new controls and set properites as shown in Table 8-13.

| Control | Property | Setting |
|---|---|---|
| Form | Caption | File Open |
| | FormName | FileForm |
| Label | Caption | Files: |
| | CtlName | Label1 |
| Label | Caption | Directories: |
| | CtlName | Label2 |
| Label | Caption | Drives |
| | CtlName | Label3 |
| File List | CtlName | FileList |
| Drive List | CtlName | DriveList |
| Directory List | CtlName | DirList |
| Command button | CtlName | OkButton |
| | Caption | OK |
| Command button | CtlName | CancelButton |
| | Caption | Cancel |

**Table 8-13** FileOpen form controls and properties

15. Add the following code to the Load event subroutine of the form.

```
Sub Form_Load ()
    '
    ' Make sure directory list is same height as files list
    '
    DirList.Height = FileList.Height
    FileList.pattern = "*.mid"
End Sub
```

16. Add the following code to the Click event subroutine of the Cancel button.

```
Sub CancelButton_Click ()
    '
    ' Change of heart    just hide form for quick restart
    '
    FileForm.Hide
End Sub
```

17. Add the following code to the Change event subroutine of the directory list box.

```
Sub DirList_Change ()
    '
    ' Directory changed    update file list
    '
    FileList.path = DirList.path
End Sub
```

18. Add the following code to the Change event subroutine of the drive combo box.

```
Sub DriveList_Change ()
  '
  ' Drive changed   update directory list
  '
  DirList.path = DriveList.drive
End Sub
```

19. Add the following code to the DblClick event subroutine of the file list box.

```
Sub FileList_DblClick ()
   OkButton_Click
End Sub
```

20. Add the following code to the Click event subroutine of the OK button.

```
Sub OkButton_Click ()
  '
  ' Ok Button clicked   If we've got a valid midi file then we'll use it
  '
  If FileList.filename <> "" Then
     FileForm.Hide
     Player.PlayMusic.Enabled = -1
     Player.Music1.filename = DirList.path + "\" + FileList.filename
  End If
End Sub
```

**How It Works**

The Music Player control plays MIDI format files. These files are laid out as a series of commands for controlling MIDI instruments. These commands come in multi-byte packets that tell each channel to do things like turn a note on or off, determine what kind of instrument to use, or increase or decrease volume. This example shows, with little overhead, how to use the Music Player control to play back these MIDI files.

When the program first starts, the Play, Stop, and Pause buttons are disabled. The File Open dialog is used to select a MIDI file to be played. After a file has been selected, the Play button is enabled. When the Play button is pressed, the currently selected file is played. The Play button is disabled and the Stop and Pause buttons are enabled.

When the Stop button is clicked, the music player is stopped by setting the Play property to False (0). The Play button is re-enabled, while the Stop and Pause buttons are disabled. When the Pause button is clicked, one of two things happen. If the music has been paused, the music is re-started and the pause button caption is set to "Pause." Otherwise, the music is paused and the button's caption is set to "Continue.".

Fade in and out values are controlled by the four scroll bars in the Fade box. They are set up with minimum and maximum values that are appropriate for the music player properties they correspond to. The fade properties are set from the scroll bar values when the Begin button is pressed. When this happens, all of the values of the scroll bars are copied to the appropriate properties, and then the Fade property is set to True (-1). This causes the music to fade (or increase in volume, as the case may be).

### Comment

Most of the code in this project supports the user interface, very little code is required to actually play the music files. The high-level interface to the MIDI music playing capabilities of the Sound Blaster provided by the Music control allows you to concentrate your effort on the design and creation of your application.

---

**8.9    How do I ...**

# Use the Sound Blaster's FM synthesizer?

Complexity: Intermediate

### Problem

I would like to add special sound effects to my programs. I know that the Sound Blaster has an FM synthesizer, and that it is very powerful, but how can I access it from within Visual Basic?

### Technique

Waite Group Software has an FM Synthesizer control that lets you manipulate all aspects of the Sound Blaster's FM synthesizer. This How-To project describes the steps required to build a complete Visual Basic interface to the Sound Blaster's FM Synthesizer.

### FM Synthesizer Control Overview

FM Synthesis is a technique used in many electronic instruments to create the timbres of instruments and other sounds. The timbre of a sound depends on the frequency and amplitude of its harmonics. Using the Sound Blaster you can program one or more of nine channels to create a specified sound. Each channel contains an Operator Cell and a Modulator Cell. The output of the Modulator is used to modulate the Carrier. This creates harmonics in the output of the Carrier. By changing the frequency of the

Modulator, you can change the timbre of the sound produced by a given channel on the Sound Blaster. There are a number of other parameters, such as attack, sustain, decay, and release level which can further modify the sound produced by a given channel. All of the parameters associated with a channel are shown in Table 8-14.

Once you have programmed a channel, either directly or by loading parameters from a file, you can set the Octave and Note properties to select the frequency of the sound played. Sounding a note requires only setting the Play property to True, the sound can later be turned off by setting Play to False. The range of sounds which can be generated by the Sound Blaster's FM Synthesizer is virtually limitless. Included on the diskette are a number of files with the extension SBI. These files contain parameters for some instruments, such as piano and organ, as well as some other special-effect sounds, such as helicopter and laser. You load an SBI file into a channel by setting the Filename property. The Creative Labs BBS has a number of SBI files which you can download (408-986-1488). You can use these files as a starting point when designing your own instruments and sounds.

| Property | Meaning |
|---|---|
| Car or ModAttackRate | Sets the rising time for a sound |
| Car or ModDecayRate | Sets the diminishing time for a sound |
| Car or ModReleaseRate | Sets rate at which sound diminishes after Play = FALSE |
| Car or ModSustainLevel | Sets the level at which sound is sustained after decay |
| Car or ModEnvelopeType | Modifies the effect of release and sustain properties |
| Car or ModKsl | Sets decrease in volume as frequency goes up |
| Car or ModKsr | Modifies length of envelope as frequency goes up |
| Car or ModMultiple | Sets output frequency which is OctaveNote * Multiple |
| Car or ModTotalLevel | Determines the amplitude of the cell's output |
| Car or ModTremelo | When set to TRUE, adds tremolo (1db at 3.7hz) |
| Car or ModVibrato | When set to TRUE, adds vibrato (6.4hz) |
| Car or ModWaveForm | Sets the waveform used |
| Connection | Determines connection between modulator and carrier |
| Feedback | Determines how much the modulator affects the carrier |
| Instrument | Loads values for a channel from a file |
| Note | Determines which note is played next |
| Octave | Determines the octave of the next note played |
| Play | Determines whether a channel is playing or not |

**Table 8-14** FM Synthesizer control properties

## Steps

Open and run FMSYNTH.MAK to get a hands-on feel for the project. The form has two columns of scroll bars: one for the carrier and one for the modulator, as shown in Figure 8-18. These scroll bars control the multivalued cell properties, such as attack and decay rate. Below each column of scroll bars is a set of options which further modify the output of a cell. The group of controls in the upper right part of the form control the type of connection between the operator cells and the amount of feedback applied to the modulator.

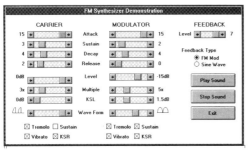

**Figure 8-18** The FM Synthesizer form at run time

Each of the waves (carrier and modulator) is defined by both its envelope (the volume of the wave) and its shape (including its frequency). The shape of the wave is determined by the waveform property, which defines the basic wave shape. Multiple modifies the basic frequency of each wave.

The envelope is defined by the attack, decay, sustain, and release scroll bars. The attack scroll bar determines how fast the volume of a note increases to the total level (as defined by the scroll bar). The decay rate determines how fast, once the maximum volume has been attained, that the volume reduces to the sustain level. The envelope can be modified by the KSR parameter, which decreases the length of the envelope as the frequency of the note goes up. The envelope can also be modified by the KSL parameter, which decreases the total volume as the frequency of the note goes up.

Finally, each wave can have tremolo (amplitude modulation) and vibrato (frequency modulation) applied to it. For some interesting effects, try setting the multiple of one wave to 0.5, 1, or 2 and setting the multiple of the other wave to 3 or above.

1. Create a new project called FMSYNTH.MAK. Create a new form and save it as FMSYNTH.FRM.

2. Add the SoundBytes demo .VBX file WGSDEMO.VBX to the project using the File menu's Add File command. Add the waveform pictures file PICTURES.FRM to the project using Add File.

3. Create an FM Channel control and set the properites as listed in Table 8-15.

| Control | Property | Setting |
|---------|----------|---------|
| Channel | CtlName | Channel |
|         | Left | 0 |
|         | Filename | CELLO.SBI |
|         | Top | 0 |

4. Create the controls used for programming the Carrier Cell.

### Carrier Scroll Bars

This array of scroll bar controls is used to set the multi-valued properties of the Carrier, such as attack and decay rates. These scroll bars have the following property values in common.

| Control | Property | Value |
|---------|----------|-------|
| Scroll bar | CtlName | CarrierHScrolls |
|            | Height | 255 |
|            | Left | 840 |
|            | SmallChange | 1 |
|            | Width | 1695 |

Be sure to set these properties for each of the following eight controls.

| Control | Property | Value |
|---------|----------|-------|
| Horizontal scroll bar | Index | 0 |
|                       | LargeChange | 4 |
|                       | Max | 15 |
|                       | Min | 0 |
|                       | Top | 600 |
| Horizontal scroll bar | Index | 1 |
|                       | LargeChange | 4 |
|                       | Max | 15 |
|                       | Min | 0 |
|                       | Top | 960 |
| Horizontal scroll bar | Index | 2 |
|                       | LargeChange | 4 |
|                       | Max | 15 |
|                       | Min | 0 |
|                       | Top | 1320 |

*Table 8-15. continued*

| Control | Property | Value |
|---|---|---|
| Horizontal scroll bar | Index | 3 |
| | LargeChange | 4 |
| | Max | 15 |
| | Min | 0 |
| | Top | 1680 |
| Horizontal scroll bar | Index | 4 |
| | LargeChange | 8 |
| | Max | 63 |
| | Min | 0 |
| | Top | 2160 |
| Horizontal scroll bar | Index | 5 |
| | LargeChange | 4 |
| | Max | 15 |
| | Min | 0 |
| | Top | 2640 |
| Horizontal scroll bar | Index | 6 |
| | LargeChange | 1 |
| | Max | 3 |
| | Min | 0 |
| | Top | 3000 |
| Horizontal scroll bar | Index | 7 |
| | LargeChange | 1 |
| | Max | 3 |
| | Min | 0 |
| | Top | 3480 |

## Carrier Check Boxes

Check boxes are used to set the Tremolo, Vibrato, Sustain, and KSR properties of the Carrier. The check boxes have the following properties in common.

| Control | Property | Value |
|---|---|---|
| Check box | CtlName | CarrierChecks |
| | Height | 255 |
| | Width | 975 |

Be sure to set these properties for each of the following four controls.

| Control | Property | Value |
| --- | --- | --- |
| Check box | Caption | Tremolo |
| | Index | 0 |
| | Left | 720 |
| | Top | 3960 |
| Check box | Caption | Vibrato |
| | Index | 1 |
| | Left | 720 |
| | Top | 4320 |
| Check box | Caption | Sustain |
| | Index | 2 |
| | Left | 1800 |
| | Top | 3960 |
| Check box | Caption | KSR |
| | Index | 3 |
| | Left | 1800 |
| | Top | 4320 |

5. Create the controls used to program the Modulator Cell.

### Modulator Scroll Bars

This array of scroll bars is used to set the multi-valued properties of the Modulator, such as attack and decay rates. These scroll bars have the following property values in common.

| Control | Property | Value |
| --- | --- | --- |
| Scroll bar | CtlName | ModulatorHScrolls |
| | Height | 255 |
| | Left | 3960 |
| | SmallChange | 1 |
| | Width | 1695 |

Be sure to set these properties for each of the following eight controls.

| Control | Property | Setting |
|---------|----------|---------|
| Horizontal scroll bar | Index | 0 |
| | LargeChange | 4 |
| | Max | 15 |
| | Min | 0 |
| | Top | 600 |
| Horizontal scroll bar | Index | 1 |
| | LargeChange | 4 |
| | Max | 15 |
| | Min | 0 |
| | Top | 960 |
| Horizontal scroll bar | Index | 2 |
| | LargeChange | 4 |
| | Max | 15 |
| | Min | 0 |
| | Top | 1320 |
| Horizontal scroll bar | Index | 3 |
| | LargeChange | 4 |
| | Max | 15 |
| | Min | 0 |
| | Top | 1680 |
| Horizontal scroll bar | Index | 4 |
| | LargeChange | 8 |
| | Max | 63 |
| | Min | 0 |
| | Top | 2160 |
| Horizontal scroll bar | Index | 5 |
| | LargeChange | 4 |
| | Max | 15 |
| | Min | 0 |
| | Top | 2640 |
| Horizontal scroll bar | Index | 6 |
| | LargeChange | 1 |
| | Max | 3 |
| | Min | 0 |
| | Top | 3000 |
| Horizontal scroll bar | Index | 7 |
| | LargeChange | 1 |
| | Max | 3 |
| | Min | 0 |
| | Top | 3480 |

Check boxes are used to set the Tremolo, Vibrato, Sustain, and KSR properites of the Modulator. The check boxes have the following properties in common.

| Control | Property | Value |
|---------|----------|-------|
| Check boxes | CtlName | ModulatorChecks |
| | Height | 255 |
| | Width | 975 |

Be sure to set these properties for each of the next four controls.

## Modulator Check Boxes

| Control | Property | Setting |
|---------|----------|---------|
| Check box | Caption | Tremolo |
| | Index | 0 |
| | Left | 3840 |
| | Top | 3960 |
| Check box | Caption | Vibrato |
| | Index | 1 |
| | Left | 3840 |
| | Top | 4320 |
| Check box | Caption | Sustain |
| | Index | 2 |
| | Left | 4920 |
| | Top | 3960 |
| Check box | Caption | KSR |
| | Index | 3 |
| | Left | 4920 |
| | Top | 4320 |

6. Add the following two labels above the columns of scroll bars, Label1 goes above the right column, Label2 goes above the left.

## Labels

| Control | Property | Setting |
|---------|----------|---------|
| Label | Alignment | 2 - Center |
| | Caption | CARRIER |
| | CtlName | Label1 |
| | Height | 255 |

*Labels (continued)*

| Control | Property | Setting |
|---------|----------|---------|
| | Left | 840 |
| | Top | 240 |
| | Width | 975 |
| Label | Alignment | 2 - Center |
| | Caption | MODULATOR |
| | CtlName | Label2 |
| | Height | 255 |
| | Left | 3960 |
| | Top | 240 |
| | Width | 975 |

7. Between the columns of scroll bars there are labels that indicate the function of the scroll bars to their right and left. As with the scroll bars themselves, there are some properties in common for this group of labels.

| Control | Property | Value |
|---------|----------|-------|
| Label | Alignment | 2 - Center |
| | Height | 255 |
| | Left | 2640 |
| | Width | 1215 |

Be sure to set these properties for the following eight controls.

| Control | Property | Setting |
|---------|----------|---------|
| Label | Caption | Attack |
| | CtlName | Label3 |
| | Top | 600 |
| Label | Caption | Sustain |
| | CtlName | Label4 |
| | Top | 960 |
| Label | Caption | Decay |
| | CtlName | Label5 |
| | Top | 1320 |
| Label | Caption | Release |
| | CtlName | Label6 |
| | Top | 1680 |
| Label | Caption | Level |
| | CtlName | Label7 |
| | Top | 2160 |

| | | |
|---|---|---|
| Label | Caption | Multiple |
| | CtlName | Label8 |
| | Top | 2640 |
| Label | Caption | KSL |
| | CtlName | Label9 |
| | Top | 3000 |
| Label | Caption | Wave Form |
| | CtlName | Label10 |
| | Top | 3480 |

8. To the left of the first seven Carrier scroll bars there are labels that display the current value of the scroll bars. The following properties are common to these labels.

| Control | Property | Value |
|---|---|---|
| Label | Alignment | 1 - Right |
| | Caption | |
| | CtlName | CarValues |
| | Height | 255 |
| | Left | 120 |
| | Width | 615 |

Be sure to set these properties for the following seven controls.

| Control | Property | Value |
|---|---|---|
| Label | Index | 0 |
| | Top | 600 |
| Label | Index | 1 |
| | Top | 960 |
| Label | Index | 2 |
| | Top | 1320 |
| Label | Index | 3 |
| | Top | 1680 |
| Label | Index | 4 |
| | Top | 2160 |
| Label | Index | 5 |
| | Top | 2640 |
| Label | Index | 6 |
| | Top | 3000 |

9. Add the following picture box control to the left of the last Carrier scroll bar. This picture control is used to display the selected wave form.

| Control | Property | Setting |
|---|---|---|
| Picture box | CtlName | CarPict |
| | Height | 495 |
| | Left | 240 |
| | Top | 3360 |
| | Width | 495 |

10. To the right the Modulator scroll bar are labels that display the current value of the scroll bars. The following properties are common to these labels.

| Control | Property | Value |
|---|---|---|
| Label | Alignment | 0 - Left |
| | Caption | |
| | CtlName | ModValues |
| | Height | 255 |
| | Left | 5760 |
| | Width | 615 |

Be sure to set these properties for the following seven controls.

| Control | Property | Value |
|---|---|---|
| Label | Index | 0 |
| | Top | 600 |
| Label | Index | 1 |
| | Top | 960 |
| Label | Index | 2 |
| | Top | 1320 |
| Label | Index | 3 |
| | Top | 1680 |
| Label | Index | 4 |
| | Top | 2160 |
| Label | Index | 5 |
| | Top | 2640 |
| Label | Index | 6 |
| | Top | 3000 |

11. Add the following picture box control to the right of the last Carrier scroll bar. This picture control displays the selected wave form.

| Control | Property | Setting |
|---|---|---|
| Picture box | CtlName | ModPict |
| | Height | 495 |
| | Left | 5760 |
| | Top | 3360 |
| | Width | 495 |

12. The next four controls are used for setting the amount of modulator feedback and setting the type of connection between the modulator and carrier.

## Feedback Controls

| Control | Property | Setting |
|---|---|---|
| Horizontal scroll bar | CtlName | FeedbackHScroll |
| | Height | 255 |
| | LargeChange | 3 |
| | Left | 7200 |
| | Max | 7 |
| | Min | 0 |
| | SmallChange | 1 |
| | Top | 600 |
| | Width | 1215 |
| Option button | CtlName | FeedbackOptions |
| | Height | 255 |
| | Index | 0 |
| | Left | 7200 |
| | Top | 1440 |
| | Width | 1455 |
| Option box | CtlName | FeedbackOptions |
| | Height | 255 |
| | Index | 1 |
| | Left | 7200 |
| | Top | 1680 |
| | Width | 1455 |
| Label | Alignment | 0 - Left |
| | Caption | |
| | CtlName | FeedbackLbl |
| | Height | 255 |
| | Left | 8520 |
| | Top | 600 |
| | Width | 255 |

13. Add the following three push buttons.

| Control | Property | Value |
|---|---|---|
| Command button | CtlName | PlaySound |
| | Caption | Play Sound |
| | Height | 495 |
| | Left | 7080 |
| | Top | 2160 |
| | Width | 1695 |
| Command button | CtlName | StopSound |
| | Caption | Stop Sound |
| | Height | 495 |
| | Left | 7080 |
| | Top | 2760 |
| | Width | 1695 |
| Command button | CtlName | Exit |
| | Caption | Exit |
| | Height | 495 |
| | Left | 7080 |
| | Top | 3360 |
| | Width | 1695 |

**Table 8-15** FM Channel Control's properties

14. Add the following code to the change event of CarrierHScrolls scroll bar. This subroutine uses the control array index to determine which property of the carrier cell is affected, sets the property from the value of the scroll bar, and updates the appropriate label by calling DisplayCarrierValues.

```
Sub CarrierHScrolls_Change (Index As Integer)
   '
   ' Carrier scroll bar value changed   update cell
   '
   Select Case Index
      Case 0
         Channel1.CarAttackRate = CarrierHScrolls(Index).Value
      Case 1
         Channel1.CarDecayRate = CarrierHScrolls(Index).Value
      Case 2
         Channel1.CarSustainLevel = CarrierHScrolls(Index).Value
      Case 3
         Channel1.CarReleaseRate = CarrierHScrolls(Index).Value
      Case 4
         Channel1.CarTotalLevel = 63 - CarrierHScrolls(Index).Value
```

```
      Case 5
         Channel1.CarMultiple = CarrierHScrolls(Index).Value
      Case 6
         Channel1.CarKSL = CarrierHScrolls(Index).Value
      Case 7
         Channel1.CarWaveform = CarrierHScrolls(Index).Value
   End Select

   DisplayCarrierValues (Index)
End Sub
```

15. Add the following code to the Load event subroutine. After centering the form on the screen this code initializes all of the controls using the Channel properties, and then calls DisplayCarrierValues and DisplayModulatorValues to update the labels associated with each scroll bar.

```
Sub Form_Load ()
   Dim I As Integer
   '
   ' Center form on screen
   '
   Top = (Screen.Height - Height) / 2
   Left = (Screen.Width - Width) / 2

   '
   ' Initialize Scroll bars with values loaded from instrument file
   '
   CarrierHScrolls(0).Value = Channel1.CarAttackRate
   CarrierHScrolls(1).Value = Channel1.CarDecayRate
   CarrierHScrolls(2).Value = Channel1.CarSustainLevel
   CarrierHScrolls(3).Value = Channel1.CarReleaseRate
   CarrierHScrolls(4).Value = 63 - Channel1.CarTotalLevel
   CarrierHScrolls(5).Value = Channel1.CarMultiple
   CarrierHScrolls(6).Value = Channel1.CarKSL
   CarrierHScrolls(7).Value = Channel1.CarWaveform

   ModulatorHScrolls(0).Value = Channel1.ModAttackRate
   ModulatorHScrolls(1).Value = Channel1.ModDecayRate
   ModulatorHScrolls(2).Value = Channel1.ModSustainLevel
   ModulatorHScrolls(3).Value = Channel1.ModReleaseRate
   ModulatorHScrolls(4).Value = 63 - Channel1.ModTotalLevel
   ModulatorHScrolls(5).Value = Channel1.ModMultiple
   ModulatorHScrolls(6).Value = Channel1.ModKSL
   ModulatorHScrolls(7).Value = Channel1.ModWaveform

   '
   ' Set other options as loaded from instrument file
   '
   FeedbackHScroll.Value = Channel1.Feedback
   FeedbackLbl.Caption = Str$(Channel1.Feedback)

   CarrierChecks(0).Value = Channel1.CarTremolo
   CarrierChecks(1).Value = Channel1.CarVibrato
```

```
    CarrierChecks(2).Value = Channel1.CarEnvType
    CarrierChecks(3).Value = Channel1.CarKSR

    ModulatorChecks(0).Value = Channel1.ModTremolo
    ModulatorChecks(1).Value = Channel1.ModVibrato
    ModulatorChecks(2).Value = Channel1.ModEnvType
    ModulatorChecks(3).Value = Channel1.ModKSR

    If Channel1.Connection Then
        FeedbackOptions(1).Value = -1
    Else
        FeedbackOptions(0).Value = -1
    End If

    For I = 0 To 7
        DisplayCarrierValues (I)
        DisplayModulatorValues (I)
    Next I
End Sub
```

16. Add the following code to the Change event of the ModulatorHScrolls scroll bar. This code is identical in form and function to CarrierH-Scrolls_Change.

```
Sub ModulatorHScrolls_Change (Index As Integer)
    '
    ' Some scrollable modulator value changed    update cell
    '
    Select Case Index
        Case 0
            Channel1.ModAttackRate = ModulatorHScrolls(Index).Value
        Case 1
            Channel1.ModDecayRate = ModulatorHScrolls(Index).Value
        Case 2
            Channel1.ModSustainLevel = ModulatorHScrolls(Index).Value
        Case 3
            Channel1.ModReleaseRate = ModulatorHScrolls(Index).Value
        Case 4
            Channel1.ModTotalLevel = 63 - ModulatorHScrolls(Index).Value
        Case 5
            Channel1.ModMultiple = ModulatorHScrolls(Index).Value
        Case 6
            Channel1.ModKSL = ModulatorHScrolls(Index).Value
        Case 7
            Channel1.ModWaveform = ModulatorHScrolls(Index).Value
    End Select

    DisplayModulatorValues (Index)
End Sub
```

17. Enter the following general subroutine. This subroutine displays the value of one Carrier scroll bar in the appropriate label.

```
Sub DisplayCarrierValues (Index As Integer)
    '
    ' Read value from scroll bar and update displayed value
    '
    Select Case Index
      Case 0 To 3
        CarValues(Index).Caption = Str$(CarrierHScrolls(Index).Value)
      Case 4
        CarValues(Index).Caption = Str$(CarrierHScrolls(Index).Value ⇐
            - 63) + "dB"
      Case 5
        Select Case CarrierHScrolls(Index).Value
          Case 0
            CarValues(Index).Caption = "0.5x"
          Case 11
            CarValues(Index).Caption = "10x"
          Case 13
            CarValues(Index).Caption = "12x"
          Case 14
            CarValues(Index).Caption = "15x"
          Case Else
            CarValues(Index).Caption = ⇐
                Str$(CarrierHScrolls(Index).Value) + "x"
        End Select
      Case 6
        Select Case CarrierHScrolls(Index).Value
          Case 0
            CarValues(Index).Caption = "0dB"
          Case 1
            CarValues(Index).Caption = "1.5dB"
          Case 2
            CarValues(Index).Caption = "3dB"
          Case 3
            CarValues(Index).Caption = "6dB"
        End Select
      Case 7
        CarPict.Picture = ⇐
            Pictures.WaveForm(CarrierHScrolls(Index).Value).Picture
    End Select
End Sub
```

18. Enter the following general subroutine. This subroutine displays the value of one Modulator scroll bar in the appropriate label.

```
Sub DisplayModulatorValues (Index As Integer)
    '
    ' Read value from scroll bar and update displayed value
    '
    Select Case Index
      Case 0 To 3
        ModValues(Index).Caption = Str$(ModulatorHScrolls(Index).Value)
      Case 4
```

```
            ModValues(Index).Caption = Str$(ModulatorHScrolls(Index).Value ⇐
               - 63) + "dB"
      Case 5
         Select Case ModulatorHScrolls(Index).Value
            Case 0
               ModValues(Index).Caption = "0.5x"
            Case 11
               ModValues(Index).Caption = "10x"
            Case 13
               ModValues(Index).Caption = "12x"
            Case 14
               ModValues(Index).Caption = "15x"
            Case Else
               ModValues(Index).Caption = ⇐
                  Str$(ModulatorHScrolls(Index).Value) + "x"
         End Select
      Case 6
         Select Case ModulatorHScrolls(Index).Value
            Case 0
               ModValues(Index).Caption = "0dB"
            Case 1
               ModValues(Index).Caption = "1.5dB"
            Case 2
               ModValues(Index).Caption = "3dB"
            Case 3
               ModValues(Index).Caption = "6dB"
         End Select
      Case 7
         ModPict.Picture = ⇐
            Pictures.WaveForm(ModulatorHScrolls(Index).Value).Picture
   End Select
End Sub
```

19. Add the following code to the Click event subroutine of the PlaySound command button. This subroutine first ensures that sound is off, then sets the Note and Octave properties, and finally sets the Sound property to True which causes the channel to play.

```
Sub PlaySound_Click ()
   Channel1.Sound = 0
   Channel1.Octave = 3
   Channel1.Note = 1
   Channel1.Sound = -1
End Sub
```

20. Add the following code to the Click event subroutine of the StopSound command button. When the click button is pressed the channel will stop playing.

```
Sub StopSound_Click ()
   Channel1.Sound = 0
End Sub
```

21. Add the following code to the Change event subroutine of the Feed-backHScroll scroll bar.

```
Sub FeedbackHScroll_Change ()
    '
    ' Feedback scroll bar changed   update cell
    '
    Channel1.Feedback = FeedbackHScroll.Value
    FeedbackLbl.Caption = Str$(FeedbackHScroll.Value)
End Sub
```

22. Add the following code to the Change event subroutine of the FeedbackOptions option button.

```
Sub FeedbackOptions_Click (Index As Integer)
    '
    ' Feedback connection type changed   update cell
    '
    If Index = 0 Then
        Channel1.Connection = 0
    Else
        Channel1.Connection = -1
    End If
End Sub
```

23. Add the following code to the Change event subroutine of the Carrier-Checks check box.

```
Sub CarrierChecks_Click (Index As Integer)
    '
    ' Carrier related check box changed   update cell
    '
    Select Case Index
        Case 0
            Channel1.CarTremolo = CarrierChecks(Index).Value
        Case 1
            Channel1.CarVibrato = CarrierChecks(Index).Value
        Case 2
            Channel1.CarEnvType = CarrierChecks(Index).Value
        Case 3
            Channel1.CarKSR = CarrierChecks(Index).Value
    End Select
End Sub
```

24. Add the following code to the Click event subroutine of the Modulator-Checks check box.

```
Sub ModulatorChecks_Click (Index As Integer)
    '
    ' Modulator related check box changed   update cell
    '
    Select Case Index
        Case 0
```

```
        Channel1.ModTremolo = ModulatorChecks(Index).Value
    Case 1
        Channel1.ModVibrato = ModulatorChecks(Index).Value
    Case 2
        Channel1.ModEnvType = ModulatorChecks(Index).Value
    Case 3
        Channel1.ModKSR = ModulatorChecks(Index).Value
   End Select
End Sub
```

25. Add the following code to the Click event subroutine of the ExitSynth command button.

```
Sub ExitSynth_Click ()
   '
   ' Exit button pushed    turn of sound and end
   '
   Channel1.Sound = 0
   End
End Sub
```

### How It Works

The code required to program the FM Synthesizer is reasonably simple, especially considering the large number of properties involved. Using scroll bars as strings helps to keep the number of lines of program minimal. The scroll bars's Min properties are set to the minimum value accepted by the corresponding channel property. Likewise, the scroll bars's Max properties are set to the maximum value accepted. This lets us set channel properties directly from the value of scroll bars. Channel True/False properties like Tremolo are easily set by directly assigning the value of a check box.

Once a channel's properties have been established, causing a sound to play is trivial. PlaySound_Click is invoked whenever the command button PlaySound is clicked. PlaySound_Click's first action is to turn off the sound by setting the Sound property to zero. When using a Channel control it is important to be sure that the channel is not playing a note at the time the octave and note properties are set. Next the note and octave for the channel are set and the statement Channel1.Sound = -1 causes the note to be played. Clicking on the Stop command button sets Channel1.Sound to zero, causing the channel to stop playing.

### Selecting Instruments

There are a number of .SBI files included on the bundled disk. The default instrument for this project is Cello. To change sounds, open the FM-SYNTH.FRM in the design mode. A button with a musical note will be visible in the top left of the form. Click on the button and the menu bar will display CtlName and Channel 1. Scroll down below CtlName to Instrument, the default CELLO will be shown. Click on the three dots (...) to the right of the instrument selection and you will be given a File Load dialog box. Select a new instrument file (SBI files are provided in the 8.9 subdirectory of the Visual Basic How-To disk). Run the project, press the Play Sound button, and you'll hear the selected instrument.

### Comment

Most of the code in this project supports the user interface, very little code is required to actually program the synthesizer. The high-level interface to the FM Synthesizer capabilities of the Sound Blaster provided by the FMSynthesizer Control allows you to concentrate your effort on the design and creation of your application.

---

**8.10    How do I ...**

## Play and record voice using the Sound Blaster?

Complexity: Intermediate

### Problem

I have a Sound Blaster card and would like to use it with Visual Basic to play and record voice, as well as other kinds of digitized sournd effects. It would be nice if my application would be able to do other things while playing and recording voice files. For example, I would like to have an animation running while a narrator explains what is happening on the screen.

**Figure 8-19** The Voice Manipulation form for the Recorder project

### Technique

You're in luck. Waite Group Software offers Voice control, a Visual Basic custom control that you can use for adding digitized sound recording and playback to your application. Files are saved in the Creative Voice .VOC file format. For this project, besides the Sound Blaster board, you'll need a standard microphone. The input impedance of the Sound Blaster's microphone input is 600 ohms and has an automatic gain control range of 10 mV to 100 mV. Any standard miniature tape recorder mike should do fine. You can also use any sound source, such as output from a radio or tape recorder. Figure 8-19 shows the form for this project.

This How-To project describes the steps required to play and record voice files. We will also list the properties of the Voice control.

### Voice Control Overview

The Voice Control has properties which allow you to play, record, pause, and continue playing a file. One thing to keep in mind while using the Voice Control is that it can be used for more than just voice. If you plug in a decent audio feed, you can digitize just about anything. Table 8-16 defines the properties of the control.

| Property | Meaning |
| --- | --- |
| Filename | What file to play or record |
| Pause | Causes playback or recording to be temporarily paused |
| Play | Starts playback of the voice file |
| Record | Starts recording the voice file |
| Rate | Sets the sampling rate for recording |

**Table 8-16** Control Masters Voice Control properties

The PlayEnd event which occurs when the voice file has played to completion can be used to signal the end of the recording mode. These properties allow you to simply start playing a voice file by setting the filename property and the play property. The voice will play until completed with no further intervention or support from within your code.

### Steps

Open and run RECORDER.MAK to get a hands-on feel for the voice control. On the form are four buttons: Play, Record, Pause, and Stop, as shown in the figure. They control the operation of the voice recorder. Only two of these buttons are enabled at a time (Play and Record are enabled if nothing is happening, Pause and Stop are enabled if playback or recording is occuring). When the Record button is pressed, a three-second count down starts. Once the countdown is complete, recording then starts.

1. Create a new project called RECORDER.MAK and add the SoundBytes demo VBX file WGSDEMO.VBX to the project using the File menu's Add File command.

2. Create a new form with the controls and properties in Table 8-17. When placing Label1, Label2, and Label3, be careful not to create the control by

double-clicking in the Toolbox. Instead, select the Label tool, move the mouse pointer to the destination on the Picture control and then create and size the label. If you create the control by double-clicking in the Toolbox, Visual Basic may at some time place the Label beneath the Picture where it will no longer be visible.

| Control | Property | Setting |
| --- | --- | --- |
| Picture box | AutoResize | True |
| | Picture | RECORDER.BMP |
| | Left | 0 |
| | Top | 0 |
| Voice | CtlName | Voice1 |
| | Filename | RECORDER.VOC |
| | Rate | 11000 |
| Timer | CtlName | Timer1 |
| | Enabled | False |
| Label | Alignment | 2-Center |
| | BorderStyle | 0-None |
| | Caption | RECORDER |
| | CtlName | Label1 |
| Label | Alignment | 2-Center |
| | BorderStyle | 0-None |
| | Caption | (None) |
| | CtlName | Label2 |
| Label | Alignment | 2-Center |
| | BackColor | &H80000005& |
| | BorderStyle | 0-None |
| | Caption | (None) |
| | CtlName | Label3 |
| | FontSize | 17.25 |
| Command button | Caption | Play |
| | CtlName | Play |
| Command button | Caption | Pause |
| | CtlName | Pause |
| Command button | Caption | Record |
| | CtlName | Record |
| Command button | Caption | Stop |
| | CtlName | Halt |

**Table 8-17** Controls and Properties for the Form

3. Resize Form1 so the picture box fills the client area of the form.

4. Place the following code in the Click event subroutine of the Play command button.

```
Sub Play_Click ()
'
' Start playing voice file, change button enables
'
   Voice1.Play = -1
   Play.Enabled = 0
   Halt.Enabled = -1
   Pause.Enabled = -1
   Record.Enabled = 0
End Sub
```

5. Place the following code in the Click event subroutine of the Pause command button.

```
Sub Pause_Click ()
'
' Pause or continue selected file, change button enables/caption
'
   If Voice1.Pause = -1 Then
     Voice1.Pause = 0
     Pause.Caption = "Pause"
     Label3.Caption = "RECORDING"
   Else
     Voice1.Pause = -1
     Pause.Caption = "Continue"
     Label3.Caption = "Paused"
   End If
End Sub
```

6. Place the following code in the Click event subroutine of the Record command button.

```
Sub Record_Click ()
'
' Record voice file
'
   CountDown = 3
   Label1.Caption = "3"
   Timer1.Enabled = -1
   Record.Enabled = 0
   Play.Enabled = 0
   Pause.Enabled = 0
End Sub
```

7. Place the following code in the Click event subroutine of the Halt command button.

```
Sub Halt_Click ()
'
```

```
' Stop playing (or recording) voice file
'
  ResetControls
End Sub
```

8. Place the following code in the Timer event subroutine of the Timer1 timer.

```
Sub Timer1_Timer ()
'
' If record is on blink RECORDING
'
  If Voice1.Record = -1 Then
    If Timer1.Interval = 900 Then
      Label3.visible = 0
      Timer1.Interval = 100
    Else
      Label3.visible = -1
      Timer1.Interval = 900
    End If
'
' Otherwise countdown until it's time to start
'
  Else
    If CountDown = 1 Then
      Timer1.Interval = 900
      Voice1.Record = -1
      Label3.Caption = "RECORDING"
      Halt.enabled = -1
      Pause.enabled = -1
    Else
      CountDown = CountDown - 1
      Label3.Caption = Str$(CountDown)
    End If
  End If
End Sub
```

9. Place the following code in the Load event subroutine of the form.

```
Sub Form_Load ()
'
' Clear all of the enables and reset any captions
'
  ResetControls
End Sub
```

10. Place the following declaration in the General section of the form.

```
Dim CountDown As Integer
```

11. Place the following code in the General subroutine ResetControls.

```
Sub ResetControls ()
'
```

```
' Reset all playback and record related controls
'
   If Timer1.Enabled Then
      Timer1.Enabled = 0
   End If
   If Voice1.Play = -1 Then
      Voice1.Play = 0
   ElseIf Voice1.Record = -1 Then
      Voice1.Record = 0
   End If


'
' Reset the button enables
'
   Record.Enabled = -1
   Play.Enabled = -1
   Halt.Enabled = 0
   Pause.Enabled = 0


'
' Reset captions
'
   Pause.Caption = "Pause"
   Label3.caption = ""

   Label2.Caption = Voice1.Filename
End Sub
```

12. Place the following code in the PlayEnd event subroutine of the Voice1 voice player.

```
Sub Voice1_PlayEnd ()
'
' Clean up after playback is complete
'
      ResetControls
End Sub
```

### How It Works

When the form first loads, the ResetControls subroutine is called. This causes the Play and Record buttons to be enabled, the Pause and Stop buttons to be disabled, disables the timer, makes sure no playback or recording is going on, and ensures the proper labeling of the Pause button.

If the Play button is clicked, voice playback is started. Along with this, the Play and Record buttons are disabled. The Pause and Stop buttons are enabled. If the voice file is allowed to completely play through (without the user stopping it via the Stop button), the PlayEnd event causes ResetControls to be called again.

If the Record button is clicked, a count down timer is started. A variable named CountDown is set to three, representing the number of seconds of the count down. Timer1 (with an interval of 1000ms) is used to keep track of the count down. Label3 is used to display the number of seconds left in the count down. Each time the Timer event is called in Timer1, CountDown is decremented. Once CountDown reaches zero, voice recording is started. Once recording has started Timer1 is used to blink a 'RECORDING' message every second. Voice recording can only be stopped via the Stop button.

If the Pause button is clicked, one of two things happens. If voice is currently being played or recorded, the voice player is paused and the Pause button has its caption changed to Continue. If the player has been paused, however, the player is un-paused and the caption is returned back to Pause.

If the Stop button is clicked, ResetControls is called. This causes the player to stop. The Pause button caption is returned to Pause. The Play and Record buttons are enabled, while the Pause and Stop buttons are disabled.

### Comment

Most of the code in this project supports the user interface, very little code is required to actually manipulate the voice file. The high-level interface to the voice playing and recording capabilities of the Sound Blaster provided by the Voice Control allows you to concentrate your effort on the design and creation of your application.

For you hardware techies, the Sound Blaster uses a technique called digital sampling. It samples the audio input waveform and converts it to a digital format suitable for storing in a file. When it is played back the reverse occurs and the digital waveform is converted back to an analogy waveform. The default sampling rate is 8000 Hz, but this can be altered by the developer to between 5000 Hz and 12000 Hz. At 8000 Hz there are 8000 samples and, hence, 8000 bytes consumed in one second. As the sample rate increases, the quality goes up and so does the storage capacity. You can refer to the Voice control documentation for more details.

# 9

# USING
# VISUAL BASIC
# WITH DLLS

# 9

One of the most powerful aspects of Visual Basic is its ability to use custom dynamic link libraries (DLL) that greatly extend the power of what you can do. This chapter will show you how to take a DLL written in another language, such as C, and get it working for Visual Basic. It will also point out the advantages of a DLL, how it can be used as a black box, and the power of Visual Basic to serve as an interface that is completely independent of the DLL's operation (adaptive programming).

The chapter is based on a fractal-generating DLL. Fractals are beautiful mathematical patterns that occur frequently in nature and can be generated on a computer screen from simple recursive formulas. Fractals occur in nature as clouds, ferns, waves, and any physical process where there is a noticeable degree of what is called self-similarity. You can learn much more about fractals by refering to *The Waite Group's Fractal Creations*, by Tim Wegner and Mark Peterson, a book/disk package that includes the fabulous Fractint program, a fold out fractal poster and a set of 3-D glasses for seeing fractals in three dimensions. The fractal DLL in this chapter was written in Borland C++ and some 386 assembly language. Details on it can be found in *The Waite Group's Borland C++ Developer's Bible* by Mark Peterson. BC++ is an object-oriented language suitable for developing complex applications that must run at the highest possible speed. The purpose of the DLL is to allow the Visual Basic user to select from a set of its built-in formulas, and then have it return a color given a certain pixel location on the screen. Visual Basic must supply the screen location to plot and the menu structure for accessing its fractal formulas. The DLL uses a concept called atoms which allow Visual Basic to poll it and find out what formulas it supports. The names of these formulas are returned to Visual Basic and used to fill its menu items. That way the DLL can be extended and no changes need to be made in the interface.

In addition you'll learn how to convert between Visual Basic's data types and the data types found in the C language and the extended data types in Windows.

## Introducing DLLs

One of the great features of Windows is its dynamic link libraries (DLLs). A DLL is a library of functions that Windows reads in and executes as the .EXE program requires them. The opposite of a dynamic link library is a static link library, where the functions and subroutines are copied from the static library into your .EXE executable program when it's compiled. There are many advantages to DLLs and only a few disadvantages.

A big advantage to DLLs is that since they're separate from your program, you can update the DLL itself without changing your compiled .EXE program. Another advantage is that since Windows manages the DLL, it's possible for several applications to use routines from the same DLL, saving memory and disk space.

The biggest disadvantage to using DLLs is that Windows must take time to load the routines from the DLL when they're needed, while routines that are linked statically to your .EXE are already in memory when the program's loaded. Another disadvantage of DLLs is that usually an entire DLL must be distributed with your .EXE program, even though you may use only a small portion of its routines. With a static link library, on the other hand, only the functions that are used by your application are included.

DLLs are so useful that they form the entire foundation of Windows itself. In the Windows SYSTEM directory, you'll find many different types of files: .DLL, .DRV, and .EXE. Contrary to the .DRV and .EXE extensions, many of them are actually DLLs that act as hardware drivers, which means that you can just plug in newer, updated versions if the manufacturer of your video board, for example, updates its video driver, or when Microsoft releases new versions of Windows.

### Visual Basic and DLLs

The Visual Basic Declare statement is used primarily to provide access to the routines in a DLL. In the Declare statement, you'll find a Lib keyword that specifies the DLL that actually contains the routine. Many of the How-Tos in this book deal with using functions from Windows' own application programming interface (API). The API functions are available in the Kernel,

GDI, and User libraries. The DLLs for those functions are in KER-NEL.EXE, GDI.EXE, and USER.EXE in the Windows SYSTEM directory, respectively.

Visual Basic custom controls are actually implemented as DLLs (regardless of the normal .VBX extension).

What about DLLs that aren't part of Windows? Visual Basic can use almost any routine from any DLL. Third party companies that want to offer extensions to Visual Basic that aren't custom controls will offer standard DLLs.

But the truly exciting thing is that Visual Basic can use DLLs created in any language, for any language, with few exceptions. A third party could write a DLL in Pascal that's usable by Pascal, C, and Visual Basic programmers. The third party doesn't need to do anything special to support so many languages. Novell, for example, offers a DLL version of its Btrieve Record Manager that's usable by almost any Windows programming language, including Visual Basic.

All is not perfect, however. Since C has dominated Windows programming for so long, the majority of DLLs available to help Windows developers is geared toward C. Indeed the DLL documentation uses C code to show how to use the DLL and even how to access the routines in the DLL. What's a non-C person to do?

## A Mini C Primer

Since Visual Basic is so popular, many companies are providing Visual Basic code examples and Declare statements for their DLLs. The problem, of course, comes up when such declarations aren't available in Visual Basic form but only C code is provided. It would seem overkill to learn C just to be able to interface your Visual Basic application with a DLL.

Luckily, you don't have to go to that extreme. By following a few simple rules, you should be able to convert declarations from C to their Visual Basic equivalents.

### C-Style Function Declarations

We'll begin with the declaration for the SendMessage function from the WINDOWS.H header file from the Windows Software Development Kit (SDK). Here is the C declaration for the SendMessage API function:

```
DWORD SendMessage(HWND hWnd, WORD wMsg, WORD wParam, DWORD lParam)
```

1. The first step in converting the declaration to Visual Basic format is to give a Declare keyword:

```
Declare
```

2. The first word in the C declaration tells you the type of value that function returns. For SendMessage, it's a DWORD. In C, some functions can be of type void, which means they don't actually return a value. In that case, Visual Basic calls them subroutines, not functions, so the next step would be to declare them as such.

`Declare Sub`

Most functions, including SendMessage, do return a value, so we must tell Visual Basic so.

`Declare Function`

We'll come back to the type of value of the function, since Visual Basic specifies the return value later.

3. The next part is easy. Just type the name of the function.

`Declare Function SendMessage`

There is a possible problem with function names. Sometimes a Visual Basic built-in statement, function, method, or property name will conflict with a function in a DLL. For example, there is an API function SetFocus, but there's also Visual Basic's SetFocus method. If there is a conflict, see step 5.

4. The next step is to tell Visual Basic in which DLL the function resides. This information isn't part of the C function declaration but it is usually part of the documentation for the DLL. SendMessage, for example, is located in the User library. (That's the USER.EXE in your WINDOWS\SYSTEM directory.) The way to specify the library is with the Lib keyword.

`Declare Function SendMessage Lib "USER"`

5. If the function name conflicts with a Visual Basic built-in statement, function, method, or property (see Step 3), here's where you need to work around the conflict. The Visual Basic Alias keyword lets you "rename" the function. For example, the API function SetFocus (which conflicts with the Visual Basic SetFocus method) could be declared like this.

`Declare Function SetFocusAPI Lib "User" Alias "SetFocus"...`

Now the name you would use to execute the function is "SetFocusAPI." With the Alias keyword, Visual Basic knows that it's really called "SetFocus" in the DLL.

6. The next step is to translate each of the parameters of the function. In C, the type of the parameter is first, followed by the parameter name. SendMessage's first parameter is

```
HWND hWnd
```

so the type is HWND and the name is hWnd. In Visual Basic a parameter is declared as

```
name As type
```

so we can say

```
hWnd As ...
```

but what would we use as the HWND type? There doesn't seem to be such a Visual Basic type.

### Windows Types

The WINDOWS.H header file defines several types that aren't native to pure C. As you've seen in other chapters, much of Windows operates on handles, which are actually just integer numbers. WINDOWS.H defines types for the various types of handles that are available—handles to windows, menus, bitmaps, etc. The idea is that it makes C programming for Windows easier.

WINDOWS.H also defines new names for some of the standard variable types, like Integer, Long, and String. Table 9-1 lists the new types that WINDOWS.H defines, along with their C and Visual Basic equivalents.

| Windows Type | C Type | Visual Basic Type | Declaration Character |
|---|---|---|---|
| BOOL | int | ByVal Integer | % |
| BYTE | unsigned char | n/a | |
| WORD | unsigned int | ByVal Integer | % |
| DWORD | unsigned long | ByVal Long | & |
| LPSTR | char far * | ByVal String | $ |
| ATOM | WORD | ByVal Integer | % |
| HANDLE | WORD | ByVal Integer | % |
| HWND | HANDLE | ByVal Integer | % |
| HICON | HANDLE | ByVal Integer | % |
| HDC | HANDLE | ByVal Integer | % |
| HMENU | HANDLE | ByVal Integer | % |
| HBITMAP | HANDLE | ByVal Integer | % |
| COLORREF | DWORD | ByVal Long | & |

**Table 9-1** Some common Windows types

Using Table 9-1, we can now complete the parameter declaration by saying

```
ByVal hWnd As Integer
```

or

```
ByVal hWnd%
```

Using the table, the rest of the parameters are also easily translated:

```
ByVal wMsg As Integer, ByVal wParam As Integer, ByVal lParam As Long
```

or

```
ByVal wMsg%, ByVal wParam%, ByVal lParam&
```

so the Visual Basic declaration for SendMessage so far is

```
Declare Function SendMessage Lib "USER" (ByVal hWnd As Integer, ByVal wMsg
As Integer, ByVal wParam As Integer, ByVal lParam As Long)
```

7. As we saw in step 2, SendMessage returns a DWORD. From Table 9-1, we know that a DWORD is a Long integer. There are two ways to tell Visual Basic what type a function returns: You can either add

```
As type
```

to the end of the declaration, as follows:

```
Declare Function SendMessage Lib "USER" (ByVal hWnd As Integer, ByVal wMsg
As Integer, ByVal wParam As Integer, ByVal lParam As Long) As Long
```

Or you can add the type specification character (for DWORD, it's an ampersand) to the function name:

```
Declare Function SendMessage& Lib "USER" (ByVal hWnd As Integer, ByVal
wMsg As Integer, ByVal wParam As Integer, ByVal lParam As Long)
```

Note that you can use either the "As *type*" method or the appropriate type specification character interchangably. They both have the same result. Which you use is mostly a matter of personal preference. Using "As *type*" can be easier to read, but the type specification character method uses less space, which can be important if you're declaring a function that takes many parameters.

As you can see, translating C-style function declarations to Visual Basic is mostly mechanical; you should be able to convert most DLL function declarations from C using the steps outlined above. There may be some more exotic declarations that don't follow the above steps. Also remember that some C parameters don't have exact matches or equivalents in Visual Basic. That's the 0.01% of DLL functions that you may not be able to use with Visual Basic. Always check with the supplier of the DLL for compatibility information.

## The Fractal DLL

How can we put our new-found knowledge to work? On the disk accompanying this book, you'll find a DLL called FRACTDLL.DLL. This DLL is developed in *The Waite Group's Borland C++ Developer's Bible*, by Mark Peterson.

FRACTDLL is a DLL that a Windows application can call to display a fractal image. We won't go into a lot of detail here about fractals, except to say that fractals are some of the most interesting and beautiful images you can create on your computer. For more information about fractals and how they're created, see *Fractal Creations*, another Waite Group Press book, with Mark Peterson as a co-author.

Looking at the chapter in the *Borland C++ Developer's Bible* that discusses the fractal DLL, we see that it's implemented as a series of files written in C++ and assembly language. The fractal DLL can perform its calculation using normal floating point math, or two special math formats: QFloat, or fixed 16-bit. The latter two math types are implemented using 386 assembly language, which means you must have a 386 (or i486) machine to use them.

How can Visual Basic use a DLL written in C++ or 386 assembly language? After all, Visual Basic doesn't have any of those features. The beauty of DLLs is that it doesn't matter how they were written. It's easiest to think of a DLL as a black box: The "internal" implementation details are hidden from view. You just throw some numbers into the box, shake it up, and the proper results come out.

The fractal DLL has an external API (application program interface), much like the Windows API. Calling one of the fractal API functions sets it in motion, executing the C++ or assembly code. As long as you stick to the fractal's API functions, it doesn't matter *how* it's done internally. Mr. Peterson could entirely rewrite how the DLL does what it does, but as long as he keeps the external API the same, your application would continue to work. The same thing holds true for any other DLLs, including those that make up Windows itself. Microsoft might very well rewrite the internals of Windows (to speed it up or make it more reliable), but as long as they keep the same external API, your application will continue to work as before.

### The Fractal DLL's API

Here's an abbreviated version of how an application using the fractal DLL should work:

- Call the NumberFractals function to determine how many fractals the DLL supports.

This is an example of adaptive programming: If a future version of the fractal DLL supports more fractals than the original version, your application will automatically be able to use them.

- Call the FractalName function to get the name of each fractal.

We call FractalName to build a Fractal menu that contains the name of every fractal the DLL supports. The value returned by NumberFractals tells you how many times to call FractalName.

- When the user has selected a fractal, call the FractalDefaults function to get the default values for the fractal.

- A fractal has parameters that tell what part of the fractal to display and how to display it. Again, that kind of detail isn't covered here, but *Fractal Creations* is an excellent resource to learn all about fractals. One interesting parameter is a fractal's symmetry; some fractals are symmetrical and have parts that are mirror images of other parts so we can speed up the fractal display by only calculating the needed parts.

- Call the CreateFractal function to have the DLL initialize the fractal.

CreateFractal actually allocates the memory needed to calculate the fractal. Mercifully, the detail is taken care of by the DLL.

- Call the ActivateFractal function to start calculating the fractal.

ActivateFractal has the DLL tell Windows it will be using the memory allocated in CreateFractal. After ActivateFractal is called, the memory used for the fractal is reserved and can't be used by another application, so you should only call ActivateFractal when you're ready to begin displaying the fractal.

- Call IdleFractal if you're temporarily not going to be displaying the fractal.

IdleFractal lets Windows have the memory that was allocated in CreateFractal. You should call IdleFractal if you call Visual Basic's DoEvent function or if you exit a subroutine.

- Call the FractalPoint function to have the DLL calculate the color of a given point.

In essence, a fractal is created by calculating how long a given point takes to exceed some formula. The specific formula actually depends on the fractal type and there are many different fractal types. Calling FractalPoint tells the fractal DLL to calculate the formula for the given point. The number returned by FractalPoint tells how long it took the point to exceed the formula for the fractal. That number is then used to pick a color for the point.

The number FractalPoint returns also indicates how long the DLL spent calculating, so the higher the number, the longer it took. Since it's not proper Windows style to "hog" the machine for a long period of time, the application should return control to Windows after it has spent a while calculating.

- Finally, when the application is done displaying the fractal, it should call the DestroyFractal function to tell the DLL it's done.

DestroyFractal releases the memory the DLL used to calculate the fractal.

We will follow all these steps to create a Visual Basic application that calls the fractal DLL to create some beautiful images.

### The Fractal DLL's Functions

Here's where we get to test out the translation steps discussed at the beginning of this chapter. The C declarations of the fractal DLL's functions are.

```
BOOL ActivateFractal(FRACTAL Fractal);
FRACTAL CreateFractal(unsigned FractNum, unsigned xdots, unsigned ydots,
   MATHTYPE MathType, double Left, double Right, double Top, double
Bottom,
   unsigned long maxit, double p1x, double p1y, double p2x, double p2y);
BOOL DestroyFractal(FRACTAL Fractal);
ATOM FractalDefaults(unsigned FractNum);
ATOM FractalName(unsigned FractNum);
unsigned long FractalPoint(FRACTAL Fractal, unsigned x, unsigned y);
BOOL IdleFractal(FRACTAL Fractal);
unsigned NumberFractals();
```

It looks like some types are missing from Table 9-1. "unsigned," "double," FRACTAL, and MATHTYPE aren't listed. "unsigned" and "double" are easy: they're other C types. "unsigned" is the same as "unsigned int," which means it translates to the Visual Basic type ByVal Integer. "double" is the Visual Basic type ByVal Double.

FRACTAL and MATHTYPE are defined by the fractal DLL. FRACTAL is the same as a Visual Basic ByVal Long and MATHTYPE is ByVal Integer.

So using this information and Table 9-1, we can translate the above C declarations to their Visual Basic equivalents:

```
Declare Function ActivateFractal Lib "FRACTDLL.DLL" (ByVal hFractal As ⇐
Long) As Integer
Declare Function CreateFractal Lib "FRACTDLL.DLL" (ByVal fractNum%, ⇐
ByVal xDots%, ByVal yDots%, ByVal mathType%, ByVal fLeft#, ByVal fRight#, ⇐
ByVal fTop#, ByVal fBottom#, ByVal maxIt&, ByVal p1x#, ByVal p1y#, ByVal
p2x#, ByVal p2y#) As Long
```

```
Declare Function DestroyFractal Lib "FRACTDLL.DLL" (ByVal hFractal As ⇐
Long) As Integer
Declare Function FractalDefaults Lib "FRACTDLL.DLL" (ByVal fractNum As ⇐
Integer) As Integer
Declare Function FractalName Lib "FRACTDLL.DLL" (ByVal fractNum As ⇐
Integer) As Integer
Declare Function FractalPoint Lib "FRACTDLL.DLL" (ByVal hFractal ⇐
As Long, ByVal x As Integer, ByVal y As Integer) As Long
Declare Function IdleFractal Lib "FRACTDLL.DLL" (ByVal hFractal As ⇐
Long) As Integer
Declare Function NumberFractals Lib "FRACTDLL.DLL" () As Integer
```

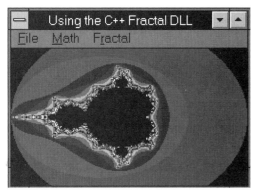

**Figure 9-1** The VFRACTAL project showing the Mandelbrot fractal

Note that in the Declare statement for CreateFractal we had to use Visual Basic's type declaration characters so the entire statement would fit on one line. Also, all the functions are in the file named FRACTDLL.DLL, so that's what we used for the Lib keyword.

So where do we go from here? Let's plunge right into creating a Visual Basic fractal interface.

**Steps**

Open and run VFRACTAL.MAK. Select a fractal type from the Fractal menu. Sit back and enjoy! A sample fractal is shown in Figure 9-1. Try some of the other fractal types to see how they look.

1. Create a new project called VFRACTAL.MAK. Since the VFRACTAL project uses the WhichCPU function, add the VBHOWTO.BAS module to the project. Create a new form with the properties listed in Table 9-2 and save it as VFRACTAL.FRM.

| Control | Property | Setting |
|---------|----------|---------|
| Form | AutoRedraw | True |
|  | Caption | Using the C++ Fractal DLL |
|  | FormName | fractalForm |
|  | Icon | WINFRACT.ICO |

**Table 9-2** VFractal form's controls and properties

2. Give VFRACTAL.FRM a menu using the Menu Design Window and the commands listed in Table 9-3.

| Caption | CtlName | Index |
|---------|---------|-------|
| &File | FileMenu | |
| &About... | FileAbout | |
| E&xit | FileExit | |
| &Math | MathMenu | |
| &Fixed point | MathFixed | |
| &Quick float | MathQuick | |
| F&loating point | MathFloat | |
| F&ractal | FractalMenu | |
| First | Fractals | 0 |

**Table 9-3**  VFractal form's menu

3. Put the following code in the Declarations section of VFRACTAL.FRM. This code declares some Windows and Fractal API functions and declares some global variables.

```
DefInt A-Z

' Fractal DLL functions -----------------
Declare Function ActivateFractal Lib "fractdll.dll" (ByVal hFractal As ⇐
Long) As Integer
Declare Function CreateFractal Lib "fractdll.dll" (ByVal fractNum%, ⇐
ByVal xDots%, ByVal yDots%, ByVal mathType%, ByVal fLeft#, ⇐
ByVal fRight#, ByVal fTop#, ByVal fBottom#, ByVal maxIt&, ByVal p1x#, ⇐
ByVal p1y#, ByVal p2x#, ByVal p2y#) As Long
Declare Function DestroyFractal Lib "fractdll.dll" (ByVal hFractal As ⇐
Long) As Integer
Declare Function FractalDefaults Lib "fractdll.dll" (ByVal fractNum As ⇐
Integer) As Integer
Declare Function FractalName Lib "fractdll.dll" (ByVal fractNum As ⇐
Integer) As Integer
Declare Function FractalPoint Lib "fractdll.dll" (ByVal hFractal As ⇐
Long, ByVal x As Integer, ByVal y As Integer) As Long
Declare Function IdleFractal Lib "fractdll.dll" (ByVal hFractal As Long) ⇐
As Integer
Declare Function NumberFractals Lib "fractdll.dll" () As Integer

Const ORIGIN = 1, X_AXIS = 2, XY_AXIS = 3

' Windows API functions -----------------
Declare Function GlobalGetAtomName Lib "User" (ByVal nAtom As Integer, ⇐
ByVal lpbuffer As String, ByVal nSize As Integer) As Integer
```

```
Const FALSE = 0, TRUE = 1, NULL = 0&

' Globals ----------------------
Const MB_ICONASTERISK = 64
Const SCALE_PIXELS = 3

Dim mathType As Integer
Dim fractal As Long
Dim numFractals As Integer
```

4. Put the following code in the StopFractal general subroutine. This code calls the fractal DLL function DestroyFractal when you're finished using it.

```
Sub StopFractal ()
   If fractal <> NULL Then
      i = DestroyFractal(fractal)
      fractal = NULL
   End If

   Cls
End Sub
```

5. Put the following line in the FileAbout_Click event subroutine. The Show method will just display the About box that we'll design in Steps 13 and 14.

```
Sub FileAbout_Click ()
   AboutForm.Show
End Sub
```

6. Put the following code in the FileExit_Click event subroutine.

```
Sub FileExit_Click ()
   End
End Sub
```

7. Put the following code in the Form_Load event subroutine. This code puts the name of every fractal that the DLL supports into the Fractal menu and selects the fastest math type that the computer can support.

```
Sub Form_Load ()
   ScaleMode = SCALE_PIXELS
   temp$ = Space$(32)

   numFractals = NumberFractals()
   For i = 0 To numFractals - 1
      atom = FractalName(i)
      If atom = NULL Then Exit For

      j = GlobalGetAtomName(atom, temp$, Len(temp$))
      If i Then Load Fractals(i)
      Fractals(i).Caption = temp$
   Next
```

```
      If WhichCPU() = 386 Or WhichCPU() = 486 Then
         MathFixed_Click
      Else
         MathFloat_Click
      End If

      ' pull down the Fractal menu
      SendKeys "%R"
   End Sub
```

8. Put the following code in the Form_Unload event subroutine. Calling the StopFractal function ensures that the DLL releases its memory.

```
Sub Form_Unload (Cancel As Integer)
   StopFractal
End Sub
```

9. Put the following code in the Fractals_Click event subroutine. This code does all the work of calling the fractal DLL functions to calculate the fractal.

```
Sub Fractals_Click (Index As Integer)
   Dim fLeft As Double, fRight As Double, fTop As Double, fBottom As ⇐
      Double, maxIt As Long, p1x As Double, p1y As Double, p2x As Double, ⇐
      p2y As Double
   Dim fColor As Long

   fractNum = Index

   For i = 0 To numFractals - 1
      Fractals(i).Checked = FALSE
   Next
   Fractals(fractNum).Checked = TRUE

   StopFractal
   temp$ = Space$(240)

   atom = FractalDefaults(fractNum)
   j = GlobalGetAtomName(atom, temp$, Len(temp$))

   file = FreeFile
   Open "VFRACTAL.DAT" For Output As #file
   Print #file, temp$
   Close #file

   file = FreeFile
   Open "VFRACTAL.DAT" For Input As #file
   Input #file, availMathTypes, fLeft, fRight, fTop, fBottom, maxIt, ⇐
      p1x, p1y, p2x, p2y, symmetry
   Close #file

   If (mathType And availMathTypes) = 0 Then
      MathFloat_Click
      MsgBox "The current math type is not supported by this fractal type.
```

```
        Floating point math has been selected", MB_ICONASTERISK, "Note!"
End If

fractalIsIdle = TRUE
n = 0
xMax = CInt(fractalForm.ScaleWidth)
yMax = CInt(fractalForm.ScaleHeight)

Select Case symmetry
   Case ORIGIN, X_AXIS
      xLimit = xMax
      yLimit = yMax \ 2
   Case XY_AXIS
      xLimit = xMax \ 2
      yLimit = yMax \ 2
End Select

fractal = CreateFractal(fractNum, xMax, yMax, mathType, fLeft, fRight,
      fTop, fBottom, maxIt, p1x, p1y, p2x, p2y)
If fractal = NULL Then
   MsgBox "Unable to create fractal", MB_ICONASTERISK, "Note!"
Else
   For y = 0 To yLimit - 1
      For x = 0 To xLimit - 1
         If fractalIsIdle Then
            If ActivateFractal(fractal) = FALSE Then
               MsgBox "Unable to activate fractal", MB_ICONASTERISK,
                  "Note!"
               End
            Else
               fractalIsIdle = FALSE
               n = 0
            End If
         End If

         fColor = FractalPoint(fractal, x, y)
         n = n + fColor

         If fColor = maxIt Then
            fColor = 1
         Else
            fColor = fColor Mod 16
         End If
         fColor = QBColor(fColor)

         PSet (x, y), fColor

         Select Case symmetry
            Case ORIGIN
               PSet (xMax - x - 1, yMax - y - 1), fColor
```

```
                Case X_AXIS
                    PSet (x, yMax - y - 1), fColor
                Case XY_AXIS
                    PSet (xMax - x - 1, yMax - y - 1), fColor
                    PSet (xMax - x - 1, y), fColor
                    PSet (x, yMax - y - 1), fColor
            End Select

            If n >= 1000 Then
                i = IdleFractal(fractal)
                i = DoEvents()
                fractalIsIdle = TRUE
            End If
        Next
      Next
    End If
End Sub
```

10. Put the following code in the MathFixed_Click event subroutine. This code sets the mathType variable to the fixed floating point math type and checks the menu item.

```
Sub MathFixed_Click ()
    mathType = 2
    MathFixed.Checked = TRUE
    MathQuick.Checked = FALSE
    MathFloat.Checked = FALSE
End Sub
```

11. Put the following code in the MathFloat_Click event subroutine. This code sets the mathType variable to the normal floating point math type and checks the menu item.

```
Sub MathFloat_Click ()
    mathType = 1
    MathFixed.Checked = FALSE
    MathQuick.Checked = FALSE
    MathFloat.Checked = TRUE
End Sub
```

12. Put the following code in the MathQuick_Click event subroutine. This code sets the mathType variable to the quick floating point math type and checks the menu item.

```
Sub MathQuick_Click ()
    mathType = 4
    MathFixed.Checked = FALSE
    MathQuick.Checked = TRUE
    MathFloat.Checked = FALSE
End Sub
```

13. Create a new form with the properties listed in Table 9-4 and save it as VFABOUT.FRM. Figure 9-2 shows how it looks.

| Control | Property | Setting |
| --- | --- | --- |
| Form | BorderStyle | 3 - Fixed Double |
| | Caption | About... |
| | FormName | AboutForm |
| | Icon | WINFRACT.ICO |
| | MaxButton | False |
| | MinButton | False |
| Picture box | AutoSize | True |
| | CtlName | Picture1 |
| | Picture | WINFRACT.ICO |
| Label | Alignment | 2 - Center |
| | Caption | Using the C++ Fractal DLL |
| | FontBold | True |
| | FontSize | 9 |
| Label | Alignment | 2 - Center |
| | Caption | The Waite Group's Visual Basic How-To |
| | FontBold | True |
| | FontItalic | True |
| | FontName | Helv |
| | FontSize | 9 |
| Label | Alignment | 2 - Center |
| | Caption | Robert Arnson |
| | FontBold | True |
| | FontName | Helv |
| | FontSize | 9 |
| Label | Alignment | 2 - Center |
| | Caption | Fractal DLL by Mark Peterson |
| | FontBold | True |
| | FontSize | 9 |
| Command button | Caption | OK |
| | CtlName | Command1 |
| | Default | True |

**Table 9-4** AboutForm's controls and properties

14. Add the following code to the Command1_Click event subroutine. This code just unloads the About box and returns to the main fractal application.

```
Sub Command1_Click ()
    Unload AboutForm
End Sub
```

### How It Works

In the Declarations section of the VFRACTAL form, there are several global variables. The mathType variable stores the currently selected math type as a global variable so the MathFixed, MathFloat, and MathQuick Click event subroutines can set it.

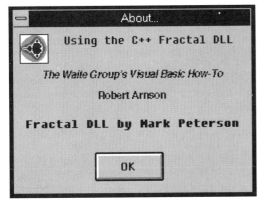

**Figure 9-2** The AboutForm displaying with the fractal icon

The fractal variable stores the FRACTAL handle type that the DLL function CreateFractal returns. Then that variable can be passed to the fractal DLL whenever we want to refer to the fractal.

The numFractals variable stores the number of fractals that the DLL supports, as the NumberFractals function returned.

The StopFractal function calls the DLL function DestroyFractal function to release the memory the DLL was using to create the fractal. The Form_Unload calls this function when the application ends.

The first thing the Form_Load event subroutine does is to set the ScaleMode property to pixels. We have to do that because the fractal DLL doesn't support Visual Basic's twips. Then, the For loop goes through each fractal the DLL supports and gets its name. The FractalName function returns a Windows atom. What the heck's an atom? An atom is a string that Windows stores globally, so any application can read it. The DLL makes an atom so that the application can read it. There's a little bit of extra work, but it also means that the DLL doesn't have to understand how Visual Basic stores strings. The Windows API function GlobalGetAtomName reads the string atom.

Since the index of the Fractal menu item is zero, it's an element of a menu control array. The Load statement makes an element in the control array for each fractal type, then Caption property is set to the fractal's name.

Calling the WhichCPU function tells us whether or not the machine will support the 386 math types. If it won't, normal floating point is selected.

Finally, using the SendKeys statement, the Fractal menu is pulled down.

The Fractals_Click event subroutine is the biggie: It's the subroutine that's executed when the user selects one of the fractal types. Since the Fractals menu is in a menu control array, Fractals_Click has the Index parameter indicating which fractal was picked.

The first For loop makes sure that the fractal that was picked is the only one with a check mark next to it.

FractalDefaults returns the fractal parameters. Again, GlobalGetAtomName is used to read the string atom. The atom that FractalDefaults returns has all the fractal default parameters in a single string, separated by commas. We cheat a little here by writing that string to a text file and reading it back in. Visual Basic's Input statement will automatically separate each part of the string and read it into a numeric variable.

Since some fractals don't support all the math types, we check to make sure. If it isn't supported by the math type selected from the Math menu, normal floating point math is selected, which all fractals support.

The symmetry parameter of the fractal is checked next to see if we really need to calculate all of the fractal. Here's what the following symmetries mean:

**ORIGIN**      The fractal is symmetrical about the origin. With this type of symmetry, the bottom half of the image is upside-down and leftside-right to the top half of the image.

**X_AXIS**      The fractal is symmetrical about the x axis. This means the bottom half is a mirror image of the top half.

**Y_AXIS**      The fractal is symmetrical about the y axis. This means the right half is a mirror image of the left half.

**XY_AXIS**      The fractal is symmetrical about both the x and y axes. This means the upper left quarter of the image can be used to generate the remaining three quarters.

Finally, the real work begins by calling the CreateFractal function with the default parameters. There's a For loop for each point along the x and y axes. If we haven't already called ActivateFractal, we do so (and display an error if it couldn't be activated).

The FractalPoint function is then called to get the color of the given x/y point in the fractal. The variable n is used to keep track of how long the fractal DLL has been calculating, so we can release control to Windows after a while.

The maxIt parameter is returned if the point exceeded the maximum of the formula. Here, we then set the color to one, which is blue. Otherwise, since Visual Basic only supports 16-color images, we use the Mod operator so a color above 15 won't cause an "Illegal function call" error. Then we display the point in the right color using the QBColor function.

Checking the symmetry parameter to see if we can update other parts of the fractal without having to recalculate those points. For example, if the symmetry is XY_AXIS, we plot four points for every one point calculated. Using symmetry is a great time saver!

Finally, we check the n variable to see if we should release control to Windows. Since we're in two tight For...Next loops, Windows would normally not get control until the subroutine ends. This would make calculating the fractal faster, but would mean that all other applications would be stopped in their tracks. We call IdleFractal before releasing control to Windows with Visual Basic's DoEvents so the memory is available. The fractalIsIdle variable keeps track of whether the fractal is idle. If it is, we call ActivateFractal to re-activate it.

## Comment

It's important to call DoEvents for more than just letting other applications get a chance to run. We set the form's AutoRedraw property to True so that we don't have to totally repaint the form, but when AutoRedraw is True, the form isn't displayed until Windows gets control. If we didn't call DoEvents, the form wouldn't be displayed until the entire fractal was created.

# Appendix A
# The Annotated WINAPI.TXT File

Many of the How-To solutions in this book rely on Windows API functions to extend the capabilities of Visual Basic. As you have seen, you must declare every Windows API function before you can use it, and you've probably noticed that the Declaration statements are long and cryptic. How do you know the parameters of each function and in which library the function can be found?

### The WINAPI.TXT File Explained

Fortunately, Microsoft has provided a file called WINAPI.TXT, although it is not supplied with Visual Basic. However, we have included this file on the disk that accompanies this book.

WINAPI.TXT contains Declare statements for almost all the API functions that Windows provides (close to 600 of them!). There are a few API functions that Visual Basic can't use because they require support for pointers to functions, something that Visual Basic doesn't provide.

The best way to use the WINAPI.TXT file is to copy the statements that relate to the API functions you intend to use to the global module of your Visual Basic program, or the Declarations section of your form. Note, however, that no single form or module in a Visual Basic application can hold over 64K of code. Since the WINAPI.TXT file is over 120K, you can't load the whole thing into a single module.

This appendix is an annotated version of the WINAPI.TXT file; throughout we have provided helpful information, tips, and references to solutions in this book that demonstrate the use of APIs.

### Global Const Statements

In addition to API function Declare statements, there are hundreds of Global Const statements to declare some mnemonic constants for the Windows messages in the text file. For example, the LB_RESETCONTENT message is declared as follows:

```
Global Const LB_RESETCONTENT = (WM_USER+5)
```

WM_USER is another constant declared as follows:

```
Global Const WM_USER = &H400
```

So the value of the constant LB_RESETCONTENT is actually &H400 + 5, which equals &H405 in hexadecimal, or 1029 in decimal. So you could actually use 1029 every time instead of LB_RESETCONTENT, but the constant LB_RESETCONTENT gives you at least a hint of what it will actually do. 1029 doesn't tell you much of anything at all!

If you're using control messages such as LB_RESETCONTENT with the SendMessageToControl function in How-To 1.6 Quickly clear a list box' you can simply use these Global Const statements in your Global module. A couple of hints: Many messages depend on the value of another; LB_RESETCONTENT, for example, depends on the value of the WM_USER constant. Be sure to include the Global Const statements for both WM_USER and LB_RESETCONTENT. The other hint: If you don't use a Global module in your Visual Basic application, you must remove the "Global" from the Const statements. Global Const statements are allowed only in the Global module.

Some other useful parts of WINAPI.TXT:

- Look for Global Const statements with WF_... constants. These constants are used in How-To 6.15 Find everything about the system configuration.

- Look for the section entitled "GDI Section." There are several Declare and Global Const statements used in How-Tos throughout this book.

- The section entitled "Virtual Keys, Standard Set" contains Global Const statements for all the key codes used in the Visual Basic KeyDown and KeyUp event subroutines.

- The section entitled "MessageBox() Flags" contains several Global Const statements for the MsgBox statement and function. For example, instead of trying to remember which number to use to display an icon in a message box, just use one of the MB_ICON... constants.

- There are several MF_ constants used in How-Tos 3.5 Draw a bitmapped picture in a menu, and How-To 3.6 Place font typefaces in a menu.

- There are many LB_ constants used to send messages to list boxes.

- There are several HELP_ constants you can use if your Visual Basic application supports online Help.

It is almost mandatory that you use a Windows reference guide; an excellent one is *The Waite Group's Windows API Bible*, James Conger, Waite Group Press, 1992.

```
' ------------------------------------
'
'    WINAPI.TXT -- Windows 3.0 API Declarations for Visual Basic
'
'        Copyright (C) 1991 Microsoft Corporation
'
' You have a royalty-free right to use, modify, reproduce and distribute
' this file (and/or any modified version) in any way you find useful,
' provided that you agree that Microsoft has no warranty, obligation or
' liability for its contents.  Refer to the Microsoft Windows Programmer's
' Reference for further information.
'
' ------------------------------------


'   General Purpose Defines
```

NULL is used throughout the API to indicate zero or an empty string.

```
Global Const NULL = 0
```

RECT is a structure holding the four corners of a rectangular screen region. Note that the coordinates are in pixels, not twips.

```
Type RECT
     left As Integer
     top As Integer
     right As Integer
     bottom As Integer
End Type
```

POINTAPI is a structure that holds the coordinates of a pixel. Note that, like the RECT structure, the coordinates are in pixels, not twips. The name of this structure in C is POINT, but that conflicts with the Visual Basic Point method.

```
Type POINTAPI
     x As Integer
     y As Integer
End Type


' ------------------------------------
'   Kernel Section
' ------------------------------------


' ParameterBlock description structure for use with LoadModule
Type PARAMETERBLOCK
     wEnvSeg As Integer
     lpCmdLine As Long
     lpCmdShow As Long
     dwReserved As Long
End Type

' Loader Routines
```

GetVersion is used in How-To 6.10 Determine which version of Windows my application is running on. GetNumTaska is used in How-To 6.1 Run a DOS program and find out when it's done. The other functions in this section are used to load other applications or DLLs and find out information about them.

```
Declare Function GetVersion Lib "Kernel" () As Integer
Declare Function GetNumTasks Lib "Kernel" () As Integer
Declare Function GetModuleHandle Lib "Kernel" (ByVal lpModuleName As ⇐
String) As Integer
Declare Function GetModuleUsage Lib "Kernel" (ByVal hModule As Integer) ⇐
As Integer
Declare Function GetModuleFileName Lib "Kernel" (ByVal hModule As Integer, ⇐
ByVal lpFilename As String, ByVal nSize As Integer) As Integer
Declare Function GetInstanceData Lib "Kernel" (ByVal hInstance As Integer, ⇐
ByVal pData As Integer, ByVal nCount As Integer) As Integer
Declare Function LoadLibrary Lib "Kernel" (ByVal lpLibFileName As String) ⇐
As Integer
Declare Function LoadModule Lib "Kernel" (ByVal lpModuleName As String, ⇐
lpParameterBlock As PARAMETERBLOCK) As Integer
Declare Sub FreeModule Lib "Kernel" (ByVal hModule As Integer)
Declare Sub FreeLibrary Lib "Kernel" (ByVal hLibModule As Integer)
Declare Function SetHandleCount Lib "Kernel" (ByVal wNumber As Integer) ⇐
As Integer
```

GetFreeSpace is used in How-To 6.13 Determine how much memory is available.

```
Declare Function GetFreeSpace Lib "Kernel" (ByVal wFlags As Integer) As Long
```

WinExec is used to create the VBHTShell function in How-To 6.7 Use the Shell function without causing run-time errors. The DebugBreak and OutputDebugString functions are used with the debugging version of Windows that comes with the SDK to aid in debugging of C and Pascal Windows applications. SwitchStackTo, SwitchStackBack, and GetCurrentPDB are used in DLLs.

```
Declare Function WinExec Lib "Kernel" (ByVal lpCmdLine As String, ByVal ⇐
nCmdShow As Integer) As Integer
Declare Sub DebugBreak Lib "Kernel" ()
Declare Sub OutputDebugString Lib "Kernel" (ByVal lpOutputString As String)
Declare Sub SwitchStackBack Lib "Kernel" ()
Declare Sub SwitchStackTo Lib "Kernel" (ByVal wStackSegment As Integer, ⇐
ByVal wStackPointer As Integer, ByVal wStackTop As Integer)
Declare Function GetCurrentPDB Lib "Kernel" () As Integer
```

The Visual Basic Open statement can duplicate all the functionality of the OpenFile structures, constants, and functions. But if you use the Open statement and an error occurs, Visual Basic will cause a run-time error that you would have to have a trap to catch; OpenFile simply returns an error code that you can process without needing an error handler.

```
' OpenFile() Structure
Type OFSTRUCT
    cBytes As String * 1
    fFixedDisk As String * 1
    nErrCode As Integer
    reserved As String * 4
    szPathName As String * 128
End Type

' OpenFile() Flags
Global Const OF_READ = &H0
Global Const OF_WRITE = &H1
Global Const OF_READWRITE = &H2
Global Const OF_SHARE_COMPAT = &H0
Global Const OF_SHARE_EXCLUSIVE = &H10
Global Const OF_SHARE_DENY_WRITE = &H20
Global Const OF_SHARE_DENY_READ = &H30
Global Const OF_SHARE_DENY_NONE = &H40
Global Const OF_PARSE = &H100
Global Const OF_DELETE = &H200
Global Const OF_VERIFY = &H400
Global Const OF_CANCEL = &H800
Global Const OF_CREATE = &H1000
Global Const OF_PROMPT = &H2000
Global Const OF_EXIST = &H4000
Global Const OF_REOPEN = &H8000

Declare Function OpenFile Lib "Kernel" (ByVal lpFileName As String, ⇐
lpReOpenBuff As OFSTRUCT, ByVal wStyle As Integer) As Integer
```

These functions would be useful if you needed to create a temporary file, for sorting, for example.

```
' GetTempFileName() Flags
'
Global Const TF_FORCEDRIVE = &H80

Declare Function GetTempDrive Lib "Kernel" (ByVal cDriveLetter as Integer) ⇐
As Integer
Declare Function GetTempFileName Lib "Kernel" (ByVal cDriveLetter as ⇐
Integer, ByVal lpPrefixString As String, ByVal wUnique As Integer, ByVal ⇐
lpTempFileName As String) As Integer
```

GetDriveType returns one of the three DRIVE_ constants for the drive you specify. It would be useful if you wanted your application to know that files are being stored on a network drive (DRIVE_REMOTE), for example.

```
Declare Function GetDriveType Lib "Kernel" (ByVal nDrive As Integer) ⇐
As Integer

' GetDriveType return values
Global Const DRIVE_REMOVABLE = 2
Global Const DRIVE_FIXED = 3
Global Const DRIVE_REMOTE = 4
```

It's usually far easier to use Visual Basic's Dim and ReDim statements to allocate memory, but the Global… and Local… memory API functions are available if you need to allocate a special type of memory for a custom DLL, for example.

```
' Global Memory Flags
Global Const GMEM_FIXED = &H0
Global Const GMEM_MOVEABLE = &H2
Global Const GMEM_NOCOMPACT = &H10
Global Const GMEM_NODISCARD = &H20
Global Const GMEM_ZEROINIT = &H40
Global Const GMEM_MODIFY = &H80
Global Const GMEM_DISCARDABLE = &H100
Global Const GMEM_NOT_BANKED = &H1000
Global Const GMEM_SHARE = &H2000
Global Const GMEM_DDESHARE = &H2000
Global Const GMEM_NOTIFY = &H4000
Global Const GMEM_LOWER = GMEM_NOT_BANKED

Global Const GHND = (GMEM_MOVEABLE Or GMEM_ZEROINIT)
Global Const GPTR = (GMEM_FIXED Or GMEM_ZEROINIT)

Declare Function GlobalAlloc Lib "Kernel" (ByVal wFlags As Integer, ByVal ⇐
dwBytes As Long) As Integer
Declare Function GlobalCompact Lib "Kernel" (ByVal dwMinFree As Long) As ⇐
Long
Declare Function GlobalFree Lib "Kernel" (ByVal hMem As Integer) As Integer
Declare Function GlobalHandle Lib "Kernel" (ByVal wMem As Integer) As Long
Declare Function GlobalLock Lib "Kernel" (ByVal hMem As Integer) As Long
Declare Function GlobalReAlloc Lib "Kernel" (ByVal hMem As Integer, ByVal ⇐
dwBytes As Long, ByVal wFlags As Integer) As Integer

'NOTE: instead of declaring the function GlobalDiscard and calling
'      GlobalDiscard(hMem), call GlobalReAlloc(hMem, 0, GMEM_MOVEABLE)

Declare Function GlobalSize Lib "Kernel" (ByVal hMem As Integer) As Long
Declare Function GlobalUnlock Lib "Kernel" (ByVal hMem As Integer) As Integer
Declare Function UnlockResource Lib "Kernel" Alias "GlobalUnlock" (ByVal ⇐
hMem As Integer) As Integer
Declare Function GlobalFlags Lib "Kernel" (ByVal hMem As Integer) As Integer
Declare Function GlobalWire Lib "Kernel" (ByVal hMem As Integer) As Long
Declare Function GlobalUnWire Lib "Kernel" (ByVal hMem As Integer) As Integer
Declare Function GlobalUnlock Lib "Kernel" (ByVal hMem As Integer) As Integer
Declare Function GlobalLRUNewest Lib "Kernel" (ByVal hMem As Integer) As ⇐
Integer
Declare Function GlobalLRUOldest Lib "Kernel" (ByVal hMem As Integer) As ⇐
Integer
Declare Function GlobalPageLock Lib "Kernel" (ByVal wSelector As Integer) ⇐
As Integer
Declare Function GlobalPageUnlock Lib "Kernel" (ByVal wSelector As Integer) ⇐
As Integer
Declare Sub GlobalFix Lib "Kernel" (ByVal hMem As Integer)
```

```
Declare Function GlobalUnfix Lib "Kernel" (ByVal hMem As Integer) As ⇐
Integer

' Flags returned by GlobalFlags (in addition to GMEM_DISCARDABLE)
Global Const GMEM_DISCARDED = &H4000
Global Const GMEM_LOCKCOUNT = &HFF

Declare Function LockSegment Lib "Kernel" (ByVal wSegment As Integer) As ⇐
Integer
Declare Function UnlockSegment Lib "Kernel" (ByVal wSegment As Integer) ⇐
As Integer

' Local Memory Flags
Global Const LMEM_FIXED = &H0
Global Const LMEM_MOVEABLE = &H2
Global Const LMEM_NOCOMPACT = &H10
Global Const LMEM_NODISCARD = &H20
Global Const LMEM_ZEROINIT = &H40
Global Const LMEM_MODIFY = &H80
Global Const LMEM_DISCARDABLE = &HF00

Global Const LHND = (LMEM_MOVEABLE+LMEM_ZEROINIT)
Global Const LPTR = (LMEM_FIXED+LMEM_ZEROINIT)

Global Const NONZEROLHND = (LMEM_MOVEABLE)
Global Const NONZEROLPTR = (LMEM_FIXED)

Global Const LNOTIFY_OUTOFMEM = 0
Global Const LNOTIFY_MOVE = 1
Global Const LNOTIFY_DISCARD = 2

Declare Function LocalAlloc Lib "Kernel" (ByVal wFlags As Integer, ByVal ⇐
wBytes As Integer) As Integer
Declare Function LocalCompact Lib "Kernel" (ByVal wMinFree As Integer) ⇐
As Integer
Declare Function LocalFree Lib "Kernel" (ByVal hMem As Integer) As Integer
Declare Function LocalHandle Lib "Kernel" (ByVal wMem As Integer) As ⇐
Integer
Declare Function LocalInit Lib "Kernel" (ByVal wSegment As Integer, ⇐
ByVal pStart As Integer, ByVal pEnd As Integer) As Integer
Declare Function LocalLock Lib "Kernel" (ByVal hMem As Integer) As Integer
'(returns a near pointer)
Declare Function LocalReAlloc Lib "Kernel" (ByVal hMem As Integer, ⇐
ByVal wBytes As Integer, ByVal wFlags As Integer) As Integer

'NOTE: instead of declaring the function LocalDiscard and calling
'     LocalDiscard(hMem), call LocalReAlloc(hMem, 0, LMEM_MOVEABLE)

Declare Function LocalSize Lib "Kernel" (ByVal hMem As Integer) As Integer
Declare Function LocalUnlock Lib "Kernel" (ByVal hMem As Integer) As Integer
Declare Function LocalFlags Lib "Kernel" (ByVal hMem As Integer) As Integer
Declare Function LocalShrink Lib "Kernel" (ByVal hSeg As Integer, ByVal ⇐
wSize As Integer) As Integer
```

```
' Flags returned by LocalFlags (in addition to LMEM_DISCARDABLE)
Global Const LMEM_DISCARDED = &H4000
Global Const LMEM_LOCKCOUNT = &HFF
```

These are low-level functions that Microsoft recommends against using.

```
Declare Function SetSwapAreaSize Lib "Kernel" (ByVal rsSize As Integer) As ⇐
Long
Declare Function ValidateFreeSpaces Lib "Kernel" () As Long
Declare Sub LimitEmsPages Lib "Kernel" (ByVal dwKbytes As Long)
Declare Function SetErrorMode Lib "Kernel" (ByVal wMode As Integer) As ⇐
Integer
Declare Sub ValidateCodeSegments Lib "Kernel" ()
Declare Function AllocDStoCSAlias Lib "Kernel" (ByVal wSelector As Integer) ⇐
As Integer
Declare Function AllocSelector Lib "Kernel" (ByVal wSelector As Integer) ⇐
As Integer
Declare Function ChangeSelector Lib "Kernel" (ByVal wDestSelector ⇐
As Integer, ByVal wSourceSelector As Integer) As Integer
Declare Function FreeSelector Lib "Kernel" (ByVal wSelector As Integer) As ⇐
Integer
```

GetDOSEnvironment returns the strings in an application's environment, just like Visual Basic's Environ$ function.

```
Declare Function GetDOSEnvironment Lib "Kernel" () As Long
```

These functions and constants are used when accessing the resources (such as bitmaps and icons) from an executable application or DLL.

```
Declare Function FindResource Lib "Kernel" (ByVal hInstance As Integer, ⇐
ByVal lpName As String, ByVal lpType As Any) As Integer
Declare Function LoadResource Lib "Kernel" (ByVal hInstance As Integer, ⇐
ByVal hResInfo As Integer) As Integer
Declare Function FreeResource Lib "Kernel" (ByVal hResData As Integer) ⇐
As Integer
Declare Function LockResource Lib "Kernel" (ByVal hResData As Integer) ⇐
As Long
Declare Function AllocResource Lib "Kernel" (ByVal hInstance As Integer, ⇐
ByVal hResInfo As Integer, ByVal dwSize As Long) As Integer
Declare Function SizeofResource Lib "Kernel" (ByVal hInstance As Integer, ⇐
ByVal hResInfo As Integer) As Integer
Declare Function AccessResource Lib "Kernel" (ByVal hInstance As Integer, ⇐
ByVal hResInfo As Integer) As Integer

' Predefined Resource Types
Global Const RT_CURSOR = 1&
Global Const RT_BITMAP = 2&
Global Const RT_ICON = 3&
Global Const RT_MENU = 4&
Global Const RT_DIALOG = 5&
Global Const RT_STRING = 6&
Global Const RT_FONTDIR = 7&
Global Const RT_FONT = 8&
```

```
Global Const RT_ACCELERATOR = 9&
Global Const RT_RCDATA = 10&


'  OEM Resource Ordinal Numbers
Global Const OBM_CLOSE = 32754
Global Const OBM_UPARROW = 32753
Global Const OBM_DNARROW = 32752
Global Const OBM_RGARROW = 32751
Global Const OBM_LFARROW = 32750
Global Const OBM_REDUCE = 32749
Global Const OBM_ZOOM = 32748
Global Const OBM_RESTORE = 32747
Global Const OBM_REDUCED = 32746
Global Const OBM_ZOOMD = 32745
Global Const OBM_RESTORED = 32744
Global Const OBM_UPARROWD = 32743
Global Const OBM_DNARROWD = 32742
Global Const OBM_RGARROWD = 32741
Global Const OBM_LFARROWD = 32740
Global Const OBM_MNARROW = 32739
Global Const OBM_COMBO = 32738


Global Const OBM_OLD_CLOSE = 32767
Global Const OBM_SIZE = 32766
Global Const OBM_OLD_UPARROW = 32765
Global Const OBM_OLD_DNARROW = 32764
Global Const OBM_OLD_RGARROW = 32763
Global Const OBM_OLD_LFARROW = 32762
Global Const OBM_BTSIZE = 32761
Global Const OBM_CHECK = 32760
Global Const OBM_CHECKBOXES = 32759
Global Const OBM_BTNCORNERS = 32758
Global Const OBM_OLD_REDUCE = 32757
Global Const OBM_OLD_ZOOM = 32756
Global Const OBM_OLD_RESTORE = 32755


Global Const OCR_NORMAL = 32512
Global Const OCR_IBEAM = 32513
Global Const OCR_WAIT = 32514
Global Const OCR_CROSS = 32515
Global Const OCR_UP = 32516
Global Const OCR_SIZE = 32640
Global Const OCR_ICON = 32641
Global Const OCR_SIZENWSE = 32642
Global Const OCR_SIZENESW = 32643
Global Const OCR_SIZEWE = 32644
Global Const OCR_SIZENS = 32645
Global Const OCR_SIZEALL = 32646
Global Const OCR_ICOCUR = 32647


Global Const OIC_SAMPLE = 32512
Global Const OIC_HAND = 32513
Global Const OIC_QUES = 32514
```

```
Global Const OIC_BANG = 32515
Global Const OIC_NOTE = 32516
```

Yield is similar to Visual Basic's DoEvent function, and gives Windows a chance to let other applications do some processing. Microsoft recommends against using Yield.

```
Declare Sub Yield Lib "Kernel" ()
Declare Function GetCurrentTask Lib "Kernel" () As Integer
```

Windows supports global atoms which are strings of information that applications can share with each other. The fractal DLL presented in Chapter 9 uses global atoms to inform applications what kinds of fractals it can do.

```
Declare Function InitAtomTable Lib "Kernel" (ByVal nSize As Integer) As ⇐
Integer
Declare Function AddAtom Lib "Kernel" (ByVal lpString As String) As Integer
Declare Function DeleteAtom Lib "Kernel" (ByVal nAtom As Integer) As Integer
Declare Function FindAtom Lib "Kernel" (ByVal lpString As String) As Integer
Declare Function GetAtomName Lib "Kernel" (ByVal nAtom As Integer, ByVal
lpBuffer As String, ByVal nSize As Integer) As Integer
Declare Function GlobalAddAtom Lib "Kernel" (ByVal lpString As String) As ⇐
Integer
Declare Function GlobalDeleteAtom Lib "Kernel" (ByVal nAtom As Integer) As ⇐
Integer
Declare Function GlobalFindAtom Lib "Kernel" (ByVal lpString As String) As ⇐
Integer
Declare Function GlobalGetAtomName Lib "Kernel" (ByVal nAtom As Integer,
ByVal lpbuffer As String, ByVal nSize As Integer) As Integer
Declare Function GetAtomHandle Lib "Kernel" (ByVal wAtom As Integer) As ⇐
Integer
```

The profile functions are used to read and write information from .INI files. See How-To 4.3 Save program settings to a file and How-To 4.4 Remember the sizes and locations of my forms, for information about using these functions.

```
' User Profile Routines
Declare Function GetProfileInt Lib "Kernel" (ByVal lpAppName As String, ⇐
ByVal lpKeyName As String, ByVal nDefault As Integer) As Integer
Declare Function GetProfileString Lib "Kernel" (ByVal lpAppName As String, ⇐
ByVal lpKeyName As String, ByVal lpDefault As String, ByVal lpReturnedString
As String, ByVal nSize As Integer) As Integer
Declare Function WriteProfileString Lib "Kernel" (ByVal lpApplicationName ⇐
As String, ByVal lpKeyName As String, ByVal lpString As String) As Integer
Declare Function GetPrivateProfileInt Lib "Kernel" (ByVal ⇐
lpApplicationName As String, ByVal lpKeyName As String, ByVal nDefault ⇐
As Integer, ByVal lpFileName As String) As Integer
Declare Function GetPrivateProfileString Lib "Kernel" (ByVal ⇐
lpApplicationName As String, ByVal lpKeyName As String, ByVal lpDefault ⇐ As
String, ByVal lpReturnedString As String, ByVal nSize As Integer, ByVal ⇐
lpFileName As String) As Integer
```

```
Declare Function WritePrivateProfileString Lib "Kernel" (ByVal ⇐
lpApplicationName As String, ByVal lpKeyName As String, ByVal lpString As ⇐
String, ByVal lplFileName As String) As Integer
```

The Get…Directory functions return the directory in which Windows was installed, and where Windows' system files are, respectively. See How-To 6.12 Determine the directory where Windows is installed

```
Declare Function GetWindowsDirectory Lib "Kernel" (ByVal lpBuffer As ⇐
String, ByVal nSize As Integer) As Integer
Declare Function GetSystemDirectory Lib "Kernel" (ByVal lpBuffer As ⇐
String, ByVal nSize As Integer) As Integer
```

Catch and Throw are low-level and should be avoided in Visual Basic application.

```
'NOTE: Catch/Throw expect a long pointer to an 18-byte buffer (lpCatchBuf)
' eg:
'     Dim Buffer(1 To 9) As Integer
'     result% = Catch (Buffer(1))

Declare Function Catch Lib "Kernel" (lpCatchBuf As Any) As Integer
Declare Sub Throw Lib "Kernel" (lpCatchBuf As Any, ByVal nThrowBack As ⇐
Integer)
```

FatalExit and SwapRecording are used while debugging with the debugging version of Windows from the SDK.

```
Declare Sub FatalExit Lib "Kernel" (ByVal Code As Integer)
Declare Sub SwapRecording Lib "Kernel" (ByVal wFlag As Integer)
```

These functions translate between the ANSI character set that Windows usually uses and the OEM character set that the PC uses when in DOS. DOS uses the OEM character set to store filenames, for example, so these functions ensure that foreign characters are translated to their OEM equivalents (if they exist).

```
' Character Translation Routines
Declare Function AnsiToOem Lib "Keyboard" (ByVal lpAnsiStr As String, ByVal ⇐
lpOemStr As String) As Integer
Declare Function OemToAnsi Lib "Keyboard" (ByVal lpOemStr As String, ByVal ⇐
lpAnsiStr As String) As Integer
Declare Sub AnsiToOemBuff Lib "Keyboard" (ByVal lpAnsiStr As String, ByVal ⇐
lpOemStr As String, ByVal nLength As Integer)
Declare Sub OemToAnsiBuff Lib "Keyboard" (ByVal lpOemStr As String, ByVal ⇐
lpAnsiStr As String, ByVal nLength as Integer)
```

These functions convert between upper- and lowercase using the ANSI character set, so international characters are properly converted.

```
Declare Function AnsiUpper Lib "User" (ByVal lpString As String) As String
Declare Function AnsiUpperBuff Lib "User" (ByVal lpString As String, ByVal ⇐
```

```
aWORD As Integer) As Integer
Declare Function AnsiLower Lib "User" (ByVal lpString As String) As Long
Declare Function AnsiLowerBuff Lib "User" (ByVal lpString As String, ByVal ⇐
aWORD As Integer) As Integer
Declare Function AnsiNext Lib "User" (ByVal lpString As String) As Long
Declare Function AnsiPrev Lib "User" (ByVal lpString As String, ByVal ⇐
lpString As String) As Long
```

These functions return information about the keyboard installed on the user's machine. See How-To 6.11 Determine how many function keys are on my user's keyboard

```
' Keyboard Information Routines
Declare Function OemKeyScan Lib "Keyboard" (ByVal wOemChar As Integer) ⇐
As Long
Declare Function VkKeyScan Lib "Keyboard" (ByVal cChar As Integer) As ⇐
Integer
Declare Function GetKeyboardType Lib "Keyboard" (ByVal nTypeFlag As ⇐
Integer) As Integer
Declare Function MapVirtualKey Lib "Keyboard" (ByVal wCode As Integer, ⇐
ByVal wMapType As Integer) As Integer
Declare Function GetKBCodePage Lib "Keyboard" ()
Declare Function GetKeyNameText Lib "Keyboard" (ByVal lParam As Long, ⇐
ByVal lpBuffer As String, ByVal nSize As Integer) As Integer
Declare Function ToAscii Lib "Keyboard" (ByVal wVirtKey As Integer, ByVal ⇐
wScanCode As Integer, lpKeyState As Any, lpChar As Any, Byval wFlags As ⇐
Integer) As Integer
```

The IsChar… functions indicate the characteristics of a given character. These functions let the language driver that Windows is using determine the characteristics, so they're essentially language-independent.

```
' Language dependent Routines
Declare Function IsCharAlpha Lib "User" (ByVal cChar As Integer) As Integer
Declare Function IsCharAlphaNumeric Lib "User" (ByVal cChar As Integer) ⇐
As Integer
Declare Function IsCharUpper Lib "User" (ByVal cChar As Integer) As Integer
Declare Function IsCharLower Lib "User" (ByVal cChar As Integer) As Integer
```

GetWinFlags returns information about how Windows is configured and the hardware it's running on. See How-To 6.15 Find everything about the system configuration.

```
Declare Function GetWinFlags Lib "Kernel" () As Long

Global Const WF_PMODE = &H1
Global Const WF_CPU286 = &H2
Global Const WF_CPU386 = &H4
Global Const WF_CPU486 = &H8
Global Const WF_STANDARD = &H10
Global Const WF_WIN286 = &H10
Global Const WF_ENHANCED = &H20
Global Const WF_WIN386 = &H20
```

```
Global Const WF_CPU086 = &H40
Global Const WF_CPU186 = &H80
Global Const WF_LARGEFRAME = &H100
Global Const WF_SMALLFRAME = &H200
Global Const WF_80x87 = &H400
```

These constants are used by DLLs when they exit. Since Visual Basic can't create DLLs, they can't be used.

```
' WEP fSystemExit flag values
Global Const WEP_SYSTEM_EXIT = 1
Global Const WEP_FREE_DLL = 0


'------------------------------------
'   GDI Section
' ------------------------------------
```

These constants are used for setting the DrawMode property setting.

```
' Binary raster ops
Global Const R2_BLACK = 1        '  0
Global Const R2_NOTMERGEPEN = 2       '  DPon
Global Const R2_MASKNOTPEN = 3        '  DPna
Global Const R2_NOTCOPYPEN = 4        '  PN
Global Const R2_MASKPENNOT = 5        '  PDna
Global Const R2_NOT = 6          '  Dn
Global Const R2_XORPEN = 7       '  DPx
Global Const R2_NOTMASKPEN = 8        '  DPan
Global Const R2_MASKPEN = 9      '  DPa
Global Const R2_NOTXORPEN = 10        '  DPxn
Global Const R2_NOP = 11         '  D
Global Const R2_MERGENOTPEN = 12      '  DPno
Global Const R2_COPYPEN = 13 '  P
Global Const R2_MERGEPENNOT = 14      '  PDno
Global Const R2_MERGEPEN = 15         '  DPo
Global Const R2_WHITE = 16       '  1
```

Some of these constants are used in How-To 5.4 Draw a transparent picture or icon on a form.

```
' Ternary raster operations
Global Const SRCCOPY = &HCC0020       ' (DWORD) dest = source
Global Const SRCPAINT = &HEE0086      ' (DWORD) dest = source OR dest
Global Const SRCAND = &H8800C6        ' (DWORD) dest = source AND dest
Global Const SRCINVERT = &H660046     ' (DWORD) dest = source XOR dest
Global Const SRCERASE = &H440328      ' (DWORD) dest = source AND (NOT dest )
Global Const NOTSRCCOPY = &H330008    ' (DWORD) dest = (NOT source)
Global Const NOTSRCERASE = &H1100A6   ' (DWORD) dest = (NOT src) AND (NOT dest)
Global Const MERGECOPY = &HC000CA     ' (DWORD) dest = (source AND pattern)
Global Const MERGEPAINT = &HBB0226    ' (DWORD) dest = (NOT source) OR dest
Global Const PATCOPY = &HF00021       ' (DWORD) dest = pattern
Global Const PATPAINT = &HFB0A09      ' (DWORD) dest = DPSnoo
Global Const PATINVERT = &H5A0049     ' (DWORD) dest = pattern XOR dest
Global Const DSTINVERT = &H550009     ' (DWORD) dest = (NOT dest)
```

```
Global Const BLACKNESS = &H42&       ' (DWORD) dest = BLACK
Global Const WHITENESS = &HFF0062    ' (DWORD) dest = WHITE

'  StretchBlt() Modes
Global Const BLACKONWHITE = 1
Global Const WHITEONBLACK = 2
Global Const COLORONCOLOR = 3

'  PolyFill() Modes
Global Const ALTERNATE = 1
Global Const WINDING = 2
```

See How-To 2.5 Align text automatically, for an example of using the TA_ constants to align text.

```
'  Text Alignment Options
Global Const TA_NOUPDATECP = 0
Global Const TA_UPDATECP = 1

Global Const TA_LEFT = 0
Global Const TA_RIGHT = 2
Global Const TA_CENTER = 6

Global Const TA_TOP = 0
Global Const TA_BOTTOM = 8
Global Const TA_BASELINE = 24

Global Const ETO_GRAYED = 1
Global Const ETO_OPAQUE = 2
Global Const ETO_CLIPPED = 4

Global Const ASPECT_FILTERING = &H1
```

These constants are used when creating Windows metafiles with the CreateMetaFile function. If you're only going to use metafiles (and not create them), you can use Visual Basic's LoadPicture function, which understands icons, bitmaps, and metafiles automatically.

```
'  Metafile Functions
Global Const META_SETBKCOLOR = &H201
Global Const META_SETBKMODE = &H102
Global Const META_SETMAPMODE = &H103
Global Const META_SETROP2 = &H104
Global Const META_SETRELABS = &H105
Global Const META_SETPOLYFILLMODE = &H106
Global Const META_SETSTRETCHBLTMODE = &H107
Global Const META_SETTEXTCHAREXTRA = &H108
Global Const META_SETTEXTCOLOR = &H209
Global Const META_SETTEXTJUSTIFICATION = &H20A
Global Const META_SETWINDOWORG = &H20B
Global Const META_SETWINDOWEXT = &H20C
Global Const META_SETVIEWPORTORG = &H20D
Global Const META_SETVIEWPORTEXT = &H20E
Global Const META_OFFSETWINDOWORG = &H20F
Global Const META_SCALEWINDOWEXT = &H400
Global Const META_OFFSETVIEWPORTORG = &H211
Global Const META_SCALEVIEWPORTEXT = &H412
```

```
Global Const META_LINETO = &H213
Global Const META_MOVETO = &H214
Global Const META_EXCLUDECLIPRECT = &H415
Global Const META_INTERSECTCLIPRECT = &H416
Global Const META_ARC = &H817
Global Const META_ELLIPSE = &H418
Global Const META_FLOODFILL = &H419
Global Const META_PIE = &H81A
Global Const META_RECTANGLE = &H41B
Global Const META_ROUNDRECT = &H61C
Global Const META_PATBLT = &H61D
Global Const META_SAVEDC = &H1E
Global Const META_SETPIXEL = &H41F
Global Const META_OFFSETCLIPRGN = &H220
Global Const META_TEXTOUT = &H521
Global Const META_BITBLT = &H922
Global Const META_STRETCHBLT = &HB23
Global Const META_POLYGON = &H324
Global Const META_POLYLINE = &H325
Global Const META_ESCAPE = &H626
Global Const META_RESTOREDC = &H127
Global Const META_FILLREGION = &H228
Global Const META_FRAMEREGION = &H429
Global Const META_INVERTREGION = &H12A
Global Const META_PAINTREGION = &H12B
Global Const META_SELECTCLIPREGION = &H12C
Global Const META_SELECTOBJECT = &H12D
Global Const META_SETTEXTALIGN = &H12E
Global Const META_DRAWTEXT = &H62F

Global Const META_CHORD = &H830
Global Const META_SETMAPPERFLAGS = &H231
Global Const META_EXTTEXTOUT = &Ha32
Global Const META_SETDIBTODEV = &Hd33
Global Const META_SELECTPALETTE = &H234
Global Const META_REALIZEPALETTE = &H35
Global Const META_ANIMATEPALETTE = &H436
Global Const META_SETPALENTRIES = &H37
Global Const META_POLYPOLYGON = &H538
Global Const META_RESIZEPALETTE = &H139

Global Const META_DIBBITBLT = &H940
Global Const META_DIBSTRETCHBLT = &Hb41
Global Const META_DIBCREATEPATTERNBRUSH = &H142
Global Const META_STRETCHDIB = &Hf43

Global Const META_DELETEOBJECT = &H1f0

Global Const META_CREATEPALETTE = &Hf7
Global Const META_CREATEBRUSH = &HF8
Global Const META_CREATEPATTERNBRUSH = &H1F9
Global Const META_CREATEPENINDIRECT = &H2FA
Global Const META_CREATEFONTINDIRECT = &H2FB
Global Const META_CREATEBRUSHINDIRECT = &H2FC
Global Const META_CREATEBITMAPINDIRECT = &H2FD
```

```
Global Const META_CREATEBITMAP = &H6FE
Global Const META_CREATEREGION = &H6FF
```

These constants are useful if you need to directly communicate with the printer. It's far easier to use Visual Basic's Printer object to manage printing.

```
' GDI Escapes
Global Const NEWFRAME = 1
Global Const ABORTDOC = 2
Global Const NEXTBAND = 3
Global Const SETCOLORTABLE = 4
Global Const GETCOLORTABLE = 5
Global Const FLUSHOUTPUT = 6
Global Const DRAFTMODE = 7
Global Const QUERYESCSUPPORT = 8
Global Const SETABORTPROC = 9
Global Const STARTDOC = 10
Global Const ENDDOCAPI = 11
Global Const GETPHYSPAGESIZE = 12
Global Const GETPRINTINGOFFSET = 13
Global Const GETSCALINGFACTOR = 14
Global Const MFCOMMENT = 15
Global Const GETPENWIDTH = 16
Global Const SETCOPYCOUNT = 17
Global Const SELECTPAPERSOURCE = 18
Global Const DEVICEDATA = 19
Global Const PASSTHROUGH = 19
Global Const GETTECHNOLGY = 20
Global Const GETTECHNOLOGY = 20
Global Const SETENDCAP = 21
Global Const SETLINEJOIN = 22
Global Const SETMITERLIMIT = 23
Global Const BANDINFO = 24
Global Const DRAWPATTERNRECT = 25
Global Const GETVECTORPENSIZE = 26
Global Const GETVECTORBRUSHSIZE = 27
Global Const ENABLEDUPLEX = 28
Global Const GETSETPAPERBINS = 29
Global Const GETSETPRINTORIENT = 30
Global Const ENUMPAPERBINS = 31
Global Const SETDIBSCALING = 32
Global Const EPSPRINTING = 33
Global Const ENUMPAPERMETRICS = 34
Global Const GETSETPAPERMETRICS = 35
Global Const POSTSCRIPT_DATA = 37
Global Const POSTSCRIPT_IGNORE = 38
Global Const GETEXTENDEDTEXTMETRICS = 256
Global Const GETEXTENTTABLE = 257
Global Const GETPAIRKERNTABLE = 258
Global Const GETTRACKKERNTABLE = 259
Global Const EXTTEXTOUT = 512
Global Const ENABLERELATIVEWIDTHS = 768
Global Const ENABLEPAIRKERNING = 769
```

```
Global Const SETKERNTRACK = 770
Global Const SETALLJUSTVALUES = 771
Global Const SETCHARSET = 772

Global Const STRETCHBLT = 2048
Global Const BEGIN_PATH = 4096
Global Const CLIP_TO_PATH = 4097
Global Const END_PATH = 4098
Global Const EXT_DEVICE_CAPS = 4099
Global Const RESTORE_CTM = 4100
Global Const SAVE_CTM = 4101
Global Const SET_ARC_DIRECTION = 4102
Global Const SET_BACKGROUND_COLOR = 4103
Global Const SET_POLY_MODE = 4104
Global Const SET_SCREEN_ANGLE = 4105
Global Const SET_SPREAD = 4106
Global Const TRANSFORM_CTM = 4107
Global Const SET_CLIP_BOX = 4108
Global Const SET_BOUNDS = 4109
Global Const SET_MIRROR_MODE = 4110

'  Spooler Error Codes
Global Const SP_NOTREPORTED = &H4000
Global Const SP_ERROR = (-1)
Global Const SP_APPABORT = (-2)
Global Const SP_USERABORT = (-3)
Global Const SP_OUTOFDISK = (-4)
Global Const SP_OUTOFMEMORY = (-5)

Global Const PR_JOBSTATUS = &H0
```

These structures and constants are used to read .BMP bitmap files and
.WMF metafiles. If all you need to do is display such a file in a picture box,
use Visual Basic's LoadPicture function.

```
'  Bitmap Header Definition
Type BITMAP '14 bytes
    bmType As Integer
    bmWidth As Integer
    bmHeight As Integer
    bmWidthBytes As Integer
    bmPlanes As String * 1
    bmBitsPixel As String * 1
    bmBits As Long
End Type

Type RGBTRIPLE
    rgbtBlue As String * 1
    rgbtGreen As String * 1
    rgbtRed As String * 1
End Type

Type RGBQUAD
    rgbBlue as String * 1
    rgbGreen As String * 1
```

```
    rgbRed As String * 1
    rgbReserved As String * 1
End Type

'  structures for defining DIBs
Type BITMAPCOREHEADER '12 bytes
    bcSize as Long
    bcWidth As Integer
    bcHeight As Integer
    bcPlanes As Integer
    bcBitCount As Integer
End Type

Type BITMAPINFOHEADER '40 bytes
    biSize As Long
    biWidth As Long
    biHeight As Long
    biPlanes As Integer
    biBitCount As Integer
    biCompression As Long
    biSizeImage As Long
    biXPelsPerMeter As Long
    biYPelsPerMeter As Long
    biClrUsed As Long
    biClrImportant As Long
End Type

'  constants for the biCompression field
Global Const BI_RGB = 0&
Global Const BI_RLE8 = 1&
Global Const BI_RLE4 = 2&

Type BITMAPINFO
    bmiHeader as BITMAPINFOHEADER
    bmiColors As String * 128 ' Array length is arbitrary; may be changed
End Type

Type BITMAPCOREINFO
    bmciHeader As BITMAPCOREHEADER
    bmciColors As String * 96 ' Array length is arbitrary; may be changed
End Type

Type BITMAPFILEHEADER
    bfType As Integer
    bfSize As Long
    bfReserved1 As Integer
    bfReserved2 As Integer
    bfOffBits As Long
End Type

'  Clipboard Metafile Picture Structure
Type HANDLETABLE
    objectHandle As String * 512 ' Array length is arbitrary; may be ⇐
    changed
End Type
```

```
Type METARECORD
    rdSize As Long
    rdFunction As Integer
    rdParm As String * 512 ' Array length is arbitrary; may be changed
End Type

Type METAFILEPICT
    mm As Integer
    xExt As Integer
    yExt As Integer
    hMF As Integer
End Type

Type METAHEADER
    mtType As Integer
    mtHeaderSize As Integer
    mtVersion As Integer
    mtSize As Long
    mtNoObjects As Integer
    mtMaxRecord As Long
    mtNoParameters As Integer
End Type
```

These structures and functions are used to determine font characteristics. It's easier to use a Visual Basic function such as TextHeight and TextWidth and properties such as FontName, FontBold, FontItalic, and Font-Underline to determine most font characteristics.

```
Type TEXTMETRIC
    tmHeight As Integer
    tmAscent As Integer
    tmDescent As Integer
    tmInternalLeading As Integer
    tmExternalLeading As Integer
    tmAveCharWidth As Integer
    tmMaxCharWidth As Integer
    tmWeight As Integer
    tmItalic As String * 1
    tmUnderlined As String * 1
    tmStruckOut As String * 1
    tmFirstChar As String * 1
    tmLastChar As String * 1
    tmDefaultChar As String * 1
    tmBreakChar As String * 1
    tmPitchAndFamily As String * 1
    tmCharSet As String * 1
    tmOverhang As Integer
    tmDigitizedAspectX As Integer
    tmDigitizedAspectY As Integer
End Type

' Logical Font
Global Const LF_FACESIZE = 32
```

```
Type LOGFONT
    lfHeight As Integer
    lfWidth As Integer
    lfEscapement As Integer
    lfOrientation As Integer
    lfWeight As Integer
    lfItalic As String * 1
    lfUnderline As String * 1
    lfStrikeOut As String * 1
    lfCharSet As String * 1
    lfOutPrecision As String * 1
    lfClipPrecision As String * 1
    lfQuality As String * 1
    lfPitchAndFamily As String * 1
    lfFaceName As String * LF_FACESIZE
End Type

Global Const OUT_DEFAULT_PRECIS = 0
Global Const OUT_STRING_PRECIS = 1
Global Const OUT_CHARACTER_PRECIS = 2
Global Const OUT_STROKE_PRECIS = 3

Global Const CLIP_DEFAULT_PRECIS = 0
Global Const CLIP_CHARACTER_PRECIS = 1
Global Const CLIP_STROKE_PRECIS = 2

Global Const DEFAULT_QUALITY = 0
Global Const DRAFT_QUALITY = 1
Global Const PROOF_QUALITY = 2

Global Const DEFAULT_PITCH = 0
Global Const FIXED_PITCH = 1
Global Const VARIABLE_PITCH = 2

Global Const ANSI_CHARSET = 0
Global Const SYMBOL_CHARSET = 2
Global Const SHIFTJIS_CHARSET = 128
Global Const OEM_CHARSET = 255

' Font Families
'
Global Const FF_DONTCARE = 0 '  Don't care or don't know.
Global Const FF_ROMAN = 16    '  Variable stroke width, serifed.

' Times Roman, Century Schoolbook, etc.
Global Const FF_SWISS = 32    '  Variable stroke width, sans-serifed.

' Helvetica, Swiss, etc.
Global Const FF_MODERN = 48  '  Constant stroke width, serifed or sans-
serifed.

' Pica, Elite, Courier, etc.
Global Const FF_SCRIPT = 64  '  Cursive, etc.
Global Const FF_DECORATIVE = 80       '  Old English, etc.

' Font Weights
```

```
Global Const FW_DONTCARE = 0
Global Const FW_THIN = 100
Global Const FW_EXTRALIGHT = 200
Global Const FW_LIGHT = 300
Global Const FW_NORMAL = 400
Global Const FW_MEDIUM = 500
Global Const FW_SEMIBOLD = 600
Global Const FW_BOLD = 700
Global Const FW_EXTRABOLD = 800
Global Const FW_HEAVY = 900

Global Const FW_ULTRALIGHT = FW_EXTRALIGHT
Global Const FW_REGULAR = FW_NORMAL
Global Const FW_DEMIBOLD = FW_SEMIBOLD
Global Const FW_ULTRABOLD = FW_EXTRABOLD
Global Const FW_BLACK = FW_HEAVY

'  Background Modes
Global Const TRANSPARENT = 1
Global Const OPAQUE = 2
```

Logical brushes and pens can be specified in Visual Basic drawing methods like Line without using these types.

```
'  GDI Logical Objects:

'  Pel Array
Type PELARRAY
    paXCount As Integer
    paYCount As Integer
    paXExt As Integer
    paYExt As Integer
    paRGBs As Integer
End Type

'  Logical Brush (or Pattern)
Type LOGBRUSH
    lbStyle As Integer
    lbColor As Long
    lbHatch As Integer
End Type

'  Logical Pen
Type LOGPEN
    lopnStyle As Integer
    lopnWidth As POINTAPI
    lopnColor As Long
End Type
```

Windows' palettes are used to support images with more than sixteen colors, something that Visual Basic itself doesn't support.

```
Declare Function CreatePalette Lib "GDI" (lpLogPalette As LOGPALETTE) As ⇐
Integer
```

```
Declare Function SelectPalette Lib "GDI" (ByVal hDC As Integer, ByVal ⇐
hPalette as Integer, ByVal bForceBackground as Integer) As Integer
Declare Function RealizePalette Lib "GDI" (ByVal hDC As Integer) As Integer
Declare Function UpdateColors Lib "GDI" (ByVal hDC As Integer) As Integer
Declare Sub AnimatePalette Lib "GDI" (ByVal hPalette As Integer, ByVal ⇐
wStartIndex As Integer, ByVal wNumEntries As Integer, lpPaletteColors As ⇐
PALETTEENTRY)
Declare Function SetPaletteEntries Lib "GDI" (ByVal hPalette As Integer, ⇐
ByVal wStartIndex As Integer, ByVal wNumEntries As Integer, ⇐
lpPaletteEntries As PALETTEENTRY) As Integer
Declare Function GetPaletteEntries Lib "GDI" (ByVal hPalette As Integer, ⇐
ByVal wStartIndex As Integer, ByVal wNumEntries As Integer, ⇐
lpPaletteEntries As PALETTEENTRY) As Integer
Declare Function GetNearestPaletteIndex Lib "GDI" (ByVal hPalette As ⇐
Integer, ByVal crColor As Long) As Integer
Declare Function ResizePalette Lib "GDI" (ByVal hPalette As Integer, ByVal ⇐
nNumEntries As Integer) As Integer

Declare Function GetSystemPaletteEntries Lib "GDI" (ByVal hDC As Integer, ⇐
ByVal wStartIndex As Integer, ByVal wNumEntries As Integer, ⇐
lpPaletteEntries As PALETTEENTRY) As Integer
Declare Function GetSystemPaletteUse Lib "GDI" (ByVal hDC As Integer) As ⇐
Integer
Declare Function SetSystemPaletteUse Lib "GDI" (ByVal hDC As Integer, ⇐
ByVal wUsage As Integer) As Integer

Type PALETTEENTRY
    peRed As String * 1
    peGreen As String * 1
    peBlue As String * 1
    peFlags As String * 1
End Type

' Logical Palette
Type LOGPALETTE
    palVersion As Integer
    palNumEntries As Integer
    palPalEntry As String * 252 ' Array length is arbitrary; may be changed
End Type

' palette entry flags
Global Const PC_RESERVED = &H1      ' palette index used for animation
Global Const PC_EXPLICIT = &H2      ' palette index is explicit to device
Global Const PC_NOCOLLAPSE = &H4    ' do not match color to system palette

' constants for Get/SetSystemPaletteUse()
Global Const SYSPAL_STATIC = 1
Global Const SYSPAL_NOSTATIC = 2

' Mapping Modes
Global Const MM_TEXT = 1
Global Const MM_LOMETRIC = 2
Global Const MM_HIMETRIC = 3
```

```
Global Const MM_LOENGLISH = 4
Global Const MM_HIENGLISH = 5
Global Const MM_TWIPS = 6
Global Const MM_ISOTROPIC = 7
Global Const MM_ANISOTROPIC = 8

' Coordinate Modes
Global Const ABSOLUTE = 1
Global Const RELATIVE = 2

' Stock Logical Objects
Global Const WHITE_BRUSH = 0
Global Const LTGRAY_BRUSH = 1
Global Const GRAY_BRUSH = 2
Global Const DKGRAY_BRUSH = 3
Global Const BLACK_BRUSH = 4
Global Const NULL_BRUSH = 5
Global Const HOLLOW_BRUSH = NULL_BRUSH
Global Const WHITE_PEN = 6
Global Const BLACK_PEN = 7
Global Const NULL_PEN = 8
Global Const OEM_FIXED_FONT = 10
Global Const ANSI_FIXED_FONT = 11
Global Const ANSI_VAR_FONT = 12
Global Const SYSTEM_FONT = 13
Global Const DEVICE_DEFAULT_FONT = 14
Global Const DEFAULT_PALETTE = 15
Global Const SYSTEM_FIXED_FONT = 16

' Brush Styles
Global Const BS_SOLID = 0
Global Const BS_NULL = 1
Global Const BS_HOLLOW = BS_NULL
Global Const BS_HATCHED = 2
Global Const BS_PATTERN = 3
Global Const BS_INDEXED = 4
Global Const BS_DIBPATTERN = 5
```

These hatch styles can be used with the FillStyle property.

```
' Hatch Styles
Global Const HS_HORIZONTAL = 0    ' ----
Global Const HS_VERTICAL = 1      ' |||||
Global Const HS_FDIAGONAL = 2     ' \\\\\
Global Const HS_BDIAGONAL = 3     ' /////
Global Const HS_CROSS = 4         ' +++++
Global Const HS_DIAGCROSS = 5     ' xxxxx
```

These pen styles can be used with the DrawStyle property.

```
' Pen Styles
Global Const PS_SOLID = 0
Global Const PS_DASH = 1          ' ------
Global Const PS_DOT = 2           ' .......
```

```
Global Const PS_DASHDOT = 3          ' _._._._
Global Const PS_DASHDOTDOT = 4       ' _.._.._
Global Const PS_NULL = 5
Global Const PS_INSIDEFRAME = 6
```

These constants are used in calls to GetDeviceCaps, generally when communicating with a printer driver or other output device. See How-To 7.1 Determine the color capabilities of a screen or printer, for an example. Using Visual Basic's Printer object is much easier and is highly recommended.

```
' Device Parameters for GetDeviceCaps()
Declare Function GetDeviceCaps Lib "GDI" (ByVal hDC As Integer, ByVal ⇐
nIndex As Integer) As Integer

Global Const DRIVERVERSION = 0      ' Device driver version
Global Const TECHNOLOGY = 2         ' Device classification
Global Const HORZSIZE = 4           ' Horizontal size in millimeters
Global Const VERTSIZE = 6           ' Vertical size in millimeters
Global Const HORZRES = 8            ' Horizontal width in pixels
Global Const VERTRES = 10           ' Vertical width in pixels
Global Const BITSPIXEL = 12         ' Number of bits per pixel
Global Const PLANES = 14            ' Number of planes
Global Const NUMBRUSHES = 16        ' Number of brushes the device has
Global Const NUMPENS = 18           ' Number of pens the device has
Global Const NUMMARKERS = 20        ' Number of markers the device has
Global Const NUMFONTS = 22          ' Number of fonts the device has
Global Const NUMCOLORS = 24         ' Number of colors the device supports
Global Const PDEVICESIZE = 26       ' Size required for device descriptor
Global Const CURVECAPS = 28         ' Curve capabilities
Global Const LINECAPS = 30          ' Line capabilities
Global Const POLYGONALCAPS = 32     ' Polygonal capabilities
Global Const TEXTCAPS = 34          ' Text capabilities
Global Const CLIPCAPS = 36          ' Clipping capabilities
Global Const RASTERCAPS = 38        ' Bitblt capabilities
Global Const ASPECTX = 40           ' Length of the X leg
Global Const ASPECTY = 42           ' Length of the Y leg
Global Const ASPECTXY = 44          ' Length of the hypotenuse

Global Const LOGPIXELSX = 88        ' Logical pixels/inch in X
Global Const LOGPIXELSY = 90        ' Logical pixels/inch in Y

Global Const SIZEPALETTE = 104      ' Number of entries in physical palette
Global Const NUMRESERVED = 106      ' Number of reserved entries in palette
Global Const COLORRES = 108         ' Actual color resolution


' Device Capability Masks:

' Device Technologies
Global Const DT_PLOTTER = 0         ' Vector plotter
Global Const DT_RASDISPLAY = 1      ' Raster display
Global Const DT_RASPRINTER = 2      ' Raster printer
```

```
Global Const DT_RASCAMERA = 3        ' Raster camera
Global Const DT_CHARSTREAM = 4       ' Character-stream, PLP
Global Const DT_METAFILE = 5         ' Metafile, VDM
Global Const DT_DISPFILE = 6         ' Display-file

' Curve Capabilities
Global Const CC_NONE = 0             ' Curves not supported
Global Const CC_CIRCLES = 1          ' Can do circles
Global Const CC_PIE = 2              ' Can do pie wedges
Global Const CC_CHORD = 4            ' Can do chord arcs
Global Const CC_ELLIPSES = 8         ' Can do ellipese
Global Const CC_WIDE = 16            ' Can do wide lines
Global Const CC_STYLED = 32          ' Can do styled lines
Global Const CC_WIDESTYLED = 64      ' Can do wide styled lines
Global Const CC_INTERIORS = 128      ' Can do interiors

' Line Capabilities
Global Const LC_NONE = 0             ' Lines not supported
Global Const LC_POLYLINE = 2         ' Can do polylines
Global Const LC_MARKER = 4           ' Can do markers
Global Const LC_POLYMARKER = 8       ' Can do polymarkers
Global Const LC_WIDE = 16            ' Can do wide lines
Global Const LC_STYLED = 32          ' Can do styled lines
Global Const LC_WIDESTYLED = 64      ' Can do wide styled lines
Global Const LC_INTERIORS = 128      ' Can do interiors

' Polygonal Capabilities
Global Const PC_NONE = 0             ' Polygonals not supported
Global Const PC_POLYGON = 1          ' Can do polygons
Global Const PC_RECTANGLE = 2        ' Can do rectangles
Global Const PC_WINDPOLYGON = 4      ' Can do winding polygons
Global Const PC_TRAPEZOID = 4        ' Can do trapezoids
Global Const PC_SCANLINE = 8         ' Can do scanlines
Global Const PC_WIDE = 16            ' Can do wide borders
Global Const PC_STYLED = 32          ' Can do styled borders
Global Const PC_WIDESTYLED = 64      ' Can do wide styled borders
Global Const PC_INTERIORS = 128      ' Can do interiors

' Polygonal Capabilities
Global Const CP_NONE = 0             ' No clipping of output
Global Const CP_RECTANGLE = 1        ' Output clipped to rects

' Text Capabilities
Global Const TC_OP_CHARACTER = &H1   ' Can do OutputPrecision   CHARACTER
Global Const TC_OP_STROKE = &H2      ' Can do OutputPrecision   STROKE
Global Const TC_CP_STROKE = &H4      ' Can do ClipPrecision     STROKE
Global Const TC_CR_90 = &H8          ' Can do CharRotAbility    90
Global Const TC_CR_ANY = &H10        ' Can do CharRotAbility    ANY
Global Const TC_SF_X_YINDEP = &H20   ' Can do ScaleFreedom      X_YINDEPENDENT
Global Const TC_SA_DOUBLE = &H40     ' Can do ScaleAbility      DOUBLE
Global Const TC_SA_INTEGER = &H80    ' Can do ScaleAbility      INTEGER
Global Const TC_SA_CONTIN = &H100    ' Can do ScaleAbility      CONTINUOUS
Global Const TC_EA_DOUBLE = &H200    ' Can do EmboldenAbility   DOUBLE
```

```
Global Const TC_IA_ABLE = &H400      ' Can do ItalisizeAbility   ABLE
Global Const TC_UA_ABLE = &H800      ' Can do UnderlineAbility   ABLE
Global Const TC_SO_ABLE = &H1000     ' Can do StrikeOutAbility   ABLE
Global Const TC_RA_ABLE = &H2000     ' Can do RasterFontAble     ABLE
Global Const TC_VA_ABLE = &H4000     ' Can do VectorFontAble     ABLE
Global Const TC_RESERVED = &H8000

' Raster Capabilities
Global Const RC_BITBLT = 1           ' Can do standard BLT.
Global Const RC_BANDING = 2          ' Device requires banding support
Global Const RC_SCALING = 4          ' Device requires scaling support
Global Const RC_BITMAP64 = 8         ' Device can support >64K bitmap
Global Const RC_GDI20_OUTPUT = &H10  ' has 2.0 output calls
Global Const RC_DI_BITMAP = &H80     ' supports DIB to memory
Global Const RC_PALETTE = &H100      ' supports a palette
Global Const RC_DIBTODEV = &H200     ' supports DIBitsToDevice
Global Const RC_BIGFONT = &H400      ' supports >64K fonts
Global Const RC_STRETCHBLT = &H800   ' supports StretchBlt
Global Const RC_FLOODFILL = &H1000   ' supports FloodFill
Global Const RC_STRETCHDIB = &H2000  ' supports StretchDIBits
```

These constants are used when creating device-independent bitmaps manually. Visual Basic picture boxes provide the same capabilities.

```
' DIB color table identifiers
Global Const DIB_RGB_COLORS = 0      ' color table in RGBTriples
Global Const DIB_PAL_COLORS = 1      ' color table in palette indices

' constants for CreateDIBitmap
Global Const CBM_INIT = &H4& '  initialize bitmap
Declare Function CreateBitmap Lib "GDI" (ByVal nWidth As Integer, ByVal ⇐
nHeight As Integer, ByVal nPlanes As Integer, ByVal nBitCount As Integer, ⇐
ByVal lpBits As Any) As Integer
Declare Function CreateBitmapIndirect Lib "GDI" (lpBitmap As BITMAP) As ⇐
Integer
Declare Function CreateCompatibleBitmap Lib "GDI" (ByVal hDC As Integer, ⇐
ByVal nWidth As Integer, ByVal nHeight As Integer) As Integer
Declare Function CreateDiscardableBitmap Lib "GDI" (ByVal hDC As Integer, ⇐
ByVal nWidth As Integer, ByVal nHeight As Integer) As Integer

Declare Function SetBitmapBits Lib "GDI" (ByVal hBitmap As Integer, ByVal ⇐
dwCount As Long, ByVal lpBits As Any) As Long
Declare Function GetBitmapBits Lib "GDI" (ByVal hBitmap As Integer, ByVal ⇐
dwCount As Long, ByVal lpBits As Any) As Long
Declare Function SetBitmapDimension Lib "GDI" (ByVal hBitmap As Integer, ⇐
ByVal X As Integer, ByVal Y As Integer) As Long
Declare Function GetBitmapDimension Lib "GDI" (ByVal hBitmap As Integer) ⇐
As Long
```

Using these constants and the DrawText function is one way to display text in a window. In Visual Basic, you can also use the Print method or label controls, both of which are easier than using DrawText.

```
' DrawText() Format Flags
Global Const DT_TOP = &H0
Global Const DT_LEFT = &H0
Global Const DT_CENTER = &H1
Global Const DT_RIGHT = &H2
Global Const DT_VCENTER = &H4
Global Const DT_BOTTOM = &H8
Global Const DT_WORDBREAK = &H10
Global Const DT_SINGLELINE = &H20
Global Const DT_EXPANDTABS = &H40
Global Const DT_TABSTOP = &H80
Global Const DT_NOCLIP = &H100
Global Const DT_EXTERNALLEADING = &H200
Global Const DT_CALCRECT = &H400
Global Const DT_NOPREFIX = &H800
Global Const DT_INTERNAL = &H1000

Declare Function DrawText Lib "GDI" (ByVal hDC As Integer, ByVal lpStr As ⇐
String, ByVal nCount As Integer, lpRect As RECT, ByVal wFormat As Integer) ⇐
As Integer
Declare Function DrawIcon Lib "GDI" (ByVal hDC As Integer, ByVal X As ⇐
Integer, ByVal Y As Integer, ByVal hIcon As Integer) As Integer
```

The constants and functions in this rather large section comprise the majority of Windows' Graphics Device Interface (GDI). The GDI is extremely powerful in that it offers many built-in graphic images, such as lines, rectangles, ellipses, arcs, chord, and even pie segments. Better yet, they're device-independent—an ellipse is an ellipse on a lowly CGA and a high-tech XGA. Visual Basic offers most of the GDI in its graphical methods: Cls, Circle, Line, Point, Print, and PSet. If you need a visual effect that Visual Basic doesn't provide, you can use API functions.

Remember that GDI requires a device context which you must provide by calling the GetDC GDI function. Also remember that device contexts are a limited resource; you should release them as soon as you're finished drawing by calling the ReleaseDC GDI function.

Various GDI functions are used in How-To 4.7 Start my applications with an animated look, How-To 2.1 Scroll all the objects in a window, How-To 2.2 Scroll text and graphics in a form or picture box, How-To 2.3 Make text and graphics roll up the screen, How-To 2.5 Align text automatically, and almost all of Chapter 5.

```
' ExtFloodFill style flags
Global Const FLOODFILLBORDER = 0
Global Const FLOODFILLSURFACE = 1

Declare Function GetWindowDC Lib "GDI" (ByVal hWnd As Integer) As Integer
Declare Function GetDC Lib "USER" (ByVal hWnd As Integer) As Integer
Declare Function ReleaseDC Lib "GDI" (ByVal hWnd As Integer, ByVal hDC As ⇐
Integer) As Integer
```

```
Declare Function CreateDC Lib "GDI" (ByVal lpDriverName As String, ByVal ⇐
lpDeviceName As String, ByVal lpOutput As String, ByVal lpInitData As ⇐
String) As Integer
Declare Function CreateIC Lib "GDI" (ByVal lpDriverName As String, ByVal ⇐
lpDeviceName As String, ByVal lpOutput As String, ByVal lpInitData ⇐
As String) As Integer
Declare Function CreateCompatibleDC Lib "GDI" (ByVal hDC As Integer) As ⇐
Integer
Declare Function DeleteDC Lib "GDI" (ByVal hDC As Integer) As Integer
Declare Function SaveDC Lib "GDI" (ByVal hDC As Integer) As Integer
Declare Function RestoreDC Lib "GDI" (ByVal hDC As Integer, ByVal nSavedDC ⇐
As Integer) As Integer
Declare Function MoveTo Lib "GDI" (ByVal hDC As Integer, ByVal X ⇐
As Integer, ByVal Y As Integer) As Long
Declare Function GetCurrentPosition Lib "GDI" (ByVal hDC As Integer) As Long
Declare Function LineTo Lib "GDI" (ByVal hDC As Integer, ByVal X ⇐
As Integer, ByVal Y As Integer) As Integer
Declare Function GetDCOrg Lib "GDI" (ByVal hDC As Integer) As Long

Declare Function MulDiv Lib "GDI" (ByVal nNumber As Integer, ByVal ⇐
nNumerator As Integer, ByVal nDenominator As Integer) As Integer

Declare Function ExtTextOut Lib "GDI" (ByVal hDC As Integer, ByVal X As ⇐
Integer, ByVal Y As Integer, ByVal wOptions As Integer, lpRect As Any, ⇐
ByVal lpString As String, ByVal nCount As Integer, lpDx As Any) As Integer

Declare Function Polyline Lib "GDI" (ByVal hDC As Integer, lpPoints As ⇐
POINTAPI, ByVal nCount As Integer) As Integer
Declare Function Polygon Lib "GDI" (ByVal hDC As Integer, lpPoints As ⇐
POINTAPI, ByVal nCount As Integer) As Integer
Declare Function PolyPolygon Lib "GDI" (ByVal hDC As Integer, lpPoints As ⇐
POINTAPI, lpPolyCounts As Integer, ByVal nCount As Integer) As Integer

Declare Function Rectangle Lib "GDI" (ByVal hDC As Integer, ByVal X1 As ⇐
Integer, ByVal Y1 As Integer, ByVal X2 As Integer, ByVal Y2 As Integer) As ⇐
Integer
Declare Function RoundRect Lib "GDI" (ByVal hDC As Integer, ByVal X1 As ⇐
Integer, ByVal Y1 As Integer, ByVal X2 As Integer, ByVal Y2 As Integer, ⇐
ByVal X3 As Integer, ByVal Y3 As Integer) As Integer
Declare Function Ellipse Lib "GDI" (ByVal hDC As Integer, ByVal X1 ⇐
As Integer, ByVal Y1 As Integer, ByVal X2 As Integer, ByVal Y2 As Integer) ⇐
As Integer
Declare Function Arc Lib "GDI" (ByVal hDC As Integer, ByVal X1 As Integer, ⇐
ByVal Y1 As Integer, ByVal X2 As Integer, ByVal Y2 As Integer, ByVal X3 As ⇐
Integer, ByVal Y3 As Integer, ByVal X4 As Integer, ByVal Y4 As Integer) As ⇐
Integer
Declare Function Chord Lib "GDI" (ByVal hDC As Integer, ByVal X1 As Integer, ⇐
ByVal Y1 As Integer, ByVal X2 As Integer, ByVal Y2 As Integer, ByVal X3 As ⇐
Integer, ByVal Y3 As Integer, ByVal X4 As Integer, ByVal Y4 As Integer) As ⇐
Integer
Declare Function Pie Lib "GDI" (ByVal hDC As Integer, ByVal X1 As Integer, ⇐
ByVal Y1 As Integer, ByVal X2 As Integer, ByVal Y2 As Integer, ByVal X3 As ⇐
Integer, ByVal Y3 As Integer, ByVal X4 As Integer, ByVal Y4 As Integer) As ⇐
```

```
Integer
Declare Function PatBlt Lib "GDI" (ByVal hDC As Integer, ByVal X As Integer, ⇐
ByVal Y As Integer, ByVal nWidth As Integer, ByVal nHeight As Integer, ByVal ⇐
dwRop As Long) As Integer
Declare Function BitBlt Lib "GDI" (ByVal hDestDC As Integer, ByVal X As ⇐
Integer, ByVal Y As Integer, ByVal nWidth As Integer, ByVal nHeight As ⇐
Integer, ByVal hSrcDC As Integer, ByVal XSrc As Integer, ByVal YSrc As ⇐
Integer, ByVal dwRop As Long) As Integer
Declare Function StretchBlt% Lib "GDI" (ByVal hDC%, ByVal X%, ByVal Y%, ⇐
ByVal nWidth%, ByVal nHeight%, ByVal hSrcDC%, ByVal XSrc%, ByVal YSrc%, ⇐
ByVal nSrcWidth%, ByVal nSrcHeight%, ByVal dwRop&)
Declare Function TextOut Lib "GDI" (ByVal hDC As Integer, ByVal X As ⇐
Integer, ByVal Y As Integer, ByVal lpString As String, ByVal nCount As ⇐
Integer) As Integer
Declare Function TabbedTextOut Lib "GDI" (ByVal hDC As Integer, ByVal X As ⇐
Integer, ByVal Y As Integer, ByVal lpString As String, ByVal nCount As ⇐
Integer, ByVal nTabPositions As Integer, lpnTabStopPositions As Integer, ⇐
ByVal nTabOrigin As Integer) As Long
Declare Function GetCharWidth Lib "GDI" (ByVal hDC As Integer, ByVal ⇐
wFirstChar As Integer, ByVal wLastChar As Integer, lpBuffer As Integer) As ⇐
Integer
Declare Function SetPixel Lib "GDI" (ByVal hDC As Integer, ByVal X As ⇐
Integer, ByVal Y As Integer, ByVal crColor As Long) As Long
Declare Function GetPixel Lib "GDI" (ByVal hDC As Integer, ByVal X As ⇐
Integer, ByVal Y As Integer) As Long
Declare Function FloodFill Lib "GDI" (ByVal hDC As Integer, ByVal X As ⇐
Integer, ByVal Y As Integer, ByVal crColor As Long) As Integer
Declare Function ExtFloodFill Lib "GDI" (ByVal hDC As Integer, ByVal X As ⇐
Integer, ByVal Y As Integer, ByVal crColor As Long, ByVal wFillType As ⇐
Integer) As Integer

Declare Function GetStockObject Lib "GDI" (ByVal nIndex As Integer) As ⇐
Integer

Declare Function CreatePen Lib "GDI" (ByVal nPenStyle As Integer, ByVal ⇐
nWidth As Integer, ByVal crColor As Long) As Integer
Declare Function CreatePenIndirect Lib "GDI" (lpLogPen As LOGPEN) As Integer

Declare Function CreateSolidBrush Lib "GDI" (ByVal crColor As Long) As ⇐
Integer
Declare Function CreateHatchBrush Lib "GDI" (ByVal nIndex As Integer, ByVal ⇐
crColor As Long) As Integer
Declare Function SetBrushOrg Lib "GDI" (ByVal hDC As Integer, ByVal X As ⇐
Integer, ByVal Y As Integer) As Long
Declare Function GetBrushOrg Lib "GDI" (ByVal hDC As Integer) As Long
Declare Function CreatePatternBrush Lib "GDI" (ByVal hBitmap As Integer) As ⇐
Integer
Declare Function CreateBrushIndirect Lib "GDI" (lpLogBrush As LOGBRUSH) As ⇐
Integer

Declare Function CreateFont% Lib "GDI" (ByVal H%, ByVal W%, ByVal E%, ByVal ⇐
O%, ByVal W%, ByVal I%, ByVal U%, ByVal S%, ByVal C%, ByVal OP%, ByVal CP%, ⇐
ByVal Q%, ByVal PAF%, ByVal F$)
```

```
Declare Function CreateFontIndirect Lib "GDI" (lpLogFont As LOGFONT) As ⇐
Integer

Declare Function SelectClipRgn Lib "GDI" (ByVal hDC As Integer, ByVal hRgn ⇐
As Integer) As Integer
Declare Function CreateRectRgn Lib "GDI" (ByVal X1 As Integer, ByVal Y1 As ⇐
Integer, ByVal X2 As Integer, ByVal Y2 As Integer) As Integer
Declare Sub SetRectRgn Lib "GDI" (ByVal hRgn As Integer, ByVal X1 As ⇐
Integer, ByVal Y1 As Integer, ByVal X2 As Integer, ByVal Y2 As Integer)
Declare Function CreateRectRgnIndirect Lib "GDI" (lpRect As RECT) As Integer
Declare Function CreateEllipticRgnIndirect Lib "GDI" (lpRect As RECT) As ⇐
Integer
Declare Function CreateEllipticRgn Lib "GDI" (ByVal X1 As Integer, ByVal Y1 ⇐
As Integer, ByVal X2 As Integer, ByVal Y2 As Integer) As Integer
Declare Function CreatePolygonRgn Lib "GDI" (lpPoints As POINTAPI, ByVal ⇐
nCount As Integer, ByVal nPolyFillMode As Integer) As Integer
Declare Function CreatePolyPolygonRgn Lib "GDI" (lpPoints As POINTAPI, ⇐
lpPolyCounts As Integer, ByVal nCount As Integer, ByVal nPolyFillMode As ⇐
Integer) As Integer
Declare Function CreateRoundRectRgn Lib "GDI" (ByVal X1 As Integer, ByVal ⇐
Y1 As Integer, ByVal X2 As Integer, ByVal Y2 As Integer, ByVal X3 As ⇐
Integer, ByVal Y3 As Integer) As Integer

Declare Function GetObject Lib "GDI" (ByVal hObject As Integer, ByVal ⇐
nCount As Integer, ByVal lpObject As Long) As Integer
Declare Function DeleteObject Lib "GDI" (ByVal hObject As Integer) As Integer
Declare Function SelectObject Lib "GDI" (ByVal hDC As Integer, ByVal ⇐
hObject As Integer) As Integer
Declare Function UnrealizeObject Lib "GDI" (ByVal hObject As Integer) As ⇐
Integer

Declare Function SetBkColor Lib "GDI" (ByVal hDC As Integer, ByVal crColor ⇐
As Long) As Long
Declare Function GetBkColor Lib "GDI" (ByVal hDC As Integer) As Long
Declare Function SetBkMode Lib "GDI" (ByVal hDC As Integer, ByVal nBkMode As⇐
Integer) As Integer
Declare Function GetBkMode Lib "GDI" (ByVal hDC As Integer) As Integer
Declare Function SetTextColor Lib "GDI" (ByVal hDC As Integer, ByVal ⇐
crColor As Long) As Long
Declare Function GetTextColor Lib "GDI" (ByVal hDC As Integer) As Long
Declare Function SetTextAlign Lib "GDI" (ByVal hDC As Integer, ByVal wFlags ⇐
As Integer) As Integer
Declare Function GetTextAlign Lib "GDI" (ByVal hDC As Integer) As Integer
Declare Function SetMapperFlags Lib "GDI" (ByVal hDC As Integer, ByVal ⇐
dwFlag As Long) As Long
Declare Function GetAspectRatioFilter Lib "GDI" (ByVal hDC As Integer) As ⇐
Long
Declare Function GetNearestColor Lib "GDI" (ByVal hDC As Integer, ByVal ⇐
crColor As Long) As Long
Declare Function SetROP2 Lib "GDI" (ByVal hDC As Integer, ByVal nDrawMode ⇐
As Integer) As Integer
Declare Function GetROP2 Lib "GDI" (ByVal hDC As Integer) As Integer
Declare Function SetStretchBltMode Lib "GDI" (ByVal hDC As Integer, ByVal ⇐
```

```
nStretchMode As Integer) As Integer
Declare Function GetStretchBltMode Lib "GDI" (ByVal hDC As Integer) As ⇐
Integer
Declare Function SetPolyFillMode Lib "GDI" (ByVal hDC As Integer, ByVal ⇐
nPolyFillMode As Integer) As Integer
Declare Function GetPolyFillMode Lib "GDI" (ByVal hDC As Integer) As Integer
Declare Function SetMapMode Lib "GDI" (ByVal hDC As Integer, ByVal nMapMode ⇐
As Integer) As Integer
Declare Function GetMapMode Lib "GDI" (ByVal hDC As Integer) As Integer
Declare Function SetWindowOrg Lib "GDI" (ByVal hDC As Integer, ByVal X As ⇐
Integer, ByVal Y As Integer) As Long
Declare Function GetWindowOrg Lib "GDI" (ByVal hDC As Integer) As Long
Declare Function SetWindowExt Lib "GDI" (ByVal hDC As Integer, ByVal X As ⇐
Integer, ByVal Y As Integer) As Long
Declare Function GetWindowExt Lib "GDI" (ByVal hDC As Integer) As Long
Declare Function SetViewportOrg Lib "GDI" (ByVal hDC As Integer, ByVal X As ⇐
Integer, ByVal Y As Integer) As Long
Declare Function GetViewportOrg Lib "GDI" (ByVal hDC As Integer) As Long
Declare Function SetViewportExt Lib "GDI" (ByVal hDC As Integer, ByVal X As ⇐
Integer, ByVal Y As Integer) As Long
Declare Function GetViewportExt Lib "GDI" (ByVal hDC As Integer) As Long
Declare Function OffsetViewportOrg Lib "GDI" (ByVal hDC As Integer, ByVal X ⇐
As Integer, ByVal Y As Integer) As Long
Declare Function ScaleViewportExt Lib "GDI" (ByVal hDC As Integer, ByVal ⇐
Xnum As Integer, ByVal Xdenom As Integer, ByVal Ynum As Integer, ByVal ⇐
Ydenom As Integer) As Long
Declare Function OffsetWindowOrg Lib "GDI" (ByVal hDC As Integer, ByVal X ⇐
As Integer, ByVal Y As Integer) As Long
Declare Function ScaleWindowExt Lib "GDI" (ByVal hDC As Integer, ByVal ⇐
Xnum As Integer, ByVal Xdenom As Integer, ByVal Ynum As Integer, ByVal ⇐
Ydenom As Integer) As Long


Declare Function GetClipBox Lib "GDI" (ByVal hDC As Integer, lpRect As ⇐
RECT) As Integer
Declare Function IntersectClipRect Lib "GDI" (ByVal hDC As Integer, ByVal ⇐
X1 As Integer, ByVal Y1 As Integer, ByVal X2 As Integer, ByVal Y2 As ⇐
Integer) As Integer
Declare Function OffsetClipRgn Lib "GDI" (ByVal hDC As Integer, ByVal X As ⇐
Integer, ByVal Y As Integer) As Integer
Declare Function ExcludeClipRect Lib "GDI" (ByVal hDC As Integer, ByVal ⇐
X1 As Integer, ByVal Y1 As Integer, ByVal X2 As Integer, ByVal Y2 As ⇐
Integer) ⇐ As Integer
Declare Function PtVisible Lib "GDI" (ByVal hDC As Integer, ByVal X As ⇐
Integer, ByVal Y As Integer) As Integer
Declare Function CombineRgn Lib "GDI" (ByVal hDestRgn As Integer, ByVal ⇐
hSrcRgn1 As Integer, ByVal hSrcRgn2 As Integer, ByVal nCombineMode As ⇐
Integer) As Integer
Declare Function EqualRgn Lib "GDI" (ByVal hSrcRgn1 As Integer, ByVal ⇐
hSrcRgn2 As Integer) As Integer
Declare Function OffsetRgn Lib "GDI" (ByVal hRgn As Integer, ByVal X As ⇐
Integer, ByVal Y As Integer) As Integer
Declare Function GetRgnBox Lib "GDI" (ByVal hRgn As Integer, lpRect As ⇐
RECT) As Integer
```

```
Declare Function SetTextJustification Lib "GDI" (ByVal hDC As Integer, ⇐
ByVal nBreakExtra As Integer, ByVal nBreakCount As Integer) As Integer
Declare Function GetTextExtent Lib "GDI" (ByVal hDC As Integer, ByVal ⇐
lpString As String, ByVal nCount As Integer) As Long
Declare Function GetTabbedTextExtent Lib "GDI" (ByVal hDC As Integer, ⇐
ByVal lpString As String, ByVal nCount As Integer, ByVal nTabPositions As ⇐
Integer, lpnTabStopPositions As Integer) As Long
Declare Function SetTextCharacterExtra Lib "GDI" (ByVal hDC As Integer, ⇐
ByVal nCharExtra As Integer) As Integer
Declare Function GetTextCharacterExtra Lib "GDI" (ByVal hDC As Integer) ⇐
As Integer

Declare Function GetMetaFile Lib "GDI" (ByVal lpFilename As String) As ⇐
Integer
Declare Function DeleteMetaFile Lib "GDI" (ByVal hMF As Integer) As ⇐
Integer
Declare Function CopyMetaFile Lib "GDI" (ByVal hMF As Integer, ByVal ⇐
lpFilename As String) As Integer

Declare Function PlayMetaFile Lib "GDI" (ByVal hDC As Integer, ByVal hMF ⇐
As Integer) As Integer
Declare Sub PlayMetaFileRecord Lib "GDI" (ByVal hDC As Integer, ⇐
lpHandletable As Integer, lpMetaRecord As METARECORD, ByVal nHandles As ⇐
Integer)

Declare Function Escape Lib "GDI" (ByVal hDC As Integer, ByVal nEscape As ⇐
Integer, ByVal nCount As Integer, lplnData As Any, lpOutData As Any) As ⇐
Integer
Declare Function GetTextFace Lib "GDI" (ByVal hDC As Integer, ByVal ⇐
nCount As Integer, ByVal lpFacename As String) As Integer

Declare Function GetTextMetrics Lib "GDI" (ByVal hDC As Integer, lpMetrics ⇐
As TEXTMETRIC) As Integer

Declare Function SetEnvironment Lib "GDI" (ByVal lpPortName As String, ⇐
ByVal lpEnviron As String, ByVal nCount As Integer) As Integer
Declare Function GetEnvironment Lib "GDI" (ByVal lpPortName As String, ⇐
lpEnviron As Any, ByVal nMaxCount As Integer) As Integer

Declare Function DPtoLP Lib "GDI" (ByVal hDC As Integer, lpPoints As ⇐
POINTAPI, ByVal nCount As Integer) As Integer
Declare Function LPtoDP Lib "GDI" (ByVal hDC As Integer, lpPoints As ⇐
POINTAPI, ByVal nCount As Integer) As Integer

Declare Function CreateMetaFile Lib "GDI" (lpString As Any) As Integer
Declare Function CloseMetaFile Lib "GDI" (ByVal hMF As Integer) As Integer
Declare Function GetMetaFileBits Lib "GDI" (ByVal hMF As Integer) As ⇐
Integer
Declare Function SetMetaFileBits Lib "GDI" (ByVal hMem As Integer) As ⇐
Integer

Declare Function SetDIBits Lib "GDI" (ByVal aHDC As Integer, ByVal hBitmap ⇐
As Integer, ByVal nStartScan As Integer, ByVal nNumScans As Integer, ByVal ⇐
lpBits As String, lpBI As BITMAPINFO, ByVal wUsage As Integer) As Integer

Declare Function GetDIBits Lib "GDI" (ByVal aHDC As Integer, ByVal hBitmap ⇐
```

```
As Integer, ByVal nStartScan As Integer, ByVal nNumScans As Integer, ByVal ⇐
lpBits As String, lpBI As BITMAPINFO, ByVal wUsage As Integer) As Integer

Declare Function SetDIBitsToDevice% Lib "GDI" (ByVal hDC#, ByVal X#, ByVal ⇐
Y#, ByVal dX#, ByVal dY#, ByVal SrcX#, ByVal SrcY#, ByVal Scan#, ByVal ⇐
NumScans#, ByVal Bits As String, BitsInfo As BITMAPINFO, ByVal wUsage#)

Declare Function CreateDIBitmap Lib "GDI" (ByVal hDC As Integer, ⇐
lpInfoHeader As BITMAPINFOHEADER, ByVal dwUsage As Long, ByVal lpInitBits ⇐
As String, lpInitInfo As BITMAPINFO, ByVal wUsage As Integer) As Integer

Declare Function CreateDIBPatternBrush Lib "GDI" (ByVal hPackedDIB As ⇐
Integer, ByVal wUsage As Integer) As Integer

Declare Function StretchDIBits# Lib "GDI" (ByVal hDC#, ByVal X#, ByVal Y#, ⇐
ByVal dX#, ByVal dY#, ByVal SrcX#, ByVal SrcY#, ByVal wSrcWidth#, ByVal ⇐
wSrcHeight#, ByVal lpBits As String, lpBitsInfo As BITMAPINFO, ByVal ⇐
wUsage#, ByVal dwRop&)

' ------------------------------------
'    USER Section
' ------------------------------------
```

wvsprintf provides formatted outputs for numbers and strings. Visual Baisc provides almost all the same capabilities with the Format$ function.

```
Declare Function wvsprintf Lib "User" (ByVal lpOutput As String, ByVal ⇐
lpFormat As String, lpArglist As Integer) As Integer
```

These are some miscellaneous constants for managing windows and controls. Visual Basic users generally don't need to worry about them.

```
' Scroll Bar Constants
Global Const SB_HORZ = 0
Global Const SB_VERT = 1
Global Const SB_CTL = 2
Global Const SB_BOTH = 3

' Scroll Bar Commands
Global Const SB_LINEUP = 0
Global Const SB_LINEDOWN = 1
Global Const SB_PAGEUP = 2
Global Const SB_PAGEDOWN = 3
Global Const SB_THUMBPOSITION = 4
Global Const SB_THUMBTRACK = 5
Global Const SB_TOP = 6
Global Const SB_BOTTOM = 7
Global Const SB_ENDSCROLL = 8

' ShowWindow() Commands
Global Const SW_HIDE = 0
Global Const SW_SHOWNORMAL = 1
Global Const SW_NORMAL = 1
Global Const SW_SHOWMINIMIZED = 2
Global Const SW_SHOWMAXIMIZED = 3
Global Const SW_MAXIMIZE = 3
```

```
Global Const SW_SHOWNOACTIVATE = 4
Global Const SW_SHOW = 5
Global Const SW_MINIMIZE = 6
Global Const SW_SHOWMINNOACTIVE = 7
Global Const SW_SHOWNA = 8
Global Const SW_RESTORE = 9

'  Old ShowWindow() Commands
Global Const HIDE_WINDOW = 0
Global Const SHOW_OPENWINDOW = 1
Global Const SHOW_ICONWINDOW = 2
Global Const SHOW_FULLSCREEN = 3
Global Const SHOW_OPENNOACTIVATE = 4

'  Identifiers for the WM_SHOWWINDOW message
Global Const SW_PARENTCLOSING = 1
Global Const SW_OTHERZOOM = 2
Global Const SW_PARENTOPENING = 3
Global Const SW_OTHERUNZOOM = 4

'  Region Flags
Global Const ERRORAPI = 0
Global Const NULLREGION = 1
Global Const SIMPLEREGION = 2
Global Const COMPLEXREGION = 3

'  CombineRgn() Styles
Global Const RGN_AND = 1
Global Const RGN_OR = 2
Global Const RGN_XOR = 3
Global Const RGN_DIFF = 4
Global Const RGN_COPY = 5
```

The following constants are key codes passed to KeyDown and KeyUp event subroutines. They're the same as the constants in the CONSTANT.TXT file.

```
'  Virtual Keys, Standard Set
Global Const VK_LBUTTON = &H1
Global Const VK_RBUTTON = &H2
Global Const VK_CANCEL = &H3
Global Const VK_MBUTTON = &H4          ' NOT contiguous with L & RBUTTON
Global Const VK_BACK = &H8
Global Const VK_TAB = &H9
Global Const VK_CLEAR = &HC
Global Const VK_RETURN = &HD
Global Const VK_SHIFT = &H10
Global Const VK_CONTROL = &H11
Global Const VK_MENU = &H12
Global Const VK_PAUSE = &H13
Global Const VK_CAPITAL = &H14
Global Const VK_ESCAPE = &H1B
Global Const VK_SPACE = &H20
Global Const VK_PRIOR = &H21
```

```
Global Const VK_NEXT = &H22
Global Const VK_END = &H23
Global Const VK_HOME = &H24
Global Const VK_LEFT = &H25
Global Const VK_UP = &H26
Global Const VK_RIGHT = &H27
Global Const VK_DOWN = &H28
Global Const VK_SELECT = &H29
Global Const VK_PRINT = &H2A
Global Const VK_EXECUTE = &H2B
Global Const VK_SNAPSHOT = &H2C
'Global Const VK_COPY = &H2C not used by keyboards.
Global Const VK_INSERT = &H2D
Global Const VK_DELETE = &H2E
Global Const VK_HELP = &H2F


' VK_A thru VK_Z are the same as their ASCII equivalents: 'A' thru 'Z'
' VK_0 thru VK_9 are the same as their ASCII equivalents: '0' thru '9'

Global Const VK_NUMPAD0 = &H60
Global Const VK_NUMPAD1 = &H61
Global Const VK_NUMPAD2 = &H62
Global Const VK_NUMPAD3 = &H63
Global Const VK_NUMPAD4 = &H64
Global Const VK_NUMPAD5 = &H65
Global Const VK_NUMPAD6 = &H66
Global Const VK_NUMPAD7 = &H67
Global Const VK_NUMPAD8 = &H68
Global Const VK_NUMPAD9 = &H69
Global Const VK_MULTIPLY = &H6A
Global Const VK_ADD = &H6B
Global Const VK_SEPARATOR = &H6C
Global Const VK_SUBTRACT = &H6D
Global Const VK_DECIMAL = &H6E
Global Const VK_DIVIDE = &H6F
Global Const VK_F1 = &H70
Global Const VK_F2 = &H71
Global Const VK_F3 = &H72
Global Const VK_F4 = &H73
Global Const VK_F5 = &H74
Global Const VK_F6 = &H75
Global Const VK_F7 = &H76
Global Const VK_F8 = &H77
Global Const VK_F9 = &H78
Global Const VK_F10 = &H79
Global Const VK_F11 = &H7A
Global Const VK_F12 = &H7B
Global Const VK_F13 = &H7C
Global Const VK_F14 = &H7D
Global Const VK_F15 = &H7E
Global Const VK_F16 = &H7F

Global Const VK_NUMLOCK = &H90
```

These constants and structures are used to install hooks or intercepts into Windows. Hooking into Windows is an advanced technique that can only be done in a more tranditional language like C or Pascal.

```
'  SetWindowsHook() codes
Global Const WH_MSGFILTER = (-1)
Global Const WH_JOURNALRECORD = 0
Global Const WH_JOURNALPLAYBACK = 1
Global Const WH_KEYBOARD = 2
Global Const WH_GETMESSAGE = 3
Global Const WH_CALLWNDPROC = 4
Global Const WH_CBT = 5
Global Const WH_SYSMSGFILTER = 6
Global Const WH_WINDOWMGR = 7

'  Hook Codes
Global Const HC_LPLPFNNEXT = (-2)
Global Const HC_LPFNNEXT = (-1)
Global Const HC_ACTION = 0
Global Const HC_GETNEXT = 1
Global Const HC_SKIP = 2
Global Const HC_NOREM = 3
Global Const HC_NOREMOVE = 3
Global Const HC_SYSMODALON = 4
Global Const HC_SYSMODALOFF = 5

'  CBT Hook Codes
Global Const HCBT_MOVESIZE = 0
Global Const HCBT_MINMAX = 1
Global Const HCBT_QS = 2

'  WH_MSGFILTER Filter Proc Codes
Global Const MSGF_DIALOGBOX = 0
Global Const MSGF_MESSAGEBOX = 1
Global Const MSGF_MENU = 2
Global Const MSGF_MOVE = 3
Global Const MSGF_SIZE = 4
Global Const MSGF_SCROLLBAR = 5
Global Const MSGF_NEXTWINDOW = 6

'  Window Manager Hook Codes
Global Const WC_INIT = 1
Global Const WC_SWP = 2
Global Const WC_DEFWINDOWPROC = 3
Global Const WC_MINMAX = 4
Global Const WC_MOVE = 5
Global Const WC_SIZE = 6
Global Const WC_DRAWCAPTION = 7

'  Message Structure used in Journaling
Type EVENTMSG
    message As Integer
    paramL As Integer
    paramH As Integer
    time As Long
End Type
```

These constants and functions are used with the GetWindowLong, GetWindowWord, GetClassLong, GetClassWord, SetWindowLong, SetWindowWord, SetClassLong, and SetClassWord functions to determine and set various characteristics of a window or control. See How-To 4-8, Prevent text typed into a text box from appearing on screen, for an example of how to use them.

```
' Window field offsets for GetWindowLong() and GetWindowWord()
Global Const GWL_WNDPROC = (-4)
Global Const GWW_HINSTANCE = (-6)
Global Const GWW_HWNDPARENT = (-8)
Global Const GWW_ID = (-12)
Global Const GWL_STYLE = (-16)
Global Const GWL_EXSTYLE = (-20)

' Class field offsets for GetClassLong() and GetClassWord()
Global Const GCL_MENUNAME = (-8)
Global Const GCW_HBRBACKGROUND = (-10)
Global Const GCW_HCURSOR = (-12)
Global Const GCW_HICON = (-14)
Global Const GCW_HMODULE = (-16)
Global Const GCW_CBWNDEXTRA = (-18)
Global Const GCW_CBCLSEXTRA = (-20)
Global Const GCL_WNDPROC = (-24)
Global Const GCW_STYLE = (-26)

Declare Function GetWindowWord Lib "User" (ByVal hWnd As Integer, ByVal ⇐
nIndex As Integer) As Integer
Declare Function SetWindowWord Lib "User" (ByVal hWnd As Integer, ByVal ⇐
nIndex As Integer, ByVal wNewWord As Integer) As Integer
Declare Function GetWindowLong Lib "User" (ByVal hWnd As Integer, ByVal ⇐
nIndex As Integer) As Long
Declare Function SetWindowLong Lib "User" (ByVal hWnd As Integer, ByVal ⇐
nIndex As Integer, ByVal dwNewLong As Long) As Long
Declare Function GetClassWord Lib "User" (ByVal hWnd As Integer, ByVal ⇐
nIndex As Integer) As Integer
Declare Function SetClassWord Lib "User" (ByVal hWnd As Integer, ByVal ⇐
nIndex As Integer, ByVal wNewWord As Integer) As Integer
Declare Function GetClassLong Lib "User" (ByVal hWnd As Integer, ByVal ⇐
nIndex As Integer) As Long
Declare Function SetClassLong Lib "User" (ByVal hWnd As Integer, ByVal ⇐
nIndex As Integer, ByVal dwNewLong As Long) As Long
```

These messages are sent by Windows to the window procedure of a traditional C or Pascal Windows application. In Visual Basic, some of them trigger a Visual Basic event subroutine. When a user moves the mouse pointer over a form, for example, Windows sends a WM_MOUSEMOVE message. Visual Basic interprets that and executes that form's MouseMove event subroutine, if one exists. Since it all happens automatically, you don't need to worry about these constants.

```
' Window Messages
Global Const WM_NULL = &H0
Global Const WM_CREATE = &H1
Global Const WM_DESTROY = &H2
Global Const WM_MOVE = &H3
Global Const WM_SIZE = &H5
Global Const WM_ACTIVATE = &H6
Global Const WM_SETFOCUS = &H7
Global Const WM_KILLFOCUS = &H8
Global Const WM_ENABLE = &HA
Global Const WM_SETREDRAW = &HB
Global Const WM_SETTEXT = &HC
Global Const WM_GETTEXT = &HD
Global Const WM_GETTEXTLENGTH = &HE
Global Const WM_PAINT = &HF
Global Const WM_CLOSE = &H10
Global Const WM_QUERYENDSESSION = &H11
Global Const WM_QUIT = &H12
Global Const WM_QUERYOPEN = &H13
Global Const WM_ERASEBKGND = &H14
Global Const WM_SYSCOLORCHANGE = &H15
Global Const WM_ENDSESSION = &H16
Global Const WM_SHOWWINDOW = &H18
Global Const WM_CTLCOLOR = &H19
Global Const WM_WININICHANGE = &H1A
Global Const WM_DEVMODECHANGE = &H1B
Global Const WM_ACTIVATEAPP = &H1C
Global Const WM_FONTCHANGE = &H1D
Global Const WM_TIMECHANGE = &H1E
Global Const WM_CANCELMODE = &H1F
Global Const WM_SETCURSOR = &H20
Global Const WM_MOUSEACTIVATE = &H21
Global Const WM_CHILDACTIVATE = &H22
Global Const WM_QUEUESYNC = &H23
Global Const WM_GETMINMAXINFO = &H24
Global Const WM_PAINTICON = &H26
Global Const WM_ICONERASEBKGND = &H27
Global Const WM_NEXTDLGCTL = &H28
Global Const WM_SPOOLERSTATUS = &H2A
Global Const WM_DRAWITEM = &H2B
Global Const WM_MEASUREITEM = &H2C
Global Const WM_DELETEITEM = &H2D
Global Const WM_VKEYTOITEM = &H2E
Global Const WM_CHARTOITEM = &H2F
Global Const WM_SETFONT = &H30
Global Const WM_GETFONT = &H31

Global Const WM_QUERYDRAGICON = &H37

Global Const WM_COMPAREITEM = &H39
Global Const WM_COMPACTING = &H41

Global Const WM_NCCREATE = &H81
Global Const WM_NCDESTROY = &H82
```

```
Global Const WM_NCCALCSIZE = &H83
Global Const WM_NCHITTEST = &H84
Global Const WM_NCPAINT = &H85
Global Const WM_NCACTIVATE = &H86
Global Const WM_GETDLGCODE = &H87
Global Const WM_NCMOUSEMOVE = &HA0
Global Const WM_NCLBUTTONDOWN = &HA1
Global Const WM_NCLBUTTONUP = &HA2
Global Const WM_NCLBUTTONDBLCLK = &HA3
Global Const WM_NCRBUTTONDOWN = &HA4
Global Const WM_NCRBUTTONUP = &HA5
Global Const WM_NCRBUTTONDBLCLK = &HA6
Global Const WM_NCMBUTTONDOWN = &HA7
Global Const WM_NCMBUTTONUP = &HA8
Global Const WM_NCMBUTTONDBLCLK = &HA9

Global Const WM_KEYFIRST = &H100
Global Const WM_KEYDOWN = &H100
Global Const WM_KEYUP = &H101
Global Const WM_CHAR = &H102
Global Const WM_DEADCHAR = &H103
Global Const WM_SYSKEYDOWN = &H104
Global Const WM_SYSKEYUP = &H105
Global Const WM_SYSCHAR = &H106
Global Const WM_SYSDEADCHAR = &H107
Global Const WM_KEYLAST = &H108

Global Const WM_INITDIALOG = &H110
Global Const WM_COMMAND = &H111
Global Const WM_SYSCOMMAND = &H112
Global Const WM_TIMER = &H113
Global Const WM_HSCROLL = &H114
Global Const WM_VSCROLL = &H115
Global Const WM_INITMENU = &H116
Global Const WM_INITMENUPOPUP = &H117
Global Const WM_MENUSELECT = &H11F
Global Const WM_MENUCHAR = &H120
Global Const WM_ENTERIDLE = &H121

Global Const WM_MOUSEFIRST = &H200
Global Const WM_MOUSEMOVE = &H200
Global Const WM_LBUTTONDOWN = &H201
Global Const WM_LBUTTONUP = &H202
Global Const WM_LBUTTONDBLCLK = &H203
Global Const WM_RBUTTONDOWN = &H204
Global Const WM_RBUTTONUP = &H205
Global Const WM_RBUTTONDBLCLK = &H206
Global Const WM_MBUTTONDOWN = &H207
Global Const WM_MBUTTONUP = &H208
Global Const WM_MBUTTONDBLCLK = &H209
Global Const WM_MOUSELAST = &H209

Global Const WM_PARENTNOTIFY = &H210
Global Const WM_MDICREATE = &H220
```

```
Global Const WM_MDIDESTROY = &H221
Global Const WM_MDIACTIVATE = &H222
Global Const WM_MDIRESTORE = &H223
Global Const WM_MDINEXT = &H224
Global Const WM_MDIMAXIMIZE = &H225
Global Const WM_MDITILE = &H226
Global Const WM_MDICASCADE = &H227
Global Const WM_MDIICONARRANGE = &H228
Global Const WM_MDIGETACTIVE = &H229
Global Const WM_MDISETMENU = &H230

Global Const WM_CUT = &H300
Global Const WM_COPY = &H301
Global Const WM_PASTE = &H302
Global Const WM_CLEAR = &H303
Global Const WM_UNDO = &H304
Global Const WM_RENDERFORMAT = &H305
Global Const WM_RENDERALLFORMATS = &H306
Global Const WM_DESTROYCLIPBOARD = &H307
Global Const WM_DRAWCLIPBOARD = &H308
Global Const WM_PAINTCLIPBOARD = &H309
Global Const WM_VSCROLLCLIPBOARD = &H30A
Global Const WM_SIZECLIPBOARD = &H30B
Global Const WM_ASKCBFORMATNAME = &H30C
Global Const WM_CHANGECBCHAIN = &H30D
Global Const WM_HSCROLLCLIPBOARD = &H30E
Global Const WM_QUERYNEWPALETTE = &H30F
Global Const WM_PALETTEISCHANGING = &H310
Global Const WM_PALETTECHANGED = &H311

' NOTE: All Message Numbers below 0x0400 are RESERVED.
```

WM_USER is the first of the "user" messages, messages that an application can define for its own use to send to another window or control.

```
' Private Window Messages Start Here:
Global Const WM_USER = &H400
```

These constants identify task switches used internally by Windows. You won't have to worry about them.

```
' WM_SYNCTASK Commands
Global Const ST_BEGINSWP = 0
Global Const ST_ENDSWP = 1
```

These constants are used with the undocumented WinWhere function, so you should avoid them (and the function).

```
' WinWhere() Area Codes
Global Const HTERROR = (-2)
Global Const HTTRANSPARENT = (-1)
Global Const HTNOWHERE = 0
Global Const HTCLIENT = 1
Global Const HTCAPTION = 2
```

```
Global Const HTSYSMENU = 3
Global Const HTGROWBOX = 4
Global Const HTSIZE = HTGROWBOX
Global Const HTMENU = 5
Global Const HTHSCROLL = 6
Global Const HTVSCROLL = 7
Global Const HTREDUCE = 8
Global Const HTZOOM = 9
Global Const HTLEFT = 10
Global Const HTRIGHT = 11
Global Const HTTOP = 12
Global Const HTTOPLEFT = 13
Global Const HTTOPRIGHT = 14
Global Const HTBOTTOM = 15
Global Const HTBOTTOMLEFT = 16
Global Const HTBOTTOMRIGHT = 17
Global Const HTSIZEFIRST = HTLEFT
Global Const HTSIZELAST = HTBOTTOMRIGHT

'  WM_MOUSEACTIVATE Return Codes
Global Const MA_ACTIVATE = 1
Global Const MA_ACTIVATEANDEAT = 2
Global Const MA_NOACTIVATE = 3

Declare Function RegisterWindowMessage Lib "User" (ByVal lpString As ⇐
String) As Integer

'  Size Message Commands
Global Const SIZENORMAL = 0
Global Const SIZEICONIC = 1
Global Const SIZEFULLSCREEN = 2
Global Const SIZEZOOMSHOW = 3
Global Const SIZEZOOMHIDE = 4
```

These constants specify which button(s) (left, middle, and right) and Shift and Ctrl keys were pressed in a mouse message. In Visual Basic, they're passed to MouseMove, MouseUp, and MouseDown event subroutines.

```
'  Key State Masks for Mouse Messages
Global Const MK_LBUTTON = &H1
Global Const MK_RBUTTON = &H2
Global Const MK_SHIFT = &H4
Global Const MK_CONTROL = &H8
Global Const MK_MBUTTON = &H10
```

These constants specify the appearance of a window—whether it has a Control-menu box or a caption (title) bar and what kind of frame (border) it has. In Visual Basic, you can change a form's appearance at design-time by changing the following properties: MaxButton, MinButton, Visible, Enabled, BorderStyle, ControlBox, and WindowState.

```
'  Window Styles
Global Const WS_OVERLAPPED = &H00000&
```

```
Global Const WS_POPUP = &H80000000&
Global Const WS_CHILD = &H40000000&
Global Const WS_MINIMIZE = &H20000000&
Global Const WS_VISIBLE = &H10000000&
Global Const WS_DISABLED = &H8000000&
Global Const WS_CLIPSIBLINGS = &H4000000&
Global Const WS_CLIPCHILDREN = &H2000000&
Global Const WS_MAXIMIZE = &H1000000&
Global Const WS_CAPTION = &HC00000& '  WS_BORDER Or WS_DLGFRAME
Global Const WS_BORDER = &H800000&
Global Const WS_DLGFRAME = &H400000&
Global Const WS_VSCROLL = &H200000&
Global Const WS_HSCROLL = &H100000&
Global Const WS_SYSMENU = &H80000&
Global Const WS_THICKFRAME = &H40000&
Global Const WS_GROUP = &H20000&
Global Const WS_TABSTOP = &H10000&

Global Const WS_MINIMIZEBOX = &H20000&
Global Const WS_MAXIMIZEBOX = &H10000&

Global Const WS_TILED = WS_OVERLAPPED
Global Const WS_ICONIC = WS_MINIMIZE
Global Const WS_SIZEBOX = WS_THICKFRAME

' Common Window Styles
Global Const WS_OVERLAPPEDWINDOW = (WS_OVERLAPPED Or WS_CAPTION Or ⇐
WS_SYSMENU Or WS_THICKFRAME Or WS_MINIMIZEBOX Or WS_MAXIMIZEBOX)
Global Const WS_POPUPWINDOW = (WS_POPUP Or WS_BORDER Or WS_SYSMENU)
Global Const WS_CHILDWINDOW = (WS_CHILD)
Global Const WS_TILEDWINDOW = (WS_OVERLAPPEDWINDOW)

' Extended Window Styles
Global Const WS_EX_DLGMODALFRAME = &H00001&
Global Const WS_EX_NOPARENTNOTIFY = &H00004&

' Class styles
Global Const CS_VREDRAW = &H1
Global Const CS_HREDRAW = &H2
Global Const CS_KEYCVTWINDOW = &H4
Global Const CS_DBLCLKS = &H8
Global Const CS_OWNDC = &H20
Global Const CS_CLASSDC = &H40
Global Const CS_PARENTDC = &H80
Global Const CS_NOKEYCVT = &H100
Global Const CS_NOCLOSE = &H200
Global Const CS_SAVEBITS = &H800
Global Const CS_BYTEALIGNCLIENT = &H1000
Global Const CS_BYTEALIGNWINDOW = &H2000
Global Const CS_GLOBALCLASS = &H4000          ' Global window class
```

These constants are used to determine and set the data in the Windows Clipboard. In Visual Basic, you can use the Clipboard object to ease use of the Windows Clipboard.

```
' Predefined Clipboard Formats
Global Const CF_TEXT = 1
Global Const CF_BITMAP = 2
Global Const CF_METAFILEPICT = 3
Global Const CF_SYLK = 4
Global Const CF_DIF = 5
Global Const CF_TIFF = 6
Global Const CF_OEMTEXT = 7
Global Const CF_DIB = 8
Global Const CF_PALETTE = 9

Global Const CF_OWNERDISPLAY = &H80
Global Const CF_DSPTEXT = &H81
Global Const CF_DSPBITMAP = &H82
Global Const CF_DSPMETAFILEPICT = &H83

' "Private" formats don't get GlobalFree()'d
Global Const CF_PRIVATEFIRST = &H200
Global Const CF_PRIVATELAST = &H2FF

' "GDIOBJ" formats do get DeleteObject()'d
Global Const CF_GDIOBJFIRST = &H300
Global Const CF_GDIOBJLAST = &H3FF

' Clipboard Manager Functions
Declare Function OpenClipboard Lib "User" (ByVal hWnd As Integer) As ⇐
Integer
Declare Function CloseClipboard Lib "User" () As Integer
Declare Function GetClipboardOwner Lib "User" () As Integer
Declare Function SetClipboardViewer Lib "User" (ByVal hWnd As Integer) As ⇐
Integer
Declare Function GetClipboardViewer Lib "User" () As Integer
Declare Function ChangeClipboardChain Lib "User" (ByVal hWnd As Integer, ⇐
ByVal hWndNext As Integer) As Integer
Declare Function SetClipboardData Lib "User" (ByVal wFormat As Integer, ⇐
ByVal hMem As Integer) As Integer
Declare Function GetClipboardData Lib "User" (ByVal wFormat As Integer) As ⇐
Integer
Declare Function RegisterClipboardFormat Lib "User" (ByVal lpString As ⇐
String) As Integer
Declare Function CountClipboardFormats Lib "User" () As Integer
Declare Function EnumClipboardFormats Lib "User" (ByVal wFormat As ⇐
Integer) As Integer
Declare Function GetClipboardFormatName Lib "User" (ByVal wFormat As ⇐
Integer, ByVal lpString As String, ByVal nMaxCount As Integer) As Integer
Declare Function EmptyClipboard Lib "User" () As Integer
Declare Function IsClipboardFormatAvailable Lib "User" (ByVal wFormat As ⇐
Integer) As Integer
Declare Function GetPriorityClipboardFormat Lib "User" (lpPriorityList As ⇐
Integer, ByVal nCount As Integer) As Integer
```

PAINTSTRUCT is a structure used for responding to the WM_PAINT message; in Visual Basic, you can simply write a Paint event subroutine.

```
Type PAINTSTRUCT
    hdc As Integer
    fErase As Integer
    rcPaint As RECT
    fRestore As Integer
    fIncUpdate As Integer
    rgbReserved As String * 16
End Type
```

CREATESTRUCT is a structure used for responding to the WM_CREATE message; the Visual Basic form Load event is similar to this message.

```
Type CREATESTRUCT
    lpCreateParams As Long
    hInstance As Integer
    hMenu As Integer
    hwndParent As Integer
    cy As Integer
    cx As Integer
    y As Integer
    x As Integer
    style As Long
    lpszName As Long
    lpszClass As Long
    ExStyle As Long
End Type
```

These constants and structures are used to support owner-drawn or customized controls. Visual Basic supports custom controls to achieve the same effect. See Chapter 8 for more information about custom controls.

```
' Owner draw control types
Global Const ODT_MENU = 1
Global Const ODT_LISTBOX = 2
Global Const ODT_COMBOBOX = 3
Global Const ODT_BUTTON = 4

' Owner draw actions
Global Const ODA_DRAWENTIRE = &H1
Global Const ODA_SELECT = &H2
Global Const ODA_FOCUS = &H4

' Owner draw state
Global Const ODS_SELECTED = &H1
Global Const ODS_GRAYED = &H2
Global Const ODS_DISABLED = &H4
Global Const ODS_CHECKED = &H8
Global Const ODS_FOCUS = &H10

' MEASUREITEMSTRUCT for ownerdraw
Type MEASUREITEMSTRUCT
    CtlType As Integer
    CtlID As Integer
    itemID As Integer
```

```
        itemWidth As Integer
        itemHeight As Integer
        itemData As Long
End Type

'  DRAWITEMSTRUCT for ownerdraw
Type DRAWITEMSTRUCT
        CtlType As Integer
        CtlID As Integer
        itemID As Integer
        itemAction As Integer
        itemState As Integer
        hwndItem As Integer
        hDC As Integer
        rcItem As RECT
        itemData As Long
End Type

'  DELETEITEMSTRUCT for ownerdraw
Type DELETEITEMSTRUCT
        CtlType As Integer
        CtlID As Integer
        itemID As Integer
        hwndItem As Integer
        itemData As Long
             End Type


'  COMPAREITEMSTRUCT for ownerdraw sorting
Type COMPAREITEMSTRUCT
        CtlType As Integer
        CtlID As Integer
        hwndItem As Integer
        itemID1 As Integer
        itemData1 As Long
        itemID2 As Integer
        itemData2 As Long
End Type
```

These functions, constants, and types are vital parts of the message processing of a C or Pascal Windows application. You generally don't need to worry about it in a Visual Basic application.

```
'  Message structure
Type MSG
        hwnd As Integer
        message As Integer
        wParam As Integer
        lParam As Long
        time As Long
        pt As POINTAPI
End Type

'  Message Function Templates
Declare Function GetMessage Lib "User" (lpMsg As MSG, ByVal hWnd As ⇐
```

```
Integer, ByVal wMsgFilterMin As Integer, ByVal wMsgFilterMax As Integer) ⇐
As Integer
Declare Function TranslateMessage Lib "User" (lpMsg As MSG) As Integer
Declare Function DispatchMessage Lib "User" (lpMsg As MSG) As Long
Declare Function PeekMessage Lib "User" (lpMsg As MSG, ByVal hWnd As ⇐
Integer, ByVal wMsgFilterMin As Integer, ByVal wMsgFilterMax As Integer, ⇐
ByVal wRemoveMsg As Integer) As Integer

' PeekMessage() Options
Global Const PM_NOREMOVE = &H0
Global Const PM_REMOVE = &H1
Global Const PM_NOYIELD = &H2
```

The lstr… functions provide the C or Pascal programmer a way to manipulate strings. The standard Visual Basic string operators (=, <, <=, >, >=, and <>) work just as well.

```
Declare Function lstrcmp Lib "User" (ByVal lpString1 As Any, ByVal ⇐
lpString2 As Any) As Integer
Declare Function lstrcmpi Lib "User" (ByVal lpString1 As Any, ByVal ⇐
lpString2 As Any) As Integer
Declare Function lstrcpy Lib "Kernel" (ByVal lpString1 As Any, ByVal ⇐
lpString2 As Any) As Long
Declare Function lstrcat Lib "Kernel" (ByVal lpString1 As Any, ByVal ⇐
lpString2 As Any) As Long
Declare Function lstrlen Lib "Kernel" (ByVal lpString As Any) As Integer
```

The following functions are used to perform disk I/O. The Visual Basic disk I/O statements perform the same functions, but you might want to use these functions to avoid Visual Basic error trapping.

```
Declare Function lopen Lib "Kernel" Alias "_lopen" (ByVal lpPathName As ⇐
String, ByVal iReadWrite As Integer) As Integer
Declare Function lclose Lib "Kernel" Alias "_lclose" (ByVal hFile As ⇐
Integer) As Integer
Declare Function lcreat Lib "Kernel" Alias "_lcreat" (ByVal lpPathName As ⇐
String, ByVal iAttribute As Integer) As Integer
Declare Function llseek Lib "Kernel" Alias "_llseek" (ByVal hFile As ⇐
Integer, ByVal lOffset As Long, ByVal iOrigin As Integer) As Long
Declare Function lread Lib "Kernel" Alias "_lread" (ByVal hFile As Integer, ⇐
ByVal lpBuffer As String, ByVal wBytes As Integer) As Integer
Declare Function lwrite Lib "Kernel" Alias "_lwrite" (ByVal hFile As ⇐
Integer, ByVal lpBuffer As String, ByVal wBytes As Integer) As Integer

Global Const READAPI = 0      ' Flags for _lopen
Global Const WRITEAPI = 1
Global Const READ_WRITE = 2
```

ExitWindows is used in How-To 6.3 Exit Windows and return to DOS to be able to shut down Windows.

```
Declare Function ExitWindows Lib "User" (ByVal dwReserved As Long, ⇐
wReturnCode) As Integer
```

```
Declare Function SwapMouseButton Lib "User" (ByVal bSwap As Integer) As ⇐
Integer
Declare Function GetMessagePos Lib "User" () As Long
Declare Function GetMessageTime Lib "User" () As Long

Declare Function GetSysModalWindow Lib "User" () As Integer
Declare Function SetSysModalWindow Lib "User" (ByVal hWnd As Integer) As ⇐
Integer
```

SendMessage is used in many How-Tos throughout this book to manipulate controls by sending messages to them.

```
Declare Function SendMessage Lib "User" (ByVal hWnd As Integer, ByVal ⇐
wMsg As Integer, ByVal wParam As Integer, lParam As Any) As Long
Declare Function PostMessage Lib "User" (ByVal hWnd As Integer, ByVal ⇐
wMsg As Integer, ByVal wParam As Integer, lParam As Any) As Integer
Declare Function PostAppMessage Lib "User" (ByVal hTask As Integer, ByVal ⇐
wMsg As Integer, ByVal wParam As Integer, lParam As Any) As Integer
Declare Sub ReplyMessage Lib "User" (ByVal lReply As Long)
Declare Sub WaitMessage Lib "User" ()
Declare Function DefWindowProc Lib "User" (ByVal hWnd As Integer, ByVal ⇐
wMsg As Integer, ByVal wParam As Integer, lParam As Any) As Long
Declare Sub PostQuitMessage Lib "User" (ByVal nExitCode As Integer)
Declare Function InSendMessage Lib "User" () As Integer
```

As their names indicate, these functions are used to retrieve and set the delay for double-clicking a mouse button. Your application shouldn't use these functions; instead, let the user use the Control Panel to change the double-click delay.

```
Declare Function GetDoubleClickTime Lib "User" () As Integer
Declare Sub SetDoubleClickTime Lib "User" (ByVal wCount As Integer)
```

These functions are used to create and destroy windows. They're not required for Visual Basic programmers, since Visual Basic takes care of creating and destroying windows for us.

```
Declare Function UnregisterClass Lib "User" (ByVal lpClassName As String, ⇐
ByVal hInstance As Integer) As Integer

Declare Function SetMessageQueue Lib "User" (ByVal cMsg As Integer) As ⇐
Integer

Global Const CW_USEDEFAULT = &H8000

Declare Function CreateWindow% Lib "User" (ByVal lpClassName$, ByVal ⇐
lpWindowName$, ByVal dwStyle&, ByVal X%, ByVal Y%, ByVal nWidth%, ByVal ⇐
nHeight%, ByVal hWndParent%, ByVal hMenu%, ByVal hInstance%, ByVal ⇐
lpParam$)
Declare Function CreateWindowEx% Lib "User" (ByVal dwExStyle&, ByVal ⇐
lpClassName$, ByVal lpWindowName$, ByVal dwStyle&, ByVal X%, ByVal Y%, ⇐
ByVal nWidth%, ByVal nHeight%, ByVal hWndParent%, ByVal hMenu%, ByVal ⇐
hInstance%, ByVal lpParam$)
```

```
Declare Function IsWindow Lib "User" (ByVal hWnd As Integer) As Integer
Declare Function IsChild Lib "User" (ByVal hWndParent As Integer, ByVal ⇐
hWnd As Integer) As Integer
Declare Function DestroyWindow Lib "User" (ByVal hWnd As Integer) As ⇐
Integer

Declare Function ShowWindow Lib "User" (ByVal hWnd As Integer, ByVal ⇐
nCmdShow As Integer) As Integer
```

FlashWindow is used in How-To 4.5 Flash the title bar of my forms, as a way of attracting attention.

```
Declare Function FlashWindow Lib "User" (ByVal hWnd As Integer, ByVal ⇐
bInvert As Integer) As Integer
Declare Sub ShowOwnedPopups Lib "User" (ByVal hWnd As Integer, ByVal fShow ⇐
As Integer)
Declare Function OpenIcon Lib "User" (ByVal hWnd As Integer) As Integer
Declare Sub CloseWindow Lib "User" (ByVal hWnd As Integer)
```

MoveWindow is one way to move a form; you can also use Visual Basic's Move method.

```
Declare Sub MoveWindow Lib "User" (ByVal hWnd As Integer, ByVal X As ⇐
Integer, ByVal Y As Integer, ByVal nWidth As Integer, ByVal nHeight As ⇐
Integer, ByVal bRepaint As Integer)
Declare Sub SetWindowPos Lib "User" (ByVal hWnd As Integer, ByVal ⇐
hWndInsertAfter As Integer, ByVal X As Integer, ByVal Y As Integer, ByVal ⇐
cx As Integer, ByVal cy As Integer, ByVal wFlags As Integer)

Declare Function BeginDeferWindowPos Lib "User" (ByVal nNumWindows As ⇐
Integer)
Declare Function DeferWindowPos Lib "User" (ByVal hWinPosInfo As Integer, ⇐
ByVal hWnd as Integer, ByVal hWndInsertAfter as Integer, ByVal x, ByVal y, ⇐
ByVal cx, ByVal cy, ByVal wFlags as Integer)
Declare Sub EndDeferWindowPos Lib "User" (ByVal hWinPosInfo As Integer)

Declare Function IsWindowVisible Lib "User" (ByVal hWnd As Integer) As ⇐
Integer
Declare Function IsIconic Lib "User" (ByVal hWnd As Integer) As Integer
Declare Function AnyPopup Lib "User" () As Integer
Declare Sub BringWindowToTop Lib "User" (ByVal hWnd As Integer)
Declare Function IsZoomed Lib "User" (ByVal hWnd As Integer) As Integer
```

These constants and functions are used to manipulate the controls in a dialog box. In Visual Basic, you can simply manipulate the properties of a control directly.

```
' SetWindowPos Flags
Global Const SWP_NOSIZE = &H1
Global Const SWP_NOMOVE = &H2
Global Const SWP_NOZORDER = &H4
Global Const SWP_NOREDRAW = &H8
Global Const SWP_NOACTIVATE = &H10
```

```
Global Const SWP_DRAWFRAME = &H20
Global Const SWP_SHOWWINDOW = &H40
Global Const SWP_HIDEWINDOW = &H80
Global Const SWP_NOCOPYBITS = &H100
Global Const SWP_NOREPOSITION = &H200

Declare Sub EndDialog Lib "User" (ByVal hDlg As Integer, ByVal nResult As ⇐
Integer)
Declare Function GetDlgItem Lib "User" (ByVal hDlg As Integer, ByVal ⇐
nIDDlgItem As Integer) As Integer
Declare Sub SetDlgItemInt Lib "User" (ByVal hDlg As Integer, ByVal ⇐
nIDDlgItem As Integer, ByVal wValue As Integer, ByVal bSigned As Integer)
Declare Function GetDlgItemInt Lib "User" (ByVal hDlg As Integer, ByVal ⇐
nIDDlgItem As Integer, lpTranslated As Integer, ByVal bSigned As Integer) ⇐
As Integer
Declare Sub SetDlgItemText Lib "User" (ByVal hDlg As Integer, ByVal ⇐
nIDDlgItem As Integer, ByVal lpString As String)
Declare Function GetDlgItemText Lib "User" (ByVal hDlg As Integer, ByVal ⇐
nIDDlgItem As Integer, ByVal lpString As String, ByVal nMaxCount As ⇐
Integer) As Integer
Declare Sub CheckDlgButton Lib "User" (ByVal hDlg As Integer, ByVal ⇐
nIDButton As Integer, ByVal wCheck As Integer)
Declare Sub CheckRadioButton Lib "User" (ByVal hDlg As Integer, ByVal ⇐
nIDFirstButton As Integer, ByVal nIDLastButton As Integer, ByVal ⇐
nIDCheckButton As Integer)
Declare Function IsDlgButtonChecked Lib "User" (ByVal hDlg As Integer, ⇐
ByVal nIDButton As Integer) As Integer
Declare Function SendDlgItemMessage Lib "User" (ByVal hDlg As Integer, ⇐
ByVal nIDDlgItem As Integer, ByVal wMsg As Integer, ByVal wParam As ⇐
Integer, lParam As Any) As Long
Declare Function GetNextDlgGroupItem Lib "User" (ByVal hDlg As Integer, ⇐
ByVal hCtl As Integer, ByVal bPrevious As Integer) As Integer
Declare Function GetNextDlgTabItem Lib "User" (ByVal hDlg As Integer, ⇐
ByVal hCtl As Integer, ByVal bPrevious As Integer) As Integer
Declare Function GetDlgCtrlID Lib "User" (ByVal hWnd As Integer) As Integer
Declare Function GetDialogBaseUnits Lib "User" () As Long
Declare Function DefDlgProc Lib "User" (ByVal hDlg As Integer, ByVal ⇐
wMsg As Integer, ByVal wParam As Integer, lParam As Any) As Long

Global Const DLGWINDOWEXTRA = 30     ' Window extra bytes needed for private
dialog classes

Declare Function CallMsgFilter Lib "User" (lpMsg As MSG, ByVal nCode As ⇐
Integer) As Integer
```

Using the Visual Basic SetFocus method (or the API function SetFocus, which here is aliased to SetFocusAPI) followed by a call to the GetFocus API function is one way of returning the window handle of a control. See How-To 1.5 Quickly send a Windows message to a control.

```
Declare Function SetFocusAPI Lib "User" Alias "SetFocus" (ByVal hWnd As ⇐
Integer) As Integer
Declare Function GetFocus Lib "User" () As Integer
```

These functions are used to determine the status of Windows, such as which window is active.

```
Declare Function GetActiveWindow Lib "User" () As Integer
Declare Function GetKeyState Lib "User" (ByVal nVirtKey As Integer) As ⇐
Integer
Declare Function GetAsyncKeyState Lib "User" (ByVal vKey As Integer) As ⇐
Integer
Declare Sub GetKeyboardState Lib "User" (LpKeyState As Any)
Declare Sub SetKeyboardState Lib "User" (lpKeyState As Any)
Declare Function EnableHardwareInput Lib "User" (ByVal bEnableInput As ⇐
Integer) As Integer
Declare Function GetInputState Lib "User" () As Integer
Declare Function GetCapture Lib "User" () As Integer
Declare Function SetCapture Lib "User" (ByVal hWnd As Integer) As Integer
Declare Sub ReleaseCapture Lib "User" ()

' Windows Functions
Declare Function KillTimer Lib "User" (ByVal hWnd As Integer, ByVal ⇐
nIDEvent As Integer) As Integer
```

EnableWindow is used to enable and disable a window or control, and IsWindowEnabled returns whether a window or control is currently enabled. In Visual Basic, you can set the value of the Enabled property and query it instead.

```
Declare Function EnableWindow Lib "User" (ByVal hWnd As Integer, ByVal ⇐
aBOOL As Integer) As Integer
Declare Function IsWindowEnabled Lib "User" (ByVal hWnd As Integer) As ⇐
Integer
```

In Visual Basic, accelerators are defined in the Menu Design window and don't have to be explicitly loaded.

```
Declare Function LoadAccelerators Lib "User" (ByVal hInstance As Integer, ⇐
ByVal lpTableName As String) As Integer

Declare Function TranslateAccelerator Lib "User" (ByVal hWnd As Integer, ⇐
ByVal hAccTable As Integer, lpMsg As MSG) As Integer
```

These constants, when used with the GetSystemMetrics function, let you determine many system-wide characteristics, such as screen size. Many such characteristics can be determined by checking the properties of the Screen object.

```
' GetSystemMetrics() codes
Global Const SM_CXSCREEN = 0
Global Const SM_CYSCREEN = 1
Global Const SM_CXVSCROLL = 2
Global Const SM_CYHSCROLL = 3
Global Const SM_CYCAPTION = 4
Global Const SM_CXBORDER = 5
```

```
Global Const SM_CYBORDER = 6
Global Const SM_CXDLGFRAME = 7
Global Const SM_CYDLGFRAME = 8
Global Const SM_CYVTHUMB = 9
Global Const SM_CXHTHUMB = 10
Global Const SM_CXICON = 11
Global Const SM_CYICON = 12
Global Const SM_CXCURSOR = 13
Global Const SM_CYCURSOR = 14
Global Const SM_CYMENU = 15
Global Const SM_CXFULLSCREEN = 16
Global Const SM_CYFULLSCREEN = 17
Global Const SM_CYKANJIWINDOW = 18
Global Const SM_MOUSEPRESENT = 19
Global Const SM_CYVSCROLL = 20
Global Const SM_CXHSCROLL = 21
Global Const SM_DEBUG = 22
Global Const SM_SWAPBUTTON = 23
Global Const SM_RESERVED1 = 24
Global Const SM_RESERVED2 = 25
Global Const SM_RESERVED3 = 26
Global Const SM_RESERVED4 = 27
Global Const SM_CXMIN = 28
Global Const SM_CYMIN = 29
Global Const SM_CXSIZE = 30
Global Const SM_CYSIZE = 31
Global Const SM_CXFRAME = 32
Global Const SM_CYFRAME = 33
Global Const SM_CXMINTRACK = 34
Global Const SM_CYMINTRACK = 35
Global Const SM_CMETRICS = 36

Declare Function GetSystemMetrics Lib "User" (ByVal nIndex As Integer) As ⇐
Integer
```

You can change a window's menu by using these functions. In Visual Basic, you create a form's menu using the Menu Design Window. How-To 3.3 Make a floating pop-up menu, How-To 3.4 Modify a form's system menu, How-To 3.5 Draw a bitmapped picture in a menu, and How-To 3.6 Place font typefaces in a menu, show how to use these API functions to modify a menu after you've created it.

```
Declare Function LoadMenu Lib "User" (ByVal hInstance As Integer, ByVal ⇐
lpString As String) As Integer
Declare Function LoadMenuIndirect Lib "User" (lpMenuTemplate As ⇐
MENUITEMTEMPLATE) As Integer
Declare Function GetMenu Lib "User" (ByVal hWnd As Integer) As Integer
Declare Function SetMenu Lib "User" (ByVal hWnd As Integer, ByVal hMenu As ⇐
Integer) As Integer
Declare Function ChangeMenu Lib "User" (ByVal hMenu As Integer, ByVal ⇐
wID As Integer, ByVal lpszNew As String, ByVal wIDNew As Integer, ByVal ⇐
wChange As Integer) As Integer
```

```
Declare Function HiliteMenuItem Lib "User" (ByVal hWnd As Integer, ByVal ⇐
hMenu As Integer, ByVal wIDHiliteItem As Integer, ByVal wHilite As ⇐
Integer) As Integer
Declare Function GetMenuString Lib "User" (ByVal hMenu As Integer, ByVal ⇐
wIDItem As Integer, ByVal lpString As String, ByVal nMaxCount As Integer, ⇐
ByVal wFlag As Integer) As Integer
Declare Function GetMenuState Lib "User" (ByVal hMenu As Integer, ByVal ⇐
wId As Integer, ByVal wFlags As Integer) As Integer
Declare Sub DrawMenuBar Lib "User" (ByVal hWnd As Integer)
Declare Function GetSystemMenu Lib "User" (ByVal hWnd As Integer, ByVal ⇐
bRevert As Integer) As Integer
Declare Function CreateMenu Lib "User" () As Integer
Declare Function CreatePopupMenu Lib "User" () As Integer
Declare Function DestroyMenu Lib "User" (ByVal hMenu As Integer) As Integer
Declare Function CheckMenuItem Lib "User" (ByVal hMenu As Integer, ByVal ⇐
wIDCheckItem As Integer, ByVal wCheck As Integer) As Integer
Declare Function EnableMenuItem Lib "User" (ByVal hMenu As Integer, ByVal ⇐
wIDEnableItem As Integer, ByVal wEnable As Integer) As Integer
Declare Function GetSubMenu Lib "User" (ByVal hMenu As Integer, ByVal nPos ⇐
As Integer) As Integer
Declare Function GetMenuItemID Lib "User" (ByVal hMenu As Integer, ByVal ⇐
nPos As Integer) As Integer
Declare Function GetMenuItemCount Lib "User" (ByVal hMenu As Integer) As ⇐
Integer

Declare Function InsertMenu Lib "User" (ByVal hMenu As Integer, ByVal ⇐
nPosition As Integer, ByVal wFlags As Integer, ByVal wIDNewItem As Integer, ⇐
ByVal lpNewItem As Any) As Integer
Declare Function AppendMenu Lib "User" (ByVal hMenu As Integer, ByVal ⇐
wFlags As Integer, ByVal wIDNewItem As Integer, ByVal lpNewItem As Any) As ⇐
Integer
Declare Function ModifyMenu Lib "User" (ByVal hMenu As Integer, ByVal ⇐
nPosition As Integer, ByVal wFlags As Integer, ByVal wIDNewItem As Integer, ⇐
ByVal lpString As Any) As Integer
Declare Function RemoveMenu Lib "User" (ByVal hMenu As Integer, ByVal ⇐
nPosition As Integer, ByVal wFlags As Integer) As Integer
Declare Function DeleteMenu Lib "User" (ByVal hMenu As Integer, ByVal ⇐
nPosition As Integer, ByVal wFlags As Integer) As Integer
Declare Function SetMenuItemBitmaps Lib "User" (ByVal hMenu As Integer, ⇐
ByVal nPosition As Integer, ByVal wFlags As Integer, ByVal ⇐
hBitmapUnchecked As Integer, ByVal hBitmapChecked As Integer) As Integer
Declare Function GetMenuCheckMarkDimensions Lib "User" () As Long
Declare Function TrackPopupMenu Lib "User" (ByVal hMenu As Integer, ByVal ⇐
wFlags As Integer, ByVal x As Integer, ByVal y As Integer, ByVal nReserved ⇐
As Integer, ByVal hWnd As Integer, lpReserved As Any) As Integer

' Menu flags for Add/Check/EnableMenuItem()
Global Const MF_INSERT = &H0
Global Const MF_CHANGE = &H80
Global Const MF_APPEND = &H100
Global Const MF_DELETE = &H200
Global Const MF_REMOVE = &H1000

Global Const MF_BYCOMMAND = &H0
Global Const MF_BYPOSITION = &H400
```

```
Global Const MF_SEPARATOR = &H800

Global Const MF_ENABLED = &H0
Global Const MF_GRAYED = &H1
Global Const MF_DISABLED = &H2

Global Const MF_UNCHECKED = &H0
Global Const MF_CHECKED = &H8
Global Const MF_USECHECKBITMAPS = &H200

Global Const MF_STRING = &H0
Global Const MF_BITMAP = &H4
Global Const MF_OWNERDRAW = &H100

Global Const MF_POPUP = &H10
Global Const MF_MENUBARBREAK = &H20
Global Const MF_MENUBREAK = &H40

Global Const MF_UNHILITE = &H0
Global Const MF_HILITE = &H80

Global Const MF_SYSMENU = &H2000
Global Const MF_HELP = &H4000
Global Const MF_MOUSESELECT = &H8000

' Menu item resource format
Type MENUITEMTEMPLATEHEADER
    versionNumber As Integer
    offset As Integer
End Type

Type MENUITEMTEMPLATE
    mtOption As Integer
    mtID As Integer
    mtString As Long
End Type

Global Const MF_END = &H80

' System Menu Command Values
Global Const SC_SIZE = &HF000
Global Const SC_MOVE = &HF010
Global Const SC_MINIMIZE = &HF020
Global Const SC_MAXIMIZE = &HF030
Global Const SC_NEXTWINDOW = &HF040
Global Const SC_PREVWINDOW = &HF050
Global Const SC_CLOSE = &HF060
Global Const SC_VSCROLL = &HF070
Global Const SC_HSCROLL = &HF080
Global Const SC_MOUSEMENU = &HF090
Global Const SC_KEYMENU = &HF100
Global Const SC_ARRANGE = &HF110
Global Const SC_RESTORE = &HF120
Global Const SC_TASKLIST = &HF130

Global Const SC_ICON = SC_MINIMIZE
Global Const SC_ZOOM = SC_MAXIMIZE
```

These functions are used to update a window when it's uncovered or needs to be repainted.

```
Declare Sub UpdateWindow Lib "User" (ByVal hWnd As Integer)
Declare Function SetActiveWindow Lib "User" (ByVal hWnd As Integer) As ⇐
Integer

Declare Function BeginPaint Lib "User" (ByVal hWnd As Integer, lpPaint As ⇐
PAINTSTRUCT) As Integer
Declare Sub EndPaint Lib "User" (ByVal hWnd As Integer, lpPaint As ⇐
PAINTSTRUCT)
Declare Function GetUpdateRect Lib "User" (ByVal hWnd As Integer, lpRect ⇐
As RECT, ByVal bErase As Integer) As Integer
Declare Function GetUpdateRgn Lib "User" (ByVal hWnd As Integer, ByVal ⇐
hRgn As Integer, ByVal fErase As Integer) As Integer

Declare Function ExcludeUpdateRgn Lib "User" (ByVal hDC As Integer, ByVal ⇐
hWnd As Integer) As Integer

Declare Sub InvalidateRect Lib "User" (ByVal hWnd As Integer, lpRect As ⇐
RECT, ByVal bErase As Integer)
Declare Sub ValidateRect Lib "User" (ByVal hWnd As Integer, lpRect As RECT)

Declare Sub InvalidateRgn Lib "User" (ByVal hWnd As Integer, ByVal hRgn As ⇐
Integer, ByVal bErase As Integer)
Declare Sub ValidateRgn Lib "User" (ByVal hWnd As Integer, ByVal hRgn As ⇐
Integer)
```

How-To 2.1 Scroll all the objects in a window, shows you how to use ScrollWindow.

```
Declare Sub ScrollWindow Lib "User" (ByVal hWnd As Integer, ByVal XAmount ⇐
As Integer, ByVal YAmount As Integer, lpRect As RECT, lpClipRect As RECT)
Declare Function ScrollDC Lib "User" (ByVal hDC As Integer, ByVal dx As ⇐
Integer, ByVal dy As Integer, lprcScroll As RECT, lprcClip As RECT, ByVal ⇐
hRgnUpdate As Integer, lprcUpdate As RECT) As Integer

Declare Function SetScrollPos Lib "User" (ByVal hWnd As Integer, ByVal ⇐
nBar As Integer, ByVal nPos As Integer, ByVal bRedraw As Integer) As Integer
Declare Function GetScrollPos Lib "User" (ByVal hWnd As Integer, ByVal ⇐
nBar As Integer) As Integer
Declare Sub SetScrollRange Lib "User" (ByVal hWnd As Integer, ByVal nBar ⇐
As Integer, ByVal nMinPos As Integer, ByVal nMaxPos As Integer, ByVal ⇐
bRedraw As Integer)
Declare Sub GetScrollRange Lib "User" (ByVal hWnd As Integer, ByVal nBar ⇐
As Integer, lpMinPos As Integer, lpMaxPos As Integer)
Declare Sub ShowScrollBar Lib "User" (ByVal hWnd As Integer, ByVal wBar ⇐
As Integer, ByVal bShow As Integer)
```

These functions control aspects of a window, such as its property data and its caption. Visual Basic programmers can directly manipulate most of that data using properties like Caption.

```
Declare Function SetProp Lib "User" (ByVal hWnd As Integer, ByVal lpString ⇐
As String, ByVal hData As Integer) As Integer
```

```
Declare Function GetProp Lib "User" (ByVal hWnd As Integer, ByVal lpString ⇐
As Any) As Integer
Declare Function RemoveProp Lib "User" (ByVal hWnd As Integer, ByVal ⇐
lpString As String) As Integer
Declare Sub SetWindowText Lib "User" (ByVal hWnd As Integer, ByVal ⇐
lpString As String)
Declare Function GetWindowText Lib "User" (ByVal hWnd As Integer, ByVal ⇐
lpString As String, ByVal aint As Integer) As Integer
Declare Function GetWindowTextLength Lib "User" (ByVal hWnd As Integer) ⇐
As Integer

Declare Sub GetClientRect Lib "User" (ByVal hWnd As Integer, lpRect As RECT)
Declare Sub GetWindowRect Lib "User" (ByVal hWnd As Integer, lpRect As RECT)
Declare Sub AdjustWindowRect Lib "User" (lpRect As RECT, ByVal dwStyle As ⇐
Long, ByVal bMenu As Integer)
Declare Sub AdjustWindowRectEx Lib "User" (lpRect As RECT, ByVal dsStyle ⇐
As Long, ByVal bMenu As Integer, ByVal dwEsStyle As Long)
```

The API function MessageBox is the same as Visual Basic's MsgBox statement and function. You can use these constants to give mnemonic names to the values you pass to the MsgBox statement and function for the command buttons and icons.

```
' MessageBox() Flags
Global Const MB_OK = &H0
Global Const MB_OKCANCEL = &H1
Global Const MB_ABORTRETRYIGNORE = &H2
Global Const MB_YESNOCANCEL = &H3
Global Const MB_YESNO = &H4
Global Const MB_RETRYCANCEL = &H5

Global Const MB_ICONHAND = &H10
Global Const MB_ICONQUESTION = &H20
Global Const MB_ICONEXCLAMATION = &H30
Global Const MB_ICONASTERISK = &H40

Global Const MB_ICONINFORMATION = MB_ICONASTERISK
Global Const MB_ICONSTOP = MB_ICONHAND

Global Const MB_DEFBUTTON1 = &H0
Global Const MB_DEFBUTTON2 = &H100
Global Const MB_DEFBUTTON3 = &H200

Global Const MB_APPLMODAL = &H0
Global Const MB_SYSTEMMODAL = &H1000
Global Const MB_TASKMODAL = &H2000

Global Const MB_NOFOCUS = &H8000

Global Const MB_TYPEMASK = &HF
Global Const MB_ICONMASK = &HF0
Global Const MB_DEFMASK = &HF00
Global Const MB_MODEMASK = &H3000
Global Const MB_MISCMASK = &HC000

' Dialog Box Command IDs
```

```
Global Const IDOK = 1
Global Const IDCANCEL = 2
Global Const IDABORT = 3
Global Const IDRETRY = 4
Global Const IDIGNORE = 5
Global Const IDYES = 6
Global Const IDNO = 7

Declare Function MessageBox Lib "User" (ByVal hWnd As Integer, ByVal lpText ⇐
As String, ByVal lpCaption As String, ByVal wType As Integer) As Integer
Declare Sub MessageBeep Lib "User" (ByVal wType As Integer)

Declare Function ShowCursor Lib "User" (ByVal bShow As Integer) As Integer
Declare Sub SetCursorPos Lib "User" (ByVal X As Integer, ByVal Y As Integer)
Declare Function SetCursor Lib "User" (ByVal hCursor As Integer) As Integer
Declare Sub GetCursorPos Lib "User" (lpPoint As POINTAPI)
Declare Sub ClipCursor Lib "User" (lpRect As Any)
```

How-To 2.10 Determine and modify the rate at which a text box's caret blinks, uses GetCaretBlinkTime and SetCaretBlinkTime.

```
Declare Function GetCaretBlinkTime Lib "User" () As Integer
Declare Sub SetCaretBlinkTime Lib "User" (ByVal wMSeconds As Integer)
Declare Sub CreateCaret Lib "User" (ByVal hWnd As Integer, ByVal hBitmap ⇐
As Integer, ByVal nWidth As Integer, ByVal nHeight As Integer)
Declare Sub DestroyCaret Lib "User" ()
Declare Sub HideCaret Lib "User" (ByVal hWnd As Integer)
Declare Sub ShowCaret Lib "User" (ByVal hWnd As Integer)
Declare Sub SetCaretPos Lib "User" (ByVal X As Integer, ByVal Y As Integer)
Declare Sub GetCaretPos Lib "User" (lpPoint As POINTAPI)
```

These functions convert between screen units and window coordinates; in Visual Basic, both are measured in twips by default.

```
Declare Sub ClientToScreen Lib "User" (ByVal hWnd As Integer, lpPoint As ⇐
POINTAPI)
Declare Sub ScreenToClient Lib "User" (ByVal hWnd As Integer, lpPoint As ⇐
POINTAPI)

Declare Function WindowFromPoint Lib "User" (ByVal Point As Any) As Integer
Declare Function ChildWindowFromPoint Lib "User" (ByVal hWnd As Integer, ⇐
ByVal Point As Any) As Integer
```

These constants and functions can be used to determine and set the colors Windows uses to display parts of a window, such as the background color or the border color.

```
' Color Types
Global Const CTLCOLOR_MSGBOX = 0
Global Const CTLCOLOR_EDIT = 1
Global Const CTLCOLOR_LISTBOX = 2
Global Const CTLCOLOR_BTN = 3
Global Const CTLCOLOR_DLG = 4
Global Const CTLCOLOR_SCROLLBAR = 5
Global Const CTLCOLOR_STATIC = 6
```

```
Global Const CTLCOLOR_MAX = 8          ' three bits max

Global Const COLOR_SCROLLBAR = 0
Global Const COLOR_BACKGROUND = 1
Global Const COLOR_ACTIVECAPTION = 2
Global Const COLOR_INACTIVECAPTION = 3
Global Const COLOR_MENU = 4
Global Const COLOR_WINDOW = 5
Global Const COLOR_WINDOWFRAME = 6
Global Const COLOR_MENUTEXT = 7
Global Const COLOR_WINDOWTEXT = 8
Global Const COLOR_CAPTIONTEXT = 9
Global Const COLOR_ACTIVEBORDER = 10
Global Const COLOR_INACTIVEBORDER = 11
Global Const COLOR_APPWORKSPACE = 12
Global Const COLOR_HIGHLIGHT = 13
Global Const COLOR_HIGHLIGHTTEXT = 14
Global Const COLOR_BTNFACE = 15
Global Const COLOR_BTNSHADOW = 16
Global Const COLOR_GRAYTEXT = 17
Global Const COLOR_BTNTEXT = 18
Global Const COLOR_ENDCOLORS = COLOR_BTNTEXT

Declare Function GetSysColor Lib "User" (ByVal nIndex As Integer) As Long
Declare Sub SetSysColors Lib "User" (ByVal nChanges As Integer, lpSysColor ⇐
As Integer, lpColorValues As Long)
```

These functions are used when painting regions; Visual Basic's graphics methods can be used more easily.

```
Declare Function FillRgn Lib "User" (ByVal hDC As Integer, ByVal hRgn As ⇐
Integer, ByVal hBrush As Integer) As Integer
Declare Function FrameRgn Lib "User" (ByVal hDC As Integer, ByVal hRgn As ⇐
Integer, ByVal hBrush As Integer, ByVal nWidth As Integer, ByVal nHeight ⇐
As Integer) As Integer
Declare Function InvertRgn Lib "User" (ByVal hDC As Integer, ByVal hRgn As ⇐
Integer) As Integer
Declare Function PaintRgn Lib "User" (ByVal hDC As Integer, ByVal hRgn As ⇐
Integer) As Integer
Declare Function PtInRegion Lib "User" (ByVal hRgn As Integer, ByVal X As ⇐
Integer, ByVal Y As Integer) As Integer

Declare Sub DrawFocusRect Lib "User" (ByVal hDC As Integer, lpRect As RECT)
Declare Function FillRect Lib "User" (ByVal hDC As Integer, lpRect As RECT, ⇐
ByVal hBrush As Integer) As Integer
Declare Function FrameRect Lib "User" (ByVal hDC As Integer, lpRect As ⇐
RECT, ByVal hBrush As Integer) As Integer
Declare Sub InvertRect Lib "User" (ByVal hDC As Integer, lpRect As RECT)
Declare Sub SetRect Lib "User" (lpRect As RECT, ByVal X1 As Integer, ByVal ⇐
Y1 As Integer, ByVal X2 As Integer, ByVal Y2 As Integer)
Declare Sub SetRectEmpty Lib "User" (lpRect As RECT)
Declare Function CopyRect Lib "User" (lpDestRect As RECT, lpSourceRect As ⇐
RECT) As Integer
Declare Sub InflateRect Lib "User" (lpRect As RECT, ByVal X As Integer, ⇐
ByVal Y As Integer)
```

```
Declare Function IntersectRect Lib "User" (lpDestRect As RECT, lpSrc1Rect ⇐
As RECT, lpSrc2Rect As RECT) As Integer
Declare Function UnionRect Lib "User" (lpDestRect As RECT, lpSrc1Rect As ⇐
RECT, lpSrc2Rect As RECT) As Integer
Declare Sub OffsetRect Lib "User" (lpRect As RECT, ByVal X As Integer, ⇐
ByVal Y As Integer)
Declare Function IsRectEmpty Lib "User" (lpRect As RECT) As Integer
Declare Function EqualRect Lib "User" (lpRect1 As RECT, lpRect2 As RECT) As ⇐
Integer
Declare Function PtInRect Lib "User" (lpRect As RECT, ByVal Point As Any) As ⇐
Integer
Declare Function RectVisible Lib "User" (ByVal hDC As Integer, lpRect As ⇐
RECT) As Integer
Declare Function RectInRegion Lib "User" (ByVal hRgn As Integer, lpRect As ⇐
RECT) As Integer

Declare Function GetCurrentTime Lib "User" () As Long
Declare Function GetTickCount Lib "User" () As Long
```

See How-To 5.8 Arrange the icons on the Windows desktop, for one use of GetDesktopWindow.

```
Declare Function GetDesktopHwnd Lib "User" () As Integer
Declare Function GetDesktopWindow Lib "User" () As Integer
```

These functions are used when manipulating parent and child windows.

```
Declare Function GetParent Lib "User" (ByVal hWnd As Integer) As Integer
Declare Function SetParent Lib "User" (ByVal hWndChild As Integer, ByVal ⇐
hWndNewParent As Integer) As Integer
Declare Function FindWindow Lib "User" (lpClassName As Any, lpWindowName ⇐
As Any) As Integer
Declare Function GetClassName Lib "User" (ByVal hWnd As Integer, ByVal ⇐
lpClassName As String, ByVal nMaxCount As Integer) As Integer
Declare Function GetTopWindow Lib "User" (ByVal hWnd As Integer) As Integer
Declare Function GetNextWindow Lib "User" (ByVal hWnd As Integer, ByVal ⇐
wFlag As Integer) As Integer
Declare Function GetWindowTask Lib "User" (ByVal hWnd As Integer) As Integer
Declare Function GetLastActivePopup Lib "User" (ByVal hwndOwnder As ⇐
Integer) As Integer

' GetWindow() Constants
Global Const GW_HWNDFIRST = 0
Global Const GW_HWNDLAST = 1
Global Const GW_HWNDNEXT = 2
Global Const GW_HWNDPREV = 3
Global Const GW_OWNER = 4
Global Const GW_CHILD = 5

Declare Function GetWindow Lib "User" (ByVal hWnd As Integer, ByVal wCmd As ⇐
Integer) As Integer
```

These cursor ID constants aren't the right values for changing the MousePointer property. Use the values 0 through 11 instead.

```
' Standard Cursor IDs
Global Const IDC_ARROW = 32512&
Global Const IDC_IBEAM = 32513&
Global Const IDC_WAIT = 32514&
Global Const IDC_CROSS = 32515&
Global Const IDC_UPARROW = 32516&
Global Const IDC_SIZE = 32640&
Global Const IDC_ICON = 32641&
Global Const IDC_SIZENWSE = 32642&
Global Const IDC_SIZENESW = 32643&
Global Const IDC_SIZEWE = 32644&
Global Const IDC_SIZENS = 32645&
```

Since Visual Basic .EXE applications don't contain normal resources like bitmaps, the only way to use these functions and constants is when loading resources from a custom DLL.

```
' Resource Loading Routines
Declare Function LoadBitmap Lib "User" (ByVal hInstance As Integer, ByVal ⇐
lpBitmapName As Any) As Integer
Declare Function LoadCursor Lib "User" (ByVal hInstance As Integer, ByVal ⇐
lpCursorName As Any) As Integer
Declare Function CreateCursor Lib "User" (ByVal hInstance%, ByVal ⇐
nXhotspot%, ByVal nYhotspot%, ByVal nWidth%, ByVal nHeight%, ByVal ⇐
lpANDbitPlane As Any, ByVal lpXORbitPlane As Any) As Integer
Declare Function DestroyCursor Lib "User" (ByVal hCursor As Integer) As ⇐
Integer
Declare Function LoadIcon Lib "User" (ByVal hInstance As Integer, ByVal ⇐
lpIconName As Any) As Integer
Declare Function CreateIcon Lib "User" (ByVal hInstance%, ByVal nWidth%, ⇐
ByVal nHeight%, ByVal nPlanes%, ByVal nBitsPixel%, ByVal lpANDbits As Any, ⇐
ByVal lpXORbits As Any) As Integer
Declare Function DestroyIcon Lib "User" (ByVal hIcon As Integer) As Integer

Global Const ORD_LANGDRIVER = 1      ' The ordinal number for the entry ⇐
point of
    ' language drivers.

' Standard Icon IDs
Global Const IDI_APPLICATION = 32512&
Global Const IDI_HAND = 32513&
Global Const IDI_QUESTION = 32514&
Global Const IDI_EXCLAMATION = 32515&
Global Const IDI_ASTERISK = 32516&

Declare Function LoadString Lib "User" (ByVal hInstance As Integer, ByVal ⇐
wID As Integer, ByVal lpBuffer As Any, ByVal nBufferMax As Integer) As ⇐
Integer

Declare Function AddFontResource Lib "GDI" (ByVal lpFilename As Any) As ⇐
Integer
Declare Function RemoveFontResource Lib "GDI" (ByVal lpFilename As Any) ⇐
As  Integer
```

' Control Manager Structures and Definitions

In this section, the constants with comments "Notification Codes" and that start with EN_, BN_, LBN_, and CBN_ are notification messages that Visual Basic handles with event subroutines.

' Edit Control Styles

See How-To 4.8 Prevent text typed into a text box from appearing on screen, and How-To 4.9 Prevent user access to a window or file, for examples of the ES_PASSWORD style.

```
Global Const ES_LEFT = &H0&
Global Const ES_CENTER = &H1&
Global Const ES_RIGHT = &H2&
Global Const ES_MULTILINE = &H4&
Global Const ES_UPPERCASE = &H8&
Global Const ES_LOWERCASE = &H10&
Global Const ES_PASSWORD = &H20&
Global Const ES_AUTOVSCROLL = &H40&
Global Const ES_AUTOHSCROLL = &H80&
Global Const ES_NOHIDESEL = &H100&
Global Const ES_OEMCONVERT = &H400&

' Edit Control Notification Codes
Global Const EN_SETFOCUS = &H100
Global Const EN_KILLFOCUS = &H200
Global Const EN_CHANGE = &H300
Global Const EN_UPDATE = &H400
Global Const EN_ERRSPACE = &H500
Global Const EN_MAXTEXT = &H501
Global Const EN_HSCROLL = &H601
Global Const EN_VSCROLL = &H602
```

' Edit Control Messages

See How-To 2.4 Scroll a text box under program control, for an example of how to use the EM_LINESCROLL message and How-To 4.8 Prevent text typed into a text box from appearing on screen, for an example of using the EM_SETPASSWORDCHAR message.

```
Global Const EM_GETSEL = WM_USER+0
Global Const EM_SETSEL = WM_USER+1
Global Const EM_GETRECT = WM_USER+2
Global Const EM_SETRECT = WM_USER+3
Global Const EM_SETRECTNP = WM_USER+4
Global Const EM_SCROLL = WM_USER+5
Global Const EM_LINESCROLL = WM_USER+6
Global Const EM_GETMODIFY = WM_USER+7
Global Const EM_SETMODIFY = WM_USER+8
Global Const EM_GETLINECOUNT = WM_USER+9
Global Const EM_LINEINDEX = WM_USER+10
Global Const EM_SETHANDLE = WM_USER+12
```

```
Global Const EM_GETHANDLE = WM_USER+13
Global Const EM_GETTHUMB = WM_USER+14
Global Const EM_LINELENGTH = WM_USER+17
Global Const EM_REPLACESEL = WM_USER+18
Global Const EM_SETFONT = WM_USER+19
Global Const EM_GETLINE = WM_USER+20
Global Const EM_LIMITTEXT = WM_USER+21
Global Const EM_CANUNDO = WM_USER+22
Global Const EM_UNDO = WM_USER+23
Global Const EM_FMTLINES = WM_USER+24
Global Const EM_LINEFROMCHAR = WM_USER+25
Global Const EM_SETWORDBREAK = WM_USER+26
Global Const EM_SETTABSTOPS = WM_USER+27
Global Const EM_SETPASSWORDCHAR = WM_USER+28
Global Const EM_EMPTYUNDOBUFFER = WM_USER+29
Global Const EM_MSGMAX = WM_USER+30

'  Button Control Styles
Global Const BS_PUSHBUTTON = &H0&
Global Const BS_DEFPUSHBUTTON = &H1&
Global Const BS_CHECKBOX = &H2&
Global Const BS_AUTOCHECKBOX = &H3&
Global Const BS_RADIOBUTTON = &H4&
Global Const BS_3STATE = &H5&
Global Const BS_AUTO3STATE = &H6&
Global Const BS_GROUPBOX = &H7&
Global Const BS_USERBUTTON = &H8&
Global Const BS_AUTORADIOBUTTON = &H9&
Global Const BS_PUSHBOX = &HA&
Global Const BS_OWNERDRAW = &HB&
Global Const BS_LEFTTEXT = &H20&

'  User Button Notification Codes
Global Const BN_CLICKED = 0
Global Const BN_PAINT = 1
Global Const BN_HILITE = 2
Global Const BN_UNHILITE = 3
Global Const BN_DISABLE = 4
Global Const BN_DOUBLECLICKED = 5

'  Button Control Messages
Global Const BM_GETCHECK = WM_USER+0
Global Const BM_SETCHECK = WM_USER+1
Global Const BM_GETSTATE = WM_USER+2
Global Const BM_SETSTATE = WM_USER+3
Global Const BM_SETSTYLE = WM_USER+4

'  Static Control Constants
Global Const SS_LEFT = &H0&
Global Const SS_CENTER = &H1&
Global Const SS_RIGHT = &H2&
Global Const SS_ICON = &H3&
Global Const SS_BLACKRECT = &H4&
Global Const SS_GRAYRECT = &H5&
```

```
Global Const SS_WHITERECT = &H6&
Global Const SS_BLACKFRAME = &H7&
Global Const SS_GRAYFRAME = &H8&
Global Const SS_WHITEFRAME = &H9&
Global Const SS_USERITEM = &HA&
Global Const SS_SIMPLE = &HB&
Global Const SS_LEFTNOWORDWRAP = &HC&
Global Const SS_NOPREFIX = &H80&      ' Don't do "&" character translation
```

C and Pascal programmers use these functions to manipulate dialog boxes; in Visual Basic, a form's methods can be used instead.

```
' Dialog Manager Routines
Declare Function IsDialogMessage Lib "User" (ByVal hDlg As Integer, lpMsg ⇐
As MSG) As Integer

Declare Sub MapDialogRect Lib "User" (ByVal hDlg As Integer, lpRect As RECT)

Declare Function DlgDirList Lib "User" (ByVal hDlg As Integer, ByVal ⇐
lpPathSpec As String, ByVal nIDListBox As Integer, ByVal nIDStaticPath As ⇐
Integer, ByVal wFiletype As Integer) As Integer
Declare Function DlgDirSelect Lib "User" (ByVal hDlg As Integer, ByVal ⇐
lpString As String, ByVal nIDListBox As Integer) As Integer
Declare Function DlgDirListComboBox Lib "User" (ByVal hDlg As Integer, ⇐
ByVal lpPathSpec As String, ByVal nIDComboBox As Integer, ByVal ⇐
nIDStaticPath As Integer, ByVal wFileType As Integer) As Integer
Declare Function DlgDirSelectComboBox Lib "User" (ByVal hDlg As Integer, ⇐
ByVal lpString As String, ByVal nIDComboBox As Integer) As Integer

' Dialog Styles
Global Const DS_ABSALIGN = &H1&
Global Const DS_SYSMODAL = &H2&
Global Const DS_LOCALEDIT = &H20&      ' Edit items get Local storage.
Global Const DS_SETFONT = &H40&        ' User specified font for Dlg ⇐
controls
Global Const DS_MODALFRAME = &H80&     ' Can be combined with WS_CAPTION
Global Const DS_NOIDLEMSG = &H100&     ' WM_ENTERIDLE message will not be ⇐
sent

Global Const DM_GETDEFID = WM_USER+0
Global Const DM_SETDEFID = WM_USER+1
Global Const DC_HASDEFID = &H534%      '0x534B

' Dialog Codes
Global Const DLGC_WANTARROWS = &H1      ' Control wants arrow keys
Global Const DLGC_WANTTAB = &H2         ' Control wants tab keys
Global Const DLGC_WANTALLKEYS = &H4     ' Control wants all keys
Global Const DLGC_WANTMESSAGE = &H4     ' Pass message to control
Global Const DLGC_HASSETSEL = &H8       ' Understands EM_SETSEL message
Global Const DLGC_DEFPUSHBUTTON = &H10 ' Default pushbutton
Global Const DLGC_UNDEFPUSHBUTTON = &H20 ' Non-default pushbutton
Global Const DLGC_RADIOBUTTON = &H40    ' Radio button
Global Const DLGC_WANTCHARS = &H80      ' Want WM_CHAR messages
Global Const DLGC_STATIC = &H100        ' Static item: don't include
Global Const DLGC_BUTTON = &H2000       ' Button item: can be checked
```

```
Global Const LB_CTLCODE = 0&

' Listbox Return Values
Global Const LB_OKAY = 0
Global Const LB_ERR = (-1)
Global Const LB_ERRSPACE = (-2)

'
' The idStaticPath parameter to DlgDirList can have the following values
' ORed if the list box should show other details of the files along with
' the name of the files;

' all other details also will be returned

' Listbox Notification Codes
Global Const LBN_ERRSPACE = (-2)
Global Const LBN_SELCHANGE = 1
Global Const LBN_DBLCLK = 2
Global Const LBN_SELCANCEL = 3
Global Const LBN_SETFOCUS = 4
Global Const LBN_KILLFOCUS = 5

' Listbox messages
Global Const LB_ADDSTRING = (WM_USER+1)
Global Const LB_INSERTSTRING = (WM_USER+2)
Global Const LB_DELETESTRING = (WM_USER+3)
Global Const LB_RESETCONTENT = (WM_USER+5)
Global Const LB_SETSEL = (WM_USER+6)
Global Const LB_SETCURSEL = (WM_USER+7)
Global Const LB_GETSEL = (WM_USER+8)
Global Const LB_GETCURSEL = (WM_USER+9)
Global Const LB_GETTEXT = (WM_USER+10)
Global Const LB_GETTEXTLEN = (WM_USER+11)
Global Const LB_GETCOUNT = (WM_USER+12)
Global Const LB_SELECTSTRING = (WM_USER+13)
```

The project in How-To 1.4 Make a file dialog box using APIs, uses the LB_DIR message to fill list boxes with file and directory names.

```
Global Const LB_DIR = (WM_USER+14)
Global Const LB_GETTOPINDEX = (WM_USER+15)
Global Const LB_FINDSTRING = (WM_USER+16)
Global Const LB_GETSELCOUNT = (WM_USER+17)
Global Const LB_GETSELITEMS = (WM_USER+18)
Global Const LB_SETTABSTOPS = (WM_USER+19)
Global Const LB_GETHORIZONTALEXTENT = (WM_USER+20)
Global Const LB_SETHORIZONTALEXTENT = (WM_USER+21)
Global Const LB_SETCOLUMNWIDTH = (WM_USER+22)
Global Const LB_SETTOPINDEX = (WM_USER+24)
Global Const LB_GETITEMRECT = (WM_USER+25)
Global Const LB_GETITEMDATA = (WM_USER+26)
Global Const LB_SETITEMDATA = (WM_USER+27)
Global Const LB_SELITEMRANGE = (WM_USER+28)
Global Const LB_MSGMAX = (WM_USER+33)

' Listbox Styles
```

```
Global Const LBS_NOTIFY = &H1&
Global Const LBS_SORT = &H2&
Global Const LBS_NOREDRAW = &H4&
Global Const LBS_MULTIPLESEL = &H8&
Global Const LBS_OWNERDRAWFIXED = &H10&
Global Const LBS_OWNERDRAWVARIABLE = &H20&
Global Const LBS_HASSTRINGS = &H40&
Global Const LBS_USETABSTOPS = &H80&
Global Const LBS_NOINTEGRALHEIGHT = &H100&
Global Const LBS_MULTICOLUMN = &H200&
Global Const LBS_WANTKEYBOARDINPUT = &H400&
Global Const LBS_EXTENDEDSEL = &H800&
Global Const LBS_STANDARD = (LBS_NOTIFY Or LBS_SORT Or WS_VSCROLL Or ⇐
WS_BORDER)

'  Combo Box return Values
Global Const CB_OKAY = 0
Global Const CB_ERR = (-1)
Global Const CB_ERRSPACE = (-2)

'  Combo Box Notification Codes
Global Const CBN_ERRSPACE = (-1)
Global Const CBN_SELCHANGE = 1
Global Const CBN_DBLCLK = 2
Global Const CBN_SETFOCUS = 3
Global Const CBN_KILLFOCUS = 4
Global Const CBN_EDITCHANGE = 5
Global Const CBN_EDITUPDATE = 6
Global Const CBN_DROPDOWN = 7

'  Combo Box styles
Global Const CBS_SIMPLE = &H1&
Global Const CBS_DROPDOWN = &H2&
Global Const CBS_DROPDOWNLIST = &H3&
Global Const CBS_OWNERDRAWFIXED = &H10&
Global Const CBS_OWNERDRAWVARIABLE = &H20&
Global Const CBS_AUTOHSCROLL = &H40&
Global Const CBS_OEMCONVERT = &H80&
Global Const CBS_SORT = &H100&
Global Const CBS_HASSTRINGS = &H200&
Global Const CBS_NOINTEGRALHEIGHT = &H400&

'  Combo Box messages
Global Const CB_GETEDITSEL = (WM_USER+0)
Global Const CB_LIMITTEXT = (WM_USER+1)
Global Const CB_SETEDITSEL = (WM_USER+2)
Global Const CB_ADDSTRING = (WM_USER+3)
Global Const CB_DELETESTRING = (WM_USER+4)
Global Const CB_DIR = (WM_USER+5)
Global Const CB_GETCOUNT = (WM_USER+6)
Global Const CB_GETCURSEL = (WM_USER+7)
Global Const CB_GETLBTEXT = (WM_USER+8)
Global Const CB_GETLBTEXTLEN = (WM_USER+9)
Global Const CB_INSERTSTRING = (WM_USER+10)
```

```
Global Const CB_RESETCONTENT = (WM_USER+11)
Global Const CB_FINDSTRING = (WM_USER+12)
Global Const CB_SELECTSTRING = (WM_USER+13)
Global Const CB_SETCURSEL = (WM_USER+14)
Global Const CB_SHOWDROPDOWN = (WM_USER+15)
Global Const CB_GETITEMDATA = (WM_USER+16)
Global Const CB_SETITEMDATA = (WM_USER+17)
Global Const CB_GETDROPPEDCONTROLRECT = (WM_USER+18)
Global Const CB_MSGMAX = (WM_USER+19)

' Scroll Bar Styles
Global Const SBS_HORZ = &H0&
Global Const SBS_VERT = &H1&
Global Const SBS_TOPALIGN = &H2&
Global Const SBS_LEFTALIGN = &H2&
Global Const SBS_BOTTOMALIGN = &H4&
Global Const SBS_RIGHTALIGN = &H4&
Global Const SBS_SIZEBOXTOPLEFTALIGN = &H2&
Global Const SBS_SIZEBOXBOTTOMRIGHTALIGN = &H4&
Global Const SBS_SIZEBOX = &H8&
```

Sound is much more complicated in a multitasking environment like Windows than normal single-tasking DOS. See How-To 7.2 Make a replacement for QuickBasic's Sound statement, and How-To 7.3 Make music in Visual Basic.

```
' Sound Functions
'
Declare Function OpenSound Lib "Sound" () As Integer
Declare Sub CloseSound Lib "Sound" ()
Declare Function SetVoiceQueueSize Lib "Sound" (ByVal nVoice As Integer, ⇐
ByVal nBytes As Integer) As Integer
Declare Function SetVoiceNote Lib "Sound" (ByVal nVoice As Integer, ByVal ⇐
nValue As Integer, ByVal nLength As Integer, ByVal nCdots As Integer) As ⇐
Integer
Declare Function SetVoiceAccent Lib "Sound" (ByVal nVoice As Integer, ⇐
ByVal nTempo As Integer, ByVal nVolume As Integer, ByVal nMode As Integer, ⇐
ByVal nPitch As Integer) As Integer
Declare Function SetVoiceEnvelope Lib "Sound" (ByVal nVoice As Integer, ⇐
ByVal nShape As Integer, ByVal nRepeat As Integer) As Integer
Declare Function SetSoundNoise Lib "Sound" (ByVal nSource As Integer, ⇐
ByVal nDuration As Integer) As Integer
Declare Function SetVoiceSound Lib "Sound" (ByVal nVoice As Integer, ⇐
ByVal lFrequency As Long, ByVal nDuration As Integer) As Integer
Declare Function StartSound Lib "Sound" () As Integer
Declare Function StopSound Lib "Sound" () As Integer
Declare Function WaitSoundState Lib "Sound" (ByVal nState As Integer) As ⇐
Integer
Declare Function SyncAllVoices Lib "Sound" () As Integer
Declare Function CountVoiceNotes Lib "Sound" (ByVal nVoice As Integer) As ⇐
Integer
Declare Function GetThresholdEvent Lib "Sound" () As Integer
Declare Function GetThresholdStatus Lib "Sound" () As Integer
```

```
Declare Function SetVoiceThreshold Lib "Sound" (ByVal nVoice As Integer, ⇐
ByVal nNotes As Integer) As Integer

' WaitSoundState() Constants
Global Const S_QUEUEEMPTY = 0
Global Const S_THRESHOLD = 1
Global Const S_ALLTHRESHOLD = 2

' Accent Modes
Global Const S_NORMAL = 0
Global Const S_LEGATO = 1
Global Const S_STACCATO = 2

' SetSoundNoise() Sources
Global Const S_PERIOD512 = 0    ' Freq = N/512 high pitch, less coarse hiss
Global Const S_PERIOD1024 = 1   ' Freq = N/1024
Global Const S_PERIOD2048 = 2   ' Freq = N/2048 low pitch, more coarse hiss
Global Const S_PERIODVOICE = 3  ' Source is frequency from voice channel (3)
Global Const S_WHITE512 = 4     ' Freq = N/512 high pitch, less coarse hiss
Global Const S_WHITE1024 = 5    ' Freq = N/1024
Global Const S_WHITE2048 = 6    ' Freq = N/2048 low pitch, more coarse hiss
Global Const S_WHITEVOICE = 7   ' Source is frequency from voice channel (3)

Global Const S_SERDVNA = (-1)   ' Device not available
Global Const S_SEROFM = (-2)    ' Out of memory
Global Const S_SERMACT = (-3)   ' Music active
Global Const S_SERQFUL = (-4)   ' Queue full
Global Const S_SERBDNT = (-5)   ' Invalid note
Global Const S_SERDLN = (-6)    ' Invalid note length
Global Const S_SERDCC = (-7)    ' Invalid note count
Global Const S_SERDTP = (-8)    ' Invalid tempo
Global Const S_SERDVL = (-9)    ' Invalid volume
Global Const S_SERDMD = (-10)   ' Invalid mode
Global Const S_SERDSH = (-11)   ' Invalid shape
Global Const S_SERDPT = (-12)   ' Invalid pitch
Global Const S_SERDFQ = (-13)   ' Invalid frequency
Global Const S_SERDDR = (-14)   ' Invalid duration
Global Const S_SERDSR = (-15)   ' Invalid source
Global Const S_SERDST = (-16)   ' Invalid state
```

Communication is also more complex in Windows than in DOS. See How-To 7.4 Create a phone dialer in Visual Basic, and How-To 7.5 Perform serial I/O in Visual Basic.

```
' COMM declarations
'
Global Const NOPARITY = 0
Global Const ODDPARITY = 1
Global Const EVENPARITY = 2
Global Const MARKPARITY = 3
Global Const SPACEPARITY = 4

Global Const ONESTOPBIT = 0
Global Const ONE5STOPBITS = 1
```

```
Global Const TWOSTOPBITS = 2

Global Const IGNORE = 0         '  Ignore signal
Global Const INFINITE = &HFFFF       '  Infinite timeout

'  Error Flags
Global Const CE_RXOVER = &H1 '  Receive Queue overflow
Global Const CE_OVERRUN = &H2          '  Receive Overrun Error
Global Const CE_RXPARITY = &H4         '  Receive Parity Error
Global Const CE_FRAME = &H8   '  Receive Framing error
Global Const CE_BREAK = &H10 '  Break Detected
Global Const CE_CTSTO = &H20 '  CTS Timeout
Global Const CE_DSRTO = &H40 '  DSR Timeout
Global Const CE_RLSDTO = &H80        '  RLSD Timeout
Global Const CE_TXFULL = &H100       '  TX Queue is full
Global Const CE_PTO = &H200  '  LPTx Timeout
Global Const CE_IOE = &H400  '  LPTx I/O Error
Global Const CE_DNS = &H800  '  LPTx Device not selected
Global Const CE_OOP = &H1000 '  LPTx Out-Of-Paper
Global Const CE_MODE = &H8000        '  Requested mode unsupported

Global Const IE_BADID = (-1) '  Invalid or unsupported id
Global Const IE_OPEN = (-2)  '  Device Already Open
Global Const IE_NOPEN = (-3) '  Device Not Open
Global Const IE_MEMORY = (-4)        '  Unable to allocate queues
Global Const IE_DEFAULT = (-5)       '  Error in default parameters
Global Const IE_HARDWARE = (-10)     '  Hardware Not Present
Global Const IE_BYTESIZE = (-11)     '  Illegal Byte Size
Global Const IE_BAUDRATE = (-12)     '  Unsupported BaudRate

'  Events
Global Const EV_RXCHAR = &H1 '  Any Character received
Global Const EV_RXFLAG = &H2 '  Received certain character
Global Const EV_TXEMPTY = &H4        '  Transmitt Queue Empty
Global Const EV_CTS = &H8    '  CTS changed state
Global Const EV_DSR = &H10   '  DSR changed state
Global Const EV_RLSD = &H20  '  RLSD changed state
Global Const EV_BREAK = &H40 '  BREAK received
Global Const EV_ERR = &H80   '  Line status error occurred
Global Const EV_RING = &H100 '  Ring signal detected
Global Const EV_PERR = &H200 '  Printer error occured

'  Escape Functions
Global Const SETXOFF = 1     '  Simulate XOFF received
Global Const SETXON = 2      '  Simulate XON received
Global Const SETRTS = 3      '  Set RTS high
Global Const CLRRTS = 4      '  Set RTS low
Global Const SETDTR = 5      '  Set DTR high
Global Const CLRDTR = 6      '  Set DTR low
Global Const RESETDEV = 7    '  Reset device if possible

Global Const LPTx = &H80     '  Set if ID is for LPT device

Type DCB
    Id As String * 1
```

```
        BaudRate As Integer
        ByteSize As String * 1
        Parity As String * 1
        StopBits As String * 1
        RlsTimeout As Integer
        CtsTimeout As Integer
        DsrTimeout As Integer

        Bits1 As String * 1 ' The fifteen actual DCB bit-sized data fields
        Bits2 As String * 1 ' within these two bytes can be manipulated by
                    ' bitwise logical And/Or operations.  Refer to
                    ' SDKWIN.HLP for location/meaning of specific bits

        XonChar As String * 1
        XoffChar As String * 1
        XonLim As Integer
        XoffLim As Integer
        PeChar As String * 1
        EofChar As String * 1
        EvtChar As String * 1
        TxDelay As Integer
End Type

Type COMSTAT
        Bits As String * 1 ' For specific bit flags and their
                    ' meanings, refer to SDKWIN.HLP.
        cbInQue As Integer
        cbOutQue As Integer
End Type

Declare Function OpenComm Lib "User" (ByVal lpComName As String, ByVal ⇐
wInQueue As Integer, ByVal wOutQueue As Integer) As Integer
Declare Function SetCommState Lib "User" (lpDCB as DCB) As Integer
Declare Function GetCommState Lib "User" (ByVal nCid As Integer, lpDCB As ⇐
DCB) As Integer
Declare Function ReadComm Lib "User" (ByVal nCid As Integer, ByVal lpBuf As
String, ByVal nSize As Integer) As Integer
Declare Function UngetCommChar Lib "User" (ByVal nCid As Integer, ByVal ⇐
cChar As Integer) As Integer
Declare Function WriteComm Lib "User" (ByVal nCid As Integer, ByVal lpBuf ⇐
As String, ByVal nSize As Integer) As Integer
Declare Function CloseComm Lib "User" (ByVal nCid As Integer) As Integer
Declare Function BuildCommDCB Lib "User" (ByVal lpDef As String, lpDCB As ⇐
DCB) As Integer
Declare Function TransmitCommChar Lib "User" (ByVal nCid As Integer, ByVal ⇐
cChar As Integer) As Integer
Declare Function SetCommEventMask Lib "User" (ByVal nCid as Integer, ⇐
nEvtMask as Integer) As Long
Declare Function GetCommEventMask Lib "User" (ByVal nCid As Integer, ByVal ⇐
nEvtMask As Integer) As Integer
Declare Function SetCommBreak Lib "User" (ByVal nCid As Integer) As Integer
Declare Function ClearCommBreak Lib "User" (ByVal nCid As Integer) As ⇐
Integer
Declare Function FlushComm Lib "User" (ByVal nCid As Integer, ByVal nQueue ⇐
```

```
As Integer) As Integer
Declare Function EscapeCommFunction Lib "User" (ByVal nCid As Integer, ⇐
ByVal nFunc As Integer) As Integer
```

Multiple Document Interface (MDI) windows are Windows' standard way of providing multiple windows in a single application. A word processor, for example, might provide MDI windows to let you open multiple documents simultaneously. Visual Basic, unfortunately, doesn't provide MDI windows, though a custom control might provide that functionality to Visual Basic applications.

```
Type MDICREATESTRUCT
    szClass As Long
    szTitle As Long
    hOwner As Integer
    x As Integer
    y As Integer
    cx As Integer
    cy As Integer
    style As Long
    lParam As Long
End Type

Type CLIENTCREATESTRUCT
    hWindowMenu As Integer
    idFirstChild As Integer
End Type

Declare Function DefFrameProc Lib "User" (ByVal hWnd As Integer, ByVal ⇐
hWndMDIClient As Integer, ByVal wMsg As Integer, ByVal wParam As Integer, ⇐
ByVal lParam As Long) As Long
Declare Function DefMDIChildProc Lib "User" (ByVal hWnd As Integer, ByVal ⇐
wMsg As Integer, ByVal wParam As Integer, ByVal lParam As Long) As Long

Declare Function TranslateMDISysAccel Lib "User" (ByVal hWndClient As ⇐
Integer, lpMsg As MSG) As Integer

Declare Function ArrangeIconicWindows Lib "User" (ByVal hWnd As Integer) ⇐
As Integer
```

As your applications get more complex, your users will demand some form of online Help so they're not stuck when they come to a problem. Microsoft provides an add-on Help compiler kit that allows you to design and write online Help.

```
'   Help engine section.

'  Commands to pass WinHelp()
Global Const HELP_CONTEXT = &H1        ' Display topic in ulTopic
Global Const HELP_QUIT = &H2 ' Terminate help
Global Const HELP_INDEX = &H3          ' Display index
Global Const HELP_HELPONHELP = &H4     ' Display help on using help
Global Const HELP_SETINDEX = &H5       ' Set the current Index for multi ⇐
```

```
index help
Global Const HELP_KEY = &H101                    '  Display topic for keyword ⇐
in offabData
Global Const HELP_MULTIKEY = &H201

Declare Function WinHelp Lib "User" (ByVal hWnd As Integer, ByVal ⇐
lpHelpFile As String, ByVal wCommand As Integer, dwData As Any) As Integer

Type MULTIKEYHELP
    mkSize As Integer
    mkKeylist As String * 1
    szKeyphrase As String * 253 ' Array length is arbitrary; may be changed
End Type
```

Microsoft provides a profiler in the Windows SDK and Borland offers its Turbo Profiler for Windows. A profiler helps you pinpoint areas in your application that take too long to execute. Once you know where a "bottle-neck" exists you can work on speeding it up.

```
'  function declarations for profiler routines contained in Windows ⇐
libraries
Declare Function ProfInsChk Lib "User" () As Integer
Declare Sub ProfSetup Lib "User" (ByVal nBufferSize As Integer, ByVal ⇐
nSamples As Integer)
Declare Sub ProfSampRate Lib "User" (ByVal nRate286 As Integer, ByVal ⇐
nRate386 As Integer)
Declare Sub ProfStart Lib "User" ()
Declare Sub ProfStop Lib "User" ()
Declare Sub ProfClear Lib "User" ()
Declare Sub ProfFlush Lib "User" ()
Declare Sub ProfFinish Lib "User" ()
```

# Appendix B
# The Visual Basic How-To Disk

This appendix lists the contents of the *Visual Basic How-To* disk that is bundled with this book.

The disk is organized by chapters and numbered How-Tos. You will find directories labeled CHAPTER1, CHAPTER2, CHAPTER3, and so on. Within those directories you will find subdirectories named 1.1, 1.2, 1.3, etc. These subdirectories correspond to the numbered How-To solutions throughout the book and contain all the .MAK files, forms, bitmaps, DLLs, and custom controls found in these pages. Most DLLs have been moved into the Chapter directories so they can be found more easily. These DLLs will need to be moved to your Windows or Windows System directory for those projects to be run.

Perceptive eyes may notice that there appear to be a few missing subdirectories. For instance, there is no subdirectory to correspond to How-To 1.4. This is because How-To 1.4 creates the VBHT.BAS file that is found at the root directory of the disk. Other "missing" subdirectories also refer to the VBHT.BAS file.

See the Introduction of this book for complete information on how to install the disk. There is also a README file on the disk that details any last minute changes. For instance, you will notice that we have added a number of .SBI (Sound Blaster Instrument) files to subdirectory 8.9 for use with the Sound Blaster FM Synthesizer project.

| **B:\** | **1.2** | ADDCTL.FRM | | HWND.BAS |
| VBHT.BAS | | ADDCTL.MAK | | TEXTBOX.BAS |
| README.TXT | **1.3** | FILEBOX.FRM | **1.8** | FILEDLG.FRM |
| | | FILEBOX.MAK | | FILEDLG.MAK |
| **CHAPTER 1** | **1.5** | CLEARAL2.FRM | **1.9** | TASKS.BAS |
| CTLHWND.DLL | | CLEARAL2.MAK | | TASKS.FRM |
| **1.1** CHECKOFF.BMP | **1.6** | FILEDLG2.FRM | | TASKS.MAK |
| CHECKON.BMP | | FILEDLG2.MAK | **1.10** | SEARCH.FRM |
| CHECKPRS.BMP | | TESTFDIA.FRM | | SEARCH.MAK |
| CUSTOM.FRM | **1.7** | EDITOR.FRM | **1.11** | SEARCH.FRM |
| CUSTOM.MAK | | EDITOR.MAK | | SEARCH.MAK |

# Appendix C
# ANSI Table

| | | | | | | | |
|---|---|---|---|---|---|---|---|
| 0 | 32 | 64 @ | 96 ` | 128 ■ | 160 | 192 À | 224 à |
| 1 ■ | 33 ! | 65 A | 97 a | 129 ■ | 161 ¡ | 193 Á | 225 á |
| 2 ■ | 34 " | 66 B | 98 b | 130 ■ | 162 ¢ | 194 Â | 226 â |
| 3 ■ | 35 # | 67 C | 99 c | 131 ■ | 163 £ | 195 Ã | 227 ã |
| 4 ■ | 36 $ | 68 D | 100 d | 132 ■ | 164 ¤ | 196 Ä | 228 ä |
| 5 ■ | 37 % | 69 E | 101 e | 133 ■ | 165 ¥ | 197 Å | 229 å |
| 6 ■ | 38 & | 70 F | 102 f | 134 ■ | 166 ¦ | 198 Æ | 230 æ |
| 7 ■ | 39 ' | 71 G | 103 g | 135 ■ | 167 § | 199 Ç | 231 ç |
| 8 * | 40 ( | 72 H | 104 h | 136 ■ | 168 ¨ | 200 È | 232 è |
| 9 * | 41 ) | 73 I | 105 i | 137 ■ | 169 © | 201 É | 233 é |
| 10 * | 42 * | 74 J | 106 j | 138 ■ | 170 ª | 202 Ê | 234 ê |
| 11 ■ | 43 + | 75 K | 107 k | 139 ■ | 171 « | 203 Ë | 235 ë |
| 12 ■ | 44 , | 76 L | 108 l | 140 ■ | 172 ¬ | 204 Ì | 236 ì |
| 13 * | 45 - | 77 M | 109 m | 141 ■ | 173 - | 205 Í | 237 í |
| 14 ■ | 46 . | 78 N | 110 n | 142 ■ | 174 ® | 206 Î | 238 î |
| 15 ■ | 47 / | 79 O | 111 o | 143 ■ | 175 ¯ | 207 Ï | 239 ï |
| 16 ■ | 48 0 | 80 P | 112 p | 144 ■ | 176 ° | 208 Ð | 240 ð |
| 17 ■ | 49 1 | 81 Q | 113 q | 145 ' | 177 ± | 209 Ñ | 241 ñ |
| 18 ■ | 50 2 | 82 R | 114 r | 146 ' | 178 ² | 210 Ò | 242 ò |
| 19 ■ | 51 3 | 83 S | 115 s | 147 ■ | 179 ³ | 211 Ó | 243 ó |
| 20 ■ | 52 4 | 84 T | 116 t | 148 ■ | 180 ´ | 212 Ô | 244 ô |
| 21 ■ | 53 5 | 85 U | 117 u | 149 ■ | 181 µ | 213 Õ | 245 õ |
| 22 ■ | 54 6 | 86 V | 118 v | 150 ■ | 182 ¶ | 214 Ö | 246 ö |
| 23 ■ | 55 7 | 87 W | 119 w | 151 ■ | 183 · | 215 × | 247 ÷ |
| 24 ■ | 56 8 | 88 X | 120 x | 152 ■ | 184 , | 216 Ø | 248 ø |
| 25 ■ | 57 9 | 89 Y | 121 y | 153 ■ | 185 ¹ | 217 Ù | 249 ù |
| 26 ■ | 58 : | 90 Z | 122 z | 154 ■ | 186 º | 218 Ú | 250 ú |
| 27 ■ | 59 ; | 91 [ | 123 { | 155 ■ | 187 » | 219 Û | 251 û |
| 28 ■ | 60 < | 92 \ | 124 \| | 156 ■ | 188 ¼ | 220 Ü | 252 ü |
| 29 ■ | 61 = | 93 ] | 125 } | 157 ■ | 189 ½ | 221 Ý | 253 ý |
| 30 ■ | 62 > | 94 ^ | 126 ~ | 158 ■ | 190 ¾ | 222 Þ | 254 þ |
| 31 ■ | 63 ? | 95 _ | 127 ■ | 159 ■ | 191 ¿ | 223 β | 255 ÿ |

■ Indicates that this character is not supported by Windows.

\* Values 8, 9, 10, and 13 convert to tab, backspace, linefeed, and carriage return characters, respectively. They have no graphical representation but they do behave appropriately in some contexts.

# Appendix D
# ASCII Table

| | **IBM Character Codes** | | | | | **IBM Character Codes** | | |
| --- | --- | --- | --- | --- | --- | --- | --- | --- |
| **DEC** | **HEX** | **Symbol** | **Key** | | **DEC** | **HEX** | **Symbol** | **Key** |
| 0 | 00 | (NULL) | (CTRL) (2) | | 29 | 1D | ↔ | (CTRL) (]) |
| 1 | 01 | ☺ | (CTRL) (A) | | 30 | 1E | ▲ | (CTRL) (6) |
| 2 | 02 | ☻ | (CTRL) (B) | | 31 | 1F | ▼ | (CTRL) (-) |
| 3 | 03 | ♥ | (CTRL) (C) | | 32 | 20 | | (SPACEBAR) |
| 4 | 04 | ♦ | (CTRL) (D) | | 33 | 21 | ! | (!) |
| 5 | 05 | ♣ | (CTRL) (E) | | 34 | 22 | " | (") |
| 6 | 06 | ♠ | (CTRL) (F) | | 35 | 23 | # | (#) |
| 7 | 07 | • | (CTRL) (G) | | 36 | 24 | $ | ($) |
| 8 | 08 | ◘ | (BACKSPACE) | | 37 | 25 | % | (%) |
| 9 | 09 | | (TAB) | | 38 | 26 | & | (&) |
| 10 | 0A | ◙ | (CTRL) (J) | | 39 | 27 | ' | (') |
| 11 | 0B | ♂ | (CTRL) (K) | | 40 | 28 | ( | (() |
| 12 | 0C | ♀ | (CTRL) (L) | | 41 | 29 | ) | ()) |
| 13 | 0D | ♪ | (ENTER) | | 42 | 2A | * | (*) |
| 14 | 0E | ♫ | (CTRL) (N) | | 43 | 2B | + | (+) |
| 15 | 0F | ¤ | (CTRL) (O) | | 44 | 2C | , | (,) |
| 16 | 10 | ► | (CTRL) (P) | | 45 | 2D | - | (-) |
| 17 | 11 | ◄ | (CTRL) (Q) | | 46 | 2E | . | (.) |
| 18 | 12 | ↕ | (CTRL) (R) | | 47 | 2F | / | (/) |
| 19 | 13 | ‼ | (CTRL) (S) | | 48 | 30 | 0 | (0) |
| 20 | 14 | ¶ | (CTRL) (T) | | 49 | 31 | 1 | (1) |
| 21 | 15 | § | (CTRL) (U) | | 50 | 32 | 2 | (2) |
| 22 | 16 | ■ | (CTRL) (V) | | 51 | 33 | 3 | (3) |
| 23 | 17 | ↨ | (CTRL) (W) | | 52 | 34 | 4 | (4) |
| 24 | 18 | ↑ | (CTRL) (X) | | 53 | 35 | 5 | (5) |
| 25 | 19 | ↓ | (CTRL) (Y) | | 54 | 36 | 6 | (6) |
| 26 | 1A | → | (CTRL) (Z) | | 55 | 37 | 7 | (7) |
| 27 | 1B | ← | (ESC) | | 56 | 38 | 8 | (8) |
| 28 | 1C | ∟ | (CTRL) (\) | | 57 | 39 | 9 | (9) |

## IBM Character Codes

| DEC | HEX | Symbol | Key | DEC | HEX | Symbol | Key |
|---|---|---|---|---|---|---|---|
| 58 | 3A | : | (:) | 97 | 61 | a | (a) |
| 59 | 3B | ; | (;) | 98 | 62 | b | (b) |
| 60 | 3C | < | (<) | 99 | 63 | c | (c) |
| 61 | 3D | = | (=) | 100 | 64 | d | (d) |
| 62 | 3E | > | (>) | 101 | 65 | e | (e) |
| 63 | 3F | ? | (?) | 102 | 66 | f | (f) |
| 64 | 40 | @ | (@) | 103 | 67 | g | (g) |
| 65 | 41 | A | (A) | 104 | 68 | h | (h) |
| 66 | 42 | B | (B) | 105 | 69 | i | (i) |
| 67 | 43 | C | (C) | 106 | 6A | j | (j) |
| 68 | 44 | D | (D) | 107 | 6B | k | (k) |
| 69 | 45 | E | (E) | 108 | 6C | l | (l) |
| 70 | 46 | F | (F) | 109 | 6D | m | (m) |
| 71 | 47 | G | (G) | 110 | 6E | n | (n) |
| 72 | 48 | H | (H) | 111 | 6F | o | (o) |
| 73 | 49 | I | (I) | 112 | 70 | p | (p) |
| 74 | 4A | J | (J) | 113 | 71 | q | (q) |
| 75 | 4B | K | (K) | 114 | 72 | r | (r) |
| 76 | 4C | L | (L) | 115 | 73 | s | (s) |
| 77 | 4D | M | (M) | 116 | 74 | t | (t) |
| 78 | 4E | N | (N) | 117 | 75 | u | (u) |
| 79 | 4F | O | (0) | 118 | 76 | v | (v) |
| 80 | 50 | P | (P) | 119 | 77 | w | (w) |
| 81 | 51 | Q | (Q) | 120 | 78 | x | (x) |
| 82 | 52 | R | (R) | 121 | 79 | y | (y) |
| 83 | 53 | S | (S) | 122 | 7A | z | (z) |
| 84 | 54 | T | (T) | 123 | 7B | { | ({) |
| 85 | 55 | U | (U) | 124 | 7C | ¦ | (¦) |
| 86 | 56 | V | (V) | 125 | 7D | } | (}) |
| 87 | 57 | W | (W) | 126 | 7E | ˜ | (~) |
| 88 | 58 | X | (X) | 127 | 7F | Δ | (CTRL) (←) |
| 89 | 59 | Y | (Y) | 128 | 80 | Ç | (ALT) 128 |
| 90 | 5A | Z | (Z) | 129 | 81 | ü | (ALT) 129 |
| 91 | 5B | [ | ([) | 130 | 82 | é | (ALT) 130 |
| 92 | 5C | \ | (\) | 131 | 83 | â | (ALT) 131 |
| 93 | 5D | ] | (]) | 132 | 84 | ä | (ALT) 132 |
| 94 | 5E | ^ | (^) | 133 | 85 | à | (ALT) 133 |
| 95 | 5F | _ | (_) | 134 | 86 | å | (ALT) 134 |
| 96 | 60 | ` | (`) | 135 | 87 | ç | (ALT) 135 |

## IBM Character Codes

| DEC | HEX | Symbol | Key | DEC | HEX | Symbol | Key |
|---|---|---|---|---|---|---|---|
| 136 | 88 | ê | ALT 136 | 175 | AF | » | ALT 175 |
| 137 | 89 | ë | ALT 137 | 176 | B0 | ░ | ALT 176 |
| 138 | 8A | è | ALT 138 | 177 | B1 | ▒ | ALT 177 |
| 139 | 8B | ï | ALT 139 | 178 | B2 | ▓ | ALT 178 |
| 140 | 8C | î | ALT 140 | 179 | B3 | │ | ALT 179 |
| 141 | 8D | ì | ALT 141 | 180 | B4 | ┤ | ALT 180 |
| 142 | 8E | Ä | ALT 142 | 181 | B5 | ╡ | ALT 181 |
| 143 | 8F | Å | ALT 143 | 182 | B6 | ╢ | ALT 182 |
| 144 | 90 | É | ALT 144 | 183 | B7 | ╖ | ALT 183 |
| 145 | 91 | æ | ALT 145 | 184 | B8 | ╕ | ALT 184 |
| 146 | 92 | Æ | ALT 146 | 185 | B9 | ╣ | ALT 185 |
| 147 | 93 | ô | ALT 147 | 186 | BA | ║ | ALT 186 |
| 148 | 94 | ö | ALT 148 | 187 | BB | ╗ | ALT 187 |
| 149 | 95 | ò | ALT 149 | 188 | BC | ╝ | ALT 188 |
| 150 | 96 | û | ALT 150 | 189 | BD | ╜ | ALT 189 |
| 151 | 97 | ù | ALT 151 | 190 | BE | ╛ | ALT 190 |
| 152 | 98 | ÿ | ALT 152 | 191 | BF | ┐ | ALT 191 |
| 153 | 99 | Ö | ALT 153 | 192 | C0 | └ | ALT 192 |
| 154 | 9A | Ü | ALT 154 | 193 | C1 | ┴ | ALT 193 |
| 155 | 9B | ¢ | ALT 155 | 194 | C2 | ┬ | ALT 194 |
| 156 | 9C | £ | ALT 156 | 195 | C3 | ├ | ALT 195 |
| 157 | 9D | ¥ | ALT 157 | 196 | C4 | ─ | ALT 196 |
| 158 | 9E | ₧ | ALT 158 | 197 | C5 | ┼ | ALT 197 |
| 159 | 9F | ƒ | ALT 159 | 198 | C6 | ╞ | ALT 198 |
| 160 | A0 | á | ALT 160 | 199 | C7 | ╟ | ALT 199 |
| 161 | A1 | í | ALT 161 | 200 | C8 | ╚ | ALT 200 |
| 162 | A2 | ó | ALT 162 | 201 | C9 | ╔ | ALT 201 |
| 163 | A3 | ú | ALT 163 | 202 | CA | ╩ | ALT 202 |
| 164 | A4 | ñ | ALT 164 | 203 | CB | ╦ | ALT 203 |
| 165 | A5 | Ñ | ALT 165 | 204 | CC | ╠ | ALT 204 |
| 166 | A6 | ª | ALT 166 | 205 | CD | ═ | ALT 205 |
| 167 | A7 | º | ALT 167 | 206 | CE | ╬ | ALT 206 |
| 168 | A8 | ¿ | ALT 168 | 207 | CF | ╧ | ALT 207 |
| 169 | A9 | ⌐ | ALT 169 | 208 | D0 | ╨ | ALT 208 |
| 170 | AA | ¬ | ALT 170 | 209 | D1 | ╤ | ALT 209 |
| 171 | AB | ½ | ALT 171 | 210 | D2 | ╥ | ALT 210 |
| 172 | AC | ¼ | ALT 172 | 211 | D3 | ╙ | ALT 211 |
| 173 | AD | ¡ | ALT 173 | 212 | D4 | ╘ | ALT 212 |
| 174 | AE | « | ALT 174 | 213 | D5 | ╒ | ALT 213 |

### IBM Character Codes

| DEC | HEX | Symbol | Key |
|-----|-----|--------|-----|
| 214 | D6 | ╥ | (ALT) 214 |
| 215 | D7 | ╫ | (ALT) 215 |
| 216 | D8 | ╪ | (ALT) 216 |
| 217 | D9 | ╛ | (ALT) 217 |
| 218 | DA | ╒ | (ALT) 218 |
| 219 | DB | ■ | (ALT) 219 |
| 220 | DC | ▄ | (ALT) 220 |
| 221 | DD | ▌ | (ALT) 221 |
| 222 | DE | ▐ | (ALT) 222 |
| 223 | DF | ▀ | (ALT) 223 |
| 224 | E0 | α | (ALT) 224 |
| 225 | E1 | β | (ALT) 225 |
| 226 | E2 | Γ | (ALT) 226 |
| 227 | E3 | π | (ALT) 227 |
| 228 | E4 | Σ | (ALT) 228 |
| 229 | E5 | σ | (ALT) 229 |
| 230 | E6 | μ | (ALT) 230 |
| 231 | E7 | τ | (ALT) 231 |
| 232 | E8 | Φ | (ALT) 232 |
| 233 | E9 | Θ | (ALT) 233 |
| 234 | EA | Ω | (ALT) 234 |

### IBM Character Codes

| DEC | HEX | Symbol | Key |
|-----|-----|--------|-----|
| 235 | EB | δ | (ALT) 235 |
| 236 | EC | ∞ | (ALT) 236 |
| 237 | ED | φ | (ALT) 237 |
| 238 | EE | ε | (ALT) 238 |
| 239 | EF | ∩ | (ALT) 239 |
| 240 | F0 | ≡ | (ALT) 240 |
| 241 | F1 | ± | (ALT) 241 |
| 242 | F2 | ≥ | (ALT) 242 |
| 243 | F3 | ≤ | (ALT) 243 |
| 244 | F4 | ⌠ | (ALT) 244 |
| 245 | F5 | ⌡ | (ALT) 245 |
| 246 | F6 | ÷ | (ALT) 246 |
| 247 | F7 | ≈ | (ALT) 247 |
| 248 | F8 | ° | (ALT) 248 |
| 249 | F9 | • | (ALT) 249 |
| 250 | FA | · | (ALT) 250 |
| 251 | FB | √ | (ALT) 251 |
| 252 | FC | η | (ALT) 252 |
| 253 | FD | ² | (ALT) 253 |
| 254 | FE | ■ | (ALT) 254 |
| 255 | FF | (blank) | (ALT) 255 |

Note that IBM Extended ASCII charcters can be displayed by pressing the (ALT) key and then typing the decimal code of the character on the keypad.

# INDEX

## ABOUT THE AUTHORS

**Robert Arnson** has been programming for eight years in BASIC, Pascal, C, and FORTRAN. He has developed several large business applications for professional insurance and statement billing, using QuickBASIC versions 2.0 through 4.5 and BASIC compilers 6.0 and 7.0. He is co-author of *The Waite Group's Microsoft QuickBASIC Bible*, and *The Waite Group's MS-DOS QBasic Programmer's Reference*, both published by Microsoft Press.

**Daniel Rosen** is Executive Vice President of Promark, a New Jersey based consulting company. He has been involved with most facets of the computer industry including the design, development, and implementation of software products, as well as the marketing, sales, and total operations and fiscal management of several computer software companies. Daniel holds graduate and undergraduate degrees in electrical engineering.

**Mitchell Waite** is President of The Waite Group, a developer and publisher of computer books. He is an experienced programmer fluent in a variety of computer languages, including Visual Basic, C, Pascal, BASIC, Assembly, and HyperTalk. He wrote his first computer book in 1976, and is co-author of many best-selling computer books including *The Waite Group's C Primer Plus, Microsoft QuickC Programming, Microsoft QuickBASIC Bible*, and *The Waite Group's Master C*.

**Jonathan Zuck** is President of User Friendly, a Washington D.C. based consulting firm specializing in Windows and database technology. He has written articles for *PC Magazine, Database Management Systems Magazine*, and is a contributing editor to the *WinTech Journal*, and *BASICPro Magazine*. His arsenal of programming languages includes BASIC, C, Pascal, Assembly, Prolog, and SmallTalk. He is also the author of a number of custom controls for Visual Basic.

## COLOPHON

Production for this book was done using desktop publishing techniques and every phase of the book involved the use of computer technology. Never did production use traditional typesetting, stats, or photos, and virtually everything for this book, from the illustrations to the formatted text, was saved on disk. Only the cover used traditional techniques.

While this book was written on IBM PC compatible computers, Apple Macintosh computers were used for desktop publishing. The following method was used to go between machines: A design template for the book was created in Aldus PageMaker for the Macintosh. This template was saved as a Microsoft Word document and then translated into Word for Windows version 1.1. The authors wrote into the WinWord files, which used style sheets to apply formatting. The finished documents were saved in an RTF format and transferred directly to a Macintosh on 3.5-inch diskettes, using Insignia's Access PC. These text files were then opened in Microsoft Word for the Macintosh, which interpreted the RTF formatting.

All book design and page formatting was done in Aldus PageMaker 4.01 on the Macintosh, using the imported Microsoft Word files. Adobe Postscript fonts were used. Line art work was created in Adobe Illustrator.

PC screen dumps were captured as .PCX files, .BMP files and .TIFF files. All screen dumps were ultimately translated to grayscale TIFFs using Hijaak by Inset Systems, and Publisher's Paintbrush, by ZSoft Corporation. The PC TIFF files were transferred to the Macintosh, again on a 3.5-inch disk opened under Access PC, and imported into PageMaker. To create the chapter opener pages, the cover painting was photographed in black and white, scanned in grey scale, and saved as a TIFF file. This file was imported into PageMaker.

Final page files were sent on Syquest data cartridges to AlphaGraphics Electronic Publishing where they were directly imposed to film through a Macintosh IIFx and Linotronic 300 phototypesetting machine, utilizing Adobe Postscript fonts. Plates were then made from the film.

AS A PUBLISHER AND WRITER WITH OVER 360,000 BOOKS SOLD EACH YEAR, I WAS SHOCKED TO DISCOVER THAT OUR RAIN FORESTS, HOME FOR HALF OF ALL LIVING THINGS ON EARTH, ARE BEING DESTROYED AT THE RATE OF 50 ACRES PER MINUTE  AT THIS RATE THE RAIN FORESTS WILL COMPLETELY DISAPPEAR IN JUST 50 YEARS  BOOKS HAVE A LARGE INFLUENCE ON THIS RAMPANT DESTRUCTION ❦ FOR EXAMPLE, SINCE IT TAKES 17 TREES TO PRODUCE ONE TON OF PAPER, A FIRST PRINTING OF 30,000 COPIES OF A TYPICAL 480 PAGE BOOK CONSUMES 108,000 POUNDS OF PAPER WHICH WILL REQUIRE 918 TREES ❦ TO HELP OFFSET THIS LOSS, WAITE GROUP PRESS WILL PLANT TWO TREES FOR EVERY TREE FELLED FOR PRODUCTION OF THIS BOOK ❦ THE DONATION WILL BE MADE TO RAINFOREST ACTION NETWORK (THE BASIC FOUNDATION, P.O. BOX 47012, ST. PETERSBURG, FL 33743), WHICH CAN PLANT 1,000 TREES FOR $250.

# NO ONE CAN DO A BETTER JOB RAVING ABOUT OUR BASIC BOOKS THAN OUR READERS.

## Here are just a few of the hundreds of comments we have received:

10) We would like to hear any additional comments you have about any portion of the book: I thought the compatibility box a major achievement! Most books don't do this for you. Excellent idea!

10) We would like to hear any additional comments you have about any portion of the book: This book was much better than the MS manuals in graphics and trapping.

10) We would like to hear any additional comments you have about any portion of the book: FANTASTIC!!

10) We would like to hear any additional comments you have about any portion of the book: I WOULD HAVE TO SAY THAT I'M VERY IMPRESSED WITH HOW YOU PUT TOGETHER THE BOOK.

10) We would like to hear any additional comments you have about any portion of the book: AS A REFRESHER OR FOR SOMEONE LEARNING OR REFERENCE - EXCELLENT SUPERB INDEXING - BEST I HAVE SEEN.

10) We would like to hear any additional comments you have about any portion of the book: VERY FINE BOOK. BEST OF MY QUICK BASI BOOKS.

10) We would like to hear any additional comments you have about any portion of the book: This is one of the most thorough and well laid out books I have ever used in programming.

10) We would like to hear any additional comments you have about any portion of the book: 1st Book I Have found That was a Complete Reference on VBASIC 4.5

10) We would like to hear any additional comments you have about any portion of the book: OUTSTANDING EFFORT. I'VE RECOMMENDED IT TO SEVERAL OF MY FRIENDS

10) We would like to hear any additional comments you have about any portion of the book: Outstanding Book

10) We would like to hear any additional comments you have about any portion of the book: Best book written on Quick BASIC by far. Superb Job By authors!

10) We would like to hear any additional comments you have about any portion of the book: I have 4 other Books on MS QB, This one is by FAR The Best of Them ALL.

10) We would like to hear any additional comments you have about any portion of the book: SUPERBLY WRITTEN. IT'S THE ONLY BOOK I NEED IN MASTERING THE BASIC LANGUAGE. PLEASE KEEP UP THE GOOD WORK

10) We would like to hear any additional comments you have about any portion of the book: The precision of the explanations is excellent.

10) We would like to hear any additional comments you have about any portion of the book: POINTS OUT COMMON PITFALLS ENCOUNTER WITH QUICK BASIC - IF I HAD THE BOOK EARLIER I WOULD HAVE SPENT LESS TIME IN THE PIT.

10) We would like to hear any additional comments you have about any portion of the book: EXCELLENT! BOOK.

10) We would like to hear any additional comments you have about any portion of the book: THIS BOOK IS BETTER THE QB 4.5 MANUAL!

10) We would like to hear any additional comments you have about any portion of the book: HAS GIVEN ME EVERY DETAIL I'VE WANTED TO KNOW THUS FAR: A VERY COMPLETE REFERENCE.

10) We would like to hear any additional comments you have about any portion of the book: I REALY LIKE THE compatibility box It was very useful THANK YOU!

10) We would like to hear any additional comments you have about any portion of the book: THIS IS THE BEST ALL AROUND BOOK ON QB THAT I AM AWARE OF. CONGRATULATIONS!

10) We would like to hear any additional comments you have about any portion of the book: Love the quick index at the front and back of the book

### THE WAITE GROUP'S
## VISUAL BASIC SUPER BIBLE

TAYLOR MAXWELL AND BRYON SCOTT

The complete reference to every command, function, statement, object, method, event, and property in the Visual Basic language detailed in Waite Group high-quality, user-friendly fashion. Each chapter begins with a lucid overview, and each entry includes purpose, syntax, an example, and in-depth descriptions. Enclosed disk contains all example projects, code resources, bit maps and complete applications developed in the book.

APRIL 1992, ISBN 1-878739-12-3, TRADE PAPER,

3.5" DISK, 744PP., 7 x 9                                    $39.95 US

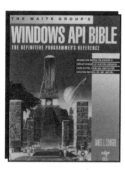

### THE WAITE GROUP'S
## WINDOWS API BIBLE
### The Definitive Programmer's Reference

JAMES L. CONGER

A single, comprehensive, easy-to-use reference with examples for the over-600 Windows Application Programming Interface (API) functions. Like all Waite Group bibles, API functions are organized into categories, preceded by lucid tutorials and features Windows version compatibility boxes. Contains the latest information on the new Windows Version 3.1.

ISBN 1-878739-15-8, TRADE PAPER, 1,158 PP.,

$7^3/_8$ X $9^1/_4$, COMPANION DISK AVAILABLE                $39.95 US

### THE WAITE GROUP'S
## FRACTAL CREATIONS
### Explore the Magic of Fractals on Your PC

TIMOTHY WEGNER AND MARK PETERSON

The best-selling book/software package that lets you create over 70 fractals with a press of a key and make them come to life. Fractint, the revolutionary software, lets you zoom in on any part of a fractal image, rotate it, do color-cycle animation, even choose accompanying sound effects and 3-D mode. For programmers, students, and amateur enthusiasts alike. "...A magical ride complete with both the mathematical background necessary to appreciate and understand fractals, and the software, which allows you to display and manipulate them, even in 3-D." *PC Magazine.*

ISBN 1-878739-05-0, TRADE PAPER,

5.25" DISK, 350PP., 7 x 9, POSTER, 3-D GLASSES            $34.95 US

### THE WAITE GROUP'S
## TURBO PASCAL HOW-TO
### The Definitive Object-Oriented Problem-Solver

GARY SYCK

Everything you need to know to begin writing professional Turbo Pascal programs including hundreds of typical programming problems, creative solutions, comments, warnings, and enhancements in an easy-to-look-up reference format. The how-to solutions are designed to work with the newest object-oriented versions Turbo Pascal 6.0, Turbo Pascal for Windows, and Turbo Vision, as well as previous versions.

ISBN 1-878739-04-2, TRADE PAPER,

500PP., 7 x 9, COMPANION DISK AVAILABLE                   $24.95 US

INNOVATION NOT IMITATION

# VBTools 2.0
## Special Discount Offer - $25 Off!

If you tried the demonstration version of VBTools included in this book, you know what custom controls can do for your program's appearance and functionality, not to mention the time you save creating the user interface. Now you know why VBTools is the best-selling add-on product for Visual Basic!

If you liked working with VBTools, you're going to love version 2.0! In addition to all the controls in the demonstration version, we've added almost 20 new ones! We've also provided access to the Windows 3.1 "common dialog" box routines so your applications will have the "standard" look and feel of Win 3.1!

As a "thank you" for purchasing this book, Waite Group Press has made special arrangements with MicroHelp so that you'll receive a $25 discount when you purchase VBTools 2.0. (Please see the next page for details on how to order it.)

## Here's a list of the controls scheduled to be in VBTools 2.00[2]

**256-Color Picture Box Control**

Loads .BMP and .PCX pictures directly. Check with us if you need other file formats, such as .TIF and .GIF.

**Spreadsheet (Grid) Control**

Write your own mini-spreadsheet or use the control for a handy database display routine.

**Toolbox/Toolbar Control**

Do you like the Visual Basic Toolbox Window? Now you can "roll you own" using whatever bitmaps you want. Bonus: Group the tools so that pressing one within a group "unpresses" all others in the group but doesn't affect the tools outside the group.

**Chart/Graph Control**

What good is a spreadsheet without charting capabilities? Includes line, scatter, pie, bar, column, etc.

**Picture/Text Enhanced List Box**

Now you can display icons and/or bitmaps along with text in a list box. Also includes multiple columns, with font characteristics settable for each line and column. Bonus: Automatic collapsing/expanding of levels, settable for the entire control or for each element in the control.

**3-D Button Control**

This is similar to the MhButton control in version 1.0, but allows mixing of bitmaps and text captions.

**Spin Control**

Think of this as combining only the arrow portions of a mouse scrollbar with a value. The user simply clicks on the arrows or uses the keyboard to change the value.

**Property Browser**

View all the properties for a control at once and change them during design mode.

**Animated Buttons**

Use this control for a variety of animation and special effects.

**Scrolling Banner**

Similar to New York's famous marquees.

## Flip Switch Control

Similar to the "switch" control in MhMulti, but has switches on both ends and a Caption property.

## Dice Control

Includes the ability to animate the dice as if they were being tossed.

## Rubber Band Control

Just like "Drag and Drop", but you can use it anywhere on the display.

## Icon/Caption Control

Lets your programs look like ProgMan, including automatic "arranging" of the controls.

## Screen Blanker Control

Blanks the screen and then entertains you. Use our bitmaps or specify your own.

## Transparent Picture Control

Lets you place irregular-shaped bitmaps on a form, with the background showing around the edges (like the way icons are displayed in ProgMan).

## Line-Drawing Control

Are you tired of the Line method? If so, you'll love this control.

## Enhanced File List Box

Includes optional date/time/size and file attribute columns.

## Telephone Dialer

Dial the phone by clicking on the phone's pushbuttons!

## More in the Works!

- - - - - - - - - - - - - - - - - - - - - - - - - - - - - - - - - - - - - - - - - -

# VBTools 2.0 Order Form
## $25 Off VBTools 2.0

Visa and MasterCard holders: For the fastest service, please call our toll-free order line at 1-800-922-3383 (In Georgia or outside the USA 404-594-1185). Be sure to mention the $25 discount, because only owners of this book are entitled to receive the discount!

If you're not in a hurry, please photocopy this form and send it to MicroHelp, Inc., 4636 Huntridge Drive, Roswell GA 30075-2012.

_____ Copies of VBTools 2.0 @$164.00 (regularly $189)  _____

Georgia residents please add sales tax for your county  _____

Please add shipping charges (see chart)  _____

Total enclosed or authorized to charge to credit card  _____

Media:  ❏ 5.25" 1.2mb     ❏ 3.5" 720k

Payment: (Circle one) VISA  MC  Check (payable to MicroHelp, Inc.)

Card No: \_ \_ \_ \_  \_ \_ \_ \_  \_ \_ \_ \_  \_ \_ \_ \_

Expiration: \_ \_ / \_ \_   Daytime Phone: (\_ \_ \_) \_ \_ \_ - \_ \_ \_ \_

Signature _____
(required for credit card orders)

Name: _____

Company: _____

Address: _____

City: _____

State:_____  Zip/Postal Code: _____

Country: _____

| SHIPPING CHART | 1st Copy | Additional Copies |
|---|---|---|
| ❏ USA via UPS ground (business address only) | $6.00 | no charge |
| ❏ USA via UPS 2nd Day | 7.00 | 3.00 each |
| ❏ Canada | 9.00 | 5.00 each |
| ❏ Other countries | 25.00 | 10.00 each |

**Call 1-800-922-3383 or 404-594-1185**

# INTRODUCING
## QUICKPAK PROFESSIONAL
# FOR WINDOWS

QuickPak Professional for Windows is the most complete collection of subroutines, functions, and custom controls for Visual Basic ever produced. It includes more than 300 services that help you improve the quality of your programs and complete them faster. All of the low-level routines are written in pure assembly language for the fastest speed and smallest code size possible. The remainder are high-level services written in Visual Basic.

## Low-level Routines For High-Level Performance

Because Visual Basic creates programs that are interpreted at runtime, assembly language routines are essential for attaining acceptable speed in many programming situations. We provide routines for searching and sorting all data types including floating point and Currency arrays. A special multi-key recursive Type sort lets you sort on any number of keys—both in memory and on disk. Other important low-level assembler routines include loading and saving entire arrays in one operation, simplified access to the Windows API services, direct access to hardware ports, extremely fast date and time arithmetic, and much more.

A wealth of string manipulation routines is included. There are InStr replacements that allow wild cards, honor or ignore capitalization, look for characters that match those in a table, and even search backwards through a string. A sophisticated parsing function lets you easily split strings such as the DOS PATH into their component parts. ParseString is much more powerful than Read and Data, and more than overcomes their omission from Visual Basic.

String encryption routines enable you to quickly secure data and passwords using any other string as a key. A unique Sequence routine advances digits and letters for controlling serial numbers and product codes.

Special UCASE$ and LCASE$ replacements let our European friends handle the unique capitalization needs of their languages.

Conversion routines translate between Hex, Binary, and Decimal numbers. A Soundex function lets you compare strings and names based on how they sound.

Many hardware services are also added to let you determine the CPU type, coprocessor, number and type of drives and if they are on a network server, printer status, monitor type, serial and parallel ports, and more.

Memory services report on the total installed memory, Windows virtual memory, and EMS/XMS memory. Windows-specific routines return the version number and operating mode, free resources, and the Windows and System directories.

Other miscellaneous routines allow you to manipulate unsigned integers, shift bits, copy blocks of memory, and compare entire Type variables in one operation.

Although Visual Basic doesn't support BASIC's CALL INTERRUPT, QuickPak Professional sure does! With DosCall you can easily access all of the low-level DOS system services.

Other important Visual Basic omissions are also provided, including the Cvi/Cvd and Mki$/Mkd$ family of functions; Peek and Poke; Inp and Out; and VarSeg, VarPtr, and SAdd. Other VB oversights we provide are Sound and Play, Swap, and Fre. Because these are no longer reserved words, we use the original names so you don't even have to change your code.

Many Visual Basic custom controls are provided:

- A unique Time Display with adjustable offset for different time zones.

- An enhanced Text Box control features masked input that lets you specify allowable characters for each position in a field. This control also features changeable tab stops, overstrike mode, enforcing a maximum field length, and definable data types.

- Enhanced Scroll Bars that provide instant updating as the sliders are moved.

- Enhanced List Boxes offering multiple columns and multiple selections.

- Keyboard and mouse controls that let you intercept those events before they are passed on to your program or other Windows applications. With these controls you can pop up a program on a hot key, or examine and filter keyboard and mouse events destined for *other* Windows programs that are currently running.

All of the low-level routines are very easy to use—we use sensible names and a simple, intuitive calling syntax. You do not have to know anything about assembly language to use QuickPak Professional for Windows. Simply specify the supplied DLL library in your Declare statements, and we do the rest!

## Don't Reinvent The Wheel

Many high-level subroutines and functions are provided including BASIC equivalents of every financial and statistical function in Lotus 1-2-3. High-level file services include file searching and encryption, and copying multiple files based on wild card specifications. A full-featured expression evaluator accepts formulas even with nested parentheses and computes the result. There's also a pop-up ASCII chart you can add to your programs.

Special enhanced dialog boxes are supplied for File Open, File Save, Search, and Search and Replace.

Contouring routines for creating an attractive sculpted look on your Visual Basic forms are included along with painting routines for filling irregularly shaped areas.

## Spectacular Demonstration Programs

Numerous demonstration programs are provided that show many of the routines in context and also serve as excellent examples of professional programming using Visual Basic. Further, QuickPak Professional for Windows includes *all* of the source code—both BASIC and assembler—so you can see how the routines really work and learn from them.

Many of the demonstration programs are complete applications in their own right. For example, the ReadDirs program shows how to search all directory levels for a given file or group of files. The SysInfo demo is a complete utility program that reports all of the system resources such as installed memory, CPU type, number and type of disk drives, and so forth. The file encryption demonstration accepts a file name and password, and actually encrypts and decrypts the file. These are but a few of the more than 50 demonstrations included.

## Windows-Specific Services

Determine if a particular program is running.

Get window handles for the whole system or one application. Although Visual Basic lets you know the handle for your own forms, without QuickPak Professional for Windows, there's no direct way to pass a control's handle to an API routine.

Functions that access the Visual Basic API Twips2Pixels and Pixels2Twips services to determine the ratio of Pixels to Twips, and vice versa.

A special function that returns a pointer to a Visual Basic HLL string. A subroutine that reports and counts all top windows, children under a given window, all tasks, and all parent tasks.

A SplitColor subroutine that splits the Windows long integer color into its component Red, Green, and Blue values.

## Get Up To Speed—Fast!

Programmers who already own QuickPak Professional for QuickBASIC or BASIC 7 PDS will be pleased to know that we use the identical calling syntax for the Windows version. This greatly simplifies converting existing applications to the new and exciting Windows environment. If you are not already a Crescent customer, you are sure to be thrilled—our products have received glowing reviews in all of the popular programming magazines.

## The Bottom Line

QuickPak Professional for Windows costs only $199 including all of the subroutines, functions, custom controls, and fully commented source code.

Crescent Software, Inc. publishes many useful products for BASIC programmers. We offer general purpose toolboxes as well as programs for graphics, screen design, database management, scientific applications, BASIC TSRs and more. All products include complete source code and royalties are never required. Please call or write for more information on our entire line.

| Name: | | Daytime Phone: | |
|---|---|---|---|
| Company: | | | |
| Address: (No P.O. Boxes please) | | | |
| City: | | State: | Zip Code |
| **PAYMENT:** ☐ CHECK (allow 10 days to clear)   ☐ VISA   ☐ MasterCard   ☐ COD | | (Cash/Certified check only) | |
| Credit Card Number: | | | Expiration Date: |
| Card Holder Name: | | | |
| Signature: | | | Date: |

| | |
|---|---|
| Subtotal | $199.00 |
| CT Residents Must Add 6.0% Sales Tax | |
| Shipping (See Below for Choices) | |
| $4.00 additional for COD | |
| **TOTAL** | |

| INDICATE DISK SIZE: ☐ 5.25″   ☐ 3.5″ | SHIPPING INFORMATION |
|---|---|
| | U.S.A.:   ☐ $7 (2nd Day)        ☐ $20 (Overnight) |
| | CANADA: ☐ $16 (Express Mail) ☐ $35 (Overnight) |
| | EUROPE: ☐ $45 (Express Mail) |
| | ALL OTHERS: ☐ $50 (Express Mail) |

CRESCENT
SOFTWARE, INC.

32 Seventy Acres, West Redding, CT 06896 Orders Only: 800-35- BASIC Technical Information: 203-438-5300 Office hours are 9 to 5 Eastern Time. All Crescent Software products require QuickBASIC 4.0 or later, or BASIC PDS. We include full commented source code, and require no royalty payments when our routines are included in your executable programs. Free Technical Support provided.

# 3-D Widgets 1/2/3   - Achieve a State of the Art 3-D Look
### - Add Professional Features to Your Apps
### - No Additional Coding Required

## 3-D Widgets/1 ( featured in the 'How-To' section of this book)

| | |
|---|---|
| **CheckBox** | 3-D version of standard CheckBox (with text alignment option) |
| **Command Button** | 3-D version of standard Command Button (with picture property) |
| **Frame** | 3-D version of standard Frame (with text alignment option) |
| **Option Button** | 3-D version of standard Option Button (with text alignment option) |
| **Panel** | An amazingly versatile new control which can be anything from a 3-D background for standard controls or text to a colored status bar with percent display |
| **Ribbon Button** | Can be used in groups to emulate the look of the Ribbon in Microsoft Excel |

## 3-D Widgets/2

| | |
|---|---|
| **ListBox** | Can be either 2-D or 3-D with all the features and capabilities that were left out of the standard VB ListBox including MultiColumn, MultiSelect, Horizontal scrolling, flexible internal tab settings, emptying list with a single VB statement at runtime.  In addition, pictures (bitmaps and icons) can be displayed for individual list items! |
| **File ListBox** | Combines the features listed above with those of the standard VB File ListBox. |
| **Directory ListBox** | 3-D version of the standard VB Directory ListBox. |
| **ComboBox** | 3-D version of the standard VB ComboBox plus support for pictures (bitmaps and icons). |
| **Drive ListBox** | 3-D version of the standard VB Drive ListBox. |

## 3-D Widgets/3

| | |
|---|---|
| **3-D Menu** | This control could not be simpler to use.  Just place it on a VB form that has a menu defined and when the form is run all of the menus will appear 3-Dimensional, including the top level menus (optional).  In addition, full support for all standard VB Font properties as well as our custom Font3D property (see below) is provided.  Additional properties allow complete flexibility as to the look of both selected and unselected menu items (raised, inset, bordered etc.). |

Note: all of the 3-D Widgets that display text include a Font3D property that allows the text to appear raised or inset .

| Name: | | | | Phone: | |
|---|---|---|---|---|---|
| Company: | | | | | |
| Address: | | | | | |
| | | | | | |
| City: | | State: | | Country: | Zip: |
| Product: | ☐ **3-D Widgets/1** $49 | ☐ **3-D Widgets/2** $39 | ☐ **3-D Widgets/3** $39 | ☐ All Three $99 | |
| Media: | ☐ 5.25" Diskette | ☐ 3..5" Diskette | | | |
| Payment: | ☐ Check Included | ☐ VISA | ☐ MasterCard | ☐ C.O.D. | |
| Card Holder: | | Card #: | | Expir.: | |
| Signature: | | | | Date: | |

| | |
|---|---|
| SubTotal | |
| New York residents add 8% Sales Tax | |
| Shipping & Handling (see below) | |
| Add $4.00 for C.O.D. | |
| Total | |

**Sheridan Software Systems, Inc.**
**65 Maxess Road**
**Melville, New York 11747**
**(516) 753-0985**

Shipping and Handling Charges: USA. $5 (2nd Day) or $20 (overnight), Canada  $16,  Europe $35, all others $40.

# We're breaking Windows programming wide open with **Windows Tech Journal,** the only magazine devoted exclusively to tools and techniques for Windows programmers.

Windows programming demands new skills, new knowledge, and new tools. That's why we've packed **Windows Tech Journal** with authoritative reviews, enlightening articles, and insightful commentary by top Windows experts. **All the Windows information you need in one place.**

Inside every issue, you'll find feature articles on innovative Windows techniques, with complete source code. Our detailed reviews of new products will help you choose the best tool for the job. Columns will keep you up-to-date on C and the SDK, C++ and class libraries, database engines, OOP languages like Actor, Pascal, and Smalltalk, and tools like Visual Basic. A "first look" section will give you advance information on the latest products. We'll tell you which books to add to your Windows library and keep you informed on industry developments.

Plan for a programming breakthrough. For a **FREE ISSUE,** call **800-234-0386** or FAX your name and address to **503-746-0071.** We'll send you a free issue and start your **no-risk** subscription. You'll get a full year—12 issues in all—of Windows tools and techniques for just **$29.95.** If you're not completely satisfied, simply write "cancel" on the invoice. The free issue is yours to keep, and you owe nothing.

Whether you're just getting started with Windows or have been developing for years, **Windows Tech Journal** is for you.

# LICENSE AND WARRANTY

# SoundBytes

## Sound Blaster® MIDI, Synthesizer, and Digitized Voice Controls from Waite Group Software

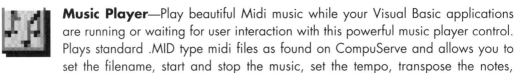

Give your Visual Basic application exciting sound effects, MIDI music, and digitized speech with Waite Group Software SoundBytes—a set of custom controls for manipulating the famous Sound Blaster audio board. Three controls allow you to play MIDI music in the background while your application is running, control up to eleven channels of the Sound Blaster FM Synthesizer, and give your applications full voice narration. Design-time only samples of the controls are provided in the disk supplied with this book and their operation is detailed in Chapter 8. If you like them, you can purchase the run-time version for only $39.95 plus postage. See ordering details on the next page.

**Music Player**—Play beautiful Midi music while your Visual Basic applications are running or waiting for user interaction with this powerful music player control. Plays standard .MID type midi files as found on CompuServe and allows you to set the filename, start and stop the music, set the tempo, transpose the notes, pause the music, and control how the music fades in and out. 22 different properties may be set with this control from Visual Basic. All music plays in the background and will not interfere with the processing of your running application.

**FM Synthesizer**—Add special sounds effects and musical notes to your VB application by controlling every detail of up to eleven Sound Blaster FM channels. Download custom instrument sounds from CompuServe so you can switch between a piano, a guitar, or an alien ship blasting off. Over 40 different properties may be set with this control. Each channel allows complete control over the carrier and modulator waveforms, so you can set the note, octave, attack, decay, sustain, and release properties as well as vibrato, tremolo, and level. Control such subtle effects as making the volume rise as the frequency goes up. The carrier waveform can be set from a sine to a rectified sine and the feedback between the carrier and the sine can be altered.

**Voice Player**—Give your applications full voice narration or record and play back any sound with this digitized recorder and player control. Voice player allows setting any of 16 properties, including the filename for the recording, pause, play, record, and more. A PlayEnd event notifies you when the recording is completed.